Systems of Care for
Children's Mental Health

Series Editors:
Beth A. Stroul, M.Ed.
Robert M. Friedman, Ph.D.

Children's Mental Health

Other Volumes in This Series

Children's Mental Health
Creating Systems of Care
in a Changing Society

Edited by

Beth A. Stroul, M.Ed.
Vice President
Management and Training Innovations
McLean, Virginia

·P A U L·H·
PUBLISHING Co.

Baltimore • London • Toronto • Sydney

Paul H. Brookes Publishing Co.
Post Office Box 10624
Baltimore, Maryland 21285-0624

Copyright © 1996 by Paul H. Brookes Publishing Co., Inc.
All rights reserved.

Typeset by PRO-IMAGE Corporation, York, Pennsylvania.
Manufactured in the United States of America by
The Maple Press Company, York, Pennsylvania.

This book is printed on recycled paper.

Library of Congress Cataloging-in-Publication Data
Children's mental health : creating systems of care in a changing
    society / edited by Beth A. Stroul.
        p.   cm.—(Systems of care for children's mental health)
    Includes bibliographical references and index.
    ISBN 1-55766-195-2
    1. Child mental health services—United States.   I. Stroul, Beth
A.   II. Series.
RJ501.A2C476   1996
362.2'083—dc20   95-52123
                                                                                CIP

British Library Cataloguing-in-Publication data are available from the British
Library.

Contents

SECTION I
A New Paradigm for Systems of Care

SECTION II
System Development at Federal, State, and Local Levels

Series Preface

In 1982, Knitzer's seminal study, *Unclaimed Children*, was published by the Children's Defense Fund. At that time, the field of children's mental health was characterized by a lack of federal or state leadership, few community-based services, little collaboration among child-serving systems, negligible parent involvement, and little or no advocacy on behalf of youngsters with emotional disorders. Since that time, substantial gains have been realized in both the conceptualization and the implementation of comprehensive, community-based systems of care for children and adolescents with serious emotional disorders and their families.

A vast amount of information has emanated from the system-building experiences of states and communities and from research and technical assistance efforts. Many of the trends and philosophies emerging in recent years have now become widely accepted as the "state of the art" for conceptualizing and providing services to youngsters with emotional disorders and their families. There is now broad agreement surrounding the need to create community-based systems of care throughout the United States for children and their families, and the development of these systems has become a national goal. Such systems of care are based on the premises of providing services in the most normative environments, creating effective interagency relationships among the key child-serving systems, involving families in all phases of the planning and delivery of services, and creating service systems that are designed to respond to the needs of culturally diverse populations.

A major need is to incorporate these concepts and trends into the published literature. This need stems from the critical shortage of staff who are appropriately trained to serve youngsters in community-based systems of care, with new philosophies and new service delivery approaches. Of utmost importance is the need to provide state-of-the-art information to institutions of higher education for use in the preservice education of professionals across disciplines, including the social work, counseling, psychology, and psychiatry fields. Similarly, there is an equally vital need for resources for the in-service training of staff in mental health, child welfare, education, health, and juvenile justice agencies to assist the staff in working more effectively with youngsters with emotional disorders and their families.

This book series, *Systems of Care for Children's Mental Health*, is designed to fulfill these needs by addressing current trends in children's mental health service delivery. The series has several broad goals:

- To increase awareness of the system-of-care concept and philosophy among current and future mental health professionals who will be providing services to children, adolescents, and their families.
- To broaden the mental health field's understanding of treatment and service delivery beyond traditional approaches to include innovative, state-of-the-art approaches.

• To provide practical information that will assist the mental health field to implement and apply the philosophy, services, and approaches embodied in the system-of-care concept.

Each volume in this continuing series addresses a major issue or topic related to the development of systems of care. The books contain information useful to planners, program managers, policy makers, practitioners, parents, teachers, researchers, and others who are interested and involved in improving systems of care for children with emotional disorders and their families. As the series editors, it is our goal for the series to provide an ongoing vehicle and forum for exploring critical aspects of systems of care as they continue to evolve.

REFERENCE

Knitzer, J. (1982). *Unclaimed children: The failure of public responsibility to children and adolescents in need of mental health services*. Washington, DC: Children's Defense Fund.

Editorial Advisory Board

Foreword

I have been involved in the mental health field for many years. My education in this field began when my husband was governor of Georgia. Knowing of my interest in the issue, he established the Governor's Commission to Improve Services to the Mentally and Emotionally Handicapped and appointed me a commissioner. Then in 1977, as president, he established the President's Commission on Mental Health, and I served as the Honorary Chairperson. I have been able to continue my work through a mental health policy program at The Carter Center in Atlanta. We hold a symposium every year and for the past few years have been closely involved in the national health care reform debate to ensure inclusion of mental health benefits on a par with physical health benefits.

The challenge that we face is finding a way to provide affordable and comprehensive mental health services to all who need them. And among our most urgent needs are those of our children.

Ever since the first White House Conference on Children in 1909, there have been meetings and conferences and commissions, all of which have told the same story—children with emotional problems have not received the help they need. There have been recommendations on how to meet their needs, and some progress has been made, but there is still an agenda to be finished.

I recently reviewed the recommendations of the President's Commission on Mental Health. The Commission recommended prevention services such as Head Start and developmental day care programs for all families, the development of a network of services organized along a continuum of care, services that respect ethnic differences and can be adapted to specific needs, the involvement of parents where services are delivered, the training of more professionals to work with children, and increased outpatient and residential care. All of these recommendations are relevant nearly two decades later, and all of them are part of the system of care concept and philosophy described in this book.

In the 1980s, we learned even more about the needs of children and how to meet them. Jane Knitzer's study, *Unclaimed Children*, showed that states did not follow children through the mental health system, and that two thirds of children with serious emotional disturbances were not receiving any services at all. As we recognized while working on the President's Commission, Knitzer contended that children were unclaimed by the public agencies that were responsible for serving them. Her report also showed that inpatient care, although more accessible to children, was more costly and restrictive, and that state systems—juvenile justice, education, child welfare, and mental health—were uncoordinated. More and more states are now experimenting with cross-agency collaboration because they have seen that the failure to collaborate is too costly in terms of both money and wasted lives.

Partly as a result of the report on "Unclaimed Children," the federal Child and Adolescent Service System Program (CASSP) was developed, and we have gained a far greater understanding about integrated systems of care through this initiative. The good news is that we have enormous knowledge and experience about what works—about the elements of successful programs for children. The bad news is that we, as a nation, are still not acting on this knowledge in a significant way. We know what we need; we know what works. The great challenge will be implementing what works, and that must be our agenda for the 1990s.

In the year 2009, we will witness the 100th anniversary of the first White House conference on the needs of America's children. If we were to hold a conference then to commemorate 100 years of progress, what goals should we work toward as an agenda for that conference? Is it beyond the realm of possibility to think of an agenda that would emphasize the strengths and abilities of children and families rather than a typical agenda of today that places so much emphasis on deficits and inabilities? Could a significant part of the 2009 agenda be devoted to sharing information about programs that are working in the prevention of emotional difficulty and the promotion of mental health? Could we have an award ceremony recognizing outstanding interagency collaboration? Is it too inconceivable to dream that in 2009 there would be systems of care for children with mental health needs in all of our nation's communities?

Without minimizing the challenge before us, I do want to encourage us to think about or to dream about what an agenda might be in 2009 and what would help us to celebrate 100 years of meaningful progress on behalf of America's children.

This book presents such an agenda—the development of comprehensive systems of care for children with emotional disturbances and their families. It calls for systems of care that are community based, family focused, and culturally competent. It calls for systems of care that include prevention and early intervention, incorporate a wide array of services, emphasize treatment in the least restrictive setting, and use flexible, individualized approaches to care. The ideas and proposals in this book can help us prepare for the future. I do believe we can make great progress for those we all care about—our children.

Let's really have something to celebrate, but let's not wait until the year 2009.

Rosalynn Carter
The Carter Center
Atlanta, Georgia

Contributors

Barbara J. Bazron, Ph.D.
Vice President
Lewin-VHI
9302 Lee Highway
Suite 500
Fairfax, VA 22031

Lenore B. Behar, Ph.D.
Head
Child and Family Services Branch
North Carolina Division of Mental
    Health, Developmental Disabilities
    and Substance Abuse Services
325 North Salisbury Street
Raleigh, NC 27603

Marva P. Benjamin, A.C.S.W.
Director
Cultural Competence Initiative
National Technical Assistance Center
    for Children's Mental Health
Director
MCH National Center for Cultural
    Competence
Georgetown University Child
    Development Center
3307 M Street, N.W.
Suite 401
Washington, DC 20007

Leonard Bickman, Ph.D.
Director
Center for Mental Health Policy
Vanderbilt Institute for Public Policy
    Studies
Vanderbilt University
1207 18th Avenue, South
Nashville, TN 37212

Suzanne M. Bronheim, Ph.D.
Associate Director for Special Projects
National Center for Networking
    Community-Based Services
Georgetown University Child
    Development Center
3307 M Street, N.W.
Suite 401
Washington, DC 20007

Scott Bryant-Comstock, M.S.
President
B-C Family Productions
16 Sagamore Place
Hillsborough, NC 27278

Hewitt B. Clark, Ph.D.
Professor
Department of Child and Family
    Studies
Florida Mental Health Institute
University of South Florida
13301 Bruce B. Downs Boulevard
Tampa, FL 33612

Robert F. Cole, Ph.D.
Project Director
National Resource Center
Washington Business Group on Health
777 North Capitol Street, N.E., #800
Washington, DC 20002

Terry Cross, M.S.W.
Director
National Indian Child Welfare
    Association
3611 SW Hood Street
Suite 201
Portland, OR 97201

Gary DeCarolis, M.Ed.
Chief
Child, Adolescent and Family Branch
Center for Mental Health Services
Substance Abuse and Mental Health
    Services Administration
Room 11-C-17 Parklawn Building
5600 Fishers Lane
Rockville, MD 20857

Neal DeChillo, D.S.W.
Associate Professor
School of Social Work
Salem State College
352 Lafayette Street
Salem, MA 01970

Karl Dennis
Executive Director
Kaleidoscope Inc.
1279 North Milwaukee Avenue
Suite 250
Chicago, IL 60622

Albert J. Duchnowski, Ph.D.
Deputy Director
Research and Training Center for
  Children's Mental Health
Florida Mental Health Institute
13301 Bruce B. Downs Boulevard
Tampa, FL 33612

Michael Foster, Ph.D.
Assistant Professor of Public Policy and
  Economics
Center for Mental Health Policy
Vanderbilt Institute for Public Policy
  Studies
Vanderbilt University
1207 18th Avenue, South
Nashville, TN 37212

Lynn Foster-Johnson, Ph.D.
NASMHPD Postdoctoral Fellow
Research and Training Center for
  Children's Mental Health
Florida Mental Health Institute
13301 Bruce B. Downs Boulevard
Tampa, FL 33612

Robert M. Friedman, Ph.D.
Chair
Department of Child and Family
  Studies
Director
Research and Training Center for
  Children's Mental Health
Florida Mental Health Institute
University of South Florida
13301 Bruce B. Downs Boulevard
Tampa, FL 33612

Barbara J. Friesen, Ph.D.
Director
Research and Training Center on
  Family Support and Children's
  Mental Health
Professor
Graduate School of Social Work
Portland State University
P.O. Box 751
Portland, OR 97207-0751

Sybil K. Goldman, M.S.W.
Associate Director
National Technical Assistance Center
  for Children's Mental Health
Georgetown University Child
  Development Center
3307 M Street, N.W.
Suite 401
Washington, DC 20007-3935

Paul E. Greenbaum, Ph.D.
Research Associate Professor
Research and Training Center for
  Children's Mental Health
Florida Mental Health Institute
13301 Bruce B. Downs Boulevard
Tampa, FL 33612

Mario Hernandez, Ph.D.
Research Associate Professor
Department of Child and Family
  Studies
Florida Mental Health Institute
13301 Bruce B. Downs Boulevard
Tampa, FL 33612

Barbara Huff
Executive Director
Federation of Families for Children's
  Mental Health
1021 Prince Street
Alexandria, VA 22314-2971

Susan Ignelzi, Ph.D.
Administrator
Office of the Governor
77 South High Street, 30th Floor
Columbus, OH 43215

Mareasa Isaacs-Shockley, Ph.D.
Partner
Human Service Collaborative
2262 Hall Place, N.W.
Suite 204
Washington, DC 20007

Judith Katz-Leavy, M.Ed.
Senior Policy Analyst
Office of Policy and Planning
Center for Mental Health Services
Substance Abuse and Mental Health
  Services Administration
Room 15-87 Parklawn Building
5600 Fishers Lane
Rockville, MD 20857

Marie L. Keefe, M.S.L.
Counterparts, Inc.
28 Fraude Circle
Cabin John, MD 20818

Betty King, M.S.
Associate Director
Annie E. Casey Foundation
701 St. Paul Street
Baltimore, MD 21202

Jane Knitzer, Ed.D.
Deputy Director
National Center for Children
  in Poverty
School of Public Health
Columbia University
154 Haven Avenue
New York, NY 10032

Paul E. Koren, Ph.D.
Research Associate
Research and Training Center on
  Family Support and Children's
  Mental Health
Portland State University
P.O. Box 751
Portland, OR 97207-0751

Nancy M. Koroloff, Ph.D.
Interim Director
Research and Training Center on
  Family Support and Children's
  Mental Health
Portland State University
P.O. Box 751
Portland, OR 97207-0751

Chris Koyanagi
Legislative Policy Director
Judge David L. Bazelon Center
Center for Mental Health Law
1101 15th Street, N.W.
Suite 1212
Washington, DC 20005

Krista Kutash, Ph.D.
Deputy Director
Research and Training Center for
  Children's Mental Health
Florida Mental Health Institute
13301 Bruce B. Downs Boulevard
Tampa, FL 33612

Ira S. Lourie, M.D.
Partner
Human Service Collaborative
2262 Hall Place, N.W.
Suite 204
Washington, DC 20007

Gary Macbeth, M.S.W., M.Ed.
125 Pinewood Place
Emerald Isle, NC 28594

Phyllis R. Magrab, Ph.D.
Director
Georgetown University Child
  Development Center
3307 M Street, N.W.
Suite 401
Washington, DC 20007

Mary McCormack, Ph.D.
Senior Scientist
Macro International, Inc.
3 Corporate Square, N.E.
Suite 370
Atlanta, GA 30329

Judith Meyers, Ph.D.
Senior Consultant
The Center for the Study of Social
  Policy
690 South Main
Geneva, NY 14456

Margaret Mezera, M.S.
Executive Director
Wisconsin Family Ties
16 North Carroll Street
Suite 630
Madison, WI 53703

Cappie C. Morgan
Counterparts, Inc.
6525 80th Street
Cabin John, MD 20818

Amelia T. Petrila, M.Ed.
Director
Community and Provider Relations
Florida Health Partnership
3014 U.S. Highway 301 North
Suite 1000
Tampa, FL 33619

Sheila A. Pires, M.P.A.
Partner
Human Service Collaborative
2262 Hall Place, N.W.
Suite 204
Washington, DC 20007

William A. Quinlan, Jr., M.P.A.
Public Health Advisor
Child, Adolescent and Family Branch
Center for Mental Health Services
Substance Abuse and Mental Health
    Services Administration
Room 11-C-17 Parklawn Building
5600 Fishers Lane
Rockville, MD 20857

Linda Reilly
Board President
Oregon Family Support Network
3668 SE Cooper
Portland, OR 97202

Judy Rinkin
Executive Director
Oregon Family Support Network
Oregon State Hospital
2600 Center Street, N.E.
Building 53, Room 207
Salem, OR 97310

Linda Roebuck
Southwest Regional Manager
Missouri Department of Mental Health
Division of Comprehensive Psychiatric
    Services
Southwest Regional Office
1515 East Pythian
P.O. Box 5030
Springfield, MO 65801

Judith Tolmach Silber, M.S.W.
Partner
Human Service Collaborative
2262 Hall Place, N.W.
Suite 204
Washington, DC 20007

Beth A. Stroul, M.Ed.
Vice President
Management and Training Innovations
6725 Curran Street
McLean, VA 22101

Wm. Thomas Summerfelt, Ph.D.
Research Associate
Center for Mental Health Policy
Vanderbilt University
1207 18th Avenue, South
Nashville, TN 37212

Naomi Tannen, M.S.
Consultant
Letsonville Road
Paradox, NY 12858

John VanDenBerg, Ph.D.
President
The Community Partnership Group
9715 Bellcrest Road
Pittsburgh, PA 15237

Michael Weber, A.M.
Director
Program for the Community Protection
    of Children
Chapin Hall Center for Children
University of Chicago
1313 East 60th Street
Chicago, IL 60637

Susan Yelton, M.S.W.
Project Director
Children First: A Global Forum
The Task Force for Child Survival and
    Development
The Carter Presidential Center
One Copenhill
Atlanta, GA 30307

Susan M. Zaro, M.P.H.
Vice President
Macro International, Inc.
3 Corporate Square, N.E.
Suite 370
Atlanta, GA 30329

Acknowledgments

This book brings together, in one volume, much of the conceptual development and practical experience achieved since the mid-1980s relative to systems of care for children with emotional disorders and their families. Given the magnitude of the undertaking, it follows that the work represents the combined effort of many individuals and organizations.

The children's mental health field owes a great debt of gratitude to Ira S. Lourie and Judith Katz-Leavy, who, in their roles at the National Institute of Mental Health, initiated the Child and Adolescent Service System Program and its attendant activities. Their leadership has been instrumental in the formation of an ever-growing network of individuals and organizations committed to the development of systems of care for children and families. Much of the work reflected in this volume is a direct result of their efforts and sponsorship at the federal level. I am pleased to acknowledge them for their vision and leadership as well as for their personal encouragement, unfailing support, and friendship over the years.

Federal efforts to assist states and communities to develop systems of care have continued under the auspices of the Child, Adolescent and Family Branch of the Center for Mental Health Services (CMHS), Substance Abuse and Mental Health Services Administration. The staff of the branch, under the direction of Gary DeCarolis, provide ongoing conceptual and financial support in the area of children's mental health to build on the efforts described in this book. I am pleased to recognize their vital contribution and thank them for their continuing leadership.

The role of CMHS has involved sponsoring a wide range of knowledge development and technical assistance activities. Three centers, all receiving federal support, have played critical roles. The work of the three centers comprises much of this volume and has contributed immeasurably to moving the field forward. I acknowledge with gratitude the expertise and contributions of the leaders and staff of the Research and Training Center for Children's Mental Health at the Florida Mental Health Institute, University of South Florida, under the direction of Robert M. Friedman, and the Research and Training Center on Family Support and Children's Mental Health at Portland State University, under the direction of Barbara J. Friesen. Special thanks are due to the National Technical Assistance Center for Children's Mental Health at the Georgetown University Child Development Center, under the leadership of Phyllis R. Magrab and Sybil K. Goldman. My affiliation with the National Technical Assistance Center has been a productive and rewarding one since its inception in 1984. Throughout the developmental stages of this volume, the center has provided both tangible and intangible supports. Deepest appreciation goes to my Georgetown colleagues for their stimulation and assistance, and particularly to Sybil K. Goldman, whose professional and personal support has meant more than words can express.

All of the chapter authors took time from their demanding schedules to contribute to this volume. It is their collective wisdom that will make this book a valuable resource to the field and will help to bring state-of-the-art ideas and approaches to students, practitioners, and policy makers. My warmest thanks to each of the contributing authors.

Members of the Editorial Advisory Board for this book series were extraordinarily helpful in reviewing individual chapters for this volume and in offering their insight and feedback. In particular, recognition and gratitude are due to Sheila A. Pires, Robert M. Friedman, Barbara J. Friesen, and Barbara J. Burns.

I am pleased to acknowledge the efforts and competence of the Paul H. Brookes Publishing Co. staff. Their assistance throughout the development of this volume has been of the highest caliber. I appreciate not only their guidance and skill, but also their excitement and commitment to continue working together to further develop the much-needed series, *Systems of Care for Children's Mental Health*. I look forward to working with Brookes and with my co-editor and long-time collaborator, Robert M. Friedman, on this series.

I also wish to acknowledge the children and their families who, on a daily basis, must cope with the challenges presented by emotional disturbances. It is their pain and courage that have inspired this work and all efforts to develop systems of care.

Finally, I am fortunate to have the unwavering support of my own family. Many thanks to Neil, Dana, and Adam Stroul and Adele Shapiro for their patience and love.

Beth A. Stroul, M.Ed.

Introduction
Progress in Children's Mental Health

Beth A. Stroul

A summary of epidemiological research conducted in the 1980s suggests that approximately 14%–20% of children ages 4–18 have some type of diagnosable mental disorder and about 7% of children in this age range have a serious disorder (Brandenburg, Friedman, & Silver, 1990). More recent research indicates that these percentages may be getting even higher (Achenbach & Howell, 1993; Kessler et al., 1994).

Calls for increased attention to the needs of youngsters with mental health disorders and their families date back to the Joint Commission on the Mental Health of Children (1969), which found that these children were typically unserved or served inappropriately in excessively restrictive settings. These findings were substantiated by numerous subsequent studies, task forces, commissions, and reports (President's Commission on Mental Health, 1978; U.S. Congress, Office of Technology Assessment, 1986).

A study published by the Children's Defense Fund, entitled *Unclaimed Children*, documented that, of the 3 million children with serious emotional disorders in this country, two thirds were not receiving the services they needed and many more were receiving inappropriate care (Knitzer, 1982). These youngsters were characterized as "unclaimed," essentially abandoned by the agencies responsible for helping them. All of these reports concurred that coordinated systems of care providing a range of services are required in order to serve these youngsters and their families effectively, and they called for concerted action to develop systems of care nationwide.

Since *Unclaimed Children* was published, remarkable progress has been achieved in improving services for children and adolescents with emotional disturbances and their families. This introduction provides a context for this book, *Children's Mental Health: Creating Systems of Care in a Changing Society*, by reviewing advances that have been achieved in the children's mental health field in a number of areas.

AREAS OF PROGRESS

Federal Leadership
In 1982, Knitzer referred to the federal role as the "unfulfilled promise," and federal leadership in the area of children's mental health was largely

missing. The few federal programs that were undertaken were either poorly funded or short lived.

As a result of a great deal of advocacy from a coalition of individuals and groups, Congress appropriated funds for a federal initiative in the area of child mental health. In 1984, the National Institute of Mental Health (NIMH) launched the Child and Adolescent Service System Program (CASSP), currently under the auspices of the Center for Mental Health Services (CMHS) of the Substance Abuse and Mental Health Services Administration, U.S. Department of Health and Human Services. The goal of the CASSP program is to assist states and communities to develop systems of care for children and youth with serious emotional disturbances. CASSP started with a very small appropriation of $1.5 million and initially provided funds to 10 states. Before its 10th anniversary, CASSP had involved all 50 states and a number of territories and had a budget that grew to almost $10 million.

CASSP is now one of a number of activities of the Child, Adolescent and Family Branch of the CMHS. In addition to providing funds to states, the branch funds local service demonstrations, research demonstrations, and family groups. A significant addition to federal children's mental health activities is the CMHS Child Mental Health Services Initiative, established in 1992, which provides grants to states and communities to develop a broad array of community-based services. This program, with a budget of $35 million in fiscal year 1994, has great potential to increase the availability of services and systems of care for children with emotional disorders.

In addition to these grant programs, a variety of technical assistance activities are supported by the Child, Adolescent and Family Branch, including the funding of three centers through interagency agreements: the National Technical Assistance Center for Children's Mental Health at Georgetown University, the Research and Training Center for Children's Mental Health at the University of South Florida, and the Research and Training Center on Family Support and Children's Mental Health at Portland State University.

Another example of federal leadership can be found in the State Comprehensive Mental Health Services Plan Act [PL 99-660]), passed in 1986, which requires states to plan for and implement community-based systems of services for persons with serious mental illness. In 1989, this law was amended to require that states not only plan for adults but submit plans and progress reports related to developing community-based systems of care for children. Most recently, the ADAMHA Reorganization Act (PL 102-321) makes comprehensive state mental health planning an integral part of the community mental health services block grant program. Plans and implementation reports focusing on both adults and children are now required as part of the application for community mental health block grant funds.

State plans and implementation progress are being reviewed with equal weight placed on progress in children's and adult's arenas, and penalties may be enforced for failure to implement plans for comprehensive community-based services for both populations.

State Leadership

With some noteworthy exceptions, at the time *Unclaimed Children* was published there was a serious gap in state-level leadership in children's mental health. In fact, in examining state mental health agencies, more than half of them (29 according to Knitzer) did not have a unit or even *one person* who focused on children.

Although it may have been a modest goal, every state mental health agency now has at least one person who is responsible for children's mental health. Many states have developed a unit of some type that is charged with the responsibility of planning and developing systems of care for children and their families (Davis, Yelton, & Katz-Leavy, 1993).

More effective leadership within states has translated into more effective national leadership. The State Mental Health Representatives for Children and Youth is a group that meets semiannually and is composed of the directors or coordinators of children's mental health services from each state. This organization plays a critical role in identifying and addressing the challenges that states face in improving systems of care.

System of Care Concept

From the time of the Joint Commission in 1969, there was a lot of discussion about a system of care for children, but much less clarity about what the system should encompass, how it might be organized, what components should comprise such a system, and what principles should guide service delivery. A project was initiated by CASSP to address these issues by adding greater definition to the system of care concept. The effort resulted in the publication of a monograph in 1986 entitled *A System of Care for Children and Youth with Severe Emotional Disturbances* (Stroul & Friedman, 1986). This document, which was revised and updated in 1994, has provided a conceptual framework for a system of care that has been widely used by states and communities to assist them in planning.

Also in 1986, the first national conference on systems of care for children was held in Boulder, Colorado. This inspiring event was dedicated to "Claiming the Unclaimed Children"; similar conferences have been sponsored by the National Technical Assistance Center at Georgetown University on a regular basis since that time.

Existence of Systems of Care

Services for children with emotional problems were clearly lacking. Many children were unserved, and many more received inappropriate services, often in excessively restrictive settings (Knitzer, 1982). Despite talk of systems of care, it was difficult to find even one example of a comprehensive, coordinated, community-based system of care.

In this area, dramatic progress has been achieved in a relatively short period of time. A number of demonstrations of systems of care have been undertaken. One of the first examples of a comprehensive community-based system of care was developed in Ventura County, California. This system development initiative was funded by the California legislature as a demonstration and is now being replicated in other areas in California (Stroul, Lourie, Goldman, & Katz-Leavy, 1992). While many struggled to find the resources to build systems of care, the Robert Wood Johnson Foundation launched a $20 million initiative in 1988, which has provided funds to eight communities to develop systems of care. These communities are demonstrating promising new ways of organizing and financing service systems (Cole & Poe, 1993).

Another demonstration is under way at Fort Bragg in North Carolina and is funded by the Civilian Health and Medical Program of the Uniformed Services. Fort Bragg has built a rich array of services and can teach a great deal about how to organize and operate a system of care (Behar, 1992). The Annie E. Casey Foundation also launched an initiative to develop systems of care. This initiative is focusing on urban neighborhoods, with the goal of bringing together all agencies and resources needed to improve outcomes for disadvantaged children.

There also have been noteworthy state initiatives to develop local systems of care, and progress is apparent in many states. Communities from the following states were selected to be part of a CASSP-sponsored descriptive study of well-developed local systems of care: California, Florida, Missouri, North Carolina, Ohio, Pennsylvania, Vermont, and Virginia (Stroul et al., 1992).

As noted, the federal government is now also funding system development following the 1992 passage of the ADAMHA Reorganization Act, which included an initiative to support the development of children's mental health services. The resulting CMHS Child, Adolescent, and Family Mental Health Services program provides funds for the development of a more complete service array in selected communities. Furthermore, health care reform may have far-reaching implications for system of care development by financing many of the services included in systems of care (Stroul, Pires, Katz-Leavy, & Goldman, 1994).

Interagency Collaboration

In 1982, there were very few attempts to collaborate among the numerous agencies that share responsibility for serving children with emotional disorders. It is axiomatic that troubled children have multiple needs and are served by education, child welfare, juvenile justice, health, mental health, substance abuse, mental retardation, and other agencies. Yet Knitzer (1982) found almost no attempts to get the range of child-serving agencies to work together either at the state or local level.

Changes began to take place when CASSP required an interagency approach to system improvement. A major boost to interagency approaches occurred when Governor Richard Celeste of Ohio issued an executive order that required all the state agencies to form an Interagency Cluster for Children. This cluster was to meet regularly to coordinate services across systems and also to review difficult cases that could not be resolved locally. The order also required that each county form a local cluster for system planning and coordination and for reviewing difficult cases. This order was translated into legislation in 1987 in Ohio, and there is similar legislation now in a number of other states.

Even where there is no legislative mandate, states and communities are creating interagency entities for system-level coordination. They are called Regional Interagency Councils, Local Coordinating Committees, Clusters, Local Interagency Teams, and other titles, and they can be found in communities ranging from Bennington, Vermont, to Ventura, California. Some of them are formalizing their structures into councils of government or corporations that can actually administer joint services. Some are beginning to pool funds to support the development of service components or to develop individualized care packages for youngsters and their families. They are overcoming longstanding turf battles among child-serving agencies, and they are proving that no one agency can meet the needs of troubled children in isolation, and that the collective efforts of child-serving agencies can be extremely effective in promoting the development of local systems of care.

Additional evidence of interagency coordination can be found in how services are planned for individual youngsters and their families. Many communities are now creating interagency teams, specific to each child, which comprise the providers and other persons most involved and influential in the child's life. The teams include the parents and youngsters themselves, depending on their ages and maturity levels. The teams are used to develop comprehensive, individualized service plans for the child and family and may meet as needed to monitor progress and reconfigure the plan based on the child's changing needs.

Knowledge About Innovative Services

The services that were available in the past were typically outpatient, inpatient, and residential treatment. Knitzer (1982) cited examples of some innovative service delivery approaches that were found scattered in a few communities around the country that provide home-based services, intensive case management, day treatment, and family support. These approaches showed promise but were known to few people in the field, and there was little or no information on how to develop and operate these services.

Since that time, there has been a tremendous growth in information and technical assistance materials about these types of services. A study of community-based services conducted by the National Technical Assistance Center at Georgetown University led to documents on home-based services, crisis services, and therapeutic foster care (Goldman, 1988; Stroul, 1988, 1989). The Research and Training Centers at the University of South Florida and Portland State University have studied and developed materials on respite, case management, transition services for older adolescents, and other services. The publication lists from these three centers alone provide a wealth of information to support system development activities, and many other organizations and entities now offer information on community-based services for children. Although all of these services are not as yet universally available, they are expanding rapidly throughout the country.

There also have been tremendous advances in techniques for providing individualized services. States including Alaska, Vermont, Idaho, and Washington have demonstrated that individualized care is a viable and highly effective approach, particularly for youngsters with the most serious and complex disorders. Individualized care can be achieved by finding or creating all the services and supports needed by a child and family, with no limits to creativity, to design a service package that is tailored to their unique needs (Katz-Leavy, Lourie, Stroul, & Zeigler-Dendy, 1992). The use of the individualized or "wraparound" services approach is expanding rapidly in both urban and rural environments.

Family Involvement

Even though parents are most often the primary caregivers for children with emotional problems, they historically have been blamed, isolated, frustrated, disenfranchised, and given the runaround from agency to agency and provider to provider. Service delivery agencies typically were not committed to supporting family functioning, to preserving families, or to helping families cope with the demands of a troubled child. Furthermore, families often were forced to relinquish custody in order to obtain expensive but needed residential treatment for their children, a practice that is still a tragic reality for many families. In 1982, families were not involved as full participants in planning and delivering services, either for their own children or at the system level.

Perhaps the greatest change has been achieved in this area. What social scientists refer to as a "paradigm shift" has occurred with respect to families. Rather than being seen as part of the problem, the cause of the problem, resistant, incompetent, or otherwise dysfunctional, families are increasingly seen as the single most important resource for a child; they are increasingly viewed as "allies" and "full partners." Policy makers and providers increasingly recognize that even the most troubled families have strengths that can be built on during the helping process. Furthermore, it is becoming more widely acknowledged and accepted that parents must be full partners not only in planning and delivering services for their own child but also in planning and overseeing services at the system level.

How has this paradigm shift occurred? Most significant in creating this shift in thinking have been the parents who have come forward, who have told their stories, and who have insisted that providers and bureaucrats listen. Parent organizations are developing in many communities and are beginning to form into statewide organizations. In fact, since 1988, CASSP has provided financial support and technical assistance to parent groups to assist them in forming statewide parent organizations. Two national parent organizations have been organized—the Federation of Families for Children's Mental Health and the National Alliance for the Mentally Ill Child and Adolescent Network (NAMI CAN). Furthermore, parents are now serving on mental health boards, advisory committees, boards of directors, and planning councils, with their input considered to be critical in developing and improving systems of care.

This process also was spurred by the fact that CASSP established the goal of family involvement and participation as a major area of emphasis for all its grantees. "Families as Allies" meetings, organized by the Portland Research and Training Center, were held all over the country to bring delegations of parents and professionals together to learn how to collaborate. Parent–professional teams have been trained and are available to provide technical assistance to others.

Cultural Competence

Children of color constitute a disproportionately large percentage of the target population of youngsters with emotional disorders, yet rarely did providers consider the unique needs created by ethnic, racial, and cultural differences. There were very few examples of programs or agencies that designed their services and procedures to respond to the cultural characteristics of the populations they served. Even if the need for cultural competence was recognized, there was little knowledge about how to achieve it. The "state of the art" in thinking about and improving cultural competence was at a very rudimentary stage.

In 1987, CASSP began a minority initiative and formed a Minority Initiative Resource Committee to implement this effort. Since then, the state of the art for achieving culturally competent systems of care has advanced dramatically. Progress started with a monograph defining what it means to have a culturally competent system of care (Cross, Bazron, Dennis, & Isaacs,

1989). Programs in the field that provide culturally competent services were subsequently identified, and representatives of these programs served as faculty at the 1990 Training Institutes organized by the National Technical Assistance Center at Georgetown and entitled "Toward Culturally Competent Systems of Care for Children of Color." A monograph describing and profiling these programs and agencies was prepared and has helped to operationalize the concept of cultural competence and to show others what can and must be done to adequately serve children and families of color (Isaacs & Benjamin, 1992). Although much remains to be done in this area, states and communities have begun to provide training on cultural competence, to recruit minority staff, to examine their system policies and approaches, and to otherwise begin the process of building systems of care that are culturally competent.

Research

Although there was clinical research in the area of children's services, there was virtually no research on some of the more innovative service delivery approaches. Because there were few, if any, examples of community-based systems of care, there was no research that examined the outcomes and benefits of systems of care.

The need for research in children's mental health was underscored by a report prepared by the Institute of Medicine (1989) that recommended a comprehensive plan to support and stimulate growth in the field of child mental health research. In response, NIMH developed a plan for children's mental health research (National Institute of Mental Health, 1990). As a result of a great deal of input from the field, the plan includes a section about research on services and systems of care. Vast increases in both attention to and funding for research on services and systems of care for children are evident both at NIMH and at CMHS.

Additionally, a number of important studies can now be identified that are exploring comprehensive, community-based systems of care, including an evaluation of the Ventura County demonstration and replications in California (conducted by the University of California at San Francisco), an evaluation of the Fort Bragg Demonstration Project (conducted by Vanderbilt University), and an evaluation of the Robert Wood Johnson Foundation's Mental Health Services Program for Youth (conducted by Brandeis University). A national evaluation of the CMHS Child Mental Health Services Initiative will focus on a set of core indicators across all of the federally funded sites.

An important annual event is the research conference sponsored by the Florida Research and Training Center. Each year, increasing numbers of researchers, policy makers, and practitioners gather in Tampa to learn the most up-to-date information and findings emanating from research on systems of care. The growing number and quality of the presentations at the research conference each year is evidence of how far the field has progressed in expanding the research base for systems of care.

Advocacy

Adults with serious and persistent mental illness found their advocacy voice through the National Alliance for the Mentally Ill, the National Mental Health Association, and consumer groups such as the National Mental Health Consumers Association and the National Association of Psychiatric Survivors. Children, however, did not have a strong and persistent advocacy voice at national, state, or local levels.

In all likelihood, it is the progress in the area of advocacy that is responsible for most of the progress in other areas. Existing advocacy groups have become increasingly involved in issues related to children's mental health. They have focused national meetings (some for the first time) on children. They have attempted to educate their memberships on the needs of children and the importance of systems of care. They have sponsored studies to highlight some of the problems and needs. They have focused lobbying activities on children's mental health issues, and they have assumed leadership and joined in coalitions to promote the development of systems of care. These groups include the National Mental Health Association, the Bazelon Center for Mental Health Law, the National Alliance for the Mentally Ill, the National Council of Community Mental Health Centers, and the Children's Defense Fund. One advocacy activity deserving special mention is the Invisible Children Project sponsored by the National Mental Health Association. This project focused on children in state hospitals and out-of-state placements, and developed a campaign to bring these children home (National Mental Health Association, 1989).

In addition to increased attention from existing advocacy groups, new advocacy groups have been formed for the sole purpose of advocating on behalf of children and adolescents with serious emotional disturbances. Although these groups are relatively new, they already have had a major impact on the field. The Federation of Families for Children's Mental Health and NAMI CAN, both formed in 1989, are playing prominent roles in shaping our nation's policy in the field of children's mental health. There can be no doubt about the critical role of advocacy in promoting development of local systems of care. It is advocacy that has been responsible for progress, and it is only through advocacy that we will be able to continue this progress in the coming years (Friedman, Duchnowski, & Henderson, 1989).

OVERVIEW OF THE BOOK

This volume is organized into five sections. Section I offers a new paradigm for systems of care and describes fundamental aspects of the system of care concept and philosophy. Included is a discussion of the core values, guiding principles, dimensions, and service components for systems of care in Chapter 1 and a description of a framework for conceptualizing and achieving culturally competent systems of care in Chapter 2. Chapter 3 further describes the concept of a family-centered system of care and discusses the needs and preferences of families for service delivery and systems of care based on a national survey. Chapter 4 discusses the population of concern, including definitions and recent epidemiological findings.

Section II reviews efforts to develop systems of care that have been undertaken at federal, state, and local levels. It begins with a review of federal activities in the area of children's mental health, including the CASSP program and the Child Mental Health Services Initiative, in Chapter 5. Chapters 6 and 7 focus on the role of the state, providing an overview of strategies used by states to promote system development and a case study of the system development approach used in Virginia. Similarly, local system development is described by first presenting a summary of system development efforts in a range of communities that were included in a descriptive study of local systems of care (Chapter 8), followed by a detailed discussion of the evolution and organization of the system of care in Ventura County, California (Chapter 9).

Section II continues with discussions, in Chapters 10 and 11, of the role of two major child-serving systems—education and child welfare—in systems of care. Finally, Chapters 12 and 13 describe the system-building initiatives sponsored by the Robert Wood Johnson Foundation and the Annie E. Casey Foundation. The philosophy, approach, progress achieved, and lessons learned from each of these initiatives are reviewed.

Section III focuses on a number of management issues that affect the development and operation of systems of care. Service coordination is discussed in Chapter 14, with an emphasis on the role and principles of case management in local systems of care. Chapter 15 focuses on human resource development and discusses workforce issues and needs that have a major impact on the ability to implement services and systems of care as well as on the quality of services provided. Trends in financing systems of care are described in Chapter 16, and a framework for evaluating systems of care is presented in Chapter 17. The final chapter in this section, Chapter 18, focuses on research on local systems of care, both summarizing the growth of research in this area and describing the evaluation of the children's mental health demonstration at Fort Bragg, North Carolina.

Family involvement in systems of care is the focus of Section IV. The evolution of the rapidly growing family movement is reviewed in Chapter 19, which also discusses the development and priorities of the two national family organizations. Chapter 20 discusses the range of roles that families can and should play within systems of care both in relation to their own children and at the system level, while Chapter 21 details a local system of care in rural New York State that has been conceptualized, planned, and implemented by families of youngsters with emotional disorders. Chapter 22 presents issues and strategies for parents and professionals to work together as allies in all aspects of the planning and delivery of services.

Section V of the volume examines service delivery within systems of care, exploring general service delivery issues as well as issues and approaches specific to particular subpopulations of youngsters. Chapter 23 discusses the concept of individualizing services and the vast potential of this approach for serving youngsters with the most serious and complex problems. Chapter 24 describes the major features of two innovative community-based service approaches based on the results of a descriptive study—home-based services and therapeutic foster care. Chapter 25 describes aspects of a number of agencies and programs that exemplify the principles of cultural competence, thus showing how these principles can be operationalized to better serve children of color and their families. Service delivery for youngsters with the dual diagnoses of emotional disturbance and substance abuse is considered in Chapter 26, while the succeeding chapters examine serving homeless and runaway youth (Chapter 27), older adolescents who are in transition to adulthood (Chapter 28), young children with or at high risk for emotional disorders (Chapter 29), and children with special health care needs (Chapter 30). The volume concludes with a discussion of factors that are likely to affect the development and maintenance of systems of care for children with emotional disorders in the future.

REFERENCES

Achenbach, T.M., & Howell, C.T. (1993). Are American children's problems getting worse? A 13-year comparison. *Journal of the American Academy of Child and Adolescent Psychiatry, 32,* 1145–1154.

ADAMHA Reorganization Act, PL 102-321. (July 10, 1992). Title 42, U.S.C. 201 et seq: *U.S. Statutes at Large, 106,* 323.

Behar, L. (1992). *Fort Bragg Child and Adolescent Mental Health Demonstration Project.* Raleigh: North Carolina Division of Mental Health, Developmental Disabilities, and Substance Abuse Services, Child and Family Services Branch.

Brandenburg, N., Friedman, R., & Silver, S. (1990). The epidemiology of childhood psychiatric disorders: Prevalence findings from recent studies. *Journal of the American Academy of Child and Adolescent Psychiatry, 29,* 76–83.

Cole, R., & Poe, S. (1993). *Partnerships for care—systems of care for children with serious emotional disturbances and their families.* Washington, DC: Washington Business Group on Health, Mental Health Services Program for Youth.

Cross, T., Bazron, B., Dennis, K., & Isaacs, M. (1989). *Towards a culturally competent system of care: Vol. I. A monograph on effective services for minority children who are severely emotionally disturbed.* Washington, DC: Georgetown University Child Development Center, National Technical Assistance Center for Children's Mental Health.

Davis, M., Yelton, S., & Katz-Leavy, J. (1993). *Unclaimed children revisited: The status of state children's mental health services.* Paper presented to the Sixth Annual Research Conference: A System of Care for Children's Mental Health: Expanding the Research Base, Tampa, FL.

Friedman, R., Duchnowski, A., & Henderson, E. (1989). *Advocacy on behalf of children with serious emotional problems.* Springfield, IL: Charles C Thomas.

Goldman, S. (1988). *Series on community-based services for children and adolescents who are severely emotionally disturbed: Vol. II. Crisis services*. Washington, DC: Georgetown University Child Development Center, National Technical Assistance Center for Children's Mental Health.

Institute of Medicine. (1989). *Research on children and adolescents with mental, behavioral, & developmental disorders*. Washington, DC: National Academy Press.

Isaacs, M., & Benjamin, M. (1992). *Towards a culturally competent system of care: Vol. II. Programs which utilize culturally competent principles*. Washington, DC: Georgetown University Child Development Center. National Technical Assistance Center for Children's Mental Health.

Joint Commission on the Mental Health of Children. (1969). *Crisis in child mental health*. New York: Harper & Row.

Katz-Leavy, J., Lourie, I., Stroul, B., & Zeigler-Dendy, C. (1992). *Individualized services in a system of care*. Washington, DC: Georgetown University Child Development Center, National Technical Assistance Center for Children's Mental Health.

Kessler, R.C., McGonagle, K.A., Zhao, S., Nelson, C.B., Hughes, M., Eshleman, S., Wittchen, H., & Kendler, K.S. (1994). Lifetime and 12-month prevalence of DSM-III-R psychiatric disorders in the United States. *Archives of General Psychiatry, 51*, 8–19.

Knitzer, J. (1982). *Unclaimed children: The failure of public responsibility to children and adolescents in need of mental health services*. Washington, DC: Children's Defense Fund.

National Institute of Mental Health. (1990). *National plan for research on child and adolescent mental disorders*. Rockville, MD: U.S. Department of Health and Human Services.

National Mental Health Association. (1989). *Invisible children project: Resource kit*. Alexandria, VA: Author.

President's Commission on Mental Health. (1978). *Report of the sub-task panel on infants, children, and adolescents*. Washington, DC: Author.

State Comprehensive Mental Health Services Plan Act, PL 99-660. (November 14, 1986). Title 42, U.S.C. 300x et seq: *U.S. Statutes at Large, 100*, 3794–3797.

Stroul, B. (1988). *Series on community-based services for children and adolescents who are severely emotionally disturbed: Vol. I. Home-based services*. Washington, DC: Georgetown University Child Development Center, National Technical Assistance Center for Children's Mental Health.

Stroul, B. (1989). *Series on community-based services for children and adolescents who are severely emotionally disturbed: Vol. III. Therapeutic foster care*. Washington, DC: Georgetown University Child Development Center, National Technical Assistance Center for Children's Mental Health.

Stroul, B.A., & Friedman, R.M. (1986). *A system of care for children and youth with severe emotional disturbances (rev. ed.)*. Washington, DC: Georgetown University Child Development Center, National Technical Assistance Center for Children's Mental Health.

Stroul, B., Lourie, I., Goldman, S., & Katz-Leavy, J. (1992). *Profiles of local systems of care for children and adolescents with severe emotional disturbances*. Washington, DC: Georgetown University Child Development Center, National Technical Assistance Center for Children's Mental Health.

Stroul, B., Pires, S., Katz-Leavy, J., & Goldman, S. (1994). Implications of the Health Security Act for mental health services for children and adolescents. *Hospital and Community Psychiatry, 459*, 877–882.

U.S. Congress, Office of Technology Assessment. (1986). *Children's mental health: Problems and services—a background paper*. Washington, DC: Author.

*This book is dedicated
to the memory of my father, Sidney Shapiro,
who devoted his life
to nurturing and educating children
and to bringing music into their lives.*

Children's Mental Health

A New Paradigm for Systems of Care

CHAPTER 1

The System of Care Concept and Philosophy

Beth A. Stroul and Robert M. Friedman

From the time of the Joint Commission on the Mental Health of Children in 1969, there has been a great deal of discussion about a system of care for children and adolescents with serious emotional disturbances and their families. However, until recently there was little clarity about such systems of care—how they might be organized, which agencies should be involved, what services should be provided, and what values and principles should guide service delivery. A project sponsored by the Child and Adolescent Service System Program (CASSP), formerly part of the National Institute of Mental Health and currently within the Center for Mental Health Services, was undertaken to define the system of care concept and philosophy in order to provide states and communities with a conceptual framework and model for planning and developing service systems for this population.

SYSTEM OF CARE VALUES AND PRINCIPLES

One of the most important results from this effort is the recognition that the concept of a system of care represents more than a network of individual service components. Rather, the system of care represents a *philosophy* about the way in which services should be delivered to children and their families. The actual components and organizational configuration of the system of care may differ from state to state and from community to community. Despite such differences, the system of care should be guided by a set of basic values and operational philosophies. It is critical that these values be clearly articulated so that they may be used to guide the character and quality of the system of care.

Not surprisingly, there is general agreement in the field and in the literature as to the values and philosophy that should be embodied in the system of care for children with serious emotional disturbances. With input and consultation from the field, including policy makers, parents, administrators, researchers, advocates, and providers, two core values and a set of 10 principles were selected to provide a philosophical framework for the system of care model.

Since the selection of the original core values, the field has moved to a greater recognition of the central role of cultural competence in the development of a system of care. A monograph describing the concept of cultural competence and establishing a framework for it was published in 1989 (Cross, Bazron, Dennis, & Isaacs, 1989) and has played a major role in promoting the development of culturally competent systems of care. In recognition of the importance of cultural competence, a third core value that specifically addresses this area has been added to the original two.

Core Values

The core values are central to the system of care and its operation. The first value is that the system of care must be driven by the needs of the child and his or her family. In other words, the system of care must be *child centered and family focused*, with the needs of the child and family dictating the types and mix of services provided. This child-centered and family-focused approach is seen as a commitment to adapt services to the child and family, rather than expecting children and families to conform to pre-existing service configurations. It is also seen as a commitment to providing services in an environment and a manner that enhances the personal dignity of children and families, respects their wishes and individual goals, and maximizes opportunities for involvement and self-determination in the planning and delivery of services.

Implicit in this value is a commitment to serving the child in the context of the family. In most cases, parents are the primary caregivers for children with serious emotional disturbances, and the system of care should support and assist parents in this role as well as involve parents in all decisions regarding service delivery. The system of care should also have a strong and explicit commitment to preserve the integrity of the family unit whenever possible. In many cases, intensive services involving the child and family can minimize the need for out-of-home treatment. Thus, a child-centered system of care is also a family-focused system of care.

The second core value holds that the system of care for children with emotional disturbances should be *community based*. Historically, services for this population have been limited to state hospitals, training schools, and other restrictive institutional facilities. There has been increasing interest and progress in serving such children in community-based programs that offer less restrictive, more normative environments. The system of care embraces the philosophy of a community-based network of services for youth with emotional disturbances and their families. Although "institutional" care may be indicated for certain children at various points in time, in many cases appropriate services can be provided in other, less restrictive settings within or close to the child's home community.

The notion of a community-based system of care extends beyond the actual services and includes the control and management of the system. Decisions about the mix of services to be offered, service coordination mechanisms, and use of resources should be made at the community level in cooperation with state government. Such flexibility and decision-making authority encourages communities to accept responsibility for serving their youngsters.

The third core value asserts that the system of care should be *culturally competent*, with agencies, programs, and services that are responsive to the cultural, racial, and ethnic differences of the populations they serve. Most child-serving agencies and systems have not addressed the structural barriers and value differences encountered by ethnic minorities, resulting in frustration, anger, and disappointment for children of color and their families (Isaacs & Benjamin, 1991). The need to create culturally competent systems of care assumes greater urgency in view of the changing demographics of the American population, with whites continuing to decline as a proportion of the population and ethnic minorities growing. Furthermore, a number of external stressors have been found to place ethnic minority children at increased risk for emotional disorders. Thus, children of color are likely to comprise an increasing proportion of the country's population of youth and an even larger proportion of youngsters receiving mental health and other services from child-serving agencies.

The concept of cultural competence is inherent in the concept of a system that emphasizes child-centered, family-focused, and community-based care. These values dictate that children and families be served within their own unique and specific contexts. Culture and ethnicity comprise a significant part of the context for children of color and their families. Isaacs and Benjamin (1991) emphasize that ethnicity shapes beliefs about what constitutes mental health and mental illness, manifestations of symptoms and patterns of coping, help-seeking patterns, and use of and response to treatment. Thus, the critical importance of culture and ethnicity necessitates the development of culturally competent systems of care.

The implementation of this value requires careful attention to such factors as location of services, culturally sensitive assessments, emphasis on the family, staffing patterns, training, and use of natural helpers. Achieving cultural competence is seen as a developmental process that involves adaptations at policy-making, administrative, and practice levels to ensure that the system of care is sensitive and responsive to the unique needs of the populations served (Cross et al., 1989).

Principles

In addition to these three fundamental values for the system of care, 10 principles have been identified that enunciate other basic beliefs about the optimal nature of the system of care. The values and principles are displayed in Table 1.1, and each principle is briefly discussed below.

1. *Children with emotional disturbances should have access to a comprehensive array of services that address their physical, emotional, social, and educational needs.* It is axiomatic that children and their families should have access to comprehensive services across physical, emotional, social, and educational domains. The Joint Commission on the Mental Health of Children (1969), the President's Commission on Mental Health (1978), and innumerable child mental health experts and advocates have stressed the conviction that a complete and comprehensive network of ser-

Table 1.1.   Values and principles for the system of care

Core Values

1. The system of care should be child centered and family focused, with the needs of the child and family dictating the types and mix of services provided.
2. The system of care should be community based, with the locus of services as well as management and decision-making responsibility resting at the community level.
3. The system of care should be culturally competent, with agencies, programs, and services that are responsive to the cultural, racial, and ethnic differences of the populations they serve.

Guiding Principles

1. Children with emotional disturbances should have access to a comprehensive array of services that address their physical, emotional, social, and educational needs.
2. Children with emotional disturbances should receive individualized services in accordance with the unique needs and potentials of each child and guided by an individualized service plan.
3. Children with emotional disturbances should receive services within the least restrictive, most normative environment that is clinically appropriate.
4. The families and surrogate families of children with emotional disturbances should be full participants in all aspects of the planning and delivery of services.
5. Children with emotional disturbances should receive services that are integrated, with linkages between child-serving agencies and programs and mechanisms for planning, developing, and coordinating services.
6. Children with emotional disturbances should be provided with case management or similar mechanisms to ensure that multiple services are delivered in a coordinated and therapeutic manner and that they can move through the system of services in accordance with their changing needs.
7. Early identification and intervention for children with emotional disturbances should be promoted by the system of care in order to enhance the likelihood of positive outcomes.
8. Children with emotional disturbances should be ensured smooth transitions to the adult service system as they reach maturity.
9. The rights of children with emotional disturbances should be protected, and effective advocacy efforts for children and adolescents with emotional disturbances should be promoted.
10. Children with emotional disturbances should receive services without regard to race, religion, national origin, sex, physical disability, or other characteristics, and services should be sensitive and responsive to cultural differences and special needs.

From Stroul, B., & Friedman, R. (1986). *A system of care for children and youth with severe emotional disturbances* (rev. ed., p. 17). Washington, DC: Georgetown University Child Development Center, National Technical Assistance Center for Children's Mental Health; reprinted by permission.

vices is necessary to meet the multidimensional needs of children and families.

Although youngsters with emotional disorders require specialized mental health services, these services are insufficient to promote proper growth and development. Mental health services can be effective only within the context of a larger child-caring network that is responsible for meeting the child's health, educational, recreational, family support, and vocational needs. Thus, the scope and array of services included in the system of care must be sufficiently broad to account for the diverse needs of the developing child. As noted by Lourie and Katz-Leavy (1986), proper care relies on proper balance and integration of services in the various domains.

2. Children with emotional disturbances should receive individualized services in accordance with the unique needs and potentials of each child and guided by an individualized service plan. Each child and family served by the system of care has unique and changing needs. These needs are related to differences in age, developmental stage, level of functioning or degree of impairment, and include special needs resulting from physical disabilities, racial or ethnic background, or other factors. Thus, the types, mix, and intensity of services must be determined for each child and family. Again, one of the basic philosophical tenets of the system of care is that children should not be expected to conform to the service system, but that services should be designed and configured to fit the child's needs.

In order to individualize services, a comprehensive diagnostic and assessment process must be an integral part of the delivery of services. The assessment process offers the opportunity to consider the child's strengths and problems, level of functioning, age and developmental stage, and any special needs that bear on service delivery. The assessment process should be "ecological," considering the child in the context of the family, school, and other relevant environments.

The culmination of the assessment process should be an individualized service plan that identifies problems, establishes goals, and specifies appropriate interventions. The individualized service plan should address the child's needs across all the major systems of care dimensions—mental health, social, educational, health, substance abuse, vocational, recreational, and operational services. Some communities have begun using multiagency teams convened by the case manager to develop a comprehensive service plan that applies across agencies and does not narrowly focus on one dimension.

The individualized service plan should be developed with the full participation of the child, family, providers, and significant others. Children and families should retain the greatest possible degree of control over their own lives, participating in the setting of their own treatment goals and in the planning and evaluation of interventions to reach those goals. Additionally, goals and expectations developed in the assessment and service planning process should be realistic and based on a thorough knowledge and acceptance of the child and family. Unrealistic goals may doom the interventions to failure and cause needless frustration for the child and family. Service goals should be regularly reassessed and revised based on the dynamic nature of the strengths, weaknesses, and needs of the child and family.

The concept of individualized services has been given new meaning over the past several years based on experiments in states including Alaska, Vermont, Washington, and Idaho (Katz-Leavy, Lourie, Stroul, & Zeigler-Dendy, 1992). The approach has involved constructing a service plan for a child and family and using flexible funds to develop a package of services and supports that are specifically tailored to address each child's and family's unique needs. This may involve enlisting existing resources in the community as well as purchasing or designing services and supports for one particular child and family. The concept of providing individualized services, also referred to as "wraparound" services, has been used in many types of environments but has been particularly successful in rural areas where services are scarce. The types of wraparound services and supports that can be provided through this approach are constrained only by the limits of the creativity of those developing the service plan. Examples of the types of wraparound services provided include training an aide in a remote village in Alaska to provide day treatment for one youngster; hiring behavioral aides, professional roommates, or mentors for the home or classroom; providing special recreational or vocational services; and purchasing reinforcers. These individually tailored service packages, designed to "surround" the child and family with a full network of resources based on their needs and wishes, are increasingly being used for youngsters with the most serious disorders.

3. Children with emotional disturbances should receive services within the least restrictive, most normative environment that is clinically appropriate. Children and adolescents should be served in as normal an environment as possible. Preferred interventions are those that provide the needed services and, at the same time, are minimally intrusive in the normal day-to-day routine of the child and family. An implicit goal of the system of care is to maintain as many children as possible in their own homes by providing a full range of family-focused and community-based services and supports. In too many cases, children are removed from their homes or placed in environments that are more restrictive than they actually need. Although out-of-home or protective placements may be indicated some of the time, frequently they are used because less restrictive, community-based alternatives are not available. Accumulating evidence indicates that, when a comprehensive system of care is available, many children with serious emotional disturbances can be maintained within their own homes and communities (Behar, 1985, 1986; Friedman & Street, 1985; Stroul, 1988, 1993).

It also is evident that the needs of a small percentage of youth with emotional disturbances cannot always be met in the less restrictive settings. In these cases, even intensive nonresidential services may not meet the therapeutic needs of the child and family, and it may not be in the child's best interest to remain with the family. Residential services should be employed *only* when more normative, nonresidential options are not effective. In these situations, residential services should be provided in the least restrictive setting possible, with the goal of rapid reintegration into the family or achievement of a stable, permanent placement.

Within the residential arena, there are a range of more normative options that attempt to approximate the child's natural environment. For example, therapeutic foster homes and family-style group homes create a family-type atmosphere and allow children to attend public schools and to remain involved in community activities. According to Friedman, these services have more potential for helping youngsters realize the goal of returning to their own family and school than do residential services that cut youngsters off from normalized family and educational environments (Friedman, 1983; Stroul, 1989).

By the same token, residential services, when indicated, should be located as close as possible to the child's home in order to cause the least disruption of the child's links to family, friends, agencies, school, and community. Services located close to home maximize the possibility of family involvement in the treatment process and are more likely to prepare the child for successful reintegration into the natural environment.

It must be acknowledged that there may be situations in which treatment in institutional settings is appropriate. In these cases, a child may need highly specialized services that are not reproducible in a community setting. Behar reported, however, that in North Carolina less than 7% of the most difficult target population (those certified as belonging to the "Willie M." class, which includes children and adolescents with serious mental, emotional, or neurological disabilities who are also violent and assaultive) is in secure treatment settings, including public and private hospitals and secure residential treatment centers, and that these placements are considered appropriate to the needs of the youngsters. The North Carolina data suggest that the vast majority of youth with serious emotional disturbances can be served in less restrictive, community-based settings, given the appropriate continuum of services and supports (Behar, 1985, 1986).

4.   *The families and surrogate families of children with emotional disturbances should be full participants in all aspects of the planning and delivery of services.*   The system of care for children with emotional disturbances should promote and encourage the involvement of families, be they natural or surrogate families. Parents and families should not be passive participants, but should be actively consulted and involved in all decision making about the child and services. Thus, the system of care should have a strong family orientation.

The President's Commission on Mental Health (1978) concluded that

> Mental health services for children must also be delivered within a system of care that insofar as possible promotes and maintains a continuing relationship between child and family. . . . We recommend that parents be partners with providers in determining a plan of treatment for every severely disturbed or handicapped child. (p. 615)

Similarly, Lourie and Katz-Leavy (1986) noted that parents are the most important resource for the child and must be given the necessary support to fulfill that role.

In order to establish parents as partners in the system of care, they should be involved in all phases of service delivery for their children, including assessment, development of the individualized service plan, service provision, service coordination, and evaluation of progress. In addition, an array of services and supports should be offered to parents and families to enhance their coping skills and their ability to care for their children effectively. These services include parent support, parent education, counseling, respite services, home aid services, and others. Recently, a number of innovative models have been developed for providing these services and supports to families. There is increasing evidence that, when adequate family support is available, many families are able to maintain children with serious emotional disturbances at home and avoid placement in residential or institutional settings.

Even when children are in out-of-home placements, the participation and involvement of parents should be encouraged. In fact, family needs are most often neglected when children are in residential settings as a result of distance or other factors. Outreach efforts should be made to contact families and engage them constructively in the service delivery process. By involving and providing supports to families, the opportunities for successful return of the child to the family are maximized. Furthermore, families should not be forced to relinquish legal custody in order to obtain expensive but needed residential treatment for their children.

Although family involvement is the goal, no child should be denied services because he or she has no traditional family or the family refuses participation. When the natural family is not involved, the system of care should engage the surrogate or substitute family in services. When this is not possible, a strategy appropriate to the youngster's particular situation should be devised.

The principle of family involvement applies not only to participation in planning and delivering services for the family's own children but to participation of the family at the system level as well. Families should be involved as full partners in policy making, planning, priority setting, and evaluating the overall system of care for children with emotional disturbances in their communities. Only when parents are active participants in decision making both for their own youngsters *and* for the overall service system will they be full partners in the system of care.

5. Children with emotional disturbances should receive services that are integrated, with linkages between child-serving agencies and programs and mechanisms for planning, developing, and coordinating services. Although states and communities may be developing more comprehensive services for children and adolescents with serious emotional disturbances, this does not ensure coordination of services or continuity of care. Nor does it ensure that the system will be able to respond to the changing service needs of children and their families. Coordination, continuity, and movement within the system are critical for youth with serious emotional disturbances who have multiple needs that cut across agency boundaries. In order to best meet the needs of children and families, *integrated, multiagency networks of services* are needed to blend the services provided by mental health, education, child welfare, health, substance abuse, juvenile justice, and other agencies. In short, the various components must be interwoven into a coherent and effective system.

In order to achieve the goal of an integrated, community-based system of care, a range of functions should be shared among the key child-serving systems. Planning, program development, administration, funding, delivering, coordinating, and evaluating services are some of the functions that should be coordinated among the agencies and programs linking together to serve children with serious emotional disturbances and their families. Furthermore, the system should be flexible in decision making and funding to allow it to respond to changing programmatic needs in the community. Many communities have created interagency entities comprised of the executives of the major child-serving systems to fulfill these system-level coordination functions. These groups focus on matters of policy, planning, resource distribution, program development, problem solving, and other strategic issues to improve the system of care for troubled children and families (Stroul, Lourie, Goldman, & Katz-Leavy, 1992).

Another critical system-level coordination function is the capacity to review difficult cases that cannot be resolved through other mechanisms within the system of care. This interagency case review and problem-solving function may be handled by the same executive-level interagency entities or by other interagency structures created in communities for this particular purpose.

6. *Children with emotional disturbances should be provided with case management or similar mechanisms to ensure that multiple services are delivered in a coordinated and therapeutic manner and that they can move through the system of services in accordance with their changing needs.* Case management has been called the backbone of the system of care and is essential to the success of the service system. Case management, therapeutic case advocacy, and a variety of similar approaches are intended to ensure that children and families receive the services they need, that services are coordinated, and that services are appropriate to their changing needs over time. Lourie and Katz-Leavy (1986) assert that without "a primary service person responsible for the coordination of the treatment plan, it is nearly impossible to assure adequate services and proper placement for an individual severely emotionally disturbed child or adolescent" (p. 169). Clearly, the case management function is critical for the effective operation of the system of care.

The organizational location of the case manager or service coordinator cannot be predetermined. It should be determined by the needs of individual children and families and by the structure and resources of the system of care within a particular community. The role of the case manager, however, has been more clearly articulated and includes a number of essential functions:

- Coordinating the comprehensive interagency assessment of the child's needs
- Planning for services to address the needs of the child and family
- Arranging for needed services
- Linking the various parts of the child's system, including family, agencies, school, and significant others
- Monitoring the adequacy and appropriateness of services
- Ensuring continuity of service provision
- Advocating for the child and family
- Establishing linkages with the adult service system to facilitate transition

These functions are essential, unifying factors in service delivery. Behar (1984) contends that case management is

> the element of planning and coordinating that has held together the workings of all the agencies concerned with the child, the energizing factor that has propelled the service plan into the reality of service delivery, the case advocacy strength that has sustained a commitment to each child and an optimism about each child's capability to change. (p. 40)

7. *Early identification and intervention for children with emotional disturbances should be promoted by the system of care in order to enhance the likelihood of positive outcomes.* Emerging evidence indicates that early identification and intervention can have a significant effect on the course of emotional disorders in children (Cowen et al., 1975; Friedman, 1984). Such early intervention can, in some cases, reverse early maladaptive patterns and prevent problems from reaching serious proportions. Thus, early identification and intervention efforts have the potential for a major impact on serious emotional disturbances in children.

One of the goals of the system of care should be to reduce the prevalence and severity of emotional disturbance through effective early identification and intervention. Although there is increasing interest in screening and intervention programs to identify and assist high-risk children and families, these services often are neglected in favor of much-needed services for children who are already demonstrating serious problems. The challenge to the system of care is to achieve an appropriate balance between early identification and intervention services and services designed for youth with serious and persistent problems.

8. Children with emotional disturbances should be ensured smooth transitions to the adult service system as they reach maturity. The transition from the system of care for children and adolescents with emotional disturbances to the adult service system is fraught with problems. Children who "age out" of the system of care become young adults who often are in need of long-term mental health care, vocational services, and a range of other support services. However, a number of factors complicate a smooth transition and make it difficult for these young adults to receive appropriate services.

First, there may be difficulties in obtaining the mental health and other needed services from the adult service system. Aging out of the system of care for children generally means moving to an entirely new set of agencies and programs. Identifying, applying to, and becoming established with the adult agencies may be a complex and cumbersome task. A second complication results from the transition from school to the world of work. Many of these youth have no prevocational or vocational skills and may not be employable. Furthermore, they may not be viewed positively by vocational rehabilitation agencies, which require substantial promise of successful outcomes. These young adults may therefore be left in a void without school, job, or opportunities to enhance their employability.

Philosophical differences also complicate the transition from the child to the adult service system. Although systems of care for children and adolescents are based on a growth-promoting, "habilitative" philosophy, adult service systems are based on the philosophy of disability and rehabilitation. This philosophical difference may present problems for aging-out youth and their families, possibly discouraging their use of needed adult services.

Finally, adult agencies may be ill prepared to serve many of the youth who have been served by the system of care for children. The adult agencies have been developing programs to serve persons with serious and persistent mental illnesses. However, only a small percentage of the aging-out youth would fit the definition of adults with serious and persistent mental illnesses. Many have not met the hospitalization criteria, and many evidence conduct disorders rather than overt psychotic disorders. Their problems often include drug and alcohol abuse. The programs offered by adult mental health and other agencies may be inappropriate to the needs and characteristics of this "youth-in-transition" population.

Clearly, the system of care for youth with serious emotional disturbances cannot address all the issues related to transition to the adult service system. Nevertheless, the system of care should establish functional linkages with relevant adult agencies. These linkages should be used to ensure continuity of services for individual youth and families as well as to work with the adult system to become responsive to the needs of youth in transition.

9. The rights of children with emotional disturbances should be protected, and effective advocacy efforts for children and adolescents with emotional disturbances should be promoted. The system of care should be an advocate for the child. The "child advocacy" function of the system of care should be evident in several areas (Friedman, Duchnowski, & Henderson, 1989). First, the system of care should adopt mechanisms to ensure the protection of client rights. Such mechanisms may include statutes, statements of the rights of children, grievance procedures, case review committees, and protection and advocacy systems.

Such mechanisms are needed to protect the rights of children in several respects. One basic right of all children is to be treated in the least restrictive, most appropriate setting. Safeguards may be necessary to ensure that this right is upheld, as well as rights on admission to hospitals and other facilities, rights of children within facilities, rights related to removal from homes, and the like. A complicating factor in protecting the rights of children occurs when the rights of the child and the rights of the parents may be in conflict.

In addition to rights protection, the system of care should actively promote advocacy activities on behalf of children and adolescents with emotional disorders. Case advocacy is defined as efforts on behalf of an individual child to ensure that the child and his or her family receive appropriate services, benefits, or protections. Class advocacy involves efforts to seek improvements in services, benefits, or rights on behalf of all children and adolescents with emotional disturbances (Knitzer, 1989). Both case advocacy and class advocacy are vital to the success of the system of care. A strong and vocal network to advocate for the needs of children with emotional disorders has been notably lacking in the past. Knitzer (1989) emphasized that the growing recognition of the need for systems of care creates a challenge and an opportunity to strengthen advocacy for children and adolescents with emotional disorders.

Currently, efforts to build support for children's mental health issues are increasing. A broad-based constituency of parents, professionals, and child advocates is growing and beginning to provide the much-needed voice in support of system of care development. Existing advocacy groups are increasingly championing the children's mental health agenda, and two national advocacy groups (the Federation of Families for Children's Mental Health and the National Alliance for the Mentally Ill–Child and Adolescent Network) are devoted exclusively to issues related to children with emotional disturbances. Similar advocacy coalitions are developing at the state and community levels and are becoming an integral part of the system of care.

10. *Children with emotional disturbances should receive services without regard to race, religion, national origin, sex, physical disability, or other characteristics, and services should be sensitive and responsive to cultural differences and special needs.* The system of care should uphold a policy of nondiscrimination in the delivery of services. All children with emotional disorders and their families, including minority children and children with special needs such as physical disabilities, should have access to quality services. Additional efforts and arrangements are needed in order to be responsive to the special needs of children and families. Without such efforts, the system of care could not truly be child centered. The President's Commission on Mental Health (1978) emphasized this principle:

> Clearly services should respect ethnic differences and preferences. Quality of services should be independent of the socioeconomic or ethnic groups being served. Services should be adapted to suit the life styles, language, and expectations of the children and families being served. (p. 615)

This principle means that services should be accessible to children and family members with physical disabilities, that interpreters should be available to those with hearing impairments, translation services should be provided for those with language barriers, and the system of care should be sufficiently flexible to remove any barriers to service delivery for children and families with special needs or from diverse ethnic groups.

Summary The task of developing a comprehensive system of care for children with serious emotional disturbances is both complex and difficult. These principles describe the characteristics of such a system of care and the values on which it is based—comprehensiveness, individualization, least restrictive setting, family orientation, service integration, case management, early intervention, smooth transitions, rights protection and advocacy, and nondiscrimination.

SYSTEM OF CARE FRAMEWORK AND COMPONENTS

A system of care is defined as *a comprehensive spectrum of mental health and other necessary services that are organized into a coordinated network to meet the multiple and changing needs of children and adolescents with serious emotional disturbances and their families.* The system of care model presented in this chapter represents one approach to a system of care. The model is designed to be a guide and is based on the best available empirical data and clinical experience to date. It is offered as a starting point for states and communities as they seek to build their systems, as a baseline from which changes can be made as additional research, experience, and innovation dictate.

The system of care model is graphically presented in Figure 1.1 and is organized in a framework consisting of eight major dimensions of service, each composed of a range of service components:

1. *Mental health services,* including a range of nonresidential services and a range of residential services
2. *Social services,* including protective services, financial assistance, home aid services, respite care, shelter services, foster care, and adoption
3. *Educational services,* including assessment and planning, resource rooms, self-contained special education, special schools, home-bound instruction, residential schools, and alternative programs

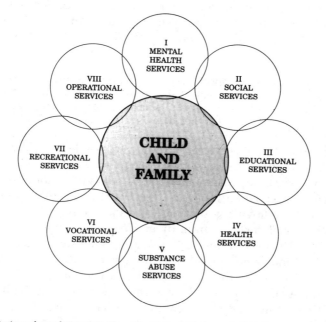

Figure 1.1. System of care framework. (From Stroul, B., & Friedman, R. [1986]. *A system of care for children and youth with severe emotional disturbances* [rev. ed., p. 30]. Washington, DC: Georgetown University Child Development Center, National Technical Assistance Center for Children's Mental Health; reprinted by permission.)

4. *Health services,* including health education and prevention, screening and assessment, primary care, acute care, and long-term care
5. *Substance abuse services,* including prevention, early intervention, assessment, outpatient services, day treatment, ambulatory detoxification, relapse prevention, residential detoxification, community residential treatment and recovery services, and inpatient hospitalization
6. *Vocational services,* including career education; vocational assessment; job survival skills training; vocational skills training; work experiences; job finding, placement and retention services; and supported employment
7. *Recreational services,* including relationships with significant others, after-school programs, summer camps, and special recreational programs
8. *Operational services,* including case management, juvenile justice services, family support and self-help groups, advocacy, transportation, legal services, and volunteer programs

Each service dimension addresses an area of need for children and families, a set of functions that must be performed in order to provide comprehensive services to meet these needs. The model is *not* intended to specify which type of agency should perform any of the particular functions. Certainly, particular agencies typically provide certain of these services. Educational services, for example, are most often provided by school systems, and social services are generally associated with child welfare or social welfare agencies. One might assume that the mental health services should be provided by mental health agencies. This, however, is often not the case.

All of the functions included in the system of care dimensions may be performed by a variety of agencies or practitioners in both the public and private sectors. Therapeutic group care, a component in the mental health dimension, is often provided by juvenile justice agencies and social service agencies as well as by mental health agencies. Day treatment is another mental health function that is frequently supplied by educational agencies, ideally in close collaboration with mental health providers. Similarly, home-based services are provided by social service agencies, mental health agencies, or jointly by both systems.

Although the roles and responsibilities of specific agencies are acknowledged, many of the services can be, and are, provided by different agencies in different communities. Furthermore, many of these services are provided not through the efforts of any single agency but through multi-agency collaborative efforts. Such collaborations are important not only in identifying needs and planning services but also in developing, funding, and operating services. It should also be recognized that services are not always provided by agencies. Some functions within the system of care may be performed by families, parent cooperatives, or other arrangements. Private-sector facilities and practitioners can play a pivotal role in the system of care, providing a wide range of services within each of the major dimensions. Additionally, juvenile justice agencies play an important role in the system of care by providing a wide range of services to children and adolescents who have broken the law (Shore, 1985).

Of primary importance is the dimension of mental health services, because these are critical services for all children with serious emotional disorders. These services are divided into seven nonresidential and seven residential categories, as displayed in Table 1.2. In the nonresidential category, many communities provide outpatient mental health services but do not offer services such as day treatment or home-based services. Emerging evidence indicates that these intensive services for youngsters and their families often can avert the need for out-of-home placement. Within the residential category, states and communities typically have concentrated on developing the more restrictive services provided in facilities such as residential treatment centers and hospitals. It is only recently that states and communities have begun to experiment with services such as therapeutic foster care. These types of programs have proven successful in treating youngsters with serious emotional disturbances in more natural family settings within the community.

When considering the individual services, it should be recalled that these are component parts of an overall system of care. Although they are listed individually, the system of care dimensions and service components cannot be operated in isolation. Only when the services are enmeshed in a coherent, well-coordinated system will the needs of youngsters with emotional disorders and their families be met in an appropriate and effective manner.

A critical characteristic of an effective system is an appropriate balance between the components, particularly between the more restrictive and less

Table 1.2. Dimension I: Mental health services

Nonresidential services	Residential services
Prevention	Therapeutic foster care
Early identification and intervention	Therapeutic group care
Assessment	Therapeutic camp services
Outpatient treatment	Independent living services
Home-based services	Residential treatment services
Day treatment	Crisis residential services
Emergency services	Inpatient hospitalization

From Stroul, B., & Friedman, R. (1986). *A system of care for children and youth with severe emotional disturbances* (rev. ed., p. 31). Washington, DC: Georgetown University Child Development Center, National Technical Assistance Center for Children's Mental Health; reprinted by permission.

restrictive services. If such a balance is not present, then youngsters and families will not have a chance to receive less restrictive services before moving to more restrictive services. For example, if within a community there are no intensive home-based services, only 20 day treatment slots, and 50 residential treatment slots, the system is not in balance. Youngsters and families most likely will not have the opportunity to participate in home-based or day treatment services because of their relative unavailability, and the residential components of the system will be overloaded with youngsters, some of whom might have been diverted from residential treatment had there been more nonresidential services available.

At the present time there are no clear, empirically based guidelines about the appropriate capacity within each component of a system of care. Implicit within a model system of service, however, is the expectation that more youngsters will require the less restrictive services than the more restrictive ones, and that service capacity should therefore diminish as one proceeds from less to more restrictive options within the system. As additional research and field experience are accumulated with respect to systems of care for children with emotional disturbances, it is becoming more feasible to define the optimal ratios of capacities in the different system components (Behar, Holland, & MacBeth, 1987; Friedman, 1987; Pires, 1990).

The operational services dimension is somewhat different from the other system of care dimensions. This dimension includes a range of support services that can make the difference between an effective and an ineffective system of care but do not fall into a specific category. Instead, they cross the boundaries between different types of services. They are called "operational services" because of their importance to the overall effective operation of the system.

Case management is a service within this dimension that can play a critical role in the system of care. Behar (1985) calls case management "perhaps the most essential unifying factor in service delivery" (p. 194). The important role that case management can play in a system of service has been increasingly recognized in recent years but has been operationalized in only a few states. Case management can be provided to youngsters in both residential and nonresidential programs. It involves brokering services for individual youngsters, advocating on their behalf, ensuring that an adequate treatment plan is developed and implemented, reviewing client progress, and coordinating services. Case management involves aggressive outreach to the child and family and working with them and with numerous community agencies and resources to ensure that all needed services and supports are in place. One important trend in serving children with emotional disorders is to combine specialized case management with the availability of flexible funds used to secure the specific mix of services and supports needed by each individual child and family on a case-by-case basis (Update, 1986–1987).

CONCLUSION

The system of care model presented in this chapter can be used as a guide in planning and policy making and provides a framework for assessing present services and planning improvements. The model can be conceptualized as a blueprint for a system of care that establishes directions and goals.

This model should not be seen as the only way to conceptualize systems of care. States and communities should revise and adapt the model to conform with their needs, environments, and service systems. The model must also be regarded as flexible, with room for additions and revisions as experience and changing circumstances dictate. Furthermore, it is important to note that not every community is expected to have every service; some highly specialized services might be made available on a regional basis. States and communities must establish priorities and identify a core set of services as a focus for their system improvement activities.

Most important is the acknowledgment that conceptualizing a system of care represents only a *preliminary step* in the service system improvement process. Development of a system of care model is a planning task that must be followed by implementation activities. Although designing a system of care is an essential and challenging task, the real challenge for states and communities is to transform their system of care plans into reality.

REFERENCES

Behar, L.B. (1984). *An integrated system of services for seriously disturbed children*. Paper presented at the ADAMHA/OJJDP "State of the Art Research Conference on Juvenile Offenders with Serious Alcohol, Drug Abuse and Mental Health Problems," Rockville, MD.
Behar, L.B. (1985). Changing patterns of state responsibility: A case study of North Carolina. *Journal of Clinical Child Psychology, 14*, 188–195.
Behar, L.B. (1986). A model for child mental health services: The North Carolina experience. *Children Today, 15*, 16–21.
Behar, L., Holland, J., & MacBeth, G. (1987). *Distribution of mental health service components and their costs within a comprehensive system of care for children and adolescents: The North Carolina plan*. Unpublished manuscript, North Carolina Department of Mental Health, Raleigh.
Cowen, E.L., Trost, M.A., Lorion, R.P., Dorr, D., Izzo, L.D., & Isaacson, R.V. (1975). *New ways in school mental health: Early detection and prevention of school maladaptation*. New York: Human Science Press.
Cross, T., Bazron, B., Dennis, K., & Isaacs, M. (1989). *Towards a culturally competent system of care: Vol I. A monograph on effective services for minority children who are severely emotionally disturbed*. Washington, DC: Georgetown University Child Development Center, National Technical Assistance Center for Children's Mental Health.
Friedman, R.M. (1983). *Children's mental health services and policy in Florida*. Unpublished manuscript, University of South Florida, Florida Mental Health Institute, Tampa.
Friedman, R.M. (1984). *Prevention, early identification and early intervention programs in Florida: A status report*. Unpublished paper, University of South Florida, Florida Mental Health Institute, Tampa.

Friedman, R. (1987). *Service capacity in a balanced system of services for seriously emotionally disturbed children.* Unpublished manuscript, University of South Florida, Florida Mental Health Institute, Tampa.

Friedman, R., Duchnowski, A., & Henderson, E. (1989). *Advocacy on behalf of children with serious emotional problems.* Springfield, IL: Charles C Thomas.

Friedman, R.M., & Street, S. (1985). Admission and discharge criteria for children's mental health services: A review of the issues and options. *Journal of Clinical Child Psychology, 14,* 229–235.

Isaacs, M., & Benjamin, M. (1991). *Towards a culturally competent system of care: Vol. II. Programs which use culturally competent services.* Washington, DC: Georgetown University Child Development Center, National Technical Assistance Center for Children's Mental Health.

Joint Commission on the Mental Health of Children. (1969). *Crisis in child mental health.* New York: Harper & Row.

Katz-Leavy, J., Lourie, I., Stroul, B., & Zeigler-Dendy, C. (1992). *Individualized services in a system of care.* Washington, DC: Georgetown University Child Development Center, National Technical Assistance Center for Children's Mental Health.

Knitzer, J. (1989). Children's mental health: The advocacy challenge. In R. Friedman, A. Duchnowski, & E. Henderson (Eds.), *Advocacy on behalf of children with serious emotional problems* (pp. 15–27). Springfield, IL: Charles C Thomas.

Lourie, I., & Katz-Leavy, J. (1986). Severely emotionally disturbed children and adolescents. In W. Menninger (Ed.), *The chronically mentally ill* (pp. 159–186). Washington, DC: American Psychiatric Association.

Pires, S. (1990). *Sizing components of care: An approach to determining the size and cost of service components in a system of care for children and adolescents with serious emotional disturbances.* Washington, DC: Georgetown University Child Development Center, National Technical Assistance Center for Children's Mental Health.

President's Commission on Mental Health. (1978). *Report of the sub-task panel on infants, children, and adolescents.* Washington, DC: Author.

Program update: Case management. (1986–1987, Winter). *Update,* 2(2), 10–12. (Available from the University of South Florida, Florida Mental Health Institute, Tampa, FL.)

Shore, M. (1985). *Mental health and the juvenile justice system: A mental health perspective.* Paper presented at the NASMHPD/NIMH Symposium "Addressing the Mental Health Needs of the Juvenile Justice Population: Policies and Programs," Washington, DC.

Stroul, B. (1988). *Series on community-based services for children and adolescents who are severely emotionally disturbed: Vol. I. Home-based services.* Washington, DC: Georgetown University Child Development Center, National Technical Assistance Center for Children's Mental Health.

Stroul, B. (1989). *Series on community-based services for children and adolescents who are severely emotionally disturbed: Vol. III. Therapeutic foster care.* Washington, DC: Georgetown University Child Development Center, National Technical Assistance Center for Children's Mental Health.

Stroul, B. (1993). *Systems of care for children and adolescents with severe emotional disturbances: What are the results?* Washington, DC: Georgetown University Child Development Center, National Technical Assistance Center for Children's Mental Health.

Stroul, B., & Friedman, R. (1986). *A system of care for children and youth with severe emotional disturbances* (rev. ed.). Washington, DC: Georgetown University Child Development Center, National Technical Assistance Center for Children's Mental Health.

Stroul, B., Lourie, I., Goldman, S., & Katz-Leavy, J. (1992). *Profiles of local systems of care for children and adolescents with severe emotional disturbances* (rev. ed.). Washington, DC: Georgetown University Child Development Center, National Technical Assistance Center for Children's Mental Health.

Willie, M. v. Hunt, Civil No. C-C-79-0294, slip op. (W.D.N.C., February 20, 1991; *See* 657 F.2d 5S, 4th Cir., 1981).

CHAPTER 2

Framework for a Culturally Competent System of Care

Mareasa Isaacs-Shockley, Terry Cross,
Barbara J. Bazron, Karl Dennis, and Marva P. Benjamin

Children of color—that is, children of African American, Latino/Hispanic, Asian American/Pacific Islander, and Native American/Alaskan Native descent—are the fastest growing population within the United States. According to the Children's Defense Fund (1991), these children comprised 30% of the population under the age of 19 years in 1990 and will comprise 33% by the year 2000. This trend is expected to continue so that, by the year 2020, children of color will constitute approximately 40% of the child population in the country. These changing demographics portend tremendous reliance on these youth for America's continued growth and prosperity in the 21st century.

The importance of children of color to our future, however, is overshadowed by the challenges they face in growing into productive and healthy citizens in a society where they are at a considerable disadvantage. For example, poverty disproportionately impacts children of color. According to the Children's Defense Fund (1994), the poverty rate for children in young families (i.e., families headed by someone younger than age 30), is 29.3% for Caucasian children, 69.3% for African American children, and 52% for Latino children. In addition, the grim litany of problems facing children of color is all too familiar. Higher proportions of children of color die before birth or during infancy; have learning, emotional, and/or physical disabilities; have higher school dropout rates and fewer higher education opportunities; become parents at an early age; enter the child welfare system and are placed out of their homes and communities; are incarcerated in youth detention facilities and "rehabilitated" into adult correctional systems; or die as a result of homicide, suicide, or unintentional injuries before reaching adulthood (Isaacs, 1993).

Any one of these conditions can have a significant impact on the emotional well-being of children and adolescents. Yet youth of color often have limited access to mental health services. The chances are good that an African American adolescent with a serious emotional disturbance will end up in the juvenile justice system rather than in the treatment setting to which his or her Caucasian counterpart would be referred (Comer & Hill, 1985; Gibbs, 1988; Hawkins & Salisbury, 1983; Lewis, Lovely, Yeager, & Femina, 1989; Lewis, Shanok, Cohen, Kligfeld, & Frisone, 1980). A Native American child with serious emotional disturbance will likely go without treatment or be removed legally and geographically from his or her family and tribe (Berlin, 1983; Blum, Harmon, Harris, Bergeisen, & Resnick, 1992; LaFromboise & Low, 1989). A Hispanic child with serious emotional disturbance will likely be assessed in a language not his or her own (Inclan & Herron, 1989; Morales, Ferguson, & Munford, 1986; Ramirez, 1989). An Asian American adolescent with a serious emotional disturbance will likely never come to the attention of the mental health system (Meinhardt, Tom, Tse, & Yu, 1986; Nagata, 1989).

In short, children and adolescents of color often do not get their needs met in the present system (Gibbs & Huang, 1989). Yet, they are more likely to be diagnosed as seriously emotionally disturbed than their Caucasian counterparts. When they do enter the system, they will experience more restrictive interventions and fewer community-based alternatives. Cultural traits, behaviors, and beliefs will likely be interpreted as weaknesses and as dysfunctional. The data are clear: Current systems of care provide differential treatment to children of color (Cummins, 1986; Katz-Leavy, Lourie, & Kaufman, 1987; Ortiz & Maldonado-Colon, 1986; Stehno, 1982). By and large, our child-serving systems, including education, have been dismal failures in meeting the needs of youth of color and helping them grow into productive adults. Those who continue to blame the "victims" rather than fix our systems are pursuing a course that is myopic, costly, and perilous (McLoyd, 1990). McLoyd and others suggest that, in order to fix child-serving systems, there is a need to understand the cultural, ecological, and structural forces that enhance or impede the healthy development of children of color.

This chapter presents a philosophical framework for improving service delivery to children of color. Although the emphasis is on those youth who suffer from serious emotional disturbances, the framework for a culturally competent system of care can be useful to any child-serving system. The framework grows out of increasing recognition that children and adolescents of color are *unserved, underserved, or inappropriately served* by most public and private sector mental health systems within the United States (Isaacs & Benjamin, 1991). This framework emphasizes an understanding of the importance of culture and building service systems that recognize, incorporate, and value diversity—a *cultural competence* model.

DEFINITION OF CULTURAL COMPETENCE

Cultural competence provides systems, agencies, and practitioners with the capacity to respond to the unique needs of populations whose cultures are different from that which might be called Eurocentric or "mainstream" American (Cross, Bazron, Dennis, & Isaacs, 1989). The word "culture" is used and defined as "the integrated pattern of human behavior that includes thoughts, communication styles, actions, customs, beliefs, values, and institutions of a racial, ethnic, religious, or social group"; the word "competence" is defined as "the capacity to function in a particular way"—the skills and abilities to perform a set of tasks successfully (Cross et al., 1989, p. 3). Thus, cultural competence can be defined as *a set of congruent behaviors, attitudes, practices, and policies that come together in a system or agency or among professionals and enable that system or agency or those professionals to work effectively in cross-cultural situations.*

As defined here, cultural competence should lead to the development of culturally appropriate prevention and treatment strategies. According to Marin (1989), such strategies should 1) be based on the cultural values of the targeted group; 2) reflect the subjective cultural characteristics of the members of the targeted group (i.e., their attitudes, expectancies, and norms regarding a particular behavior); and 3) reflect the behavioral preferences and expectations of the members of the group.

Five essential elements contribute to a system, agency, or professional becoming more culturally competent (Cross et al., 1989; Isaacs & Benjamin, 1991): valuing diversity, undertaking cultural self-assessment, understanding the dynamics of difference, institutionalization of cultural knowledge, and adaptation to diversity.

Valuing Diversity

The first essential element is to value diversity. To value diversity is to see and respect its worth. A mental health service is strengthened when it accepts that the people it serves are from very different backgrounds and will make different choices based on culture. Although all people share common basic needs, there are vast differences in how people of various cultures go about meeting those needs. These differences are as important as the similarities. We must begin to see differences as something positive and as something that has value. In valuing diversity, we acknowledge cultural differences and become aware of how these differences affect the helping process.

Because American society operates predominantly out of a Eurocentric framework, and its institutions—including those for mental health—are established based on the values inherent in such a framework, it has been particularly difficult for children and families of color, who often have a differing value base, to be effectively served and assisted by American institutions. There are assumptions of cultural blindness and assimilation inherent in these institutional values and practices that fail to recognize the richness and values of other cultures. An approach that values diversity would assure that these differences between groups, as well as within groups, are acknowledged and incorporated into programs and services.

Cultural Self-Assessment

In order to understand the role that culture plays in another's life, it is important that each individual become aware of the role it plays in his or her own life. Many people never acknowledge how their day-to-day behaviors and attitudes have been shaped by their own cultural values and reinforced by families, peers, and social institutions.

Agencies and systems also have cultures that are reflected in the way they are structured, the kinds of staff they seek, and the policies and practices that are implemented. Thus, agencies also must undertake a self-assessment process to gain a clearer understanding of the values and attitudes that are at the roots of the organization. When personnel understand how their agency is shaped by its culture, then it is easier for them to assess how the agency interfaces with other cultures. For example, if "family" refers to immediate families in one culture and in another culture denotes extended family or kinship networks, then concepts such as "family involvement" will mean something different. Recognition and involvement of kinship networks will require some adjustments in agency policies and interventions for an agency that thinks "immediate" when family is discussed. Otherwise, their services simply will not work for populations that conceptualize family in a different way.

Thus, in order to provide sensitive and competent care to clients from cultures that are different from one's own, there must be 1) an awareness of one's own cultural values and beliefs and a recognition of how these influence one's attitudes and behaviors, and 2) an understanding of the cultural values and beliefs of one's clients and how these influence their attitudes and behaviors (Randall-David, 1990).

It should be noted that often staff from the same ethnic group as a client assume that they understand the client's culture and that there is no need for this type of cultural self-assessment. However, cultural competence is not a given because there are as many variations *within* cultures as *between* cultures. For example, in African American professional–client relationships, there are cultural differences based on geographical locations as well as on socioeconomic and educational differences. Although there is a tendency to "lump" all Asian Americans or Hispanics into one category, there are many different cultures and languages represented within these groups. Therefore, this need for cultural self-assessment must occur at the individual and agency levels even when there is a common ethnicity with the client/consumer groups.

Dynamics of Difference

The third essential element of cultural competency is that of understanding and acknowledging the dynamics of difference. When professionals of one culture interact with a population from another, both may misjudge the other's actions based on learned expectations. Each brings to the relationship unique histories and the influence of current political relationships between the two groups. Both will bring culturally prescribed patterns of communication, etiquette, and problem solving. Both may bring stereotypes or underlying feelings about serving or being served by someone who is different. African Americans, for example, may exhibit behaviors expressing stress, anger, and frustration that may make the agency staff uncomfortable. The agency and its staff must be constantly vigilant about the dynamics of difference in order to avoid misinterpretation and misjudgment.

Historical distrust is one such dynamic that often occurs between a helper from the dominant culture and a client from an ethnic minority community. Historical discrimination and racism are some of the core underpinnings of the relationship between people of color and the dominant Eurocentric culture. Nickens (1990) states that "many minority communities feel substantial mistrust of the government, its agents and its information" (p. 134). For example, just as Native Americans view the introduction of alcohol into their culture as a form of genocide, so do many African Americans view the level and types of illegal drugs in their communities as a modern-day form of genocide. They often distrust those who preach a "war on drugs" because the war seems to result in a disproportionate number of deaths and incarcerations for young African American males and females (Isaacs, 1993).

Such dynamics of difference must be clearly understood so that effective strategies can be developed to mitigate the impact of historical distrust and other dynamics of difference that can significantly impede a positive interaction between groups from different cultures. It is important to note that the dynamics of difference are always a two-way process in a cross-cultural situation. By incorporating an understanding of these dynamics and their origins into service systems, the chances for productive cross-cultural interventions are enhanced.

Institutionalization of Cultural Knowledge

An agency must sanction, and in some instances mandate, the incorporation of cultural knowledge into the service delivery framework. This knowledge must be available at every level of the organization. This knowledge base should include information about a culture, such as critical attitudes, values, communication patterns, and history. It is also important to explore how cultural values are related to mental health and help-seeking patterns, concepts of health and wellness, and attitudes toward services and programs.

Agencies can institutionalize cultural knowledge through such approaches as required in-service training for staff; collection of journal articles and other print resources; use of consultants, natural helpers, healers, key community leaders, and advisory committees; and linkages with advocacy groups. In other words, an agency must develop specific mechanisms to secure the cultural knowledge it requires to be effective in its interactions with clients. The development of knowledge through culturally competent research and demonstration projects must also be included in strategies to institutionalize cultural knowledge.

Adaptation to Diversity

The final element of a culturally competent delivery system is the adaptation of services and programs to reflect cultural specificity and diversity. The first four elements mean little if organizations do not change the way they work with people or the ways in which they provide services. Agencies can adapt or adjust their helping approaches to compensate for and acknowledge cultural differences. Styles of interviewing, focusing on strengths rather than deficits, changing and accepting other definitions of "family," and changing approaches and types of services offered are all ways that agencies can adapt in order to become more culturally competent.

THE CULTURAL COMPETENCE CONTINUUM

Mason (1989), Cross (1992), and others have developed cultural competence assessment instruments that can be used by individuals and agencies to assess their levels of cultural competence, based on the five essential elements previously discussed. It is important to understand that cultural competence is a developmental process. In our society, everyone must work toward this goal, and there is little that prepares us to acknowledge or appreciate multiculturalism. Rather, the primary goal in American society has been assimilation and acculturation. Thus, cultural competence is not something that occurs because one reads a book, or attends a workshop, or goes to an ethnic festival, or happens to be a member of an ethnic group. It is a process born of a commitment to provide quality services and to make a positive difference for clients and communities of color.

To better understand where one is in the process of becoming more culturally competent, it is useful to think of the possible ways of responding to cultural differences. If one imagines a continuum that ranges from cultural destructiveness to cultural proficiency, there are a variety of possibilities between these two extremes. Cross et al. (1989) describe six points along the continuum and the characteristics that might be exhibited by an agency or an individual at each level of the continuum.

Cultural Destructiveness

The most negative end of the continuum is represented by attitudes, policies, and practices that are destructive to cultures and consequently to the individuals within these cultures. The most extreme example of this orientation is programs and policies that promote or actively participate in cultural genocide—the purposeful destruction of a culture. The institution of American slavery is a dominant example for African Americans. Another example is the Exclusion Laws of 1885–1965 (Hune, 1977), which prohibited Asians from bringing spouses to this country, imposed immigration quotas, and denied them basic human rights on the state and federal levels. Equally destructive is the process of dehumanizing or subhumanizing clients of color. Historically, some agencies have been actively involved in services that have denied people of color access to their natural helpers or healers, removed children of color from their families on the basis of race, or purposely risked the well-being of minority individuals in social or medical experiments without their knowledge or consent.

A system that adheres to this extreme assumes that one race is superior and should eradicate "lesser" cultures because of their perceived subhuman position. Bigotry coupled with vast power differentials allows the dominant group to disenfranchise, control, exploit, or systematically destroy the minority population. Although such overt practices had disappeared from the American scene, there is increasing concern that this type of approach is again on the upswing (e.g., the resurgence of the Ku Klux Klan, white supremacy groups, skinheads).

Cultural Incapacity

The next position on the continuum is one at which the system or agencies do not intentionally or consciously seek to be culturally destructive but rather lack the capacity to help clients and communities of color. At this level, the agency or individual remains extremely biased, believes in the racial superiority of the dominant group, and assumes a paternal posture toward "lesser" races. These agencies may disproportionately apply resources, discriminate against people of color on the basis of whether they "know their place," and believe in the supremacy of dominant culture helpers. Such agencies may support segregation as a desirable policy. They may act as agents of oppression by enforcing racist policies and maintaining stereotypes. Such agencies often are characterized by ignorance and an unrealistic fear of people of color. The characteristics of cultural incapacity include discriminatory hiring practices, subtle messages to people of color that they are not valued or welcome, and generally lower expectations of minority clients.

Cultural Blindness

At the midpoint on the continuum, the system and its agencies provide services with the express philosophy of being unbiased. They function with the belief that color, race, or culture make no difference and that we are all the same. Culturally blind agencies are characterized by the belief that helping approaches traditionally used by the dominant culture are universally applicable; if the system worked as it should, all people—regardless of race or culture—would be served with equal effectiveness. This view reflects a well-intentioned liberal philosophy. However, the consequences of such a belief are to make services so ethnocentric as to render them virtually useless to all but the most assimilated people of color. Ethnocentrism refers to misinterpretation and misjudgment based on looking at another person's behavior from one's own cultural reference point and a belief that one's culture is the best and only way to interpret reality.

Such services ignore cultural strengths, encourage assimilation, and blame the victims for their problems. Members of minority communities are viewed from the cultural deprivation model, which asserts that problems are the result of inadequate cultural resources. Outcome is usually measured by how closely the client approximates a middle-class nonminority existence. Institutional racism restricts minority access to professional training, staff position, and services.

These agencies may participate in special projects with minority populations when monies are specifically available or with the intent of "rescuing" people of color. Unfortunately, such projects are often conducted without community guidance and are the first casualties when funds run short. Culturally blind agencies suffer from a deficit of information and often lack the avenues through which they can obtain needed information. Although these agencies often view themselves as unbiased and responsive to minority needs, their ethnocentrism is reflected in attitude, policy, and practice.

Cultural Precompetence

As agencies move toward the positive end of the scale, they reach a position called "cultural precompetence," a term chosen because it implies movement. The precompetent agency realizes it has weaknesses in serving people of color and attempts to improve some aspect of its services to a specific population. Such agencies try experiments, hire minority staff, explore how to reach people of color in their service areas, initiate training for their workers on cultural sensitivity, enter into needs assessments concerning minority communities, and recruit minority individuals for their boards of directors or advisory committees. Precompetent agencies are characterized by the desire to deliver quality services and a commitment to civil rights. They respond to minority communities' cry for improved services by asking, "What can we do?"

One danger at this level is a false sense of accomplishment or of failure that prevents the agency from moving forward along the continuum. An agency may believe that the accomplishment of one goal or activity fulfills its obligation to minority communities or may undertake an activity that fails and is therefore reluctant to try again.

Another danger is tokenism. Agencies sometimes hire one or more (usually assimilated) workers of color and believe they are then equipped to meet the need. Although hiring staff of color is very important, it is no guarantee that services, access, or sensitivity will be improved. Because professionals of color are trained in the dominant society's frame of reference, they may be little more competent in cross-cultural practice than their co-workers. These professionals, like all others, need training on the function of culture and its impact on client populations. The precompetent agency, however, has begun the process of becoming culturally competent and often only lacks information on what is possible and how to proceed.

Basic Cultural Competence

Culturally competent agencies are characterized by acceptance and respect for difference, continuing self-assessment regarding culture, careful attention to the dynamics of difference, continuous expansion of cultural knowledge and resources, and a variety of adaptations to service models in order to better meet the changing needs of minority populations. The culturally competent agency works to hire unbiased employees, seeks advice and consultation from the minority community, and actively decides what it is and is not capable of providing to clients of color. Often, there is ongoing dialogue and input from the minority community at all levels of the organization and a network with other formal and informal supports within the community.

Advanced Cultural Competence or Cultural Proficiency

The most positive end of the scale is advanced cultural competence or proficiency. This point on the continuum is characterized by holding culture in high esteem. The culturally proficient agency seeks to add to the knowledge base of culturally competent practice by conducting research, developing new therapeutic approaches based on culture, evaluating and disseminating the results of demonstration projects, and experimenting with changes in organizational structures that support critical cultural values and beliefs. The culturally proficient agency hires staff who are specialists in culturally competent practice. Such an agency advocates for cultural competence throughout the system and for improved relations between cultures throughout society.

Summary

The degree of cultural competence an agency achieves is not dependent on any one factor. Attitudes, policies, and practices are three major arenas where development can and must occur if an agency is to move toward cultural competence. Attitudes change to become less ethnocentric and biased. Policies change to become more flexible and culturally sensitive. Practices become more congruent with the culture of the client from initial contact through termination.

MAJOR CULTURAL COMPETENCE PRINCIPLES

A core set of principles underlie the concept of cultural competence and act as guidelines for developing culturally competent delivery systems (Cross et al., 1989; Isaacs & Benjamin, 1991):

- The family as defined by each culture is the primary system of support and preferred intervention.
- The system must recognize that minority populations must be at least bicultural and that this status creates a unique set of psychological/emotional issues to which the system must be equipped to respond.
- Individuals and families make different choices based on cultural forces; these choices must be considered if services are to be helpful.
- Practice is driven by culturally preferred choices, not by culturally blind or culture-free interventions.
- Inherent in cross-cultural interactions are dynamics that must be acknowledged, adjusted to, and accepted.
- The service system must sanction, and in some cases mandate, the incorporation of cultural knowledge into practice and policy-making activities.
- Cultural competence involves determining a client's cultural location in order to apply the helping principle of "starting where the client is" and includes understanding the client's level of acculturation and assimilation.
- Cultural competence involves working in conjunction with natural, informal support and helping networks within the minority community (e.g., neighborhood organizations, churches, spiritual leaders, healers, community leaders).
- Cultural competence embraces and extends the concept of "self-determination" to services offered in communities of color.
- Culturally competent services seek to match the needs and help-seeking behavior of the client population.
- Beyond services, culturally competent agencies recognize that they also have a role of advocacy and empowerment in relationship to their clients and the minority community in which they attempt to deliver highly responsive services. (Isaacs & Benjamin, 1991, pp. 52–54).

BARRIERS TO CULTURAL COMPETENCE

Although cultural competence appears to be a natural and effective approach to the increasing concern about providing acceptable and quality services to clients of color in a cost-effective manner, there are many resistances and barriers to agencies adopting a cultural competence philosophy and framework. Bernard (1992) and other authors have identified several major barriers to implementation of cultural competence in health and human services agencies. These include

- The "isms"—racism, sexism, classism, and other such "isms"
- "It's not culture, it's poverty"—the inability to accept culture as a factor and arguing against giving it prominence, although there is also great inertia in addressing poverty as well. This attitude keeps discussion on an intellectual and conceptual level so that actions to address either are not taken
- Cultural blindness—that is, the belief that color or culture makes no difference in assessment and treatment and, therefore, there is no need for change
- "What's in it for me?"—insufficient motivation or will to initiate or participate in changes
- "Full plate"—the claim of a lack of time
- "Too many demands"—jumping from crisis to crisis, with a lack of energy to deal with new changes
- "No extra funding"—viewing bilingual, bicultural, and ethnic-specific services as "luxury" items
- "Too much, too fast"—being overwhelmed and paralyzed by the dramatic increase of many groups of color; there is an inability to set priorities or know "where to begin"
- "Too difficult to change"—insufficient leadership in the organization and inadequate management skills to cope with change
- "Powerless"—a lack of political support and/or resources to implement change

Some of these barriers and resistances will be recognized through the cultural self-assessment process; others will only become visible when the agency embarks on a course of action to increase its level of cultural competence. It is usually helpful to provide outside facilitation and consultation regarding known and unknown resistances to change. It has become very clear that, in order for cultural competence to occur, there must be buy-in from the top leaders in the agency, and there should be specific activities undertaken so that buy-in by lower-level staff occurs.

INFUSING CULTURAL COMPETENCE AT ALL LEVELS OF AN AGENCY

When many people think of cultural competence, they think only in terms of the direct service provider–client relationship. Although this is certainly an extremely important relationship, most direct service providers do not work in a vacuum. Rather, they work in agencies that have policy makers and administrators who play a very important role in setting the policies and program directions for the agency. If direct service providers are expected to be the only staff to incorporate cultural competence in their practice, without supportive policies, supervision, and program adaptations, then they are being set up to fail. To be effective, cultural competence must have commitment and attention from all levels of an organization: its policy makers, its administrators/managers, its direct service providers, and its consumers/clients.

Policy-Making Level

The policy makers or planners of services may be board members of private agencies, public agency officials, legislators, commissioners, and/or task force or advisory board members. Anyone who has a voice in the shaping of policy might be included. At this level, there are a number of actions that would enhance cultural competence. These actions may include the following:

1. *Involve communities of color.* Persons of color, living within the affected community, can be recruited and asked to serve on boards, advisory committees, and commissions that already exist in the agency or system. The agency could also create special task forces or advisory groups that are representative of the minority community to study and address issues of that particular community.
2. *Set standards for cross-cultural services.* An agency board may develop standards it expects its employees to follow. Standard-setting bodies can incorporate cultural competence into existing standards for services. States having licensing requirements for professionals might add cultural competence to the required skills of a profession.
3. *Sanction, and in some cases require, participation in training that builds cultural knowledge and skills.* It is not enough to require that direct service providers receive training; it is also important that policy makers themselves receive and participate in such training as well.
4. *Incorporate cultural competence into executive orders and legislation at the state and local government levels.* Policy can be both integrated into existing laws and formulated in new laws.
5. *Use research and data to guide decision making.* Policies can be implemented that ensure that adequate and accurate data and information are collected on groups of color, that research is monitored to avoid cultural bias or intrusion, that minority researchers are utilized and supported, and that the minority community is involved in the research and data-collection process and receives feedback about results and findings.
6. *Create a decision-making structure that allows minority participation in the process.* A decision-making structure that is flexible and empowers less

powerful segments of the community contributes to the minority voice being heard.

7. *Use funding mechanisms to improve service access and incentives for developing culturally competent programs.* Through the use and expansion of contracting, more funding can be directed at minority service providers and agencies. Funding agencies also can develop service and staffing requirements (through performance contracting) that provide incentives for agencies to become more culturally competent.

8. *Develop written mission statements that specifically address a commitment to cultural competence at all levels.* Actions such as incorporating cultural competence development into an agency's 5-year plan can help the policy maker break the process into manageable parts with reasonable timelines. There also may be a need to develop a specific cultural competence action plan.

9. *Participate in resource development and program fostering.* Agencies can actively work in conjunction with communities of color to enable the creation and healthy growth of a service. Established agencies can assist in the start-up and nurturance of new specialized programs for groups of color and then spin them off to full community self-control.

Administrative/Management Level

The administrative level of service delivery is composed of agency directors, managers, department heads, supervisors, and a variety of other people in both public and private organizations. This level interprets and implements policy in addition to creating it. It is at the administrative level of an organization that cultural competence must be fully embraced. The administrator's primary role is to set the context for the development of cultural competence. Some of the actions that can be taken at this level include

1. Establishing and sanctioning some form of agency self-assessment
2. Ensuring that persons of color are recruited and retained on staff
3. Ensuring that cultural competence training and skill development are included in the agency's staff orientation and in-service training
4. Adapting personnel policies to make an agency more culturally competent
5. Developing program evaluation mechanisms that specifically target clients of color to determine their perceptions of the agency's effectiveness and their satisfaction with services offered
6. Adapting physical facilities to be more inviting to clients of color
7. Ensuring that adequate and accurate data regarding services to clients of color are collected and used in planning and evaluation
8. Using the capacity to develop new approaches or adjust existing ones

Although actions at the administrative level alone cannot bring an agency to cultural competence, administrators are in key positions to jump start the process.

Direct Service Provider Level

Sound cross-cultural practice begins with a commitment from the direct service provider to offer culturally competent services. Throughout the intake, assessment, diagnosis, treatment, referral, and termination process, the cultural competence of the worker is crucial for determining the success of the intervention.

Wilson (1982) listed personal attributes, knowledge, and skills that are essential for a culturally competent service provider:

1. Personal Attributes

   - Personal qualities that reflect genuineness, accurate empathy, nonpossessive warmth, and a capacity to respond flexibly to a range of possible solutions
   - Acceptance of ethnic differences between people
   - A willingness to work with clients of different ethnic minority groups
   - Articulation and clarification of personal values, stereotypes, and biases related to one's own and others' ethnicity and social class, and ways these may accommodate or conflict with the needs of minority clients
   - Personal commitment to change racism and poverty
   - Resolution about one's professional image in fields that have systematically excluded people of color

2. Knowledge

   - Knowledge of the culture (history, traditions, values, family systems, artistic expressions) of minority clients
   - Knowledge of the impact of class and ethnicity on behavior, attitudes, and values
   - Knowledge of the help-seeking behaviors of minority groups
   - Knowledge of the role of language, speech patterns, and communication styles in ethnically distinct communities
   - Knowledge of the impact of social policies on minority clients
   - Knowledge of the resources (agencies, persons, informal helping networks, research) that can be utilized on behalf of minority clients and communities
   - Knowledge of power relationships within the community, agency, or institution and their impact on minority clients

3. Skills

   - Techniques for learning the cultures of minority client groups
   - Ability to communicate accurate information on behalf of minority clients and their communities
   - Ability to openly discuss racial and ethnic differences and issues and to respond to culturally based cues
   - Ability to assess the meaning ethnicity has for individual clients
   - Ability to differentiate between the symptoms of intrapsychic stress and stress arising from the social structure
   - Interviewing techniques reflective of the worker's understanding of the role of language in the client's culture

- Ability to utilize the concepts of empowerment on behalf of minority clients and communities
- Capability of using resources on behalf of minority clients and their communities
- Ability to recognize and combat racism, racial stereotypes, and myths in individuals and in institutions
- Ability to evaluate new techniques, research, and knowledge as to their validity and applicability in working with minorities

The direct care provider can gain these skills and this knowledge through training and experience. The personal attributes can be developed through exposure to the positive aspects of cultures. Information is a strong tool in the development of cultural competence, and workers should avail themselves of every opportunity to build their cultural knowledge. Such knowledge must, however, be coupled with a willingness to let clients and cultural groups determine their own future.

Client/Consumer Level

Families, as service consumers, also have a role in the development of the cultural competence of the system. Families can become more effective advocates for their children when they gain the skills to articulate the importance of their culture. Families also can be resources in the system's training process by talking about the natural networks and insisting that significant parts of their networks be included in the helping process for their children. Families encountering insensitive services can turn to each other for aid in interfacing with the system. Families linked with other families can provide mutual support and help define issues from their perspectives.

CONCLUSION

There are many challenges associated with the development of more effective systems of care for responding to the mental health needs of children and adolescents of color and their families. We must begin to meet these challenges through more thoughtful attention to cultural variations (even within our own cultural groups), increased cultural knowledge, attitudinal changes, and the development of more effective programs.

Cultural competence has a critical role to play in systems of care and the agencies and services that comprise them. Unless our systems devise a more appropriate way to prevent and intervene in mental health problems among youth of color, we will continue to hinder and restrict healthy development. We must begin to direct our energies and resources toward the development of interventions that work for the populations we need to reach. We cannot develop effective mental health services for children and families of color until we understand the important role that culture plays and until we examine our own attitudes and those of the agencies in which we work. Therefore, it is imperative that we all become more culturally competent.

REFERENCES

Berlin, I.N. (1983). Prevention of emotional problems among Native American children: Overview of developmental issues. In S. Chess & A. Thomas (Eds.), *Annual progress in child psychiatry and development* (pp. 320–333). New York: Brunner/Mazel.

Bernard, J.A. (1992). *Cultural competence training handbook.* Ventura County, CA: Ventura County Health Care Agency—Mental Health.

Blum, R.W., Harmon, B., Harris, L., Bergeisen, L., & Resnick, M. (1992). American Indian–Alaskan Native youth health. *JAMA, 267,* 1637–1644.

Children's Defense Fund. (1991). *The state of America's children.* Washington, DC: Author.

Children's Defense Fund. (1994). Young families: Suffering an economic freefall. *CDF Reports, 15*(10), 6.

Comer, J.P., & Hill, H. (1985). Social policy and the mental health of black children. *Journal of the American Academy of Child Psychiatry, 24,* 175–181.

Cross, T. (1992). *Organizational self-study on cultural competence for agencies addressing child abuse and neglect.* Prepared for the People of Color Leadership Institute, Center for Child Protection and Family Support, Washington, DC.

Cross, T., Bazron, B., Dennis, K., & Isaacs, M. (1989). *Towards a culturally competent system of care: A monograph on effective services for minority children who are severely emotionally disturbed.* Washington, DC: Georgetown University Child Development Center, National Technical Assistance Center for Children's Mental Health.

Cummins, J. (1986). Psychological assessment of minority students. In A.C. Willig & H.F. Greenberg (Eds.), *Bilingualism and learning disabilities: Policy and practice for teachers and administrators* (pp. 3–14). New York: American Library Publishing Company.

Gibbs, J.T. (Ed.). (1988). *Young, black and male in America: An endangered species.* Dover, MA.: Auburn House Publishing Company.

Gibbs, J.T., & Huang, L.N. (Eds.). (1989). *Children of color: Psychological interventions with minority youth.* San Francisco: Jossey-Bass.

Hawkins, J.D., & Salisbury, B.R. (1983). Delinquency prevention programs for minorities of color. *Social Work Research and Abstracts, 19*(4), 5–12.

Hune, S. (1977). U.S. immigration policy and Asian Americans: Aspects and consequences. In *Civil rights issues of Asian and Pacific Americans: Myths and realities* (pp. 283–291). Washington, DC: Government Printing Office.

Inclan, J., & Herron, D. (1989). Puerto Rican adolescents. In J.T. Gibbs & L.N. Huang (Eds.), *Children of color: Psychological interventions with minority youth* (pp. 251–278). San Francisco: Jossey-Bass.

Isaacs, M. (1993). Developing culturally competent strategies for adolescents of color. In A. Elster, S. Panzarine, & K. Holt (Eds.), *Adolescent health promotion (State-of-the-art conference)* (pp. 35–54). Chicago: American Medical Association.

Isaacs, M., & Benjamin, M. (1991). *Towards a culturally competent system of care: Programs which utilize culturally competent principles.* Washington, DC: Georgetown University, Child Development Center, National Technical Assistance Center for Children's Mental Health.

Katz-Leavy, J., Lourie, I.S., & Kaufman, R. (1987). Meeting the mental health needs of severely emotionally disturbed minority children and adolescents: A national perspective. *Children Today, 16*(5), 10–14.

LaFromboise, T.D., & Low, K.G. (1989). American Indian children and adolescents. In J.T. Gibbs & L.N. Huang (Eds.), *Children of color: Psychological interventions with minority youth* (pp. 114–147). San Francisco: Jossey-Bass.

Lewis, D.O., Lovely, R., Yeager, C., & Femina, D.D. (1989). Toward a theory of the genesis of violence: A follow-up study of delinquents. *Journal of the American Academy of Child and Adolescent Psychiatry, 28,* 431–436.

Lewis, D.O., Shanok, S.S., Cohen, R.J., Kligfeld, M., & Frisone, G. (1980). Race bias in the diagnosis and disposition of violent adolescents. *American Journal of Psychiatry, 137,* 1211–1216.

Marin, G. (1989). AIDS prevention among Hispanics: Needs, risk behaviors, and cultural values. *Public Health Reports, 104,* 411–415.

Mason, J. (1989). *The cultural competence self-assessment questionnaire.* Portland, OR: The Portland State University Research and Training Center for Children and Youth with Serious Emotional Handicaps and Their Families.

McLoyd, V. (1990). Minority child development: The special issue. *Child Development, 61,* 263–266.

Meinhardt, K., Tom, S., Tse, P., & Yu, C.Y. (1986). Southeast Asian refugees in the "Silicon Valley": The Asian health assessment project. *Amerasia Journal, 12,* 43–66.

Morales, A., Ferguson, Y., & Munford, P.R. (1986). The juvenile justice system and minorities. In G.J. Powell (Ed.), *The psychosocial development of minority group children* (pp. 515–537). New York: Brunner/Mazel.

Nagata, D. (1989). Japanese children and adolescents. In J.T. Gibbs & L.N. Huang (Eds.), *Children of color: Psychological interventions with minority youth* (pp. 67–113). San Francisco: Jossey-Bass.

Nickens, H. (1990, Summer). Health promotion and disease prevention among minorities. *Health Affairs,* pp. 133–143.

Ortiz, A.A., & Maldonado-Colon, E. (1986). Reducing inappropriate referrals of language minority students in special education. In A.C. Willig & H.F. Greenberg (Eds.), *Bilingualism and learning disabilities: Policy and practice for teachers and administrators* (pp. 37–52). New York: American Library Publishing Company.

Ramirez, O. (1989). Mexican American children and adolescents. In J.T. Gibbs & L.N. Huang (Eds.), *Children of color: Psychological interventions with minority youth* (pp. 224–250). San Francisco: Jossey-Bass.

Randall-David, E. (1990). *Strategies for working with culturally diverse communities and clients.* Washington, DC: Association for the Care of Children's Health.

Stehno, S.M. (1982). Differential treatment of minority children in service systems. *Social Work, 27*(1), 39–46.

Wilson, L. (1982). *The skills of cultural competence.* Unpublished resource paper, University of Washington, Seattle.

CHAPTER 3

Family Perspectives on Systems of Care

Barbara J. Friesen and Barbara Huff

Professional planners, administrators, and service providers share with families many common goals about improving systems of care for children with serious emotional, behavioral, or mental disorders. People who occupy different positions in groups, organizations, or larger systems, however, often have different perspectives. For example, managers and supervisors tend to estimate that line workers have more opportunity to participate in decision-making authority than the workers themselves think they have (Packard, 1993). Therapists and clients have been shown to have different views of the progress made in treatment (Lishman, 1978; Maluccio, 1979). Also, children and their parents often have contrasting views of family structure and process (Gehring, Marti, & Sidler, 1994). It should be no surprise, therefore, that family members may have different views of services and supports than those who provide or administer them, or that they might identify different priorities for system reform.

Chapter 1, by Stroul and Friedman, outlines the history of reform in children's mental health and presents a set of principles that have served as a framework for much system redesign and improvement since 1986 (Stroul & Friedman, 1986). This chapter complements Stroul and Friedman's work by offering views of the system of care in children's mental health from the perspectives of the families who are primary customers of services.

Viewing the system of care from the perspectives of families whose children have emotional, behavioral, or mental disorders involves looking through a lens that allows the viewer to understand the practical and emotional experiences of families—to "walk in their shoes." Often families' perspectives are not incompatible with those of services providers, administrators, researchers, or policy makers, but rather are complementary. When this is the case, families' viewpoints may suggest additional issues that should be considered when approaching system reform or may result in innovative solutions to problems.

To illustrate, consider the fact that it is difficult for many working parents to leave their jobs to attend meetings during the work day. This "fact" becomes a "problem" when there is a need for frequent meetings between family members and school personnel to plan and coordinate services for children with emotional disorders. Is this problem primarily related to the parent's situation (cannot afford to take time off, or not allowed to leave the workplace by employers)? Or, is it a problem of the school (meetings are held during times when many parents cannot reasonably be expected to attend, and union contracts often do not permit frequent evening hours for teachers)? If we define the problem primarily as related to the parents' situation, and the goal as "getting parents to meetings at the school during business hours," strategies might include providing subsidies for lost wages, intervening with employers to allow parents to use personal or medical leave to attend meetings related to their child's disability, or promoting workplace policies that encourage family members to be involved in school affairs (Mannan & Blackwell, 1992). If the problem is judged to be primarily school related, then possible solutions might include scheduling evening meetings (which may necessitate renegotiating union contracts) or allowing teachers to visit parents' workplace during their (family members') lunch break. Clearly, in this example, consideration of multiple perspectives might result in better problem solving.

Although families' perspectives may often complement or expand the perspectives of system planners and service providers, at times they may be quite different from, or even in conflict with, prevailing attitudes and practices. One example of this situation is the continuing practice in many states of requiring parents to relinquish custody of their children in order to gain access to services (Cohen, Harris, Gottlieb, & Best, 1991; Ervin, 1992; McManus & Friesen, 1989a, 1989b). This requirement is seen by some administrators and service providers as a means of gaining access to federal funds, increasing parental cooperation, or assuring that children receive the services they need. Most family members, in contrast, view this practice as negative and coercive, and are overwhelmingly opposed to it (Friesen, 1989; Thomas & Friesen, 1990). Family members, along with like-minded professionals, have worked in many states and at the federal level toward legal remedies to this problem (McManus & Friesen, 1989b; Research and Training Center, 1990). Other differences may arise because of the dissimilarities between the cultural backgrounds of service providers and family members. These differences may be evident in areas such as beliefs about child rearing or health practices or in ideas about what is considered appropriate or polite behavior.

In this chapter, family perspectives, both about their concerns as family members and caregivers and about their experiences with seeking and using services, are explored. Following a brief history of the development of a family perspective in children' mental health, themes of concern to family members are presented, illustrated with quotations from parents and other caregivers. The chapter concludes with a framework for thinking about family-centered systems of care.

VIEWING THE SYSTEM THROUGH THE EYES OF FAMILIES: A SHORT HISTORY

This chapter could not have been written in 1984, when the Child and Adolescent Service System Program (CASSP) was first funded by Congress to assist states in improving services for children with serious emotional disorders (Lourie, Katz-Leavy, & Jacobs, 1985). The original CASSP goals did not address family issues, and early system change guidelines reflected a top-down, professional-dominated view of the system. Furthermore, there was virtually no conceptual or empirical literature or even practice wisdom that provided information about families' concerns about their circumstances or their views of the children's mental health system. One important exception was the work of Jane Knitzer, who provided insightful glimpses of obstacles faced by families in her landmark book, *Unclaimed Children* (Knitzer, 1982). At that time, Knitzer summarized the problems faced by families as follows:

- Parents receive little assistance in finding services for their children and are either ignored or coerced by public agencies.
- Respite and support services to relieve the stress on parents are unavailable.
- Parents with children needing residential care must often give up custody to get them placed.
- Few advocacy efforts are aimed at relieving their problems. (p. xi)

Along with the lack of published literature in 1984 was the absence of any mechanism or forum for family perspectives to be expressed and heard. Families were largely isolated, and there was no organized national family voice on behalf of children needing mental health services. These three interrelated elements—family-related values and goals, knowledge about family perspectives, and an organized family voice—have all been developed and strengthened since the mid-1980s.

Values and Goals

By 1985, the second year of the CASSP program, evidence of the potential contribution that individual family members and family organizations could make to system reform efforts resulted in the addition of a family-related CASSP goal. This new goal read, "to develop family input into the planning and development of service systems, treatment options, and individual service options" (Lourie, Katz-Leavy, & Jacobs, 1986, p. 2). The inclusion of family participation as a CASSP goal required that state applications for federal CASSP funds demonstrate how families would be included in service planning efforts at the child and family, program, and system levels. In November 1986, Congress passed the State Mental Health Services Comprehensive Plan (PL 99-660), which mandated family participation in the development of state mental health plans. This mandate created the opportunity for family input regarding child mental health needs. (It should be noted, however, that in many states only family members representing the interests of adults with mental illnesses were initially appointed to serve on state planning councils.) Stroul and Friedman's inclusion of one of the CASSP principles—"The families and surrogate families of emotionally disturbed children should be full participants in all aspects of the planning and delivery of services" (Stroul & Friedman, 1986, p. vii)—also served to legitimize the family perspective. These supports for family participation were crucial to creating and maintaining a climate in which the perspectives of family members were considered to be relevant and important to the system reform effort.

There has also been considerable activity at the level of the states to increase family involvement in service planning. This increased acknowledgment of family perspectives has come about as a result of a variety of forces, including the federal legislation mandating family involvement in state mental health planning bodies, voluntary changes implemented by forward-looking state administrators, and policy change stimulated by advocates of family organizations and other advocates.

Knowledge about Family Perspectives

As family members were included in state and local planning processes, planners, administrators, and service providers had opportunities to hear about family members' experiences and concerns. Thus, one important source of information for many professionals charged with creating system reform was personal interaction, listening to first-person accounts of family members' attempts to locate, obtain, finance, and use services that are appropriate for their children. For some professionals, the experience was transforming. One service provider recalled:

> [W]hen I started this experience, when I met with the first group of parents in Topeka one year ago, it became my biggest, most significant career change. What Cindy said and what the other parents said in that meeting probably had the most profound impact . . . that I've ever had in my life. I'm a clinician and an administrator with 15 years of experience in the field of mental health, specifically with children and adolescents and their families. I had to sit there and listen to the experiences that these parents were sharing and bite my tongue. It wasn't very pleasant to think about the fact that as a professional who had always thought that I was doing what was helpful, that many times what I had done or what I hadn't done may not have been helpful at all. (McManus & Friesen, 1986, p. 11)

One organized mechanism for family members to express their perspectives was five regional "Families as Allies" conferences held between

1986 and 1988. The overall purpose of these conferences was to promote family–professional collaboration in undertaking service delivery and system reform. These meetings brought planners, administrators, and services providers from various systems (e.g., mental health, child welfare, education, juvenile justice) together with equal numbers of family members to exchange information and make plans for further action in their states (McManus & Friesen, 1986; Research and Training Center, 1987). One of the most important features of these conferences was the opportunity for family members to speak directly about their experiences and hopes. For example, at the first Families as Allies conference, one family member told conference participants:

> I guess my biggest hope and one of the biggest reasons I'm here today is that you professionals are sitting out there . . . please, please give us parents a break. Listen to what we have to say. Help us if you can. We live with these kids. We know what it feels like. We need your help, but you need ours, too. You can't possibly know what it's like to live in [our] home and not know from day to day what's going to happen and not know where to go for help. (McManus & Friesen, 1986, p. 11)

In addition to the regional Families as Allies conferences, a number of states held statewide conferences during 1987 and 1988 that featured family perspectives. Family members were featured speakers at each of these conferences, where they described their attempts to obtain appropriate assessments and locate, access, and pay for services. These regional and state conferences provided a public forum for family members to share their views of services and their hopes and dreams for their children. The conferences also illustrated the tremendous strength and courage of family members in the face of very complex and troublesome situations.

Between 1984 and 1989, when the first state and regional conferences promoted the gathering and exchange of information among families and between families and professionals, a few family-oriented research projects were also undertaken. These studies were designed to collect information from family members about their experiences with seeking and using services, their needs and resources, and their recommendations for system improvement (Friesen, 1989; Hosick, 1988; Kotsopoulos, Elwood, & Oke, 1989; Robin, 1989; Tarico, Low, Trupin, & Forsyth-Stephens, 1989). These early studies provided a beginning empirical foundation for themes that were already being communicated by families in first-person accounts: lack of clear and accurate information about emotional disorders of children, lack of appropriate services, the impact on the entire family of struggling to address the needs of a child with serious behavior problems, the importance of informal as well as formal support, and the dire consequences when such support was lacking.

Since the CASSP program began in 1984, there has been a steady increase in information about the perspectives of families from a variety of sources. A large number of family groups and organizations produce newsletters or regularly contribute articles to newsletters of other advocacy organizations. Another important source of information for and about families is materials produced either entirely by families and family organizations or in collaboration with professionals. These materials include manuals about how to start and maintain family support and advocacy groups (Donner & Fine, 1987); handbooks for families that address the nature of emotional, behavioral, and mental disorders in children and/or provide guidance about navigating the education, social service, and mental health systems (Anderson, 1994; Binkard, Goldberg, & Goldberg, 1984; Kelker, 1987); and first-person accounts about living with a child who has serious emotional problems (Gattozzi, 1986; McElroy, 1988; Zeigler-Dendy, 1994). In addition, family members contribute to newsletters, articles, and books addressing system reform issues in children's mental health (e.g., Donner et al., 1995; Fine & Borden, 1989; Friesen & Huff, 1990; Friesen & Wahlers, 1993; Mayer, 1994).

The number of articles in the professional literature that view the system from the perspectives of families is also growing. These documents address topics such as relationships with professionals (Collins & Collins, 1990; Cournoyer & Johnson, 1991; DeChillo, 1993; DeChillo, Koren, & Schultze, 1994; Friesen, Koren, & Koroloff, 1992), family empowerment (Heflinger, 1995; Koren, DeChillo, & Friesen, 1992), effect of the child's disability on the family (Asarnow & Horton, 1990), and family members' evaluation of services (Byalin, 1990; DeChillo & Lebow, 1991; Greenley & Robitschek, 1991; Kotsopoulos et al., 1989).

Taken together, these research reports, conference proceedings, book chapters, family newsletters, and articles in professional journals constitute a rich source of information about how family members view their situations and the service delivery system.

Development of an Organized Family Voice

In 1985, a national study undertaken to describe the degree to which families of children with serious emotional disorders were organized for the purposes of support, education, and advocacy located only nine organizations focused solely on children's mental health (Friesen, 1991). The other 200 organizations that participated in the study either addressed mental health issues for both children and adults or provided services to families whose children had a wide variety of emotional, physical, and cognitive disabilities. Between 1984 and 1988, there was dramatic growth in local and statewide organizations focused on children's mental health issues, related in part to increased support from state mental health authorities, local and state mental health associations, state and local chapters of the Alliance for the Mentally Ill, and private foundations (Friesen, Griesbach, Jacobs, Katz-

Leavy, & Olson, 1988). By 1993, there were more than 30 statewide family organizations and hundreds of local groups focused on children's mental health issues (Wagner, 1993). Much of the development at the state level was stimulated by funding provided by the federal CASSP program to stimulate the growth and capacities of statewide family networks.

In December 1988, 60 family members and professionals from 20 states met together to consider "next steps" in addressing issues urgently needing attention: 1) family support services, 2) access to appropriate educational services, 3) relinquishing custody as a means of obtaining services, and 4) coordination of services at the individual family level (case management) (Thomas & Friesen, 1990). At that meeting, participating family members voted to form a steering committee to consider what form a "national voice for children" should take (see Friesen, 1993, for a more complete history of this organizing process). The steering committee subsequently voted to form a new national organization, and the Federation of Families for Children's Mental Health was legally incorporated in August 1989. This organization now has an office in Washington, D.C., sponsors an annual meeting attended by hundreds of families each year, provides technical assistance to families and professionals across the country, publishes a newsletter (*Claiming Children*) in English and Spanish, and addresses policy issues in children's mental health. The National Alliance for the Mentally Ill (NAMI), a family organization founded in 1979 to address issues related to adults with mental illness, also sponsors and supports the Child and Adolescent Network (NAMI CAN), which emphasizes issues of concern to families whose children have neurobiological disorders. NAMI provides valuable information about issues of concern to families whose children have mental illnesses and works to promote research, advocacy, and better services for these children and their families (Howe, 1995).

A number of other state and national organizations addressing specific disorders (e.g., attention-deficit/hyperactivity disorder, learning disabilities, pervasive developmental disorders, and attachment disorders) also provide support to families whose children are broadly defined as having emotional, behavioral, or mental disorders (Wagner, 1993). Bryant-Comstock, Huff, and VanDenBerg provide a more detailed history of the family advocacy movement in children's mental health, education, juvenile justice, and child welfare (see Chapter 19).

CONCERNS OF FAMILY MEMBERS

This section presents a set of themes that represent some central concerns of family members whose children have emotional, behavioral, or mental disorders. The impact of dealing with the myriad issues associated with a child's emotional disorder is most eloquently expressed by family members' descriptions of their own experiences. One source of such information is a study conducted by Friesen (1989) that gathered information from more than 900 family members across the United States, called the Parent Survey. In this study, family caregivers completed a written questionnaire exploring issues such as their experiences with professionals, their use of services, information needs, and formal and informal sources of support (see Koroloff & Friesen, 1991, for a description of the overall study methodology). At the end of the questionnaire, family members responded to an open-ended question, "What's the most important issue that you have had to face in raising a child with an emotional disorder?" The written responses to this question were transcribed and then examined to identify themes expressed by the family members who responded to the survey. Once the themes were identified, the narrative was then coded by two members of the research team and their work was reviewed to examine interrater reliability, which was judged to be acceptable. Differences were arbitrated by a third member of the research team. The following discussion of these themes includes verbatim quotations from respondents to the question about their "most important concerns" gathered in the Parent Survey (Friesen, 1989). These family members' descriptions of their circumstances and experiences with trying to obtain services provided a window into their lives that had not previously been available.

Impact on the Family

One clear concern that emerges from both research and first-person accounts is the profound impact on the entire family when services to help the child with an emotional disorder are lacking or inappropriate. Growing awareness on the part of both family members and professionals about the difficulties faced by families has led to a call for services that address the needs of all family members and the need to support families' efforts to keep their children at home (Federation of Families for Children's Mental Health, 1992; Friesen & Koroloff, 1990). This shift in children's mental health, from a focus solely on the child to consideration of the needs of the entire family, parallels developments in fields such as child welfare (Frankel, 1988; Stehno, 1986; Whittaker, 1991), developmental disabilities (Summers, 1988), and health (Brewer, McPherson, Magrab, & Hutchins, 1989; Shelton, Jeppson, & Johnson, 1987).

In response to the question in the Parent Survey about their "most important issue" (Friesen, 1989), a number of respondents identified impact on their families and trying to maintain a balanced family life as most important to them. Family members identified the immediate impact on the family of dealing with the child's difficult emotions and behavior, and the consequences of the lack of appropriate response from the service delivery system, in the following quotations:

"Trying to keep a marriage and family together in a healthy environment for the other children when one child creates havoc."

"The effect on family life in general. Constant stress and cannot have friends over for fear of an incident. Also house is in poor condition due to his destructive tantrums."

"Lack of respite care or relief, no time off. No breaks, social life is nil. No time together for me and my spouse. Child's needs dominate time, conversation, all consuming, so much energy is necessary for day-to-day living."

"Probably the most disconcerting thing is that no one understood that there was a family involved."

"If a system could be designed to support and assist families rather than to punish and/or supplant them, we would have a lot more functional families, kids, and societies."

"Family-centered service" involves a response to the needs of the whole family, including the child with a health or mental health problem (Shelton et al., 1987). Essential to the development of family-centered service is the concept of family support. The need to include family support services as a fundamental part of designing mental health services and a clearly articulated philosophy is contained in the statement of principles developed by the Federation of Families for Children's Mental Health (1992):

> Family support is a constellation of formal and informal services and tangible goods that are defined and determined by families. It is "whatever it takes" for a family to care for and live with a child or adolescent who has an emotional, behavioral, or mental disorder. It also includes supports needed to assist families to maintain close involvement with their children who are in out-of-home placement and to help families when their children are ready to return home. (p. 1)

Karp and Bradley (1991) review the values that guide family support programs and the types of supports that may be offered to families. Guiding values include 1) focusing on the family and community, 2) putting decision-making control in the hands of families, 3) involving families throughout the process, and 4) ensuring program flexibility. Family support may include services such as respite and child care, support from another family member when visiting a hospitalized child or attending an agency meeting, in-home assistance, transportation, cash assistance, training, and recreation.

Addressing Stigma and Blame

Another clear concern of families is related to the stigma that is attached to mental health problems in our society and the blame that parents and other caregivers may experience because of their children's emotional, behavioral, or mental disorders. In the Parent Survey (Friesen, 1989), many family members identified stigma and blame as their biggest challenge. Some family members addressed the lack of understanding about mental and emotional disorders on the part of the general public: "[There is a] lack of support from the community as a whole, there is lack of knowledge on the subject, treating us like we had a disease that was catching." One mother described how lack of public understanding about her child's disability led to intervention by the child welfare system:

"I have had child abuse charges brought on me . . . when a rage or tantrum would occur in public and all I could do was keep him safe (from traffic) or from hurting himself. What we go through as parents—we don't need this too."

Lack of public understanding about their children's behavior also led many families to curtail their social activities. One family member commented:

"Lack of social acceptance for our child is difficult for us to deal with. It limits our activities and public appearances. It's easier to just stay home than take him out. We have even stopped vacations."

In addition to the general public, many respondents also identified a lack of understanding on the part of family, friends, or neighbors:

"My mother and father were not supportive. They thought my son was spoiled. My ex-husband and his family blamed my parenting for all of my son's problems. I had nowhere to turn and had no idea what would become of us."

This mother's theme, that of being blamed for her child's behavior because she had "spoiled" him, was echoed by many family members. One mother used professional services to educate those around her:

"Extended family and close friends do not understand or accept what they perceive as a spoiled child that 'just needs better discipline.' Much blame is placed (and felt by) parents. . . . We were blamed by grandparents and friends. We also experienced problems with school nurses, secretaries, and teachers who didn't understand the emotional problems. . . . The authority of our psychiatrist was helpful in dealing with them."

Still other family members commented that professional attitudes and behaviors constituted the most difficult issue that they faced:

"Instead of supporting families emotionally and financially, some professionals tend to view the cause as the family and use adversarial processes. This further discourages those people who must find the energy to deal with the child, advocate, and case manage and parent. The consequences of the lack of support for families can be devastating for all."

Many parents also blamed themselves for their children's problems. Some cited specific instances, such as remaining too long with an abusive spouse, whereas for others feelings of remorse were not tied to specific issues. One mother wrote about how her self-blame persisted despite reassurance from professionals:

"I blame myself and always have, although doctors and social workers say I don't have any reason to. I have tried to get a solid diagnosis for many years and have not. I feel I have failed in some way to give my son the best start. I feel terrible for him. I love him very much. I wish someone could help me and help him."

Lack of Services

Many family members focused on the lack of services and the difficulty of locating appropriate services. As one parent commented, "[The most important issue I faced was] learning what is available, discovering what is appropriate, and learning how to obtain these necessary services for my child." Some family members said that they were better able to get services when their insurance coverage allowed them to use private services, and that their access to services became severely limited when their insurance benefits were exhausted. This problem was addressed by a family member who said:

"In the private system parents have greater freedom to choose professionals who will relate to them in the way they want. While not perfect, my experiences in the private system were much more supportive than they have been in the public system."

Problems associated with lack of resources were identified by many family members, including one frustrated parent who said:

"We are told at every turn that there is no money available for services, no services in place even if there was money, my child doesn't fit this criterion or that."

Other respondents focused on the lack of local resources, often appearing to believe that services were available in other parts of the state or country and that their situation was especially bad. This belief was expressed by one family member in this way:

"Services in our county/state are poor. We don't have a child psychiatrist here in the county, or an adolescent psychiatric unit. I travel nearly 100 miles round trip for my child's therapy in a neighboring county."

In order to seek appropriate services, family members must know what to look for. Many families had difficulty obtaining a diagnosis and getting a clear recommendation about what service package was most appropriate for their children. One mother described her search over many years, stating that the most important issue she faced was finding appropriate treatment:

"Although there have been problems since early childhood, I had been unable to obtain effective treatment. . . . Last year, after consulting a psychiatrist and child psychologist, I was able to have my son entered into day treatment. Some improvement occurred. . . . Although my son finally received the needed care, I am still angry about the ordeal of obtaining it."

Many family members commented about the difficulty they had finding community-based services, sometimes resulting in an out-of-home placement. One mother wrote this about the problem:

"I feel angry that I had to send my son away. I feel that if our county had the proper programs, we could have made it with my son at home. We needed a day treatment center and respite care. The only options we had . . . were the state hospital or residential care."

Parenting Issues

Many family members also had questions about how to address the needs of their children with mental or emotional disorders. As one mother noted, "I would like any information that I can get to help raise [my son]." For some, concerns focused on dealing with day-to-day situations:

"What to do to help him with his disability. How to explain it to him so he understands, 'Why me?' "

"Trying to find a way to help him so he can function as a happy and confident person."

"Understanding what he is going through and being patient enough with his shortcomings and frustrations."

"I am always seeking new ways to handle him, a cure, a new method of dealing with problems, new medication, any promising hint of help for him or me."

"Trying to teach him how to live in the world with less anger and frustration and getting along with others' values and morals."

"Trying to preserve my beautiful, creative son, while just about everyone else (teachers, principles, neighbors, family, "friends," etc.) beats down his spirit, ego, and self-worth."

"Trying to keep his self-esteem from going down the drain."

Other family members identified long-range concerns as most important. Examples of concerns about transitions are reflected in the following responses:

"How to prepare children for adulthood. How to have a mentally healthy family in spite of this disability."

"Trying to help my child make a transition to be a healthy, happy, well-balanced person."

Family–Professional Relationships

In addition to sometimes feeling blamed for their children's problems, family members' concerns about their interaction with service providers focused on three areas. The first has to do with wanting to be listened to and acknowledged as experts. The second theme is related to family members' feelings that professionals do not always know how to help. The third area of concern reflects families' experiences with service quality.

Family members' statements about wanting to be heard and acknowledged included the following:

> "Getting him the help he so desperately needed, getting a professional to believe us as parents in order to have him diagnosed . . ."

> "Every time I asked to see the guidance counselor I was told it wasn't necessary and [my son's] actions were purely deliberate . . ."

> "I would like to see professionals listen to the insights I have about my child. Many times my ideas were pushed aside because they were "educated" and I was not. The professional can shrug and walk away when he or she is wrong and my family is left to pick up the pieces."

> "Getting respect and proper services and not condescension about my parenting and his problem. Turns out it never was his problem. Simply, more services need to be made available for schizophrenic children and their families."

> "I am very happy to see someone doing research and asking for parent participation. Many, not all [professionals], have been so insensitive to the pain of the parent. I hope we can work together to change this."

Many family members expressed their chagrin about service providers' not having the answers they sought, or sufficient training to adequately address the problems that they and their children encountered. Examples of this theme are evident in the following statements made by family members in their response to the Parent Survey:

> "Many professions, especially the school system, lack training and knowledge of emotional disturbance."

> "I called the hospital back three times after his release to say that I was very frightened of his continued depression. I related he was screaming that he hated himself. I was told to leave him alone, he was fine and was just doing his thing. He killed himself four days after my third call back, within a week of his release."

> "Our pediatrician should have informed us of the services available, but never did. We found an adolescent residential and day hospital almost by accident."

> "We find that regular education teachers and some special education teachers don't know how to adapt regular curriculum and assignments to meet our child's learning style."

Some who responded to the Parent Survey felt that the services they received were inappropriate or ineffective. They identified problems such as a lack of direction in counseling or therapy, lack of coordination among professionals or agencies, and treatments or programs that were not tailored to their children's needs. Some examples of these responses include

"The social worker we counseled with was good to a point. Then sessions became redundant. Communication of direction she was leading us was extremely poor."

"An unqualified instructor was in one of the programs my child was placed in and the other program was very inappropriate. Three years of my child's life [were] wasted in these programs."

"Too many people involved and no one seeing the problem. At one time people who were seeing my son with no results: L.C. [licensed counselor], S.W. [social worker], psychologist, psychiatrist—private, probation officers, two neurologists—private. Hospitalized for 4 days (S.W., psychiatrist, M.D.). Diagnosis obtained—atypical psychosis."

"Professionals knowledgeable to help in real life settings . . ."

The day-to-day challenges facing families whose children have emotional disorders provide an important counterpoint to the view of the system often held by policy makers, planners, and administrators.

A FRAMEWORK FOR A FAMILY-CENTERED SYSTEM OF CARE

This section contrasts a "program-centered" view of the system with a "family-centered" perspective and offers suggestions for increasing the extent to which family viewpoints can be incorporated into the current system of care. Moving toward a family-centered system of care involves blending two contrasting perspectives of the system. The first perspective, which is the dominant "program-centered" way of thinking, is exemplified in virtually all mental health and social service planning processes and often results in what VanDenBerg (1993) calls "categorical services." This perspective involves a focus on a program, organization, or entire system, and, although children and families are seen as the primary beneficiaries of services, they still constitute only one of many considerations in program planning and development. In a program-centered planning process, there may be an emphasis on creating a system of care that is responsive to the needs of children and families, but such planning is by necessity based on estimates of common needs, with choices made according to rational planning strategies (York, 1982). This approach makes it difficult to ensure that the needs of all children with emotional disorders and their families are addressed, and emphasis on programs may impede the ability to individualize services.

To illustrate, an in-home respite program might be developed based on the fact that two thirds of families surveyed said that they would prefer that type of respite service. The one third of the families who would not use that option would simply not benefit from the program. From the program's perspective, this situation could be quite acceptable because of limited resources and a waiting list for respite services that would ensure that the new program will be used. The program would be full, and the needs of families who preferred in-home respite would be satisfactorily addressed. Over time, many families would move in and out of the program, and a program evaluation would assess how well the program was doing in terms of variables such as the appropriateness, timeliness, and quality of services, and child and family satisfaction.

The perspective that we call "family-centered" shifts the focus from the system, organization, or program to the level of children and families. The approach views the environment, and indeed the passage of time, from the perspective of the individual child and family. From this point of view, any given program or agency may or may not be relevant now or in the future to the needs, aspirations, and preferences of children and families. In addition to the formal services that comprise the formal service delivery system, each family's environment also contains informal relationships and resources that are very important to them but may not be a part of the general resource pool for all families. Furthermore, concern is focused on how well the needs of children and families are met over time; children and families may use a wide variety of formal and informal services as their needs change. This "bottom-up" view of the system is apparent in Burchard and colleagues' (1995) discussion about using case-level data to monitor system-level operations and is also represented in the few published discussions of individualized services (Burchard & Clarke, 1990; Katz-Leavy, Lourie, Stroul, & Zeigler-Dendy, 1992; VanDenBerg, 1992, 1993).

If one is concerned both about the health of children and families and the health of the service delivery system, neither of these two perspectives is sufficient. The current dominant program-centered perspective has difficulty taking individual needs into account—families can rarely get what they need in one location or from one organization, and coordination of services is often problematic. The family-centered perspective does not include organizational issues, except as they pertain to addressing the needs of individual families while operating within a "whatever it takes" approach to service planning. The logical outcome of this latter approach, carried to its extreme, would be fewer resources committed to ongoing programs and more flexible resources available. Fully implemented, this approach could lead to great uncertainty and chaos within the service delivery system. VanDenBerg (1993) discusses the advantages and disadvantages of categorical and individualized services and suggests strategies to increase the ability of categorical services to provide individualized services.

In Table 3.1, some differences between the program-centered and family-centered perspectives are summarized in relation to five major issues: 1) the focus, or unit of attention; 2) access to services; 3) assessment of child and family needs; 4) service design decisions at the agency and

Table 3.1.   Comparing the program-centered and family-centered perspectives

Variables	Program-centered perspective	Family-centered perspective
Unit of attention	Program, organization, or system	Child and family
Major access issues	Eligibility (Do this child and family qualify for our services on the basis of diagnosis, geography, income level, etc?)	Availability, timeliness, appropriateness of services (How do families get what they need when they need it?)
Assessment of child and family needs	Need–program match (Do this child and family need what we have? How well do our services fit their needs?)	"Whatever it takes"—focus on unique needs of child and family; family defined
Service design decisions		
Agency level	Majority rule (What do most of the clients/families who come to our agency need and/or want?)	Case-by-case decision (What do this child and family need now?)
Community or state levels	Comprehensiveness (Do we have in our community a full range of services?)	Focus on family ecology and individualization (What role do formal services play in addressing the needs of families? How can we design a system that is flexible and responsive?)
Family participation	Role of families (What role should families have in the planning process or in the services that we provide?)	Family-driven planning (How can service planning processes maximize the extent to which the expertise and wisdom of family members are taken into account? What role should service providers have in the planning process?)

community or state levels; and 5) family participation. These contrasts are briefly discussed for each category.

Unit of Attention

When the focus is on the program, agency, or set of services that comprise the system in a given community or state, children and families are seen not only as the primary beneficiaries of services but also as the raw materials, "inputs," or part of the organization's "task environment" (Hasenfeld, 1983). From this perspective, children and families may constitute important resources needed for organizational survival, along with other elements such as space, adequate numbers of competent staff, and community support. Children and families who need services may also constitute a source of burden, if a given organization, or an entire system, does not have sufficient control over the nature or number of referrals and does not have sufficient resources to respond to need. Thus, as Kirk and Kutchins (1992) point out, "regulating client flow" is a central concern of mental health and other social service organizations. Concerns about regulating the flow of children and families and distributing scarce resources lead to mechanisms such as eligibility requirements, limitations on location or time, or other access-related program elements as a way of attempting to keep a balance between organizational capabilities and client (child and family) demand.

When the unit of attention is the individual child and family, or small groups of children and families who face similar challenges, concerns are quite different. Emphasis is placed on addressing the problems and needs associated with each child's emotional disorder, including the needs of the family. From this perspective, a service organization's efforts to manage client flow may impede the ability of children and families to locate, access, and use needed services. The family-centered perspective also takes a broader view of the family system. For example, when thinking about the environment of any given family, it becomes apparent that formal service organizations are just some of the sources of important services and supports. Others, such as extended family, friends, church, school, employers, and social clubs, also may provide resources, support, and "services," perhaps as a part of a system of exchange.

Access to Services

Eligibility requirements constitute the major filter by which agencies regulate access to and use of their resources. When a child and family first come in contact with an agency, eligibility determination is often the first order of business. In this regard, agency personnel ask questions such as, "Do this child and family qualify for our services on the basis of age, diagnosis, geography, income level, or other requirements?" A positive answer to the eligibility question is usually required before other assessment is undertaken and before any services are provided.

In contrast, a family-centered approach focuses not on eligibility, but rather on obtaining needed services for a child and family in a timely manner. The question here becomes, "Can this child and family get what they need when they need it?" This perspective obviously goes beyond questions of eligibility to include issues such as the availability, timeliness, appropriateness, and acceptability of services, in addition to access questions such as location, hours, cost, and other factors associated with accessibility.

Assessment of Child and Family Needs

In the program-centered perspective, there is a concern from the first contact about whether there is a match between program resources and the needs of children and families. This is, of course, reasonable in a system in which programs do not have much flexibility and the emphasis is on en-suring that children and families get connected to the services that come closest to addressing their needs. In program management terms, the con-cern is with maximizing appropriate referrals (i.e., the people referred need what the organization has to offer). So the central questions become, "Do this child and family need what we have?" or "How well do our services fit their needs?" If the needs of the child and family are a reasonable fit with the agency mission, once they are accepted for service, services may be tailored through the selection and adaptation of treatment strategies or referrals to more appropriate programs.

A focus on the unique needs of children and families involves discov-ering these needs and then providing, or helping to locate, "whatever it takes" to address those needs. As Friesen and Koroloff (1990) suggest, family-centered service should also centrally involve the family in defining their needs and in selecting or designing services. It is here, in the definition of need, that families often feel at odds with, or come into conflict with, service providers. For example, one mother described the discrepancy be-tween what she needed and what she could get (Thomas & Friesen, 1990):

> As an example, the service that I most needed when my son was younger was someone to come into my home at 6:30 in the morning, get him up, and get him ready for school. Just support and encourage him to get ready for school. That would have made a tremendous difference to our family. In fact, I called the local social service agency at one point and said, "Can I get this?" because I knew that the developmental disability agency had that service. . . . They said, "No, we can give you counseling." We didn't need any more counseling about that issue. Counseling was not solving our problem. (p. 9)

In a study involving families whose adult children had psychiatric dis-abilities, Spaniol, Jung, Zipple, and Fitzgerald (1987) found similar discrep-ancies between what families said they needed and professionals' views of family needs.

Agency-Level Service Design Decisions

As illustrated in the respite care example earlier in this chapter, programs and agencies often do their best to maximize the extent to which their re-sources are directed to the needs of a majority of the clients that they serve. Because their focus is on building programs and program capacity, this decision making often involves a "majority rule" approach. From a pro-grammatic point of view, this may be sensible decision making. For the children and families for whom this program is not appropriate, the ap-proach is unsatisfactory and disappointing.

Family-centered services involve decision making on a case-by-case basis, addressing questions such as, "What do this child and family need now? What strengths and resources do they bring, including informal sources of support? How can we pull together resources from a variety of formal and informal sources to help this family cope and thrive? Especially for families of color, attention to the importance of extended families and other social relationships acknowledges the strengths and resources of families, rather than focusing exclusively on problems. Slaughter (1988) proposes a "cultural-ecological" approach to family program design that builds on family strengths and existing coping strategies. In our experience, family support and advocacy organizations are less likely than established mental health and social service agencies to have fixed eligibility criteria and are more able to implement a flexible approach to serving families, even when the mental health needs of their children may not be their initial concern. Over time, however, family organizations, too, will face questions about how to distribute their scarce resources and may be faced with the dilemma of matching their capacities to the demands of the families who ask for help (i.e., developing service guidelines and/or eligibility criteria).

Community or State-Level Service Design Decisions

A commitment to comprehensive services, and to addressing the needs of the "whole child" and family, often leads community planners to ask the question, "Do we have in our community a full range of services?" Over the years, concern about how to distribute scarce resources, combined with an agenda to reduce reliance on restrictive placements, has resulted in attention to such issues as "sizing the system of care" (Friedman, 1987; Pires, 1990) through deciding what proportion of resources should be devoted to service components such as inpatient, outpatient, day treatment, therapeutic foster care, and other service categories. Attention has also been devoted to addressing related staffing and training needs (Pires, 1992).

From the family-centered perspective, the true test of the system will always be whether a given child and family can get what they need in a timely manner. Considering the entire life circumstances of children and families, it is clear that formal services may play a large role or may constitute a very small portion of the support and resources that any given family may need. Furthermore, although a focus on the entire population of children with emotional disorders and their families emphasizes the need for comprehensiveness, a focus on individual children and families leads us to a primary emphasis on flexibility and responsiveness. A more individualized approach to service planning is common in rural areas, where population density does not support the development of a wide spectrum of specialized services. Perhaps we have much to learn from successful approaches to rural mental health service delivery.

Family Participation

From a program-centered perspective, staff and administrators are likely to struggle with the question, "What role should families have in the planning process or in the implementation and evaluation of the services we provide?" Even as individuals and organizations have increased their commitment to the involvement of family members in planning and policy making, implementation of this goal poses many challenges (Hunter, 1994; Koroloff, Hunter, & Gordon, 1995). Service organizations and family members alike confront issues such as the need for training and support for family members' participation in decision making, how to avoid tokenism, and the importance of creating effective patterns of communication and information exchange between family and professional committee members.

A family-centered system of care seeks to maximize the extent to which the expertise and experience of family members is utilized in planning and decision making. Although the program-centered perspective dominates throughout most of the country, a few examples exist in which the influence of family members in planning and decision making is well established. One such example is the Finger Lakes Family Support Program (Friesen & Wahlers, 1993), in which family members screen and train respite providers, have decision-making authority over a portion of the budget, and make day-to-day decisions about the program.

The most well-developed example of a system in which families have considerable decision-making clout is in the Families First project in Essex County, New York (see Chapter 20). This effort began with intensive discussions with families regarding their ideas about how services could be improved. Based on this need assessment, the Families First organization was begun to provide services at no cost to families whose children have emotional disorders. Seventy-five percent of the organization's board is composed of family members. Services include a wide range of family support resources, including an office where families may visit without an appointment, parent-to-parent support, a resource library, respite programs, social events for families, and flexible dollars to address service gaps. Other components include advocacy, case management, and youth activities. Families First emphasizes interagency collaboration as a way to increase resources and create a family-friendly system of care. Although Families First is leading the way in implementing a family-centered approach to system reform, this project, too, faces many challenges. These include resource constraints as well as skepticism and resistance from established service providers.

BLENDING TWO PERSPECTIVES: STRATEGIES FOR CHANGE

Blending the rational planning approach with a family-centered perspective of the system should present advantages both to families and children and to the current stewards of the system (legislators, planners, administrators, and service providers). The advantages to families include reduction or elimination of barriers to service, increased appropriateness of services, and attention to the ecology of each family (considering strengths as well as problems and taking informal resources into account). This should result in greater satisfaction with services and better service results for children and families.

These positive outcomes for families should be mirrored by advantages to "the system." Although reduction of barriers to service may raise the specter of overwhelming demand, in fact, use of a family-centered planning process should result in more focused use of formal services, a reduction of "inappropriate" referrals, and more efficient use of resources. When family members are involved in planning and selecting services, they should be more likely to complete services, reducing the current inefficiencies associated with a dropout rate in children's mental health that approaches 50% (46.8% according to a meta-analysis by Wierzbicki & Petarik, 1993). This prediction is supported by Elliott's (1994) finding that a significant relationship existed between the extent to which parents' expectations were met and their children's continuance in mental health services.

VanDenBerg's (1993) suggestions for increasing the ability of the existing system to individualize services focus on the availability of flexible funds, a careful assessment and planning process, and combining traditional and nontraditional services to fill in service needs. Other strategies for moving toward family-centered services include the following:

1. *Include family members in service design, implementation, and evaluation of services.* First, this involvement of family members should be at all levels—with respect to their own children and families, but also in organizational and system-level planning and decision-making. Second, this involvement must avoid tokenism. It must allow families to be *in charge* of decisions with respect to their own families, and to have *substantial* influence at the organizational and system levels. Families chosen to participate in planning must represent diverse backgrounds, cultures, and experiences. Such diversity will help maintain a focus on the need for individualization and flexibility.
2. *Create ways to maintain a focus on the experiences and preferences of individual families, even in "top-down" planning processes.* Strategies such as conducting focus groups with families to "market test" program proposals or to anticipate implementation issues could greatly increase system responsiveness.
3. *Involve family members in the evaluation of programs, services, organizations, and systems.* Once family members identify the outcomes that are important to them, these should be combined with evaluation questions that reflect system concerns such as cost and

efficiency. This process should also be very useful in identifying areas where the interests of planners and administrators and those of families converge.

4. *Develop mechanisms to keep the "minority" view represented in program planning processes.* Many creative strategies exist that may be used to balance the traditional "funnel" approach to decision making. Systematically building in questions such as, "What effect will this choice have on those for whom this service is not appropriate?" and "Is there a way to increase options within a fixed budget?" will help to keep in mind those who may not benefit from specific decisions.

5. *Build in flexibility and choice as basic program planning principles.* Flexible funds constitute a necessary resource for individualized services, but creative planning that takes into account the strengths and informal resources of families may reduce or eliminate the need for additional funds. For example, family members in Washington State receive training about case management in exchange for their provision of case management services to one other family (P. Miles, personal communication, 1994), and family members frequently exchange child care (respite) services. Churches and service organizations may be willing to adapt and extend their programs and resources to children with mental health problems and their families once the need is explained, especially when training and support are provided.

6. *Consider employing family members as service providers, either by contracting with family organizations or by hiring parents and other family members directly.* This suggestion is currently being implemented in some service systems. It is apparent that there are many advantages to having family members on staff. They often have an understanding of and empathy for difficult family situations beyond that provided by professional training and work experience alone, and they may have access to families not available to other staff. Other advantages include having a spokesperson for the family-centered perspective present at staff meetings and available for other planning and decision-making processes. Along with these advantages are potential challenges such as licensing and certification hurdles, family members' feeling co-opted or inhibited (especially with respect to advocacy for the families they serve), and potential torn loyalties of family members when the needs and demands of their employing organization conflict with their best judgment about family-centered services. The trend toward hiring family members as service providers clearly begs for systematic examination.

7. *Take advantage of opportunities to participate in research and evaluation activities specifically focused on family issues.* For example, researchers at the University of Kansas (Petr, 1995) have developed a measure that assesses programs and organizations with regard to the degree that they reflect family-centered principles. This and other family-oriented research efforts will advance knowledge about how to increase program responsiveness and will help to bring family issues into the mainstream of child mental health research.

CONCLUSION

This chapter addresses the system of care through the eyes of family members who, on behalf of their children, are the primary customers of services. As family-centered principles become adequately represented in program and system planning processes, the relevance and quality of services should greatly improve. Although much system change has occurred in the last decade, persistence will be necessary to achieve a more responsive, flexible, and family-centered system. Reviewing the change that has occurred since 1984, and considering the family members, professionals, advocates, and policy makers who are dedicated to further improvement, we are optimistic about the future.

REFERENCES

Anderson, C. (1994). *Finding help— finding hope.* Alexandria, VA: Federation of Families for Children's Mental Health.

Asarnow, J.R., & Horton, A.A. (1990). Coping and stress in families of child psychiatric inpatients: Parents of children with depressive and schizophrenia spectrum disorders. *Child Psychiatry and Human Development, 21,* 145–157.

Binkard, B., Goldberg, M., & Goldberg, P. (1984). *A guidebook for parents of children with emotional disorders.* Minneapolis, MN: Pacer Center, Inc.

Brewer, E.J., McPherson, M., Magrab, P.R., & Hutchins, V.L. (1989). Family-centered, community-based, coordinated care for children with special health care needs. *Pediatrics, 83,* 1055–1060.

Burchard, J.D., & Clarke, R.T. (1990). The role of individualized care in a service delivery system for children and adolescents with severely maladjusted behavior. *Journal of Mental Health Administration, 17*(1), 48–60.

Burchard, J.D., Hinden, B., Carro, M., Schaefer, M., Bruns, E., & Pandina, N. (1995). Using case-level data to monitor a case management system. In B.J. Friesen & J. Poertner (Eds.), *Systems of care for children's mental health: Vol. 1. From case management to service coordination for children with emotional, behavioral, or mental disorders: Building on family strengths* (pp. 169–187). Baltimore: Paul H. Brookes Publishing Co.

Byalin, K. (1990). Parent empowerment: A treatment strategy for hospitalized adolescents. *Hospital and Community Psychiatry, 41,* 89–90.

Cohen, R., Harris, R., Gottlieb, S., & Best, A.M. (1991). States' use of transfer of custody as a requirement for providing services to emotionally disturbed children. *Hospital and Community Psychiatry, 42,* 526–530.

Collins, B., & Collins, T. (1990). Parent-professional relationships in the treatment of seriously emotionally disturbed children and adolescents. *Social Work, 35*(6), 522–527.

Cournoyer, D.E., & Johnson, H.C. (1991). Measuring parents' perceptions of mental health professionals. *Research on Social Work Practice, 1,* 399–415.

DeChillo, N. (1993). Collaboration between social workers and families of patients with mental illness. *Families in Society: The Journal of Contemporary Human Services, 74,* 104–115.

DeChillo, N., Koren, P.E., & Schultze, K.H. (1994). From paternalism to partnership: Family/professional collaboration in children's mental health. *American Journal of Orthopsychiatry, 64,* 564–576.

DeChillo, N., & Lebow, W. (1991). *Help when it's needed: Community mental health crisis services for children and youth.* Portland, OR: Regional Research Institute for Human Services, Portland State University.

Donner, R., & Fine, G.Z. (1987). *A guide for developing self-help/advocacy groups for parents of children with serious emotional problems.* Washington, DC: Georgetown University Child Development Center, National Technical Assistance Center for Children's Mental Health.

Donner, R., Huff, B., Gentry, M., McKinney, D., Duncan, J., Thompson, S., & Silver, P. (1995). Expectations of case management for children with emotional problems: A parent perspective. In B.J. Friesen & J. Poertner (Eds.), *Systems of care for children's mental health: Vol. 1. From case management to service coordination for children with emotional, behavioral, or mental disorders: Building on family strengths* (pp. 27–36). Baltimore: Paul H. Brookes Publishing Co.

Elliott, D.J. (1994). *Children's mental health treatment in rural and urban communities: Do parental expectations affect treatment initiation and continuance?* Doctoral dissertation, Ohio State University, Columbus.

Ervin, C.L. (1992). Parents forced to surrender custody of children with neurobiological disorders. In E. Peschel, R. Peschel, C.W. Howe, & J.W. Howe (Eds.), *Neurobiological disorders in children: New directions for mental health services* (no. 54, pp. 111–116). San Francisco: Jossey-Bass.

Federation of Families for Children's Mental Health (1992). *Family support statement.* Alexandria, VA: Author.

Fine, G., & Borden, J.R. (1989). Parent Involved Network project: Outcomes of parent involvement in support group and advocacy training activities. In R.M. Friedman, A.J. Duchnowski, & E.L. Henderson (Eds.), *Advocacy on behalf of children with serious emotional problems* (pp. 68–78). Springfield, IL: Charles C Thomas.

Frankel, H. (1988). Family-centered, home-based services in child protection: A review of the research. *Social Service Review, 62*(1), 137–157.

Friedman, R. (1987). *Service capacity in a balanced system of services for seriously emotionally disturbed children.* Tampa: University of South Florida, Florida Mental Health Institute.

Friesen, B.J. (1989). *Survey of parents whose children have serious emotional disorders: Report of a national study.* Portland, OR: Portland State University, Research and Training Center on Family Support and Children's Mental Health.

Friesen, B.J. (1991). *Organizations for parents of children who have serious emotional disorders: report of a national study.* Portland, OR: Portland State University, Research and Training Center on Family Support and Children's Mental Health.

Friesen, B.J. (1993). Creating change for children with serious emotional disorders: A national strategy. In T. Mizrahi & J. Morrison (Eds.), *Community organization and social administration* (pp. 137–146). New York: The Haworth Press.

Friesen, B.J., Griesbach, J., Jacobs, J.H., Katz-Leavy, J., & Olson, D. (1988). Family support as a central component in the system of care: Improving services for families whose children have serious emotional disorders. *Children Today, 17*(4), 18–22.

Friesen, B.J., & Huff, B. (1990). Parents and professionals as advocacy partners. *Preventing School Failure, 34*(3), 31–36.

Friesen, B.J., Koren, P.E., & Koroloff, N.M. (1992). How parents view professional behaviors: A cross-professional analysis. *Journal of Child and Family Studies, 1,* 209–231.

Friesen, B.J., & Koroloff, N.M. (1990). Family-centered services: Implications for mental health administration and research. *Journal of Mental Health Administration, 17,* 13–25.

Friesen, B.J., & Wahlers, D. (1993). Respect and real help: Family support and children's mental health. *Journal of Emotional and Behavioral Problems, 2*(4), 12–15.

Gattozzi, R. (1986). *What's wrong with my child?* New York: McGraw-Hill.

Gehring, T.M., Marti, D., & Sidler, A. (1994). Family System Test (FAST): Are parents' and children's family constructs either different or similar, or both? *Child Psychiatry & Human Development, 25,* 125–138.

Greenley, J.R., & Robitschek, C.G. (1991). Evaluation of a comprehensive program for youth with severe emotional disorders: An analysis of family experiences and satisfaction. *American Journal of Orthopsychiatry, 61,* 291–297.

Hasenfeld, Y. (1983). *Human service organizations.* Englewood Cliffs, NJ: Prentice-Hall.

Heflinger, C. (1995). Studying family empowerment and parental involvement in their child's mental health treatment. *Focal Point, 9*(1), 6–8.

Hosick, J. (1988). *Coping among the parents of hospitalized emotionally disturbed adolescents: The role of attributions and expectations.* Master's thesis, Virginia Commonwealth University, Richmond.

Howe, C. (1995). A history of NAMI CAN. *NAMI CAN News, 2*(5), 1–3.

Hunter, R.W. (1994). *Parents as policy-makers: A handbook for effective participation.* Portland, OR: Portland State University, Research and Training Center on Family Support and Children's Mental Health.

Karp, N., & Bradley, V. (1991). Family support. *Children Today, 20*(2), 28–31.

Katz-Leavy, J., Lourie, I., Stroul, B., & Zeigler-Dendy, C. (1992). *Individualized services in a system of care.* Washington, DC: Georgetown University Child Development Center, National Technical Assistance Center for Children's Mental Health.

Kelker, K. (1987). *Taking charge: A handbook for parents whose children have emotional handicaps.* Portland, OR: Portland State University, Research and Training Center to Improve Services for Seriously Emotionally Handicapped Children and Their Families.

Kirk, S.A., & Kutchins, H. (1992). Diagnosis and uncertainty in mental health organizations. In Hasenfeld, Y. (Ed.), *Human services as complex organizations* (pp. 163–183). Newbury Park, CA: Sage.

Knitzer, J. (1982). *Unclaimed children: The failure of public responsibility to children and adolescents in need of mental health services.* Washington, DC: Children's Defense Fund.

Koren, P.E., DeChillo, N., & Friesen, B.J. (1992). Measuring empowerment in families whose children have emotional disabilities: A brief questionnaire. *Rehabilitation Psychology, 37,* 305–321.

Koroloff, N.M., & Friesen, B.J. (1991). Support groups for parents of children with emotional disorders: A comparison of members and non-members. *Community Mental Health Journal, 27,* 265–279.

Koroloff, N., Hunter, R., & Gordon, L. (1995). *Family involvement in policy making: A final report on the Families in Action project.* Portland, OR: Portland State University, Research and Training Center on Family Support and Children's Mental Health.

Kotsopoulos, S., Elwood, S., & Oke, L. (1989). Parent satisfaction in a child psychiatric service. *Canadian Journal of Psychiatry, 34,* 530–533.

Lishman, J. (1978). A clash in perspective? A study of worker and client perceptions of social work. *British Journal of Social Work, 8,* 301–311.

Lourie, I.S., Katz-Leavy, J., & Jacobs, J.H. (1985). *The Office of State and Community Liaison (OSCL) Child and Adolescent Service System Program fiscal year 1985.* Washington, DC: National Institute of Mental Health.

Lourie, I.S., Katz-Leavy, J., & Jacobs, J.H. (1986). *The Office of State and Community Liaison (OSCL) Child and Adolescent Service System Program fiscal year 1986.* Washington, DC: National Institute of Mental Health.

Maluccio, A.N. (1979). Perspectives of social workers and clients on treatment outcome. *Social Casework, 60,* 394–401.

Mannan, G., & Blackwell, J. (1992). Parent involvement: Barriers and opportunities. *Urban Review, 24,* 219–226.

Mayer, J.A. (1994). From rage to reform: What parents say about advocacy. *Exceptional Parent, 4*(5), 49–51.

McElroy, E. (Ed.). (1988). *Children and adolescents with mental illness: A parents guide.* Kensington, MD: Woodbine House.

McManus, M.C., & Friesen, B.J. (1986). *Families as Allies conference proceedings.* Portland, OR: Portland State University, Research and Training Center to Improve Services to Emotionally Handicapped Children and Their Families.

McManus, M.C., & Friesen, B.J. (1989a). Barriers to accessing services: Relinquishing legal custody as a means of obtaining services for children with serious emotional disabilities. *Focal Point, 3*(3).

McManus, M.C., & Friesen, B.J. (1989b). *Relinquishing legal custody as a means of obtaining services for children who have serious mental or emotional disorders. Proposals to improve the foster care and child welfare programs.* Hearing before the subcommittee on Human Resources of the Committee on Ways and Means, U.S. House of Representatives. Washington, DC: U.S. Government Printing Office.

Packard, T. (1993). Managers' and workers' views of the dimensions of participation in organizational decision making. *Administration in Social Work, 17*(2), 53–65.

Petr, C. (1995). Helping professionals and programs become more family centered. *Focal Point, 9*(1), 10–11.

Pires, S.A. (1990). *Sizing components of care.* Washington, DC: Georgetown University Child Development Center, National Technical Assistance Center for Children's Mental Health.

Pires, S.A. (1992). *Staffing systems of care for children and families: A report of the Southern Human Resource Development Consortium for Mental Health on Workforce Issues Related to Community-Based Service Delivery for Children and Adolescents with Serious Emotional Disturbances/Mental Illness and Their Families.* Washington, DC: Human Service Collaborative.

Research and Training Center. (1987). Families as Allies conferences. *Focal Point, 1*(2).

Research and Training Center. (1990). *Focal Point, 4*(2).

Robin, S.C. (1989). *Family-based services: "Success" as defined and experienced by families and providers.* Doctoral dissertation, University of Minnesota, Minneapolis.

Shelton, T.L., Jeppson, E.S., & Johnson, B.H. (1987). *Family-centered care for children with special health care needs.* Washington, DC: Association for the Care of Children's Health.

Slaughter, D.T. (1988). Programs for racially and ethnically diverse American families: Some critical issues. In H.B. Weiss & F.H. Jacobs (Eds.), *Evaluating family programs* (pp. 461–476). New York: Aldine De Gruyler.

Spaniol, L., Jung, H., Zipple, A., & Fitzgerald, S. (1987). Families as a resource in the rehabilitation of the severely psychiatrically disabled. In A. B. Hatfield & H.P. Lefley (Eds.), *Families of the mentally ill: Coping and adaptation* (pp. 167–190). New York: Guilford Press.

State Comprehensive Mental Health Services Plan Act, PL 99-660. (November 14, 1986). Title 42, U.S.C. 300 et seq: *U.S. Statutes at Large, 100,* 3794–3797.

Stehno, S.M. (1986). Family-centered child welfare services: New life for a historic idea. *Child Welfare, 65*(3), 231–240.

Stroul, B.A., & Friedman, R.M. (1986). *A system of care for severely emotionally disturbed children and youth* (rev. ed.). Washington, DC: Georgetown University Child Development Center, National Technical Assistance Center for Children's Mental Health.

Summers, J.A. (1988). Family adjustment: Issues in research on families with developmentally disabled children. In V.B. Van Hasselt, P.S. Strain, & M. Hersen (Eds.), *Handbook of developmental and physical disabilities* (pp. 79–90). New York: Pergamon Press.

Tarico, V.S., Low, B.P., Trupin, E., & Forsyth-Stephens, A. (1989). Children's mental health services: A parent perspective. *Community Mental Health Journal, 25,* 313–326.

Thomas, N.E., & Friesen, B.J. (1990). *Next steps: Conference proceedings.* Portland, OR: Portland State University, Research and Training Center on Family Support and Children's Mental Health.

VanDenBerg, J.E. (1992). Individualized services for children. In E. Peschel, R. Peschel, C.W. Howe, & J.W. Howe (Eds.), *Neurobiological disorders in children, New directions for mental health services* (no. 54, pp. 97–100). San Francisco: Jossey-Bass.

VanDenBerg, J.E. (1993). Integration of individualized mental health services into the system of care for children and adolescents. *Administration and Policy in Mental Health, 20,* 247–257.

Wagner, C. (Ed.). (1993). *National directory of organizations serving parents of children and youth with emotional and behavioral disorders* (3rd ed.). Portland, OR: Portland State University, Research and Training Center on Family Support and Children's Mental Health.

Whittaker, J.K. (1991). The leadership challenge in family-based services: Policy, practice and research. *Families in Society, 72,* 294–300.

Wierzbicki, M., & Petarik, G. (1993). A meta-analysis of psychotherapy dropout. *Professional Psychology: Research and Practice, 24*(2), 190–195.

York, R.O. (1982). *Human service planning: Concepts, tools, & methods.* Chapel Hill, NC: University of North Carolina Press.

Zeigler-Dendy, C.A. (1994). *Teenagers with ADD: A parents' guide.* Bethesda, MD: Woodbine House.

CHAPTER 4

The Population of Concern
Defining the Issues

Robert M. Friedman,
Krista Kutash, and Albert J. Duchnowski

In 1984, the National Institute of Mental Health (NIMH) initiated a new federal program targeted specifically at children with serious emotional disturbances. The program, called the Child and Adolescent Service System Program (CASSP), has had a major influence on the entire children's mental health field and on other child-serving systems. This influence comes in part from the policy decision made at that time to have a primary focus on those children with the most serious problems.

There were compelling reasons for this policy decision. First and foremost is the fact that serious emotional disturbances have a major impact on the lives of the children who are affected and on their families. Second, children with serious emotional disturbances frequently require extensive services over an extended period of time that are beyond the financial reach of almost all families. Because of the inability of families to finance the services, the cost to public service systems becomes considerable. Given these factors, and the documentation provided by Knitzer (1982) in *Unclaimed Children* that children with serious emotional disturbances were either being underidentified or inappropriately served, the decision was made by NIMH, in partnership with state children's mental health directors, that public mental health systems should declare those children with the most serious problems as their priority.

At the time this decision was made, there were a number of important and somewhat basic questions that needed to be addressed about the group of youngsters who were now established as a priority:

- Given that "serious emotional disturbance" is not a diagnostic category, how should it be defined?
- Within what service systems are these youngsters found, and how are they currently served?

- What is the prevalence of serious emotional disturbance in children and adolescents?
- What are the diagnostic and other characteristics of this group of youngsters and their families?

The purpose of this chapter is to explore these issues. The chapter begins with a discussion of definitions for "serious emotional disturbance." The focus is not only on definitions developed within the mental health system but on related definitions in other systems, particularly the education system. The research on the prevalence of serious emotional disturbance in children and adolescents is then reviewed, and the characteristics of these children, as determined through clinical, epidemiological, and services research, are described. A framework for considering the seriousness of the problem is presented, and the chapter concludes by briefly examining the implications of the definition, prevalence, and descriptive information for the development of effective supports and services for children with serious emotional disturbances and their families.

DEFINING THE POPULATION OF CONCERN

Although there are many barriers to achieving a comprehensive and effective system of care for children who have serious emotional disabilities, the problem of defining the target population is one of the most formidable. At present, there is no universally accepted definition of this condition among the various disciplines, agencies, and interest groups who advocate for or have responsibility to serve the children who have emotional disabilities and their families. The research community also has experienced the effects of the lack of clarity in the definition. For example, Kavale, Forness, and Alper (1986) reviewed over 200 studies of children with behavioral and emotional problems and concluded that growth in the knowledge base was inhibited by the inconsistent definitions used in these studies. The problem continues to challenge researchers who conduct studies of the service system for these children and their families (Burns & Friedman, 1990).

The effects of the lack of a valid and reliable definition, however, are more than academic. Since the late 1960s, there have been reports issued by blue ribbon panels (Joint Commission on the Mental Health of Children, 1969), advocacy groups (Knitzer, 1982), government agencies (U.S. Department of Education, 1993), and many researchers (see Brandenburg, Friedman, & Silver, 1990, for a review) documenting the continual under-identification and underserving of children with emotional disabilities. There is a consensus that the confusion in terminology and definition plays a central role in the failure of the service delivery system to identify and serve a realistic number of children (Forness & Knitzer, 1992).

As the results of research efforts continue to increase and refine our knowledge about children who have emotional disabilities, some findings have emerged that help explain some of the confusion associated with defining the target population. Several studies have clearly indicated that children who have serious emotional disabilities are an extremely varied group in terms of diagnostic characteristics, strengths and needs, level of functioning, family issues, and past histories of service (Duchnowski, Johnson, Hall, Kutash, & Friedman, 1993; Greenbaum, Prange, Friedman, & Silver, 1991; McConaughy & Skiba, 1993; Silver et al., 1992). The results of these studies highlight the varied and often complex problems found in this group of children and, consequently, the array of agencies that have become involved in caring for them and their families.

Because the development of integrated systems of care, employing effective interagency collaboration, is only in the initial stages across the country, there are currently many fragmented systems that are attempting to serve this varied group of children and their families (Stroul & Friedman, 1986). It is not unusual for agencies to use narrow criteria in defining eligibility for service, or to provide limited services, and fail to consider the multiple needs of children with serious emotional disturbances. At present, children who have emotional disabilities may receive funding, services, or both from any combination of the following agencies: education, child welfare, mental health, vocational rehabilitation, developmental disabilities, social security, public health, and substance abuse programs. The confusion that may ensue from so many agencies with differing goals and traditions is illustrated in Table 4.1 in which definitions of three major child-serving agencies are presented. This table also includes a proposed revision of the federal definition used by the U.S. Department of Education that is intended to reduce some of the current confusion surrounding this issue.

An in-depth discussion of these various definitions is contained in a report produced by the Bazelon Center for Mental Health Law (1993). The definition developed by the Center for Mental Health Services (CMHS) was in response to the Alcohol, Drug Abuse, and Mental Health Administration (ADAMHA) Reorganization Act (PL 102-321), which was enacted into federal law on July 10, 1992. This law required that CMHS develop a definition of "children with serious emotional disturbances" to be used by states in their mental health planning, and particularly in developing their request for federal block grant funds for mental health services.

As indicated in Table 4.1, this definition requires the presence of a "diagnosable mental, behavioral, or emotional disorder of sufficient duration to meet diagnostic criteria specified within the DSM-III-R" (Substance Abuse and Mental Health Services Administration, 1993, p. 29425), and also requires that the disorder has "resulted in functional impairment which substantially interferes with or limits the child's role or functioning in family, school or community activities" (p. 29425).

This emphasis on functional impairment is present in the other definitions in Table 4.1 as well. The definition of "seriously emotionally dis-

Table 4.1. Four federal definitions of children who have serious emotional disabilities

---

Center for Mental Health Services Definition
Children with a serious emotional disturbance are persons:

• from birth up to age 18
• who currently or at any time during the past year,
• have had a diagnosable mental, behavioral or emotional disorder of sufficient duration to meet diagnostic criteria specified within the DSM-III-R, that resulted in functional impairment that substantially interferes with or limits the child's role or functioning in family, school or community activities.

These disorders include any mental disorder (including those of biological etiology) listed in the DSM-III-R or its ICD-9-CM equivalent (and subsequent revisions), with the exception of DSM-III-R "V" codes, substance use, and developmental disorders, which are excluded, unless they co-occur with another diagnosable serious emotional disturbance. All of these disorders have episodic, recurrent, or persistent features; however, they vary in terms of severity and disabling effects.

Functional impairment is defined as difficulties that substantially interfere with or limit a child or adolescent from achieving or maintaining one or more developmentally appropriate social, behavioral, cognitive, communicative, or adaptive skills. Functional impairments of episodic, recurrent, and continuous duration are included unless they are temporary and expected responses to stressful events in the environment. Children who would have met functional impairment criteria during the referenced year without the benefit of treatment or other support services are included in this definition

Developmental Disabilities Definition
The term "developmental disability" means a severe, chronic disability of a person 5 years of age or older that—
(A) is attributable to a mental or physical impairment or combination of mental and physical impairments;
(B) is manifested before the person attains age 22;
(C) is likely to continue indefinitely;
(D) results in substantial functional limitations in three or more of the following areas of major life activity: (i) self-care, (ii) receptive and expressive language, (iii) learning, (iv) mobility, (v) self-direction, (vi) capacity for independent living, and (vii) economic self-sufficiency; and
(E) reflects the person's need for a combination and sequence of special, interdisciplinary, or generic care, treatment, or other services that are lifelong or of extended duration and are individually planned and coordinated; except that such a term, when applied to infants and young children, means individuals from birth to age 5, inclusive, who have substantial developmental delay or acquired conditions with a high probability of resulting in developmental disabilities if services are not provided.

Definition of "Seriously Emotionally Disturbed" under Individuals with Disabilities Education Act

The current Federal Definition [34 CFR 300.5(b)(8)] is:

"Seriously emotionally disturbed" is defined as follows:

"(i) The term means a condition exhibiting one or more of the following characteristics over a long period of time and to a marked degree, which adversely affects school performance:

(A) An inability to learn which cannot be explained by intellectual, sensory, or health factors;
(B) An inability to build or maintain satisfactory interpersonal relationships with peers and teachers;

(continued)

Table 4.1. *(continued)*

(C) Inappropriate types of behavior or feelings under normal circumstances;
(D) A general pervasive mood of unhappiness or depression; or
(E) A tendency to develop physical symptoms or fears associated with personal or school problems.

The term includes children who are schizophrenic. The term does not include children who are socially maladjusted, unless it is determined that they are seriously emotionally disturbed."

Proposed New Federal Department of Education Definition

Delete the term "serious emotional disturbance" and replace it with "emotional or behavioral disorder" defined as follows:

(i) The term emotional or behavioral disorder means a disability characterized by behavioral emotional responses in school programs so different from appropriate age, cultural, or ethnic norms that they adversely affect educational performance. Educational performance includes academic, social, vocational, or personal skills. Such a disability—

(A) is more than a temporary, expected response to stressful events in the environment;
(B) is consistently exhibited in two different settings, at least one of which is school-related; and
(C) is unresponsive to direct intervention applied in general education, or the child's condition is such that general education interventions would be insufficient.

(ii) Emotional or behavioral disorders can coexist with other disabilities.
(iii) This category may include children or youth with schizophrenic disorder, affective disorders, anxiety disorders, or other sustained disorders of conduct or adjustment when these adversely affect educational performance in accordance with section (i).

From Bazelon Center for Mental Health Law. (1993). *Federal definitions of children with serious emotional disturbance* (pp. 25–29). Washington, DC: Author; reprinted with minor revisions by permission.

turbed" included under the Individuals with Disabilities Education Act (IDEA) of 1990 (PL 101-476) requires more specifically that the disturbance adversely affect school performance. The proposed new U.S. Department of Education definition, developed by the National Mental Health and Special Education Coalition (Forness & Knitzer, 1992), recommends that the term "serious emotional disturbance" be replaced with the term "emotional or behavior disorder." This proposed definition also requires that educational performance be adversely affected, and that the disability be exhibited in two different settings, at least one of which is school related. The developmental disabilities definition requires that the disability result in functional limitation in three or more areas of activity, including self-care, receptive and expressive language, learning, mobility, self-direction, capacity for independent living, and economic self-sufficiency.

Despite the fact that the issue of definition has been reexamined recently at the federal level within both the mental health and education domains, there remain important differences. The CMHS, in deciding on its definition, indicated that it recognized that "it makes sense that definitions used by federal child-serving agencies conform to one another" (Substance Abuse and Mental Health Services Administration, 1993, p. 29424). However, it pointed out that terms may be used for different purposes. For example, the Department of Education definition is intended to be used to determine eligibility for special education services funded under IDEA, whereas the CMHS definition is intended to be used as a basis for comprehensive system planning.

PREVALENCE OF SERIOUS EMOTIONAL DISTURBANCE

This section presents a brief summary of research findings on the prevalence of serious emotional disturbance. The summary is based primarily on the definition of the CMHS, which requires both a clinical diagnosis and functional impairment. Most epidemiological research has used the presence of a clinical diagnosis as an essential part of its case identification process. As E.J. Costello and Tweed (1994) and Hodges and Gust (1995) have pointed out, the most challenging aspect of assessing the prevalence of serious emotional disturbance is the measurement of functional impairment.

Gould, Wunsch-Hitzig, and Dohrenwend (1980), as part of the work done by the President's Commission on Mental Health during the Carter administration, reviewed the epidemiological research in children's mental health in the United States and concluded that at least 11.8% of children showed a "clinical maladjustment" at any point in time. This conclusion, although based almost exclusively on studies in school settings rather than on community studies and on studies that neither assessed functional impairment nor included clinical diagnoses, provided a general estimate that was used extensively by the field for about 10 years.

Based on studies done in the United States and elsewhere in the 1980s, E.J. Costello (1989) estimated that the prevalence of diagnosable emotional or mental disorders in children was between 17% and 22%. Brandenburg et al. (1990), basing their estimates on a slightly different set of community studies, concluded that the prevalence was between 14% and 20%. However, there was very little information on functional impairment to use, and so very little basis for determining the prevalence of *serious* emotional disturbance.

E.J. Costello et al. (1988) conducted a study at two primary care pediatric clinics in Pittsburgh in the mid-1980s with children 7–11 years of age. To determine the presence of a diagnosable mental disorder, they used the Diagnostic Interview Schedule for Children (DISC), a newly developed structured interview with a parent and child version (A. Costello, Edelbrock, Kalas, Kessler, & Klaric, 1984). To assess functional impairment, they used the Children's Global Assessment Scale (CGAS) (Bird, Canino, Rubio-

Stipec, & Ribera, 1987; Shaffer et al., 1983). This instrument gives one overall score for functional impairment, with a score of 100 indicating no impairment. Bird et al. (1993) has indicated that, "Empirical work has demonstrated that the optimal cut-off score on the CGAS that demonstrates definite impairment is a score lower than 61" (p. 173). Although there is some disagreement about this conclusion by Bird et al., and data are frequently presented for CGAS scores of 70 or lower, scores of 60 or lower typically are used as the criteria for significant impairment.

E.J. Costello et al. (1988) found that 22% of their sample had a diagnosable disorder on the DISC and 13.3% had a CGAS score of 60 or lower. They also found that 9.1% had both a diagnosis and a CGAS score of 60 or lower. This constitutes a group that can reasonably be considered to meet the definition of children with a serious emotional disturbance. This same group of youngsters was studied again by Costello and her colleagues (E. J. Costello & Tweed, 1994) when the youngsters were between 12 and 18 years of age. In that analysis, 10.8% were determined to have both a diagnosable disorder and a CGAS of 60 or lower.

Both the DISC and the CGAS were used by Bird et al. (1988) in a two-stage community epidemiological study in Puerto Rico with youngsters between 4 and 17 years of age. Clinicians interviewed parents and children separately using the DISC, made a diagnosis based on the combined information, and assigned a CGAS score. In this sample, 17.9% of the youngsters had both a diagnosis and a CGAS score of 60 or below, therefore meeting the criteria for serious emotional disturbance.

NIMH sponsored a major four-site study with 9- to 17-year-olds to develop the methodology for conducting epidemiological research in children's mental health in the early 1980s (Lahey et al., in press). Called the Methodological Epidemiological Catchment Area (MECA) study, the effort focused on Westchester County, New York; the New Haven, Connecticut, area; Atlanta, Georgia; and Puerto Rico. The DISC was used in this study, and a youngster was considered to have a disorder if either the youth or parent version of the DISC indicated a diagnosis. This procedure obviously results in higher prevalence estimates than procedures that require agreement by both informants. It has become the most commonly used procedure, given the high degree of different information obtained from difference sources.

The MECA study used three different approaches to assessing impairment: the CGAS, a recently developed psychometric instrument called the Columbia Impairment Scale (Bird et al., 1993), and questions concerning impairment that were incorporated within the DISC itself. The prevalence rate of a diagnosis plus a CGAS of 60 or below for all four sites combined was 12.82%. The prevalence rate of a diagnosis plus a CGAS of 70 or below was 24.7%, and the corresponding prevalence rate for a CGAS of 50 or below was 6.2%. The prevalence rate for a diagnosis based on the *Diagnostic and Statistical Manual of Mental Disorders,* Third Edition, Revised (DSM-III-R) (American Psychiatric Association, 1987) plus impairment on the measure of impairment internal to the DISC was 32.8%, and the prevalence rate for a diagnosis plus a CGAS of 60 or below plus impairment on the internal measure was 11.5% (Shaffer et al., in press).

There was considerable variability between MECA sites in prevalence rate. For example, with a CGAS of 60 or below, the range of prevalence rates was from a high of 17.8% in the New Haven site to a low of 2.5% in the Puerto Rico site. This 2.5% figure is not due to differential rates of DSM-III-R diagnosis in Puerto Rico compared to the other sites but rather to scores on the CGAS for the Puerto Rico site that showed markedly less impairment than in the other sites, according to Canino (personal communication, July 20, 1994). This prevalence rate from Puerto Rico is highly discrepant with the other data.

Several other studies have used different approaches to assessing functional impairment. Kashani et al. (1987), in a study of 14- to 16-year-olds, found that 18.7% of this community sample both had a diagnosis, using the Diagnostic Interview for Children and Adolescents (Herjanic & Reich, 1982), and were considered to need treatment. In a second study of 8-, 12-, and 17-year-olds by Kashani, Ezpeleta, Dandoy, Doi, and Reid (1991), 17.6% of the youngsters had a diagnosis and also were judged as requiring care. The diagnoses were determined using the Child Assessment Schedule (Hodges, Kline, Stern, Cytryn, & McKnew, 1982).

Jensen et al. (1995) studied the prevalence of disorders in 6- to 17-year-old military dependents in a military installation in the Washington, D.C., area. They reported that 15.8% of the sample received a diagnosis on the DISC and were either in treatment or considered to need treatment. Jensen and colleagues also used an internal measure of impairment within the DISC and obtained a prevalence rate of diagnosis plus impairment of 26.3%. Therefore, when a measure of treatment need was used as the indicator of impairment, they arrived at a prevalence rate similar to those obtained by Kashani et al. (1987, 1991). When the internal measure of impairment within the DISC was used, the prevalence rate was higher and more comparable to the 32.8% figure obtained in the MECA study, in which the internal measure of impairment also was used.

Kessler et al. (1994) conducted a national prevalence study on 15-through 54-year-olds. The presence of a disorder was measured by a specially developed survey instrument, and the measure of impairment was a set of questions about whether the individual had been unable to perform his or her normal activities during the last month. Using this approach, Kessler and colleagues reported a prevalence rate of diagnosis plus impairment of 15% in 15- to 17-year-olds (R. C. Kessler, personal communication, July 20, 1994).

An important addition to the research is a study conducted by Costello and her colleagues (E.J. Costello et al., in press), initially on children 9, 11, and 13 years of age in the Great Smoky Mountain region of North Carolina. Referred to as the Great Smoky Mountain Study, it is the first study in the group to use the Child and Adolescent Psychiatric Assessment (CAPA) as the structured diagnostic interview. The CAPA generates DSM-III-R diagnoses for a 3-month time period in contrast to the DISC, which establishes 6-month prevalence rates.

The Great Smoky Mountain Study used multiple methods of assessing functional impairment. These included a process of determining the extent to which individual symptoms interfere with functioning that is built into the CAPA, the CGAS, and the Child and Adolescent Functional Assessment Scale (CAFAS), developed by Hodges (1990). This study, therefore, provides data on the prevalence of serious emotional disturbance with several different methods of assessing impairment.

The prevalence rate for serious emotional disturbance in the Great Smoky Mountain study (DSM-III-R diagnosis plus significant impairment) was 6.8% using an incapacity rating of 2 or more on the measure internal to the CAPA; 3.8% using CAFAS cutoff score of 20 specifically on the Role Performance or Behavioral subscales of the CAFAS; 7.6% for the CAFAS overall, with a score of 10 (indicating any impairment); 4.2% with a CGAS cutoff score of 70 or below; and 1.8% with a CGAS cutoff score of 60 or below.

In the Great Smoky Mountain Study, similarly to the MECA study, lay interviewers were used to conduct the interviews and to make the global assessments of impairment that are required by the CGAS. Based on reports from Puerto Rico that showed comparable rates for the CGAS and for other studies when clinicians rather than lay interviewers were used, and based on the findings of her own Great Smoky Mountain Study that showed discrepant rates using the CGAS in comparison to more structured measures of impairment, Costello raises questions about possible biases in the use of the CGAS, particularly by lay interviewers. She indicates that

> a single global impression of level of functioning used by lay interviewers may be subject to a range of distortions depending on such factors as how long the interviewer has spent with the subject, what local attitudes are to children's emotional and behavioral problems, and the interviewer's background, training, and experience with children. (E.J. Costello, personal communication, August 21, 1995).

This conclusion seems to be consistent not only with the findings in the field but also with general concerns about the degree to which global measures may be subject to cultural biases. Costello recommends that, to assess impairment, a measure that examines functioning in several key areas, using standard ratings, be used rather than methods such as the CGAS that yield a single score. Measures that examine functioning in several key areas include the CAFAS, the Columbia Impairment Scale, and the Global Level of Functioning, patterned after the CGAS but designed by Hodges to include specific training procedures and to focus on functioning at home, with the family, with peers, and in the community.

The findings from the Great Smoky Mountain Study clearly differ from those of the other studies reviewed. The prevalence rates are lower than all of the other rates reported (except, as already indicated, for the Puerto Rico site of the MECA study). It is not possible at this point to adequately explain this discrepancy. Among the differences between this study and the others are the diagnostic interview used (the Great Smoky Mountain Study is the only study to use the CAPA); the length of time for which prevalence rates were established (the CAPA provides a 3-month prevalence rate, whereas the DISC provides a 6-month prevalence rate); the measures of impairment used (the CAFAS has not yet been used in any community epidemiological studies other than the Great Smoky Mountain Study, and the measure of incapacity built into the CAPA is of course unique to that instrument); and the population studied (largely a pre-adolescent rural population). It will require further research to help unravel the reasons for the differences in findings.

Based on the findings reviewed here, it may be estimated that the prevalence of serious emotional disturbance is likely to be between 9% and 19%. There are only two findings that are below this level. The first is the Puerto Rico site of the MECA study, in which a major part of the discrepancy may be due to a tendency of lay interviewers, using a global measure of impairment such as the CGAS, to give lower estimates than clinicians or lay interviewers in other sites give. In fact, when the measure of impairment internal to the DISC is used (a measure that is anchored more specifically to particular areas of impairment), the findings for rates of impairment in the Puerto Rico MECA site are much more similar to the other three sites than when the CGAS is used (G. Canino, personal communication, 1994). The second finding that is below 9% is the Great Smoky Mountain Study, which used 3-month prevalence estimates. The prevalence rate for this study varies depending on the cutoff point used, and, because there are no prior community studies done using the CAPA or the CAFAS, it is difficult to determine the appropriate cutoff point.

The findings of Bird et al. (1987), Jensen et al. (1995), Kashani et al. (1987, 1991), and Kessler et al. (1994), using a variety of measures of impairment, all produced estimates in the 15%–19% range, as did two of the four MECA sites (with a CGAS of 60 or below, the prevalence rate for both the New Haven and Atlanta sites was about 17%, for the New York site it was about 11%, and, as already indicated, for the Puerto Rico site it was 2.5%). Costello, in her Pittsburgh health maintenance organization study (E.J. Costello et al., 1988), derived estimates between 9% and 11%. The highest estimates were from the MECA study, in which the most lenient criteria for impairment were used on the measure contained within the DISC (32.8%), and the Jensen study, also using the internal DISC measure (26.3%).

It is important, partly from a public policy perspective, to note some of the differences between this prevalence rate for serious emotional disturbance and general prevalence rates for DSM-III-R diagnoses. The prevalence rate for serious emotional disturbance was approximately one third of the overall prevalence rate for DSM-III-R diagnosis in the Great Smoky Mountain Study (E. J. Costello et al., in press). The likelihood of impairment, and therefore meeting the criteria for serious emotional disturbance, was particularly high if there were multiple diagnoses or a diagnosis of a behavior disorder.

The MECA study found that half of the youngsters in the sample received a DSM-III-R diagnosis (Shaffer et al., in press). However, not all diagnoses were strongly related to impairments in functioning. For example, the diagnoses of anxiety disorders and enuresis were least likely to be associated with significant impairment in functioning (Shaffer et al., in press). Although the prevalence of these disorders was high (e.g., 21.6% for simple phobia, 15.1% for social phobia, and 4.9% for nocturnal enuresis), thereby contributing to a high prevalence of DSM-III-R disorders in general, the rate of impairment associated with these disorders was low, thereby contributing very little to the prevalence of serious emotional disturbance. Less than 10% of the youngsters in the MECA study with a diagnosis of simple phobia obtained a CGAS of 60 or below and obtained at least a score of 1 for impairment on the internal measure included within the DISC. In contrast, almost half of the youngsters with a diagnosis of major depression, 43% of youngsters with an attention deficit diagnosis, and 43% of youngsters with a conduct disorder had a CGAS of 60 or lower.

This is important from a policy and public education perspective. Although the numbers of youngsters with diagnosable mental disorders are far greater than those with serious emotional disorders, the 9%–19% with serious disorders clearly show an important impairment in functioning as well as the disorder. They have been identified as a top priority for services at a federal level since the initiation of CASSP in 1984, and remain so, as evidenced in the Children's Mental Health Services Program included in the ADAMHA Reorganization Act (PL 102-321). They also are a top priority within most states.

WHO ARE THE CHILDREN AND WHAT ARE THEIR CHARACTERISTICS?

Although little consensus has been achieved in defining and measuring emotional or mental disorders in children, a knowledge base is beginning to emerge on the characteristics of the population currently being served in the public mental health and social service arenas. This section will review the emerging empirical knowledge base documenting the characteristics of youngsters with serious emotional disturbances who are served within public systems, with a summary of these characteristics presented in Table 4.2.

California's AB377 Evaluation Project

In a report describing the 3-year results of the California AB377 Evaluation Project, the characteristics of the youth receiving services were described (Rosenblatt & Attkisson, 1993). The goal of this project was to examine the implementation and cost savings of replicating an innovative system of care for youth with serious emotional disabilities, which had been demonstrated in Ventura County, in three other California counties: Santa Cruz, San Mateo, and Riverside. Project data were collected in four areas relating to criteria established by legislative mandate. These criteria were 1) to document that the target population was served as intended, 2) to reduce the use of restrictive levels of care such as state hospital and group home care, 3) to reduce the likelihood of rearrest for youth in the target population, and 4) to improve the educational performance of the target population. The target population for this initiative was restricted to those youth considered "most in need," generally defined as youth who were in, or "at risk" for, an out-of-home-placement. A total of 8,834 youths were served from January 1990 to June 1992, representing 1.57% to 1.84% of the youth under 18 years of age in these three counties.

In general, the youth served were male, were older (average age = 13.57 years), had low Global Assessment of Functioning scores (52% had scores of 50 or lower), and predominantly received clinical diagnoses of mood disorders (23%) and disruptive behavior disorders (34%). As depicted in Table 4.3, in Santa Cruz County, the youth served were representative of the ethnic breakdowns of the general population under 18 years of age. However, in San Mateo and Riverside counties, the youth served were less reflective of the total population. San Mateo's served population reflected an underrepresentation of Asian Americans and an overrepresentation of African Americans. In both San Mateo and Riverside counties, Latino youth were underserved. Furthermore, Latino youth had different referral patterns in that they were more often referred through the legal system (Rosenblatt & Attkisson, 1994).

National Sample of Students Served in the Public School System

Males were also found to be the predominant gender served in public school systems as having serious emotional disturbance, according to a national, representative sample of 269 youth between the ages of 12 and 17 described in a survey conducted by Cullinan, Epstein, and Sabornie (1992). Although 24% of the total sample was non-Caucasian (i.e., either Hispanic or African American), more non-Caucasian students were likely to be found

Table 4.2. Summary of characteristics of youth being served as having severe emotional disabilities

Name of study	N	Age	Gender	Diagnosis	Ethnicity	Level of impairment	Other findings
The California AB377 Evaluation (Rosenblatt & Attkisson, 1993)	8,334	Older, with 39% being between 15–20 years of age; the mean age on admission was 13.57 years	Predominantly male (approximately 60%)	Most frequent clinical diagnoses: disruptive behavior disorders (34%), mood disorders (23%), and adjustment disorders (15%)	Overrepresentation of African Americans in two of the three counties, while Asian Americans and Latinos are slightly underrepresented	Frequency of GAF scores: 51–60: 17% 41–50: 30% 31–40: 22%	
National sample of adolescents with serious emotional disturbance served in the public school system (Cullinan, Epstein, & Sabornie, 1992)	269 randomly selected and representative	Between 12 and 17 years of age	79% male	Not reported	24% non-Caucasian (22% African American, 2% Hispanic)		98% of the youths had IQ scores between 70 and 130 (mean of 92.6, standard deviation of 14.4)
Mental health service utilization by cluster of children with serious emotional disturbance in Texas (Berndt et al., 1995)	4,299	0–5 yr: 5% 6–12 yr: 41% 13+ yr: 54%	62% male	Most frequent clinical disorders: adjustment disorder (17%), ADHD (13%), oppositional defiant disorder (12%), major depression (11%), conduct disorder (10%)	Caucasian: 58% Hispanic: 25% African American: 16% Other: 1%	Frequency of GAF scores: 51–60: 16% 41–50: 52% 31–40: 18%	Frequency of CBCL scores: <60: 16% 60–63: 8% >63: 76%

(continued)

Table 4.2. (continued)

Name of study	N	Age	Gender	Diagnosis	Ethnicity	Level of impairment	Other findings
National Adolescent and Child Treatment Study (Silver et al., 1992)	812 youth identified with severe emotional disabilities and served in either schools or residential settings	Three age cohorts: 8–11 (N = 198) 12–14 (N = 323) 15–18 (N = 291) Average age 13 years 11 months	75% male	Most frequent diagnosis was conduct disorder, followed by anxiety disorders	Caucasian: 71% African American: 22% Hispanic: 5% Other: 2%	73% were reading below grade level Vineland Adaptive Behavior Scales scores: Daily Living Skills, 85.6; Socialization, 76.6; Communication Skills, 76.6	
Alternatives to Residential Treatment Study (ARTS) (Duchnowski et al., 1993)	150 youth in 5 different community-based programs	Average age 14.2 years	64% male	92% in clinical range on the CBCL; further 56% scored in the clinical range on both internalizing and externalizing scales	Caucasian: 72% African American: 9% Hispanic: 9% Native American: 7% Other: 3%	81% were below grade level in reading; 56% deficient in math skills	
National Longitudinal Transition Study (NLTS; Wagner, 1995)	552–777 youth with SED	Ages 13–21	For youth with SED: 76% male	Serious emotional disability (SED)	For youth with SED: Caucasian: 67% African American: 25% Hispanic: 6% Other: 2%		For youth with SED: 38% annual income <$12,000 32% $12,000–$24,999 44% from single-parent households 40% urban 34% suburban 27% rural

Table 4.3. Percentage of youth served in AB377 Project by ethnicity as well as percentage of ethnicity in general population for youth under 18 years of age

| | County | | | | | |
| | Santa Cruz | | San Mateo | | Riverside | |
Ethnicity	% in general population	% served	% in general population	% served	% in general population	% served
Caucasian	74	70	48	45	54	61
African American	3	3	6	20	6	11
Latino	17	22	25	20	36	24
Asian American	3	2	20	4	4	2

in high-density population areas. On the average, measured intelligence scores were in the low-normal range (mean = 92.6) on the WISC-R (Wechsler, 1974), with males and Caucasian students having higher measured scores than females and non-Caucasian students.

Only 35% of the students identified and being served as having serious emotional disturbance lived in two-parent homes, whereas 56% lived with only one parent or relative and 9% lived in foster care or some other living arrangement. Nearly all the students spent time in more than one type of educational placement, but the placement where the student spent the *majority* of time was a self-contained classroom (39%), a resource room (23%), a regular classroom with consultation (19%), an alternative public school (14%), a residential or homebound situation (2%), and some other placement option (3%). These placements resulted in nearly a third of the students spending more than half of their school day with peers without emotional disturbance, whereas 19% of the students had no mainstream placement time. Furthermore, measured intelligence was related to time spent in regular education, with those students with higher scores tending to spend more time in regular education.

Mental Health Services Utilization in Texas

Data from 14 community mental health centers have been collected on 4,299 youth being served in an integrated service system in Texas (L. Rouse, personal communication, August 9, 1994; Berndt et al., 1995). The majority of youth served were male (62%), Caucasian (58%), and over 13 years of age (mean age of 15.5 years) (54%) and lived in a single-parent–headed household (56%). The most frequent diagnostic categories were adjustment disorder (17%), attention-deficit/hyperactivity disorder (13%), oppositional defiant disorder (12%), major depression (11%), and conduct disorder (10%). On the Child Behavior Checklist (CBCL) (Achenbach & Edelbrock, 1983), 76% of those served were in the clinical range, and the mean overall score was 69. The youth also exhibited low general functioning, as reflected in the majority (75%) scoring 50 or below on the Global Assessment of Functioning scale.

National Adolescent and Child Treatment Study

In a 7-year, longitudinal study of youth ages 8–18, identified as having a serious emotional disability and being served in either a residential ($n = 378$) or school ($n = 434$) setting, the National Adolescent and Child Treatment Study (NACTS) (Silver et al. 1992) had the primary goal of describing these youths and their outcomes over time. The sample as a whole was predominantly male (75%) and Caucasian (71%), with an average age of 13 years 11 months; however, youth in residential settings tended to be older than their school-based peers (14 years, 5 months and 13 years, 11 months, respectively) and more likely to be female. Furthermore, there were fewer African Americans in residential settings than in school-based settings.

Parents of the youth reported the mean age of onset for emotional or behavioral problems as 6 years, 3 months. Females in residential treatment had a later age of onset than females in school settings, whereas the age of onset for males in the two settings did not differ. The most common diagnosis for the sample using the child version of the Diagnostic Interview Schedule for Children (DISC-C) (A. Costello et al., 1984) was conduct disorder, with two thirds of the sample meeting the criteria for this disorder. Twenty-six percent of the children met the criteria for anxiety disorders, and 19% met the criteria for depression. Parent ratings of psychopathology using the CBCL revealed that the sample, on average, was in the clinical range on this scale, with more frequent externalizing and internalizing problems found in the residential sample than the school-based population (mean = 72.9 and 69.8 for externalizing problems, respectively, and 71.6 and 66.6 for internalizing problems, respectively).

Measures of intelligence revealed a mean of 86 on the Slosson Intelligence Test with a standard deviation of 16.9. This places about 51% of the sample within 1 standard deviation of the mean (e.g., 100) in intelligence, while 30% of the sample had scores between 1 and 2 standard deviations below the mean (70–85). Overall, standard scores on the Vineland Adaptive Behavior Scale (Sparrow, Balla, & Cicchetti, 1984) revealed daily living skills to be 1 standard deviation below the mean. Mean scores for the communication and socialization domains (76.6 for each) were within 2 standard deviations of the mean or average score.

A separate investigation of older youth in this sample (i.e., ages 18–22; $n = 215$) was undertaken to examine the outcomes for these youth as they made the transition from adolescence to young adulthood. These youth tended to live on their own (38%) or with their parents (45%), with most (74%) not completing high school. For the 60% of the youth who were employed, most (66%) were service workers, handlers and laborers, and machine operators with a median income of $700 per month. In addition to these youth in the community, approximately 9% of the youth were in jail or prison and another 8% were in mental health facilities during this investigation (Silver, Unger, & Friedman, 1994).

In a sample of the NACTS group of youngsters, Greenbaum et al. (1991) found a high prevalence of comorbidity of substance abuse and psychiatric disorders. Factors significantly associated with severe alcohol or marijuana abuse/dependency diagnoses included a diagnosis of conduct disorder or depression, age, and placement in a residential mental health program.

Alternatives to Residential Treatment Study

The Alternatives to Residential Treatment Study, a descriptive study of youth in five exemplary community-based programs that serve children with serious emotional disturbances and their families, examined the clinical, social, and academic functioning of the participants over a period of 2 years (Duchnowski et al., 1993). On admission to these programs, it was documented that these youth had problems of long duration, in that the average age of the sample was 14.2 years with a reported average age of onset of problems of 7 years of age. Reading scores for 81% of the sample were below expected grade level, and 56% were in the borderline or deficient ranges in math relative to a standardized sample. On the CBCL, 92% of the youth had total behavior scores in the clinical range (T scores > 63). Furthermore, 54% scored in this range on the internalizing as well as the externalizing symptom scales. On the Social Skills Scale of the Social Skills Rating System (Gresham & Elliott, 1990), two thirds of the group was found to be functioning at a social level below their same-age peers.

National Longitudinal Transition Study (NLTS)

In a national longitudinal study of students with disabilities served in special education, Wagner (1995) reported the characteristics of more than 8,000 young persons with disabilities ages 13–21 who were special education students during the 1985–1986 school year in more than 300 school districts nationwide. Data for youth with serious emotional disturbances indicated that 76.4% were male and 67.1% were Caucasian. Over one third (38.2%) came from households with an annual income of under $12,000, and 32.1% came from households with an income of $12,000 to $24,999. Furthermore, 44.3% came from single-parent households, and about equal percentages were from urban (39.5%) and suburban communities (34%).

Summary

Overall, these studies point to a group of youngsters with serious problems in many domains. These include emotional and behavioral functioning, educational performance, social behavior, and overall level of functioning. DSM-III-R diagnoses are varied and often multiple and show a high prevalence both of mood disorders and disruptive behavior disorders. Furthermore, there is a high percentage of youngsters from low-income families and from single-parent households.

SERIOUSNESS OF THE PROBLEM

From both a social policy and a humanitarian perspective, it is useful to consider the significance or "seriousness" of the problem of serious emotional disturbance in children and youth. This is particularly the case at the current time, when policy makers at all levels of government find themselves struggling to establish priorities amid a growing number of important problems, for each of which there are passionate, articulate, and persuasive advocates.

Manis (1974) has offered one framework for assessing the seriousness of social problems. This framework examines three dimensions, the first of which is the incidence and/or prevalence of the problem. Obviously, the greater the incidence and/or prevalence of a problem, the more serious it is. Within the mental health field, the primary focus is placed on determining the prevalence of disorders within a specified population for a particular period of time rather than the incidence of disorders (number of new cases).

The second dimension proposed by Manis is the magnitude or impact of a problem. According to this formulation, conditions that result in mild discomfort, for example, or temporary inability to carry out particular functions, are less serious than conditions that cause significant pain or discomfort, interfere with functioning in a major way for an extended period of time, or both. The third dimension has to do with primacy, or the extent to which a problem contributes to other problems. Teen pregnancy, for example, is partly viewed as an extremely serious problem because it often leads to a range of other child, family, and social problems.

A modification of the Manis framework is proposed here for examination of the seriousness of the problem of serious emotional disturbance in children and adolescents. This modified framework begins by focusing on *prevalence*, as Manis proposed. Then, as one means of assessing magnitude, the *persistence* of serious emotional disturbance is considered. Next, the *relationship* of serious emotional disturbance *to other problems* is examined from both concurrent and longitudinal perspectives. However, the concept of primacy, as defined by Manis, is avoided, because it implies a linear set of causal relationships between conditions; it is believed that the relationships between problems affecting the human condition are complex and multidirectional and cannot be accounted for adequately by a linear model. Finally, the *financial cost* of serious emotional disturbance is discussed, a dimension that must be considered when assessing the seriousness of a problem.

Prevalence

As noted previously, the best current estimate, based on a number of studies using different measures and different populations, is that the 6-month prevalence rate of serious emotional disturbance is in the range of 9%–19%. It is important to note that there are several indications that these prevalence rates are increasing. In an article entitled, "Are American Children's Problems Getting Worse? A 13-Year Comparison," Achenbach and Howell (1993) presented compelling data to suggest that the problems *are* getting worse. These researchers gathered data from parents and teachers on nearly the same behavior checklists for very similar samples of youngsters at two points in time. There was a 13-year time period between data collections from parents (1976 to 1989) and a 7-year time period between data collections from teachers (1981–1982 to 1989). The research showed "small but pervasive increases in reported problems and decreases in competencies" (p. 1153). It also showed that, even though Achenbach and Howell excluded 8.3% of their potential sample because they had received mental health services in the previous year, 18.2% of the remaining 1989 youngsters scored in the clinical range on the CBCL, compared to 10.0% of the 1976 subjects.

The research of Kessler et al. (1994) and Robins (1986) also suggests a trend toward increasing prevalence of problems. Although both Kessler and Robins focused primarily on adults in their research, they consistently found large "cohort" effects. In Kessler's study, younger groups (including 15- to 24-year-olds) more frequently experienced emotional or mental disorders than older groups. In Robins's work, younger groups of adults reported higher rates of problems as adolescents than did older groups of adults, suggesting a secular trend toward increasing prevalence with successive generations.

In a longitudinal study of 386 Caucasian youngsters, primarily from working class backgrounds, Reinherz, Giaconia, Lefkowitz, Pakiz, and Frost (1993) found prevalence rates at age 18 for alcohol abuse/dependence, phobias, and depression that are strikingly higher than earlier research suggested. Although acknowledging that the finding may be due to many different things, Reinherz et al. also suggest that it may reflect the finding "that prevalence rates of depression and substance abuse are increasing for younger generations, and shifting toward earlier ages of onset in more recent birth cohorts" (p. 374). Therefore, in beginning to assess the seriousness of the problem of serious emotional disturbance in children and adolescents, recognition must be given not only to the high prevalence estimates

(9%–19%) but also to the indications that there is a trend toward increasing rates.

Persistence

The issue of persistence of emotional and mental disorders of children and adolescents is complex. The purpose of this section is not to comprehensively review the research on persistence, but to provide enough information to shed additional light on the seriousness of the problem of serious emotional disturbance.

It is important to note at the outset that there is considerable support for the general finding that, for a substantial portion of children and adolescents, the presence of an emotional or mental disorder persists over time, both from preadolescence to adolescence and from adolescence to adulthood. For example, Verhulst, Eussen, Berden, Sanders-Woudstra, and Van Der Ende (1993) followed 936 children in the Netherlands over a 6-year time period, administering the CBCL every 2 years. Despite a general trend for test scores on the CBCL to decrease over time, they found that one third of their sample who had scored over the 90th percentile during the first test administration still scored over the 90th percentile 6 years later. Using the Youth Self Report, this same group of investigators found that about 40% of youngsters who scored in the clinical range at age 15 still scored in the clinical range 4 years later (Ferdinand, Verhulst, & Wiznitzer, 1995). Of particular interest is the likelihood of persistence of problems in youngsters who can be identified as having a serious emotional disturbance. As pointed out earlier, E.J. Costello et al. (in press) found that youngsters with multiple diagnoses were more likely to show the impairment in functioning included in the definition of serious emotional disturbance than were youngsters with only a single diagnosis. It is noteworthy in this regard that, in a 4-year follow-up in Ontario of youngsters who were 4–12 years of age at the point of original data collection, 43.5% of those with multiple disorders had one or more disorder 4 years later, compared to 27.6% of those who had only one disorder earlier (Offord et al., 1992).

The findings on persistence of disorders are most meaningful when examined for specific diagnoses. This is particularly the case because several diagnoses are most common in youngsters with serious emotional disturbance. In a summary of findings on persistence of conduct disorder, Offord and Bennett (1994) concluded that "there is enough known now to conclude that children with conduct disorder, as a group, have a poor adult outcome" (pp. 1072–1073). They indicated that the presence of a conduct disorder in children or adolescents not only predicts similar problems in adulthood but also predicts widespread social dysfunction, including alcohol abuse and dependence. In their 4-year follow-up in Ontario, Offord et al. (1992) concluded that children with conduct disorders had increased rates of other disorders 4 years later compared to children with no disorders.

Robins and Price (1991) reached a similar conclusion, based on an analysis of data from the adult Epidemiological Catchment Area study. Although the primary focus of this study was on disorders in adults, retrospective information was gathered on conduct problems prior to age 15. Based on their analysis of these data, Robins and Price concluded that conduct problems in adolescence have a direct and strong link to externalizing disorders of adults, and they are also connected to other adult disorders.

Another of the most prevalent disorders of youngsters with serious emotional disturbance is depression. One of the most significant longitudinal studies of the persistence of adolescent depression was conducted by Kandel and Davies (1986), who followed up a group of 15- to 16-year-olds 9 years later. They found that depressive symptoms "were relatively stable over time" (p. 261), with individuals reporting such symptoms in adolescence being more likely to do so as young adults. Similarly, in the Ontario 4-year follow up, Fleming, Boyle, and Offord (1993) found that one quarter of depressed adolescents experienced a serious major depressive disorder in the 6-month period preceding the follow-up. In comparison, 6.9% of the control group had a major depressive disorder at the 4-year follow-up.

Based on a review of the literature on the long-term effects of depression among adolescents, Lewinsohn, Hops, Roberts, Seeley, and Andrews (1993) reiterate that having an episode of depression early in life substantially increases the risk for future episodes both during adolescence and later in life. They further point out that "Adolescent depression predicts future adjustment problems in the area of marriage, dropping out of school, unemployment status, involvement with drugs, delinquent behavior, being arrested, being convicted of a crime, and being in a car accident" (p. 133).

Similar results have been found with another of the disorders that contribute to the high prevalence of serious emotional disturbance—attention-deficit/hyperactivity disorder (ADHD). Herrero, Hechtman, and Weiss (1994) conclude, based on a review of the research, that "there is a growing consensus that attention-deficit hyperactivity disorder is one of the most stable syndromes in child psychiatry, continuing into late adolescence and adulthood in over half of patients. . . . Moreover, the continuing hyperactive syndrome is associated with a much higher frequency of antisocial behavior and personality disorders than occurs in nonhyperactive adults" (p. 510).

Offord et al. (1992) found that one third of hyperactive children still retained that diagnosis 4 years later, and that a similar percentage earned a diagnosis of conduct disorder 4 years later. Most (73.9%) of the youngsters in this study who received a diagnosis of conduct disorder 4 years later had earlier received a diagnosis of both conduct disorder and hyperactivity.

Overall, this brief review of the literature indicates that not only is there a high 6-month prevalence rate of serious emotional disturbance, but there is a high persistence rate for several of the most common diagnoses, a particularly high persistence rate for youngsters with multiple diagnoses, and a tendency for youngsters with any diagnosis to be more likely to receive at least one other diagnosis later in life. In addition, the research suggests a link between serious emotional disturbance and other negative outcomes, be they educational, social, or psychological.

Relationship to Other Problems

To analyze this component of the framework for establishing the seriousness of a problem, two major issues are considered. First, the issue of comorbidity of disorders is discussed. Second, the historical, concurrent, and prospective relationships between serious emotional disturbances and other problems are considered.

One of the most thoughtful discussions of the issue of comorbidity of disorders in children and adolescents is by Nottelmann and Jensen (1995). They begin by emphasizing, as others have done (Caron & Rutter, 1991; Friedman, 1996; Greenbaum et al., 1991) that comorbidity of emotional and behavioral disorders is extremely common, and that such patterns should be identified and examined both for their treatment implications and to advance knowledge in the field. As already indicated, youngsters with more than one diagnosis are more likely to show functional impairment than youngsters with only one disorder (E.J. Costello et al., in press) and therefore are more likely to meet the definition of serious emotional disturbance; youngsters with more than one diagnosis also are more likely to show persistence of their disorders (Offord et al., 1992).

Nottelman and Jensen (in press) not only review the findings on comorbid psychiatric disorders but explore the meaning of such disorders. In particular, they approach the issue from a developmental standpoint, seeking to determine whether, for example, comorbid disorders represent more nonspecific expressions of psychopathology in childhood, in contrast to more clearly presented disorders of older children and adolescents. They also examine the issue of whether problems with boundaries between diagnostic categories may be contributing to the high rate of comorbidity, perhaps because diagnostic criteria for frequently comorbid disorders may not be sufficiently clear or may not adequately discriminate between the disorders. As important as these issues are, the most important finding for the discussion of serious emotional disturbances is the generally accepted fact that there is a high degree of comorbidity in diagnosis among this population.

From a public health and prevention perspective, it is important to understand the historical relationship between serious emotional disturbance and other conditions. Such an understanding contributes to identification of risk and protective factors and to the description of developmental pathways that frequently lead to a psychiatric diagnosis and an accompanying functional impairment. With this knowledge, the development of effective preventive interventions becomes more feasible.

However, from the perspective of determining the overall seriousness of a problem, it is more important to understand both the concurrent problems that are associated with it and the problems that are associated with it prospectively. In this regard, the co-occurrence of other psychiatric diagnoses has already been discussed, as has the likelihood that other diagnoses will occur in the future.

Our own research on youngsters with serious emotional disturbances (Duchnowski et al., 1993; Silver et al., 1992) supports the fact that there are many problems associated with this condition. These include poor academic achievement, failure to complete high school, involvement with the correctional system, poor success vocationally, and frequently an inability to live independently. There are even indications that youngsters with serious emotional disturbances and a history of having been abused not only have high rates of having children at early ages but that the children frequently are removed at early ages to foster care (Silver et al., 1992). Other indications of poor functioning in many important life domains have been identified by many others, such as Lewinsohn et al. (1993), Offord and Bennett (1994), Reinherz et al. (1993), and Robins and Price (1991).

In attempting to highlight the interrelatedness of many negative conditions of adolescents, Schorr (1988) uses the term "rotten adolescent outcomes." Without question, the research on level of functioning in many domains both at the time of diagnosis and in the future indicates sizeable problems for youngsters with serious emotional disturbances that includes not only rotten adolescent outcomes but "rotten adult outcomes."

Financial Cost

The focus up to this point has been on the human toll exacted by serious emotional disturbances in children and adolescents. An important part of determining the seriousness of this problem from a social policy standpoint is determining the financial cost. This is a complex task for which the data are totally inadequate. Although it is possible to estimate costs in, for example, a particular system, the total cost of serious emotional disturbance to individuals and families, to different levels of government, to different categorical agencies (e.g., mental health, education, health, child welfare, substance abuse, corrections), and to employers has not yet been even grossly estimated. This task is made even more complicated by the close relationship between serious emotional disturbance and functioning in the home, school, and general community, and by the need to look not just at the present level of functioning but also at future functioning. For present purposes, it is important to recognize that this is a major component of the framework for estimating the seriousness of a problem, that the cost is likely to be very substantial, and that no good estimates exist at the present time.

IMPLICATIONS FOR SERVICE SYSTEM DEVELOPMENT

The information contained within this chapter has important implications for service system and policy development. Many of these implications are already being acted on, as reflected throughout this book.

First, all of the data presented on prevalence, persistence, and relationship to other problems indicate that the problem of serious emotional disturbance in children and adolescents is large, important, and costly in many ways and, perhaps most disturbing, seems to be growing. Individuals working with this population are all too aware of the importance of the problem, so it is hoped that the framework presented here and the accompanying data for examining the seriousness of the problem will be helpful in advocating for the resources needed to effectively address this important area.

Second, there is very little about this whole area that fits into neat and clear categories. Serious emotional disturbance takes many forms, frequently involves multiple diagnoses, and typically involves interactions with a range of family, educational, social, and community issues. Although it is sometimes useful to discuss serious emotional disturbance as if it were a separate and self-contained problem, long-term progress in educating the public about the need, in securing resources, and in developing effective services and service systems will only come when there is a full recognition of the interrelatedness of so many of the problems affecting children and adolescents.

Third, although the concept of impairment in functioning has been a part of the definition of serious emotional disturbance in both mental health and education settings since at least the mid-1980s, this concept has never received the focus that it deserves. It is important from a policy and public education standpoint to emphasize that youngsters with serious emotional disturbances not only have a diagnosable disorder but also show significant impairment in functioning in important life domains. There is a need to ensure that treatment programs and systems of care adequately attend to the need to improve functioning in domains such as education, family, peers, overall social network, and work, and there are similar needs for researchers and evaluators to ensure that there is continued development of measures of life functioning and that these measures are used in assessing effectiveness of services.

Fourth, the data on persistence of difficulties in youngsters with serious emotional disturbances underscore the fact that there are no quick fixes.

The need is to develop services and systems that will provide youngsters and their families with the supports and help that they need, with an expectation that this will be a long-term endeavor in many instances.

Finally, the combined data on prevalence, persistence, and interrelationship with other problems suggest the need to better explore preventive strategies to avoid problems in children at the same time that systems of care are developed to focus on children with serious problems (Friedman, 1994). Such efforts at prevention and family support should focus both on risk and protective factors that affect individual children and families and on broader neighborhood and community factors that affect large groups of youngsters and families. Unless careful efforts at prevention are developed, the data clearly suggest that serious emotional disturbance and all of the interrelated problems are only likely to increase.

REFERENCES

Achenbach, T.M., & Edelbrock, C. (1983). *Manual for the Child Behavior Checklist and Revised Child Behavior Profile*. Burlington, VT: University of Vermont, Department of Psychiatry.

Achenbach, T.M., & Howell, C.T. (1993). Are American children's problems getting worse? A 13-year comparison. *Journal of the American Academy of Child and Adolescent Psychiatry, 32,* 1145–1154.

ADAMHA Reorganization Act, PL 102-321. (July 10, 1992). Title 42, U.S.C. 201 et seq: *U.S. Statutes at Large, 106,* 323.

American Psychiatric Association. (1987). *Diagnostic and statistical manual of mental disorders* (3rd ed., rev.). Washington, DC: American Psychiatric Press.

Bazelon Center for Mental Health Law. (1993). *Federal definitions of children with serious emotional disturbance*. Washington DC: Author.

Berndt, D., Ellmer, R.M., Toprac, M.G., Rouse, L.W., Mason, M., & MacCabe, N. (1995). Mental health service utilization by clusters of children with serious emotional disturbance. In K. Kutash & C. Liberton (Eds.), *Seventh annual research conference proceedings, A system of care for children's mental health: Expanding the research base* (pp. 3–8). Tampa: University of South Florida, Florida Mental Health Institute.

Bird, H.R., Canino, G., Rubio-Stipec, M., Gould, M.S., Ribera, J., Sesman, M., Woodbury, M., Huertas-Goldman, S., Pagan, A., Sanchez-Lacay, A., & Moscoso, M. (1988). Estimates of the prevalence of childhood maladjustment in a community survey in Puerto Rico. *Archives of General Psychiatry, 45,* 1120–1126.

Bird, H.R., Canino, G., Rubio-Stipec, M., & Ribera, J.C. (1987). Further measures of the psychometric properties of the Children's Global Assessment Scale. *Archives of General Psychiatry, 44,* 821–824.

Bird, H.R., Shaffer, D., Fisher, P., Gould, M.S., Staghezza, B., Chen, J.Y., & Hoven, C. (1993). The Columbia Impairment Scale (CIS): Pilot findings on a measure of global impairment for children and adolescents. *International Journal of Methods in Psychiatric Research, 3,* 167–176.

Brandenburg, N.A., Friedman, R.M., & Silver, S. (1990). The epidemiology of childhood psychiatric disorders: Recent prevalence findings and methodologic issues. *Journal of the American Academy of Child and Adolescent Psychiatry, 29,* 76–83.

Burns, B.J., & Friedman, R.M. (1990). Examining the research base for child mental health services and policy. *Journal of Mental Health Administration, 17,* 87–98.

Caron, C., & Rutter, M. (l991). Comorbidity in child psychopathology: Concepts, issues, and research strategies. *Journal of Child Psychopathology and Psychiatry, 32,* 1063–1080.

Costello, A., Edelbrock, C., Kalas, R., Kessler, M., & Klaric, S. (1984). *NIMH diagnostic interview schedule for children (DISC-C)*. Rockville, MD: National Institute of Mental Health.

Costello, E.J. (1989). Developments in child psychiatric epidemiology. *Journal of the American Academy of Child and Adolescent Psychiatry, 28*, 836–841.

Costello, E.J., Angold, A., Burns, B.J., Erkanli, A., Stangl, D., & Tweed, D. (in press). The Great Smoky Mountains Study of Youth: II. Functional impairment and severe emotional disturbance. *Archives of General Psychiatry.*

Costello, E.J., Edelbrock, C., Costello, A.J., Dulcan, M.K., Burns, B.J., & Brent, D. (1988). Psychopathology in pediatric primary care: The new hidden morbidity. *Pediatrics, 82*, 415–424.

Costello, E.J., & Tweed, D.L. (1994). *A review of recent empirical studies linking the prevalence of functional impairment with that of emotional and behavioral illness in children and adolescents.* Unpublished paper prepared for the Center for Mental Health Services.

Cullinan, D., Epstein, M.H., & Sabornie, E.J. (1992). Selected characteristics of a national sample of serious emotionally disturbed adolescents. *Behavior Disorders, 17*, 273–280.

Duchnowski, A.J., Johnson, M.K., Hall, K.S., Kutash, K., & Friedman, R.M. (1993). The Alternatives to Residential Treatment Study: Initial findings. *Journal of Emotional and Behavioral Disorders, 1*, 17–26.

Ferdinand, R.F., Verhulst, F.C., & Wiznitzer, M. (1995). Continuity and change of self-reported problem behaviors from adolescence into young adulthood. *Journal of the American Academy of Child and Adolescent Psychiatry, 34*, 680–690.

Fleming, J.E., Boyle, M.H., & Offord, D.R. (1993). The outcome of adolescent depression in the Ontario Child Health Study follow-up. *Journal of the American Academy of Child and Adolescent Psychiatry, 32*, 28–33.

Forness, S.R., & Knitzer, J. (1992). A new proposed definition and terminology to replace "serious emotional disturbance" in the Individuals with Disabilities Education Act (IDEA). *School Psychology Review, 21*, 12–20.

Friedman, R.M. (1994). Restructuring of systems to emphasize prevention and family support. *Journal of Clinical Child Psychology, 23*, 40–47.

Friedman, R.M. (1996). Child mental health policy. In B. L. Levin & J. Petrila (Eds.), *Mental health services: Public health perspective* (pp. 234–248). New York: Oxford University Press.

Gould, M.S., Wunsch-Hitzig, R., & Dohrenwend, B.P. (1980). Formulation of hypotheses about the prevalence, treatment and prognostic significance of psychiatric disorders in children in the United States. In B.P. Dohrenwend, B.S. Dohrenwend, M.S. Gould, B. Link., R. Neugebauer, & R. Wunsch-Hitzig (Eds.), *Mental illness in the United States* (pp. 9–44). New York: Praeger.

Greenbaum, P.E., Prange, M.E., Friedman, R.M., & Silver, S.E. (1991). Substance abuse prevalence and comorbidity with other psychiatric disorders among adolescents with severe emotional disturbances. *Journal of the American Academy of Child and Adolescent Psychiatry, 30*, 575–583.

Gresham, F.M., & Elliott, S.N. (1990). *The Social Skills Rating System.* Circle Pines, MN: American Guidance Service.

Herjanic, B., & Reich, W. (1982). Development of a structured psychiatric interview for children: Agreement between child and parent on individual symptoms. *Journal of Abnormal Child Psychology, 10*, 307–324.

Herrero, M.E., Hechtman, L., & Weiss, G. (1994). Antisocial disorders in hyperactive subjects from childhood to adulthood: Predictive factors and characterization of subgroups. *American Journal of Orthopsychiatry, 64*, 510–521.

Hodges, K. (1990). *Manual for the Child and Adolescent Functional Assessment Scale.* Unpublished manuscript, Eastern Michigan University.

Hodges, K., & Gust, J. (1995). Measures of impairment for children and adolescents. *Journal of Mental Health Administration, 22*, 403–413.

Hodges, K., Kline, J., Stern, L. Cytryn, L., & McKnew, D. (1982). The development of a child assessment interview for research and clinical use. *Journal of Abnormal Child Psychology, 10*, 173–189.

Individuals with Disabilities Education Act of 1990, PL 101-476. (October 30, 1990). Title 20, U.S.C. 1400 et seq: *U.S. Statutes at Large, 104*(Part 2), 1103–1151.

Jensen, P.S., Watanabe, H.K., Richters, J.E., Cortes, R., Roper, M., & Liu, S. (1995). Prevalence of mental disorder in military children and adolescents: Findings from a two-stage community survey. *Journal of the American Academy of Child & Adolescent Psychiatry, 34*, 1514–1524.

Joint Commission on the Mental Health of Children. (1969). *Crisis in child mental health: Challenge for the 1970s.* New York: Harper & Row.

Kandel, D.B., & Davies, M. (1986). Adult sequelae of adolescent depressive symptoms. *Archives of General Psychiatry, 43*, 255–262.

Kashani, J.H., Beck, N.C., Hoeper, E.W., Fallahi, C., Corcoran, C.M., McAllister, J.A., Rosenberg, T.K., & Reid, J.C. (1987). Psychiatric disorders in a community sample of adolescents. *American Journal of Psychiatry, 44*, 584–589.

Kashani, J.H., Ezpeleta, L., Dandoy, A.C., Doi, S., & Reid, J.C. (1991). Psychiatric disorders in children and adolescents: The contribution of the child's temperament and the parents' psychopathology and attitudes. *Canadian Journal of Psychiatry, 36*, 569–573.

Kavale, K.A., Forness, S.R., & Alper, A.E. (1986). Research in behavioral disorders and emotional disturbance: A survey of subject identification criteria. *Behavioral Disorders, 11*, 159–167.

Kessler, R.C., McGonagle, K.A., Zhao, S., Nelson, C.B., Hughes, M., Eshleman, S., Wittchen, H., & Kendler, K.S. (1994). Lifetime and 12-month prevalence of DSM-III-R psychiatric disorders in the United States. *Archives of General Psychiatry, 51*, 8–19.

Knitzer, J. (1982). *Unclaimed children: The failure of public responsibility to children and adolescents in need of mental health services.* Washington, DC: The Children's Defense Fund.

Lahey, B.B., Flagg, E.W., Bird, H.R., Schwab-Stone, M., Canino, G., Dulcan, M.K., Leaf, P.J., Davies, M., Brogan, D., Bourdon, K., Horwitz, S.M., Rubio-Stipec, M., Freeman, D.H., Lichtman, J., Shaffer, D., Goodman, S.H., Narrow, W.E., Weissman, M.M., Kandel, D.B., Jensen, P.S., Richters, J.E., & Regier, D.A. (in press). The NIMH methods for the epidemiology of child and adolescent mental disorders (MECA) study: Background and methodology. *Journal of the American Academy of Child and Adolescent Psychiatry, 34*.

Lewinsohn, P.M., Hops, H., Roberts, R.E., Seeley, J.R., & Andrews, J.A. (1993). Adolescent psychopathology: I. Prevalence and incidence of depression and other *DSM-III-R* disorders in high school students. *Journal of Abnormal Psychology, 102*, 133–144.

Manis, J.G. (1974). Assessing the seriousness of social problems. *Social Problems, 13*, 1–15.

McConaughy, S., & Skiba, R. (1993). Comorbidity of externalizing and internalizing problems. *School Psychology Review, 22*, 421–436.

Nottelmann, E., & Jensen, P.S. (1995). Comorbidity of disorders in children and adolescents: Developmental perspectives. In T. Otterdick & R. Prinz (Eds.), *Advances in Clinical Child Psychology, 17*, 109–155. New York: Plenum.

Offord, D.R., & Bennett, K.J. (1994). Conduct disorder: Long-term outcomes and intervention effectiveness. *Journal of the American Academy of Child and Adolescent Psychiatry, 33*, 1069–1078.

Offord, D.R., Boyle, M.H., Racine, Y.A., Fleming, J.E., Cadman, D.T., Blum, H.M., Byrne, C., Links, P.S., Lipman, E.L., MacMillan, H.L., Rae-Grant, N.I., Sanford, M.N., Szatmari, P., Thomas, H., & Woodward, C.A. (1992). Outcome, prognosis, and risk in a longitudinal follow-up study. *Journal of the American Academy of Child and Adolescent Psychiatry, 31*, 916–923.

Reinherz, H.Z., Giaconia, R.M., Lefkowitz, E.S., Pakiz, B., & Frost, A.K. (1993). Prevalence of psychiatric disorders in a community population of older adolescents. *Journal of the American Academy of Child and Adolescent Psychiatry, 32*, 369–377.

Robins, L.N. (1986). Changes in conduct disorder over time. In D.C. Farran & J.D. McKinney (Eds.), *Risk in intellectual and psychosocial development* (pp. 227–259). New York: Academic Press.

Robins, L.N., & Price, R.K. (1991). Adult disorders predicted by childhood conduct problems: Results from the NIMH epidemiologic catchment area project. *Psychiatry, 54*, 116–132.

Rosenblatt, A., & Attkisson, C.C. (1993, October). *The California AB377 Evaluation: Three-year summary.* San Francisco: University of California.

Rosenblatt, A., & Attkisson, C.C. (1994, October). *The ethnicity, age, gender, and language of youth served in three innovative care systems in California.* Paper presented at the 122nd annual meeting of the American Public Health Association, Washington, DC.

Schorr, L.B. (1988). *Within our reach: Breaking the cycle of disadvantage.* New York: Anchor.

Shaffer, D., Fisher, P., Dulcan, M., Davies, M., Piacentini, J., Schwab-Stone, M., Lahey, B.B., Bourdon, K., Jensen, P., Bird, H., Canino, G., & Regier, D. (in press). The NIMH Diagnostic

Interview Schedule for Children (DISC 2): Description, acceptability, prevalences, and performance in the MECA study. *Journal of the American Academy of Child and Adolescent Psychiatry.*

Shaffer, D., Gould, M.S., Brasic, J., Ambrosini, P., Fisher, P., Bird, H., & Aluwahlia, S. (1983). A Children's Global Assessment Scale (CGAS). *Archives of General Psychiatry, 40,* 1228–1231.

Silver, S.E., Duchnowski, A.J., Kutash, K., Friedman, R.M., Eisen, M., Prange, M.E., Brandenburg, M.A., & Greenbaum, P.E. (1992). A comparison of children with serious emotional disturbance served in residential and school settings. *Journal of Child and Family Studies, 1,* 43–59.

Silver, S.E., Unger, K.V., & Friedman, R.M. (1994). *Transition to young adulthood among youth with emotional disturbance.* Unpublished manuscript, University of South Florida, Florida Mental Health Institute.

Slosson, R.L. (1984). *Slosson Intelligence Test.* East Aurora, NY: Slosson Educational Publications.

Sparrow, S.S., Balla, D.A., & Cicchetti, D.V. (1984). *Vineland Adaptive Behavior Scales: Interview Edition. Survey from manual.* Circle Pines, MN: American Guidance Service.

Stroul, B.A., & Friedman, R.M. (1986). *A system of care for severely emotionally disturbed children and youth.* Washington, DC: Georgetown University Child Development Center, National Technical Assistance Center for Children's Mental Health.

Substance Abuse and Mental Health Services Administration. (1993, May 20). Definition of mental illness and emotional disturbance in children. *Federal Register, 58*(96), 29422–29422.

U.S. Department of Education. (1993, April). *Together we can: A guide for crafting a profamily system of education and human services.* Washington, DC: Author.

Verhulst, F.C., Eussen, M.L.J.M., Berden, G.F.M.G., Sanders-Woudstra, J., & Van Der Ende, J. (1993). Pathways of problem behaviors from childhood to adolescence. *Journal of the American Academy of Child and Adolescent Psychiatry, 32,* 388–396.

Wagner, M.M. (1995). The outcomes of youth with serious emotional disturbance in secondary school and early adulthood: What helps? What hurts? *The Future of Children, 5*(2), 90–112.

Wechsler, D. (1974). *Wechsler Intelligence Scale for Children–Revised.* New York: Psychological Corporation.

SECTION II

SYSTEM DEVELOPMENT AT FEDERAL, STATE, AND LOCAL LEVELS

CHAPTER 5

The Role of the Federal Government

Ira S. Lourie, Judith Katz-Leavy,
Gary DeCarolis, and William A. Quinlan, Jr.

Accounts of federal efforts to increase the level and availability of services for children and adolescents date back to the first White House Conference on Children in 1909. This and subsequent conferences on children were held periodically throughout the early 20th century, and issues related to children with emotional problems were included on their agendas. A report on the 1930 White House Conference on Child Health and Protection states:

> The emotionally disturbed child has a right to grow up in a world which does not set him apart, which looks at him not with scorn or pity or ridicule—but which welcomes him exactly as it welcomes every child, which offers him identical privileges and identical responsibilities. (Joint Commission on the Mental Health of Children, 1969, p. 5)

Although these were admirable goals, there was no real movement toward them for many years. Data from the National Institute of Mental Health in 1966 estimated that, out of the 1.4 million children who needed mental health care, 1 million were not receiving it (Joint Commission on the Mental Health of Children, 1969, p. 5). This was true despite the fact that, in 1963, legislation (PL 88-164, the Mental Retardation Facilities and Community Mental Health Centers Construction Act of 1963) creating a national movement to develop local community mental health centers had been passed and was in its early stages of implementation.

The modern era of system building for children and adolescents with serious emotional disturbances and their families began in 1965 with the Joint Commission on the Mental Health of Children. This national commission was established by Congress to assess the care the nation provided to children with emotional and mental disturbances and to develop recommendations. When it completed its work in 1969, the Joint Commission recommended the creation of systems of care that would meet the needs of all children and adolescents in the country. To accomplish this, the Joint

Commission offered the theory that there should be a national child advocacy system operating simultaneously at the national, state, and local levels. A President's Advisory Committee was proposed to aid in the formulation of child development policy for the President and Congress. The Joint Commission suggested that the U.S. Department of Health, Education and Welfare create a unit in which all children's programs would be housed and coordinated. At the state level, it recommended creating state child development agencies that would be charged with developing comprehensive state plans for children and youth, and, at the community level, establishing local child development councils. These three levels of system coordination and planning were envisioned as working together to assure that the needs of children would be responded to not only in the community but also at the state and national levels (Joint Commission on the Mental Health of Children, 1969, pp. 9–25). The Joint Commission also recommended 1) an array of services that included mental health, health, and public assistance; social services (including juvenile justice); education; and approaches to work, leisure, and preparation for adult roles; 2) training; and 3) a research agenda. With these recommendations, the Joint Commission set the tone for changes in child-serving systems, many of which are just beginning to occur 20-odd years later.

The federal response to the Joint Commission report was disappointing. Legislation to implement the basic recommendations was introduced in Congress and defeated in both 1973 and 1974. However, the role of the Children's Bureau in the U.S. Department of Health, Education and Welfare was increased in scope, and the Bureau was incorporated into a new Office of Child Development. This action purportedly addressed the Joint Commission's recommendation for federal coordination; however, the agency never fulfilled that role. In fact, in 1980, the Department of Education became a separate department, and the other federal child-serving agencies became part of the newly created U.S. Department of Health and Human Services, making coordination even more difficult.

The most successful response to the Joint Commission's report was federal funding for about 10 local child advocacy demonstration projects. An initial round of such projects was jointly funded in 1971 by the National Institute of Mental Health, the Bureau for the Educationally Handicapped, and the Rehabilitation Services Administration, all three of which were then part of the Department of Health, Education and Welfare. These were followed in the next year by similar demonstration projects funded by the Office of Child Development. Funding for these demonstration projects lasted for 3 years and focused on the creation of local agencies to develop service priorities and assure access. Although all these projects appeared to be successful, none of them was picked up for state funding after the federal funding ended, and all were gone several years later. Incredibly, as states were developing Child and Adolescent Service System demonstrations based on the same child advocacy principles in 1983, involved state officials apparently lacked any knowledge of the child advocacy demonstration projects that had taken place in their states some 10 years earlier.

Within the mental health arena, the federal response was more promising: It went beyond funding for advocacy projects and involved the development of increased systems capacity for serving children. This response came from the National Institute on Mental Health, which created an internal Ad Hoc Committee on Child Mental Health in 1971 to set a course for increased priority on children within the agency. In fact, child mental health was designated as the Institute's number one priority. The report of the Ad Hoc Committee (1971) mimicked the Joint Commission report and set directions in all three of the Institute's areas of interest: services, research, and training. The primary result of this report was increased funding for research and training for child mental health.

Changes in the actual delivery of services were equally significant and resulted from congressional mandate. By 1972, the Community Mental Health Centers program, enacted into law in 1963, had created a national revolution in the delivery of public-sector mental health services in communities. It not only resulted in increased service capacity but also led to a shift of state priority from inpatient state hospital programs toward the support of community-based services. In its first 9 years, close to 50% of the country's catchment areas (the Mental Retardation Facilities and Community Mental Health Centers Construction Act divided the United States into over 1,000 "catchment areas," or geographical areas based upon population characteristics that were intended as ideal service areas) were covered by community mental health centers. However, only about half of these centers had specialized child mental health service capacity (Ad Hoc Committee, 1971, p. 13). In 1972, Congress responded to this deficiency by amending the authorizing statute to include a provision making grants to centers and freestanding clinics for specialized children's services. This amendment to the 1963 authorizing legislation was called Part F; through it, close to 400 centers and children's service agencies were given funds expressly for the development of specialized children's mental health services. This led to a huge increase in service capacity. Even more exciting was the broad scope and creativity of these new services.

Ironically, Part F was so successful that it rapidly led to its own demise. After 3 years of funding, Congress, impressed by the growth of child mental health services, repealed Part F and replaced it with a requirement that all community mental health services offer specialized children's mental health services. Unfortunately, Congress also added 6 other new required services but no new money. Although each program under Part F lived out its complete 8-year funding cycle, there were no new specialized children's programs funded. In addition, the new requirement proved unenforceable, and the growth of community child mental health programs came to a halt. The lack of specialized children's services has persisted to the present, even though the Mental Health Block Grant, which replaced the Community Mental Health Centers program in 1981, has a specific 10% set-aside for child mental health services.[1]

About the same time as the development of Part F, Congress also enacted into law the Education for All Handicapped Children Act of 1975 (PL 94-142). This law assured access to free and appropriate education in the least restrictive environment for all children with a disability, including children and adolescents with serious emotional disturbances. Under this law, and under the subsequent Individuals with Disabilities Education Act (PL 101-476, enacted in 1990), which expanded on it, new child mental health services have been developed in schools and the capacity to serve the children with the most difficult problems has been expanded. However, the potential of this legislation has been muted by state and local implementation policies that have tended to exclude many children in need of mental health care.

In 1978, President Jimmy Carter established the President's Commission on Mental Health. One of its major findings was that children and adolescents with serious emotional disturbances were one of several underserved populations in the nation, a population to which the National Institute of Mental Health had not responded well. The other major underserved population included persons with chronic mental illness, representing, in large part, deinstitutionalized adults whose service needs had not been adequately addressed. The federal response was a multi-million-dollar appropriation leading to the Community Support Program. For children, the federal response was the development of a program at the National Institute of Mental Health called the Most-In-Need Program.

Most-In-Need was an innovative local system-building approach in which communities were to identify those children who were the most troubled and had not been well served and to create a multiagency response to meet their needs. The foundations for this program went back to the principles of the Joint Commission and embodied the type of program development that was to have evolved from the negotiations of local child

---

[1]Under Section 300x-3 of Title 42 of the U.S. Code, states must, as a condition of receiving block grants for community mental health services, expend not less than a certain amount each year for a system of integrated services for children with a serious emotional disturbance, as defined in Section 300x-2. The statutory formula for calculating these amounts stipulates that, in fiscal years 1993 and 1994, states must expend at least 10% of block grants to increase funding from the prior year for such a system. Section 300x-3 also requires that such state spending in fiscal year 1995 and beyond shall at least equal the amount expended in fiscal year 1994.

development councils. Most-In-Need, however, suffered the fate of most federal child mental health programs. First, there was no commitment by Congress or the Institute to ensure that this newest mental health program for children reached its potential through adequate funding; in fact, it was not funded at all for the first 2 years after its enactment into law. Second, when funding did materialize, it came only from the Indian Health Service, which offered $800,000 over 4 years for 12, three-year Most-In-Need demonstration projects in Native American, Hawaiian, and Native Alaskan communities. Although Most-In-Need never was adequately funded and lived a short life, the experience was useful in conceptualizing and preparing for current child mental health programs (Stroul, 1983).

In 1980, Congress responded to the President's Commission on Mental Health by passing the Mental Health Systems Act (PL 96-398), legislation that completely restructured the Community Mental Health Centers program. The act reauthorized community mental health center operations, planning, consultation and education, and financial distress programs and also created several categorical programs designed to reach individuals with chronic mental illnesses and other underserved population groups. The act recognized that care for populations that had been designated as underserved (children and adolescents with serious mental and emotional disturbances, as well as adults with chronic mental illnesses) required multiagency approaches using intervention mechanisms not usually available in community mental health centers. For children and adolescents, this meant including child welfare, juvenile justice, and education agencies, as well as mental health, in an integrated system. This ambitious new program was seen as the vehicle to take the principles of the Joint Commission and apply them nationwide. Unfortunately, 8 months after its passage, the Mental Health Systems Act was repealed and replaced by block grants to states under President Ronald Reagan's "New Federalism." The Omnibus Budget Reconciliation Act of 1981 (PL 97-35) consolidated federal funding for services related to mental health, alcoholism and alcohol abuse, and drug abuse into a state-administered block grant, the Alcohol, Drug Abuse, and Mental Health Services Block Grant. This program was designed to permit each state to carry out its own program within very general and flexible parameters and with minimal federal oversight. Not surprisingly, there is little or no information to suggest that this program provided a vehicle for promoting and providing integrated services for children and adolescents with serious emotional disturbances.

In 1982, Jane Knitzer wrote her scathing national report on mental health services for children and adolescents, *Unclaimed Children: The Failure of Public Responsibility to Children and Adolescents in Need of Mental Health Services*, in which she described the federal efforts summarized above as the "shadowy presence" and the "unfulfilled promise." Knitzer's study helped to crystallize a growing dissatisfaction in the child-serving community and spurred the appropriation to the National Institute of Mental Health of $1.5 million in 1984 for the creation of a national program for the development of a response to the needs of children and adolescents with serious emotional disturbances. It is interesting to note that, as with prior congressional appropriations, this one was not specifically aimed at improving services for children. Rather, it was attached to the legislation for the continuation of the then 6-year-old Community Support Program, and appeared not in the legislation itself but as a short phrase placed by an aide in the congressional report that described Congress' intent that $1.5 million be expended on a similar program for children and adolescents with serious emotional disturbances. This program, the Child and Adolescent Service System Program (CASSP), has utilized the ideas and experiences derived from the Joint Commission, Child Advocacy, Part F, Most-In-Need, and the Mental Health Systems Act, and blended them into a new model for delivering services to children and their families.

CASSP: THE CHILD AND ADOLESCENT SERVICE SYSTEM PROGRAM

In 1984, the Child and Adolescent Service System Program was initiated to address the lack of priority, services, and interagency coordination for children and adolescents with severe emotional disturbances and their families. The program was located within the National Institute of Mental Health until October 1992, when it became part of the newly created Center for Mental Health Services.[2] In 1994, the program was renamed the Planning and Systems Development Program, and it remains one of the programs within the Child, Adolescent and Family Branch of the Center for Mental Health Services.

Developed in close collaboration with the State Mental Health Representatives for Children and Youth, a Division of the National Association of State Mental Health Program Directors, this program became a catalyst for service system change. It assisted states and communities in planning and developing comprehensive, coordinated, community-based, family-centered, and culturally competent systems of care for children and adolescents with serious emotional disturbances and their families. The goals of the program are

---

[2]The Center for Mental Health Services was created, effective July 10, 1992, under the ADAMHA Reorganization Act (PL 102-321). Its service programs previously had been a part of the National Institute of Mental Health, which, under the act, was transferred to the National Institutes of Health. This reorganization of mental health and substance abuse programs within the U.S. Public Health Service separated service programs from research programs, housed the service programs in the newly created Substance Abuse and Mental Health Services Administration, and transferred the research programs to the National Institutes of Health.

- To improve access to and the availability of a continuum of care for children and adolescents with serious emotional disturbances and their families
- To develop leadership capacity and increase funding priority for child and adolescent mental health services
- To promote more and better coordination and collaboration among child-serving agencies
- To promote full family participation in all aspects of planning and service delivery
- To ensure that services are structured and delivered so as to maximize their efficacy within the cultural context of the client
- To evaluate the progress of states and communities in improving systems of care for this population

The central concept of the Planning and Systems Development Program is "system," a term that merits elaboration. The kind of system the program has promoted is a truly integrated set of services within which children and adolescents and their families can move easily as their evolving needs dictate. This means systems within which bureaucratic turf and other organizational barriers do not get in the way of meeting their needs. It means systems within which agency budgets and funding sources are designed so as to meet their needs. Also, it means systems that are sufficiently flexible to adjust frequently as the needs of rapidly growing children and adolescents change. It means systems that meet the special challenge of pulling together agencies, such as child welfare, education, social services, juvenile justice, and mental health, that often have very different perspectives. In short, it means systems that revolve around the needs of children and families and not around the needs of agencies and service providers.

The program has used various strategies to promote its philosophy and goals. These include 1) providing grants to states and communities to promote the development of systems of care as well as grants to family organizations and to support research demonstrations; 2) supporting a wide range of technical assistance activities, including the development and publication of many resource materials to aid in various aspects of system development; 3) disseminating information and encouraging information exchange and networking through national meetings, regional meetings, professional meetings, and on-site technical assistance; and 4) collaborating and planning with public federal and state agencies and other national groups concerned with improving services for children with serious emotional disturbances and their families.

First at the state level and then at the local level, the program has emphasized the development of the infrastructure required for improving systems and developing an expanded array of community-based services. Infrastructure development efforts have focused on creating structures and processes for system management and interagency coordination at both state and local levels. Such activities are intended to demonstrate the efficacy of various approaches to organizing systems and laying the foundation for services capacity expansion.

The target population for this effort is children and adolescents with or at risk of serious emotional disturbance, and their families. To be included, children and adolescents must meet the following conditions:

- *Age:* They must be under 22 years of age.
- *Diagnosis:* They must have an emotional, behavioral, or mental disorder diagnosable under the categories of the *Diagnostic and Statistical Manual of Mental Disorders* (Fourth Edition (*DSM-IV;* American Psychiatric Association, 1994) or their equivalents in the *International Statistical Classification of Diseases and Related Health Problems* (10th Revision) (World Health Organization, 1992) or subsequent revisions (with the exception of DSM-IV "V" codes, substance use disorders and developmental disorders, unless they co-occur with another diagnosable serious emotional disturbance).
- *Disability:* They must have functional impairment that substantially interferes with or limits adaptive functioning in family, school, or community activities. States may further define what level of impairment is required for eligibility.
- *Multiagency need:* They should have service needs in two or more community agencies, such as mental health, substance abuse, health, education, juvenile justice, or social welfare.
- *Duration:* They must have a disability that has been present for at least a year or, on the basis of a diagnosis, have one that is expected to last at least a year.

This population includes children and adolescents who, as a result of environmental or biological factors, already have experienced significant problems and who, without outreach, identification, and early intervention, are very likely to become more seriously emotionally disturbed.

Although funding for the program has been minuscule compared to that for many federal programs, beginning with $1.5 million in fiscal year 1984 and growing to $12.1 million in 1994, the dollars have had an impact far beyond their monetary value. They have provided states and communities with the flexibility to engage in a process of participatory planning that crosses agency boundaries and includes family members as equal partners. Planning dollars have been used by states as a catalyst to leverage other funding streams and, in many cases, to begin a process of blended funding across child-serving systems.

By fiscal year 1993, the program's infrastructure development grants were funded at a level of $4.3 million, its statewide family network grants at $1.5 million, and its research demonstrations grants at $4.3 million. In addition to its grants, the program has funded three support centers since 1984. Two of these centers, one at Portland State University in Portland, Oregon, and the other at the University of South Florida in Tampa, provide research and training and are funded jointly with the National Institute on Disability and Rehabilitation Research of the U.S. Department of Education. The third, at Georgetown University in Washington, D.C., provides technical assistance and is funded jointly with the Maternal and Child Health Bureau (part of the Health Services and Resources Administration within the Public Health Services, U.S. Department of Health and Human Services).

Results have been impressive in many states. A 1995 survey by Davis, Yelton, Katz-Leavy, and Lourie (1995) revealed that every state and the District of Columbia now has at least one full-time person assigned to child mental health. Thirty-four of these have an identifiable child and adolescent mental health unit, 5 have consolidated agencies serving children, and the remaining 12 have a full-time person assigned to children's programs but not in a separate unit expressly for children. Significantly, the proportion of states with separate child mental health budgets has gone from 18% in 1982 to 70% in 1993 (Davis et al., 1995).

Interagency collaboration is another critical area in which substantial progress has been made. Twenty-seven states now report that they have legislatively mandated interagency planning councils, 23 report legislatively mandated interagency case review processes, and 25 have defined in law their systems of care for youth. Many states have mandated specific child and adolescent mental health projects, such as pooled funding at specific demonstration sites. Many states report mandates for specific clinical services and broadened Medicaid options for children's mental health services. Twenty-two mandate parental involvement in policy making, program planning, or treatment planning. Finally, every state reports at least one family-run advocacy group focused on children's mental health issues and offering support to family members of children with emotional disturbances (Davis et al., 1995).

CASSP also addressed early in its development the need to support research, training, and knowledge dissemination. With program funding, the Research and Training Center on Children's Mental Health at the University of South Florida and the Research and Training Center on Family Support and Children's Mental Health at Portland State University have played critical roles in these areas. In fact, they have advanced the state of the art in service system research across child-serving systems, as well as in developing new approaches to conceptualizing and designing family-centered research methodologies. The Florida center sponsors an annual research conference attended by researchers, policy officials, and families.

In 1989, the need for research, especially clinical research, into children's mental health issues was highlighted in a report prepared by the Institute of Medicine (1989). At the request of the House Appropriations Committee, the National Institute of Mental Health Advisory Council (1990) developed a national plan to implement the recommendations of this study. This plan, the National Plan for Research on Child and Adolescent Mental Disorders, called for the inclusion of research on services and service systems in the area of child mental health. CASSP played a role in responding to this challenge by initiating the Child Mental Health Research Demonstration program to study the effectiveness of innovative models of organizing, delivering, and financing mental health services for children and their families. The program continues under the Center for Mental Health Services.[3]

In addition, there has been considerable effort to ensure that children's mental health research continues to be supported in a significant way by the National Institute of Mental Health, the Office of Special Education Programs in the U.S. Department of Education, and other federal agencies. As a result, federal research on critical issues affecting children's mental health is slowly expanding. The Child, Adolescent and Family Branch of the Center for Mental Health Services works closely with the National Institute of Mental Health and other agencies to continuously refine and support this research agenda.

The CASSP research and training and technical assistance program has been a critically important element of the program, providing invaluable research, training, and technical assistance not only to the general public and the child mental health field, but also to the program's grantees. It has provided a vehicle for the expansion and promotion of the program's goals through five specific initiatives known as System of Care for Children with Serious Emotional Disturbances, Families as Allies, Development of Culturally Competent Services, the High Risk Program, and Coalition Building. The National Technical Assistance Center for Children's Mental Health at Georgetown University has taken a lead role in the technical assistance effort, working closely with the Child, Adolescent and Family Branch at the Center for Mental Health Services. The research and training centers at

---

[3]Under the ADAMHA Reorganization Act (PL 102-321), effective July 10, 1992, the research program previously carried out by the National Institute of Mental Health was split into two coordinated programs. One, tending to focus on basic research issues, is carried out by the National Institute of Mental Health, which now is a part of the National Institutes of Health. The other, tending to focus on applied research issues, is carried out by the Center for Mental Health Services, a part of the Substance Abuse and Mental Health Services Administration, a new agency created under PL 102-321.

Portland State University and the University of South Florida also have been utilized in these efforts.

THE CHILD, ADOLESCENT, AND
FAMILY MENTAL HEALTH SERVICES PROGRAM

Fiscal year 1993 signaled a new era of federal involvement in addressing the mental health needs of children who are experiencing serious emotional disturbances and their families. The Child, Adolescent and Family Mental Health Services Program, authorized in law and funded beginning in that year, represents a new federal commitment to the provision of services simply because of the desperate need for such services, and not solely to demonstrate their effectiveness.[4]

In addition to CASSP, an important and related initiative also advanced the state of the art and played an important role in the enactment of this new federal services program. In 1989, the Robert Wood Johnson Foundation launched a children's mental health initiative that greatly contributed to the field of knowledge concerning community-based systems of care. The Foundation's Mental Health Services Program for Youth chose eight sites throughout the country to see if the strategic plans developed by CASSP could yield positive clinical gains for children while also being cost-effective when compared to more traditional service delivery models, which relied primarily on outpatient therapy, inpatient psychiatric care, and residential treatment programs. The sites included city, county, and state agencies.

The funded sites each implemented a range of flexible services that were designed to meet the unique needs of each child served. At the core of this new service provision was an individualized treatment plan and intensive case management. The populations of children targeted to be served were those in out-of-state placements or at risk for such placements. In most sites, the targeted children were the most troubled and the most costly to serve; current practice had failed them within their communities and states. Individualizing each care package, or service plan, was an attempt to see if better outcomes could be achieved for these needy and difficult-to-treat children. Results to date are positive both in terms of clinical gains made by the children served, and in terms of the cost-effectiveness of the service programs. Other key results of the initiative have been achieved with respect to financing, administrative structuring, and program development (Cole & Poe, 1993).

---

[4]Enacted effective July 10, 1992, as part of the ADAMHA Reorganization Act (PL 102-321), the new program of Comprehensive Community Mental Health Services for Children With Serious Emotional Disturbances is Sections 561—565 of the Public Health Service Act, codified at 42 U.S.C. 290-ff.

CASSP and the Robert Wood Johnson Foundation initiative have demonstrated very well the tremendous potential value of reform, which empowers states and communities to plan, develop, and begin to operate community-based systems of care. These initiatives, in fact, resulted in an informal but powerful national coalition of families, service providers, and key advocacy groups that played a critical role in convincing Congress that it was time to invest in community-based systems of service delivery nationwide for children and adolescents experiencing serious emotional disturbances and their families. Together, these groups mounted a successful campaign to convince Congress to authorize and fund implementation of community-based systems of care. This watershed event, the funding of services built on the model that had heretofore been implemented only through demonstrations on a limited scale, occurred in 1992 as part of the ADAMHA Reorganization Act (PL 102-321). The effort took nearly 2 years. Congress authorized $100 million dollars in fiscal year 1993 for the new Child, Adolescent and Family Mental Health Services Program and such sums as might be necessary in fiscal year 1994. In actuality, the program began with an appropriation of $4.9 million dollars in fiscal year 1993, but this grew rapidly to $35 million in 1994, and $60 million in fiscal year 1995.

The Services Program establishes several mechanisms for creating community-based systems of care. Under the new law, each child and adolescent served through these grants must have an individualized service plan developed and carried out with the participation of the family and the child. Required services include crisis outreach; diagnosis and evaluation; outpatient treatment, including family counseling; intensive home-based services for families in which a child is at imminent risk of out-of-home placement; intensive day treatment; therapeutic foster care; therapeutic care in facilities with 10 or fewer beds; respite care for families; and special assistance for adolescents making the transition into adulthood. Optional services include preliminary assessments to determine whether a child is eligible for services; training in administration of the system, in the development of individual care plans, and in the provision of home-based care, day treatment, and foster care; recreational services for children and adolescents in the system; and such other services as may be appropriate.

Case management is required for each child or adolescent in the system. Case managers must assure that services are coordinated and periodically reassessed; that the family is kept apprised of progress in meeting the objectives of the individualized service plan; and that the child and the family receive appropriate assistance in establishing eligibility for and receiving other needed services, including health, educational, and social services.

Funded entities must assure state- or local-level matching funds in cash or in kind in accord with a statutory formula that provides for an increasing state and local share over a 5-year period. As of fiscal year 1994, 5-year awards were made to 22 entities. These state and local government agencies are in geographical areas dispersed widely around the United States and provide services to sharply varying populations. Two grantees, Rhode Island and Vermont, provide services statewide. Other grantees serve heavily urbanized areas, sparsely populated rural or frontier areas, primarily suburban areas, and areas that are partly urban and partly rural. Several of the geographical areas served include Native American communities, and one grantee is a Native American Tribal Organization.

A new technical assistance capacity designed specifically to assist the service sites was created in fiscal year 1994 through award of a cooperative agreement to the Washington Business Group on Health. The National Resource Network for Child and Family Mental Health Services established under the agreement must address the unique service needs of rural, frontier, county, and urban areas; integrate the principles of family involvement and cultural competence into all aspects of the project; and address various clinical issues, program development, health care reform, and leadership issues. The effort involves the creation of a national center and three demographically unique "hubs" under its aegis. Each hub works with specific service sites to develop site-specific technical assistance plans. Based on needs at each site, the hub coordinator contracts with a cadre of consultant experts in the subject areas in which sites request help. Joint funding for the national center and hubs comes from the Child, Adolescent and Family Branch of the Center for Mental Health Services; the Office of Special Education Programs within the U.S. Department of Education; and the National Center for Child Abuse and Neglect within the Administration for Children, Youth and Families, U.S. Department of Health and Human Services. The Center for Mental Health Services continues to pursue the possibility of adding other federal and private-sector partners for this endeavor.

The Child, Adolescent and Family Branch also continues to pursue an agenda of services research and evaluation of systems of care for children and adolescents with serious emotional disturbances, as well as of more specific related issues. In carrying out that responsibility, the Branch issued a contract through which to carry out its statutory mandate to evaluate the effectiveness of services provided under the new services program. In addition, the Branch continues to work with the National Institute of Mental Health to define and carry out its agenda of research on services for children and adolescents with serious emotional disturbances. Finally, the Branch issued a Request for Applications jointly with the National Institute of Mental Health to provide for more in-depth research at the 22 sites into various aspects of these projects.

STATE PLANNING PROGRAM

A related development in building comprehensive and integrated systems of care for children and adolescents with serious emotional disturbances has occurred in the state planning arena. Since 1981, states have received their federal community mental health funds through a block grant mechanism. During the decade that followed, states stopped using these funds to develop new community mental health centers and instead used them to support existing mental health centers and services. Through amendments in the block grant legislation, Congress has attempted to impose controls to create incentive for the use of these funds in order to stimulate program growth in vital areas of need. At different times states were required to spend at least 10%–25% of the money on new programs for children and adolescents. Although few states rushed to implement this new provision, some successfully used it to fund new programs that embodied system of care principles.

By the mid-1980s, the block grant program was funded at about $250 million per year, but Congress remained dissatisfied with the results, particularly with the slow progress in many states toward the development of community-based systems of care for persons with serious and persistent mental illnesses. Further legislation amending the block grant statute was enacted, in 1986 (State Comprehensive Mental Health Services Plan Act, PL 99-660) and again in 1992 (the ADAMHA Reorganization Act, PL 102-321), to make block grant funding conditional upon an acceptable state plan detailing how the state was to develop and improve community-based systems of services. Moreover, these amendments provided for withholding significant amounts of block grant funding from states that failed to make satisfactory progress in implementing these plans. The state planning legislation mandates that states address 12 criteria to demonstrate progress in implementing their plans to develop systems of care for both adults and children with serious mental and emotional disorders:

1. Specifically for children and adolescents with serious emotional disturbances, development of a system of integrated social, educational, juvenile justice, and substance abuse services
2. Establishment of an organized community-based system of care
3. Targets for number of people to be served
4. Description of available services, treatment options, and resources
5. Description of health, mental health, rehabilitation, employment, housing, educational, and other services to be provided to enable individuals to function outside of institutions
6. Description of available financial and staff resources
7. Provision of activities to reduce hospitalization
8. Provision of case management services to each individual receiving substantial amounts of publicly funded services
9. Outreach to and services for homeless individuals
10. Description of how needs will be met in rural areas

11. Estimates of the incidence and prevalence of serious emotional disturbance among children and serious mental illness among adults
12. Description of the state's spending plan

When the state planning program was first implemented, its impact on the development of services for children and adolescents was extensive. For the first time, states were required to create and implement plans for the development of community-based systems of care. Furthermore, advocates had a vehicle to hold states accountable for addressing these issues. As a result of the state planning process, many of the CASSP and system of care principles are becoming solidified in state practice. Thus, the state planning requirements have played a major role in enhancing the use of systematic approaches to caring for children and adolescents with serious emotional disturbances nationwide.

CONCLUSION

The process of building community-based systems of care for children and adolescents with serious emotional disturbances and their families is becoming a truly shared and coordinated mission within the federal government. Beginning in late 1993, a broad array of federal child-serving agencies have been meeting regularly to collaborate in various ways to create a common agenda for federal involvement in building systems of care. Outgrowths of this collaboration have been joint funding of technical assistance and research and training centers, requirements in various requests for proposals that funded grantees collaborate as appropriate with specific agencies, joint funding of various requests for proposals, and joint sponsorship of important conferences. Perhaps the most significant aspect of this collaboration is the development of a common approach at the federal level to addressing the mental health needs of children and adolescents and their families throughout the United States.

The future looks bright as public-sector partners at the federal, state, and local levels join together and join with private-sector providers, family organizations, and others in order to address these crucial issues. The future depends, in part, on the success of these efforts.

REFERENCES

Ad Hoc Committee on Child Mental Health. (1971). *Ad Hoc Committee on Child Mental Health: Report to the Director, National Institute of Mental Health*. Rockville, MD: National Institute of Mental Health.

ADAMHA Reorganization Act, PL 102-321. (July 10, 1992). Title 42, U.S.C. 201 et seq: *U.S. Statutes at Large, 106*, 323.

American Psychiatric Association. (1994). *Diagnostic and statistical manual of mental disorders* (4th ed.). Washington, DC: American Psychiatric Press.

Cole, R., & Poe, S. (1993). *Patnerships for care—systems of care for children with serious emotional disturbances and their families.* Washington, DC: Washington Business Group on Health, Mental Health Services Program for Youth.

Davis, M., Yelton, S., Katz-Leavy, J., & Lourie, I. (1995). Unclaimed children revisited: The status of state children's mental health service systems. *Journal of Mental Health Administration, 22*(2), 142–166.

Education for All Handicapped Children Act of 1975, PL 94-142. (August 23, 1977). Title 20, U.S.C. 1401 et seq: *U.S. Statutes at Large, 89,* 773–796.

Individuals with Disabilities Education Act of 1990, PL 101-476. (October 30, 1990). Title 20, U.S.C. 1400 et seq: *U.S. Statutes at Large, 104* (Part 2), 1103–1151.

Institute of Medicine. (1989). *Research on children and adolescents with mental, behavioral, and developmental disorders.* Washington, DC: National Academy Press.

Joint Commission on the Mental Health of Children. (1969). *Crisis in child mental health.* New York: Harper & Row.

Knitzer, J. (1982). *Unclaimed children: The failure of public responsibility to children and adolescents in need of mental health services.* Washington, DC: Children's Defense Fund.

Mental Health Systems Act of 1980, PL 96-398. (October 7, 1980). Title 42, U.S.C. 210 et seq: *U.S. Statutes at Large, 94,* 1564–1613.

Mental Retardation Facilities and Community Mental Health Centers Construction Act of 1963, PL 88-164. (October 31, 1963). Title 42, U.S.C. 2670 et seq: *U.S. Statutes at Large, 77,* 282–298.

National Institute of Mental Health Advisory Council. (1990). *National plan for research on child and adolescent mental disorders.* Rockville, MD: Author.

Omnibus Budget Reconciliation Act of 1981, PL 97-35. (August 31, 1981). Title IX, U.S.C. 3393 et seq: *U.S. Statutes at Large, 95,* 560–572.

State Comprehensive Mental Health Services Plan Act, PL 99-660. (November 14, 1986). Title 42, U.S.C. 300x et seq: *U.S. Statutes at Large, 100,* 3794–3797.

Stroul, B. (1983). *Improving service systems for children and adolescents: Analysis of the NIMH Most-In-Need Program.* Rockville, MD: National Institute of Mental Health, Office of State and Community Liaison.

World Health Organization. (1992). *International statistical classification of diseases and related health problems* (10th revision). Geneva: Author.

CHAPTER 6

The Role of the State in System Development

Sheila A. Pires and Susan Ignelzi

States play a variety of roles to promote the development of community-based systems of care for children and their families. Particularly since the mid-1980s, they have used a wide range of strategies to educate, persuade, assist, and/or require key constituencies (such as legislatures, local governments, providers, and others) to develop systems of care. These include such mechanisms as launching strategic planning processes, funding new types of services, creating demonstration programs, enacting legislation, changing state policies and regulations, providing training and technical assistance, implementing new standards, changing financing processes, creating new interagency relationships, building new or stronger constituencies, changing state administrative structures, altering standard operating procedures, and supporting research and evaluation. State decisions as to which particular mechanisms to use are influenced by political, fiscal, organizational, technical capacity, and other environmental factors, including prevailing values in the state (Stroul, 1982, 1985).

Developing new systems or changing traditional ones can be a difficult and long-term undertaking. Systems tend to have lives of their own and resist change. State entities interested in system development must develop a process of change powerful enough to overcome many layers of resistance. The focus of this chapter is on the positive roles that states have played, and continue to play, in promoting system development.

FACTORS STIMULATING STATE INTEREST IN SYSTEM DEVELOPMENT

Since the mid-1980s, a number of factors have stimulated states' interest in developing systems of care for children with emotional disorders and their families. These have included federal initiatives, private foundation initiatives, internal budgetary pressures, concerns regarding the number and cost of children in out-of-home or out-of-state care, class action and other lawsuits, parent and advocacy groups, and concerned and enlightened leadership at both state and local levels.

The Child and Adolescent Service System Program (CASSP), launched by the National Institute of Mental Health in 1984, has been the key federal initiative in the past decade to assist states to promote the development of systems of care for children with serious emotional disturbances and their families. CASSP has funded all 50 states, U.S. territories, and multiple local jurisdictions to develop systems of care for children and their families.

The momentum begun by CASSP was strengthened by the 1986 State Comprehensive Mental Health Services Plan Act (part of PL 99-660). This legislation, which was amended in 1990 specifically to include children, required all states to develop and implement plans to create community-based systems of care for persons with serious mental illness. In 1992, federal support for state efforts expanded further with passage of the Comprehensive Community Mental Health Services Program for Children with Serious Emotional Disturbances, which provides funds to state and local jurisdictions for development of community-based services for children and their families.

Private foundation initiatives also have stimulated state activities in systems development since the mid-1980s. In 1987, the Robert Wood Johnson Foundation launched its Mental Health Services Program for Youth, which builds on CASSP concepts and progress in the states, with a particular focus on local system building. In 1991, the Annie E. Casey Foundation also built on CASSP principles and activities in starting its Mental Health Initiative for Urban Children, which focuses on system building in inner city neighborhoods. Both of these foundation initiatives require active state involvement.

Budgetary pressures within states also have been instrumental in stimulating state involvement in system of care development. States have focused particularly on the significant amount of funds spent on residential treatment and psychiatric hospitalization of children and adolescents. State analyses during the last decade typically found that many children in very expensive residential treatment or inpatient units appeared to be in need of less intensive care. States' findings suggested that many of these children could have been more appropriately treated, at less cost, in community- or home-based programs had those been available.

Another focus of state budgetary concern is the notable cost of a few very expensive children to the system. These children usually are not eligible for federal Medicaid or Title IV-E (child welfare) funds of the Social Security Act, and, often, their families have expended all of their resources (including third-party funds) attempting to provide adequate services. These few children tend to cost states a significant amount of state dollars. Many states have sought to build systems of care that "wrap" community-

and home-based services around these children and their families to provide more appropriate, less costly care and have attempted to redirect funds to support community-based services.

In addition to budgetary pressures, concern over the large numbers of children in out-of-home or out-of-state care also has been a factor in encouraging states to develop community-based service systems. In 1989, the National Mental Health Association released its "Invisible Children" report, showing that states across the country tended to overuse out-of-home placements for children with serious emotional disorders. The study documented that many of these children could be served as effectively in their own homes and communities if appropriate services were available. Many states have initiated system development activities specifically to reduce the numbers of children in out-of-home and out-of-state care.

National attention and the growing body of literature throughout the 1980s on the needs of children with serious emotional disorders and their families have encouraged enlightened leadership at both state and local levels. The development of leadership capacities at state and local levels has itself been a major factor in system of care development.

Leadership has been a key factor not only within state and local governments but also with respect to the development and maturation of family and advocacy groups. Efforts by families, in particular, over the last decade to come together to advocate for their children have furthered states' interest in system development. In addition, advocates have brought a number of key lawsuits to pressure states to develop systems of care for children and families.

STRATEGIC PLANNING AND IMPLEMENTATION PROCESS

The role of the state in the development of systems of care is, first and foremost, to provide the leadership to launch and sustain the process. The challenge to states is to develop a process that weaves the needs of the target population, resources, strategies, and outcomes into a purposeful plan and implementation endeavor that is sufficiently flexible to allow for adjustments while staying focused on long-term goals.

In the past decade, virtually all states have engaged in strategic planning and implementation processes to develop systems of care. Effective state planning and implementation processes share a number of common elements (Pires, 1991):

- Effective processes *ensure the development and promotion of a shared vision* that defines the essential values and characteristics of an ideal system of care. State leadership to articulate and promote a vision for system change is critical. A shared vision is the glue that brings and holds together diverse and often competing constituencies.

- Effective processes *are staffed, carefully organized, and managed.* Staff anticipate what the process needs to accomplish and in what time frame, what the milestones are along the way, and who needs to be involved in what ways and at what points.
- Effective processes *involve key stakeholders,* such as family members, local providers, other child-serving system representatives, judges, and elected officials. Effective state processes recognize that the involvement and investment of key stakeholders in system planning and implementation are essential to create a constituency for change, to establish or strengthen relationships needed for implementation, and to minimize resistance to change.

  It is unquestionably a challenge to states, particularly large states, to reach out to and involve multiple constituencies. Ohio provides one example of a large state that actively sought and achieved broad-based participation in planning and implementation. Forums were held across the state to create awareness, holding the meetings on Saturdays to make it easier for working families and others to attend, and utilized over 50 committees with over 700 members to plan and implement system changes.
- Effective processes *involve families early in the process* and in ways that are meaningful. Virginia provides one example of a state that successfully involved families early in its planning and implementation process. The state joined forces with an existing parent advocacy and support organization to apply for a CASSP grant, involve family members on key state planning bodies, facilitate the development of multiple local parent support groups throughout the state, and keep parents informed through a newsletter and other public education activities.
- Effective processes *ensure meaningful attention to the needs of children and families of color.* In most states, children of color are overrepresented in the most restrictive placements and tend to have limited access to treatment services, even in states with small minority populations as a whole. Effective processes recognize this as a fundamental systemic problem and take steps to involve organizations representing persons of color and families of color early in the process. In Alaska, for example, Alaskan Native villagers developed ideas for culturally relevant approaches to care for Alaskan Native youth with emotional disturbances, which became an integral part of the state's system development strategy.
- Effective processes *develop and maintain an interagency focus,* recognizing that children with emotional disorders and their families usually require the services of more than just the mental health agency. A number of states, such as Tennessee, Louisiana, Virginia, and Ohio, have mandated, through executive order or legislation, interagency planning and implementation bodies.

- Effective processes *involve local planning, administrative, and service entities.* Depending on the state structure, counties, cities, regions, local service boards, and a range of community-based providers and local parent groups need to be integrated into the planning and implementation of systems of care. Vermont, for example, which is a small state with a centralized administrative structure, put in place 12 local interagency teams across the state, which were comprised of district child welfare directors, children's coordinators from community mental health centers, local special education administrators, private service providers, and parents. The teams were used to plan and implement systems of care. In Pennsylvania, a large state with a strong county structure, grants were given to counties to develop planning and implementation processes that involved key county constituency groups.
- Effective processes *ensure that there is a needs assessment* to determine who the target population is, its size, its needs, and the implications of its size and needs for system development. Again, state leadership to implement this needs assessment is critical. The needs assessment process, like that of defining values and a vision, is an essential early part of the overall process for system change, which can serve to bring people together, generate interest, and build consensus for system change objectives.
- Effective processes *establish clear goals and objectives* that provide a road map for system development. Although most states have successfully articulated and promoted a vision for system change, far fewer states have articulated concrete objectives that specify what is to be done, by when, and by whom in order to implement the vision, particularly objectives that fundamentally alter traditional system tendencies. Those states that have specified and built consensus for concrete objectives tend to be more actively engaged in meaningful system development.
- Effective processes *articulate strategies to achieve objectives.* Because the process of identifying strategies forces those involved in system planning and development to gauge the feasibility of implementing objectives, it is an important aspect of a state's leadership role. The question of feasibility must take into account financial, staffing and other operational realities, programmatic and technical capacity, and political concerns, as well as the need to balance competing interests. The process of identifying strategies and weighing feasibility provides a way for states to educate the various stakeholders as to the realities informing, constraining, and aiding systems change.
- Effective processes *track and monitor progress* toward achieving objectives, as well as the quality of progress, over time. Evaluation of progress serves to alert key stakeholders as to where revisions are needed or contingencies warranted. It can provide invaluable data documenting the

advantages of system development. Most important, by creating evaluation processes, states assure key constituencies that they are serious about system development and recognize that it is a long-term, dynamic process requiring assessment and readjustments over time. Some states, such as Alaska and Vermont, have formed linkages with universities to assist them in evaluating the progress and quality of their system change objectives. Other states, such as Ohio, utilize state planning bodies composed of key constituencies to evaluate progress.

EXAMPLES OF STATE SYSTEM DEVELOPMENT STRATEGIES

The most difficult, and most critical, issues for states to tackle in system development are those that relate to structural problems in the traditional system. Making structural, or systemic, change requires strong state leadership over time.

Structural change concerns itself with those aspects of current state operating procedures (usually the most entrenched) that seem most irrational in light of the values, vision, and goals of systems of care. In the world of public child mental health service delivery, the "irrational" may be that

- There is no mandate, or designated funding, for the state mental health system to provide community-based children's services.
- Three-quarters of state child mental health dollars are spent on inpatient care.
- Block grant funds for community-based services are allocated by states to community mental health centers (CMHCs) whose services are not responsive to the needs of children with serious emotional disturbances and their families.
- Minority children are overrepresented in inpatient and residential treatment facilities and underrepresented in services provided by CMHCs.
- Administrators with operational and budgetary control over child mental health services at state and local levels are predominantly adult focused.
- Parents are viewed by administrators and clinicians in the system as "part of the problem."
- The child mental health, child welfare, juvenile justice, education, health, and substance abuse systems do not collaborate, although they share caseloads.
- There is no state requirement or mechanism to collect child-specific utilization data or to develop child-specific standards either within the mental health system or across child-serving agencies.
- The state mental health agency has a policy of reducing inpatient beds, but the state's Certificate of Need process, managed by another depart-

ment, keeps approving applications for new beds from for-profit providers.
- Most of the state's population of children in out-of-state residential care have serious emotional disturbances, but the mental health system plays no role in the placement of these children (or prevention of placement), monitoring of their care, or development of aftercare plans.

The above list is by no means exhaustive, nor does it characterize all states. However, it is illustrative of the kinds of structural, or systemic, problems often found in states.

A great deal of rigor and tenacity on the part of states is required to identify and achieve consensus on structural change approaches to address these and other problems. For example, funding a newsletter for parents would not generate the same degree of anxiety within the system as requiring all state hospitals and local service boards to include parents as equal participants on treatment planning and discharge planning teams. Although both approaches may be worthwhile, it is the latter (if implemented with the same degree of rigor and tenacity) that would lead to more enduring systemic change.

Similarly, creation of a bureau of child and adolescent services within a state mental health agency, with operational and budgetary authority for children's services, will lead to more enduring systemic change than creation of a special assistant for children's services with no operational authority. Changes in a state's Medicaid plan from the clinic to the rehabilitation services option, so that a range of community-based services for children can be covered, will create greater structural change than creation of a one-time set-aside of state monies to fund local community-based services demonstrations (although, again, both approaches may be worthwhile). Enactment of legislation to mandate state and local interagency policy formulation and individual service planning teams will produce greater systemic change than a mandate for quarterly meetings of child-serving agency representatives.

The following subsections describe structural change strategies, across a number of key areas affecting children's services, in which states have been engaged.

Strategies Related to Infrastructure

The term "infrastructure" is used to refer to the underlying foundation or basic framework of a state's mental health system. Knitzer (1982) found that the infrastructure of most state mental health systems was heavily adult oriented. Central operations, such as data systems, planning offices, training, budget development, standard setting, human resource development, and basic organizational structures, were predominantly focused on adult services (Knitzer, 1982). Regional or area offices, local service boards, and CMHCs tended to have similar adult-oriented structures and staff.

Since Knitzer's findings, a number of states have focused on changing their infrastructures to make them more "child friendly" and to give children's issues greater visibility and clout within the system. The following examples illustrate the range of strategies used.

The *District of Columbia* created within its Commission on Mental Health a Child and Youth Services Administration with operational and budgetary authority for the entire continuum of child mental health services, inpatient through community-based services. *North Carolina* pursued a number of strategies related to infrastructure. The state sought to develop, over a 5-year period, synchronicity between the mental health system's data system and those of the other major child-serving systems. It mandated its central Office of Human Resource Development to develop a 6-year plan to support the child mental health system, including preservice education, recruitment, distribution, utilization, career systems, orientation, on-the-job training, continuing education, retention, certification, credentialing, and licensing.

Early in its system development process, *Virginia* focused on a strategy to change the structure and mandate of its local service boards by requiring that each designate a child and adolescent services director (see Chapter 7 for more information on the strategies used in Virginia). *Ohio* augmented the capacity of its central research and evaluation office to evaluate and conduct research in the children's mental health area. It also required that the planning process conducted by mental health boards at the community level focus directly on children's needs and integrate a specific children's plan into the larger community plan.

Pennsylvania created CASSP projects in all 45 county (or joinder) programs, which have the authority in Pennsylvania to administer core mental health services. By instituting CASSP projects in each county, the state sought to ensure that its counties have the capacity to participate in and manage a coordinated system of care. Pennsylvania also required that all Office of Mental Health policy bulletins regarding admission to and discharge from state hospitals and continuity of care agreements between state mental hospitals and county programs contain specific requirements applicable and appropriate to children and families.

Strategies Related to Financing Structures

Funding structures in a state often are themselves irrational, given the values, vision, and goals of integrated systems of care. For example, a goal may be the development of an array of accessible community-based services, but the state's Medicaid plan is structured in such a way that only inpatient care for children and clinic-based outpatient services are covered. A value may be that services should be provided in the least restrictive, most normalized setting, yet Title IV-E (child welfare) or the Individuals with Disabilities Education Act (PL 101-476) (education) monies are used to pay for out-of-state residential care for children with serious emotional disturbances, instead of in-home crisis and respite services or community-based day treatment. Recognizing that financing plays a major role in influencing the types of services provided and who receives them, many states have focused on strategies to change financing structures as a way to support the development of community-based systems of care.

A number of states have changed state Medicaid plans. For example, *Mississippi* (along with other states) changed its state Medicaid plan to cover case management and day treatment as eligible services. Some states, such as *Oregon*, switched from the clinic to the rehabilitation services option to cover a broader range of community services. A few states, such as *Pennsylvania*, broadened the scope of services and the size of the population covered by Early Periodic Screening, Diagnosis and Treatment (EPSDT) under Medicaid. Another financing system change is to alter the allocation of federal block grant monies. *Kentucky*, for example, diverted a larger share of block grant dollars to children's services.

Some states have changed the way in which the state allocates state dollars to the regions, counties, or local service boards to give local entities greater fiscal incentives and control to shift dollars from inpatient to community-based services or to target services to those most in need. *North Carolina*, for example, implemented the Pioneer Project to restructure the funding of services delivered by its area mental health authorities to target services to those with *serious* mental illness or emotional disturbance (and, in the case of children, also to those at risk of serious emotional disturbance, reflecting an important early intervention goal of the North Carolina plan) and to encourage local authorities to develop and provide the array of services called for in a system of care. The Pioneer Project establishes a purchase of services model of funding in which state dollars are earned by area programs based on the delivery of specific types of services to the designated target population.

Pennsylvania has pursued a strategy to change its county funding and reimbursement structures to create a unified system at the county level. Counties would be given control over both community mental health and state hospital dollars, as well as Medicaid expenditures. Counties thus would have the option of using dollars currently spent on state hospital care to develop community-based alternatives to hospitalization. Counties would control client flow by acting as gatekeepers to the unified system. *North Carolina* and *Pennsylvania* also are implementing "managed care" demonstrations as a means of controlling dollars spent on restrictive placements and encouraging spending on alternative (and less expensive) community-based services.

Blending funding across child-serving agencies, or utilizing the funding streams of other agencies, such as Title IV-E (child welfare) or Individuals with Disabilities Education Act (PL 101-476) (education) dollars, is another strategy states have used to make financing mechanisms more conducive to supporting community-based services for children with serious emotional disturbance. *Alaska,* for example, created a "new" pot of flexible funding, made up of mental health, education, and social services dollars, to support individualized assistance and case management (also called "wraparound" services) for children with serious emotional disturbances. *Ohio* utilized Title IV-E (child welfare) dollars for family preservation services to prevent out-of-home placement of children with serious emotional disturbances. The *District of Columbia* used education dollars to pay for the education components in its inpatient, residential treatment, day treatment, and therapeutic preschool components.

Some states, such as *Kentucky* and *Texas,* have increased state appropriations for child mental health services by getting legislation enacted to create new service mandates for children with serious emotional disturbances. Kentucky enacted legislation to provide intensive family-based services or wraparound services, and the Texas legislation supports a range of community-based services, including day treatment, in-home, and crisis services.

A number of states, such as *Oregon,* have mandated that private insurance plans cover mental health services or, if already covered, include a wider array of community-based services.

Several states, such as *Pennsylvania,* have increased access to income supports and entitlements, such as Supplemental Security Income (SSI) and Title IV-A (emergency assistance) dollars, which can help low-income children and families offset the cost of care. This approach may involve placing benefit acquisition specialists at local service sites; providing training for case managers, families, and others on entitlement criteria and application procedures; and improving coordination between the state mental health and public assistance agencies.

Strategies Related to Interagency Collaboration

Since the 1970s, the literature on children's services has described the fragmentation and needless duplication that characterize children's services delivery as a result of the categorical nature of child-serving systems and their lack of coordination. The literature also has described the need for holistic, comprehensive services for children and families with multiple problems, which can only be achieved by effective interagency collaboration.

No one child-serving agency has either the technical or the financial capacity to provide the array of services needed in a system of care. Effective state planning and implementation processes seek to identify cross-system collaboration mechanisms that are meaningful and enduring. These may include collaboration in regard to policy and budget formulation, program development and service provision, financing, case management, individual treatment planning, research, evaluation, and data systems. Their common feature is the objective of breaking down categorical approaches to service delivery to create more holistic systems of care. The process of identifying meaningful interagency strategies serves to help clarify where the mental health system needs to assume a lead responsibility, with other agencies providing supportive services, and where the mental health system needs to play the supportive role with other agencies taking the lead.

A number of states, such as *Ohio, Kentucky, Virginia, Vermont,* and *Texas,* enacted legislation to create state- and local-level interagency teams with responsibility for joint policy development and problem resolution and interagency case planning and service provision for children with multiple problems, including serious emotional disturbances. Virginia pursued a number of strategies, which included establishing common definitions of "serious emotional disturbance" and "high risk" across child-serving systems, establishing common entry processes at the local level for coordination of services, and creation of an Interagency Consortium Funds Pool to assist localities to keep children in their own homes (see Chapter 7).

North Carolina took the approach of sharing staff, funds, and programs across its three divisions of mental health, developmental disabilities, and substance abuse, including development of common screening instruments, single points of entry at local service levels, and decategorization of services. *Pennsylvania* adopted a strategy whereby the mental health system provides supportive services for children predominantly involved in other systems. For example, it increased the mental health system's support for the Student Assistance Program, which is a school-based program to identify, intervene with, and refer students at risk for chemical abuse, suicide, or other major mental health problems. The state also took steps to ensure that a mental health assessment would be included in EPSDT examinations provided to children who have been physically or sexually abused.

Strategies Related to Utilization of Community-Based Services

States have focused on a variety of approaches to encourage greater utilization of community-based services. Some states, such as *New Jersey*, enacted legislation prohibiting state hospitalization of children under age 11, closed state hospital beds, and diverted inpatient dollars to community-based services. Other states, such as *North Carolina* and *Kansas*, reduced inappropriate hospitalization and ensured that children are referred to community-based services by creating "single portals of entry" at the local level. The single portal of entry concept often is accompanied, as in North Carolina, by strategies to give local offices greater financial incentive to divert children from hospital to community-based care. Kansas enacted state legislation to 1) mandate 100% screening of all admissions to state hospitals by CMHCs and assign the gatekeeping responsibility and authority to CMHCs, 2) mandate joint discharge planning between state hospitals and CMHCs, 3) establish a free flow of clinical information between state hospitals and CMHCs and mutual clinic staff privileges, and 4) provide additional community-based services in a phased approach.

Another approach is for states to prioritize development of community-based services by local, regional, or area agencies. *Virginia*, for example, required each local service board to establish at least one of the less restrictive, nontraditional services, including intensive in-home services, day treatment, and individualized residential treatment (see Chapter 7). *Ohio* expanded development of "core" community-based services, including day treatment, therapeutic foster care, home-based services, and case management, by earmarking funds for these services to be given to its local service boards.

A number of states, such as *Ohio*, used CASSP, foundation, and state dollars to develop local demonstrations of community-based services as a means of "testing" and marketing new system concepts. These local demonstrations were evaluated and the outcomes brought to the attention of state legislators for consideration for broader implementation. Other states, such as Virginia and Alaska, as discussed in the financing section, have blended funds from several child-serving agencies to develop community-based services.

Strategies Related to Case Management

Closely related to the development of community-based services is the development of case management services. Case management is broadly recognized as a critical mechanism to create continuity and coordination of care for children and families who are involved with several service components and agencies and whose needs change over time.

The process of developing case management requires states to define carefully both who is to receive case management and what those services are. In addition, changes to state Medicaid plans to cover case management services necessitate definition of both the service and the eligible target population.

Many states have developed *intensive* case management services, which are targeted to those who are most seriously ill. Some states, such as *Virginia* and *North Carolina*, developed curricula in intensive case management and are training local service staff. As discussed in the financing section, many states changed state Medicaid plans to cover case management services.

Strategies Related to Family Involvement

Researchers and practitioners in the field of children's mental health agree that quality services and successful treatment for children with emotional disturbance must involve the family. Almost every state plan cites the creation of a "child-centered system of care" as both a core value and a primary goal. As Stroul and Friedman note

> Implicit in this value is a commitment to serving the child in the context of the family. In most cases, parents are the primary caregivers for severely emotionally disturbed children, and the system of care should support and assist parents in this role as well as involve parents in all decisions regarding service delivery. The system of care should also have a strong and explicit commitment to preserve the integrity of the family unit whenever possible. In many cases, intensive services involving the child and family can minimize the need for residential treatment. *Thus, a child-centered system of care is also a family-focused system of care.* [Emphasis added.] (Stroul & Friedman, 1986, p. 16)

National family advocacy groups, such the Federation of Families for Children's Mental Health and the National Alliance for the Mentally Ill Child and Adolescent Network, describe a family-focused system of care as one that provides an array of comprehensive services that strengthens and supports family life, the encouragement and authority for families to plan and evaluate their child's treatment, and meaningful opportunities to participate in state-level policy planning and service reform (Friesen & Koroloff, 1990). A number of states have taken steps to operationalize family-focused values and goals.

Virginia pursued several approaches intended to strengthen existing parents' organizations so that they have the ability and the power to become enduring, effective, informed, and visible advocacy entities in the state. For example, the state enabled Parents and Children Coping Together (PACCT) to have a key role in state-level planning, policy formation, and legislative education through participation on key committees, such as the Virginia Treatment Center for Children Planning Council, the State Consortium on Child Mental Health, and the Mental Health Advisory Committee (see Chapter 7). The state made a commitment to ensure that there is an effective voice for children in the state. One strategy, for instance, obligates the Department of Mental Health to assist PACCT, the Mental Health Association, the Virginia Association for the Mentally Ill, and the League of Women Voters to launch a collaborative advocacy campaign to educate legislators and the general public about children's mental health service needs.

Vermont envisioned an equally substantive role for parents in its reorganization of children's services. For example, Vermont created 12 Local Interagency Teams charged with reviewing and developing treatment plans for difficult-to-serve youth and settling disputes concerning treatment plans. The parents of the child under discussion sit on the Local Interagency Team, along with an additional parent who is a permanent team member. Other permanent members include representatives from the key agencies that provide services to children, such as the special education administrator and the coordinator for children's services at the community mental health center. In addition to reviewing individual treatment plans, the teams also develop priorities for local services needs. Parents also participate on an advisory board that Vermont has established to advise the Secretary of Human Services and the Commissioners of Mental Health, Education, and Rehabilitative Services on matters relating to children who have serious emotional disturbances. Five parents of children with serious emotional disturbances sit on the board, along with five advocates and five providers. The board reviews and evaluates current budgets and makes recommendations to the commissioners for new service initiatives.

Strategies Related to Cultural Competence

Although state mental health systems affirm their commitment to providing services without regard to race, religion, or national origin, few states have actually developed specific approaches to ensure that children and families of color have access to culturally competent services. The need to focus on strategies for achieving cultural competence has intensified in many states where the number of minority children has grown but the percentage of those children who receive services has not increased at the same rate. At the same time, children of color who *are* in state care frequently are found in the most restrictive, out-of-home settings, suggesting that the relatively few minority children who are receiving services may not be receiving appropriate care.

In response to this challenge, *Alaska*, with its large population of Alaskan Native children living in remote villages far from urban treatment centers, developed specific strategies to make its system more responsive. State planners did not attempt to impose their own solutions on the native population but, rather, collaborated with village leaders in an interactive planning and implementation process to identify culturally relevant service approaches. A major strategy was the Alaska Youth Initiative (AYI) (see Chapter 22). AYI empowers local teams, unconstrained by traditional solutions, to devise their own village-based treatment plans, which are then reviewed by state mental health planners. These treatment plans are based on an "environmental assessment" that takes into account not only the child's strengths and weaknesses but also the resources and stresses in the environment. Flexible funding mechanisms enable the state to underwrite the cost of village-based wraparound services that allow treatment to take place within the native cultural community. AYI seeks to achieve cultural competence and to avoid "placement" in service components out of state or otherwise far from villages, except as a last resort.

Ohio also focused specifically on minority concerns. The state, for example, required that local mental health boards address minority issues in the plans that the boards submit to the state along with their requests for funding. The local plan must include a section specifying strategies and objectives for improving the quality of culturally competent treatment.

Mississippi took the approach of training additional mental health staff in cultural competence in an effort to increase the utilization of mental health services by minority populations. To accomplish this, the Division of Community Services, the Division of Children and Youth Services, and the Division of Human Resources collaborated with the University of Mississippi on the development of a training program to "address the Southern culture in general and minority populations of this culture in particular." The effectiveness of the new curriculum will be evaluated in a study to determine if, as a result of increased cultural competence, there has been an increase in the number of minority children and youth who utilize mental health services.

In addition to its training efforts, Mississippi also established a Minority Affairs Advisory Committee within its Division of Human Resources to monitor statewide progress in achieving cultural competence. Mississippi's Division of Children and Youth Services also has initiated a Minority Mental Health Planning Committee with particular interest in improving services, advocacy efforts, and support networks for African Americans, Vietnamese, and Native American children and their families.

SUMMARY

The state role in the development of systems of care for children and families is multifaceted and vital. State entities are in a unique position to champion the vision of systems change across the state, to build coalitions, and to create opportunities for key stakeholders from across the state to share information and ideas. States also have powers not available at local levels to require system development through legislation, regulation, financing mechanisms, and operating procedures. They also have resources to provide training and technical assistance on a statewide basis to facilitate system development, and they often are in a position to support research and data collection that demonstrate the need for and effectiveness of systems change.

An important lesson to be learned from the experience of states is that there is no step-by-step approach, no single right way to develop systems of care. However, it also is clear from system change experiments that state leadership is a critical component.

REFERENCES

Friesen, B., & Koroloff, N. (1990). Family-centered services: Implications for mental health administration and research. *Journal of Mental Health Administration, 17,* 1.

Individuals with Disabilities Education Act of 1990 (IDEA), PL 101-476. (October 30, 1990). Title 20, U.S.C. 1400 et seq: *U.S. Statutes at Large, 104*, 1103–1151.

Knitzer, J. (1982). *Unclaimed children: The failure of public responsibility to children and adolescents in need of mental health.* Washington, DC: Children's Defense Fund.

National Mental Health Association. (1989). *Invisible children project: Final report and recommendations.* Alexandria, VA: Author.

Pires, S. (1991). *State child mental health planning.* Washington, DC: Georgetown University Child Development Center, National Technical Assistance Center for Children's Mental Health.

State Comprehensive Mental Health Services Act, PL 99-660. (November 14, 1986). Title 42, U.S.C. 300x et seq: *U.S. Statutes at Large, 100*, 3794–3797.

Stroul, B. (1982). *Community support program: Analysis of state strategies.* Boston: Boston University Center for Rehabilitation, Research and Training in Mental Health.

Stroul, B. (1985). *Child and Adolescent Service System Program (CASSP) system change strategies: A workbook for states.* Washington, DC: Georgetown University Child Development Center, National Technical Assistance Center for Children's Mental Health.

Stroul, B., & Friedman, R. (1986). *A system of care for children and youth with severe emotional disturbances.* Washington, DC: Georgetown University Child Development Center, National Technical Assistance Center for Children's Mental Health.

CHAPTER 7

A Statewide Approach to System Development

Virginia

Gary Macbeth

Virginia, like many states, has embraced the system of care model (Stroul & Friedman, 1986) to guide mental health service system development and practice. The passage of the Comprehensive Services Act by the Virginia legislature in 1992 was the culmination of 6 years of smaller steps toward the implementation of a statewide interagency system of care for troubled and at-risk youth and their families. At the same time, the passage of the act marks the beginning of a new set of implementation challenges for Virginia. This chapter details the early stages of system reform in Virginia and the structural and financing changes being carried out through the Comprehensive Services Act. Lessons learned to date, as well as continuing challenges, are discussed.

EARLY STAGES OF SYSTEM REFORM IN VIRGINIA

The early stages of mental health system reform in Virginia can be traced back to a 1987 forum on children's mental health. From that time, a number of strategies were used that furthered the system development agenda. These strategies comprise the early stages of system reform that laid the foundation for the statewide structural and financial reform that followed.

The First Lady's Forum on Child Mental Health

Prior to 1987, there was little focus on interagency collaboration in Virginia regarding children and adolescents with serious emotional and behavioral problems and their families. In 1987, the Department of Mental Health, Mental Retardation and Substance Abuse Services, in conjunction with parents, advocates, child-serving departments (Education, Health, Social Welfare, and Juvenile Justice), and the governor sponsored the First Lady's Forum on Child Mental Health. In preparation, agency staff and constituency groups developed three consensus papers on the direction that services in Virginia should take. These papers discussed a model system of services, interagency collaboration, and prevention/early intervention. At the First Lady's Forum, agency executives made commitments to implement the strategies outlined in the papers. This was the first step toward a collaborative, community-based system of care for Virginia's children. Funds were committed by the agency executives to move forward with the collaborative system-building process.

State Interagency Consortium—
Funds Pool and Local Interagency Service Projects

The first collaborative venture among agencies and parents was the formation of the State Interagency Consortium in the fall of 1987 with $450,000 in blended funding. The Consortium operated through an interagency memorandum of agreement and set two goals:

1. To provide financial incentives for local agencies to do comprehensive interagency assessments, planning, and service provision for their most troubled children and families, without regard to "who pays" for services
2. To encourage localities to develop innovative service packages to meet the needs of these children and their families in their home communities

A "funds pool" was established with contributions from state agencies. Funds were then allocated to applying localities for services to individual children and families. These services had to be based on service plans developed collaboratively by interagency child and family planning teams and signed by all four participating local child-serving departments (mental health, child welfare, juvenile courts, and education) and the family. Services that were unavailable locally could be developed or purchased with funds pool dollars. A state-level committee composed of staff of five agencies, parents, and private providers reviewed funding applications.

The funds pool had an immediate impact on increasing local collaboration. In addition, consensus was developed at the state and local levels on a definition of children and adolescents who were considered "children of all agencies," those for whom responsibility was clearly shared across agency lines. The success of the funds pool resulted in a $1.15 million appropriation by the 1988 General Assembly to increase the funds pool to $650,000 and to add a second initiative, Local Interagency Services Projects.

The goals for the Local Interagency Service Projects and the funds pool were the same. Six Virginia localities were each awarded up to $200,000 to develop interagency-managed and -operated services that complemented existing local services. For the first time, local interagency management teams focusing on system-building issues were formed to complement interagency child and family planning teams. The projects were intensively evaluated for 3 years (Rowe, 1991a, 1991b), and positive outcomes were documented.

Parents and Children Coping Together and the Mental Health Association in Virginia

The Virginia Department of Mental Health, Mental Retardation and Substance Abuse Services recognized very early that successful promotion of child and family mental health services and a commitment by agencies to collaborate could occur only through strong advocacy voices for system improvements. Virginia successfully competed for a federal Child and Adolescent Service System Program (CASSP) grant in 1986, enabling the state to actively pursue the objective of empowering parents and advocates.

Parents and Children Coping Together (PACCT), formed by a Richmond father in 1985 as a support group for parents of hospitalized children, was strengthened as a statewide umbrella organization for parent support groups and for advocacy. PACCT has grown to comprise a network of 23 support groups statewide. PACCT continues to publish the quarterly *Parent Watch* newsletter, to link and inform parents, and to provide minigrants to cover expenses of local support group operations.

The Mental Health Association in Virginia adopted children and families as a major priority beginning in 1989. Through its government affairs committee, the Mental Health Association began lobbying the General Assembly on bills affecting children and families. The association began representing the interests of children and families on state-level policy boards, the Coalition for the Mentally Ill, and the Council on Community Services. It also provided office space and support services for PACCT, enabling that organization to develop an independent identity.

As PACCT and the Mental Health Association grew, so did their roles as advocacy organizations. Parents and advocates became vital and effective voices for service funding at Department of Mental Health, Mental Retardation and Substance Abuse Services budget hearings, at General Assembly committee meetings, and at local mental health center board meetings. In addition, PACCT quickly became involved on policy boards and on the State Interagency Consortium. The leadership of parents and advocates has resulted in improved services for Virginia children and their families and has led to the inclusion of parents by law, as of 1992, on all state and local teams implementing systems reform in Virginia.

Invisible Children's Study

At the same time that the State Interagency Consortium was attempting to move the service system toward nonresidential services and community ownership of troubled children, the Mental Health Association in Virginia and the four major child-serving departments began to study issues concerning children in group residential care. The results were predictably discouraging. *The Study of Invisible Children* (Mental Health Association in Virginia, 1989) documented that many children were placed in group residential care without less restrictive services being attempted and with little evidence of collaborative service planning. When these children returned home, they often quickly experienced difficulties because of a lack of supportive services. This study received immediate attention and results. Policy makers noted the difficulty in obtaining accurate data on the numbers of children and the costs of their care, prompting a formal study of the issue initiated in 1989 by the Governor's Planning and Budget Office.

Interagency Guidance on Services

Increased collaboration among agencies and the expansion of nonresidential services in Virginia pointed to the need for common guidance for localities on service models. Agency staff, parents, and service providers developed guidance packages for localities on in-home services, case planning, and case management in order to reinforce high-quality, collaborative service delivery. The publication of these papers in 1990 was followed by interagency training across the state on innovative service modalities. This marked a new step toward a collaborative system—establishing joint service expectations and providing cross-system staff training.

Use of Title IV-E and Federal Block Grant Funds

Virginia also began the practice of sending interagency and parent teams to national conferences and in-state training events. This provided additional incentives for communities to work together, reinforced the collaborative service system direction in Virginia, and made available high-quality training. Title IV-E funds were accessed for this training whenever appropriate. For example, 62 persons from Virginia, most in teams from local communities, attended the 1992 Training Institutes sponsored by CASSP on developing local systems of care.

The proportion of the federal block grant dollars allocated for children's services increased each year. In 1992, additional state general funds and federal block grant funds were awarded to localities, based on their unfunded state budget requests, for in-home and individual therapeutic home services. Requirements for collaboration in the provision of services were part of the awards.

Study of Children's Residential Services

The Department of Planning and Budget was asked by the governor, in 1989, to study issues associated with the Commonwealth of Virginia's use of residential care and to make policy recommendations (Department of Planning and Budget, 1990). This study was welcomed by public agencies, parents, and advocates as validation of the direction set for system reform in Virginia. For private residential care providers, the study was threatening because they believed that the commonwealth was moving to put them out of business.

With high-level backing from the governor and his cabinet, the study was comprehensive and examined issues identified since the mid-1980s by legislative committees, state agencies, provider organizations, parents, and advocates. The following issues surfaced:

- Children with serious emotional and behavioral problems frequently have multiple needs that require the involvement of several agencies.
- Children who have emotional and behavioral problems are too frequently treated outside of their home environment or outside of their community.
- Community resources and financial incentives to treat children in their home communities are inadequate.
- The type of treatment received depends on the system the child enters: juvenile justice, mental health, foster care, or special education.
- The costs of group residential care in Virginia are high and are increasing quickly.

The study examined data on group residential care utilization by four Virginia public agencies and on the delivery of services and funding of service delivery in Virginia. The results of the study confirmed the seriousness of the issues:

- Examination of the 14,000 child cases in group residential care across four agencies in fiscal year 1989 only found 4,993 children actually in care, revealing considerable overlap in agency caseloads.
- At least 80% of the children received services from more than one agency, and 50% were involved with three or more agencies.
- A total of $93 million in fiscal year 1989 and $110 million in fiscal year 1990 in state and local dollars was spent on group residential care. For fiscal years 1992–1994, the commonwealth would have to spend $42 million in new dollars to maintain current levels of care.
- Costs of residential care were increasing at the rate of 22% per year.

The necessity for change was clear, and this study had a major impact on continuing system development efforts in the state.

STATEWIDE IMPLEMENTATION OF A SYSTEM OF CARE IN VIRGINIA

In the spring of 1990, the secretaries of Health and Human Resources, Education, and Public Safety called for major changes in the delivery and funding of services for troubled and at-risk youth and their families. A cross-secretarial interagency Council on Community Services for Youth and Families was formed to recommend creative and realistic changes for state-wide implementation. The Council on Community Services was given the charge to

- Improve services for youth with emotional and behavioral problems and their families.
- Control the escalating costs of residential group care for state and local governments.

The council was to accomplish this charge by recommending a new system that would expand community nonresidential services, improve inter-agency collaboration and service delivery, and adapt the state's funding streams and management structures to this new system. Significant from a strategic point of view, the council was given an 18-month time limit to produce a plan for General Assembly action.

Planning Virginia's System of Care

The Council on Community Services began its work in the spring of 1990 and established the working structure shown in Figure 7.1. The council included key stakeholders at each level of work (Table 7.1). This inclusive process was necessary in order to gain maximum energy for change and as much consensus as possible on the shape of the new service system. Over 145 state and local government and public agency staff, private providers, parents, judges, and advocates were involved in the planning. For 18 months the Executive Management Committee, Steering Committee, and work groups discussed the goals, structure, design, and funding of a new interagency service delivery system.

Process The planning process was characterized by high energy, enormous commitments of time, considerable conflict over agency turf and private interests, and relentless efforts to mold the various pieces of a pro-posed service system and its funding. Several lessons were learned in this process. First, a clear direction had to be set by the Steering Committee and reinforced by the Executive Management Committee and cabinet secretar-ies. This required negotiations on:

- What a collaborative system means
- The belief in community approaches to care
- The willingness to subordinate agency interests to the interests of chil-dren and families
- The equal involvement of parents in the process
- The willingness to decategorize funding streams and to change funding incentives to support community services
- Incorporating a public/private partnership
- The importance of early intervention in the service system

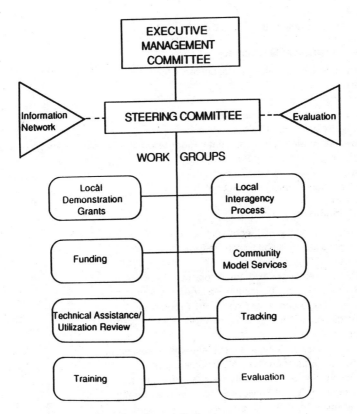

Figure 7.1. Organization of the Council on Community Services.

Second, with the addition of each new group of people to the process, the belief in the benefits of collaboration had to be discussed again. Every work group struggled with this basic belief.

Third, the council realized quickly that a new system of services and funding is threatening and that communities across the state had to be included in the development process. The council used a multitude of inclusion strategies:

- All documents produced by the work groups, once agreed on by the Steering Committee and the Executive Management Committee, were distributed to constituent organizations for reaction.
- An initial draft of a proposed system of care was circulated throughout the commonwealth for public comment in the summer of 1991 (Council on Community Services, 1991b).
- Public hearings were held across the state on the draft proposal, and parents were encouraged to voice their opinions.

Table 7.1. Membership of the Council on Community Services

Executive Management Committee

Secretary of Health and Human Resources, Chair
Secretary of Education
Secretary of Public Safety
Executive Secretary of the Supreme Court
Commissioner of Social Services
Commissioner of Mental Health, Mental Retardation and Substance Abuse Services
Director of Youth and Family Services
Superintendent of Public Instruction
Budget Manager, Planning and Budget

Steering Committee[a]

Council Staff Director, HHR Secretariat, Chair
Youth Services Commission Executive Director
DSS Director of Service Programs
DMHMRSAS Director of Child and Adolescent Services
DOE Director of Special Education Management & Programs
DYFS Chief of Operations for Community Programs
DOH Coordinator of Child Development Services Programs
DPB representative
Virginia Association of School Superintendents representative
Virginia Special Education Directors representative
Virginia Association of Community Services Board representative
Virginia League of Social Services Executives representative
Virginia Juvenile Court Directors Association representative
Juvenile & Domestic Relations Judges representative
Private Residential Providers Associations representative
Parent representative

Work Group Members

State and local staff of five child-serving agencies
Departments for Medical Assistance, Criminal Justice Services, Planning and Budget,
    Information Technology, Rights of Disabled, and Council on Child Day Care and Early
    Childhood Programs
Judges, Office of the Supreme Court, legislative staff
Local officials, Municipal League, Association of Counties
Commonwealth Institute for Child & Family Studies
Parent and advocate representatives
Public/private residential and nonresidential providers
State Interagency Consortium, Rate Setting Council

[a]Abbreviations: HHR, Health and Human Resources; DSS, Department of Social Services; DMHMRSAS, Department of Mental Health, Mental Retardation and Substance Abuse Services; DOE, Department of Education; DYFS, Department of Youth and Family Services; DOH, Department of Health; DPB, Department of Planning and Budget.

- State agency executives began to meet with key legislators, advocacy groups, local government organizations, and private provider organizations to overcome differences and to develop positive momentum going into the 1992 General Assembly.

Fourth, the council knew that massive change would be criticized, and even attacked, if there was no proof that it could work. Despite the many previous successful smaller efforts, the concepts had to be tested further. Six localities were competitively awarded demonstration grants, totaling $2.4 million, to test models of collaborative systems of care. In each locality, some funding was blended, interagency management structures were put into place, interagency child and family planning teams were formed, parents were included as partners, and services were provided. Pressure was extensive for these localities to improve services and outcomes and to reduce the use of group residential care. The demonstration grant sites were extensively evaluated and the results published; the outcomes supported system reform (Koch, Page, & Watts, 1993; Office of Comprehensive Services, 1993b).

Products of the Planning Process   As a result of the council's work in 1990–1991, the Comprehensive Services Act for At-Risk Youth and Families (1992) was introduced in the 1992 Virginia General Assembly. The intent of the Comprehensive Services Act is to establish a system of service delivery and funding in Virginia that will

- Preserve and strengthen families.
- Provide services in the least restrictive environment while protecting the welfare of children and adolescents, consistent with public safety.
- Require increased collaboration among the child-serving agencies and parents in the management, operation, and funding of services.
- Combine and decategorize many current state and federal funding streams of the child-serving state agencies and provide greater community control and flexibility in the use of those funds.
- Identify children in need of services and intervene as early as possible.
- Create services that meet the needs of individual youths and their families.
- Encourage a public–private partnership.

The planning process produced two other important products. The first was a document entitled *Improving Care for Troubled & "At Risk" Youth & Their Families* (Council on Community Services, 1991a). This document summarized the 18 months of Council work and provided detail on the changes outlined in the Comprehensive Services Act. The second product was a funding formula that enabled each of 124 Virginia localities to understand the potential impact of the fiscal changes proposed by the Comprehensive Services Act.

Legislative Compromise The General Assembly deliberations on the Comprehensive Services Act again raised all the same concerns that were voiced during the 18-month planning process. Many localities embraced the concepts of the new system of services but could not accept the funding formula. Some localities wanted implementation to be delayed until results of the demonstration grant sites were more conclusive. A major private residential care association threatened to oppose passage of the act, which it had previously agreed to, unless it was granted certain changes.

After lengthy debate, compromise, and tremendous displays of support by parents and advocates, the General Assembly passed the Comprehensive Services Act. However, the General Assembly rejected the funding formula and required that a new formula be presented to the 1993 General Assembly. This delayed full implementation of the act until July 1993. However, this delay also provided significant time in 1992 and 1993 to begin to implement the structural changes included in the act. A new challenge began—to implement the new system.

Implementing Virginia's New System of Care

With the passage of the Comprehensive Services Act, a 14-month implementation process (from April 1992 through June 1993) was used to put the system into operation. The implementation process and structure looked very similar to the planning structure illustrated in Figure 7.1. The name of the effort changed to Comprehensive Services for Youth and Families, new persons were appointed to the State Management Team (formerly the Steering Committee), and new work groups were formed.

The Comprehensive Services Act is a major restructuring of the Virginia service delivery system and its funding. The new interagency system is depicted in Figure 7.2.

Population Eligible for Services Children and adolescents (and their families) who are targeted for services under the act have serious emotional or behavioral problems that

- Have persisted over a significant period of time or, although only in evidence for a short period of time, are of such a critical nature that intervention is warranted; and
- Are significantly disabling and are present in several community settings; and
- Require services or resources that are unavailable or inaccessible, or that require coordinated intervention by at least two agencies (Comprehensive Services Act for At-Risk Youth and Families, 1992, Section 2.1-758).

Children with serious emotional and behavioral problems who are in residential group care or who are at risk of placement, and who require

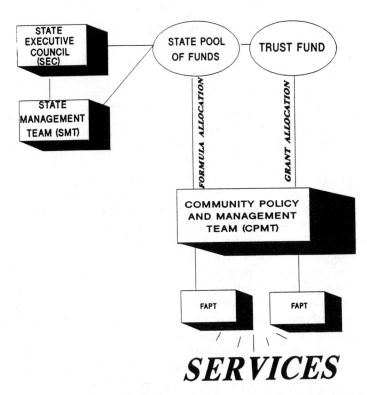

Figure 7.2. Comprehensive Services Act interagency structures and funding. (FAPT, Family Assessment and Planning Team.)

coordinated services, are a priority. Children served are from ages birth to 18. However, youth may be served until age 22 if already involved with social services or special education. A second part of the act targets young children at risk of later serious emotional or behavioral problems and their families.

Financial Resources

State Pool of Funds   The major funding is provided through a state pool of funds totaling about $101 million in FY 96 federal and state dollars, formally administered at the state level, and the historical local matching funds for those dollars. The pool consolidates and decategorizes eight funding streams across four agencies:

- Department of Juvenile Justice funds for special placements of court-involved youth
- Department of Social Welfare state/local foster care funds, foster care Supplemental Block Grant funds, and foster care Purchase of Services Block Grant funds

- Department of Education private tuition assistance funds and inter-agency assistance funds
- Department of Mental Health, Mental Retardation and Substance Abuse Services private hospital bed purchase funds
- The State Interagency Consortium Funds Pool

Funds are allocated by formula to each locality for use in purchasing or developing services for the eligible population and their families. The intent of this pooled funding is to provide more local responsibility in the management of funds and greater flexibility in the use of funds to meet individual needs of children and families. The incentives, therefore, are for localities to contain high-cost residential placements and to provide community services alternatives in order to maximize the numbers of children and families who can receive services. Communities are required to contribute local matching funds for all state pool funds, which provides further encouragement to maximize treatment choices.

Localities are first expected to serve those children and adolescents who are mandated by federal foster care and special education laws to receive services. Once a locality has carved out funding to cover anticipated needs for mandated children and their families, remaining pooled funds are available for others in the eligible population.

Funding Formula The development of an acceptable funding formula and local match requirements was accomplished by a task force chaired by the Secretary of Health and Human Resources and that involved many local government officials. The funding formula adopted by the 1993 General Assembly has three parts:

- Each locality receives its fiscal year 1992 historical use of the combined funding streams, regardless of equity issues, and contributes the fiscal year 1992 historical local match for these funds.
- All new funds are awarded to localities based on a formula that includes three equally weighted local factors: population under age 18; poverty (households on food stamps with children under age 18); and risk (child protective services, juvenile justice, and special education indicators).
- Localities must contribute matching funds for all new funds received. The local match is a single rate that is a composite index of community wealth currently used by the Virginia Department of Health.

On July 1, 1993, every locality received additional state funds—a minimum of $25,000 up to a maximum amount equivalent to the difference between their total allocation, based on application of the formula, and their historical use.

State Trust Fund A trust fund has also been established to provide seed funds to communities to develop community-based services for troubled youth and their families and to develop early intervention services for young children at risk of developing emotional or behavioral problems. The trust fund helps localities to increase their service base and emphasizes the goal of shifting dollars toward early intervention with young children. For 1993–1994, $3.4 million was competitively made available to 20 localities, with 27% of the funds going to early intervention.

Interagency Structures

State Executive Council This council is the highest decision-making body for the system of care and consists of six state agency heads (the commissioners of Health, of Mental Health, Mental Retardation and Substance Abuse Services, and of Social Services; the Superintendent of Public Instruction; the Executive Secretary of the Virginia Supreme Court; and the Director of the Department of Youth and Family Services) and a parent representative. The council oversees program and fiscal policies and provides direction to the State Management Team.

State Management Team This is the main body at the state level for implementing the system of care. The State Management Team is appointed by the State Executive Council and includes representatives from five state agencies and their local counterparts, a private provider of children's and family services, a judge, and a parent representative. The State Management Team develops policies to promote collaboration in providing services; governs the use, distribution, and monitoring of monies in the state pool of funds and trust fund; provides training and technical assistance at the state and local level; and oversees data collection and evaluation.

Over the 14-month implementation period, approximately 10 statewide work groups operated at any given time to assist the State Management Team. This enabled the implementation process to be inclusive of all stakeholders and ensured that all issues and strategies were debated thoroughly. Many major tasks were accomplished by the State Management Team:

- Policies and procedures were developed related to the target population, service requirements for localities, rules for the use of funds, and appeals mechanisms for families.
- Communities were oriented to the values, principles, and operation of the new system.
- Communities developed their management teams, their child and family planning teams, and their operating procedures.
- Communities were certified that they were ready to receive funding on July 1, 1993.
- A new funding formula was developed and approved by the 1993 General Assembly.
- Fiscal procedures were put into place.
- $6 million was allocated from existing department budgets to provide training and technical assistance for localities.

- The planning for a statewide data system was begun.
- A major plan for the evaluation of outcomes was developed and implemented.

Each of these tasks required enormous commitments of staff time and work. The implementation of the act demonstrated that, with every new step, old struggles emerged and had to be resolved. Systems change continued to be difficult. Improving the level of coordination among five major child-serving systems even further was critical to the implementation process, along with strong leadership exercised by the state agency heads and the Secretary of Health and Human Resources to overcome conflicts and difficulties.

Community Policy and Management Teams   In each local jurisdiction, Community Policy and Management Teams have been formed to develop local operations policy, plan for and implement services, and disburse funds. The community teams include local agency heads of the departments of social services and health, the community services board, the local school division, and the juvenile court services unit, as well as a parent representative and a representative of private providers of children and family services.

The community team manages its allocation of the state pool of funds to maximize local service provision. This often includes reviewing decisions made by the child and family planning teams and deciding how to best coordinate existing services across agencies. Because not all funding streams are in the pool of funds, the team must ensure that other, nonpooled resources are accessed. Over time, it is hoped that community teams across the state will reshape local service delivery systems to be more family friendly, comprehensive, and efficient.

Family Assessment and Planning Teams   In each locality, one or more Family Assessment and Planning Teams have been developed to assess the strengths and needs of individual troubled youth and their families, develop family service plans, identify and obtain a complement of individualized services to meet their needs, recommend funding for services, and monitor provision of services for each child and family. When current available services do not meet the needs of individual children, teams are encouraged to use pooled funds to create "wraparound" services that are child and family specific. The teams consist of representatives of the same five agencies as the Community Policy and Management Teams and a parent representative. Other key individuals or organizations also may be included. Families must be invited to participate fully in the assessment, planning, and implementation of services.

The skill levels of the Family Assessment and Planning Teams are a critical variable in systems change. Where these teams have strong system of care values and are creative, the Comprehensive Services Act allows tremendous flexibility to wrap services around children and their families. These teams, through their recommendations to the Community Policy and Management Teams, will be central to molding system reform at the local level. Therefore, the State Management Team is beginning to invest significant resources in training these teams on collaboration, effective assessment and planning, alternative service modalities, and effective parent involvement.

Data and Evaluation   Two essential components of the Virginia system of care are data collection and evaluation in order to monitor progress, measure outcomes, and provide feedback that can be used to modify the system. Work has been progressing slowly but steadily on developing a statewide interagency information management system on children and families served. The difficulties with setting up interacting multiple data systems across agencies and modifying their capabilities means that the system will take a number of years to become operational. In the meantime, a modified data and evaluation system is being phased in to gather necessary information (Office of Comprehensive Services, 1993a). The plan includes a number of key components:

- A minimum data set is being collected statewide on a quarterly basis on children and families served, by broad categories of services.
- Ten sites are collecting more comprehensive data on children, families, services, collaboration, and parental satisfaction. The five demonstration grant sites continue to provide extensive data.
- The trust fund grantees that provide early intervention services are providing data and evaluation information.
- Special surveys are being used statewide to measure collaboration and parent satisfaction.
- Information from the reimbursement system is being used to track expenditures by broad service categories and population types.

CHALLENGES STILL AHEAD

States engaging in system of care reforms, like Virginia, will find continuing challenges. For Virginia, five major challenges lie ahead over the next several years for the system changes to become most effective.

First, it is important for the system managers to take a flexible view of change. As implementation progresses, obstacles and difficulties are encountered that require adjustments and refinements as localities provide feedback to the State Management Team and Executive Council. Flexibility on the part of these management bodies is necessary to address those concerns.

Second, real differences have emerged between those persons best characterized as "visionaries" and those who are "implementers." Both are needed at different times. Often implementers have difficulty grasping the vision and, although they think they grasp it, they continually attempt to inject troublesome aspects of the old system into new practice. Visionaries, in contrast, have limitations in the other direction; they often think that "anything is possible." The key is to maintain a balance between the vision and practical realities.

Third, team building and communications are essential, ongoing parts of the system reform effort—team building with those who are designing and managing the system at the state and local levels as well as continual communications with everyone who is a part of implementing the system. This process requires special attention in order to keep the system evolving effectively.

Fourth, when existing dollars are blended and decategorized, a host of problems arise. The tendency in Virginia has become to protect those children and families who are "mandated" by federal law for services, or who are currently being served by the funding streams that were blended, and to make this net as wide as possible. Although certain mandates are clear, the size of the net has a lot to do with turf protection. It is difficult not to substitute one type of categorization, based on funding stream eligibility, with another, based on mandates, in order to protect traditional agency turf. Virginia must continue to struggle with the long-term goal of providing services for children and families in a noncategorical manner, based on their needs and characteristics.

Finally, training and technical assistance is a major component that must be built into continuing systems change efforts. Training is necessary to expose people to new ideas. At the same time, despite exposure to extensive training, many people do not know how to translate that training to their day-to-day practice. The quality and availability of good technical assistance to individual Community Policy and Management Teams and Family Assessment and Planning Teams will likely determine how successful the systems change effort in Virginia will be in the future.

STRATEGY FRAMEWORK FOR SYSTEM CHANGE

The experience of the Commonwealth of Virginia in promoting the development of systems of care has yielded much information about effective strategies. Other states and communities can benefit by examining some of the strategies used in Virginia that have had clear benefits and results in furthering the system change agenda. These strategies include the following.

Setting a Clear Direction

At each step of system change, it is essential to set a clear direction or road map of the desired system. This includes defining what is meant by a collaborative service system and how each effort, program, or project will assist in reaching that vision. Once clear goals are set, the job of the innovators becomes marketing the goals and reinforcing any positive examples of local efforts that embrace the goals.

Believing in the Benefits of Collaboration

System reform in child and family services involves collaboration. It is important to establish a cadre of people across agencies and among parents and advocates who believe that collaboration benefits everyone. This core group must be committed to its belief in the benefits of collaboration and in the directions collaboration should take, if there is to be long-term system impact. This group then becomes a vehicle for moving system change forward given the inevitable problems, disagreements, and resistances that arise.

Taking Many Small Steps

Collaborative service and financing development requires that many small steps be taken. Each effort, program, or initiative must be seen as contributing to the larger system reform agenda and must not become an end unto itself. Small, successful steps set the foundation for larger changes. The system changes currently being implemented in Virginia are the product of many smaller steps.

Using Multiple Strategies

It is very difficult to predict which strategies will result in successful system change. It is essential to incorporate as many strategies as possible in the effort to reach any one goal. The system that emerges from multiple strategies is likely to be better and stronger than one built on single-strategy methods. Using many strategies also increases the number of people committed to system change and the variety of programs or projects that are put into place.

Using Financial Incentives to Support the Direction

Incentive approaches encourage people to "do the right thing" more quickly than they might otherwise do it. Even small amounts of money can develop collaborative service processes and reinforce the directions set to achieve system change. Because it is often easier for people to embrace concepts than to carry them out, financial incentives tend to speed the pace of translating new concepts into practice.

Taking a Long-Term View

Finally, change takes time. Each effort, program, or project brings successes and some new challenges as well. Often the realized outcomes of each effort are not as great as the innovators had hoped. It is important to take a long-term view and realize that, with every step forward, new people must be convinced and new challenges overcome.

CONCLUSION

Virginia has been engaged in system reform efforts for children and adolescents with serious emotional and behavioral problems and their families since 1987. The implementation of the Comprehensive Services Act in Virginia moves system change in the delivery and funding of services to a statewide level. In this process, much has been learned about strategies and challenges that may benefit other states engaged in similar efforts.

REFERENCES

Comprehensive Services Act for At-Risk Youth and Families. (1992). *Code of Virginia*, Chapter 46, Section 2.1-745–2.1-759. Richmond: General Assembly of Virginia.

Council on Community Services. (1991a). *Improving care for troubled & "at risk" youth & their families*. Richmond, VA: Department of Planning and Budget.

Council on Community Services. (1991b). *Proposed draft of a system of services for troubled and at-risk youth and their families*. Richmond, VA: Department of Planning and Budget.

Department of Planning and Budget. (1990). *Study of children's residential services*. Richmond, VA: Author.

Koch, R., Page, M., & Watts, A. (1993). *Research notes: comprehensive services for at-risk youth and families demonstration projects interim evaluation report*. Richmond, VA: Office of Research and Evaluation, Department of Mental Health, Mental Retardation and Substance Abuse Services.

Mental Health Association in Virginia. (1989). *Study of invisible children*. Richmond, VA: Author.

Office of Comprehensive Services. (1993a). *Comprehensive services act for at risk youth and families: evaluation plan*. Richmond, VA: Office of Research and Evaluation, Department of Mental Health, Mental Retardation and Substance Abuse Services.

Office of Comprehensive Services. (1993b). *Comprehensive services for at-risk youth and families demonstration projects: interim evaluation report*. Richmond, VA: Office of Research and Evaluation, Department of Mental Health, Mental Retardation and Substance Abuse Services.

Rowe, K. (1991a). *Research notes: evaluation of the local interagency service projects initiative; part I*. Richmond, VA: Office of Research and Evaluation, Department of Mental Health, Mental Retardation and Substance Abuse Services.

Rowe, K. (1991b). *Research notes: evaluation of the local interagency service projects initiative; part II*. Richmond, VA: Office of Research and Evaluation, Department of Mental Health, Mental Retardation and Substance Abuse Services.

Stroul, B., & Friedman, R. (1986). *A system of care for children and youth with severe emotional disturbances*. Washington, DC: Georgetown University Child Development Center, National Technical Assistance Center for Children's Mental Health.

CHAPTER 8

Profiles of Local Systems of Care

Beth A. Stroul

This chapter presents the results of a descriptive study of local systems of care that was initiated in 1990 by the National Technical Assistance Center for Children's Mental Health at Georgetown University and funded by the federal Child and Adolescent Service System Program (CASSP) (Stroul, Lourie, Goldman, & Katz-Leavy, 1992). The project involved identifying and studying communities that have made substantial progress toward developing comprehensive, coordinated, community-based systems of care for children and adolescents with serious emotional disturbances and their families.

Until recently, there were few, if any, examples of local systems of care that combined an array of community-based services with other essential elements, including interagency collaboration and case management. Today, there is what might be described as an explosion of activity related to system of care development. Many communities now have evolving systems of care that can be studied and described. Descriptions of the system-building approaches and experiences of these communities are designed to assist other communities that are attempting to develop such systems.

Potential sites for inclusion in this study were identified through a process of consultation with key informants, including individuals at national and state levels who had extensive knowledge of developments in the children's mental health field and in the development of local systems of care in particular. Through these initial discussions, approximately 20 communities were identified. These localities were characterized as having made significant progress toward the development of community-based systems of care consistent with the philosophy and principles that have been promoted by CASSP (Stroul & Friedman, 1986). Accordingly, an attempt was made to locate local systems that are family focused, emphasize treatment in the least restrictive environment, involve multiple agencies, individualize services, and so forth. Similarly, an attempt was made to locate systems that have moved beyond the more traditional outpatient, inpatient, and residential treatment services and have begun to develop a

more complete and balanced array of nonresidential and residential services, including components such as home-based services, day treatment,
crisis services, therapeutic foster care, respite care, and case management.

The second phase of the selection process involved extensive telephone
interviews with a representative from each site to obtain detailed information about the array of services available in the community, the nature
and functioning of the system-level coordination mechanisms, and the nature and functioning of the client-level coordination or case management
mechanisms. In addition, information was collected about any special system activities related to such issues as financing the system, evaluating the
system, involving families in planning and delivering services, and enhancing the cultural competence of the system of care.

Selection of a smaller sample of sites for more in-depth study was
accomplished with the assistance of an advisory committee and was based
on the following set of criteria:

- Must have a range of services in place.
- Must have interagency coordination mechanisms in place.
- Must have client-level coordination mechanisms in place (e.g., case man-
  agement).
- Must be a sufficiently well-developed local system to be able to serve as
  a useful example to the field and to receive national attention.
- Should have some noteworthy activities in one or more areas, including
  family involvement, cultural competence, financing, and evaluation.

A group of five communities was selected for site visits by the project
team: Norfolk, Virginia; Northumberland County, Pennsylvania; Richland
County, Ohio; Stark County, Ohio; and Ventura County, California. It
should be noted that the exercise of choosing systems of care to visit would
be far more arduous today than it was only a few years ago. Because of an
enormous increase in system development activities in communities across
the nation, there currently are many more noteworthy examples of local
systems of care that would meet the above criteria.

The site visits generally involved spending 3–4 days in each community engaged in a variety of activities designed to provide insight into the
functioning of the system of care. These activities included interviews with
a number of individuals and groups, such as key system managers, senior
management representatives of the major child-serving agencies (mental
health, child welfare, education, and juvenile justice), case managers,
youngsters, parents, and advocates. Additionally, the schedules included
visits to three or more service components in the system of care, where
activities were observed and discussions held with program managers,
staff, and, in some cases, clients.

An important aspect of the site visits was observing the functioning of interagency entities. Site visitors attended meetings of interagency groups focusing on system-level coordination as well as meetings of interagency teams organized for the purpose of creating individualized service plans for specific youngsters and their families. The site visits provided a wealth of information about each system of care—its developmental milestones, strengths, and obstacles yet to be overcome.

It should be emphasized that none of the communities selected for study has fully developed systems of care, and all are struggling to overcome financial and other obstacles to system development. Rather, they are communities that have succeeded in putting some basic building blocks into place and have demonstrated progress toward achieving system development goals. It should also be noted that the systems of care have continued to evolve in response to changing circumstances. Invariably, various details about the systems of care have changed since the site visits. Although details may change, examination of these communities yields valuable insights into the process of building systems of care.

This chapter examines the communities studied as a group, synthesizing information about their systems of care. Key aspects of these systems of care are described and analyzed, including the history of system development, target population, philosophy, service array, mechanisms for system-level coordination, mechanisms for client-level coordination, evaluation activities, financing strategies, approaches for involving families, and efforts to enhance cultural competence. The chapter concludes with an analysis of the major strengths across communities that appear to be critical variables in the system development process and the major challenges facing these systems of care as they continue to evolve.

HISTORY OF SYSTEM DEVELOPMENT

The development of each of the community systems has followed its own unique evolutionary path. Analysis of the history of system development in the communities revealed that certain critical events were instrumental in moving the process forward. Three types of events appear in the histories of most of the communities studied and played significant roles in furthering the development of their systems of care.

The first of these critical events is the creation of an interagency entity for cross-system planning and collaboration. Each of the communities identified this as a turning point in the development of its system of care. The Norfolk Youth Network, Northumberland County Children's Clinic, Richland County Interagency Cluster (which later became a Council of Governments), Stark County Interagency Cluster, and Ventura County Interagency Juvenile Justice Council are examples of the interagency entities identified by sites. Despite their different names and varying roles, these interagency entities have been pivotal in the system development process.

Another type of critical event common to most of the sites is the receipt of some type of funding that enabled the development of new services in the system of care. Ventura County received a demonstration grant from the California legislature to develop a comprehensive, community-based system of care; Norfolk also received a demonstration grant from the Commonwealth of Virginia to develop a range of services using an interagency pool of funds. Stark County received grants for the development of home-based services, day treatment, and case management. Similarly, Richland County received a grant that allowed for the development of key service components. Although system development in the communities proceeded prior to receiving the grants, these funding opportunities clearly had a positive impact on the development of their systems of care.

A third critical event reported by the communities is perhaps less obvious than the development of an interagency entity or the receipt of funding. Several communities reported that, at some point in the system development process, leaders made the decision to move beyond traditional approaches and to invest in an array of community-based services. These decisions were significant in that they set the precedent for continued system development as opportunities and funding became available.

In all of the communities, the state has influenced the system development process. States have spurred system development in a variety of ways, including emphasizing and requiring interagency collaboration in service delivery, passing legislation related to system of care development, providing funding for systems of care, and providing technical assistance to communities. For example, through an executive order and subsequently through legislation, Ohio required the formation of interagency clusters at the local level. Pennsylvania required each county to prepare plans for system development and provided grants to counties, coupled with technical assistance, to stimulate system building. Virginia funded a series of demonstrations related to system development, leading to the passage in 1992 of the landmark Comprehensive Services Act, which requires community-based systems of care, blended funding, and an interagency approach to planning and service delivery (see Chapter 7). In these and other examples, the state has played a leadership role in system development, including setting the tone and goals, creating demonstrations and funding opportunities, and legislating elements of systems of care statewide. For the study communities, the states were credited with establishing a climate conducive to the growth of systems of care. Some individuals involved in the local systems of care reported that, without the positive state influence, critical changes would not have occurred at the local level or would have taken substantially more time and effort.

TARGET POPULATION

The communities included in the study take somewhat different approaches to defining the target populations for their efforts. For instance, Richland County made a deliberate attempt to avoid establishing a restrictive population definition and defined its target population as "children with multiple needs and their families." This approach is said to reduce categorical thinking among agencies and to promote the concept of shared ownership of the population of children and families needing services. In Northumberland County, a similarly broad definition was adopted to reflect the philosophy of the system that each child and family can receive the amount and intensity of services that they require and that a child does not have to have a particular level of need in order to be eligible for services and related coordination.

The opposite approach has been taken by Ventura County, where defining the target population is one of the essential elements of the "Ventura Planning Model" and is considered critical to the success of the system (see Chapter 9). A clear and specific definition is thought to ensure public agency accountability, achieve multiagency support, focus limited public resources on those most in need, and enable program development to be tailored to the population to be served. Thus, the target population in Ventura County is specifically defined to include children with emotional or behavioral disorders who are court dependents, court wards, or special education students or are at risk of out-of-home placements.

Whether a broad or more explicit target population definition is used, in practice all of the communities appear to focus on similar priority groups. The communities emphasize serving youngsters who have multiple needs and are involved with multiple systems, youngsters who are in or at risk of out-of-home placements of various types, those with serious problems who require intensive services, and those for whom current or existing services have been inadequate or unsuccessful.

PHILOSOPHY

Respondents in each of the sites emphasized the importance of basing the system of care on a vision and philosophy that is shared among the leaders and participating agencies. Accordingly, each of the communities has articulated a system of care philosophy that guides the way in which services are provided to children and their families. Remarkable commonality across communities was found with respect to the central elements of their philosophies. Although additional elements are included in the philosophies of the various sites, three elements appear to be universal.

Home- and Community-Based Services

The communities expressed a strong philosophical commitment to providing services within the least restrictive setting, keeping youngsters with their families to the greatest possible extent, and keeping youngsters within their communities to the greatest possible extent. This commitment reflects widespread agreement that keeping youngsters in their homes and communities is preferable on philosophical as well as economic grounds based on the skyrocketing costs of out-of-home and out-of-community placements. The community-based service approach is thought to offer the greatest benefit to children, their families, and the community at the lowest possible cost to the public sector.

Interagency Collaboration

A second philosophical element common to the study communities is the belief that child-serving agencies cannot operate in isolation and that no single agency can be effective in serving youngsters with emotional disturbances. The communities espoused a belief in collective ownership of multineed children and families and emphasized the contention that child-serving agencies must share responsibility for developing, funding, providing, and overseeing service delivery. Consistent with this philosophy, the communities included in the study all have developed viable interagency partnerships at both policy and service delivery levels.

Family Focus

Another common philosophy is the belief that children cannot be served outside of the context of their families and that families represent the most important influence and resource for children. This conviction results in interventions that are oriented toward families, delivery of home- and community-based services, efforts to avert out-of-home placements and reunify families to the greatest possible extent, involvement of families in planning services for their children, and involvement of families in policy development and planning at the system level. Most of the communities emphasized their commitment to maximizing the potential of families to care for their children and to strengthening and supporting families as they cope with the demands of caring for children with emotional disturbances.

SERVICE ARRAY

The communities included in the study have developed many new services, moving well beyond the traditional outpatient, inpatient, and residential treatment that was typically available to children in the past. The communities have invested in a range of additional service components that often are used as alternatives to hospital and residential treatment. The services found most often in the study communities include the following:

- *Outpatient services*: All of the communities offer individual, group, and family therapy as well as psychiatric services. Respondents reported that their outpatient services are shifting from a more traditional concept to greater flexibility as to the location, intensity, scheduling, and approaches used in treatment. Services can be provided in the home or school as well as in an office setting, and they often involve consultation with parents and with staff from other agencies. Several of the communities are targeting the population of youngsters with more serious disturbances, and several are emphasizing a time-limited, problem-focused approach for their outpatient services. The reconceptualization of their outpatient service capacities is an area that most of the communities continue to struggle with as they attempt to shift traditional services to fit the new system of care concept.

- *Home-based services*: All of the communities offer short-term, crisis-oriented, home-based services that are directed primarily at averting the need for out-of-home placement. These services are characterized by small caseloads for staff, highly intensive support, and limited durations. Several of the communities also offer longer-term home-based services for children and families with multiple and complex problems or services aimed at assisting children who are returning from institutional placements to reunify with their families.
- *Day treatment*: Most of the communities offer several day treatment options designed for different age groups or client populations. For example, one day treatment program in Northumberland County is designed primarily for the juvenile justice population. The day treatment programs typically are collaborative efforts between mental health agencies and the schools and have both mental health and educational components. Extended day and summer programs are provided in several communities.
- *Crisis services*: A range of crisis services is provided by the communities, including 24-hour telephone crisis services and mobile outreach crisis services. Some communities offer crisis residential services, which are crisis beds in nonhospital settings that can be used for short-term crisis intervention and stabilization.
- *Respite services*: Most communities offer some type of respite care on both a planned and an emergency basis. Respite services are provided both in the child's home and in out-of-home settings, utilizing trained respite providers. In several communities, some respite providers' homes are certified as foster homes so that children can stay overnight when necessary. Respite services are invaluable in offering families a much-needed break from the physical and emotional demands of caregiving.
- *Therapeutic foster care*: In several communities, therapeutic foster care services are jointly administered by the mental health and child welfare agencies. The approaches used vary, but generally involve training treatment parents to be primary agents of treatment for the child and pro-

viding professional staff support to the treatment parents, child, and natural parents.

- *Substance abuse services*: All of the communities offer a range of substance abuse treatment services, including such components as detoxification services, intensive outpatient services, continuing care, and residential treatment options.
- *Case management*: The communities offer varying levels of case management services depending upon the needs of the child and family. Basic levels of service coordination are provided, as well as intensive case management services for those youngsters with the most serious or complex problems.

Services found less frequently but that were available in some of the communities include

- Individualized "wraparound" services using flexible funds
- School-based services that bring mental health professionals into the schools
- Early intervention programs that include youngsters at risk for emotional disorders
- Therapeutic nursery programs
- Therapeutic camps
- A central intake, assessment, and case management program
- Recreational after-school and summer programs
- A parent center that provides support and education
- A therapeutic program for victims of child sexual abuse
- A therapeutic program for youth sex offenders

In addition, the communities still have access to therapeutic group homes, residential treatment centers, and inpatient facilities. Some of these residential services are available within the community; in some cases it is necessary to use programs outside of the community to meet highly specialized needs. These residential services are still used by the communities when necessary and appropriate. However, respondents reported that these types of facilities have been used much less frequently following the addition of the array of community-based services.

Although this list of services may appear impressive, it is important to recognize that these communities are not resource rich and do not necessarily have unlimited funds. Rather, they are communities that have thought strategically about where to place their resources, and they have invested in services such as home-based services, day treatment, respite care, and the others. In most of the communities, these services have been added sequentially, often in a planned and strategic manner. They have been added either as funding opportunities presented themselves or as the agencies made decisions about which services were the priorities for development.

The service arrays in the study communities are not by any means complete. Each community identified a number of service gaps that it is working to address. Mentioned most frequently as being high-priority needs are services such as therapeutic foster care, crisis residential services, transition services for older adolescents, and specialized services for youth sex offenders. Additional capacity in nearly all of the existing service components was a need identified by all of the study communities.

MECHANISMS FOR SYSTEM-LEVEL COORDINATION

The systems of care in the study communities typically have evolved from a history of approaching problems through collaborative problem-solving strategies involving multiple agencies. The communities reported previous instances of organizing interagency task forces or committees to address such diverse problems as at-risk children, sexual abuse, early intervention, and economic recovery. Given this context, it is not surprising that the study communities have chosen to address the needs of troubled children and their families with interagency approaches and have implemented well-designed mechanisms for system-level coordination across the major child-serving agencies and systems.

In most of the communities, this coordination takes the form of one or more interagency entities that were formed specifically to plan and administer the comprehensive, community-based system of care for children and their families. The structure common to the study communities is an entity composed primarily of the executives of the major child-serving agencies. These entities assume responsibility for policies, joint planning, priority setting, service development, financing, resource allocation, resource development, system management, problem solving, and any other concerns of mutual interest to the participating agencies. These executive-level interagency entities represent, to a great extent, the locus of leadership for the system of care and the foundation for all other system development activities. It is at this level that decisions can be made and resources committed in response to systemic issues and problems. These entities also may become involved in reviewing cases when particularly challenging issues cannot be resolved at lower levels of the system of care. The Norfolk Interagency Consortium, Northumberland Human Services Management Team, Richland County Council of Governments, Stark County Interagency Cluster, and Ventura County Interagency Juvenile Justice Council are the executive-level interagency entities for their respective communities.

The interagency entities typically meet on a monthly basis. In several of the communities, the role of chairperson rotates among the membership to reflect the true interagency nature of the effort and to avoid the dominance of any one agency in the process. Some communities, such as Ventura County, specify that only the agency executives may attend and that no substitutes may serve on the council. The importance of the individual executives to the collaborative process was emphasized by many system participants. It was noted that the process is most effective when agency administrators are predisposed to collaboration and believe in the concept and philosophy of a community-based system of care. Furthermore, strong personal relationships among the agency executives are helpful in the resolution of the inevitable conflicts that arise.

In addition to a formalized structure to ensure interagency collaboration at the highest levels of system leadership, some communities have created one or more additional layers of interagency activity. These often take the form of a standing committee of midlevel agency managers who meet regularly for purposes of case review and problem solving. In several communities, these midmanagers are vested with the authority to commit the resources of their particular agency to meet the needs of an individual child and family. The ACCORD (A Creative Community Options Review Decision) in Stark County is an example of such a standing committee of midmanagers. The ACCORD, which is considered a subcommittee of the Interagency Cluster, reviews cases, solves problems, and monitors treatment in especially difficult situations. If consensus on a plan of care for a particular child and family cannot be reached at the ACCORD level, the case may be referred to the Interagency Cluster for resolution. The ACCORD, like other similar interagency entities, is in an excellent position to feed information about system needs, gaps, and problems to the executive-level group for appropriate systemic solutions.

Several of the communities have full- or part-time coordinators to organize the activities and work of the interagency entities. For example, a grant from the state enabled Richland County to hire a cluster coordinator who oversees and manages the system planning and coordination efforts. Prior to this grant, the coordinating role was fulfilled by a staff person from one of the participating agencies who also had full-time responsibilities within his own agency. Most communities reported that handling the logistics, agenda, follow-up assignments, and other work emanating from the system-level coordination efforts is at least a full-time job.

The communities consistently expressed the view that these interagency entities have begun to break down the barriers between the child-serving systems and have made steady progress toward more integrated systems of care. Despite such remarkable progress, a number of barriers to effective system-level coordination were noted:

- Difficulty in balancing the mission of the system of care with the missions of individual agencies

- Dependency on key individuals for the success of the collaborative system development process
- Differences in philosophy and approach among the various participating agencies
- Reluctant or uninvolved agencies

MECHANISMS FOR CLIENT-LEVEL COORDINATION

The primary mechanism used by the sites to ensure coordination and continuity of service delivery at the client level is case management. The range of functions performed is consistent with those commonly associated with case management, including assessment, developing a service plan, accessing or brokering services, coordinating services, monitoring services, and advocating for children and their families. In most of the communities, direct clinical services per se are not considered part of the case manager's role, but it is clear that case managers do provide high levels of support, crisis intervention, and educational services.

Most of the communities studied have some capacity to provide specialized case management services. Specialized case management involves the use of full-time case managers, often housed within the mental health agency, who have been hired and trained to work with youngsters with emotional disturbances and their families. These services often are reserved for youngsters with the most serious problems, those at risk for out-of-home placements, or those in both categories.

In Ventura County, case managers specialize even further through their organization into subteams (see Chapter 9). Subteams of case managers are designated to work exclusively with youngsters with emotional disorders who are in the juvenile justice, child welfare, and special education systems. These small teams develop specialized knowledge and expertise in navigating their respective systems and are therefore able to maximize interagency coordination regarding the interagency service plan for each child. This approach reportedly facilitates close working relationships with the staff of the respective agencies as well.

Caseloads for specialized case managers appear to range from approximately 15–25 cases per case manager, including both active and follow-up cases. Although this range appears commonplace, case managers in the various sites tended to agree that 10–12 cases would be a more optimal caseload size. Flexible funds are available to the case managers in several of the communities for use in meeting identified needs for a particular child and family. In Stark County, for example, flexible funds have been used for taxi fares, school supplies, scouting organization memberships, music and karate lessons, camp, after-school activities and classes, food, clothing, cleaning and household items, and repairs. The funds also have been used for utility bills and rent, with agreements from clients for repayment.

Several of the communities reported that their philosophy of case management revolves around the notion of "empowering" families. This philosophy is reflected in an approach that involves assisting families to select their own goals and priorities, providing families with options for services and supports, allowing families to make decisions and assume responsibility, providing families with information and skills, and teaching families how to advocate for themselves. In addition to this commitment to family empowerment, the case management services provided in the sites clearly reflect and support the systemic commitment to maximize the use of community-based alternatives and minimize the use of out-of-home and out-of-community placements. When children are in hospitals or other out-of-home settings, the case managers in most communities continue to work with the child and family as well as with the staff of the particular treatment setting.

The case managers in the sites work very closely with the various child-serving agencies on a formal and informal basis. Case managers do not have the authority to compel agencies to provide services in any of the communities studied. However, they appear to successfully use alternative methods to maximize the cooperation and participation of the agencies in the care of individual youngsters. Personal relationships reportedly play an important role in enabling case managers to involve and coordinate the services with staff from other involved agencies and systems.

A number of advantages to using this specialized case management approach were identified by respondents. Specialized case managers develop considerable expertise in working with children with emotional disturbances and their families, as well as in-depth knowledge of the services and resources available in the community. Furthermore, they become skilled at providing community support to this population and at advocating on their behalf.

Despite the many advantages of using specialized case managers, most of the sites lack the resources to provide these services to all youngsters who could benefit from the approach. Thus, in addition to specialized case management for some youngsters, most communities also use the "lead case management" approach. This approach involves assigning case management responsibilities to the most logical or most involved provider agency. Thus, a child welfare worker, mental health therapist, probation officer, or any other staff person fulfills the case management functions in addition to performing the other responsibilities involved in his or her agency role. In some communities, a parent may be assigned the lead case management role when appropriate and desirable.

Respondents in the study communities reported that lead case managers typically have in-depth knowledge of the youngster's primary area of need and of the resources available in that area. However, using the lead case management approach involves some challenges and complexities stemming from the following factors:

- Staff with varying backgrounds and skills may become lead case managers. They may be experienced and skilled in their own fields, but are not likely to have training specific to case management skills or activities.
- Lead case managers may not have adequate time for case management responsibilities because of conflicting demands from the other aspects of their jobs in their own agencies. These competing demands and responsibilities may frustrate their efforts to adequately fulfill case management functions.

Despite these potential problems, sites reported that lead case managers can be highly effective in coordinating services for children and families, particularly if the entire system of care is committed to a multiagency approach to service delivery. The study communities tend to use a combination of the specialized case management and lead case management approaches.

Another approach to client-level coordination involves the use of multiagency teams to assist in planning and overseeing services to individual youngsters and their families. These teams typically are organized by the case manager and are composed of the persons most involved and influential in the child's life, including the parents, the youngsters themselves as appropriate, and all professionals who are serving or will potentially serve the child. With the case manager playing a facilitative leadership role, the team meets and works together over time to develop and implement a comprehensive, individualized service plan for the youngster and family that addresses all of the child's life domains. At the instigation of the case manager, the team continues to meet as needed to monitor progress and to reconfigure the service plan and approaches based upon the child's changing needs. These types of service planning teams are increasingly being used as an integral part of the case management process.

Consistent with this trend, most study communities use service planning teams of some type to plan and coordinate services for youngsters, generally for those with the most complex and challenging problems. Stark County refers to this process as a "Creative Community Options" meeting. The meeting is chaired by the case manager and is designed to examine creatively what might work for a child and family and to develop a written service plan that details strategies to address treatment, living, educational, and recreational needs. The process used to structure the meeting involves reviewing the child's and family's history, strengths, and needs and proceeding to identify options for services and supports.

A similar process used in Richland County is referred to as a "network meeting." Also organized and chaired by the case manager, the network meeting results in a coordinated service plan with clearly defined roles and responsibilities for all involved agencies and professionals. Respondents in Stark and Richland counties, as well as other sites, noted that, as a result of their participation in interagency service planning meetings, line staff from agencies throughout the system of care become increasingly aligned with the system of care philosophy, particularly with respect to the need for interagency collaboration and a family focus in service delivery.

A variation on the use of these child-specific teams involves the use of one or more standing multiagency groups for the purpose of service planning and coordination for individual youngsters with intensive or complex needs. Northumberland County, for example, uses its Children's Clinic for this purpose. The Children's Clinic is comprised of representatives from each child-serving system who meet on a regular basis to plan, coordinate, and monitor services for youngsters and their families. When an individual child is discussed, the parents and workers involved with the child participate in the process; the result is a "family service plan" that presents the goals of intervention, services to be provided, and responsible staff. Consistent with their system of care philosophy, the family service plan includes a section called "methods used to involve parents" and a section that requires substantial documentation should an out-of-home placement be used. The need for, appropriateness of, and goals of such placements must be specified, along with documentation of efforts to prevent this placement and reunification plans, if appropriate.

Norfolk created Community Assessment Teams to formulate and coordinate case plans for individual youngsters. Ten such teams exist in the city, each comprised of supervisory-level workers from the various child-serving agencies. Parents and involved direct service workers join the team for discussion of specific youngsters. In Ventura County, the Interagency Case Management Council was created to enable interagency planning for especially difficult cases. The sites reported that these approaches encourage agencies and families to see themselves as part of a unified team with shared responsibility for the challenges of providing services and support to multineed youngsters.

For situations, service delivery challenges, or disputes that cannot be resolved at the level of these various service planning groups, the sites typically utilize higher-level interagency entities for case review and problem resolution. This case review and resolution function may be fulfilled by an interagency entity formed specifically for this purpose (such as the ACCORD in Stark County) or by the system-level coordinating body. In some cases, a state-level interagency group is the final recourse for problems that cannot be resolved locally.

It should be noted that concerns about maintaining confidentiality have not proven to be an impediment to coordinated treatment planning and service delivery in the communities studied. Most of the communities have developed a common release form that allows participating agencies to share information. Typically, the case manager or a staff person from one of the involved agencies takes the lead in approaching the parents to explain the interagency service planning and intervention process and requests that they sign the release. System participants reported that rarely, if ever, have parents refused permission for information sharing when they have been educated as to the necessity for doing so in order to effectively plan and coordinate services. Although the need to share information across agencies is clear, the communities are cognizant of the need to protect sensitive client information. In Richland County, for example, copies of case records that have been shared in preparation for service planning meetings or case review are placed in the center of the table to be shredded following the discussion.

EVALUATION ACTIVITIES

With a few exceptions, evaluation generally has not been a high priority for the systems of care included in the study. Communities reported that service development and direct service have taken precedence over devoting time and resources to evaluation activities. Thus, although the importance of evaluation information is recognized, most of the communities have not undertaken any formal evaluations of their systems of care.

Regardless of the lack of formalized or systematic evaluation efforts, the site visits revealed noteworthy agreement across sites regarding the indicators that should be used to assess the effectiveness of their systems of care. The sites reported that the following indicators are most relevant to an assessment of their systems:

- Reduction in out-of-home placements
- Reduction in out-of-community placements
- Reduction in the use of restrictive treatment environments

Some data relative to these indicators were provided by the sites. For example, Ventura County reported that 85% of its children at imminent risk of out-of-home placement remained at home. Stark County reported a 73% decline in the use of out-of-county psychiatric placements from 1985 to 1991. The state hospital census for Stark County declined by 79%, from an average of 7 beds in 1989 to an average of 1.5 in 1992. Ventura County reported a 58% reduction in the rate of state hospitalization from its baseline period to 1992, as well as a 44% reduction in average inpatient days per year. Northumberland County reported a 100% decline in hospital and residential treatment center placements, from 12 in 1985 down to none in 1990 and 1991.

In Ventura County, evaluation has been given somewhat higher priority (see Chapter 9). Evaluation activities have emphasized aggregated systemic changes and have focused specifically on youth remaining in their homes and communities, recidivism of juvenile offenders, effects on school attendance and performance, and costs to the public sector. Positive findings were reported in each of these areas for youngsters participating in the system of care. For example, Ventura County documented not only significant cost avoidance within the mental health system, but savings accrued by reducing youngsters' involvement in the child welfare, juvenile justice, and special education systems as well, primarily by reducing placement rates and lengths of stay.

In addition, Ventura County, along with the three replication sites in California, participated in an evaluation of their systems of care conducted by the University of California at San Francisco. One of the most noteworthy findings of this evaluation was that the group home (i.e., residential treatment center) placement rate in Ventura and the three replication counties was significantly lower than the group home placement rate for the state of California as a whole. Evaluators calculated that these counties saved over $35 million in costs for residential care from 1989 to 1992 and that the state could have saved a total of approximately $50 million in residential costs if it had followed the trend of these counties instead of the actual trend in the state for the same time period.

Norfolk also participated in an evaluation of Virginia's system of care demonstration sites. With respect to Norfolk, the evaluation found that the community's capacity for providing community-based services increased and collaboration among child-serving agencies increased. Although psychiatric admissions have remained at about the same level from 1990 to 1993, the cost of these admissions has dropped by more than 50%, indicating shorter hospital stays. Child welfare placements decreased over the same 4-year period.

FINANCING STRATEGIES

The communities included in the study typically weave together the funding needed for their systems of care from a variety of sources. The primary funding streams they rely on include state block grants, state categorical grants, local tax revenues, and reimbursements from Medicaid and other third-party sources. The communities agreed that, overall, funding levels are insufficient to support services at adequate levels to meet the need. Furthermore, the categorical nature of the various funding streams often inhibits the flexibility and creativity of the communities in their attempt to build effective service systems.

Despite serious concerns and challenges regarding the financing of systems of care, several of the communities have developed creative strategies to maximize their use of available resources and to focus resources to meet system priorities. The financing strategies used by study communities include the following:

- *Joint funding of service components*: Several communities have blended funds to support the development and operation of specific components of their systems of care. Home-based services, day treatment, therapeutic foster care, and case management are examples of services funded by two or more agencies in some sites.
- *Interagency funding of service plans for individual youngsters*: In several communities, provisions have been made for multiple agencies to participate in financing the service plan designed for a specific youngster and family. In Richland County, for example, agreement is reached among the participating agencies regarding their relative contributions to support a service plan designed for a child and family. In Northumberland County, treatment plans are jointly funded by the various agencies, with each picking up the costs of care falling within its jurisdiction. Another approach has been adopted in Stark County, involving the creation of an interagency funding pool (with a formula to govern contributions from participating agencies) that is used to fund plans of care and to cover the administrative costs of the Interagency Cluster.
- *Maximizing third-party resources*: Nearly all of the communities studied were exploring strategies for increasing third-party reimbursements for services included in their systems of care. The primary focus of these efforts has been on Medicaid, with communities working diligently to increase the range of services and providers eligible for Medicaid reimbursement. Sites have reported considerable success in this endeavor.

At the time of the site visits, nearly all communities were engaged in some type of planning process related to the long-term fiscal viability of their systems of care. In Richland County, for example, the Council of Governments was planning a retreat to address long-term financing and was establishing a finance committee to explore all potential funding options for the system of care. Similarly, Ventura County developed a consortium of public agencies to develop interagency fiscal strategies.

In addition to fiscal planning at the local level, efforts to address system financing were being undertaken by several state governments. In 1992, California adopted a state policy of "realignment" that transferred resources for health, social services, mental health, and substance abuse from the state general fund to a local trust fund. This strategy is expected to provide counties with a greater degree of financial control and stability. In Virginia, an innovative new funding mechanism was adopted with the passage of the Comprehensive Services Act in 1992 (see Chapter 7). This legislation combines eight major funding streams for services to children and adolescents and gives communities the flexibility to determine how resources are spent. The funding pool is to be administered by local interagency teams. Additionally, a new state trust fund was established to support localities in expanding their service arrays.

APPROACHES FOR INVOLVING FAMILIES

In all of the communities, the notion of working with children in the context of their families is emphasized as a central element of their philosophies. Respondents in all sites consistently expressed strong convictions that children cannot be isolated from their families, that services should focus on the entire family, that families should be involved in all phases of the planning and delivery of services, and that the system of care should be committed to family preservation and reunification. Respondents further reported that their systems of care are based on this philosophy and on the belief that families are the most important resource for children and adolescents and should be supported and empowered in every way possible.

Overall, the communities involved in the study have been able to translate this philosophy into practice at the service delivery level. They do, in fact, involve families in the planning and delivery of services for their own youngsters. Evidence of family involvement is seen in many of the service components within the systems of care. For example, outpatient services in Northumberland County are provided from a family perspective, parent centers in several of the communities provide support and enhance parenting skills, treatment parents in therapeutic foster care programs work with natural parents to facilitate reunification, and day treatment programs have family components that offer services and supports to the parents and siblings of participating youngsters.

In addition to having service components that are family focused, all of the communities studied involve parents in the process of developing individualized service plans, whether this involves working in partnership with case managers, participating fully on the interagency service planning teams organized for this purpose, or both. Families are considered essential participants in the various types of service planning meetings. Beyond the fact that parents have a basic right to be involved in planning and decision making for their children, communities noted a range of other reasons underlying the inclusion of parents in this process. For example, respondents indicated that, the greater the involvement of the family in service planning, the greater the family's investment and commitment to the intervention process. Furthermore, respondents stated that, if families are expected to take part in solving problems, then solutions cannot be imposed on them by agencies and professionals. Rather, families and professionals must work together collaboratively to design solutions.

Although family participation is accepted as the goal across sites, implementing this is not without problems. Unless precautions are taken, parents may find attending service planning meetings with numerous professionals to be an intimidating experience. Steps are taken in some communities to help parents feel more at ease. Parent volunteers who have previously been through the process are used to brief the family in advance, case managers orient parents before the meetings, and written materials or videotapes are used for orientation and training purposes. Even those parents who were initially wary and apprehensive about this process reported leaving these meetings feeling that, for the first time, their needs were addressed and their input was valued.

Communities reported that staff from the various participating agencies may feel uncomfortable with parents present and may resist. Furthermore, some staff persons may have difficulty fully accepting the role of parents, may appear patronizing or condescending, and may dictate to the family what the service plan should be rather than working together to create a service plan. The experience of the communities studied is that this initial resistance is reduced once the individual staff persons have participated in a few service planning meetings involving parents. Staff appear to quickly recognize the value of parent participation and the enhanced commitment and results that ensue.

Although the communities successfully involve parents on the service delivery level, they have made less progress in involving parents at the system level. Few of the study communities afford parents a meaningful role in planning, policy making, or evaluating their systems of care. Stark County provides an example of a community that has attempted to involve parents at the system level—parents serve on boards and planning committees, they have participated in a strategic planning process for the system of care, and they have input in the design and development of any new programs. Additionally, support is provided for parents to attend statewide and national meetings. Although most communities recognize the need to involve families at the system level, this remains an area of relative weakness across sites.

Another gap in most communities is the lack of parent support and advocacy groups. Although this is widely recognized as a need, the study communities are struggling to find ways to support the development of support and advocacy groups for parents of youngsters with emotional disorders.

EFFORTS TO ENHANCE CULTURAL COMPETENCE

All communities acknowledged the importance of creating a culturally competent system of care. However, most conceded that this is an area in which comparatively little progress has occurred. Some strategies have been used by the study communities to enhance cultural competence. These have focused primarily on staff recruitment, staff training, and outreach to minority communities; the success of these strategies has been variable. Examples of the activities used in the communities to improve the cultural competence of their systems of care include

- Attempting to recruit and hire minority staff
- Providing staff training related to cultural competence
- Holding retreats devoted to the issue of cultural competence
- Locating programs or satellite offices in areas that are accessible to minority communities
- Accommodating the needs of the client population by staying open in the evenings, bringing medical personnel to the program to perform physicals, and the like
- Developing programs with a cultural emphasis (e.g., a mentor program in Norfolk that selects and assigns mentors in order to build on the cultural and ethnic strengths in the child's background)
- Ensuring outreach to minority communities by going to minority agencies, churches, and community organizations to educate people about available services
- Involving key minority community leaders and groups in the system of care in an advisory capacity
- Establishing a task force comprised of staff interested in issues of cultural awareness and cultural competence
- Hiring a consultant to assist in the planning process to meet the needs of a particular cultural group (e.g., Native Americans)

One community that has made significant strides in improving cultural competence is Ventura County (see Chapter 9). The Ventura County Mental Health Department recognized that, to better serve the growing minority population in the area, the system would have to undergo major institutional changes. The department hired a minority services coordinator to work with the administration and staff to develop and implement a master plan to improve the cultural competence of Ventura County's system of care. The Cultural Competence Master Plan, developed in 1991, addresses four key areas and includes specific objectives, activities, and timelines. The four areas, and examples of the activities included in each, are as follows:

- *Policy and administration*: Incorporate cultural competence in the agency's mission, policies, and procedures; establish a Minority Advisory Planning Subcommittee of the Mental Health Advisory Board.
- *Human resource development*: Provide orientation and training in cultural competence for new and current staff; implement recruitment incentives such as differential pay for staff with bilingual skills; establish liaison

with schools of social work for staff recruitment purposes; implement a minority staff retention program.
- *Services for clients and families*: Establish a priority on outreach and informing the public about available services and how to access them.
- *Research and evaluation*: Develop a database with information on ethnicity; examine differential outcomes across ethnic groups.

MAJOR STRENGTHS

Throughout the study, attempts were made to ascertain why these particular communities have succeeded at system of care development while other communities struggle to achieve similar progress. A number of strengths were identified that may begin to explain the advances in the study communities. The following strengths are common to most or all of the sites and appear to be critical variables in the system development process.

Leadership

The importance of strong and committed leadership for system of care development is evident in all of the study communities. One community emphasized the importance of a single individual, a strong and powerful leader, who was instrumental in the development of the system. Most of the communities studied, however, reported that a core group of committed leaders were instrumental in the early stages of system building and continue to be essential in maintaining the focus and momentum of the system development process.

In most of the communities, the system leaders are agency executives who are committed to the development of a system of care. The involvement and commitment of the executives of the child-serving agencies seem to be essential in providing the impetus to develop and sustain the system of care. In most of the communities, agency executives participate closely and directly in planning and overseeing the system.

Respondents in several communities noted that stability of some of the key agency executives in the system has been an asset. A number of individuals have filled various positions in the community over the years, have served together on a host of task forces and committees, have developed personal relationships, and have worked together to make the system more responsive to the needs of children and families. This has enhanced their ability to work together as well as their ability to assume leadership roles. Regardless of the issue of stability, all of the communities studied have a core group of committed leaders who have pushed the system-building agenda.

Shared Responsibility and Vision

A clear acceptance of mutual responsibility for the target population of children and youth across agencies is a common feature of the communities studied. Participants at all levels of the systems of care expressed a sense of collective ownership of troubled children and a belief that no one agency can meet their needs in isolation.

In addition to this pervasive sense of shared responsibility, the vision of a community-based system of care appears to be shared among the various participating agencies in the study communities. Agency executives, as well as many managers and providers throughout the systems, appear to widely accept the system of care concept and philosophy and to agree on system development goals. This common vision across agencies provides a shared understanding of what service delivery for children and families should be and a clear sense of purpose for system-building activities. Thus, a sense of shared responsibility and vision characterizes the study communities and appears to have moved the system development process forward.

Meaningful Interagency Structure and Processes

All of the communities studied have interagency structures and processes that are meaningful and have tangible results. They do not merely have pro forma interagency groups that meet regularly but have a negligible impact. Rather, at various levels of the systems of care, the communities have created vital collaborative structures—structures that have important roles and contributions, focus on critical issues, and yield results. The interagency structures in these communities have resulted in new programs, pooled funds, jointly administered services, interagency agreements, multiagency contracts, communitywide plans for system development, individualized service plans for children with complex needs, and other outcomes. The interagency structures and processes in the study communities have made real strides in overcoming turf barriers and in creating an attitude of shared ownership of the children in the community and of the system of care that serves them.

Proactive Attitude

The communities appear to share a proactive approach to system development. They do not wait for state or federal governments to tell them what to do, nor do they wait for extra funding or special grants, although they take advantage of any opportunities that arise. Moreover, they have not been stymied by disappointments such as unsuccessful grant applications, failed service delivery experiments, political obstacles, or even seemingly overwhelming economic or social problems. When problems arise in these communities, they tend to be seen as challenges that require creative and collaborative solutions and not as intractable barriers to progress. System participants focus more on what they *can* do rather than on what is not possible. This proactive attitude and emphasis on what can be accomplished appears to propel these communities into action.

Cooperative Approach to Problem Solving

In the communities studied, there seems to be a willingness among agencies to confront and resolve problems openly and in good faith. Turf issues, disagreements, and conflicts occur in these communities as they inevitably do in most other communities. However, when problems and disagreements arise, the players in the study communities do not leave the table. Rather, they appear willing to negotiate and to work on problems until they are resolved, even if this involves confrontation. In several communities, retreats have been used effectively to create a structure for problem solving, and outside facilitators have proven valuable to help the various participants reach consensus at critical junctures in the system development process.

Service Implementation

All of the communities studied have been able to expand the range of services available to children and families. This creation and expansion of the array of services in the system of care has been accomplished in a gradual and strategic manner by many of the communities. It has been accomplished by leveraging resources, reallocating resources, obtaining new resources, or blending resources across agencies. Whatever the timetable or mechanism, the communities moved beyond planning to the implementation of services. This ability to translate plans into actual service capacity is perhaps the most important factor in the system-building process. Respondents emphasized that the accomplishment of something concrete, such as the addition of services, in turn creates momentum and motivation to continue the system development process and to create additional service components.

MAJOR CHALLENGES

Although the communities studied clearly have many noteworthy strengths that have expedited system development, they face many problems and challenges as well. The challenges confronting these communities are most likely identical to those facing most communities that are attempting to develop systems of care.

Funding

Most communities reported that financing presents the most significant barrier to system development. Financing problems emanate from two significant issues. First, the funding available to date has been insufficient to create the needed service capacities. The communities have used a patchwork of funding sources to begin the system development process. Although they have achieved a great deal of progress, the lack of sufficient resources has prevented the communities from implementing all of the needed service components. Creative approaches have been used by some of the communities to blend funds from the participating agencies in order to create service capacities and fund individualized service plans. Nevertheless, the lack of funds has slowed progress and prevented full implementation of system of care plans. Some of the communities reported that serious deficits in their states have resulted in local budget cutbacks that further threaten their service systems. Respondents in all of the communities expressed concern about the long-term financial viability of their systems of care because of the lack of a coherent, stable, reliable funding base.

A second major financing problem stems from the constraints presented by inflexible, categorical funding streams. The communities indicated that the allocation of most of their resources is governed by a host of mandates, restrictive regulations, and reimbursement rules. These prevent them from investing resources in the service priorities established locally and hinder the provision of nontraditional services and supports that may be included in individualized service plans. The communities agreed that more substantial pools of flexible funds are needed in order to allow greater creativity in system development and in implementing responsive service plans. Additional funding opportunities, creative funding strategies, and greater flexibility will all be needed in order to address these financing challenges.

Human Resource Needs

The need for qualified personnel to provide services within systems of care is another critical challenge. Most of the communities reported difficulty in recruiting specialists in children's mental health, particularly those who are trained in and prepared to work with nontraditional approaches such as home-based services, case management, or therapeutic foster care. These difficulties stem both from the limited pool of mental health professionals who specialize in children's services and from the inadequate preservice training currently provided by most colleges and universities. Potential staff typically are not educated about the system of care concept and philosophy, nor are they exposed to the newer service technologies. Some states and communities are beginning to work in partnership with universities to develop curricula, create internship opportunities in systems of care, establish recruitment programs and incentives to attract graduates, and otherwise address this need. Still, the lack of a sufficient pool of qualified and trained staff for systems of care remains a profound problem that has obvious implications for continued system development as well as for the quality of the services provided.

Educating Line Staff

The system of care philosophy may be clearly articulated and well accepted at higher levels of the service system, but does not always filter down to line workers. The communities reported that executives and managers in the participating agencies generally are well versed in the system philosophy and in the new service approaches. However, it is a continual challenge to ensure that line staff in all child-serving agencies are equally well educated and committed to the system's mission, goals, and service approaches. Respondents emphasized that it is unrealistic to assume that these ideas will permeate the system of care. Rather, concerted efforts must be devoted to selling the new ideas at all levels of the system until they become ingrained.

The process of educating line staff throughout the system is complicated by the reality of staff turnover. Because line staff positions often are subject to high turnover rates, educational efforts must be continuous and managers must regularly model and reinforce the system of care philosophy and approaches. Further complications may stem from the resistance of some staff to system reform. For example, several communities noted difficulties in shifting the emphasis of their outpatient services to more flexible and intensive treatment approaches. Educational strategies coupled with firsthand experience with the new philosophies and service technologies are necessary to bring staff in line with the system of care.

Service Gaps

Filling service gaps represents another challenge for systems of care. One aspect of this challenge is developing missing service components. None of the communities studied considers its service array to be complete. All reported that there are a number of missing components; those mentioned most frequently as priority needs include therapeutic foster care, crisis residential services, day treatment for all age groups, respite services, transition services for older adolescents, and services for youth sex offenders.

A second aspect of this challenge relates to insufficient capacity in many of the existing services in the systems of care. Most of the communities reported that, even when services are in place, they rarely have sufficient capacity to adequately meet the demand. Waiting lists are common for some services, and few programs have the resources to serve all youngsters who are eligible and in need. This situation proves troubling and frustrating for the communities, and the threat of additional cuts in funding in some areas leaves little hope for major expansion of service capacities in the foreseeable future.

Family Support and Advocacy Groups

Despite the remarkable progress in the communities studied, many were without parent support and advocacy groups. This gap was evident even though many of these systems of care are based on the premise of family involvement and family empowerment. Despite the high priority given to parent involvement, parent networks have not as yet developed. The communities uniformly recognize and understand the need for parent support and advocacy groups but are struggling to find ways to stimulate their development. An important challenge for these systems of care is to devise effective strategies to stimulate and facilitate the development of parent groups that may fulfill both support and advocacy functions.

A related challenge is to find more effective ways of involving families in decision making at the system level. Although the communities generally have succeeded in including parents as partners in planning and delivering services for their own youngsters, they have been less successful in fully involving families in planning and policy making for the entire system of care. Identifying and including parents in system-level decision making, as well as stimulating the development of parent groups, are essential tasks facing the communities studied.

Cultural Competence

With some noteworthy exceptions, the communities studied have not demonstrated substantial achievements in the area of cultural competence. Although one community developed a cultural competence plan and is in the process of implementing its objectives and action steps, the others typically have made only modest attempts to enhance the cultural competence of their systems of care. Staff training and staff recruitment are the two approaches mentioned most frequently for improving cultural competence. However, the need for more concerted efforts to recruit minority staff, to provide training on cultural issues, and to adapt policies and services to account for diverse client populations is evident across the study communities. The need to improve cultural competence is widely acknowledged, and much remains to be done to meet the needs of minority children and their families in these systems of care.

Involvement of All Agencies

In creating coordinated systems of care, most of the communities have encountered one or more agencies that are reluctant to fully participate in interagency entities and activities. These less committed agencies can be a source of frustration for the other agencies that are dedicated to an interagency approach to the development and operation of a system of care. Respondents indicated that these "reluctant" agencies have not been allowed to impede progress; system building efforts have moved ahead without their participation when necessary. Several noted that an agency that declines a meaningful role in system development and coordination efforts may ultimately see the system developed without its involvement and expertise. Although not allowing hesitant agencies to slow the collaborative process, respondents emphasized the need for continual attempts to encourage their participation. Pilot programs, opportunities for cost sharing, reaching out to key individuals, and other strategies were mentioned as potential approaches and incentives for engaging agencies that are less enthusiastic system participants. In some instances, lagging agencies have become more active partners in the system of care over time when the successes of the system and the benefits of participation have become apparent.

CONCLUSION

As noted, none of the communities selected for this study has a fully developed system of care. These communities have made noteworthy progress in many areas. Yet, like most communities, they continue to struggle with many aspects of system development, including obtaining adequate funding, recruiting qualified staff, filling service gaps, involving families, and achieving cultural competence. An important strength in these communities, however, is the ability to recognize the deficits in their systems of care and to continue the system-building process in order to overcome them. In fact, since the time of the site visits, the communities have begun to address many of the identified challenges and have continued to make progress.

It is important to recognize that the development of a system of care is an evolutionary process—one that does not occur overnight. Respondents depicted a process that entails an enormous investment of time and energy, that proceeds through various stages of development, and that continually learns from and builds on its successes and failures. Hard work, constant negotiation, patience, and nurturance were noted as necessary ingredients for a successful system-building initiative. Furthermore, evolving systems of care must be able to constructively respond to changes in the community, the target population, the service system, funding streams, and state and federal requirements that inevitably occur over time.

There is much to be learned from these communities. They have ably demonstrated that the vision of a comprehensive, coordinated, community-based system of care is within reach. They have demonstrated strategies for developing a broad range of services coupled with system-level and client-level coordination mechanisms. They have demonstrated some of the key elements that appear to underlie successful system-building efforts as well as the principal challenges that lie ahead. Many other communities have learned from them, and there are now countless other examples of communities that are in the process of developing similar systems of care.

These systems of care are dynamic; they continue to change, develop, and adapt to changing environments. As a result, some of the specifics may change—the precise array of services, the financing approaches used, or the title of the interagency structure. Despite these changes, these communities remain steadfast in their commitment to the basic concept and philosophy of a community-based system of care and in their determination to continue building their systems.

REFERENCES

Stroul, B., & Friedman, R. (1986). *A system of care for children and youth with severe emotional disturbances* (rev. ed.). Washington, DC: Georgetown University, Child Development Center, National Technical Assistance Center for Children's Mental Health.

Stroul, B., Lourie, I., Goldman, S., & Katz-Leavy, J. (1992). *Profiles of local systems of care for children and adolescents with severe emotional disturbances.* Washington, DC: Georgetown University, Child Development Center, National Technical Assistance Center for Children's Mental Health.

CHAPTER 9

A Local Approach to System Development

Ventura County, California

Mario Hernandez and Sybil K. Goldman

The Ventura County Mental Health Department has developed and evaluated an innovative, comprehensive, locally planned and implemented children's mental health system. The system was built on what has become known as the "Ventura Planning Model," a framework that has been used to guide system development. The Ventura Planning Model has been described as offering a new way of doing business for public mental health agencies, other child-serving public agencies, and communities interested in helping their highest risk and most vulnerable children live independent and productive lives (Feltman, 1987). The application of this model in Ventura County has resulted in the creation of an interagency system of care along with the ability for continual modification and improvement.

HISTORICAL BACKGROUND

The development of the Ventura County system of care for children and adolescents has been an interesting process and demonstrates the importance of leadership, coalition building, accountability, and support at the state level. As is so often the case, individuals with vision and leadership abilities have been the catalysts for producing system change. In Ventura County, the combined forces of a member of the county's Board of Supervisors, a local mental health children's coordinator, a state assemblywoman, and a state children's mental health administrator provided the vision and brought together the necessary elements and support to create system reform.

The development of Ventura County's system occurred in three phases. The first phase, from 1980 to 1984, consisted of early successful efforts to reduce the county's population of children in the state hospital. This led to legislation establishing Ventura County as a demonstration site to reduce

177

placement of children into residential care in California. The second phase occurred from 1984 to 1987 and consisted of the actual implementation of the demonstration project and the development of an outcome-based planning approach for delivering human services. The third phase began in 1987 with legislation leading to replication of the planning approach in other California counties and continues to the present.

Phase 1

In the late 1970s and early 1980s, there were few services for children within the Ventura County Mental Health Department. Most of these services were limited to an hour a week of psychotherapy and rarely touched the lives of the county's most distressed children and families. Instead, community mental health primarily served whoever arrived at the door first. County agencies worked separately and rarely thought of serving children collaboratively. Various providers and community leaders began to realize that these traditional approaches were no longer viable and that a reconceptualization of services was needed if the county's most troubled children were to be adequately served within the community.

During the early 1980s, the California Department of Mental Health allowed counties to "buy out" state hospital beds. Counties at that time could propose alternatives to state hospitalization and receive dollars that would otherwise purchase hospital beds. At that time, Ventura County had an average of 12 hospitalized children and adolescents. A share of the cost for five of these beds was transferred to the county, and a community-based, 5-day-per-week residential program was created. In addition, three case management positions were created to facilitate the transfer of children from the hospital and to divert new children from entering the hospital. At the time, this approach was not considered appropriate by those professionals who believed that many of these children were too dangerous for community-based care.

During the first 5 years of operation, the number of children in the state hospital was reduced from an average daily census of 14 to 3. Children were staying in the alternative program for a year living with their families on weekends and experiencing successful reintroductions into their homes and local schools. Most of these children entered either local special education programs or alternative community-based schools.

Much of the success of this alternative program was due to its philosophy of focusing on the strengths of children and their families. This philosophy influenced the efforts of case managers and family therapists who worked with families during evenings and weekends or at other times depending on a family's particular needs. These professionals linked families to services, advocated for needed services, monitored services, provided emergency response during times of family crisis, and provided direct treatment as needed.

Special education, juvenile justice, child welfare, and mental health agencies as well as the private sector all collaborated in creating community-based services for individual children rather than having them enter the state hospital. Memoranda of understanding were written, mechanisms for interagency planning were created, and information about children began to be shared across the various agencies. This early collaborative work eventually led to the building of cooperative agency relationships that formed the foundation for what would later become Ventura County's interagency system of care.

The county learned several lessons from implementing the state hospital buyout plan. First, it discovered that, through aggressive case management, the community could identify and create services for children previously thought to require restrictive care. Second, less restrictive services such as community residential care not only were beneficial to children and families but also resulted in less expense to the state and county. Third, through the combined effort of multiple agencies, obstacles to serving children in the community were overcome. Fourth, it was learned that the benefits of saving money while serving children close to home were powerful tools in convincing policy makers that a new direction in allocating service dollars was needed.

Phase 2

The second phase in the development of Ventura County's system of care commenced in 1984 with the passage of the Mental Health Services for Children bill (AB 3920), which identified Ventura County as a demonstration county to develop and test the cost–benefit of a comprehensive interagency system of care. AB 3920 supplemented an existing $2 million spent annually within Ventura County for children's mental health services with an additional $1.5 million of state funding. This legislation came about through an unorthodox alliance between those interested in cost containment and advocates for improving the quality of children's services. AB 3920 directed Ventura County to develop a community-based continuum of care that could provide alternatives to the residential placement of children. During this phase, California's public agencies had removed from their families more than 11,000 children and adolescents who were adjudicated either delinquent or dependent and placed them into group homes and residential care (Jordan & Hernandez, 1990.) The annual residential costs for these children were approaching $500 million. Since 1980, those costs had risen annually at a rate of 15%–20%. As placements in residential treatment were growing in California, community-based mental health services for these children were either absent, limited in scope, or being eliminated through funding cuts. The assumption underlying AB 3920 was that mental health care, if provided in a goal-directed, interagency manner, could reduce the residential costs to other public sector agencies and thereby justify the expense of increasing community-based mental health services (Jordan & Hernandez, 1990).

The surge in residential care costs, in combination with Ventura County's prior successful experience in reducing state hospitalization of children, led to the development of an array of community-based interagency services for all children at risk of out-of-home placement. As a result of AB 3920, the county had the opportunity to demonstrate that not only children in state hospitals but also children in residential care could be served in the community through innovative system reform.

When AB 3920 implementation began, mental health managers were focused primarily on mental health program development. They believed that the best solution to inadequate community-based care was in the creation of additional mental health programs such as day treatment or outpatient services. Collaboration across agencies was seen as necessary but secondary to increased mental health treatment. After the first year, however, it became apparent that collaboration among child-serving agencies was fundamentally changing both the delivery and effectiveness of mental health programs and the operation of other agencies. The "magic bullet" generating results was actually the influence and synergism of collaboration and the focus on outcomes.

These insights led to a shift in agency planning from developing specific programs to a new structured strategic planning framework that emphasized both interagency partnerships and outcomes and became known as the Ventura Planning Model (Essex, Jordan, & Feltman, 1989). This new approach to planning system reform replaced the earlier focus on more and larger independent mental health programs. Instead, it required collaborative planning, joint administration and gatekeeping, records and information integration, and a new shared accountability for measurable goals. This planning approach required agencies to tailor their service development around the needs of children rather than having children fit into existing services.

The planning model consisted of five essential characteristics or elements:

1. Identifiable target populations
2. Measurable goals
3. Coalitions or interagency partnerships
4. An array of services tailored to the needs of the target populations
5. Evaluation and continuous monitoring of client outcomes

These five characteristics provided a step-by-step planning process and defined the essential components of a system of care (Essex et al., 1989).

Phase 3

As a result of Ventura County's successful experience implementing AB 3920, the Mental Health Services for Children bill (AB 377) was passed in 1987. This legislation required that Ventura County continue to achieve measurable client and cost outcome goals during the third year of system implementation. These legislated outcomes were incorporated into a performance contract between the state and the county. Given Ventura County's experience at achieving positive results, AB 377 also declared legislative intent to expand and replicate the planning model, as developed in Ventura County, statewide to all 58 counties.

During 1987, Ventura County exceeded all of the client outcome goals set in AB 377. According to Jordan and Hernandez (1990), out-of-county court-ordered placements dropped by 47%, the rate of state hospitalization dropped by 68%, and out-of-county nonpublic school placements declined 21%. Significant gains were made in school attendance and academic performance for the system's day treatment program. The cost avoidance acknowledged by the State Department of Finance through reductions in group home, state hospital, nonpublic school, and incarcerations expenditures was 66% of Ventura County's AB 377 annual budget of $1,528,265.

In 1989 Ventura County's success in achieving the AB 377 outcomes led to the funding of three other California counties: Santa Cruz, San Mateo, and Riverside. An independent evaluation by Rosenblatt and Attkisson (1992) found that the replication of the planning model in these three counties has achieved similar successful outcomes. The researchers reported that the replication counties generated substantially lower per capita, inflation-adjusted rates of expenditures and per capita group home placements than California as a whole. In addition, foster home and state hospital utilization and expenditures were lower for the replication counties than for the state as a whole. The evaluators concluded, "the cumulative evidence supports the conclusion that the replication counties are utilizing restrictive levels of care at lower rates than would be expected, given state-wide patterns" (p. 285).

In 1992, the Children's Mental Health Services: County Contract (AB 3015) was passed and signed by the governor in order to add more definition and clarity to the requirements for a system of care model. It also expressed the governor's commitment to the model's statewide expansion. The bill states that "an interagency system of care for children with serious emotional and behavioral disturbances provides comprehensive, coordinated care based on the Ventura Planning Model" (Section 5852, Article 2). Furthermore, the bill directs that "the State Department of Mental Health adopt as part of its overall mission the development of community-based, comprehensive, interagency systems of care that target seriously emotionally and behaviorally disturbed children separated from their families, or at risk of separation from their families" (Section 5851a, Article 1). Seven additional counties were selected from a pool of 29 counties to receive additional funding necessary to implement a system of care in accordance with what is now known as the California System of Care Planning Model.

The outcome-driven nature of Ventura County's planning model created true interagency system reform, which enables the system to evolve in response to the changing needs of children and families. The system also has expanded from a single focus of providing children with alternatives to out-of-home placement to a broader focus that includes specific early intervention and prevention efforts. This ability to change over time is the result of Ventura County's outcome-oriented information system that provides feedback to policy makers, managers, public stakeholders, and direct service workers that guides system refinements and continued evolution.

DESCRIPTION OF PLANNING CHARACTERISTICS

The planning model offers policy makers and managers the clarity and simplicity required for accomplishing the major changes that Ventura and other California counties have experienced in creating community-based systems. The model has maximized existing resources by bringing together vital public services, including social services, corrections, mental health, and education. As a result, a broad array of cost-beneficial services for the county's most troubled children has been established. The planning model organizes agency thinking about children with multiple problems and the services they need from a perspective that views children holistically rather than categorically by problem or legal class. The difficulties encountered by children become problems for the whole interagency system rather than problems delegated to one agency or another. Ventura County has adopted the credo, "Multiproblem children and families require interagency solutions."

The model utilizes five simple and commonsense planning steps as a framework to understand problems, provide focus and direction, and demonstrate accountability for child and family outcomes. The five planning steps are described below.

Targeted Populations

One of the earliest tasks in Ventura County's development was reaching a common understanding among agencies about which children would become the focus of interagency efforts. For mental health, this meant a shift from serving children on a "first come, first served" basis in outpatient settings during 9:00 A.M. to 6:00 P.M. office hours to serving those children who were most in need and who required flexibility in service hours, service location, and treatment approaches.

Determining the target populations for Ventura County's system was critical to its success. One of the first concerns was developing a definition acceptable to the multiple agencies involved. Unlike the Mental Health Department, the social services, education, and juvenile justice systems all have mandates specifying the populations they serve. The consensus among agencies that was reached for the target population definition included the following children and adolescents with emotional/behavioral disorders:

- Court dependents whose histories include neglect, physical or sexual abuse or both, multiple foster home placements, residential treatment, and psychiatric hospitalization
- Court wards whose histories include delinquent behavior, risk of out-of-home placement, residential placement, psychiatric hospitalization, and/or incarceration
- Special education pupils who require mental health services in order to benefit from their individualized education program (IEP) and who are at risk of nonpublic school or residential placement or both
- Children who are not part of a formal agency other than the Mental Health Department and are at risk of placement in a psychiatric hospital or other mental health–funded residential facility

The difficulties encountered by these children put them at the highest risk of becoming long-term public responsibilities. All of these children are either at risk of out-of-home placement or are already in out-of-home placements and represent existing public sector legal responsibility and financial liability.

Generally, the targeted children who have emerged in Ventura County have three common characteristics. First, they have a diagnosis from the *Diagnostic and Statistical Manual of Mental Disorders*, Fourth Edition (American Psychiatric Association, 1994). Second, the children exhibit functional impairments in daily living that place them at risk of out-of-home placement. Third, they may exhibit serious problems, such as psychotic symptoms, suicidal risk, or risk of causing injury to others, as a result of a mental disorder.

Ventura County's general population of 700,000 includes about 225,000 children and adolescents. Approximately 12,000 children are identified as requiring special education, approximately 2,000 are arrested and enter the corrections system each year, and approximately 2,000 enter the county's dependency system each year. From this population, and the others at risk of hospitalization but not identified by these agencies, Ventura County's mental health system serves approximately 800 at any point in time, with about 1,600 served annually.

There are vital reasons to target specific populations. Ventura County developed its skill to define and measure outcomes because of its ability to specify a specific group of children. By having targeted populations, Ventura County has been able to increase its efficiency in tracking children and costs across agencies and time. This, consequently, has facilitated advocacy for increasing fiscal support of services to the targeted populations. As a result of demonstrable benefit to high-risk children and reduced out-of-home costs, the Ventura County's Children's Mental Health Program has grown from less than 10 to over 70 full-time staff members during a time of declining fiscal support for public services.

System Goals

Ventura County has defined clear and measurable goals. Family preservation, school attendance, academic achievement, and delinquency prevention are the primary goals for the system. Having clearly stated goals reflecting a common mission has facilitated the development of a consensus on the direction and purpose of interagency efforts.

Another primary goal for the system is to maximize a child's effective functioning while minimizing public sector costs (Essex et al., 1989). This goal seeks to reduce the transfer of legal responsibility and fiscal liability for out-of-home care from the family to the state. The fiscal liability includes costs for group home placements paid by federal, state, and local dollars. It also includes the costs for nonpublic schools and the costs associated with incarceration. Specifically, Ventura County's goals include

- Reduction in out-of-home placements
- Reduction in juvenile justice recidivism
- Reduction in psychiatric hospitalization
- Reduction in out-of-county nonpublic school placements
- Improved school performance and attendance

The ability of Ventura County to communicate its goals in measurable ways is an improvement over how the system previously functioned. Prior to the adoption of clearly stated goals, there was no way to track success, discuss the appropriateness of interventions, and change services that were not effective. Establishing measurable outcomes that are defined in practical terms requires agencies to become accountable, allows the public to be better informed, and increases the probability that interventions will affect children's lives.

Partnerships and Coalitions

The third planning characteristic involves the identification of public and private agencies that form the system's foundation. These agencies, in close collaboration, determine policy, develop plans, create fiscal and service delivery agreements, and form work groups for implementation. Overall, the system of partnerships provides for interagency coordination of services from the highest administrative levels to the level of interaction between direct service workers.

These interagency partnerships are driven by the philosophy that children with multiple problems require interagency solutions. Ventura County believes that coordinating and integrating multiagency expertise and resources to treat the full range of problems affecting children at risk for out-of-home placement is more effective than single-agency approaches.

Ventura County's system relies on the development of written interagency agreements. These agreements facilitate interagency communication and integration of resources. They provide a "rulebook" to service providers on how to maneuver within the system of care; new employees are able to refer to these agreements when obtaining services.

Ventura County's primary interagency agreements are between the Ventura County Mental Health Department and the following agencies: Social Services, Corrections Services, Special Education, and Public Health. There are also memoranda of understanding between the various agencies that do not involve the Mental Health Department. These memoranda often address specific issues, such as the expectations between the Corrections Services Agency and Social Services when a child is legally within both agencies' jurisdictions.

Another essential partner of the Ventura County system is the private sector. The Youth Connection is a bank of goods and services donated by the private sector for use by public-sector children. Services include private counseling, dental services, dance lessons, and tutoring. Goods include clothing, recreational equipment, and school supplies. The worth of goods and services is over $1 million. The Youth Connection is operated and staffed by a local nonprofit human services agency, Interface.

The Casa Pacifica Board is another private-sector initiative serving children in need of emergency shelter care. This private initiative has raised both public and private-sector funds to build and maintain an emergency shelter care facility in the county. The shelter will provide housing, schooling, child-friendly medical/legal examinations, and other services to children entering the child welfare system.

Service Array

In the Ventura County system, mental health services are designed to help children and their families attain their personal goals and to complement the goals of other public agencies. All services are designed as a continuum of alternatives to restrictive, intrusive, and costly care. Systematically, interagency screening of children and case management are added for all children who are at highest risk of out-of-home placement. The resulting array of services fills the wide gap between once-a-week office therapy and hospital admission.

Ventura's service system development alters the way agencies conduct their "business" (Wright, 1989). Ventura's method of service integration requires an understanding of each major agency's processes and how decisions about a child's life are made over time. For example, when working in a correctional setting where a child is sent after arrest, an interagency team must know what court proceedings will affect future service decisions and what legal time lines must be met by all involved.

The broad array of interagency services accomplishes a balance between meeting the needs of individual children and their families and complementing and supporting the mandated goals of agencies. Standards have been developed to guide the quality of the services delivered through the system of care:

- Services are designed to meet cultural, linguistic, and special needs of the targeted populations.
- Each child has a single specified person or interagency team that is responsible for his or her care across programs and agencies over time.
- Families, extended families, and foster families fully participate in all aspects of service planning and service delivery.
- Services are offered in locations that are natural settings for children, such as in their schools and in their homes.
- Services are flexible and focus on child and family strengths.
- Communities have local control of service system design but are held accountable for outcomes.

The services are organized into five subsystems: special education/mental health, juvenile justice/mental health, child welfare/mental health, case management, and outpatient. The specific services provided by each subsystem are detailed in a subsequent section of this chapter.

Evaluation and Monitoring

This final planning characteristic focuses on maintaining an interagency information system that provides feedback to all stakeholders. The system monitors children and outcomes across agencies and over time. The resulting information is used for staff supervision, programmatic decision making, and reporting the system's progress to the state.

The Ventura County Mental Health Department is responsible for collecting and summarizing data from each agency and for maintaining a centralized database. Information is collected and reported monthly on the number of children in out-of-home placement. Although it is possible to track individual children within the database, this is not the focus of monitoring because of cost and time constraints. Rather, the emphasis is on systemwide indicators that measure both child benefit and cost. The number of children in all categories of publicly funded out-of-home placements is one example of a benefit measure. Examples of cost measures include

- Group home costs paid by Aid to Families with Dependent Children– Foster Care
- State hospital expenditures
- Nonpublic school costs
- Costs associated with juvenile justice incarceration
- Other short- and long-term costs in public funds

SYSTEMWIDE COORDINATING FUNCTIONS

Ventura County's interagency network is coordinated both at the system level and at the child/family level. Coordinating mechanisms at all levels are essential to the maintenance of Ventura County's collaborative system. The commitment of both time and resources from managers and direct service personnel facilitates these mechanisms.

System-level coordination occurs across various interagency domains, including policy making, fiscal planning, information sharing, and troubleshooting. At the policy level, the Presiding Court Judge of the Juvenile Court chairs the Interagency Juvenile Justice Council. The Council's executive members include the Chief Administrative Officer, the Superintendent of Schools, the Director of Social Services, the Director of the Health Care Agency, the Mental Health Director, the Chief Probation Officer, the Public Defender, the District Attorney, and a member of the elected County Board of Supervisors. No substitutes can serve on the Council or be sent to meetings. The Council has been meeting monthly since 1980, when it began as a "brown bag" task force meeting during lunch.

Gradually the Council's focus has evolved. Initially, the emphasis was on learning about each other's agencies, building trust, and developing a systemwide philosophy. Over time, these meetings came to focus on solving service delivery problems and identifying service strengths and gaps. Decisions could be made and resources committed to address issues because of the authority of each of the Council's members. Currently, the Council still serves as a vehicle for identifying problems, developing interagency solutions, and working through interagency conflicts.

At the middle management level, coordination occurs through the Interagency Case Management Council. In addition to facilitating the implementation of interagency agreements, this group provides a forum for direct service staff to discuss problems related to particularly difficult child and family situations. Systemic problems that become apparent over time are communicated back to the Juvenile Justice Council for review and possible recommendations for change of existing policies and procedures.

Other more recently developed system-level coordinating work groups have formed in the county. One of the more significant groups addresses the coordination of the system's fiscal resources. This committee is chaired by the fiscal officer of the Social Services Agency. Discussions have ranged from enhancing federal financial participation to rethinking how local and state agency monies can be used to create cross-agency pools of dollars. Over the last 2 years, Ventura County has been able to significantly improve each agency's ability to capture available federal dollars as well as to create new community-based services through reinvesting dollars from savings in residential expenditures. One significant result has been the ability of many county human services agencies and schools to claim Title XIX (Medicaid) administrative costs. This resulted in approximately $3 million in unanticipated revenue for the county for the 1992–1993 fiscal year.

At the child/family level, Ventura has several coordination mechanisms. Multiagency screening and placement committees function within the child welfare and juvenile justice systems. This interagency gatekeeping is designed to review all candidates for out-of-home residential placement, monitor treatment plans, and offer service recommendations. Within each agency, review by committee is a prerequisite for obtaining more intensive levels of care.

Joint programming, in which multiagency staff co-locate to provide services, is another child/family level coordinating mechanism. These staffing arrangements involve the blending of personnel and program management. Services such as therapeutic foster care, school-based day treatment, and facility-based residential treatment services are examples of joint programming in Ventura County.

For pupils receiving special education services, child/family coordination occurs through the pupil's educational plan. In Ventura County, a child's IEP, as established by the Education for All Handicapped Children Act of 1975 (PL 94-142), is the legally defined mechanism that brings multiple agencies together to conduct a single planning process. Any child who is being considered for home teaching, day treatment, or out-of-home placement as a result of behavioral or emotional problems or both is assigned a mental health case manager who becomes part of the pupil's IEP team.

Finally, for children most at risk of out-of-home placement or already in placement, a case management system assists them and their families to maneuver within the system across agencies and over time. This service is provided by the Mental Health Department and includes assessment, planning, linkage, monitoring, and advocacy.

SUBSYSTEMS OF CARE AND SERVICE APPROACH

Ventura County's Mental Health Department is organized by five subsystems of care. Two of these are service subsystems providing case management and outpatient services. The remaining three are interagency based and are defined by the lead agency having the legal responsibility for children in the particular targeted population. Specifically, these interagency subsystems are: special education/mental health, juvenile justice/mental health, and child welfare/mental health.

Each of the five subsystems has a Mental Health Department supervisor who is responsible for both direct supervision and maintenance of the particular interagency relationship. These five managers report to the Mental Health Chief of Service, who ensures that all five subsystems are coordinated.

Within each subsystem, a flexible service approach is used. For example, each subsystem has the ability to increase service intensity within a child's treatment plan before increasing service restrictiveness. Higher levels of service or additional services can be offered before moving a child to a more restrictive level of care. In this manner, a child's problem behaviors become related to the intensity or variety of service, or both, that they are receiving rather than solely to the level of service restrictiveness.

The Special Education/Mental Health Subsystem

The special education/mental health subsystem integrates each agency's resources by co-locating staff to optimize accessibility and effectiveness (Hernandez, 1989). Service options include outpatient treatment (in-home, at school, and clinic based), school-based day treatment, case management, respite care, emergency inpatient services, and intensive in-home services. The primary purpose that drives this service array is to assist a child in meeting his or her educational needs in the most appropriate, least restrictive setting. Emphasis is placed on keeping children in local schools or on returning them to their schools as quickly as appropriate. Within local schools, desired outcomes include enhancing school attendance and academic achievement.

The Phoenix School and Phoenix Elementary Program are examples of co-administered and co-funded day treatment services provided by the Special Education and Mental Health agencies. To enter these programs, children must first be eligible for special education services and have an IEP recommending the service. Eight children are assigned to each of four classrooms. The academic as well as the therapeutic elements of the programs are based on the acquisition of adaptive life skills. This approach supports the goal of reintegrating students back to their neighborhood schools.

Enhanced Special Day Classes are also part of this subsystem. These services are offered in neighborhood schools and involve the co-location of a mental health professional with a special education teacher. This core team assists students in achieving their academic and personal goals. In addition to the educational curriculum, the therapeutic component provides individual, group, and family therapy; case management; and crisis response. These Enhanced Special Day Class programs are currently growing and are now offered to over 100 students across 12 campuses.

Juvenile Justice/Mental Health Subsystem

The juvenile justice/mental health subsystem includes services provided by the county's Juvenile Probation and Mental Health departments. The driving philosophy for this subsystem has been to move away from simply detaining minors to intervening in ways that prevent future delinquent behavior (Kaplan, 1989). Specifically, the focus of this subsystem is to reduce recidivism and residential placement. Services include community-based sex offender treatment, short-term community-based residential treatment, suicide screening and crisis intervention following arrest, case management, outpatient services, intensive in-home services, and school-based day treatment.

The Colston Youth Center is a 45-bed, medium-security residential facility that offers an example of a program that balances issues of treatment and security needs. A screening conducted by both a mental health professional and an investigating probation officer provides recommendations to the court regarding a youth's appropriateness for the residential facility. Youth enter Colston after sentencing by the Juvenile Court. Colston serves youth ages 13–17 who have lengthy delinquency histories as well as a number of mental health needs. Youth are committed to Colston for 120-, 150-, or 180-day periods. Each youth is assigned to an interagency treatment team consisting of a social worker, teacher, corrections services officer, psychologist, and probation officer. Each team has the primary responsibility for developing and implementing the youth's individualized service plan.

Another example of interagency service collaboration is found in the Visions Interagency Program (VIP). This is a school-based day treatment program for adjudicated delinquents developed by Corrections Services, Children's Protective Services, the Ventura County Superintendent of Schools, and the Mental Health Department. Staff from all four agencies work on site at VIP. Referrals come from the Corrections Service Agency and are screened for admission by the entire interagency team. Youths often are ordered into the program through the Juvenile Court following the recommendation of the interagency team. Many youth who enter VIP are transitioning from secure detention back into the community. The school provides academic instruction, therapeutic services, and community supervision. A special focus is on job training and job hunting. Sixteen adolescents are served at any given time in an independent study format and remain in the program for 6–10 months. Youth attend the program 3 days a week and are expected to have jobs during the remaining days.

Child Welfare/Mental Health Subsystem

The child welfare/mental health subsystem serves children who have been physically abused, sexually molested, neglected, or abandoned and who have been removed from their homes by the court. The primary goals of services in this subsystem are family preservation and family reunification. For children in long-term foster care, the goal is stability of placement or adoption. Several primary services are available, including assessment within 72 hours of a child entering shelter care following removal from the home, assessment of children to determine the need for services, outpatient services, therapeutic foster care, school-based day treatment, case management, and emergency mental health inpatient care. The service approach within this subsystem requires that the mental health professional negotiate the therapeutic relationship with the child and the relationships between and with the Child Protective Services social worker, foster parents, and natural parents or guardian (Juday, 1989).

The Shomair Program brings the foster parents, Child Protective Services, and Mental Health Department resources together to implement a collaborative plan based on the individual needs of foster children. Shomair is a network of foster homes with the added support of field-based mental health professionals. The caseload per worker is no more than 10 children, and the expectation is that the originally assigned professional remain involved throughout a child's placement in Shomair and for 6 months after discharge when a child returns home. Staff are available to participating foster families 24 hours a day on an on-call basis.

Case Management Subsystem

The primary goal of the case management subsystem is to ensure both continuity of care across agencies and the availability of services in the most appropriate, least intrusive manner (Brown, 1989). Prevention of inappropriate out-of-home placements and the return of children to the community is a primary task of Mental Health Case Management. Case managers are required to develop a thorough knowledge of public and private sector services and have good social skills and flexibility. Generally, the case manager is the entire system's "broker" who assists families in obtaining needed services.

Ideally, each of Ventura County's 10 mental health case managers serves 25 children and families at any point in time. However, caseloads have grown to between 30 and 40 children. This situation has increased time pressures, making it more difficult to provide the ideal level and intensity of services (Brown, 1989). As a result of this increased responsibility, the case management subsystem has undergone reorganization. Three interagency teams have been formed in which case management responsibilities are shared with professionals from Corrections Services, Social Services, and Special Education. These teams meet regularly to coordinate their activities as well as to keep track of children in residential placements, children who are at high risk for placement, and children who are returning home from placements.

Case managers maintain a countywide tracking system for children moving into or out of placements and between placements. Case managers document these changes, and the information is entered into a computer database. A monthly report providing a summary of children in placement is generated and serves as Ventura County's primary indicator for system effectiveness.

Outpatient Services Subsystem

The outpatient services subsystem is referred to as the "Options Program," and it provides services across all of the major subsystems. Services include assessment; home, clinic- and school-based treatment; and family treatment. Because the targeted population of children creates more challenges for Options workers than do children with fewer problems, innovative and specialized outpatient approaches have been developed. Children and families are offered services in their homes, and the frequency of contacts has become more flexible relative to the more common once-a-week therapy services found in many more traditional outpatient programs. Additionally, frequent collaboration with other agencies and professionals such as schools, physicians, social service workers, and probation officers, occurs to make the Options intervention as pervasive as possible (Akimoto, Saum, & Wellwood, 1989). Despite these service adaptations, it should be noted that Options staff struggle with turning away children who could benefit from services but who do not meet the target population criteria. The number of families who are accepted for services and the severity of their needs press the limits of staff and at times exceed their capacities.

CULTURAL COMPETENCE

Ventura County is committed to developing a service system that is responsive to and respectful of different cultural groups in the community. Although Ventura County is predominantly Caucasian (65.9%), it does have a culturally diverse population: 26.5% Latino, 4.9% Asian American, 2.2% African American, and 0.5% Native American. In three of Ventura County's 10 cities, Latinos comprise almost 60% of the population.

The county recognized that, to better serve this diverse population, the agency and the system would have to undergo major institutional changes. In 1990, the Mental Health Department hired a Minority Services Coordinator to work with administrators and staff to develop and implement a cultural competence master plan. In 1991, a cultural competence master plan was developed that targets four key areas for improvement: policy and administration, human resource development, services to clients and families, and research and evaluation. For each of these areas, objectives, activities, resources, staff responsibilities, timelines, and monitoring procedures are delineated. Objectives for each of the four areas are highlighted below:

- *Policy and administration*: Develop a mission statement that includes cultural competence, develop and maintain communication with managers and supervisors throughout the master planning process, identify revenues for implementation, and develop a policy statement for performance expectations for organizations that subcontract with the Mental Health Department.
- *Human resource development*: Establish interpreter training, create a resource list of training materials, establish a staff recruitment coordinator, develop a minority staff retention program, conduct ongoing orientation and training in cultural competence for current and new staff, and develop a cultural mentor program.
- *Services*: Improve outreach and information for the public about services, develop service approaches that are field based, and create service environments that are culturally appropriate to the population being served.
- *Research and evaluation*: Develop a client data base with information on client ethnicity, diagnosis by ethnicity, years in the United States, and bilingual status; develop a tracking and monitoring process for the ethnicity of staff across divisions and classifications; and develop methods to examine differential treatment outcomes across ethnic groups.

SUMMARY OF STRENGTHS

The Ventura Planning Model has served as a leader and forerunner for the development of local systems of care for children and adolescents who have serious emotional disturbances. When many national experts in the children's services field were discussing the need for a new approach to serving troubled children and families in this country, Ventura County was operationalizing these concepts. The country has learned a great deal from the Ventura County experience. A number of initiatives, including the Child and Adolescent Service System Program and the Robert Wood Johnson Foundation's Mental Health Services Program for Youth, have looked to Ventura County for guidance in the development of local systems of care. States and communities across the country have studied the Ventura Planning Model in their own efforts to develop systems.

The Ventura County experience is not only about creating a system of care; it is about creating system change. This effort has been successful because the strengths Ventura County has developed dovetail well with the crucial elements necessary for system change. These critical elements include the following:

- *Leadership*: The importance of leadership cannot be underestimated. Ventura County has demonstrated an understanding of the value of obtaining and fostering multiple sources of leadership to develop a power base of support. Individuals have been willing to take risks and bring others together to explore ways to serve youth differently.
- *Vision and clarity of goals*: The Ventura Planning Model has had a strong philosophical underpinning and vision from the outset. The core value for Ventura County is that a community-based, interagency system of mental health care that targets the children with the most emotional/behavioral disturbance will provide the greatest benefit to children, their families, and the community at the lowest cost to the public sector. This mission statement and the essential elements of the Ventura Planning Model drive all the activities of the system and, over time, have permeated all levels of decision making.
- *Planning*: The leaders of Ventura County have been highly skilled strategic planners. They believe in and have operationalized a planning model to achieve goals for mental health care reform.
- *Meaningful collaboration*: From the outset, Mental Health Department staff was committed to working with other child-serving agencies. These staff members physically go to or work in these agencies and become part of the culture of these other service systems. Staff of the Mental Health, Special Education, Child Welfare, and Juvenile Justice agencies work together as teammates. There are also numerous mechanisms at multiple levels that provide a forum for discussion and problem solving.
- *Dedicated staff*: The project has changed how mental health staff provide treatment, and, for the most part, staff have demonstrated a willingness to make changes. They are believers in the vision, they understand system issues, and they are committed to collaboration.
- *Service array*: By leveraging resources, reallocating dollars, and blending personnel across agencies, Ventura County has been able to expand the array of available services and make them fit children and families flexibly.
- *Legislative mandate*: One of the strengths of the system is its statutory sanction. Many of the critical elements of the system are established in law. This mandate gives Ventura County the political and legal clout to implement its system of care and institutionalizes the concept of an interagency, community-based system of care.
- *Evaluation capability and successful outcomes*: Because the Ventura Planning Model was started as a demonstration project and was mandated to

document cost avoidance and successful outcomes, it has set up an evaluation and tracking system that enables the mental health agency to collect data and report progress in achieving goals. This approach for tracking both system and client outcomes has been enormously valuable to improving services. Ventura County leadership maintains that outcome data are a prerequisite for any system, for future decision making, and for political and financial survival.

- *Cultural competence*: Ventura County has made a major commitment to cultural competence and actively promotes its application throughout California. Ventura County has developed a cultural competence master plan, regularly conducts specialized training of staff, and initiates numerous other activities to improve services to minority groups. The county is in a leadership role in the area of cultural competence and strongly believes that cultural competence is a key to system effectiveness and future success.
- *Continuous planning*: Ventura County accepts change as a constant and seeks to plan and direct its services with an evolving vision for system of care development.

REFERENCES

Akimoto, M., Saum, K., & Wellwood, D. (1989). Intensive outpatient services. In D. Essex, D. Jordan, & R. Feltman (Eds.), *The Ventura planning model for mental health services* (p. 10). Ventura, CA: Ventura County Mental Health.

American Psychiatric Association. (1994). *Diagnostic and statistical manual of mental disorders* (4th ed.). Washington, DC: American Psychiatric Press.

Brown, J. (1989). Case management and services for other at-risk children and youth. In D. Essex, D. Jordan, & R. Feltman (Eds.), *The Ventura planning model for mental health services* (p. 5). Ventura, CA: Ventura County Mental Health.

Children's Mental Health Services Act, AB 377, Wright. (September 29, 1987). Chapter 1361.

Children's Mental Health Services: County Contracts, AB 3015, Wright. (September 29, 1982). Chapter 1229, Section 5850, Part 4.

Education for All Handicapped Children Act of 1975, PL 94-142. (August 23, 1977). Title 20, U.S.C. 1401 et seq: *U.S. Statutes at Large, 89*, 773–796.

Essex, D., Jordan, D., & Feltman, R. (Eds.). (1989). *The Ventura planning model for mental health services*. Ventura, CA: Ventura County Mental Health.

Feltman, R. (1987, July 14). *Testimony before the Select Committee on Children, Youth, and Families: Hearings on Children's Mental Health: Promising Responses to Neglected Problems*, 100th Congress, 171–175.

Hernandez, M. (1989). Services for mentally disordered special education pupils. In D. Essex, D. Jordan, & R. Feltman (Eds.), *The Ventura planning model for mental health services* (p. 5). Ventura, CA: Ventura County Mental Health.

Jordan, D., & Hernandez, M. (1990). The Ventura planning model: A proposal for mental health reform. *Journal of Mental Health Administration, 1*, 26–47.

Juday, M. (1989). Services for mentally disordered dependents. In D. Essex, D. Jordan, & R. Feltman (Eds.), *The Ventura planning model for mental health services* (p. 4). Ventura, CA: Ventura County Mental Health.

Kaplan, S. (1989). Services for mentally disordered juvenile offenders. In D. Essex, D. Jordan, & R. Feltman (Eds.), *The Ventura planning model for mental health services* (p. 4). Ventura, CA: Ventura County Mental Health.

Mental Health Services for Children, AB 3920. (September 25, 1984). Chapter 1984.

Rosenblatt, A., & Attkisson, C. (1992). Integrating systems of care in California for youth with severe emotional disturbance: Initial group home expenditure and utilization findings from the California AB377 evaluation project. *Journal of Child and Family Studies, 1,* 263–286.

Wright, C. (1989). Extending the model to adults and seniors. In D. Essex, D. Jordan, & R. Feltman (Eds.), *The Ventura planning model for mental health services* (p. 1). Ventura, CA: Ventura County Mental Health.

CHAPTER 10

The Role of Education in Systems of Care

Jane Knitzer

The increasing policy and service attention to the needs of children with behavioral and emotional disorders and their families has underscored the important role schools can potentially play in operationalizing these new values and service directions. This chapter highlights the challenge the schools face in serving these troubled and troubling children and adolescents and examines the roles that schools and educational agencies are playing in organized systems of care.

THE CHALLENGE

The picture from the schoolhouse door with respect to children with emotional and behavioral disorders is disturbing (Knitzer, Steinberg, & Fleisch, 1990; Koyanagi & Gaines, 1993). The problems center in five areas. First, based on epidemiological estimates, too few children are identified. Studies suggest that 14%–20% of all children have emotional or behavioral problems warranting intervention, with 3%–5% defined as having severe problems (Brandenburg, Friedman, & Silver, 1990). Yet, nationally, fewer than 1% of all schoolchildren are identified by the schools as having emotional and behavioral problems, with many states overall and individual districts significantly below this level (U.S. Department of Education, 1991).

Second, the educational programs and, to the limited extent they are offered, related support services provided to the children are often inadequate or inappropriate, marred by minimal emphasis on social skills or academics and an overemphasis on behavioral controls—so much so that the real curriculum for this population has been described as "a curriculum of control" (Knitzer et al., 1990). Furthermore, even if students do receive mental health services, because they are not typically part of the children's individualized education programs (IEPs), these services are often totally disconnected from their school lives. In one community, even when the school made the referrals, in only 4 of 80 instances did the therapist and the teacher share information (Knitzer et al., 1990).

Third, families are typically seen as adversaries, not partners, in the process of helping identified students—called to the schools, for example, when there is a crisis that the school cannot handle and often either explicitly or implicitly blamed for the problems of the student (Knitzer et al., 1990). Fourth, under the Individuals with Disabilities Education Act (IDEA) of 1990 (PL 101-476), one of the major federal special education laws, this population of children is disproportionately placed in segregated settings, including high-cost residential placements.

Fifth, studies of youth postschooling reveal that whatever monies are spent on this population are spent badly. Outcomes are poor: graduation rates are lower than for other groups of children with disabilities (36% compared to 54%); job prospects are dimmer; and the likelihood of involvement with the criminal justice system is two and one half times as great (SRI, 1991).

Emerging system of care efforts are yielding new insights about both roles for education in collaboration with other agencies and specific strategies to improve the school-related life of troubled children and their families. This chapter considers first the general ways in which education has been involved and, second, how this is translated into specific systems of care.

EMERGING ROLE OF EDUCATION IN SYSTEMS OF CARE

As systems of care develop to better meet the needs of children and adolescents with identified emotional and behavioral disabilities, individual schools, school districts, and state departments of education have been involved in at least four major ways.

Developing Collaborative Child- and Family-Specific Plans

At the most basic level, school personnel participate in the development of common, cross-agency service plans to ensure consistency of approach across all domains of a child's life and to maximize the resources any one system can provide. For example, in an effort to prevent the long-term residential placement of a child who at age 5 had already been hospitalized, a single interagency service plan was created in which the schools played a key role. Special education funds were used so that school personnel were able to offer the grandparent and parent caring for the child at home a specialized course in limit setting, discipline, and behavior management. (School personnel had developed the course for another purpose.) In addition, the family and the teacher developed a close working relationship that included almost daily contact not just about problems, but about how to build on the positive behaviors of the child. Both of these strategies were part of an overall plan that also included respite care provided (and paid for) by the mental health agency, along with psychiatric supervision of medication. This careful approach to wrapping intensive services around the child and family led to dramatic reductions in problem behaviors and healing for a family that was almost disrupted. In this instance, as is often the case where there is a strong cross-agency commitment to school involvement, the team meetings were held at the school to make it easier for the teachers to participate.

Participating in Community-Based Governance Structures

Characteristic of virtually all organized systems of care is the involvement of community schools or school districts at the governance/management level, often through the ongoing participation of special education directors. (It has been estimated that, in the systems of care funded by the Robert Wood Johnson Foundation, close to half of all enrolled students are in special education [Stroul, 1993].) The willingness of the schools to play a leadership role in these governance or system-level coordination structures and take a proactive stance varies considerably, and the experience has been that often school "buy-in" in more than name is difficult, at least initially. However, recognition is growing within the special education community that the school-related response to children and adolescents with behavioral and emotional disabilities has been marginal, and, hence, a new openness within special education to explore ways to be more effective is increasingly apparent (Center for Policy Options in Special Education, 1993).

Providing Dollars

Given the importance of maximizing increasingly scarce human services dollars, and ensuring that existing dollars are used as flexibly as possible for "wraparound" services tailored to specific needs of children and families (Burchard & Clark, 1990), the value systems of care place on managing dollars more effectively is high. To that end, systems of care have sought ways to decategorize state and federal dollars through waivers, to reallocate dollars from residential services to community-based services, and to pool dollars to create "no strings" monies to meet individual family needs such as respite care (Cole & Poe, 1993; Kutash, Rivera, Hall, & Friedman, 1993). Education has participated unevenly as a fiscal partner in system of care efforts, but, as interest spreads and the benefits are more carefully documented, greater fiscal contributions from education are likely.

Developing New Services

One of the key challenges in serving children with emotional and behavioral disorders within a school context is to strengthen the therapeutic/mental health perspective. This does not necessarily mean providing "pull-out" therapy to students outside of the classroom. Instead, it means supporting a student's strengths within the context of a school day; supporting the capacity of the teacher to use the classroom/school to help the student test out and practice new social skills, new emotional responses, and new academic competencies; and ensuring adequate resources to cope with predictable crises and disruptions.

Embedding practices and approaches reflecting this orientation, however, is difficult. The fact is that schools start in a deficit position. Teachers are ill prepared to cope with this population (Nichols, 1991; Steinberg & Knitzer, 1992). Furthermore, there has been an erosion of school mental health personnel, and those who remain often spend their time evaluating and testing students rather than developing classroom-based or other interventions (Knitzer et al., 1990). For example, a recent study found that only 59% of all schools have any kind of in-school counseling capacity *for any students* (Moore, Strang, Schwartz, & Braddock, 1988). That systems of care have been the catalyst for the development of new, often collaborative, mental health/education strategies is therefore significant.

SYSTEMS OF CARE IN ACTION

To capture the uniqueness of community responses to their particular needs and politics, this section presents brief descriptions of system of care efforts that highlight variations in both the role of education (and its evolution over time) and the general approach to the system of care challenge.

Ventura County, California

The oldest system of care effort in the country targets youth with identified disorders who are in or at risk of out-of-home placement from multiple systems: mental health, juvenile justice, child welfare, and special education. These are children who, taken together, represent a major fiscal liability for the county. The Ventura County system of care is governed by a series of interagency agreements, a system-level interagency entity called the Juvenile Justice Council, a middle-management case management council, and a Youth Connection board that includes leaders from the business, religious, and professional communities. The mental health agency provides case management. Community-based services range from in-home family preservation services (i.e., intensive crisis intervention services) to special programs in the juvenile justice facilities (Jordan & Hernandez, 1990; Stroul, Lourie, Goldman, & Katz-Leavy, 1992). During the demonstration period, the county offset project costs through placement avoidance, including a 21% reduction in nonpublic school residential placements for special education students, a total decrease in out-of-county placements of 47%, and a decrease in hospitalization rates of 68% (Jordan & Hernandez, 1990) (see Chapter 9).

The education strategy initially involved participation both at the governance level and in the development of new programs—specifically, the creation within the public schools of a specialized day treatment program with a strong family component and creative behavior management alternatives (Jordan & Hernandez, 1990; Knitzer et al., 1990). As that effort evolved, an additional school program was created for youth at risk, particularly for youth already in custody but not necessarily identified as having emotional or behavioral disturbances. Furthermore, mental health workers from the clinic were based in special education classes within regular schools, and, to supplement intensive home-based services, reimbursement for intensive, off-site clinical services was developed.

In 1992, building on these working relationships, a new initiative was undertaken to reduce the growing reliance on group homes that had occurred as an unanticipated consequence of state reform legislation for students with emotional disturbances. The effort entailed using a collaborative, multiagency approach. In addition, social services dollars were used to seed alternative school-based services while a longer-term reimbursement strategy through Medicaid was generated. Through this strategy, Ventura County again was able to demonstrate the power of a unified, cross-system approach to increasing school-based support services, developing a day treatment program for elementary-age students, and enhancing school-based case management, all resulting in countywide placement cost avoidance (Ichinose, Kingdon, & Hernandez, 1994).

The Robert Wood Johnson Foundation Mental Health Services Program for Youth

In 1990, the Robert Wood Johnson Foundation began a 5-year, $20.4 million system of care initiative designed explicitly to emphasize managed care and fiscal reform in the context of individualized, family focused, and normalized services (Beachler, 1990; Cole & Poe, 1993). In two of the seven funded sites, education-related issues and systems have been central.

In Cleveland, Ohio, the Robert Wood Johnson Foundation project known as Connections has brought case management to and in through the schoolhouse door. There, under the auspices of the Positive Education Program (PEP), a longstanding, innovative program based on the "re-education" philosophy (Knitzer, 1982), 16 case managers (10 of whom are based directly in the schools) develop community-based service plans that include flexible services authorized pursuant to a voucher system. Unlike the Ventura County system, the project does not yet reflect significant cross-system pooling of funds. School personnel, however, do participate in the individual treatment or service teams and are part of the project management team. PEP has found that the school-based mental health strategy is particularly useful given the highly mobile school population in the city.

In Portland, Oregon, the schools have played a more central role by providing significant funds as well as leadership to the entire project. Interestingly enough in view of the PEP strategy, the Portland project is a successor initiative to a pilot case management project developed by the Multnomah County School System (Knitzer et al., 1990). The more direct impetus for the Partners Project, however, was the realization that the schools were contributing a disproportionate share (an average of $14,000 per child and over half of the dollars) of the county costs for children's mental health. Through the Partners Project, the schools agreed to commit $4,000 per child as part of a pool of funds to be used as a match for Medicaid and to participate in the development of individualized, family-focused services such as respite care and wraparound services. The link between the project and the schools was further enhanced when the former director of programs for children with emotional and behavioral disorders became the project manager.

Although there are no systematic data as yet, the Partners Project is deemed very effective in controlling the overuse and inappropriate use of residential and other segregated placements and in providing supportive services to individual children and families. In addition, there also has been significant spinoff within the schools. IEPs have become more flexible and more attuned to the clinical significance and potential impact of more individualized school interventions. In one instance, for example, a behavior coach was hired by the schools to help a student meet the tasks necessary to work in a family business as an alternative to a more standard vocational education placement. Through the common plan development process, which included the family, the school staff recognized that this issue had been a source of longstanding family conflict and that a carefully tailored and supported placement in the family business could (and did) have a major significant impact on the youth's and family's functioning.

In addition, the school system has made a much stronger commitment within the schools to diverting children not involved in the Partners Project from segregated placements. To that end, special education teachers have been redeployed in regular education classrooms to be "early interventionists." Furthermore, the school social worker has been asked to help as a behavior management specialist on behalf of children who otherwise might be placed in day treatment. The schools, in other words, are making a commitment to wrap supports around children in regular classrooms as well as to provide more intensive on-site interventions to those students who are more seriously troubled.

La Grange, Illinois

In most system of care efforts, the school's role has been carved out in response to invitations from mental health agencies. In 1990, however, the U.S. Department of Education's Office of Special Education Programs, based on an amendment to IDEA, established a system change grant program on behalf of children with serious emotional and behavioral disorders. The La Grange, Illinois, Project WRAP, with funds from this grant program as well as state funds, is yielding important insights about how to stretch the role of education for students with emotional and behavioral disorders. Project Wrap, under the direction of the Deputy Director of Special Education, encompasses a number of distinct components built on the lessons of first-generation system of care efforts (Eber, 1993), including

1. A multiagency community council, led by the schools, to identify systemic barriers to serving troubled children and adolescents and to redeploy resources
2. A resource network that provides consultation to *any* community provider seeking help in serving children and families whose needs cut across systems (and that, by design, is composed of the same individuals who are on the council in order to ensure that policy making is not disconnected from the hard work of changing direct services)
3. Pooled funds for wraparound services not otherwise funded
4. Two innovative support programs—the Buddy Program, which pairs an identified student with a nonidentified student in activities that foster interaction, and the Parent to Parent Support Program, a parent mentoring program for parents whose children are experiencing difficulties
5. The newest component, WAIS (Wrap Around in School), which is an effort to bring wraparound services into the school using a special support team that includes a family service manager, a WAIS team teacher, and in-school respite workers to convert self-contained programs into wraparound models that include students with emotional and behavioral disorders in in-school and after-school activities (Project WRAP is currently testing the WAIS concept on a small number of youths from elementary, middle, and high schools.)

Several aspects of this educationally driven system of care effort are particularly interesting. One aspect that is unique to this effort is that there has been a concerted effort to test the concept of "inclusion" for this population of students—the proposition that even the most troubled children, with appropriate supports, can be served in regular classrooms and/or have more opportunities for interaction with other peers.

Second, there has been a commitment to parent collaboration and empowerment that goes far beyond what most schools are able to tolerate. In Project WRAP, for example, a goal is to eventually have parents serve as paid case managers. The project also has seeded a parent support network that has helped develop the Illinois Federation for Families, an organization linked directly to a national parent support and advocacy group, the Federation of Families for Children's Mental Health.

Third, there has been a conscious commitment to use the multiagency network as a vehicle to provide easy access to training and technical assistance for the local provider community, at their own pace and centered around individual children and families (Eber, 1993). Fourth, there has been an immediate effort to spread the knowledge and experience. The director of the project is now providing technical assistance and support to several other educationally based reform projects around the state that also rely on community networking and wraparound services.

Fifth, the state of Illinois, which has long used a mechanism called an Individual Care Grant to pay for high-cost and, very often, out-of-state residential placement is now granting waivers to enable school districts to use those same monies for in-district packages of service, based, in part, on the experience of La Grange. Because children with serious emotional and behavioral disorders are especially likely to be in residential placements at school expense, this is an important precedent for the reallocation of residential dollars through education, paralleling the much more widespread efforts to reallocate mental health, Medicaid, and child welfare dollars (Cole & Poe, 1993).

The Family Preservation Initiative of Baltimore City

In Baltimore, the system of care effort has its most direct roots not in the mental health or education systems but in the child welfare system. Therefore, the initial core service of the system of care was Maryland's intensive family preservation services. These services were seeded with support from the Annie E. Casey Foundation and have been expanded statewide over the course of the last few years in the face of escalating foster care and residential placements. To supplement this family preservation strategy, Baltimore has adopted the concept of wraparound services, particularly for those children being reintegrated into the community.

As with the other system of care development efforts, there is a multiagency governance structure that includes the education system and a commitment to redeploy resources. In fiscal year (FY) 1992, approximately $3.8 million was redirected to community-based services; in FY 1993, the figure was expected to be $7 million (Family Preservation Initiative, n.d.). The Baltimore effort has been particularly significant for education because, in Maryland in general and in Baltimore in particular, the education system spends large amounts of money on what are called "level V and VI" placements, the most restrictive (and often out-of-state) placements for children with emotional and behavioral disorders. (Estimated costs for out-of-state care funded by education statewide in FY 1992 were $30.7 million, with 46% of the children from Baltimore.) Motivated by the hopes of reducing those costs, and through new state legislation that increased the local share of placement costs from 0% to 20%, the schools have had a strong incentive to collaborate. So, for example, in FY 1992, of the 70 children receiving wraparound services, education funds were used for close to half, with wraparound costs approximately 11% less than residential costs (Staff of Family Preservation Initiative, personal communication based on data for 1993 annual report). As the initiative evolves, current plans are to use shared resources to develop more therapeutic foster homes and behavior aides for the schools.

North Idaho System of Care

The challenge of meeting the needs of troubled children and their families who live in rural areas has long been recognized. In north Idaho, using both state funds and special federal research and demonstration funds, there has been a systematic effort to create an organized system of care that is sensitive to rural challenges, particularly the absence of specialized services and providers and the transportation difficulties that face families and service providers alike. There, in a variation on a theme, the system is under the leadership of the local office of the state Division of Services to Children, Youth and Families, a single state agency for children created in 1989 that combines responsibility for child mental health, child protection, juvenile justice, and runaway youth. Building on this integrated system, the local public agency staff, through its "intensive treatment and support teams," provide the entry point to the system as well as the core family-focused services: intensive family treatment, family case management, and family support services to children at risk of removal from their homes. In addition, the system of care uses flexible wraparound dollars and two types of paraprofessional "service extenders," treatment and respite families and classroom companions. The classroom companions have been developed as a deliberate alternative to day treatment. They provide individualized educational, emotional, and behavioral support to children across school districts, enabling them to remain in their regular classrooms. Preliminary results, based on over 50 families, show reduced use of hospitalization and residential placement and greater family satisfaction (Lubrecht, n.d.).

Taking Stock

It is too early to draw any firm conclusions about the impact of these systems of care on the general well-being of children and families or specifically on education-related outcomes, although efforts to compile disparate data have been undertaken and show trends in the right direction (Stroul, 1993). However, several points do seem clear. First, the involvement of education as a key player is central to the success of transforming existing fragmented delivery systems, whether serving rural, urban, or suburban students. Second, the systems of care highlighted here have been initiated by different agencies (e.g., mental health, child welfare, or education), but all use basically the same strategies, all have had strong leadership, and all have paid attention to fiscal as well as service and governance issues. Third, there appear to be important spinoffs in a number of system of care efforts that positively affect what has been described as the "bleakness" of the school day for students with emotional and behavioral disorders (Knitzer et al., 1990; Nichols, 1991). Put differently, system of care reform appears to be a vehicle for underscoring the need for, and developing strategies for, substantive school-based change.

MOVING FORWARD

The new developments highlighted in this chapter signify meaningful progress since the release of *At The Schoolhouse Door*, a report documenting the policy and programmatic problems related to serving children with emotional and behavioral disorders (Knitzer et al., 1990). At the same time, it is important not to minimize the critical issues and challenges that schools and other agencies continue to face, both in creating systems of care for children with emotional and behavioral disorders and in addressing the explicitly school-related agenda on behalf of this population. This section highlights key challenges at both the practice and policy levels.

Practice-Level Challenges

Although practice and policy are not so neatly separated (i.e., policy strategies can be used to promote practice changes and practice changes can stimulate policy innovations), three direct service–level issues are critical to improving outcomes for troubled children and adolescents.

Respecting the Culture of the School Critical to the collaborative framework of systems of care is the premise that no one agency or system can do it alone (Boyd, 1992; Kamerman & Kahn, 1992; Stroul & Friedman, 1986). At the practice level, this means enabling mental health professionals and educators to work more effectively in partnership with families and with each other. In particular, for mental health professionals working in the school, sensitivity to the school culture is critical. At the very least, this often unacknowledged dimension involves respecting the leadership role of the principal and working to support him or her, as well as appreciating what it takes to be a teacher and paying careful attention to what teachers say they need and what works and does not work for them.

Getting Beyond the Constraints of the IEP Process Under IDEA, children age 5 and above who are identified as having emotional or behavioral disorders and are eligible for special education must have an IEP. Although initially seen as a way to develop meaningful service plans, instead, the IEP is often an assembly line (sometimes even computer-generated) formality. For students with emotional and behavioral disorders, two constraints are particularly problematic: "the payor of last resort" provision, which means that the schools are ultimately responsible for funding any service on the IEP, and the absence of a family focus. The former often has a chilling effect on school interest in collaborating across systems, particularly in developing shared plans of care. The latter makes the IEP process inconsistent with the family-focused, "whatever it takes" orientation of the emerging children's mental health system of care paradigm. However, in the interest of breaking the gridlock, strategies such as holding two consecutive meetings, one to develop the common plan and the other to meet the formal requirements of the IEP, have developed.

Paying Attention to the Life of the Classroom   The schools have a twofold agenda with respect to children with emotional and behavioral disorders. One, the focus of this chapter, is to become active participants in system of care efforts. The other, closely related to the success of the system of care efforts but broader in scope, is to focus on what happens to children while they are in school, particularly behind classroom doors. The agenda for this effort has been spelled out elsewhere, and new models and strategies are emerging (Jones, 1992; Knitzer et al., 1990; Nichols, 1991). However, the importance of attending to the quality and content of the school life of a child with behavioral and emotional disabilities must be emphasized.

Policy-Level Challenges

Except in isolated programs, classrooms, or community mental health systems, widespread practice does not typically change without policy-driven catalysts. The following five issues all have particular implications for system of care effectiveness, and all have the potential to serve as those catalysts.

Changing the Federal Definition   During the past several years, national momentum has been mounting to replace the term "serious emotional disturbance" with the term "emotional and behavioral disorder." The proposed definition makes significant conceptual changes (Forness & Knitzer, 1992). It requires that the disability be more than temporary, be exhibited in two settings (one of which is school related), be different from the cultural norms of the group, and be unresponsive to direct intervention in regular education (unless there is strong evidence that such interventions would be insufficient). The proposed language also explicitly includes children who are now sometimes excluded, largely for cost rather than clinical reasons. Children with conduct disorder, for example, are sometimes excluded, although conduct disorder is a clear psychiatric diagnostic category and, furthermore, conduct disorders often coexist with other disorders, especially anxiety or depression (Forness, Kavale, & Lopez, 1993). Similarly, the proposed definition eliminates the "maladjustment" exclusion, a cause for confusion and dumping under the current structure (Weinberg & Weinberg, 1990). Finally, the proposed language clarifies that the intent of the law is not to focus solely on academic competence.

At the time of this writing, Congress has not yet acted, although individual states are moving in this direction. Furthermore, recently promulgated federal regulations for the definition of disability in Head Start use the term "emotional and behavioral disorders" and incorporate many of the concepts in the proposed change for IDEA. Given recent political changes, the likelihood that these changes will be enacted is minimal—the very survival of IDEA is at stake.

Developing Comprehensive Statewide Education Change Strategies Typically, state departments of education have focused little strategic attention on children with emotional and behavioral disorders (Knitzer et al., 1990). There is, however, at least one example of a comprehensive, state-led educational initiative on behalf of children with emotional and behavioral disorders (Phillips, Nelson, & McLaughlin, 1993). Kentucky, recognizing the significant underidentification of this population in its schools (in 1986, the state identified only 0.36% of the population as having emotional and behavioral disorders) and concerned about the escalating use and cost of hospitalization, began a multiyear initiative in close collaboration with the Department of Mental Health to restructure its approach. This has resulted in a demonstration effort to test a careful, teacher-driven, multiphase screening process designed not only to benefit children but also to serve as a tool to help teachers understand and identify early patterns of behavior and affect that signal potential problems. Once the demonstration was completed, the initiative became a statewide strategy. The state then developed a range of technical assistance materials and strategies for the schools (EBD Task Force, 1992). Finally, the state modified its rules and regulations, adopting a careful new definition of emotional and behavioral disorders consistent with the proposed federal change.

Buttressing these efforts, in 1990 Kentucky enacted legislation encouraging state, regional, and local cross-system collaboration on behalf of children with serious emotional and behavioral disorders and then successfully competed for a Robert Wood Johnson Foundation grant to develop a local system of care demonstration, known as Bluegrass IMPACT (Cole & Poe, 1993) (see Chapter 12). Furthermore, the state enacted a broad general educational reform law that included a mandate to develop Family Resource Centers, thus providing a potentially powerful laboratory to test, in one state, many of the emerging constructs of how best to help children and families with multiple and complex needs.

Assessing State and Local School-Related Fiscal Incentives During the past several years, as is reflected in many of the systems of care described above, much attention has been paid to the refinancing of children's mental health, largely in recognition of the fact that available public dollars (from all the systems) typically act as incentives for out-of-home, high-cost placement (Cole & Poe, 1993). Significantly less attention, however, has been paid to the implicit incentives and disincentives in educational funding formulas. Following both the Maryland and Illinois examples, this should be an area for further scrutiny and action.

Ensuring that Children with Emotional and Behavioral Disorders are Part of District Inclusion Efforts Increasingly, under the impetus of several decades of advocacy, pressure is mounting to dismantle the largely segregated special education system that has emerged in favor of "inclusion"—serving a child with special needs in his or her regular classroom and providing, in that context, whatever additional supports the child needs. For children with behavioral and emotional disorders, which are often called "invisible" disabilities, the inclusion movement holds both special challenges and special pitfalls and, as a result, has been controversial (Kauffman & Smucker, 1995). There is fear, for example, on the part of teachers, some parents, and others that children will be dumped and that the tendency to see them as "bad" or "mad" rather than in need of help will be worsened. In contrast, proponents argue that inclusion represents the possibility of reducing the isolation that children with emotional and behavioral disorders frequently experience, an isolation bred of the lack of opportunity to engage in normal developmental activities and to build friendships with children who are not "labeled." Beyond that, as classroom environments change to accommodate the needs of identified students, and as regular teachers, aides, special education teachers, and support personnel are redeployed in regular classrooms, experience suggests that the new partnerships and transfer of skills across regular and special education will also work to the benefit of the many children who manifest behavioral and emotional problems but who are not necessarily identified.

Only systematic data will help to sort out the conditions under which inclusion is positive or harmful (or neutral). It is, however, clear that regular education is now on notice, including through court decisions, that serious efforts must be made to provide services and supports to children in regular education. Therefore, the field must work more vigorously to develop models for supports to teachers and children to enable a meaningful test of the power of the reform ideology.

Promoting Early Intervention This chapter has focused on children and adolescents with already identified, typically long-visible, and severe emotional and behavioral disabilities, just as systems of care are focused on this population. However, perhaps the most important set of policy reforms that need to be given new priority on both the educational and mental health agendas has to do with the early identification of and intervention with children showing signs of problems. To fail to do so is to invite the need for long-term, high-cost interventions for too large a pool of children. This is a major policy-level challenge yet to be addressed.

Several strategies appear to be promising vehicles for such early intervention. The first strategy involves what is known as "prereferral" interventions. Partly as a corrective to the inappropriate identification of students for special education and partly as a cost-containment strategy, state legislators, school districts, or both are increasingly requiring that specific efforts be made prior to referral to special education to determine if such referral can be avoided (Carter & Sugai, 1989). However, Knitzer and her colleagues (1990) found that, although prereferral interventions represent a potentially important strategy for children with emotional and behavioral problems, in reality, most of the prereferral strategies are targeted to academic issues, and neither classroom teachers nor teacher support teams (which are often used to help generate the interventions after a teacher makes a referral) are skilled at developing interventions dealing with emotional or behavioral problems. More sophisticated approaches are emerging, and these need to be nurtured, evaluated, and expanded (Knitzer et al., 1990; Knoll, Kamps, & Seaborn, 1993).

In addition to prereferral interventions, school-linked support services represent a promising strategy to ensure early access to services before system of care levels of service are needed (Center for the Future of Children, 1992). To this end, there has been growing interest in using the school as a "hub" for service delivery, sometimes called a one-stop or full-service school. In a variant of this, a number of states, including Kentucky, as noted above, are supporting the development of Family Resource Centers attached to schools. These resource centers can help broker services for individual children and families; develop specific and sustained parent involvement strategies; and seed collaborative ventures with hospitals, social service agencies, and the like for on-site services. Additionally, particularly for adolescents, school-based health and mental health clinics may also be an important first line of defense for early identification and intervention for students experiencing stresses and problem behaviors (Paavola, Hannah, & Nichol, 1989). Available data, albeit limited, suggest that mental health issues are a major reason for self-referral for adolescents.

A third strategy for prevention and early intervention is to build on the growing knowledge about risk factors, particularly risk factors predisposing children to conduct disorders, and to develop more early, comprehensive, intensive, and evaluated interventions. In this light, the learning from the FAST Track Program promises to move the field forward (Conduct Problems Prevention Research Group, 1992). In that research effort, funded by the National Institute of Mental Health, four sites are testing an intervention with five components (each of which has been singly tested but not integrated):

1. Parent training to minimize harsh parenting styles and disciplinary practices
2. Home visiting carried out by family coordinators to help families problem solve and, as necessary, gain access to services

3. Social skills training, targeted not just to the identified at-risk group of children but to the entire classroom (and eventually school)
4. Academic tutoring to forestall the downward trajectory that is so typical
5. Classroom interventions that both provide support to teachers and use them as key agents in changing the interaction patterns and sense of self of the target children

These ecologically sound interventions, consistent with the best knowledge from child and family development and developmental psychopathology, set a standard that should be widely adopted elsewhere.

CONCLUSION

Since the 1980s, there has been significant changes in services for children and adolescents with emotional and behavioral disorders. For much of the time, schools have been limited and often reluctant partners, but this too is changing. Across the country there is a sense, particularly among special educators, that the strategies they have used are no longer working; hence they are searching for new models, new syntheses, new partners, and new policies. These efforts must be nurtured, expanded, and carefully evaluated to continue the quest to claim children with emotional and behavioral disorders and their families, by improving services and options for them.

REFERENCES

Beachler, M. (1990). The Mental Health Services Program for Youth. *Journal of Mental Health Administration, 17,* 115–121.

Boyd, L.A. (1992). *Integrating systems of care for children and families: An overview of values, methods and characteristics of developing models with examples and recommendations.* Tampa: University of South Florida, Florida Mental Health Institute.

Brandenburg, N., Friedman, R., & Silver, S. (1990). The epidemiology of childhood psychiatric disorders: Prevalence from recent studies. *Journal of the American Academy of Child and Adolescent Psychiatry, 29,* 76–82.

Burchard, J., & Clarke, R. (1990). The role of individualized care in a service delivery system for children and adolescents with severely maladjusted behavior. *Journal of Mental Health Administration, 17,* 48–60.

Carter J., & Sugai, G. (1989). Survey of referral practices: Responses from state departments of education. *Exceptional Children, 55,* 298–302.

Center for Policy Options in Special Education. (1993). *Issues in the education of students with severe emotional and behavioral disorders* [mimeo]. Deliverable #22. College Park: University of Maryland.

Center for the Future of Children. (1992, Spring). School-linked services. In *The Future of Children* (pp. 4–144). (Available from the Lucille and David Packard Foundation)

Cole, R., & Poe, S. (1993). *Partnerships for care: Systems of care for children with serious emotional disturbances and their families.* Interim report of the Mental Health Services Program for Youth. Washington, DC: Washington Business Group on Health.

Conduct Problems Prevention Research Group. (1992). A developmental and clinical model for prevention of conduct disorder: The FAST Track Program. *Development and Psychopathology, 4,* 509–527.

EBD Task Force. (1992). *Emotional and behavioral disability technical assistance manual.* Lexington: Kentucky Department of Education.

Eber, L. (1993). *Project WRAP: Interagency systems change through a school-based model.* La Grange, IL: La Grange Area Department of Special Education.

Family Preservation Initiative. (n.d.). Introduction [mimeo]. Baltimore, MD: Author.

Forness, S., Kavale, K., & Lopez, M. (1993). Conduct disorders in school: Special education eligibility and co-morbidity. *Journal of Emotional and Behavioral Disorders, 1,* 101–108.

Forness, S., & Knitzer, S. (1992). A new proposed definition and terminology to replace "Serious Emotional Disturbance" in Individuals With Disabilities Act. *School Psychology Review, 21*(1), 12–20.

Ichinose, C., Kingdon, D., & Hernandez, M. (1994). *Developing community alternatives to group home placement for SED Special Education Students in the Ventura County system of care.* Ventura, CA: Ventura County Department of Mental Health.

Individuals with Disabilities Education Act of 1990 (IDEA), PL 101-476. (October 30, 1990). Title 20, U.S.C. 1400 et seq: *U.S. Statutes at Large, 104,* 1103–1151.

Jones, V. (1992). Integrating behavioral and insight-oriented treatment in school-based programs for seriously emotionally disturbed students. *Behavioral Disorders, 17,* 225–236.

Jordan, D., & Hernandez, H. (1990). The Ventura planning model: A proposal for mental health reform. *Journal of Mental Health Administration, 17,* 26–47.

Kamerman, S., & Kahn, A. (1992). *Integrating services integration: An overview of initiatives, issues and possibilities.* New York: Columbia University, National Center for Children in Poverty.

Kauffman, J.M., & Smucker, K. (1995). The legacies of placement: A brief history of placement options and issues with commentary on their evolution. In J.M. Kauffman, J.W. Lloyd, D.P. Hallahn, & T.A. Astuto (Eds.), *Issues in educational placement: Students with emotional and behavioral disorders* (pp. 21–44). Hillsdale, NJ: Lawrence Erlbaum Associates

Knitzer, J. (1982). *Unclaimed children: The failure of public responsibility to children and adolescents in need of mental health services.* Washington, DC: Children's Defense Fund.

Knitzer, J., Steinberg, Z., & Fleisch, B. (1990). *At the schoolhouse door: An examination of programs and policies for children with behavioral and emotional problems.* New York: Bank Street College of Education.

Knoll, M.B., Kamps, D., & Seaborn, C. (1993) Prereferral intervention for students with emotional or behavioral risks: Use of a behavioral consultant model. *Journal of Emotional and Behavioral Disorders, 1*,(4), 203–214.

Koyanagi, C., & Gaines, S. (1993). *All systems failure: An examination of the results of neglecting the needs of children with serious emotional disturbances.* Washington, DC: National Mental Health Association and The Federation of Families for Children's Mental Health.

Kutash, K., Rivera, V., Hall, K., & Friedman, R. (1993). *Public sector financing of community-based services for children with serious emotional disabilities and their families: Results of a national survey.* (Paper #828) Tampa: University of South Florida, Florida Mental Health Institute.

Lubrecht, J. (n.d.). *North Idaho rural system of care: Continuation grant application* [mimeo]. Boise, ID: Division of Family and Children's Services.

Moore, M.T., Strang, E., Schwartz, M., & Braddock, M. (1988). *Patterns in special education service delivery and cost.* Washington, DC: Decision Resource Corporation.

Nichols, P. (1991, May). Through the classroom door: What teachers and students need. *Mountain Plains Information Bulletin.* Des Moines, IA: Mountain Plains Regional Resource Center.

Paavola, J.C., Hannah, F.P., & Nichol, G.T. (1989). The Memphis city schools mental health center: A program description. *Professional School Psychology, 4*(1), 61–74.

Phillips, V., Nelson, C.M., & McLaughlin, J.R. (1993). Systems change and services for students with emotional/behavioral disabilities in Kentucky. *Journal of Emotional and Behavioral Disorders, 1,* 155–164.

SRI. (1991). *Youth with disabilities: How are they doing? The first comprehensive report for the longitudinal transition study of special education students.* Menlo Park, CA: SRI International.

Steinberg, Z., & Knitzer, J. (1992). Classrooms for emotionally and behaviorally disturbed students: Facing the challenge. *Behavioral Disorders, 17,* 145–156.

Stroul, B. (1993). *Systems of care for children with severe emotional disturbances: What are the results?* Washington, DC: Georgetown University Child Development Center, National Technical Assistance Center for Children's Mental Health.

Stroul, B., & Friedman, R. (1986). *A system of care for severely emotionally disturbed youth.* Washington, DC: Georgetown University Child Development Center, National Technical Assistance Center for Children's Mental Health.

Stroul, B., Lourie, I., Goldman, S., & Katz-Leavy, J. (1992). *Profiles of local systems of care for children and adolescents with severe emotional disturbances.* Washington, DC: Georgetown University Child Development Center, National Technical Assistance Center for Children's Mental Health.

U.S. Department of Education. (1991). *Fourteenth annual report to Congress on the implementation of IDEA.* Washington, DC: U.S. Department of Education, Office of Special Education.

Weinberg, L., & Weinberg, C. (1990). Seriously emotionally disturbed or socially maladjusted? A critique of interpretations. *Behavioral Disorders, 15,* 149–158.

CHAPTER 11

The Role of the Child Welfare System in Systems of Care

Michael Weber and Susan Yelton

The child welfare system in the United States, with its 100-year history, and the children's mental health system, with its shorter history, have become increasingly close partners, an astonishing accomplishment to the observers of some of the conflicts between the two systems in the 1970s and 1980s. Increasingly, stakeholders of the child welfare and the children's mental health systems are recognizing the mutual benefits of collaborative relationships, and increasingly their efforts are resulting in joint commitments to establishing and sustaining a single, collaborative system of care responsive to the needs of the children and families who are the responsibility of both systems.

This chapter examines today's child welfare system, its policies and programs, and the role it currently plays in today's society, and it explores the role the child welfare system might play in the system of care. The policy and program issues and challenges that would accompany the implementation of this desired role are identified and promising resolutions are proposed.

THE CHILD WELFARE SYSTEM OF TODAY

The child welfare system emerged toward the end of the last century with a role very similar to the role it plays today, the protection of children from parental abuse and neglect. The earliest child welfare system intervened when parents crossed the unclear but understood societal boundary between what is acceptable parenting and what is unacceptable cruelty or neglect of the child's needs. The "child savers" tended to focus on the behavior of the parents to determine the extent to which the child's safety was at risk, to judge the acceptability of the parents as parents, and to intervene through removal of the child from the parents' custody. Minimal attention was provided to changing the parenting capacity of the child's birth parents; rather, substitute parenting was found for the child through the establishment of foster care and orphanages.

During this century of development, the child welfare system has progressed from this origin and has made a transition through many stages. Early in this century, the field of social work developed as a profession with the assumptions that family behavior can change through social service intervention and that communities can develop as environments fostering desired citizen behavior. The inclusion of Aid to Families with Dependent Children in the Social Security Act of 1935 (PL 74-271) brought with it a view that the factors leading to poverty can be remedied through social work intervention. The earliest federal child welfare programs emerged from this policy environment in the form of programs to provide assistance to families, particularly to families in poverty, in changing their behavior and style of parenting.

The child welfare field flourished during the Johnson administration's Great Society days, with federal funds supporting the establishment of a wide variety of social services ranging from child care to parenting programs to teen pregnancy prevention initiatives. This new federal matching funding provided the stimulation for the commitment of public and private dollars to establish a plethora of new community-based nonprofit organizations offering a wide range of services to families in the social work tradition. Many of these organizations began as grass roots organizations, with program approaches supporting family involvement and voluntary participation in services and with governance structures very close to the community. The residential institutions established in the early part of the century continued, often converting from orphanages to residential treatment centers, and family foster homes were supplemented by group homes for adolescents not amenable to family-style living. However, these out-of-home substitutes for parental care were becoming a smaller percentage of the rapidly growing child welfare "pie."

The fiscal limitations imposed by the federal government in 1980 and the budget shortfalls experienced by many states and counties in 1980–1982 radically reversed these more recent trends in the child welfare system. Federal funds to match local and state expenditures were no longer unlimited and were increasingly attached to rigid "categories" of eligible services. There was a growing interest in accountability for the use of federal funds, and this accountability took the form of federal audits examining whether the federal funds were expended in accord with the increasingly prescriptive procedural requirements contained in the categorical funding statutes and regulations. State and local public funds also became increasingly scarce and were often limited to the minimum amount required to match the federal funds, furthering the extent to which funds were available for only specifically funded categories of services. Foundations, the United

Way, and other philanthropic groups were inundated with additional requests to sustain the programs losing public funding and, in an effort to demonstrate effective results through expenditure of their funds, adopted the federal and state trends toward narrowly restricting the programs for which allocated funds could be used.

The Adoption Assistance and Child Welfare Act of 1980 (PL 96-272) exerted a major impact on the child welfare system nationally in this time frame. The law originated from a concern about the unnecessary use of foster care, a concern heightened by research from the late 1970s demonstrating that many children in foster homes would not have to be there if sufficient support were provided to their parents in lieu of foster care or if more attention were paid to recruiting adoptive homes for children whose parental rights had been terminated. This law required public child welfare agencies to make "reasonable efforts" to avoid the use of foster care, to seek speedy "reunification" with birth parents if foster care was used, and to aggressively seek "permanency" opportunities for children whose parental rights were terminated. A number of specific procedural requirements were included in the legislation, such as the content of case plans and periodic administrative and judicial review of placements, reflecting an increasing federal skepticism about whether states would appropriately implement programs if given great discretion.

The cumulative impact of these trends was major devastation for the child welfare system during the last half of the 1980s. Funds were reduced, and remaining funds were closely tied to categorical programs. By 1989, Child Protective Services constituted the typical urban public child welfare program (Kamerman & Kahn, 1989). A large number of highly publicized children's deaths resulted in statutory prescription about how child protection investigations should be conducted, mandating an intrusive, accusatory response to all maltreatment reports received by child protection agencies. By 1990, the only three child welfare services available in each of the 50 states were child protection, foster care, and special needs adoptions (American Public Welfare Association, 1990). The additional federal funds envisioned in the passage of the Adoption Assistance and Child Welfare Act for prevention and early intervention services to reduce the reliance on foster care had not been realized. On the contrary, foster care was the only categorical service entitled to federal reimbursement, providing states with a perverse fiscal incentive assuring federal funding for only the most extreme form of intervention in families. Child advocates, seeking better services for children, filed class action lawsuits against half of the states, concentrating on the failure of states to comply with the protections of the Adoption Assistance and Child Welfare Act and on states' insufficient compliance with the undefined "reasonable efforts," "reunification," and "permanency" requirements.

A time of crisis for the child welfare system was beginning.

THE CHILD WELFARE SYSTEM AND THE
CHILDREN'S MENTAL HEALTH SYSTEM OF CARE

It was during this decade of narrowing for the child welfare system that the children's mental health system rapidly expanded as a result of Jane Knitzer's publication in 1982 of *Unclaimed Children* and the resulting 1984 federal grants for developing systems of care for children with serious emotional disturbances (Stroul & Friedman, 1986). The concept of a system of care represented a broadening of the traditional mental health services offered to children, which typically had been limited to outpatient services, inpatient hospitalization, and residential treatment. The system of care movement recognized the hazards of relying extensively on hospital and residential care and emphasized the necessity for a full array of services, including a range of intensive nonresidential treatment options as well as prevention and early intervention services. Since the early stages of the evolution of systems of care, family members have played an increasingly significant role in determining which services would be provided and in setting the style and philosophy of those services. Additionally, the system of care concept was predicated on the establishment of collaborative relationships with other services and systems, relationships particularly significant in view of the limited funding for systems of care within public mental health systems and the need to secure both public and private resources for system development. Because no legal authority was established in the children's mental health system (except in the rare instance of civil commitment), services could not be imposed involuntarily; on the contrary, mental health services for children were aggressively demanded by parents.

Not surprisingly, tensions emerged between the expanding children's mental health system and the contracting child welfare systems. Often the tension was between professionals within the two systems, perhaps because of a lack of understanding of the history, tradition, and authorizing legislation of each other's system. Often the tension was between the two conflicting systems and parents who were seeking services for their children but were being bounced back and forth between the two systems. The latter was often the case for parents of children with serious emotional disturbances who attempted to access services from multiple agencies without getting either an adequate diagnosis or services, who might be able to access residential care (not necessarily treatment) for their children in the child welfare system only by giving up legal custody (ordinarily temporarily) of their children, and who might be charged with neglect for failure to obtain needed services or with abuse as a result of parental behavior stemming from the child's untreated behavior. This intersystem tension is well described by the typical comment of the child welfare staff person who says of the children's mental health system, "they won't serve our kids, they want only children whose families are anxious for services and who can afford services." It is equally well described by the typical comment of the mental health professional who says of the child welfare system, "they intrude into families, don't understand the stress parents are under, and just take kids away."

In the mid-1980s, the national organizations representing each of these two systems—the National Association of Public Child Welfare Administrators (NAPCWA) and the State Mental Health Representatives for Children and Youth (SMHRCY)—recognized that this nationally observed tension was counterproductive both to the systems and to the families in the systems, focusing particularly but not exclusively on families of children with serious emotional disturbances. The leadership of the two organizations made a commitment to establish a national partnership to resolve national issues and to model a collaborative relationship for their counterparts at the state and local levels. There was explicit discussion of the need for also including the juvenile justice and the special education systems in this collaboration, but the greatest need and therefore the initial focus was on the two systems. Mutual representation on the executive committees was established, and the organizations held a joint national meeting to explore the differences between the systems. An introductory session entitled "A Tale of Two Systems" provided a bridge for the two sets of participants. The expectation of child protection investigators for cooperation encountered the mental health professionals' strong tradition of protecting client privacy. The mental health system's reliance on patient willingness to receive services faced statutory mandates for reporting abuse and neglect and for investigating all such reports. The mental health system's reliance on family members as allies in treatment encountered the child welfare experience with families in an adversarial relationship. The child welfare system's comparatively large budget faced the children's mental health system's ability to stop admitting new families when at capacity. The overall impact was something of a "eureka" experience—an informed recognition that what often appeared as hostile bureaucratic barriers were predictable and understandable outcomes of different histories and professional traditions.

A series of NAPCWA–SMHRCY committee efforts led to the joint publication of a monograph on child welfare–children's mental health collaboration (Miller & Yelton, 1991). This monograph emphasized the need for collaboration:

> The consensus is clear. Services for children and families are fragmented, uncoordinated, and unable to meet the multiple need of youth and families who are multiproblemed entering the public human services system.
>
> The consensus is clear. A coordinated human service system that meets the needs of troubled children and families can only be developed through a de-

liberate process of interagency collaboration—implemented with unswerving commitment from all levels of the service delivery system. . . .
What is not clear, however, is how to collaborate. (p. 3)

The balance of the monograph answered that introductory challenge, presenting the key components of intersystem collaboration and featuring state and local examples of such collaboration.

More recently, the same two national organizations, this time with family members as full partners, published a second monograph (NAPCWA, SMHRCY, and families, 1994) articulating the common basis for partnerships. This second monograph presents the core values, guiding principles, and core practices shared by the two systems, building on the children's mental health system's Child and Adolescent Service System Program (CASSP) system of care concept and philosophy (Stroul & Friedman, 1986). The monograph also identifies five program areas urgently requiring joint action by the two systems.

The collaborating efforts of these two national organizations have both influenced and reflected the growing recognition that both the child welfare and the children's mental health systems will benefit from joint involvement in a community-based system of care. Three major reasons for this joint involvement quickly emerge. First, the two systems have programmatic and statutory responsibility for many of the same children and their families, and these responsibilities would be better implemented jointly. For each system to maintain its own comprehensive service system would be duplicative; for each system to maintain unique and specialized but uncoordinated services would necessitate that families navigate two disjointed systems and implement two potentially contradictory service plans each designed to help resolve their needs. Moreover, the increasingly complex problems facing many of the families participating in both systems require a response of a complexity unlikely to be available in a single system.

A second reason for collaborative partnerships between the two systems is that children in each system are highly likely to need the services of the other system. For example, research indicates that children with disabilities are at increased risk of child abuse (Groce, 1988). For the children's mental health system (or the developmental disabilities system) to ignore this risk as the responsibility of another system is tantamount to knowingly submitting a child to unnecessary risk. Conversely, research also indicates (although less decisively) that abused and neglected children are at higher risk of future mental health and behavioral problems as a result of the trauma experienced (National Research Council, 1993). However, the typical response of child protection programs is limited to removing the child from the risk of further abuse without addressing the predictable mental health impact from the abuse already experienced.

A final reason for joint program efforts is the increasingly explicit expectations of consumers of services, of funding sources, and of the community at large. Numerous stories are heard of inhumanely and un-necessarily complex responses of bureaucratic systems to what should be cooperative and consumer-friendly systematic provision of care. In a society increasingly expecting and demanding accountability, efficiency, and effectiveness, the systems of care for families and children must respond or face diminishing consumer and public support.

The widespread recognition of these advantages of joint children's mental health–child welfare system involvement in a community-based system of care and the readiness of the child welfare system to be a contributing partner in a system of care are but two reflections of the major reform occurring in the public child welfare system.

THE CHILD WELFARE SYSTEM IN REFORM

By 1990, there was widespread recognition that the child welfare system emerging from the 1980s was badly in need of reform. The National Commission on Children concluded:

> We are deeply disturbed that a nation so captivated by youth is leaving so many of its young behind. Few subjects inspire more soaring rhetoric than children. Yet in their individual and collective actions, Americans fall short of their words . . . In the halls of government, public investments in strong families and healthy, whole children are grudging and piecemeal, guided by neither a common vision nor a sense of shared responsibility. (1991, p. 7)

Similarly, the U.S. Advisory Board on Child Abuse and Neglect observed of the child protection system, the primary component of the child welfare system, that "child abuse and neglect in the United States now represents a national emergency" (1990, p. 2). The National Commission on Child Welfare and Family Preservation, convened by the American Public Welfare Association (APWA) to develop recommendations on child welfare, commented on

> deep and widely shared concerns about the status of the family in contemporary society and the need to establish a strong family policy. Ours is a special perspective grounded in first-hand knowledge of the nation's failure to address the many diverse problems facing troubled families and their children. As public human service commissioners and child welfare administrators, we see the ways families can hurt rather than nurture their children; we are witnesses to the failure of a system that intends and seeks to help protect children from abuse and neglect and prepare families to care competently for their children. (National Commission on Child Welfare and Family Preservation, 1990, p. 1)

From 1990 to 1992, over 60 national commissions and study groups developed recommendations for major reform of the child welfare system, reflecting a consensus about the need for reform and about the direction such reform should take (Weber, 1992). In June 1991, the Children's Division of the American Humane Association convened a National Policy Leadership Institute to forge a common agenda for reform from the numerous independent commissions and study groups calling for reform (England, 1991). This Institute identified seven "underlying principles" that were common to most of the reform recommendations and acceptable to the 70 national, state, and local child welfare leaders participating. The final principle called for vigorous advocacy for "an agenda for change." The Institute participants also identified 11 "areas of commonality" that emerged in the national reform recommendations as the most frequently recommended priorities (American Humane Association, 1991). These priorities included

- Maintaining a comprehensive system of support assuring every family adequate housing, nutrition, health care, education, and economic security
- Creating a comprehensive array of services for all children and families
- Including prevention and early intervention services in addition to crisis responses in the service array
- Ensuring that services are culturally relevant, accessible, coordinated, community based, and outcome oriented
- Ensuring that services are responsive to the needs of families and appropriately tailored to each community

These themes became the common agenda for child welfare reform during the early 1990s.

This reform was launched most visibly by the enactment of the Family Preservation and Support Services Program (FPSSP) as part of the Omnibus Budget Reconciliation Act of 1993 (PL 103-66). This program included a major commitment to family support services, reflecting congressional interest in prevention efforts to complement the existing system's concentration on crisis response. The implementing regulations defined family support services as

> community-based services to promote the well-being of children and families designed to increase the strength and stability of families (including adoptive, foster, and extended families), to increase parents' confidence and competence in their parenting abilities, to afford children a stable and supportive family environment, and otherwise to enhance child development. (Federal Register, 1994, p. 50666).

The program also included a major commitment to family preservation services, reflecting congressional frustration that the intent of the Adoption Assistance and Child Welfare Act of 1980 to reduce the reliance on foster care and other out-of-home placements had not been realized. The implementing regulations defined family preservation services as "services for children and families designed to help families (including adoptive and extended families) at risk or in crisis" (Federal Register, 1994, p. 50666).

The Family Preservation and Support Services Program required state child welfare agencies to plan for the use of the $1 billion in new dollars committed by Congress over a 5-year period to accomplishing the purposes of the program. The legislation required that the planning be conducted by a diversely inclusive group representing the entire community; that the planning for the newly allocated child welfare funds (Title IV-B, Part II) be coordinated with the planning for other categorical federal child welfare funds (particularly the preexisting child welfare grants, Title IV-B, Part A) and funds available through the Child Abuse Prevention and Treatment Act of 1978 (PL 93-247), reauthorized as part of the Child Abuse, Domestic Violence, Adoption, and Family Services Act of 1992 (PL 102-295); and that there be expansions of family support and family preservation services. In addition to these requirements of the legislation and regulations, an opportunity was available for much more significant reform, a reform of the magnitude envisioned in the child welfare reform commissions, in the 1991 Leadership Institute, and in the congressional hearings on child welfare begun in 1988 and culminating in the passage of the Family Preservation and Support Services Act.

An Ad Hoc Family Preservation and Support Work Group of over 20 national child welfare organizations urged their members and colleagues to aggressively pursue this rare opportunity for a major reform of the child welfare system and formally recommended, in a letter to Joe Mottola, Acting Commissioner of the Administration for Children, Youth and Families of the U.S. Department of Health and Human Services (DHHS), that the implementing regulations for the FPSSP and the leadership opportunities for DHHS's Administration for Children, Youth and Families (ACYF) promote this major reform (Ad Hoc Work Group, personal communication, October 18, 1993). Although the program regulations could require only the components included in the authorizing legislation, the tone of the regulations and the exhortations of ACYF leadership urged states and communities to fully use the FPSSP implementation as an opportunity to launch major child welfare reform. The Ad Hoc Work Group developed a manual to assist states in designing major reform (Center for the Study of Social Policy and Children's Defense Fund, 1994) and convened a national meeting in November 1994 during which representatives from 44 states and territories and American Indian tribes were exhorted to jointly pursue the discretionary but real opportunity for major system reform.

Although there is no single written source of the elements that would constitute this major system reform, the following components are quite universally included in the reform discussions and in the activities of states most aggressively pursuing reform:

- The planning for the system (not yet referred to as a system of care) will be conducted by a diverse group representing the community and the group of families served.

- The planning will include all available public child welfare funds, and will be coordinated with planning for other children's systems funds (children's mental health, juvenile justice, special education, developmental disabilities and early childhood services, and public health).
- The emerging system will include a comprehensive array of services, such as some supports universally available for all families, prevention services for families at identifiable risk of problems in child rearing, early intervention services for families beginning to exhibit problems in child rearing, and crisis intervention services to stabilize families and protect children during times of imminent danger.
- The services offered will be family centered, culturally appropriate and delivered by culturally competent staff, and easily accessible to families.
- The system will be community based, reflecting the individualized needs and strengths of each community, with the community actively involved in the planning and governance of the system and in the delivery of services.
- The child welfare system's services will be integrated and coordinated with the services available through other systems serving families and children, and the collaborative delivery of services will be facilitated by intersystem case management and joint family service planning.
- The system will be accountable to funding sources, to consumers, and to the public, and accountability will be for results and outcomes rather than for compliance with process and procedures.
- The funding mechanism will enable available resources to be expended to meet the identified needs of families and communities, rather than restricted to narrow categorical programs to which families and children must adjust.

It is this reformed child welfare system that would be welcomed as an active partner in a community-based system of care for families and children, and not only in the system of care for families with children with serious emotional disturbances. This reformed system would bring numerous, significant contributions to any system of care, and participating as a collaborating partner in a system of care would be truly characteristic of the reformed child welfare system. This contrasts with the current child welfare system, which is seen (to a large extent appropriately) as unwilling or unable to share resources beyond its own system, as limited to involvement in crisis responses, as disrespectfully intrusive in family life, and as unwilling to invest in collaboration efforts with communities, other social service agencies, or other family and children's service systems.

A REFORMED CHILD WELFARE SYSTEM IN THE SYSTEM OF CARE
Child welfare systems nationally, statewide, and locally that reflect the above-mentioned characteristics of reform bring significant and probably

essential contributions to any system of care for families and children. For the system of care for families with children with serious emotional disturbances, these contributions include

- Access to an array of services often not available within the children's mental health system, including child care, respite care, parenting support, perinatal home visiting, and postadoption supports
- Access to major financial resources that can more effectively meet children's and families' needs through flexible funding strategies than can categorical funding restricted to the most expensive resources, such as residential treatment
- Access to federal entitlement revenue streams, such as Emergency Assistance (Title IV-A of the Social Security Act), often used for family preservation programs, and Foster Care (Title IV-E), often used for prevention programs and training, as is being launched in Colorado's child welfare–children's mental health initiative
- The readiness and authority to intervene decisively when parental abuse or neglect threatens a child's safety
- A vehicle for comprehensive planning incorporating all other major systems attempting to meet the needs of families and children, through the FPSSP
- Numerous cooperative programs, such as Virginia's therapeutic foster home initiative, in which the child welfare system recruits foster homes and the children's mental health system provides the training for foster parents to enable them to meet the needs of children with mental health issues
- A set of values compatible with and complementary to the most positive values of the children's mental health system, particularly the family-centered values of the system and the commitment to intervention at as early a stage as possible

The reformed child welfare system would bring these contributions to any system of care in which it participates, but it will also be necessary for the reformed child welfare system to develop its own system of care. For example, reform efforts in Child Protective Services (CPS) recognize as one of the major problems with this subsystem of the child welfare system the extent to which communities look to CPS agencies to solely implement society's responsibility for protecting children and the extent to which these agencies attempt to implement this impossible role unilaterally. To appropriately and comprehensively meet the needs of the abused and neglected children who are the responsibility of CPS agencies, those agencies will have to become collaborating partners in a community-based child protection system of care, just as children's mental health agencies meet the needs of children with serious emotional disturbances through a community-based system of care. A system of care for abused and neglected children would presumably have most of the characteristics of the system of care developed by the children's mental health system since the 1980s. The policy and pragmatic question, then, becomes whether the CPS–child welfare system should develop its own system of care for abused and neglected children, a system that would serve many of the same families, would operate in most of the same communities, would involve the same community agencies, would participate in the same planning process, and would look to the same funding sources as the children's mental health system does for its system of care, or whether the CPS–child welfare system can develop a system of care for abused and neglected children that is part of the same network as the children's mental health system of care.

The obvious answer for both efficiency and effectiveness, as well as for most appropriately meeting the needs of families and children involved in both systems, is that these two systems should be part of a larger network. The conceptual framework of a network of systems of care would readily allow for the development of systems of care for multiple sets of families and children, such as children with developmental delays or children committing delinquent acts, both of whom are often involved with either the child welfare or children's mental health systems or both.

NATIONAL, STATE, AND LOCAL POLICY ISSUES AND IMPLICATIONS FOR SYSTEMS OF CARE

A variety of policy issues and implications arise as the child welfare and children's mental health systems explore collaborating as partners in a community-based system of care or in a network of multiple systems of care. As federal policy shifts to provide states and local communities greater discretion in service delivery, and in view of the importance of systems of care being tailored to the needs and resources of each community, these issues must be addressed at the federal, state, and local levels.

Identifying Common Missions

An essential first step in mutual collaboration in a system of care is the articulation of the shared mission that provides the basis for collaboration. Because multiple systems do not have identical missions (this is why they are multiple systems), the common ground will not be coincident with either system's mission and might best be graphically displayed as intersecting circles. For example, the protection of children is traditionally associated with the CPS component of the child welfare system. Nevertheless, the children's mental health system has a clear—but often unexpressed—responsibility for protecting children. The children's mental health system's role in this protection is different from that of CPS; for example, it does not have the statutory responsibility to receive or investigate reports of abuse or neglect. However, the mission of the children's mental health system does include treating the mental health problems that present the increased risk of abuse, seeking the intervention and protection that some child clients will require, and providing the clinical treatment that many abused and neglected children need. Similarly, the child welfare system has the responsibility to assure the treatment as well as the protection of abused and neglected children and to provide for the mental health needs of foster children along with their need for a safe family environment. The articulation of these intersections of the missions of both systems lays a necessary foundation for collaboration.

Comprehensive, Multisystem Planning

The needs of families and children seldom occur in the neat, separate organizational boxes that represent the service delivery system, and no system can be designed so that the organizational structure directly meets the needs of the entire consumer population. Therefore, there must be provision for planning across the children's mental health, child welfare, juvenile justice, special education, and developmental disabilities systems to assure multisystem responsiveness to the needs of families and children through responsive, community-based systems of care. This planning must include the financial resources and program responsibilities of at least child welfare block grants and the Family Preservation and Support Services Program (Title IV-B of the Social Security Act), the Child Abuse Prevention and Treatment Act, the Social Services Block Grant (Title XX of the Social Security Act), and the federal mental health block grants available to states (ADAMHA Reorganization Act). The FPSSP presents the ideal opportunity for such planning if the state child welfare leadership pursues it and if consumers and the wider community expect it.

Prevention and Early Intervention

Both the children's mental health system and the child welfare system must explore how resources can be invested more strategically to prevent the occurrence of or the intensification of problems that are reasonably predictable. No one has a functional crystal ball, as is apparent the morning after a child dies as a result of parental abuse or after an adolescent explodes in violent behavior. Therefore, although empirical research has already identified some high-risk factors associated with abuse and neglect and with serious emotional disturbance, continued investment in research will enable systems of care to better direct their resources to high-need, high-opportunity children and families. Policy makers and program administrators at all levels must incorporate available empirical findings in the ongoing redesign of systems of care.

The child welfare system is currently wrestling with the issue of targeted prevention efforts in its reform initiatives. In response to an increasing reliance on foster care, family preservation services were developed to prevent the unnecessary removal of children from their homes. Although these services did prevent many foster placements, early initiatives emphasized keeping children with their families and did not constantly articulate the importance of attending to child safety. Therefore, the mistaken impression arose in some jurisdictions that family preservation meant keeping children with their parents irrespective of the safety of the children. In response, belated efforts to identify which families and children will benefit from family preservation services are underway, and the importance of pursuing child safety along with family preservation is being reemphasized. For example, in its 1995 report on fatal child abuse and neglect, the U.S. Advisory Board on Child Abuse and Neglect presented guidelines for the appropriate use of family preservation services until research efforts can develop more empirically based guidelines.

Although family preservation services were an early intervention compared with foster care, child welfare advocates were still concerned that access to these services was usually available only after a report of abuse or neglect, a CPS investigation, and a determination of the need for foster care unless another crisis intervention strategy was employed. In response, the next phase of child welfare reform emerging is child protection reform, such as that reflected in 1993 Florida and 1994 Missouri reform legislation. These child protection reform efforts call for communities to share the responsibility for protecting children, for aggressive community outreach efforts to provide support and services to families with the characteristics associated with the incidence of abuse and neglect, and for CPS agencies to have the capacity to systematically respond differentially to the widely different reports received by these agencies. The community efforts bring existing and new services, such as the Healthy Families America program offering home visiting after the birth of a child, to families at high risk of abuse or neglect. The changes within the CPS agencies move beyond the "one-size-fits-all" investigative response incorporated in most state child protection legislation, which is appropriate for only the most severe reports. This reform offers additional CPS agency responses more appropriate for the majority of reported families in which severe abuse or neglect has not yet occurred. These other responses ordinarily include at least the capability of diverting some families back to community agencies that can more appropriately meet the family's needs while still attending to the child's safety, and the capability of providing the family with services able to remove or ameliorate the impact of the factors associated with the incidence of abuse or neglect.

Fiscal Incentives

The existing perverse incentive providing unlimited federal funding for foster care but limited funding for prevention and early intervention services has already been discussed, but it is a prime example of fiscal incentives that must be corrected. Congressional action in 1995 proposed reducing the federal reliance on narrow categorical funding streams through the use of block grants, but this process was contaminated by the accompanying reduction in federal funds. At the national level, the level of funding appropriated must be separated from the issue of how appropriated funds will be channeled to states and communities. Then the policy parameters for channeling appropriated funds must foster the development of community-based, integrated, collaborative systems of care responsive to the needs and strengths of the children, families, and communities served. Because states are increasingly channeling federal and state funds to local communities for allocation, care must be taken to avoid replicating the federal experience of categorical funding streams with counterproductive incentives and to establish policy parameters that will predictably develop the systems of care intended.

Community Governance

The trend in both child welfare and children's mental health is toward community-based systems of care, but what constitutes a "community-based" system is an amorphous, ephemeral issue. Increasingly, communities are recognizing that a truly community-based system cannot be owned or governed from a state capital or exclusively by governmental bodies. The Annie E. Casey Foundation and Chicago Community Trust initiatives and the Minneapolis Neighborhood Redevelopment Program have committed major resources to exploring how communities can most effectively be involved in their own redevelopment. One necessary ingredient emerging from such experiences is that a broad-based, diverse representation of the community must be involved in governance structures. How to achieve representative, accountable, effective community governance with the continuity necessary for maintaining a system of care remains a challenging question.

PROGRAMMATIC ISSUES AND IMPLICATIONS FOR SYSTEMS OF CARE

In addition to the policy issues that challenge national, state, and local leadership, a variety of programmatic issues challenge communities establishing systems of care.

Providing a Balanced Array of Services

Many communities currently have a heavy concentration of available resources for crisis situations and a void in the prevention and early intervention arenas. Because there will never be sufficient staff, financial, or other resources to fully meet the demands in any single component of the system, and because communities will likely be dealing with reduced rather than increased resources, the focus must be on maintaining a balanced system of care. This process must begin with an assessment of children's, families', and community needs and strengths and with an inventory of how available resources are currently allocated. The opportunity and the tools for these efforts are available through the FPSSP. No recipe exists for the next step, that of reallocating resources to most appropriately respond to existing needs and strengths; however, the FPSSP's planning process provides the opportunity for communities to accomplish this reallocation. Conceptual programmatic frameworks such as the CASSP system of care model (Stroul & Friedman, 1986) and the array of services presented by the National Commission on Child Welfare and Family Preservation (1990) provide, as a context for the reallocation, an array ranging from supports for all families to prevention programs, to early intervention and treatment efforts, and finally to crisis responses.

Comprehensive Assessment, Service Planning, and Service Delivery

A system of care is premised on multiple agencies being able to bring together their resources and expertise to families and children in an integrated, coherent manner. Currently, in both the child welfare and the children's mental health systems, most agencies have their own protocol for taking family histories, for assessing family strengths and needs, for developing a responsive service plan, and for conveying this information to the professional staff involved in service delivery. Each protocol might be independently very functional but, for families involved in a system of care undergoing multiple intake and planning processes and in contact with more that one service provider, the repetition, complexity, and inconsistency are more than an irritant.

The operation of an effective, family-friendly system of care requires a level of collaboration among service providers that will enable the development of a single, comprehensive information-gathering and conveyance protocol enabling families to tell their stories only once. Traditionally, both the child welfare and the children's mental health system have raised confidentiality issues as prohibiting such a protocol. However, as is indicated by the San Francisco Youth Law Centers (Soler, Shotten, & Bell, 1993), actual legal barriers are minimal. As long as service consumers retain the authority to authorize the sharing of information and the choice to repeat the information multiple times rather than to authorize its conveyance, a system-wide protocol is feasible and legal. As computer and communication technology emerges, such a protocol can be incorporated into high-technology systems for extremely efficient service coordination, as the Macro International Corporation is demonstrating in a number of communities through its Community Services Workstation project.

Out-of-Home Placements of Children

Both the child welfare and children's mental health systems expend huge percentages of their financial resources on placing children outside their homes. Whereas historically the question asked was often "What type of placement facility will be most appropriate?" the question now is "Is it feasible to maintain this child in his or her family and home community while still meeting the child's treatment needs and attending to the child's safety?" This shift results from the budgetary crises precipitated by expensive placements, from the development of new service methodologies, and from renewed commitments to preserving families.

The resolution of this question is inherently connected to what constitutes a community's system of care. Since the 1980s, child welfare systems have been increasingly adding intensive family preservation services to their service continuum. Less uniformly, mental health systems have also been adding family preservation services. As individual communities plan for a balanced system of care, it will be critical that the two systems develop a joint strategy for making family preservation services available to children in either system and for assuring that intensive family preservation services are not the only available alternative to foster placement.

Providing Quality Services

Quality improvement has pervaded the corporate sector since the 1980s, and is increasingly moving into the human services sector. To maintain credibility within society and to assure effectiveness for participating families, the children's mental health and child welfare systems must make an equal commitment to quality. A major component of such a commitment will be the articulation of the standards by which the quality of services should be judged. The characteristics that have almost become a mantra within child welfare reform and children's mental health discussions—that services be community based, comprehensive, coordinated, collaborative, culturally competent, accessible, family centered, integrated, and outcome oriented—provide a good start. In addition to these value-based standards, quality services must also be empirically based, building on the scarce research findings available regarding service effectiveness. To accompany the adoption of expressed standards of quality, a system of care must also maintain a quality improvement process to continually increase the quality of its services and an ongoing self-assessment process that will enable the system to continually track the achievement of its intended outcomes and the compliance with its own standards of quality.

Involvement of and Support for Family Members

From its inception, the children's mental health system has made a major commitment to including family members in system planning and implementation, a commitment gaining new prominence in the child welfare system. Many children's mental health systems of care have also helped to stimulate the development of support groups for family members, often through chapters of the Federation of Families for Children's Mental Health. As the child welfare system increases its commitment to families, it will make sense for existing family support networks to broaden their purview to include this additional system rather than for communities to attempt to replicate existing networks.

CONCLUSIONS

Perhaps the establishment of a single common network for involving and supporting families will serve as the pervasive force bringing the children's mental health and child welfare systems together into a network of systems of care able to respond well to the children, families, and communities served. These are the clients whose needs must be met and whose strengths must be increased. These are the consumers whose satisfaction will be an increasing component of accountability mechanisms. These are the stakeholders who will increasingly be in decision-making roles. These are the stakeholders who do not have to attend to federal and state regulations and organizational structures, but who will experience the usefulness—or the nonproductiveness—of the systems of care.

As the children's mental health system recognizes the value of involving the child welfare system in the system of care, as the reforming child welfare system perceives itself as a collaborating partner in systems of care, and as child welfare reform initiatives increasingly depend on the establishment of community-based systems of care, a constant and consistent focus on the children and families in the systems of care will perhaps be the most important component of success.

REFERENCES

ADAMHA Reorganization Act, PL 102-321. (July 10, 1992). Title 42, U.S.C. 201 et seq: *U.S. Statutes at Large, 106,* 323.

Adoption Assistance and Child Welfare Act, PL 96-272. (June 17, 1980). Title 42, U.S.C. 67 et seq: *U.S. Statutes at Large, 94,* 500–535.

Alcohol, Drug Abuse, and Mental Health Administration Reorganization Act, PL 102-321. (July 10, 1992).

American Humane Association. (1991). Working toward an agenda for change: A summary. *Protecting Children, 8*(2), 21.

American Public Welfare Association. (1990). *Factbook on public child welfare services and staff.* Washington, DC: Author.

Center for the Study of Social Policy and Children's Defense Fund. (1994). *Making strategic use of the Family Preservation and Support Services Program* Washington, DC: Center for the Study of Social Policy.

Child Abuse Prevention and Treatment Act of 1978, PL 93-247. (January 31, 1974). Title 42, U.S.C. 5101 et seq: *U.S. Statutes at Large, 88,* 4–8.

Child Abuse, Domestic Violence, Adoption, and Family Services Act of 1992, PL 102-295. (May 28, 1992). Title 42, U.S.C. 5101 et seq: *U.S. Statutes at Large, 106,* 187–214.

England, P. (1991). National Policy Leadership Institute—summary of proceedings. *Protecting Children, 8*(2), 3–9.

Federal Register. (1994, October 4). *59*(191).

Groce, N.E. (1988). Special groups of children at risk of abuse: The disabled. In M. Straus (Ed.), *Abuse and victimization across the life span* (pp. 223–239). Baltimore: The Johns Hopkins University Press.

Kamerman, S., & Kahn, A. (1989). *Social services for children, youth, and families in the U.S.* Greenwich, CT: The Annie E. Casey Foundation.

Knitzer, J. (1982). *Unclaimed children: The failure of public responsibility to children and adolescents in need of mental health services.* Washington, DC: Children's Defense Fund.

Miller, J., & Yelton, S. (1991). *The child welfare/children's mental health partnership: A collaborative agenda for strengthening families.* Washington, DC: American Public Welfare Association.

National Association of Public Child Welfare Administrators, State Mental Health Representatives for Children and Youth, and Families. (1994). *A partnership for action.* Washington, DC: American Public Welfare Association.

National Commission on Child Welfare and Family Preservation. (1990). *A commitment to change.* Washington, DC: American Public Welfare Association.

National Commission on Children. (1991). *Beyond rhetoric: A new American agenda for children and families.* Washington, DC: National Commission on Children.

National Research Council. (1993). *Understanding child abuse and neglect.* Washington, DC: National Academy Press.

Omnibus Budget Reconciliation Act of 1993, PL 103-66. (August 10, 1993). Title 42, U.S.C. 629 et seq: *U.S. Statutes at Large, 107,* 649–658.

Social Security Act, PL 74-271. (August 14, 1935). Title 42, U.S.C. 301 et seq: *U.S. Statutes at Large, 15,* 687–1774.

Soler, M., Shotten, A., & Bell, J. (1993). *Glass walls: Confidentiality provisions and interagency collaboration.* San Francisco: San Francisco Youth Law Center.

Stroul, B., & Friedman, R. (1986). *A system of care for severely emotionally disturbed youth.* Washington, DC: Georgetown University Child Development Center, National Technical Assistance Center for Children's Mental Health.

U.S. Advisory Board on Child Abuse and Neglect. (1990). *Child abuse and neglect: Critical first steps in response to a national emergency.* Washington, DC: Author.

U.S. Advisory Board on Child Abuse and Neglect. (1995). *A nation's shame: Fatal child abuse and neglect in the United States.* Washington, DC: Author.

Weber, M. (1992). Collaboration does not mean consorting with the enemy. *Protecting Children, 9*(2), 3–9.

CHAPTER 12

The Robert Wood Johnson Foundation's Mental Health Services Program for Youth

Robert F. Cole

The Mental Health Services Program for Youth (MHSPY) is a $20.4 million initiative of the Robert Wood Johnson Foundation to provide services to children and adolescents with serious emotional, mental, and behavioral disorders through service delivery systems involving partnerships between states and communities and the collaboration of all the responsible categorical agencies—child welfare, mental health, substance abuse, education, public health, and juvenile justice. The program began in 1988, and 40 applications were received from the eligible states and territories. In 1989–1990, the program provided 1-year funding for 12 state and community partnerships to develop their applications for full implementation; eight sites—in California, Oregon, Wisconsin, Kentucky, Ohio, North Carolina, Pennsylvania, and Vermont—were funded for 4-year implementation for the period 1990–1994. The Delaware County site in Pennsylvania, even though it had provided the model for a major $10 million statewide initiative, withdrew from the second 2-year phase of implementation funding because of a change of leadership in the county government. The seven MHSPY sites are completing their 4-year implementation on uneven schedules and are in the process of positioning their delivery systems so that their achievements will become a permanent part of the community's evolving delivery system under health care reform and managed care.

The context for MHSPY was provided by the Child and Adolescent Service System Program (CASSP) initiated in the early 1980s by the National Institute of Mental Health (NIMH) and now administered by the Center for Mental Health Services. CASSP articulated a vision for a multiagency system of care for children's mental health and spurred a national movement that has influenced constructive programming initiatives in many communities throughout the country, including the MHSPY sites. The

experience and achievements of the MHSPY sites, and the lessons they have
learned, provide some practical guidelines for other communities attempting to develop systems of care.

The MHSPY sites have primarily provided individualized services to
a targeted group of children and their families. To do so, they have had to
grapple with a set of core issues, adapting solutions to the politics, context,
and needs of their state or region. The solutions implemented by the sites
are a study in variation. They deal both uniquely and unevenly with the
following core issues:

- The designation of an *authority and governance structure* that integrates
  the efforts of all the responsible categorical agencies
- The development of *organizational mechanisms* at the local level to marshal
  resources and to ensure that services are flexible, individualized, culturally sensitive, and delivered in normal environments
- The implementation of *rational financing policies* and administrative mechanisms to implement and monitor these service approaches

California's Family Mosaic Project in San Francisco moved quickly to integrate its efforts by building the case management function from a genuinely multiagency team. Wisconsin's Project FIND in Madison linked an
effective crisis intervention capacity with an intensive case management
unit. Vermont's statewide New Directions program and North Carolina's
Children's Initiative in the state's 11 westernmost counties built interdependent service networks capable of creating individualized services out of
sparse resources spread across thinly populated rural counties. The Partners
Project in Portland, Oregon, jumped ahead with an administrative and financing mechanism that streamlined the joint efforts of all the agencies on
behalf of the child and family. No single site has done everything, because
of the challenges each faced and their unique environments.

Because of the wide variations in public administration practice and
organizational and political realities, the specific approaches used by each
site differ and a strict model prescribing how to organize a system of care
could not be applied to each site. Nevertheless, the experience of the
MHSPY sites as a group yields much information about the types of structures, processes, and policies that support the development of effective systems of care. Thus, a composite picture of an entire group of MHSPY sites
provides useful information about the types of policy structures used to
develop systems of care, the organizational components of local service
delivery systems, and the types of financing mechanisms that support system development. This chapter explores the policy structures, organizational components, and financing models used by a MHSPY composite system
of care, with illustrations from the specific approaches used by individual

sites. The chapter concludes with a discussion of accountability, an essential feature of the MHSPY program.

POLICY STRUCTURES FOR A SYSTEM OF CARE

To a greater or lesser degree, the MHSPY sites have 1) integrated financing; 2) caused agencies to collaborate in service planning and implementation; and 3) delivered individualized, intensive care in home and community settings. These service delivery systems at the community level depend upon certain policy structures—at both the local operating agency level and in their central state bureaucracies. These necessary policy structures include the following:

1. An *interagency compact* among the state's central categorical bureaucracies that is consistent with a shared set of values and goals for serving children with serious behavioral and emotional disorders, and by which authorization is given to modify agency procedures and practices as appropriate to allow flexible service provision and to formulate a joint policy of single-stream funding. Vermont had established under its CASSP initiative a statewide interagency planning body defined in its children's mental health statute; North Carolina established a state-level interagency committee which has been active throughout, overseeing the effort in the Blue Ridge and Smoky Mountain area programs; Kentucky established a State Interagency Committee (SIAC) as part of its Cabinet for Human Resources to oversee its IMPACT program in the Bluegrass region—17 counties around Lexington and Frankfort.

2. A *local interagency consortium of operating categorical agencies*, each with its own broader mission and mandate, through which collaborative commitments of resources are made (e.g., pooled funding as in the Partners Project in Portland, Oregon, where two school districts, mental health, child welfare, and juvenile justice budgets were pooled), and operational cooperative arrangements are planned and implemented (e.g., the structure of integrated governance, the organization of unitary case management, as in San Francisco's Family Mosaic Project where the program was organized out of the Mayor's office and staffed by professionals from all the categorical agencies).

3. A *service delivery organization or system of care*, organized on a scale appropriate to a given community, that delivers, through a network of associated providers and voluntary community resources, integrated services for children with serious mental, emotional, and behavioral disturbances and their families. Of course, the MHSPY sites all have some form of service delivery organization, but these range from a nonprofit corporation organized as the management center of a network of

"preferred provider" community agencies (such as Children Come First in Madison, Wisconsin) to the more traditional interagency collaboration, as orchestrated in the Blue Ridge and Smoky Mountain areas of North Carolina through a web of 66 interagency agreements among all the categorical agencies in each of 11 mountainous counties and the sovereign nation of the Eastern Band of the Cherokees.

However the local delivery system is organized at the community level, it requires *formal agreements* among the responsible public agencies at the local and regional levels and the central bureaucracies. These agreements are commitments that financing, funding, policy, and service provision decisions will be made in response to the individualized child's and family's plan of care prepared by the child's clinical team. The system of care is a cross-agency initiative, and thus it can marshal a range of services that is eclectic, original, and unconstrained by the orientation or regulatory boundaries of a given agency—a service package responsive to the needs of the child and family. It is a mental health program only insofar as the children's needs stem from their mental and emotional disturbances and the mental health methods (diagnostic expertise and clinical quality assurance practices) are integral to the management of the system. In keeping with the goals of interagency support, the system of care should assume and emphasize a "decategorized" identity.

COMPONENTS OF THE LOCAL ORGANIZED SYSTEM OF CARE

At the community level, the MHSPY system of care has common elements that compose a functioning service delivery organization. These elements include 1) the steering committee representing the governance authority of the local consortium, 2) the agency base that houses the management function for the system, 3) a unitary case management function, 4) the clinical team, 5) the common plan created by the multiagency care team, and 6) the provider network. How these elements are configured in each site varies, but the term *local system of care* summarizes this basic pattern in the sites' organizations.

The Governance Authority: The Steering Committee of the Multiagency Consortium of Categorical Agencies

The steering committee is the governing authority of the local multiagency consortium and may be the consortium's executive committee or may be designated managers from each of the agencies in the consortium. For example, in Ohio's Connections program in Cleveland, "agency liaisons" are senior supervisors from the participating agencies supporting the Connections cross-agency efforts. They control referrals from their agencies and guarantee support from their agencies when needed. In Kentucky's Bluegrass IMPACT Program, local interagency coordinating committees fulfill this role and support the individual planning teams. And in Oregon, the Partners Project has an executive committee of the contributing agencies (public systems) and a finance committee that focuses on day-to-day operations.

The Agency Base: The Care Management Entity

The multiagency consortium must identify an agency base for the system of care to house, support, and manage the joint effort. This agency is sometimes referred to as a *care management entity* and provides the consistent clinical control and centralized decision making on which the responsible agencies rely to carry out effective care for a child and family.

Typically, the agency base designates a *management team* whose responsibilities include overall direction, the support of an administrative manager, supervision of care coordinators, and access to a group of consulting clinicians who guide the treatment of individual children and families independently from the concerns of each agency. The designated agency is responsible for clinical and professional liability for services provided by the system of care and, especially under capitation arrangements, financial liability.

The selection of an agency base allows for variation and might take the form of 1) a host public agency, such as a county social services agency or mental health authority like the Cuyahoga County Community Mental Health Board in Cleveland; 2) an established nonprofit agency such as a mental health center, a family and children's agency, or a special educational collaborative agency; or 3) a special purpose nonprofit agency with a public character—a "public benefit corporation" created by the consortium of local operating agencies specifically to do their common work for a shared target population.

In North Carolina's Blue Ridge and Smoky Mountain area mental health programs, two state-designated mental health centers built the system of care through a complex web of interagency agreements with county categorical agencies. Each serves as a Medicaid coordinated care entity to provide prepaid, capitated services under the new Carolina Alternatives initiative, which will carve out children's mental health services. Wisconsin's Children Come First, a freestanding, nonprofit corporation created by Project FIND, serves as Medicaid's coordinated care entity, receiving a prepaid capitated rate. This agency base provides care through a network of provider agencies and participating solo practitioners, functioning much as a preferred provider organization. In California, Family Mosaic has become a program unit within the San Francisco County/City Health Department and serves as Medicaid's coordinated care entity for the prepaid capitation program to children and their families in their target population.

Unitary Case Management: Care Coordinators

The multiagency consortium identifies a group of care coordinators to whom a target population of children with serious needs and their families are assigned and for whom the participating agencies share responsibility. These care coordinators take the lead role in fulfilling many of the case management functions, even though other agency professionals may need to keep open records on the children and families to meet their agency's requirements. Through the agency base, the multiagency care coordinators receive central clinical supervision and training and have direct access to independent clinical consultation. While it may be possible to spread some care coordination functions to different workers in different agencies, it appears to be critical, based on the experience of the MHSPY sites, that basic coordination functions are centralized—especially to meet the needs of the most challenging children and their families identified for the MHSPY target populations. The Wisconsin Children Come First program delegates the principal care coordination functions to the participating provider agencies, but does so while retaining final authorization of the plan of care and under the conditions of shared risk with its network providers.

The Multidisciplinary Clinical Team

The multidisciplinary clinical team includes the caregivers, clinical consultants, agency representatives, and—always—the child, his or her family, and their care coordinator. The care coordinator, in most instances, serves as the convener, organizer, and orchestrator of the clinical team. Often others may chair the meeting—in Kentucky's Bluegrass IMPACT program, the child welfare agency representative routinely chairs the team meetings—but the background preparation for the meeting and deliberate organization of follow-up activities are the responsibility of the care coordinator.

The clinical team can become the care coordinator's most effective tool for effecting care and treatment of the child and family. The primary purpose of the care team is to formulate informed, expert *judgments* on behalf of patients and to build a *working consensus for action*. The child and family should be appropriately involved in the team's deliberations and an integral part of its consensus building process for a plan of care.

The MHSPY sites have used the care team as a means to integrate the efforts and resources of all the responsible agencies. In Wisconsin's Children Come First program, the care team is organized by the participating preferred provider agency and is responsible for constructing a package of individualized services financed by decategorized dollars drawn from all the agencies, including residential treatment and inpatient funds, making it possible to achieve genuinely intensive care in home and community settings. Special education services are provided in a manner closely coordinated with the team's strategies. In North Carolina's Blue Ridge and Smoky Mountain areas, the care teams are formed in each rural county by bringing together county child welfare, court, and school representatives to organize coordinated activities and services by each agency under the consensus strategy.

The MHSPY sites also have tried to make the care team the locus of stability for treatment and support over time. There is relatively little turnover in the sites' caseloads, and the sites have tried to establish the care teams as a long-term resource for the child and family throughout the child's developmental years. It is reasonable to consider that a child for whom mental or emotional disturbance threatens to result in lifetime disability needs a stable, interdisciplinary team that is committed to staying with him or her throughout the developmental years (until ages 18–22). The care coordinator assembles a team, maintains its involvement with the child and family, records its deliberations in the clinical record, and informs the team of measured progress by monitoring the outcomes of the services the team prescribes. At points at which the child is stabilized and growing and the family feels confident, the team can appropriately withdraw its support. But for children whose needs are particularly great, the team should be available to be reconvened as a familiar panel of experts to support a child and family as they are confronted with new problems or challenges.

The Common Plan of Care: Central Clinical Record

The image of the multiagency care team that creates a common plan of care, integrating the efforts of all the categorical agencies, has become the theoretical center for "organized systems of care" created by the MHSPY sites. The common plan serves as a sine qua non condition of true integration of effort on behalf of the categorical agencies and is indispensable for the "full court press" that truly intensive care in the normal settings of home and community requires.

The common plan focuses all the functions of the system of care. It is the repository of diagnosis and assessment—not as a labeling procedure, but as an ongoing process of ever deepening insight into the nature of the child's disabilities. It is the "work room" for the clinical strategy where clearly articulated goals are crafted that lead coherently to specified treatment interventions and integrate the efforts and the purposes of all the responsible agencies. And it serves as the ledger of accountability, both by charting progress through predefined outcome measures of functional performance and by managing service expenditures through service authorizations derived from the clinical strategy.

It is not easy for the agencies to commit to a common plan of care, and several issues typically arise when a common plan of care is instituted. It is difficult to make the common plan coincident with the individualized education program (IEP) required for special education, since, in a major "catch-22," schools are financially liable for everything within the IEP and so cannot technically cooperate in a broader, multiagency effort for these children and their families. Court records and otherwise unreported illegal activity on the part of the child or family must be isolated from both clinical and treatment issues—even though resolution must obviously be coordinated with the common plan. The confidentiality requirements of each agency usually conflict in explicit ways, making it exceedingly difficult for agencies to work together on behalf of the child and family.

These problems remind one of the terse advice of the old Maine farmer to the traveler asking for directions that "you just can't get there from here!" If all the rules are followed exactly, it is not possible to effectively serve child and family. Nevertheless, if there is a commitment to serve, ways can be found. Acceptable procedures can be invented, releases sharing confidential records among responsible participating agencies can be drafted and executed, and separate parallel records can be kept as an accommodation to a particular agency's requirements.

Because of their early work together on the design of an automated, client-tracking clinical record—the CareTrack project—the MHSPY sites have developed nearly parallel formats for their clinical plans. In general, they follow the standard conventions for clinical records that meet medical quality assurance requirements. The Ohio Connections project started out with an effort to create a common form that would meet the needs of all the participating agencies. The forms have become the focus of the meetings of the care teams and their content is recorded in a database management system called PEPTrack, which provides aggregate reports and includes a systematic record of progress in treating presenting problems. Most of the MHSPY sites developed paper-based record systems that have served as the common plan. Kentucky and Vermont piloted the use of the automated CareTrack system, and California's Family Mosaic program is beginning to manage their capitation program by generating service authorizations and billing from the CareTrack Plan of Care. As the MHSPY sites have opened up new financing resources and streamlined administrative mechanisms, it has become apparent that the degree of flexibility in developing individualized services depends upon the degree of completeness in the documentation of the clinical record.

The Provider Network

Working from an individualized plan of care created by a multiagency care team under a centralized administrative entity that consolidates the resources and the missions of a consortium of the local categorical agencies, there remain the direct care providers, which need to be organized into a network that can effectively coordinate and consolidate service efforts. The experience of the MHSPY sites has been that, although provider agencies have had to make significant adjustments in their philosophy, organization, and administrative practices, they have gained in effectiveness through the exercise of the flexibility demanded by individualized care.

In the MHSPY sites, the network of provider services has been built around necessary capacities: the capacity for clinical assessment and consultation, some kind of crisis response capacity, and the basic supportive service capacity that can take a variety of forms. The role of senior clinicians in the regular workings of the care teams and consultation with care coordinators has developed in all of the MHSPY sites. Six of them developed affiliations with child and adolescent psychiatric residency programs. The Wisconsin crisis intervention service was enhanced in order to be able to meet the special needs of children and families in crisis; Vermont developed a crisis capacity that could work in sparsely populated rural areas; and, as North Carolina has introduced its prepaid children's mental health program making its area programs responsible for inpatient care, they have enhanced the programs' ability to respond immediately to crisis situations.

Kentucky developed early on a flexible response team in order to respond immediately to the needs of children and families for supportive services. This unit consisted of a group of experienced child care workers who were prepared to go into school, home, or community situations and help the child to manage and perform appropriately. In developing its network, Wisconsin's Children Come First program brought in a respected child placement agency, which ran a series of therapeutic foster homes and other in-home services. In order to meet the needs of minority youth and their families, the program asked an African American church to start a social services agency that could provide effective family support services in that community. The big change as the provider networks have developed has been the shift from the fee-for-service format for narrowly defined procedures to a whole package of interconnected services. A clinic that works in a fee-for-service format, or under a purchase of service contract format, must operate somewhat rigidly in order to survive financially. Under the authority of an authorized plan of care, especially in prepaid capitation formats, there is every incentive to tailor and modify services to meet the specific needs of the child and family.

RATIONAL FINANCING MODELS: MECHANISMS AND MANAGEMENT

Funding has always been in the background, shaping the problem of children's mental health care as it has grown into a national issue since the mid-1980s. There is too little money when it is most needed for early and effective intervention; there has been too much money badly spent on expensive and restrictive services when a child's troubles escalate to crises. Caring professionals often complain that children have to follow the money rather than the reverse.

No jurisdiction has articulated a financing policy for services to children with serious mental, emotional, and behavioral disturbances and their families. These children and families constitute a small portion (in terms of numbers) of the work of the child welfare, education, mental health, juvenile justice, substance abuse, and public health agencies; the missions of these agencies are directed toward the larger mainstream of disadvantaged children. Just as responsibility for the care of these children has been fragmented, so has financing policy. But this oversight is tragic. Even though the numbers of children are small, the numbers of dollars spent on them are enormous—spent primarily in response to crises, in irrational spending patterns, and with minimal interagency coordination.

Each MHSPY site needed to find new sources of revenue to meet its obligation to the Robert Wood Johnson Foundation that the new initiatives will be maintained after the grant funds are phased out. Creative means to finance the new services initiatives in the long run became necessary. And, as funding was pursued, the need to formulate new financing policies for these children and their families became clear. The MHSPY composite system of care provides some guides for a rational financing policy.

When considering financing policy, it is essential that the starting point be the vision of the system of care. If a financing policy focuses simply on generating new federal dollars or replacing state dollars with federal dollars, a significant opportunity to realize genuine savings will be lost. The focus must be on the system of care itself. Changes in financing policies can and should be used to enable an improvement of the delivery system, not simply to leverage more federal money into a state's general fund. With health care reform that may occur at federal or state levels or both in the future, the effectiveness of the service delivery system is even more important because the intergovernmental fiscal relationships for health care will change substantially.

Based on the experience of the MHSPY sites, an effective revision of a financing policy must try to preserve six values that are closely linked to the values of the system of care.

- *Sovereignty of the clinical strategy.* The needs of the child and family and the clinical strategy should drive financing. The plan of care serves as the authorizing document where clinical direction and financial control meet.
- *Ability to fund flexible services.* Once a serious effort is launched to serve this target population, it becomes obvious that a traditional set of ser-

vices alone cannot serve their needs. The system of care must command a broad range of services and be able to respond with timeliness and agility to sustain them in normal settings. Funding policy and funding mechanisms will serve as key factors in enabling that flexibility.

- *Simplicity of record keeping.* Another value is to eliminate duplication and parallel record-keeping systems (e.g., clinical records paralleled by financial records) and to create one common record and make it the operating document for all clinical and financial decision making. The common plan, of which the records are part, should integrate quality assurance and financial control functions. The outcome shifts the responsibility and accountability away from higher bureaucratic levels and to the provider/care management entity.

- *Full accountability.* One delivery system should be responsible for all services, from early intervention to intensive care. Mental health benefits have been both unreasonably limited and hopelessly fragmented. Indemnity plans (public and private), characterized by fee-for-service billing, artificially limit traditional outpatient and inpatient services; when the benefit is exhausted, there is a long gap before public sector programs are initiated for the most seriously ill. The system of care will have every incentive to extend their resources better, and more cost effectively, if it is responsible for the full range of care.

- *Single-stream financing.* The more simple and straightforward the administrative mechanisms that pay for services are, the easier the provision of services will be. Various forms of single-stream financing have been used, from fund transfers at the state level to pooling categorical funds to pay for prepaid capitation rates. Again, the process of achieving single-stream financing supports the integration of effort on the part of the responsible categorical agencies.

- *Reallocation of funds.* Making money that is currently locked into restrictive placements available to provide wraparound services for children in their homes and communities has immediate appeal. However, the process of displacement or diversion can be dauntingly complex. Reallocating funds must be driven by a clear financing policy initiative.

These values emerged as the MHSPY sites struggled with the issues of permanent financing streams for their new programs. Most of the sites started out with traditional funding mechanisms: purchase-of-service contracting for new capacity in programs that were designed to meet licensing requirements, meet rate-setting guidelines, and provide a prescribed number of "slots." The MHSPY experience led to experimentation with other financing approaches. Ohio and Oregon began with two variations of capitation funding. Cleveland's Connections program used a prepaid mechanism to expand Medicaid financing of respite services and clinical services offered in therapeutic foster homes in the geographical limits of the program without changing the state's Medicaid plan. This effectively expanded the potential for flexible services, although it was administered by the county mental health board with the same constraints as a fee-for-service billing system. In Oregon, a prepaid mechanism was employed with the full flexibility associated with risk-sharing capitation contracting, and five of the responsible categorical agencies pooled their resources in order to expand the Medicaid match base. San Francisco's Family Mosaic Project developed a prepaid rate that included responsibility for inpatient care and has elaborated care coordination by introducing a kind of team case management as well as delegation of care coordination functions to community partner agencies in their provider network. Wisconsin's Children Come First program developed along the same lines, targeting children at risk of out-of-county placement and using decategorized county funds to expand the Medicaid match base. As noted, the Wisconsin care management entity is a nonprofit, public benefit corporation that is related to its network of traditional provider agencies in a manner similar to a preferred provider organization (PPO), in that it provides administrative control and oversight delegating most clinical decision making to member providers. These capitation experiments opened new possibilities for establishing the preeminence of the clinical strategy, flexibility, accountability, and single-stream financing. Vermont achieved a form of single-stream financing by setting up a system whereby representatives of the various state agencies reviewed individual plans of care and arranged for joint funding of them through fund transfers at the state level. This arrangement is driven by the individualized needs of the child and family and also has been used to expand the Medicaid match base.

The most dramatic reallocation of resources has been achieved in the North Carolina site, which has inspired a statewide initiative called Carolina Alternatives. That state had used the "psych under 21" provision of Medicaid, whereby a hospitalized child can, after the family's private insurance runs out, be considered Medicaid eligible in order to pay for extended psychiatric hospitalization. This had become a $40 million problem, and, although the process was controlled by a utilization review company that assured timely and appropriate discharges, both providers and families were unhappy because youth were being discharged into homes and communities without supportive services. Under Carolina Alternatives, the $40 million projected to be used for inpatient care has begun to be distributed to the state's area mental health programs in the form of a prepaid capitation for all Medicaid-eligible children. This is a mental health carve-out requiring all Medicaid recipients to go to these area programs—care management entities—for mental health services and, as such, has required a waiver of Medicaid's requirement of freedom of choice of providers. The advantage to the area mental health programs is that they have the substantial hospitalization money up front, and, because they are responsible for paying for any hospitalizations that may be necessary, they have every incentive to intervene early and to provide the children and their families with the services and support that will make hospitalization unnecessary.

A strategic logic for financing policy emerges from MHSPY experiences in improving children's mental health service delivery. By changing financing policy to take advantage of all applicable funds, it is possible to integrate the efforts of the responsible agencies in a community so that they organize a delivery system that can respond directly and flexibly to the unique needs of a troubled child and his or her family. Simultaneously, the new system of care can be given the leeway to reallocate resources from restrictive forms of care to intensive care in home and community settings and to earlier and more effective interventions. There are, over time, savings that can be realized by the effectiveness and efficiency of this kind of care management. There are new resources that can be captured through full leveraging of federal entitlements. With these new resources, the system of care has incentive to extend its reach to provide early intervention and to avert crisis situations that lead to expensive, restrictive placements. Starting with a focus on the children with the most critical needs, resources can be shifted to individualized wraparound services that will shape resource allocation and the delivery system permanently.

ACCOUNTABILITY: THE IMPORTANCE OF COHERENCE IN THE SYSTEM OF CARE

One of the great assets brought to the MHSPY sites by the Robert Wood Johnson Foundation was the participation of the eminent child psychiatrist Albert Solnit, as a part of the program's evaluation team. Dr. Solnit led a team from the Yale Child Study Center on site visits to review the clinical content of a necessarily small sample of the service plans for children and families in care. This experience has been greatly appreciated by the sites, for whom these meetings were an occasion to have their work reviewed in depth and to receive confirmation and encouragement, as well as receive the benefit of the views of highly respected clinicians. At one point, Dr. Solnit was asked what in particular he was looking for when he reviewed a child's plan of care. "Coherence," he replied. "I want to see that it makes sense and holds together."

"Coherence" does sum up the achievements and lessons offered by this effort. It becomes the operative word in what the MHSPY sites have tried to achieve and in the agenda for future efforts. There is a fundamental "holding together" or "fitting together" that one should look for at the level of direct care:

• The *strategy* or package of services must fit with the *needs* of the child and family.
• The *actual delivery* of services must fit or reflect the *strategy* in the plan.

- The *expected outcomes* of services must fit the actually *measured outcomes.*
- The *renewal* of the plan of care must fit the *changing needs* of the child and family.

The coherence of need, plan, services, and outcomes at the direct care level is essentially a test of accountability. Are services undertaken for specific and appropriate reasons? Do they have the intended benefit for the children and their families? That same coherence must be reflected and supported at the administrative and policy levels if the system of care is to be accountable. The local interagency consortium needs to demonstrate its commitment to the coherence of the individualized services process in its resource allocation and program operations decisions and policies; the central bureaucracies of the categorical agencies similarly need to confirm this commitment in budget priorities, operational policies and regulations, financing policies, and administrative mechanisms under which the state agencies operate. The MHSPY sites have made some progress on these different fronts, and, probably more important, they have discovered the critical questions to ask if we are to achieve accountable systems of care for children with serious emotional, mental, and behavioral disturbances and their families.

REFERENCES

Burchard, J.D., & R.T. Clark. (1990). The role of individualized care in a service delivery system for children and adolescents with severely maladjusted behavior. *Journal of Mental Health Administration, 17,* 48–98.

Cole, R.F., & Knitzer, J. (1993). Children's mental health: Paradigms and precedents for managed competition. Unpublished working paper. Washington, DC: Washington Business Group on Health.

Cole, R.F., & Poe, S. (1993). *Partnerships for care: Systems of care for children with serious emotional disturbances and their families.* Washington, DC: Washington Business Group on Health.

Goldman, S.K. (1988). *Community-based services for children and adolescents who are severely emotionally disturbed: Vol. 2. Crisis services.* Washington, DC: Georgetown University Child Development Center, National Technical Assistance Center for Children's Mental Health.

Knitzer, J. (1982). *Unclaimed children: The failure of public responsibility to children and adolescents in need of mental health services.* Washington, DC: Children's Defense Fund.

Knitzer, J. (1993). Children's mental health policy: Challenging the future. *Journal of Emotional and Behavioral Disorders, 1*(1), 8–16.

Knitzer, J., Steinberg, Z., & Fleisch, B. (1990). *At the schoolhouse door: An examination of programs and policies for children with behavioral and emotional problems.* New York: Bank Street College of Education.

Stroul, B.A., & Friedman, R.M. (1986). *A system of care for children and youth with severe emotional disturbances.* Washington, DC: Georgetown University Child Development Center, National Technical Assistance Center for Children's Mental Health.

CHAPTER 13

The Annie E. Casey Foundation's Mental Health Initiative for Urban Children

Betty King and Judith Meyers

There is virtually universal agreement that service delivery systems in children's mental health have grown increasingly ineffective because of a variety of limitations:

- Services are untimely and reactive, with insufficient attention to prevention and early intervention.
- Services are fragmented and uncoordinated and fail to address the multiple and interrelated problems frequently experienced by disadvantaged children.
- Services are too institutional, office bound, and expensive.
- Services to minority children are culturally and linguistically incompetent.
- Services are indifferent to the family and neighborhood context in which they are provided.

There is also widespread agreement that adequately meeting the needs of disadvantaged children and their families requires services that are flexible, family focused, and comprehensive. The successful delivery of such services, in turn, requires a fundamental restructuring of the established systems to allow for the divesting of institutionalized authority, decision making, standard setting, and resources to communities and families.

Through its Mental Health Initiative for Urban Children, the Annie E. Casey Foundation is attempting to demonstrate the potential for such a reformed system of services in four of the poorest urban minority communities in the country. The initiative builds on the principles of the federal Child and Adolescent Service System Program (CASSP), the Ventura County, California, system of care, and the Robert Wood Johnson Foundation's Mental Health Services Program for Youth, as well as on the principles of reform and governance that guide all Casey Foundation efforts.

Given this broader system reform agenda, the Mental Health Initiative for Urban Children is a significant departure from other initiatives that are exclusively targeted to children with serious emotional disorders and their families. The characteristics of the selected neighborhoods are such that most of the children are at risk of poor outcomes and are therefore included in the target population.

THE CASEY INITIATIVE

The goal of the Mental Health Initiative for Urban Children is to improve outcomes for troubled children, adolescents, and their families through demonstrating new ways of delivering culturally appropriate, family-focused mental health services in high-poverty, inner-city neighborhoods and to work with states to improve policies and practices supporting these services. The initiative focuses on all children and families within selected neighborhoods. It is designed to address the needs of a broad range of families, including those with a child already receiving or in need of services from a public child-serving agency, as well as those with children who are considered to be at risk because of the conditions in their neighborhoods. Although recognizing that not all children living in poor, urban environments are at risk for developing serious mental health problems, the initiative is built upon the recognition that such environments have a high number of risk factors associated with negative outcomes for children and families, thus threatening the healthy development of a great number of children. The focus of the initiative is intended to be on the promotion and protection of the emotional well-being and behavioral health of children and their families, not just the prevention or treatment of mental illness.

Figure 13.1 depicts the model that serves as the basis for the initiative. As shown in the model, neighborhood-based control of service planning and delivery is the central mechanism for developing systemwide changes, with the neighborhood working in cooperation with the state and city. System change is to be achieved through three primary strategic interventions. State and local systems that serve children and families are 1) to be restructured to be neighborhood based, with more local control over the design, development, and implementation of services; 2) to be integrated across multiple systems; and 3) to focus a greater proportion of resources on pre-

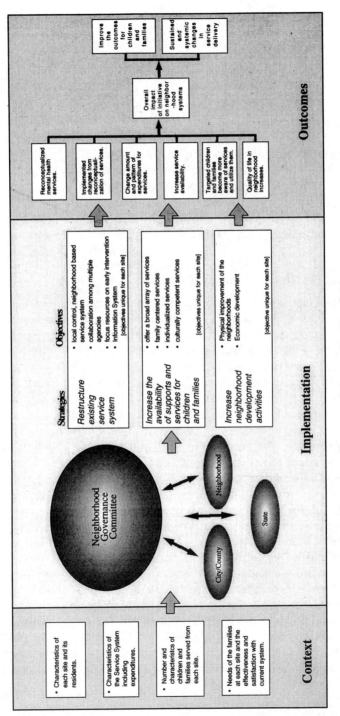

Figure 13.1. Logic model of the Annie E. Casey Foundation's Mental Health Initiative for Urban Children.

vention and early intervention to keep problems from becoming so severe that out-of-home care or out-of-community placements are the only alternatives. Supports and services for children are to be expanded to include a full array of services that are more family centered, flexible, and culturally competent. Mental health services are to be integrated into existing community settings and activities that offer greater access to needy children and families and offer these services in locations where they are less stigmatizing, such as in schools, community health centers, churches, and recreation centers. Neighborhood development activities, including physical improvement and economic development, are to be increased. In addition to the overarching strategies for all participating sites, each site will develop its own set of objectives, in response to local needs.

Although the focus of this initiative is initially on one neighborhood in each of the participating states, the intent is that state and local decision makers will reform policies and practices so that the work can be replicated in other neighborhoods and communities within each of the states. It is also anticipated that the states will ultimately serve as models for other states.

Target Population and Neighborhood-Scale Focus

The Casey Foundation seeks to create a multiagency system of care scaled to an urban neighborhood that will bring together community leaders and representatives to assess and meet the needs of troubled children and their families. The initiative is intended to reach children in those neighborhoods who are at high risk for developing serious emotional disturbances leading to such poor outcomes as a suicide or suicide attempt; school failure or dropping out of school; abuse of drugs, alcohol, or other substances; treatment in a hospital or residential center; or violent behavior. Although mental health, broadly defined, is the principal focus, it is clearly recognized that success depends on the participation and commitment of many service systems and other key groups within a local community and state, including health, education, child welfare, and juvenile justice agencies.

The neighborhood focus envisioned by the Casey Foundation is rooted in the conviction that interventions centered only on children do little to change the factors that give rise to, or increase the incidence of, mental health problems. By building on existing strengths in a neighborhood, and working toward neighborhood ownership and support of a community-based system of care, there is greater likelihood of sustained change over the long term—long after the Casey Foundation's role has ended. A neighborhood focus also provides the opportunity to target efforts on critical aspects of children's lives that are seldom addressed by large public service systems. Such critical factors that are central to preventing mental health problems among urban children include

- Opportunities to interact one-to-one with caring adults in informal learning and recreational settings

- Safe, clean facilities for informal and organized sports and recreation
- Protection from exposure to violent crimes and victimization by criminal elements in the community
- Formal and informal support systems that reinforce positive values and avoidance of risky behavior, and buffer the impact of negative peer pressure and stressful adult relationships
- Caring adults to advocate for youth and to train them in self-advocacy
- Opportunities for voluntary community service that develop leadership skills and teach young people to value community building
- Experiences and information that teach young people the value of work and economic enterprise

The initiative is designed to build on the strengths of residents and traditional community institutions, such as churches, social clubs, fraternal organizations, parent groups, and business associations, which are viewed as important neighborhood resources for support to children and families. The Casey Foundation looks to the neighborhood sites to create innovative, flexible, and integrated systems that provide the necessary interventions while reducing reliance on the formal service delivery systems. It is expected that the resulting service system will be responsive to the poverty, crime, violence, racism, family disruption, and other stressors that place children at risk for emotional disturbance. Services are expected to be responsive, accessible, convenient, comprehensive, and culturally appropriate. Services for children identified as having more serious mental health problems are to be family and community based, with a reduction in the need for more restrictive placement through hospitalization or incarceration evident over time.

SELECTED SITES

Six states originally were awarded $150,000 planning grants in July 1992. Based on the results of their planning, four of these states—Florida, Massachusetts, Texas, and Virginia—were awarded $3 million grants over a 4-year period to implement their plans. Each state selected a city and then, together, the city and state selected the neighborhoods for the demonstration. The selected neighborhoods are described below.

Florida

Miami's East Little Havana, with a population of 33,900, is a low-income, high-density, high-crime community covering the eastern 1.3 square miles of Little Havana. The poverty rate is twice the county average, with close to 50% of the children living in poverty. East Little Havana has been the point of entry for many Hispanic/Latino immigrants, in part because of its low income housing and Hispanic/Latino businesses. Named after its predominantly Cuban immigrant population of the 1960s and 1970s, the community is now home to families from many Spanish-speaking countries, including Cuba, Nicaragua, Honduras, Puerto Rico, and Guatemala. Many residents are transient because most seek to relocate to other communities as soon as they can afford to move. Few of the residents are property owners, with most renting from absentee landlords. Fear of crime is high, with the police department reporting 10 street or drug gangs operating in East Little Havana. The most serious challenges in the neighborhood stem from a large number of undocumented residents. Census reports do not count many undocumented persons, who often find themselves unwelcome, in hiding, and afraid to seek services. Conservative population estimates by city officials place the actual neighborhood population 16% higher than the census reports.

Within the neighborhood, an organization entitled Vecinos en Accion (VEA) has been created to involve community residents in the planning. VEA has already undertaken some short-term projects, such as reclaiming a local park for recreational use by children and families, organizing a series of volunteer recreational activities, and organizing a Juvenile Violence Forum for the neighborhood. Florida's plan for services includes a neighborhood service center, implementation of many of the model programs that exist in other parts of the state but not in East Little Havana, school-based services, and neighborhood-based early intervention programs.

Massachusetts

The area of Mission Hill, Highland Park, and Lower Roxbury in Boston, with a population of 30,200 was for many decades considered home to Boston's African American community. Changing demographics now reflect a multiethnic/multicultural community consisting of African Americans, Hispanics, and Cape Verdean, Haitian, and other African/Caribbean ethnic groups. According to the 1990 census, 55% of the population is African American, 20% is Hispanic, 20% is Caucasian, and 4% is Asian. Five public housing developments are located in this area, accounting for 21% of the public housing in Boston. Twenty-one percent of the area's residents live in these public developments. Forty-four percent of the children live in poverty.

The Casey Initiative is being operated in coordination with the Healthy Boston Initiative, headed by the Boston Department of Health and Hospitals, which seeks to develop and support neighborhood coalitions to address the economic, social, mental, and physical well-being of their communities. Their plan includes the establishment of a Family Resource Center staffed with Family Resource Teams, a commitment of flexible funds to support wraparound services from two state agencies, and a commitment from state agencies to fund community-based services for children in lieu of residential or institutional placements, using redirected funds.

Texas

The Third Ward of Houston is located 2.5 miles south of the central business district and has a population of 24,800. The neighborhood is 85% African American, 9% Caucasian, and 3% Hispanic. Seventy percent of the children live below the federal poverty level. The area has a number of community resources, including seven public schools, 50 churches, a university, health care facilities, four community centers, and a number of civic organizations.

The service delivery design proposed for the Third Ward is referred to as a "community-based, community-linked model," and includes a Family Resource Center, therapeutic school teams at a middle school and two elementary schools, and the reintegration of children placed out of the community using wraparound services.

Virginia

The East End of Richmond is one of nine city planning districts and is composed in part of three of the oldest and most historic districts in Richmond, dating back to 1609. The community has a population of about 27,700. Approximately 90% of the population is African American. Sixty percent of the children live below the poverty level. Four of the city's seven public housing developments are in the East End. There are many programs and services in the East End, but they reportedly serve only a small number of youth and there is very little collaboration among them.

Virginia proposes a number of new services in the East End, including preschool, after-school, and summer programs; parent support groups in each of the four housing developments and in five other locations; in-home, foster care, respite care, and therapeutic foster care with residents trained and hired as providers; case management and interagency coordination; and an interagency Youth Service Assessment Team.

COMPONENTS OF THE INITIATIVE

The Mental Health Initiative for Urban Children is based on the premise that every level of government needs to be involved. Although the focus is on the neighborhoods, policy makers in state and local governments are expected to examine and be ready to modify state laws, local ordinances, regulations, policies, and practices that impede the reform effort. At every level of this process, commitment to reform is essential to the successful completion of the following tasks:

- Integrating planning and programming across child-serving systems
- Restructuring financial practices and policies with necessary flexibility to provide for the development of a system of care at the neighborhood level
- Developing new ways of delivering services

- Developing the necessary information systems
- Involving families in a significant way
- Evaluating and tracking client and system outcomes

Integrating Planning and Programming across Systems

To carry out this work, state, local, and neighborhood coordinating or collaborative groups have been established in each state.

- *State interagency compact*: At the state level, the child-serving and financing agencies are working together to integrate programming efforts, reform funding practices, and restructure other policies and practices in order to support a system of care in the targeted neighborhood.
- *Local interagency consortium*: Government agencies at the city or county level are working together to rearrange their resources on a collaborative basis to support the creation of a system of care in the neighborhood. Similar to the responsibilities at the state level, key players at the local level are responsible for 1) aiding in the needs assessment, planning, and design of the service system in the neighborhood; 2) eliminating policy barriers across local agencies as needed; 3) eliminating funding barriers; 4) ensuring planning, coordination, and collaboration among local services; 5) facilitating the creation of joint databases; 6) providing technical assistance to the neighborhood governing board; 7) revising local procedures and practices as needed; and 8) ensuring the involvement of city officials and other key players.
- *Neighborhood governance structure*: Within the neighborhood, governance groups are being established to design and develop a set of services based on assessed needs and to provide administrative oversight and fiscal accountability for the new system of care.

As planning has evolved, several states have formed policy or executive planning committees with representation from the state, city, and neighborhood groups to oversee and coordinate the work of the initiative.

Restructuring Finances

A basic premise of the Casey Foundation's initiative is that existing public investments can be more effectively utilized. Currently, the greatest portion of public dollars is spent on the fewest children, to pay for institutional and residential treatment center placements for children with the most serious disturbances. The least amount is spent for prevention and family support services. The Casey Foundation envisions a markedly different pattern of resource allocation in an effective multiagency system of care, with a shift in spending from the most expensive placement to "front-end" services, such as early intervention programs. The effort to reform funding policies and practices is perceived by the Casey Foundation to be closely tied to the development of a plan for a local system of care. Fiscal reform is central to achieving long-term change in the structure and delivery of services at the neighborhood level and will pave the way for future replication in other areas within the state.

Close cooperation between the state, city, and neighborhood is necessary to achieve and sustain such reform. Based on an analysis of all sources of public and private investment spent in serving the neighborhood's children and families, and the barriers to creating an integrated service system, states will identify strategies for redirecting or more effectively using resources. Financing reforms may include 1) the decategorization of funding; 2) the development of community funding pools that include both public- and private-sector funds; 3) the development of flexible funding for wraparound services; 4) the maximization of federal, state, and third-party reimbursement mechanisms; 5) managed care/capitation mechanisms; and 6) reinvestment of funds from out-of-home placements to community services. Collaboration among state agencies and the legislature in refinancing services will be significant in determining how new dollars, particularly those received as the result of maximizing federal funding, will be reinvested to support the reform of child and family services.

It is anticipated that the restructuring of finances will result in more resources targeted to supporting community-based services, which will lead to a reduction of revenue outflow from the neighborhoods. Most of the money currently spent on children in poor urban areas tends to go to agencies and services located in other parts of the city or state and, therefore, is of no economic benefit to the neighborhood. By redirecting the dollars to community-based services, the money can be used to support jobs for neighborhood residents and benefit businesses in the community, thus helping to bolster the local economy.

Developing New Ways of Delivering Services

The traditional office-based or institutional approach to delivering mental health services to children is not effective in meeting the needs of children living in poor, urban neighborhoods. The Mental Health Initiative provides an opportunity for the development of neighborhood systems of care based on the system of care model promoted by CASSP, with a range of services that are flexible enough to tailor services to meet individual needs, are community based and family focused, and embrace the cultural values and practices of the communities. With residents and parents as active participants in the planning and design of services, the initiative provides an opportunity to learn what services will be most responsive to local needs. Furthermore, the sites have the opportunity to develop nontraditional approaches that use a range of helpers beyond existing service providers; that are provided in a range of sites, including the home, school, and family centers; and that are available during a range of hours throughout the day, evenings, weekends, and summers. It is anticipated that states and cities will also use the initiative as an opportunity to pilot some of their most innovative approaches, such as home-based family preservation services to prevent out-of-home placement, therapeutic foster care in the community to prevent institutional placement, school-based mental health services, outreach and education, universal screening at an early age, parent skill training through home visiting, and youth development and recreational activities.

Developing Information Systems

To develop better interventions and more responsive policies, communities need reliable information about trends in indicators relevant to the well-being of the children and families in the community. A fundamental principle of the Mental Health Initiative is that an integrated data management system is essential to a well-designed and well-functioning service system. Such a system should have the capacity to combine information about children and families across service systems, to be accessed by the various service systems so that families do not have to be subjected to multiple intakes and assessments, and to track the services received by children and families over time. Only with a managed data system will communities succeed in accurately defining their problems, establishing meaningful and measurable goals, and gaining the feedback needed to modify and strengthen their interventions. Each state is expected to design and develop a management information system that will support a family-focused, community-based model of services.

Involving Families

The Casey Foundation places a high value on the involvement of family members in all aspects of this initiative, from the initial planning to the design of service systems and the evaluation. As a part of the initiative, the Casey Foundation has supported the enhancement of national and state family advocacy organizations, with specific emphasis on the increased participation of minority and disadvantaged families.

Specifically, the Casey Foundation has awarded a grant to the Federation of Families for Children's Mental Health to provide technical assistance to states and communities to develop family support networks in the demonstration communities. The Federation of Families is a national, parent-run organization dedicated to improving research, training, services, and policies that pertain to children with emotional, behavioral, and mental disorders, and to support their families. The Federation of Families is working with the states and communities so that they can 1) assist families to become aware of the concept of family-centered services and approaches, 2) enable families to advocate for family-centered services and approaches, 3) enhance the ability of families to provide ongoing support for each other through local support groups, 4) provide information to families to improve their abilities to obtain resources, and 5) enable families to identify their strengths and decide what support and services will enhance those strengths.

Evaluating the Initiative

A comprehensive, independent evaluation conducted by the Florida Mental Health Institute of the University of South Florida in collaboration with the Casey Foundation, and with input and participation from each of the sites, will quantitatively and qualitatively describe the initiative and measure outcomes. The primary focus for the implementation evaluation will be on the specific strategies selected at the sites to achieve their goals, the rationale for the selection of these strategies, and the manner in which these strategies are employed. The role of the neighborhood governance structures will also be closely examined. As noted in Figure 13.1, the evaluation will focus on a series of questions about changes in how mental health services are conceptualized; how services are organized, financed, and delivered; the pattern of expenditures; the availability of services and the pattern of their use by children and families; and the quality of life in the neighborhood. Ultimately these changes are intended to lead to improved outcomes for children and families living in the project sites and to sustained changes in the service delivery system in the state, city, and neighborhood.

LESSONS LEARNED

Although this multiyear initiative is still in its early stages, some lessons have been learned from the planning period.

The Stigma of Mental Health

In the conceptual stage of this initiative, the Casey Foundation was advised against targeting a mental health initiative for poor urban America for two basic reasons: 1) the difficulty of developing a mental health service system in areas where people are preoccupied with problems of daily living, and 2) the stigma associated with mental health services in the predominantly minority populations who live in these cities. Because the initiative defines mental health as a positive human and group condition to be promoted and protected, the Casey Foundation has basically ignored the first issue and has planned to address the second through education and the development of culturally competent services.

It is interesting to note how much easier it has been for our communities to use the word "Casey" than the "MH" word. In early discussions about services, community residents clearly preferred talking about the need for employment and training services, even neighborhood landscaping, rather than mental health. After a year, an enlightened mayor still referred to the initiative as the "Casey project on poverty." In addition to education efforts, it will be a continuing challenge to blend mental health services into the spectrum of other "acceptable" human services.

Governance Structures

Although it was relatively simple to develop interagency compacts at state and city levels and to create governing bodies at the neighborhood level, it has been more difficult to develop appropriate structures to integrate work at these three levels and to share authority and responsibility. The states initially pursued the line of least resistance (and change) by viewing this as a neighborhood project and interpreting their role as a "pass through" for the Casey Foundation's resources to the sites. The neighborhood residents, having had decades of bad experiences with those who govern them, were basically distrustful of any state and city involvement and wanted *all* the money passed on to them. It mattered little that the funds from the Casey Foundation were both temporary and insignificant compared to government resources. Despite institutionalized structures, roles, and attitudes that are inflexible and difficult to change, the Casey Foundation remains hopeful that the notion of pushing the system from both ends—top and bottom—will have some impact. The enormity of the task is underscored by the fact that, in most communities, the mere presence at the same table of the people who design, deliver, and pay for services, as well as the people who utilize the services, is regarded as significant progress.

Concept of Neighborhood

In asking states and cities to select neighborhood sites of approximately 6,000 children, the Casey Foundation was concerned not only about ensuring a large enough population base for a system of care but also about ensuring a community size that is small enough to be manageable. In several states, however, neighborhoods actually had much smaller populations. As a result, three or four traditional communities were merged to create unnatural alliances and much conflict—conflict that was further exacerbated when the alliances comprised multiethnic groups. Although experts in the field of community development note that community organization, by its very nature, is complicated, the work of this initiative progressed more quickly in the states where the neighborhoods were more "naturally occurring" communities, rather than several smaller communities that were blended together to create the required critical mass.

System Reform

The Casey Foundation predicted from the start that the most difficult challenge was likely to be the reform of the system itself. Difficulties were anticipated in efforts to extract the resources—both human and financial—from the current system and redeploy them in a reformed system. As a result, neighborhood governance was considered to be a significant part of the innovation of this initiative. The creation of viable neighborhood organizations that have both the capacity and the credibility to develop and deliver services is considered a prerequisite for the genuine movement of authority and decision making from centralized state and city bureaucracies to neighborhood-level communities. Bureaucrats, in turn, must understand that such a devolution fundamentally restructures, but does not make obsolete, their own jobs.

Although the complexity of these changes was understood, the extent of the difficulty was underestimated. Additional training and consultation has been arranged to work closely with the four states to assist them in plans to build improved systems that not only enhance services within the neighborhood sites but also link service enhancement to reform of the existing service delivery systems, including redirection of resources; centralized and integrated management information systems; centralized assessment and referral systems; and redefinition of the functions of frontline workers who can identify a range of needs within a family, respond in ways that are comprehensive as well as tailored to individual circumstances, and adjust services as a family's needs change.

On the positive side, the Casey Foundation is encouraged by the increasing numbers of people who speak a common language and who understand and believe in the concepts of family-centered, comprehensive, culturally competent, community-based, and decategorized services. The success of the initiative will, in large measure, be attributable to the coincidence of its agenda and the agendas of the states that are participating. For, in the final analysis, the Casey Foundation's presence simply provides the reinforcement, the opportunity, and the encouragement for states to pursue an agenda to which they are already committed. Why else would states with billions of dollars of resources pay attention to people bearing $3 million gifts?

MANAGEMENT ISSUES FOR SYSTEMS OF CARE

Service Coordination in Systems of Care

Beth A. Stroul

The notion of "coordination" is intrinsic to the system of care concept based on the recognition that children with emotional disturbances and their families have multiple needs that cut across agency and system boundaries. One of the system of care principles calls for "linkages between child-caring agencies and programs and mechanisms for planning, developing, and coordinating services" (Stroul & Friedman, 1986). This principle refers to the need for structures and mechanisms to ensure coordination at the *system level*. In order to best meet the needs of children and families, integrated, multiagency networks are needed to blend the services provided by mental health, education, child welfare, health, juvenile justice, substance abuse, and other agencies. These components must be interwoven into a coherent system with provisions for joint planning, service development, problem solving, funding, and evaluation of services. Communities have designed various types of interagency entities to accomplish these system-level coordination functions (Stroul, Lourie, Goldman, & Katz-Leavy, 1992).

Another level of coordination is reflected in the principle calling for case management in systems of care. Case management focuses on *client-level coordination* and is intended to ensure that children and families receive the services they need, that services are coordinated, and that services are appropriate to their changing needs over time. The importance of case management in a system of care is evidenced by the way it has been described in the literature. Case management has been characterized as the "backbone of the system of care," the "glue that holds the system together," and essential to the success of the service system (Stroul & Friedman, 1986). Case management also has been portrayed as "perhaps the most essential unifying factor in service delivery" (Behar, 1985) and as the "key to systemic success" in a complex system of services (Behar, 1991).

Lourie and Katz-Leavy (1986) asserted that it is nearly impossible to assure adequate services for an individual youngster without a primary service person responsible for coordination of the treatment plan and service delivery. Case management appears to play an especially critical role in individualized service approaches in which the case manager is responsible for facilitating the planning and implementation of an individualized plan of care, including wraparound services, for each youngster and family (Katz-Leavy, Lourie, Stroul, & Zeigler-Dendy, 1992). Thus, in all systems of care, some form of case management or care coordination plays a critical role in planning, orchestrating, monitoring, coordinating, and adjusting services.

TERMINOLOGY AND DEFINITION

A review of the literature is likely to leave the reader confused by the endless variety of terms used to describe the set of functions typically associated with case management. Terms such as "care coordination," "service coordination," "therapeutic case management," "clinical case management," and "therapeutic case advocacy" abound, and few clear and consistent distinctions have been drawn to clarify their use. Many of these terms often are used interchangeably. It has been suggested that the term "case management" is gradually being replaced by other terms, most notably "service coordination" (Doel, 1991). This shift may be associated with the negative, depersonalizing connotation sometimes attached to the term "case management." Preference for the term "service coordination" was expressed by Illback and Neil (1995) based on two biases—that individuals do not like to be referred to as cases to be managed and that case management cannot occur outside of the context of a service system.

In addition to the diversity of terms, confusion is created by the plethora of implicit and explicit definitions of case management that can be found in the literature and in the field. In fact, the disparate definitions of case management led Schwartz, Goldman, and Churgin (1982) to suggest that the concept represents a Rorschach test on which is projected any image one wishes. Despite the multiplicity of both terms and associated definitions, there appears to be growing consensus as to the basic definition and purposes of case management.

In its broadest sense, case management refers to a set of functions designed to mobilize resources to meet client needs (Doel, 1991). Rubin (1992) defines case management as an approach that attempts to ensure that individuals receive all of the services they need in a timely, appropriate, and coordinated fashion; Solomon (1992) similarly states that case management is a coordinated strategy on behalf of clients to obtain the services that they need, when they need them, and for as long as they need them. A definition used by Weil and Karls (1985) portrays case management as a set of logical steps and a process of interaction within a service network that assure that a client receives an array of services in a supportive, effective, efficient, and cost-effective manner. These and other commonly used definitions are based upon the premise that case management is a "boundary-spanning approach" through which case managers link clients to the multiple providers, agencies, services, and resources and are responsible for ensuring that the service delivery system is responsive to clients' needs (Rubin, 1992). Most definitions share two major features, specifying that case management is 1) *a set of functions* and 2) intended to *mobilize, coordinate, and maintain an array of services and resources* in order to meet the needs of individuals over time.

HISTORICAL PERSPECTIVE

The origins of case management have been traced to the 1960s, a period of extraordinarily rapid growth of a wide range of human services programs (Rose, 1992). Many specialized programs began to emerge during this time, often serving a narrowly defined target population or responding to a narrowly defined problem. In time, the resulting network of services was increasingly perceived as highly complex, fragmented, duplicative, and uncoordinated (Intagliata, 1982; Rubin, 1987). Particularly for individuals with multiple and complex needs and disabilities, the challenges inherent in navigating the maze of agencies, providers, and services became overwhelming. By the early 1970s, case management approaches began to emerge in order to assist clients to access and coordinate services and to assist them in "managing" their involvement with the service delivery system (Rose, 1992). The role of case managers as "systems agents" or brokers of services received increasing attention and was increasingly seen as a critical aspect of service systems, leading to a large number of federally funded demonstration projects experimenting with various approaches (Raiff & Shore, 1993). These approaches generally involved holding one worker accountable for the overall care of a client and for the responsiveness of the entire service delivery system. This designation of a case manager as a strategy for overcoming the neglect and fragmentation of the service system was characterized by Rubin (1987) as an "attempt to ensure that there is somebody who is accountable and who is helping the client hold the service delivery system accountable, someone who cannot pass the buck to another agency or individual when and if services are not delivered quickly and appropriately" (p. 212).

The use of case management rapidly spread, with such techniques applied to a range of populations, including individuals who are elderly, have developmental disabilities or chronic health conditions, or are involved with the child welfare system. In the field of mental health, the deinstitutionalization movement contributed to the growth of case management.

When the primary locus of care was moved from institutions to the community, individuals with serious and persistent mental illnesses needed a wide range of services and supports that often were unavailable, inaccessible, or restricted by complex and confusing eligibility requirements, policies, or procedures. It became increasingly apparent that these individuals were not receiving the services and supports they needed and that they often were unable to negotiate complex and unresponsive service delivery systems (General Accounting Office, 1977; Rose, 1992). Case management has evolved in the mental health arena in response to these systemic problems and has been conceptualized as an essential component of a comprehensive community support system for adults with serious and persistent mental illnesses (Chamberlain & Rapp, 1991; Stroul, 1989). Whereas case management became firmly established in adult mental health services, little attention was given to the need for case management for children and adolescents with emotional disturbances until the 1980s. As the system of care concept and philosophy were defined (Stroul & Friedman, 1986) and experimentation with the development of such systems proceeded, the role and importance of case management for children and their families gained prominence.

The federal government has played a crucial role in the growth of case management through federally funded demonstrations and legislative mandates for case management services for a variety of target populations. In mental health, the critical role of case management in service delivery systems has been recognized in several recent federal laws. The Omnibus Health Act of 1986 (PL 99-660; amended by the ADAMHA Reorganization Act of 1992 [PL 102-321]) requires states to create plans to develop and deliver community-based services for individuals (both adults and children) with serious mental illnesses. The legislation mandates the provision of case management services to individuals receiving substantial amounts of publicly funded services. The Education of the Handicapped Act Amendments of 1986 (PL 99-457) is intended to improve services (including mental health services) for infants and toddlers with special needs and their families. Individualized family service plans are required, along with case managers who are responsible for implementation of the plan and service coordination.

Public Law 102-321 authorized the new Child Mental Health Services Initiative, which is being implemented by the Center for Mental Health Services. The program provides grants to develop a broad array of community-based services for children with serious emotional disorders as part of coordinated local systems of care. The legislation identifies case management as a critical function and requires case management services for all youngsters offered access to the system of care. Furthermore, Medicaid waivers and provisions for targeted case management have enabled states to use Medicaid as a source of financing for case management services for individuals with mental illnesses.

In this context, case management has proliferated with great diversity in emphasis, approach, philosophy, intensity, and more. Recent applications of case management have emphasized its potential role in system management and cost containment. Raiff and Shore (1993) discuss "the new case management" in which case managers have great authority to "drive the service package" and are viewed as powerful forces for system change. Similarly, case management is increasingly seen as a tool for cost containment in mental health service delivery, with case managers responsible for ensuring cost-effective services and for minimizing the current rampant overutilization and inappropriate utilization of the most expensive treatment environments. These variations, which add a "system-focused" dimension to case management along with the more traditional "client-focused" stance, contribute to the intriguing varieties and blends of case management approaches that are evolving in the 1990s.

CASE MANAGEMENT FUNCTIONS

The functions associated with case management have roots in such fields as social work and public health nursing. In fact, there has been considerable debate as to whether case management functions represent something new or are simply rediscovered interventions that are part of the longstanding history of the profession of social work (Raiff & Shore, 1993; Rose, 1992). Despite this discussion, there appears to be considerable consensus that case management is composed of a core set of functions that include assessment, service planning, service implementation, service coordination, monitoring, and advocacy.

- *Assessment*: The assessment function involves determining the comprehensive needs of children and their families as well as current and potential strengths that can be built on through the helping process. Assessment often involves convening and facilitating a multidisciplinary or multiagency team (which includes the parents and, often, the youngsters) to complete a broad-based, ecological assessment of strengths and needs.
- *Service planning*: The planning function involves coordinating the development of an individualized service plan to address identified needs. This process is accomplished in close partnership with the child and family, and case managers are responsible for assisting families to become involved in the service planning process. The development of the service plan or plan of care also is often accomplished within the context of a multiagency team for which the case manager typically is the facilitator.

- *Service implementation*: The service implementation function involves ensuring that the individualized service plan is executed as intended in a timely and appropriate manner. Implementing the service plan entails referring and linking the child and family to appropriate agencies and providers as well as arranging for, procuring, and brokering needed services and resources. Service implementation extends beyond accessing formal services to include informal and nontraditional supports. In some instances, case managers become "resource developers" who must creatively locate or design the services and supports needed by a child and family. On many occasions, this function also involves troubleshooting in order to overcome obstacles to the utilization of services and resources.
- *Service coordination*: The coordination function involves linking the various agencies, systems, and individuals who may be involved with the care of the youngster, including the family, school, mental health providers, child welfare or juvenile justice workers, health care providers, and any other involved individuals or programs. For older adolescents, establishing linkages with the adult service system in order to facilitate transition becomes a critical aspect of this activity. Effective service coordination requires ongoing contact with the child and family and with other providers to ensure that services are implemented in a logical manner and that multiple services and interventions are consistent and directed at the same goals. The case manager often serves as the hub of all service-related interaction among involved providers.
- *Monitoring and evaluation*: The monitoring and evaluation function involves monitoring the adequacy and appropriateness of services over time. Monitoring is directed toward ensuring the continuity of service provision as well as the continuing appropriateness of the services being delivered in view of changes in the youngster's functioning at home, in school, and in the community. Continuous evaluation of the effectiveness of services and progress toward treatment objectives also is an integral part of the case manager's role, resulting in necessary adjustments in service plans and interventions.
- *Advocacy*: The advocacy function involves serving as an advocate for the child and family to ensure that they receive needed services, resources, and entitlements. The case manager works to address and overcome barriers and deficiencies that clients encounter when interacting with the service delivery system. An integral part of this function involves helping to empower families with the skills and knowledge to serve more effectively as their own advocates. Moving beyond case advocacy for individual youngsters and families, case managers often become involved in "class advocacy," or promoting changes in the service delivery system that will benefit all children and families.

These functions are not discrete, but should be seen instead as a process with sequential and often overlapping tasks (Raiff & Shore, 1993). All of these functions are performed within a context of a warm, supportive, caring, and collaborative relationship with the child and family. In fact, the case manager–client relationship represents the "core" of the case management process, ensuring that case management services are not mechanistic but are rather a highly personal form of helping (Modrcin, Rapp, & Chamberlain, 1985; Stroul & Friedman, 1986). In addition to considering the quality of the relationship between the case manager and child and family, Raiff and Shore (1993) advocate the use of a set of "quality standards" by which to assess the caliber of the case management services, including such standards as the degree of cultural competence, the level of consumer empowerment, and the quality of the family–professional partnership.

This set of functions can be performed in a variety of ways and by a variety of individuals within a system of care. Rose (1992) noted that not everyone who is called a case manager performs all of these core functions and that, conversely, not everyone who performs some or all of these functions is called a case manager. Some agencies and programs assign these functions to other service providers and clinicians, whereas agencies with specialized case managers may expand upon these core functions and assign additional roles and functions to their case management staff. In many cases, the parents of youngsters with emotional disorders perform case management functions. With variability inherent in the field, these core elements of case management currently are widely accepted as essential functions to be performed on behalf of and in collaboration with youngsters with emotional disorders and their families (Katz-Leavy et al., 1992; Raiff & Shore, 1993; Rose, 1992; Stroul & Friedman, 1986).

Two newer roles are increasingly ascribed to case managers—clinical services and financial management. Clinical services such as training in daily living skills, crisis intervention, medication management, supportive counseling, and individual and family therapy are functions that case managers may fulfill in some systems of care. Financial management of services and interventions also is an expanding role for some case managers, involving functions such as developing and managing a "budget" for the care of individual youngsters and families, overseeing the expenditure of flexible funds for service delivery, gatekeeping for the most expensive services and settings, and cost containment (Applebaum & Austin, 1990). These aspects of case management are among the most significant variables among case management services in the field.

MAJOR CASE MANAGEMENT VARIABLES

Although most case management services share similar goals and a set of core functions, such services differ significantly in many respects. The following discussion reviews the major variables accounting for these differences in the implementation and delivery of case management services for children with emotional disturbances and their families.

Clinical Services

The debate as to whether "clinical services" per se should be part of the case management role or remain separate is longstanding, and the inclusion of clinical services in the role of case managers varies widely. Some programs emphasize the clinical nature of their activities and refer to their services as "clinical case management" or "therapeutic case management" (Roberts, Mayo, Alberts, & Broskowski, 1986). These programs tend to view case management itself as a therapeutic intervention. The opposite point of view has been argued—specifically, that the requirements of case management are extensive and most likely beyond the capabilities of clinicians who are providing direct treatment at the same time. Furthermore, it has been argued that case managers who are not the primary treatment agents are in a position to review clients' progress more objectively and independently and to advocate more effectively.

It has become increasingly apparent over time that it is difficult, if not impossible, to separate clinical functions entirely from case management. Supportive counseling, crisis intervention, parent education, and medication management are functions of a clinical nature that are closely bound with the core case management functions. However, vast differences still exist as to the degree to which clinical services are included and encouraged and as to the acceptance of the case manager as the primary treatment provider or therapist. Those professionals with a "clinical case management" perspective see case management as a treatment in its own right, with the case manager viewed as an "outreach therapist"; others see case managers as brokers and enablers rather than agents of personal growth and therapeutic change (Bachrach, 1989).

Financial Management

One of the most significant variables affecting the delivery of case management services is whether a financial management function is included among the other core functions. This financial management function has been described as a "system-oriented fiduciary focus," generally directed at the goal of cost containment (Raiff & Shore, 1993). This financial management function often is associated with insurance companies and other health care organizations that are attempting to manage the care provided to consumers in order to promote more efficient service delivery and contain costs. A rapidly increasing array of both public- and private-sector systems of services are including a financial management role among the other responsibilities of case managers to respond to the escalating costs of service delivery. According to Raiff and Shore (1993), the addition of this function is considered by some to be the "advance guard of future case management programming," whereas others express profound concern about the "seductive promise" of being able to both contain costs and ensure the delivery of needed services.

The addition of the financial management function may create a tension among the various goals of case management, specifically in terms of the relative emphasis on improved access to services versus resource allocation and gatekeeping (Austin, 1983; Loomis, 1988). Is the case manager to be primarily an advocate for the client or a resource manager acting in the interests of the larger society? Case management with a financial management (or managed care) focus has been characterized as "client unfriendly" and as reflecting the interests of payers rather than of consumers. However, positive aspects of this function have also been identified, including enhancing collaboration with providers, forcing the service system to provide alternatives to costly (and often inappropriate) care in restrictive service environments, and adding provisions for ensuring appropriate and high-quality service delivery (Raiff & Shore, 1993). Although concerns persist about the effect of the financial management function on access to services and quality of care, examples in the field have shown that financial management functions can coexist with other, more traditional, case management functions.

Intensity

Case management services vary according to intensity, generally referring to the amount of time and resources devoted to serving each individual youngster and family. As case management services increase in intensity, they generally are characterized by more frequent contact with clients, more time spent with each client and family, smaller caseloads, more "in vivo" approaches, an expanded range of roles and functions, and expanded services and supports to family members and significant others.

A trend noted by Raiff and Shore (1993) is to target high levels of case management services to the most high-risk populations—persons with the most serious and persistent disorders, those with complex and multiple needs, those who are the most difficult to serve, and those who are high utilizers of services and, therefore, are expensive to serve. The term "intensive case management" refers to the many examples of such services that have recently emerged to serve these individuals. The individualized service approach, typically used for youngsters with the most serious disorders, centers around an intensive form of case management performed by highly skilled case managers, based upon the challenges presented by the youngsters served and the complexity and uniqueness of their intervention plans (Katz-Leavy et al., 1992).

Caseload

The size of the caseload assigned to each case manager is highly variable, ranging from as few as 4 to as many as 75 or more clients per case manager.

The dangers of large caseloads have been emphasized in the literature. For example, Rose (1992) stated that large caseloads may impair the quality and effectiveness of services by reducing case managers' contact with clients, diminishing opportunities to build close relationships, and predisposing them to respond to crises rather than anticipating problems. Stroul and Friedman (1986) warned that, although it may appear cost-effective to have higher caseloads, it is important to keep caseloads small when serving a population of children with serious emotional disturbances because of their multiple needs, the severity and complexity of their problems, the frequency with which crises develop, and the high cost of failure. Case management for individualized services, in particular, requires small caseloads because of the complexity of the function that case managers must perform and the fact that they are serving the most needy target population.

Suggested optimal caseload sizes range from 5 to 15 (Katz-Leavy et al., 1992; Raiff & Shore, 1993; Santarcangelo, 1989). Caseload size may depend on the intensity of the needs of the youngsters to be served; youngsters and families in the initial stages of service provision require more time and effort, whereas those in maintenance or transition phases need lower levels of services and support. Some regions in Kentucky have developed a weighting system for limiting caseload size, with weights assigned to each case based upon the level of intensity of the services required (Illback & Neill, 1995).

Philosophy

The philosophy guiding case management services varies across programs. Two convictions appear to be emerging as essential philosophical underpinnings of effective case management services—the belief in a family-centered approach and the belief in a strengths-based approach. The degree to which these precepts have been accepted and incorporated into service delivery differentiates case management programs at the present time.

The adoption of a family-centered philosophy of care is based on the recognition that the family is the most important resource for a child and that it is the family that plays the primary role in the care of youngsters with emotional disorders, a very difficult and demanding task. A family-centered approach to case management is built around seeing families (or surrogate caregivers) as full partners in all aspects of the planning and delivery of services. In addition, an array of services and supports (such as parent education, counseling, respite care, and home aid services) are offered to families to support and enhance their ability to care for their children effectively.

The strengths-based approach involves careful analysis of the skills, resources, and other strengths that the child and family may have and building intervention plans around these strengths. This philosophy of care emphasizes existing strengths and resources rather than focusing solely on deficits, problems, and needs—an approach that has typified much service delivery in the past. The strengths-based approach is considered to be less stigmatizing and demoralizing and recognizes that even the most troubled youngsters and families have assets that can be enlisted and utilized in the helping process.

Specialization

Another variable affecting case management services is whether they are provided by specialized case managers or by staff who have other treatment or service delivery responsibilities in addition to fulfilling case management functions. Some systems utilize specialized case managers who are hired and trained for this role and who serve as full-time case management specialists. A number of advantages to using specialized case managers have been identified. They can provide case management services without competing priorities resulting from other responsibilities; they become experienced in working with youngsters with difficult and complex problems and skilled at managing individual intervention plans; and they develop an intimate knowledge of the resources available in the community for children and families and become adept at assisting families to obtain these resources (Stroul et al., 1992).

Although there are clear advantages to using specialized case managers, many systems of care do not have sufficient resources to provide specialized case managers to all the youngsters who may need case management services. Thus an approach often used involves assigning case management responsibilities to a staff person in a provider agency. This approach often is described as using a "lead case manager" from the most logical agency, the agency with the longest relationship with the child and family or the one with the primary or greatest level of service responsibility. Most often, systems of care use some combination of these approaches to meet the need for case management services.

Staff Qualifications

The level of education of case managers is another significant variable, with the educational background of staff ranging from high school diplomas to doctoral degrees. This variability reflects differences in the perception of case management. Some perceive it as a type of intervention that requires well-educated and highly skilled and experienced staff; others see case management as a transitioning profession that is amenable to more alternative hiring approaches (Raiff & Shore, 1993). Rose (1992) discussed the dilemma related to case managers' educational background. He noted that most programs require bachelor's degrees, but that questions have been raised regarding the sufficiency of this level of training in view of the range and complexity of the required activities, the need to work independently, and the need to establish credibility with other professionals and administrators who may regard them as "paraprofessionals." However, more highly educated professionals may be less willing and enthusiastic about performing case management functions, particularly those that involve more mundane tasks such as accompanying and transporting clients. Prior experience is also considered in hiring decisions by case management programs, but there is little current consensus as to the relative importance of professional training and experience. This lack of consensus is reflected in the variability with respect to staff qualifications across programs. Many assert that preservice education, at whatever professional level, has not adequately prepared staff for case management roles. Educational programs and curricula focusing specifically on the skills and knowledge needed for case management are a fairly recent phenomenon and are not yet widely used. As a result, the need for on-the-job and in-service training for case managers is especially critical, and there has been an increasing emphasis on case management training.

Another recent trend is the employment of consumers and parents as case managers. Raiff and Shore (1993) state that this practice is built on the acknowledgment that persons with extensive experience as users of services bring a unique level of understanding and skill to the delivery of case management services to others. Their first-hand experience with the system of care contributes a pragmatic perspective to the process, and they may be better able to establish rapport and serve as role models for clients. Thus, at the same time that some systems are raising professional requirements for case managers, others are becoming more open to innovations such as the hiring of parents and consumers for case management roles.

Use of Teams

Some case management services involve using teams in various ways to help to accomplish the goals of planning and coordinating service delivery for youngsters and their families. There is wide variability in both the types of teams that are used and the general purposes that such teams serve. One approach involves the use of a "case management team" that is composed of a group of case managers who share responsibility for a caseload of youngsters. There are many possible variations in the size of the team, the extensiveness of sharing of clients, and the level of mutual backup provided. Raiff and Shore (1993) cite a number of practical considerations favoring the use of such case management teams including enhancing continuity of care, facilitating 24-hour on-call availability and coverage during sick leave and vacation, allowing for flexible management of crises, accommodating staff turnover more efficiently, and facilitating mutual support and consultation among staff. A review of research indicates that neither the team nor the individual approach to case management is more effective (Rothman, 1992).

Another use of teams as part of case management services involves the use of multidisciplinary or multiagency teams to assist in planning and overseeing services to individual youngsters and their families. These teams typically are organized by the case manager and are composed of the persons most involved and influential in the child's life, including the parents and youngsters themselves as appropriate and all professionals who are serving or will potentially serve the child. With the case manager playing a facilitative leadership role, the team meets and works together over time to develop and implement a comprehensive, individualized service plan for the youngster and family that addresses all of the child's life domains. At the instigation of the case manager, the team continues to meet as needed to monitor progress and to reconfigure the service plan and approaches based upon the child's changing needs (Katz-Leavy et al., 1992). These types of service planning teams are increasingly being used as an integral part of the case management process.

Organizational Context

Case management programs and services are offered under a wide variety of organizational auspices and locations. Such services may be part of a freestanding agency or program, may be housed within a particular provider agency, or may be provided under the auspices of an interagency team. Examples of all of these organizational arrangements, and others, can be found in systems of services for children with emotional disorders and their families. Problems and challenges have been noted with respect to all types of organizations. For example, Illback and Neill (1995) stated that case managers do not fit neatly into traditional niches within mental health organizations and experience such problems as turf battles, questions of competence, regulatory gridlock, and a general devaluation of their role. Case managers in freestanding agencies may be too far removed or isolated from other providers to establish effective working relationships and secure needed resources.

Placement of case managers within an organization is also an important factor affecting their ability to influence decisions and secure resources within their own agency and from other agencies. Stroul and Friedman (1986) emphasized the importance of placing case managers in a position that accords them considerable influence within the overall system. Without such placement, the ability of case managers to effectively advocate for clients, to coordinate and broker services, and to monitor intervention plans becomes limited.

Authority

The amount of authority and autonomy given to case managers in planning and implementing the intervention plan for a youngster and family varies tremendously. In some systems, case managers have considerable authority to make decisions, to access both traditional and nontraditional services and supports, and to influence agencies and providers. The authority of case managers in some systems has been extended to controlling funds that can be used to purchase services for youngsters and their families. In some program examples, case managers control a capitated budget that is used to purchase all needed services; in other examples, case managers are able to obtain flexible funds to be used on an individual-case basis to purchase specialized services or supports.

The extent of the authority of case managers may be a crucial factor in determining the effectiveness of case management services (Rose, 1992). Strategies for enhancing the authority of case managers include clarifying and codifying the authority of case managers in interagency agreements, giving case managers greater discretion over funds used to purchase services, and enhancing the credibility of case managers through informal working relationships with administrators and providers.

CONCLUSION

The implementation of case management services, with many variations, continues to progress at a rapid pace. Systems of care for children and adolescents with emotional disorders and their families are reporting that case management is vital to their service delivery approach. Illback and Neill (1995) conclude that case management "remains compelling as an essential mechanism to ensure comprehensive, high quality, and integrated services for this population" (p. 26).

Despite these reports, some skepticism remains as to whether case management can overcome the serious deficiencies in service delivery systems for persons with disabilities. Rose (1992) argues that service integration strategies alone will not ameliorate these deficiencies and that much greater expenditures of resources to enhance services are needed. He calls for research to determine whether case management is a viable strategy or whether scarce funds might be better spent by directly filling service gaps rather than by creating boundary-spanning mechanisms.

Continued research surely is needed to firmly establish the value and effect of case management, recognizing that the wide variations in definitions and functions of case management make it difficult to isolate the effects of the core case management functions and case management approaches that incorporate additional functions, particularly clinical services. However, the value of case management services cannot be established outside of the context of a system of care that includes all of the essential elements—an array of service options, mechanisms for system-level coordination, and mechanisms for client-level coordination (i.e., case management). In the context of the system of care, case management does play a vital role in ensuring the continuous, effective, and efficient delivery of services.

REFERENCES

ADAMHA Reorganization Act, PL 102-321. (July 10, 1992). Title 42, U.S.C. 201 et seq: *U.S. Statutes at Large, 106,* 323.

Applebaum, R., & Austin, C.D. (1990). *Long-term case management: Design and evaluation.* New York: Springer-Verlag.

Austin, C. (1983). Case management in long-term care: Options and opportunities. *Health and Social Work, 8*(2), 16–30.

Bachrach, L. (1989). Case management: Toward a shared definition. *Hospital and Community Psychiatry, 40,* 883–884.

Behar, L. (1985). Changing patterns of state responsibility: A case study of North Carolina. *Journal of Clinical Psychology, 14,* 188–195.

Behar, L. (1991). Fort Bragg demonstration project: Implementation of the continuum of care. In *Close to home: Community-based mental health for children.* Raleigh: North Carolina Division of Mental Health, Mental Retardation, and Substance Abuse Services.

Chamberlain, R., & Rapp, C. (1991). A decade of case management: A methodological review of outcome research. *Community Mental Health Journal, 27,* 171–188.

Doel, M. (1991). *Early intervention systems change: A review of models.* Portland, OR: Association of Retarded Citizens.

Education of the Handicapped Act Amendments of 1986, PL 99-457. (October 8, 1986). Title 20, U.S.C. 1400 et seq: *U.S. Statutes at Large, 100,* 1145–1177.

General Accounting Office. (1977). *Returning the mentally disabled to the community: Government needs to do more.* Washington, DC: Author.

Illback, R., & Neill, T.K. (1995). Service coordination in mental health systems for children, youth, and families: Progress, problems, and prospects. *Journal of Mental Health Administration, 22*(1), 17–28.

Intagliata, J. (1982). Improving the quality of community care for the chronically mentally disabled: The role of case management. *Schizophrenia Bulletin, 8,* 655–674.

Katz-Leavy, J., Lourie, I., Stroul, B., & Zeigler-Dendy, C. (1992). *Individualized services in a system of care.* Washington, DC: Georgetown University Child Development Center, National Technical Assistance Center for Children's Mental Health.

Loomis, J. (1988). Case management in health care. *Health and Social Work, 13,* 219–225.

Lourie, I., & Katz-Leavy, J. (1986). Severely emotionally disturbed children and adolescents. In W. Menninger (Ed.), *The chronically mentally ill* (pp. 159–185). Washington, DC: American Psychiatric Association.

Modrcin, M., Rapp, C., & Chamberlain, R. (1985). *Case management with psychiatrically disabled individuals: Curriculum and training program.* Lawrence: University of Kansas, School of Social Welfare.

Omnibus Health Act of 1986, PL 99-660. (November 14, 1986). Title 42, U.S.C. 300x et seq: *U.S. Statutes at Large, 100,* 3794–3797.

Raiff, N., & Shore, B. (1993). *Advanced case management: New strategies for the nineties.* Newbury Park, CA: Sage Publications.

Roberts, C., Mayo, J., Alberts, F., & Broskowski, A. (1986). *Child case management for severely disturbed children and adolescents.* Unpublished manuscript, Northside Center, Tampa, FL.

Rose, S. (1992). *Case management and social work practice.* New York: Longman Publishing Group.

Rothman, J. (1992). *Guidelines for case management: Putting research to professional use.* Itasca, IL: F.E. Peacock.

Rubin, A. (1987). Case management. In A. Minahan (Ed.), *Encyclopedia of social work* (pp. 212–222). Silver Spring, MD: National Association of Social Workers.

Rubin, A. (1992). Is case management effective for people with serious mental illness? A research review. *Health and Social Work, 17,* 138–150.

Santarcangelo, S. (1989). *Case management for children and adolescents with a severe emotional disturbance and their families.* Waterbury: Vermont Department of Mental Health and Mental Retardation, Child and Adolescent Service System Programs.

Schwartz, S., Goldman, H., & Churgin, S. (1982). Case management for the chronically mentally ill: Models and dimensions. *Hospital and Community Psychiatry, 33,* 1006–1009.

Solomon, P. (1992). The efficacy of case management services for severely mentally disabled adults. *Community Mental Health Journal, 28,* 163–180.

Stroul, B. (1989). Community support systems for persons with long-term mental illness: A conceptual framework. *Psychosocial Rehabilitation Journal, 12*(3), 9–26.

Stroul, B., & Friedman, R. (1986). *A system of care for children and youth with severe emotional disturbances* (rev. ed.). Washington, DC: Georgetown University Child Development Center, National Technical Assistance Center for Children's Mental Health.

Stroul, B., Lourie, I., Goldman, S., & Katz-Leavy, J. (1992). *Profiles of local systems of care for children and adolescents with severe emotional disturbances.* Washington, DC: Georgetown University Child Development Center, National Technical Assistance Center for Children's Mental Health.

Weil, M., & Karls, J. (Eds.). (1985). *Case management in human service practice.* San Francisco: Jossey-Bass.

CHAPTER 15

Human Resource Development

Sheila A. Pires

Much has been accomplished since the mid-1980s to heighten awareness, articulate a vision and values, and define a conceptual framework for a system of care for children with emotional disorders and their families. The challenge of the 1990s is to translate these advances into operational realities. Workforce, or human resource development (HRD), issues pose one of the most important challenges to operationalizing systems of care for children and their families.

The term "human resource development" is defined by the National Institute of Mental Health (NIMH) as "the explicit and coordinated efforts of an organization to achieve the right number and right kinds of people in the right places at the right times doing the right things to carry out its mission effectively" (NIMH, 1992). HRD is further defined by NIMH as encompassing a broad set of activities that include *planning and evaluation* (i.e., assessing workforce issues as they relate to the mission of an organization, particularly in the context of systems change); *workforce management*, including recruitment, retention, distribution, and utilization of staff; *education and training*, including both preservice preparation and in-service training; and *sanctions and regulations*, such as standards and licensure.

The implications for the workforce of the developments in the child mental health field since the 1980s are enormous:

- The types of less restrictive, community-based services included in most state plans today (such as therapeutic foster care, different types of in-home services, intensive case management, "wraparound" services, respite and crisis services) involve new, still evolving technologies in which the vast majority of staff have not been trained. Indeed, with many of the new technologies, there is continuing experimentation with what staffing patterns ought to look like.
- The interagency collaboration and service integration called for in most state plans today is complex, involving staff from multiple systems with different mandates, financing streams, training, and orientation.

- Meaningful involvement of families often requires staff both to acquire new skills and to change existing attitudes. Families themselves need training to be effective participants in systems of care, including functioning in staff roles.
- Few staff have been trained in cultural competencies, yet the population served is increasingly ethnically and culturally diverse.
- Many state plans encompass both children with serious emotional disorders and those at risk. Staff must have the capacity to understand a wide spectrum of disorders as well as risk factors.
- Many state plans emphasize the importance of early intervention services for infants and toddlers, ages birth to 3, as well as transition services for young adults, ages 18–22. Thus, staff capacity must cover a broad developmental range.
- The infrastructure to implement community-based systems of care requires major adjustments in management information systems, financing, and other central support structures (including human resource development), which pose challenges for managers and administrative support staff.
- Health care reform, with its emphasis on managed, cost-effective service networks, will precipitate further the need for a workforce trained in community-based systems and settings.
- Since the mid-1980s there has been some formal documentation and much anecdotal corroboration from state and local administrators that academic curricula and practica across all of the disciplines are not keeping pace with developments in public service systems for children and families (Kravitz, 1991). Too often, the academic preparation of those entering child-serving systems has failed to give them the knowledge, skills, or attitudes needed to implement effective community-based systems of care.

In addition to this complexity of workforce issues, many states face a far more basic workforce challenge in that they have a gross insufficiency of staff members trained to work with children and adolescents (regardless of how appropriately trained they are). Shortages may be limited to certain disciplines, such as child psychiatry, or apply across all areas. They may be limited to certain parts of a state, such as rural areas, or exist statewide. Shortages may be aggravated by limited funding or supply or both. Mandates to redeploy staff from adult components to children's services, particularly staff from downsized state hospitals, may take precedence over the hiring of new child-trained staff.

Assessment of workforce issues is a critical step in the implementation of community-based systems of care. It is crucial to understand a variety of workforce issues, specifically

- Staffing requirements (i.e., the numbers, mix, and skills of staff required for community-based service systems)
- Limitations and strengths of existing staff capacity to implement community-based systems
- Strengths and weaknesses of academic curricula and practica, as well as in-service training, to provide staff with the required knowledge, skills, and attitudes
- Recruitment, retention and distribution issues
- Similarities in workforce issues nationally and regionally, as well as important differences across states

With this understanding, policy makers and practitioners can begin to identify strategies to ensure adequate numbers of appropriately trained staff who are effectively deployed and utilized.

This chapter describes the results of a regional needs assessment of workforce issues related to the delivery of community-based services for children and adolescents with serious emotional disturbances and their families (Pires, 1992). The study was conducted in 1992 for the Southern Human Resource Development Consortium for Mental Health, a coalition of 12 southern states, by Human Service Collaborative, a research and consulting group specializing in children's systems, with input from the National Technical Assistance Center for Children's Mental Health at Georgetown University. Although the study was confined to the southern region of the United States, the diversity of states in the region, as well as anecdotal information from policy makers and practitioners in other parts of the country, suggests the results have national applicability.

METHODOLOGY

Survey Instrument

The principal instrument used for the needs assessment was a written survey, which addressed 10 major areas of interest:

1. The *goals and objectives* of the public mental health system serving children and adolescents and their families in each of the states in the region (This section sought to identify the most important directions in which states wish to head over the next 5 years.)
2. *Major HRD issues* associated with the development of community-based services for children and adolescents with serious emotional disturbances/mental illness and their families (This section was intended to provide an overview of the key HRD concerns in each state in the region, as well as an indication of the importance states attach to HRD issues.)

3. *Staffing requirements* (This section sought to shed light on the extent to which states have identified the staffing requirements for implementation of priority areas.)
4. The question of whether states have access to *sufficient numbers* of staff, regardless of how appropriately trained they are, and the *appropriateness of preservice training*—that is, whether states have access to appropriately trained staff, regardless of whether there are adequate numbers of staff available
5. *In-service training* issues, including strengths and deficiencies in staff skills
6. *Recruitment* issues
7. *Retention* issues, including the ability of states to retain staff in nontraditional services
8. *Staff distribution and utilization* issues, such as difficulty in deploying staff to rural areas or to nontraditional service locations
9. *Relationships between the child mental health system and HRD offices* in each state
10. *Linkages between the child mental health system and higher education* in each state

In addition to identifying issues in each of these areas, the survey also sought to identify existing HRD strategies and resources to assist states to address workforce issues.

All of the survey questions addressed service and HRD issues in the public child mental health system. "Public mental health system" was defined to include both publicly operated programs and services and private programs with which the public sector may contract. Respondents were asked to include in their answers HRD issues affecting both publicly operated programs and private agencies providing services on behalf of the public system.

Most survey questions required respondents to check relevant answers from a list and then rank the top three. All sections also included open-ended questions to identify other relevant issues, as well as strategies.

The survey was sent to 84 key informants in 11 of the 12 states that are members of the Southern HRD Consortium (Florida did not participate in the survey). Key informants were identified by state mental health commissioners and HRD managers in each of the states in the region, at the request of the Southern HRD Consortium. Those identified to receive the survey included parents of children and adolescents with emotional disturbance/mental illness; state mental health commissioners; HRD managers; state mental health representatives for children and youth; Child and Adolescent Service System Program directors; other state mental health agency officials; local service providers (public and private); state legislators; university representatives; representatives from other child-serving systems, such as child welfare and education; and state and local advocates. The four largest categories of key informants were local mental health service providers (public and private), state mental health agency officials, parents, and advocates. Copies of the survey also were sent to key individuals at the national level to encourage their interest and assistance in maximizing response to the survey.

Several rounds of follow-up telephone calls were made to all those who received the survey to ensure receipt and understanding of the survey and to encourage response. A 58% rate of response was obtained.

Survey returns were analyzed to identify 1) central tendencies (pointing to central issues) regionwide; 2) central tendencies by state; 3) central tendencies by four major groups of respondents, which included state mental health agency officials, local service providers, parents, and advocates; 4) similarities, if any, in central tendencies between states, as well as between types of respondents; 5) critical differences, if any, in central tendencies between states, as well as between types of respondents (e.g., do parents tend to view training needs or service shortage areas differently from state agency officials; are certain states raising critical issues unique to their situations, but not necessarily true regionwide?); and 6) HRD strategies and resources identified by respondents as effective. "Central tendencies" is defined as those items on the survey checked most frequently by respondents and assigned the highest rankings.

Survey Caveats

In most states in the country, including those in the southern region, there has been minimal systematic data gathering with respect to HRD issues related to services for children and families. It was recognized that those participating in this survey, for the most part, would be offering at best their *impressions* of key workforce issues, rather than necessarily factual data. Also, given the diversity of the group of key informants participating in the survey, it was not expected that every respondent would be able to answer every question. Respondents were encouraged both to leave questions blank that they did not feel comfortable answering and to offer an opinion even if they felt they did not know "the answer" per se.

Survey results thus convey the impression of key stakeholders with respect to HRD issues, rather than fact. Impressions, of course, particularly those of key stakeholders, are in themselves vitally important—especially where there is an absence of factual data. Impressions suggest areas where additional data gathering needs to occur and add weight to fact where the two coincide. Impressions also must be dealt with if the facts differ. The survey results must be considered in this context.

A second caveat is that not every conceivable type of key stakeholder was represented among the participants. Line workers, for example, were not surveyed, nor were youth, and there are undoubtedly others. Survey results therefore represent the impressions of some, but by no means all, key stakeholders in the region.

The third caveat concerns the variable number of respondents by state and by type of respondent. The number of respondents by state fluctuated from a high of 7 to a low of 1; in other words, as discussed in detail in the next section, as many as 7 individuals responded to the survey from some states and as few as 1 from other states. The number of respondents by the four major groups of respondents fluctuated from a high of 16 to a low of 7 (i.e., 16 local service providers from across the region, but only seven parents responded to the survey). The analysis did not give more or less weight to answers because they represented higher or lower numbers of respondents; for example, it did not give more weight to the answers from local service providers than from parents because more local providers responded, nor did it discount a state because only one individual from the state participated. However, the results should be considered in this context.

MAJOR FINDINGS

The following discussion describes the major workforce issues and needs identified through the southern regional study.

Directions of Child Mental Health Systems and Related Workforce Issues

The major directions in which state child mental health systems in the region are heading in the late 1990s are

- Development of more and new types of community-based services (identified by 94% of respondents)
- Joint initiatives between child mental health and other child-serving systems, particularly the child welfare system (identified by 88% of respondents)
- Development of new financing mechanisms (i.e., expansion of Medicaid, use of Title IV-E, blended funding, etc.) (identified by 80% of respondents)
- Development of state- and local-level coordinating bodies (identified by 71% and 73% of respondents, respectively)
- Development of family advocacy and support programs (identified by 69% of respondents)
- Development of culturally competent services (identified by 65% of respondents)

The new types of community-based services states are developing are

- Therapeutic foster care or family treatment homes (identified by 82% of respondents)
- In-home services, either crisis or longer term (identified by 78% of respondents)

- Day treatment or psychoeducational programs (identified by 73% of respondents)
- Therapeutic group homes (identified by 73% of respondents)
- Intensive case management services (identified by 69% of respondents)
- Crisis intervention services (identified by 67% of respondents)
- Respite services (identified by 67% of respondents)
- Community-based residential treatment centers (identified by 65% of respondents)

There is a high level of concern throughout the region over a wide array of workforce issues related to the directions in which states are heading. These issues include ability to recruit appropriately trained staff; geographic distribution of staff; racial, ethnic, and cultural diversity among staff; staff retention; in-service training; knowledge about staffing requirements; sufficient numbers of staff; and capacity to assess, address, and track workforce issues. The overriding concern is ability to recruit appropriately trained staff. This was ranked as a top-three concern by 61% of respondents overall, in every state but one and among all of the major respondent groups. This was the only workforce issue to be ranked in the top three by a majority (or greater) of respondents. Consensus regarding the next most frequently ranked top three workforce concerns drops to 47%; that issue is ability to achieve desired geographic distribution of staff. The third most frequently ranked top-three issue (ranked by 22% of respondents) is ability to achieve desired racial, ethnic, and cultural diversity among staff.

Sixty-nine percent of those surveyed consider workforce issues to be at least as important as, or more important than, securing adequate funding for the successful implementation of community-based services for children and adolescents with serious emotional disturbances and their families.

The majority of respondents regionwide either do not know whether or do not believe there is adequate knowledge in their respective states about staffing requirements for implementing community-based services for children, including knowledge about the numbers of staff needed, the skills that are required, the types of staff needed, the mix of staff, and staff distribution requirements. If knowledge does exist, it is most likely related to identification of required skills; knowledge is least likely to exist in the area of staff distribution (i.e., where and how staff should be deployed). Nearly two thirds of respondents indicate that their states do not have information available related to staffing requirements that would be useful to other states in the region.

Access to Sufficient Numbers of Staff and Appropriately Trained Staff

A large majority (80%) of those surveyed do not believe their states have access to sufficient numbers of staff to implement community-based services for children. Respondents cite a variety of reasons for staff shortages.

The top-ranked reasons are insufficient funding to hire staff (ranked as a top-three reason by 59% of respondents); salaries are too low (ranked by 53%); insufficient numbers of persons being trained (ranked by 37%); and too few who are trained are entering the public system (ranked by 35%).

Those surveyed believe staff shortages exist in every discipline, and types of shortages vary across states. Majority (or greater) consensus as to the most critical shortage areas occurs only with respect to child psychiatry: 73% of respondents, all states but one, and all major respondent groups consider child psychiatry to be the most critical shortage area. Regional consensus as to the next most critical shortage area drops to 20%; those areas are parents in staff roles and psychiatrists. Sixty-five percent of respondents could identify no strategies in their respective states to address staff shortages.

A large majority (76%) of those surveyed do not believe their states have access to adequately prepared staff to implement community-based services for children. Respondents believe this is especially a problem in three major areas: working with families, understanding emotional disturbance in children and adolescents, and understanding and having the skills to implement the newer community-based service technologies.

Respondents believe lack of adequate preparation and training is a problem with all of the disciplines. There was no majority consensus as to which of the disciplines are least adequately prepared. Those most frequently cited are mental health technicians (cited by 39%), special educators (cited by 36%), and child psychiatrists (cited by 29%). There also was no consensus as to which of the disciplines are most adequately prepared. Most frequently cited are master's-level social workers and doctoral-level psychologists (by 18%; however, 20% also cite these groups as least prepared).

A large majority (71%) believe that the major reason staff are not adequately prepared is because university curricula are not relevant to state priority areas. This was ranked as a top-three reason by all states but one and by all respondent groups. The next most highly ranked reasons are limited faculty exposure to and understanding of state priority areas (ranked by 65% overall); child mental health system relies on staff from the adult mental health system who are not trained in the children's area (ranked by 41%); and insufficient opportunities for students to do practica and internships in the public child mental health system (ranked by 41%).

In-Service Training

Respondents rank highly (8–10 on a scale of 1 to 10) the need for in-service training to improve staff skills to implement community-based services for children. The most frequently cited new skills that are needed are working with families, understanding the newer community-based service technologies and the system of care concept, interagency competencies, appropriate use of behavior management, and cultural competence.

The majority also rank highly (7–10 on a scale of 1 to 10) the need for in-service training because of inappropriate staff attitudes toward working with children with serious emotional disturbances and their families. However, there is greater inconsistency among respondent groups on this issue than with respect to staff skills. Eighty percent of parents rank this a "10" on a scale of 1 to 10, as do 71% of state agency officials, but only 38% of local providers give it this high a ranking. The most frequently cited areas in which staff attitudes are an issue are working with families; resistance to interagency collaboration; overreliance on hospitalization or traditional, clinic-based psychotherapy; and lack of cultural awareness.

A majority of respondents indicate that appropriate in-service training curricula, methods, and personnel are not available in their respective states, primarily because of lack of funding. Major pieces of curricula are available throughout the region but not necessarily implemented. Perceptions as to the extent states are conducting in-service training vary considerably by state and by respondent group, as well as within states and respondent groups. However, 61% of respondents overall rank the extent to which states are conducting in-service training at 5 or below on a scale of 1 (none) to 10 (extensive).

Staff Recruitment

With respect to recruitment, respondents indicate that the public child mental health system is most likely to draw staff from higher education graduating students (respondents estimate, on average, that 37% of children's staff come from this source; it is cited as the first major source of staff by all states except one, which cited the adult mental health system); from the adult mental health system (estimated to provide 26% of children's staff on average; it is a top-three source of staff in every state except three); and from other public child-serving systems, such as child welfare (estimated to provide 24% of child mental health staff; is a top-three source in all states). Staff for the public system are least likely to come from the for-profit sector, higher education faculty, and parents.

Respondents estimate that staff coming from higher education are drawn, roughly, half and half from the bachelor's and master's levels (each is estimated at about 45%), with the remainder coming from the associate (11%) and doctoral (7%) levels. Students predominantly come from in-state, 4-year public colleges and universities.

A solid majority (57%) of those surveyed believe that clinical staff are the most difficult to recruit and that administrative support staff are the least difficult. An overwhelming majority (73%) rank child psychiatrists as the most difficult discipline to recruit. Beyond child psychiatry, however, there is no majority consensus as to which are the next most difficult disciplines to recruit. The next most frequently ranked are psychologists, especially at the doctoral level (ranked by 27%), and psychiatrists (ranked by 20%). There is no majority consensus regarding the disciplines that are the least difficult to recruit. Those most frequently ranked are social workers at the bachelor's level (ranked by 37%) and mental health technicians (ranked by 24%).

In-home services was cited most frequently (by 41% of respondents) as the community-based service for which states have the most difficulty recruiting staff. Clinic outpatient services is most frequently cited (by 33%) as the component for which states have the least difficulty recruiting staff.

In response to the question of who does recruitment for the public child mental health system, respondents tend to identify a central personnel office in the state mental health agency or in an umbrella human services agency. Those surveyed describe few strengths of their state's recruitment process and a variety of weaknesses, most having to do with a lack of a specialized focus on children's services, bureaucratic obstacles, and lack of funding. All respondents, but especially parents and advocates, had difficulty answering questions related to recruitment. The few recruitment strategies that are identified, mainly by local providers, have to do with individual local agency efforts rather than statewide initiatives.

Staff Retention

Respondents had even greater difficulty answering questions related to retention; again, parents and advocates had the most difficulty and local providers, relatively speaking, had the least. Regarding the extent to which retention of children's staff is a problem in the states, the response is inconsistent. Rankings on a scale of 1 (low) to 10 (high) range from 2 to 10. Some respondents suggest that the child mental health system is too new for experience with retention issues to exist.

Those surveyed indicate numerous reasons that staff leave public systems, with no one reason receiving a majority response. They most frequently cite better salaries (ranked by 49%); more manageable caseloads (ranked by 33%); frustration with the bureaucracy (ranked by 24%); and staff feeling ineffective with clients because of lack of access to resources (ranked by 24%).

One of the few questions dealing with retention that received a majority or greater consensus response was with respect to where staff go when they leave public child mental health systems. Fifty-three percent of respondents say staff go to the private, for-profit sector, such as a for-profit hospital, or into private practice. (The private, for-profit sector, however, is not identified as a place from which staff come.) The other most frequently cited places where staff go when they leave public child mental health systems are the private nonprofit sector (ranked by 37%) and other public child-serving systems, such as child welfare (ranked by 20%).

A solid majority (61%) of respondents identify clinical staff as the most difficult to retain and administrative support staff and senior managers as the least difficult. (These are also cited as the most and least difficult types of staff to recruit, respectively.) There is majority consensus as to the most difficult discipline to retain only with respect to child psychiatry (ranked by 53%). (This discipline is also ranked as the most difficult to recruit.) The next most frequently cited disciplines that are difficult to retain are psychologists, especially at the doctoral level (ranked by 29%), psychiatrists (ranked by 20%), and social workers (ranked by 20%). Doctoral-level psychologists and psychiatrists, like child psychiatrists, also are ranked as most difficult to recruit. Social workers are not ranked as difficult to recruit, however.

In-home services is cited most frequently as the most difficult service component for which to retain staff. In-home services also is cited as the component for which states have the most difficulty recruiting staff. Clinic outpatient services is cited most frequently as the least difficult component for which to retain staff and the component for which states have the least difficulty recruiting staff. Few retention strategies are identified. Those strategies that are cited typically pertain to individual local agency efforts rather than reflecting statewide initiatives.

Staff Distribution

Those surveyed also had difficulty answering questions related to staff distribution issues. With respect to understaffing concerns, respondents indicate that the types of services for which states have the most difficulty recruiting and retaining staff are crisis services, in-home services, and therapeutic foster care. Those surveyed indicate these are difficult components to staff and keep staffed because they tend to be characterized by high levels of stress, irregular hours and schedules, low pay, lack of back-up supports, high caseloads, and inadequate training.

Those surveyed indicated that the service component for which states have the least difficulty recruiting and retaining staff is clinic outpatient services. Respondents believe it is less difficult to recruit and retain staff for this component because it is less stressful; has regular, office-based hours and back-up supports; and is most like private practice.

Those surveyed believe it is most difficult to recruit and retain staff for nontraditional service locations, particularly juvenile corrections and child protective services settings, and least difficult to recruit and retain staff for clinic outpatient services. Every state in the region cites rural communities as the most geographically understaffed areas. Very few strategies are cited to address staff distribution issues. Again, strategies that were cited tend to pertain to individual agency, not statewide, efforts.

Human Resource Development Capacity

A large majority (82%) of those surveyed either do not know whether there is or indicate there is not a HRD office or other capacity in their respective states that is focused on the child and adolescent system, although almost half (49%) indicate that there is a HRD office focused on the adult mental health system. An equally large percentage (84%) either do not know whether their states have had or indicate that their states have not had a NIMH grant targeted to workforce issues in the children's system, although about a third (31%) indicate that their states have had NIMH grants targeted to adult services. Again, a large majority (88%) either do not know whether there is or indicate there is no collaboration between the children's mental health system and their state's HRD office. Respondents in most states cannot identify who is responsible for HRD issues related to the children's system. Over one third (35%) of state agency officials and one quarter of local providers say "no one" is responsible.

Nearly two thirds (60%) of those surveyed either do not know whether there are or indicate there are no linkages between the children's system and higher education in their respective states to address workforce issues. Barriers to state–university linkages are described as lack of time, lack of resources (staff and dollars), lack of leadership and vision on the part of both sectors, and lack of communication and understanding. Eighty percent of parents and 81% of local providers believe there are no linkages or do not know.

OBSERVATIONS

There are a number of observations to be drawn from the survey results.

1. There is a high level of awareness and remarkable consistency across all states and types of respondents about the directions in which states are heading. These new directions represent a major departure in service delivery for children and adolescents with serious emotional disturbances/mental illness and their families, and raise critical workforce issues.
2. Although all states in the region are moving in similar directions, some are further along than others, are engaged on more multiple fronts, or both. This suggests opportunity for peer-to-peer technical assistance among states in the region.
3. There exists a high level of concern in every state and among every type of respondent about HRD issues. This concern covers

a wide variety of HRD areas, including ability to recruit appropriately trained staff; geographic distribution of staff; racial, ethnic, and cultural diversity among staff; retention; in-service training; knowledge about staffing requirements; sufficient numbers of staff; and capacity to assess, address, and track HRD issues.

4. The HRD issue that generates the greatest degree of consensus is ability to recruit appropriately trained staff. This concern is integrally tied to the perception that university curricula are not relevant to state priority areas; that not enough of those being trained have the requisite knowledge, skills, and attitudes; and that not enough of those trained are entering public systems. In several states, the issue also is tied to the fact that the child mental health system must rely on staff from the adult system, who do not have the necessary training in children's services.

5. Given the lack of capacity in most states to focus on children's workforce issues, and the fact that, in some states, children's systems are at an early developmental stage, it is not surprising that a limited body of knowledge seems to exist with respect to staffing requirements for implementing community-based services. State mental health officials, who are the most aware of what knowledge does exist, are also the most pessimistic about the state of that knowledge, with a very high percentage (79%) saying there is no information available in their respective states that would be useful to other states in the region.

6. Concern over access to sufficient numbers of staff (regardless of how appropriately trained they are) is, first of all, related to funding issues (insufficient funding to hire staff and low salaries) and, second, related to training deficits (insufficient numbers being trained and not enough who are trained entering public systems). Those surveyed believe staff shortages exist in every discipline, and the nature of the shortages seems to vary considerably from state to state, except for child psychiatrists, who are in short supply in virtually every state. To move beyond speculation, the determination of why types of shortages may vary from state to state requires further exploration, which might also yield information about effective approaches to alleviate shortages.

7. Although a majority are concerned, local providers do not express the same *degree of concern* over issues related to inadequate skills, inappropriate attitudes, and inadequate academic preparation as do all of the other major respondent groups. Large majorities (86%–100%) of state agency officials, parents, and advocates, for example, express concern over states being able to access appro-

priately trained staff, whereas only 56% of local providers indicate this concern. One hundred percent of parents and state officials believe that university curricula are not relevant to state priority areas, whereas only 56% of local providers share this view. One hundred percent of parents and 71% of state officials believe inappropriate staff attitudes are an issue, whereas only 38% of local providers have this view. The other respondent groups most frequently cite staff skills and attitudes toward working with families as problem areas, but these are not concerns often cited by local providers. Although additional data are needed to understand the reasons for these differences in levels of perception, they are troubling if they suggest that local providers are less in touch with fundamental system issues. (One reason may be that system of care concepts that have taken several years to develop at state levels are only now beginning to move to local levels.)

8. Lack of in-service training seems to be related primarily to lack of funding rather than lack of curricula. Although gaps still exist in curricula in some states and some subject areas, major pieces of relevant curricula do exist or are being developed—such as in the areas of working with families, interagency skill-building, cultural competence, system of care concepts, and many of the new treatment modalities, such as in-home services and intensive case management—that could be implemented more widely if funding were available.

9. Responses related to recruitment and retention indicate a fair amount of staff movement among public child-serving systems, suggesting the usefulness of an interagency approach to HRD issues in the children's area.

10. Responses suggest there is only one-way traffic, however, between the public system and the for-profit sector. Staff leave public systems to enter the for-profit world, including private practice, but there apparently is little reciprocity. This raises issues for both sectors: Are public systems serving as "training grounds" for the for-profit sector with little return benefit? How can public systems become more attractive to for-profit practitioners? What is the responsibility of the for-profit sector to the public system?

11. Recruitment and retention responses also suggest that public system staff rarely are drawn from the ranks of higher education faculty, nor do public system staff tend to join faculties when they leave public service. This lack of exchange perpetuates the gap that exists between the public system and higher education.

12. The absence of parents in staff roles also is cause for concern. If understanding and working with families is indeed a priority for

states, involvement of parents in meaningful staff roles, much like adult systems have begun to involve consumers in staff roles, would help to foster understanding, reduce the isolation that families feel, and enhance the skills of providers and parents alike.

13. Recruitment, retention, and staff distribution responses all suggest a need for HRD strategies targeted to the newer types of services and to nontraditional service locations, which might include pay differentials, specialized training, smaller caseloads, more intensive on-the-job supports and back-up systems, and "time off" periods through rotation into other assignments. There also is a need regionwide for strategies targeted to staffing rural areas and retaining staff in inner cities. The Community Support Program in adult services, which is a decade older than the child and adolescent community-based services movement, may offer examples of strategies adaptable to the children's system.

14. Responses suggest that, in most states, there is minimal systematic attention devoted to children's workforce issues, nor is there a structure at state levels to focus on this area beyond the traditional state personnel agency, which most respondents describe as marginally effective at best. The responses of parents, local providers, and advocates, who left blank most questions dealing with HRD capacity, suggest that, even where states do have a focus, large groups of key stakeholders do not know about it.

15. Respondents strongly believe that universities are not playing a role in encouraging persons to train in child mental health–related fields, nor to enter public systems if they do, nor are universities working to ensure that curricula and practica are relevant to public system needs. By the same token, respondents also believe that states are not exerting the leadership to engage and support universities to help meet public sector demands. Even the relatively painless step of establishing a dialogue has not occurred in most states in the region. State–university linkages are critical, and a logical starting point is with public colleges and universities, which, according to respondents, are supplying the majority of staff to public systems and which have a mission to support public concerns.

NEXT STEPS

There is a critical need for state and local officials, providers, parents, other key stakeholders, and university representatives to come together to address child workforce concerns and explore common ground for addressing them. Public awareness campaigns, targeted to communities at large and to college campuses, are needed to raise consciousness about children with serious emotional disturbances and their families and the opportunities that exist in public systems, particularly those undertaking innovative change.

It is especially critical that the major child-serving systems—child welfare, mental health, health, education, and juvenile justice—join forces to develop coordinated workforce strategies. It is also critical that the family "movement," much like the consumer movement in adult services, become an integral part of HRD strategies across children's systems. This requires both consciousness raising and identification and dissemination of effective ways of involving families in the HRD area, such as family members assuming paid staff roles, teaching in preservice and in-service training programs, having roles in public awareness and recruitment campaigns, and serving on task forces to assess workforce issues.

Peer-to-peer technical assistance among states is needed, bringing together states that have developed effective HRD strategies in either the child or adult areas with states that need assistance. An information clearinghouse would be helpful to systematically identify, "package," and disseminate major pieces of curricula relevant to community-based services for children, and identify where gaps still exist, to save states from having either to track down examples or develop material on their own.

In addition to the identification and dissemination of curricula, a clearinghouse could explore other approaches to the issue of in-service training needs. Identification of a corps of trainers that states could tap into is another possibility, particularly if this corps takes a "train the trainers" approach at state levels. A clearinghouse could also identify, catalog, and disseminate information related to staffing requirements for community-based services and systematically identify the gaps in knowledge that exist nationally.

There needs to be greater dialogue between child-serving systems and medical colleges, medical societies, and professional associations to explore approaches to increasing the numbers of persons entering child psychiatry, which seems to be a critical shortage area in virtually every state. A similar dialogue needs to occur with historically African American colleges and universities to start a process for involving those institutions in training, recruiting, and preparing culturally competent staff for public systems.

Policy makers, in general, need assistance to understand the importance of HRD issues to implementing community-based systems of care for children and families and to determine the most effective structures for incorporating a HRD focus in the children's mental health area.

REFERENCES

Kravitz, S. (1991, Summer). Professional social work education and public child welfare: Where do we stand? Where are we going? *Future Choices, 3,* 1.

National Institute of Mental Health. (1992). *Human Resource Development Program National Task Force strategic plan*. (Draft report). Rockville, MD: Author.

Pires, S. (1992). *Staffing systems of care for children and families: A report of the Southern Human Resource Development Consortium for Mental Health on workforce issues related to community-based service delivery for children and adolescents with serious emotional disturbance/mental illness and their families*. Columbia, SC: Southern Human Resource Development Consortium for Mental Health/Center for Mental Health Services.

CHAPTER 16

Financing Systems of Care

Lenore B. Behar

Although financing strategies have always been essential to the planning and operation of service delivery systems, this aspect of managing service systems has become more challenging as managers have become aware of the multiplicity of funds available for services to children with mental health problems. Until the 1980s, public agencies that provided mental health services to children and families received financial support primarily from state appropriations, augmented by local tax dollars, federal grants, and some first- and third-party payments. In the 1980s, states began to experiment with a variety of approaches designed to finance mental health services for children. In particular, states sought mechanisms to finance the emerging vision of community-based systems of care for children with serious emotional disturbances and their families (Stroul & Friedman, 1986). These efforts have involved identifying new sources of funding such as Medicaid, accessing funding streams such as child welfare entitlement funding, and integrating services and funding streams across child-serving agencies. This chapter describes these efforts to enhance and restructure financing mechanisms. Examples of the use of a range of financing strategies in North Carolina follow.

ENHANCING AND RESTRUCTURING FINANCING MECHANISMS

The first major effort to identify other sources of funding for services focused on the federal Medicaid program, which is authorized under Title XIX of the Social Security Act of 1935 (PL 74-271) to provide funds for medical services to low-income and other needy individuals. Although Medicaid is a federal program, its use by each state is governed by a State Medicaid Plan, resulting in substantial variations in the types of services covered and in the rates paid by the states to providers of services. Thus, states have considerable latitude in how this federal program is implemented.

During the 1980s, state mental health agencies developed strategies to improve the use of Medicaid for funding services both to children and adults. Nationally, children represent 50% of the population receiving Medicaid, and, within the states, their use of public mental health services represents approximately 30%–40% of the children served. Thus enhancement of the Medicaid programs within the states has been an important strategy to expand the funding base for systems of care.

The attractiveness of the Medicaid program was increased through the opportunities made available through expansion of a part of the Medicaid program, the Early Periodic Screening, Diagnosis and Treatment (EPSDT) program, in 1989 (Omnibus Budget Reconciliation Act of 1989 [PL 101-239]). This expansion allowed for 1) screening to occur at any time and not be confined to the specific screening periods designated to meet the minimum requirements of the program, and 2) partial screening to identify specific problem areas in addition to the full screening designated to meet the minimum requirements of the program. There was an increased emphasis on screening for behavioral health problems. Furthermore, any problem identified through screening and diagnosis could be treated using any federally approved service, whether or not it was part of the state's Medicaid Plan. Beginning in the late 1980s, the public child mental health programs benefited from the technical assistance efforts of the federal Child and Adolescent Service System Program (CASSP), followed by technical assistance from the Robert Wood Johnson Mental Health Services Program for Youth (MHSPY). State mental health agencies have improved substantially their use of Medicaid and EPSDT for children with mental health problems. However, because of the complicated and changing nature of both Medicaid and EPSDT, most states have not used these programs maximally. The requirement of the states to provide matching funds to draw down the federal share of Medicaid (and EPSDT) funds has appeared costly to some states, and the current focus on containing the Medicaid program has, in some states, limited the full realization of the program's potential to finance children's mental health services.

Beyond the use of Medicaid funds for children's mental health services, accessing other funding sources has been a complex process. The complexity stems from the fact that many of the funding sources for children with mental health problems are the province of other agencies, such as the child welfare entitlement funds, including Titles IV-A, IV-B, and IV-E of the Social Security Act (DeWoody, 1994). Access to these funding streams requires joint planning, which in turn requires considerable trust and goodwill among the agencies. Although the requisite joint planning could serve as a mechanism for better coordination of services, such joint planning may not come easily. To address the sharing of resources, some states have moved toward more comprehensive plans for integrating services for children, particularly those children with emotional or behavioral problems and those who are at risk for separation from their families through out-of-home placement. These children are an important focus for such integration because they simultaneously receive services from, and are frequently the legal responsibility of, several public agencies, or because they move from one system to another as their needs or legal status change. Appropriately addressing the needs of these children is critical not only to the children and their families but to the state as well. There is substantial risk that, if these children do not receive needed services or are inappropriately treated, their lives can be seriously affected and the costs of their services will become a greater financial burden to the state.

Thus, states have moved to improve services for children and to develop mechanisms for the maximal use of federal funding. In order to maximize the service capacity of public agencies and to pay for these services with funds to which certain groups of children are entitled by nature of their demonstrated needs and status in life, states have moved to restructure the financing of children's services (Koyanagi & Brodie, 1994). Such restructuring includes serious attention to the federal entitlement programs to determine how best to obtain these funds for the benefit of children. One reason to restructure financing may be for states to recover federal funds that they have already earned but not collected. A second reason to restructure is so that, in the future, greater use of federal funds can be made. The successful restructuring of financing mechanisms for the future requires a planned strategy, coordinated across several agencies.

As states have developed plans to improve their use of federal entitlement programs, it has become apparent that integrating services and funding streams and maximizing revenue are more easily discussed than done. Changes in the use of entitlement programs are difficult to implement sometimes because current practices within a state are based on what staff have believed to be the correct and maximal application of complicated federal requirements; any proposed changes are suspect. Any changes in application must occur at many levels of state government and must involve many levels of staff.

To effect a broader use of federal funding, the agencies involved in the process should have similar goals for their clients. Generally, the child-serving agencies aspire to the goals of 1) keeping families together; 2) serving children in the least restrictive settings possible, that is, in community-based settings; 3) developing service plans that are family centered and having parents participating as partners with the professionals; and 4) delivering services that are respectful of and sensitive to the cultural backgrounds of the children and families. In practice, these beliefs may only be partially actualized as agencies strive to fully reach these goals. As professionals who are responsible for programs and services work toward these common goals, it should be emphasized that these goals supersede the goal of revenue enhancement. Programmatic conflict could arise, for example, if one agency places priority on residential services because its revenues are earned that way, while another agency places priority on non-residential services for the same reason. Conflict occurs, and the revenue enhancement expectations of the state may be thwarted if differing priorities lead to increased conflicts among the agencies rather than increased cooperation. Thus, it is important to articulate the programmatic goals at the beginning, lest revenue enhancement become the driving force.

FINANCING STRATEGIES USED IN NORTH CAROLINA

In an effort to uphold the principles stated above, professionals in North Carolina have worked to increase interagency policy development, programming, and funding. A variety of strategies have been used, ranging from innovations resulting from a class action suit to using federal and foundation grants to test new financing approaches and to piloting the use of managed care through a Medicaid waiver. Each strategy is discussed below.

Willie M. Program

Beginning in 1980, with the implementation of the settlement agreement in the *Willie M. et al. v. James B. Hunt, Jr., et al.* case, the North Carolina Division of Mental Health, Developmental Disabilities and Substance Abuse Services (DMH/DD/SAS) forged a partnership with the other child-serving agencies to develop a full array of coordinated services for children with serious disturbances accompanied by assaultive behavior. Because these children were the responsibilities of multiple agencies, particularly schools, juvenile court, and the child welfare agencies, the development of cross-agency service plans for this population represented the first step toward an integration of services. The *Willie M.* program was confined to a small part of the child mental health population, focusing on approximately 1,200 children per year who were identified as class members. However, the changes required in service delivery for this population had an impact on providers throughout the state; the way of delivering services changed for much of the child population. There was a greater emphasis on planning collaboratively across agencies, to work toward community-based service plans, and to use case management services to integrate the efforts of multiple agencies for the non–*Willie M.* children as well.

Federal Grants

In 1987, it seemed highly desirable for North Carolina to seek a federal CASSP grant to focus on a very different part of the child population, the preschool child, and to develop an infrastructure for infant and toddler mental health services. The interest in this very young population of children with mental health problems, or at risk for such, grew out of the services to preschool children that had been a part of the mental health system since the early 1970s. Much of the original funding for these services came from Part F of the Community Mental Health Center Act Amendments of 1975 (PL 89-105) and was later supplemented by state allocations. A second source of interest in this population stemmed from the emerging implementation of the Education of the Handicapped Act Amendments of 1986 (PL 99-457), which mandated that states provide education and other services to populations of children ages birth to 5 who are at risk of or have developmental disabilities. In North Carolina, the responsibility for services to 3- to 5-year-old children rested with the state education agency, as in most other states. However, responsibility for the birth to 3-year-old children was placed with the DMH/DD/SAS, a unique decision on the part of North Carolina's governor. The importance of establishing a focal point of responsibility for young children needing mental health services could not be overestimated, given the earlier failures across the country of including this population in services provided under the Education for All Handicapped Children Act of 1975 (PL 94-142).

The CASSP project involved coordinating services with the already established in-home parent training services provided through the Developmental Disabilities Section within the same state agency. By adding a mental health professional to the in-home team, services were provided to infants and toddlers and mental health support services were available to their parents.

A substantial change in state policy resulting from the early childhood mental health initiative was the decategorization of children under the age of 3. The impact of this change was that services designated and funded for youngsters with disabilities could be provided to infants and toddlers who did not have a specific diagnosis but rather met the more broad definition of "atypical development" or "at risk for atypical development." The decategorization was in response to the recognition that diagnoses may be difficult to make in emerging conditions, and the need to label very young children was avoided. As a result of this sound programmatic change, the funding streams of the Education of the Handicapped Act Amendments and Medicaid became more available to this younger population who had nonspecific or emerging disabling conditions.

A second CASSP grant funded a local demonstration that provided a concentrated in-home service with a research component that studied the pre–post impact on mother–child relationships. This grant also provided for training of community providers to better identify emerging mental health problems in this very young population. The service network for infants and toddlers was further enhanced by the use of crisis nursery demonstration funds for four projects from the Administration for Children, Youth and Families (ACYF) in the federal Department of Health and Human Services. These federal funds became the stimulus for using state and local funds for services to infants, toddlers, and their families, and, through the refinancing initiatives described below, Medicaid and Title IV-A (Emergency Assistance) funds also became sources of support for such activities.

A major benefit of the infant and toddler programs has been the interagency emphasis of the Education of the Handicapped Act Amendments, which have expanded the networking and have provided a good model for services to older children. Furthermore, parents who have participated in the infant and toddler services have become a strong core group in the development of parent involvement in the state's child mental health system.

Robert Wood Johnson Foundation Project

Although efforts during the 1980s had laid the foundation for stronger interagency ties, the new directions of the 1990s enhanced these efforts and resulted in greater progress. Several events can be recognized as making substantial contributions to such progress. These are provided as examples of strategies designed to help states move forward toward improved programming and financing of services.

In 1989–1990, the Robert Wood Johnson Foundation had designated $20.4 million for grants to state mental health agencies for local projects to focus on the development of innovative strategies to integrate services and to prevent the out-of-home placement of children. The intent was that these local demonstrations would impact state-level policies regarding the financing and delivery of services for children with mental health problems. From the 41 applicants, 12 states were awarded 1-year planning grants and, subsequently, 8 states—California, Kentucky, North Carolina, Ohio, Oregon, Pennsylvania, Vermont, and Wisconsin—were awarded implementation grants for a 4-year period (Cole & Poe, 1993).

The North Carolina Robert Wood Johnson Project, called the Children's Initiative, was located in the Blue Ridge and Smoky Mountain Area Programs, covering the 11 most western counties in one of the most rural parts of the state. The project was designed to serve children with the most serious mental health problems in community-based services with the goal of minimizing the use of out-of-home placements. The primary focus was on children with mental health problems who were also receiving services from county departments of social services or from the juvenile court. Both of the area programs had substantial parts of the continuum of mental health services in place; thus the project expanded intensive case management services and in-home crisis stabilization services (also referred to as home-based services or family preservation services) to decrease the use of residential services. However, a new focus for the area programs was the joint case planning with the other child-serving agencies. Through the use of interagency treatment teams, joint treatment plans were developed and progress was reviewed, resulting in realization of the project's goals to decrease out-of-home placements to residential mental health facilities, foster care, and juvenile justice training schools. These sites developed collaborative, cross-agency programming to serve as a foundation for expanding the revenue base for children's mental health services.

A second focus of the Children's Initiative was on the financing of services. Through this project, national consultants who reviewed the state's use of Medicaid made recommendations for strengthening the use of Medicaid statewide, particularly through improved claims submissions and broadening of the provider groups that could be covered to include employees of other agencies. Simultaneously, the state office responsible for child mental health services expanded the applicability of a Medicaid-approved service called "High Risk Intervention," which essentially provided reimbursement for "wraparound" services. These two efforts resulted in a 1993 statewide increase of over 400% in Medicaid reimbursements for child mental health services. More recently, High-Risk Intervention has become the single most widely used child mental health service in the Medicaid program being applied to the treatment portion of therapeutic foster care and other residential services. High-Risk Intervention also has become the service that is most frequently contracted to other public and private agencies. In 1995, the service was divided into two parts to allow for reimbursement for services provided by nonprofessional staff as well, creating the service category of "Community Based Intervention," which is reimbursed at a lower rate than High-Risk Intervention. Claims for Medicaid reimbursement are paid by the fiscal intermediary directly to the area programs and therefore are not at risk of being diverted to the state's general fund. These reimbursements can be used for support of continuing services or for service expansion.

In addition to improving the use of Medicaid for the child mental health population, consultants to the Children's Initiative helped the state to restructure its use of Title IV-E reimbursements for services to a part of the foster care population. The Division of Social Services and its county agencies experienced the major financial benefits of improved claiming under Title IV-E, resulting in an annual increase of approximately $20 million. However, the benefits to DMH/DD/SAS were an immeasurable increase in goodwill for having identified such financial improvements for its sister agency. Additionally, child mental health services realized modest reimbursements for residential services provided to children eligible for IV-E services.

Reimbursement for training under Title IV-E has been more beneficial than the reimbursements for residential services. This reimbursement has resulted in a revolving training fund of approximately $500,000 per year for children's mental health services. Training funds are being used to support ongoing training in case management in communities (Weil, Zipper, & Dedmon, 1995), as well as supporting staff development and in-service training in local agencies and graduate education at the University of North Carolina at Chapel Hill and East Carolina University, the latter being a part of the PEN-PAL Project described below. The focus of the graduate education programs is to better prepare new practitioners in the fields of child psychiatry, psychology, social work, nursing, special education, and marriage and family therapy. These funds also are used to address a range of in-service training needs related to systems of care.

Medicaid Waiver/Managed Care

The above-described improvements in reimbursements for community-based services generated by the Children's Initiative led to a serious study of how such services are delivered statewide. Addressing the state's Medicaid program, both the Division of Medical Assistance (the state Medicaid agency) and the DMH/DD/SAS focused attention on the startling increase in the costs of psychiatric inpatient services for children and adolescents, an increase from $19 million to $35 million in the 2-year period between 1989 and 1991. To address the unbridled access to psychiatric hospital services, the two agencies have planned and implemented a Medicaid waiver program under section 1915(b), allowing for the introduction of a managed care pilot program.

This waiver program, called Carolina Alternatives, uses a single portal of entry into the mental health system through the area programs for children under age 18 with mental health or substance abuse problems. As in the Children's Initiative and another demonstration of a system of care implemented at the Fort Bragg military base (Behar et al., 1995; see also Chapter 18), initial assessments are completed and treatment plans are developed by the area program jointly with the family and with other providers involved with the child and family; treatment is then provided either by the area program or through an organized network of private providers and public agencies. Thus, through the use of contracts, the area programs provide a vehicle for integrating services across agencies and provide access to Medicaid reimbursement for those services delivered by other agencies as part of a comprehensive service plan for the child and family.

In Carolina Alternatives it is the area program's responsibility to authorize services, manage the care, and manage the Medicaid funds, which are prepaid on a capitated basis; the capitation payment is based on the entire eligible population. The savings realized from decreasing the use of inpatient services are used to broadened the array of community-based public and private services to provide alternatives to hospital services and to improve early access to services for the treatment of emerging problems. In determining the capitated rates to be paid to the area programs for inpatient services, the basis was the utilization history expanded by antici-pated growth and inflation. However, recognizing that nonhospital services had been underdelivered and therefore underutilized, it did not seem rea-sonable to base the capitation rate only on history because the resulting rate would have been too low to adequately fund needed services. Thus a plan was developed jointly by the state agencies and the participating area pro-grams to base the capitation rate on utilization history *and* provide pay-ments for any increases in services using the fee-for-service rate. This approach has provided the incentive to expand community-based services to enable a decrease in inpatient utilization. After 18 months of experience and an increase of approximately $40 million per year for the 10 pilot sites, there is sufficient information to establish a fair nonhospital rate.

Carolina Alternatives has been initiated in 10 of the 41 DMH/DD/SAS area programs covering 30 of the state's 100 counties. Plans are to add groups of area programs over the next year in order to achieve statewide implementation by 1997. As with other major changes in service delivery in child mental health in the state, the planning for this initiative has been shared by the participating area programs and the state agencies. Over a 14-month period, the program was crafted to avoid pitfalls and to ensure the likelihood of success. The goals to improve access, to improve mental health and substance abuse services to children and families, and to curb inappropriate growth of hospital use were supported by efforts to ensure that sufficient funds and technical assistance were available. The DMH/DD/SAS and the Division of Medical Assistance worked at the state level to effect changes in laws and policies that the planning group found im-portant for successful implementation.

When the program was in danger of being discontinued, the directors of the county departments of social services were some of the strongest advocates for its continuation, stating that the expansion in services bene-fited their clients substantially. The area programs have begun planning with the DMH/DD/SAS to amend the waiver request to implement a sim-ilar program for adults. The area directors believe that this method of or-ganizing mental health and substance abuse services represents a major and positive approach to health care reform and carves out a clear role for the public mental health/substance abuse agency as an organizer and manager of services across the public and private sectors (Kirkpatrick, Knisley, Shear, & Blum, 1995).

Use of Title IV-A (Emergency Assistance)
In addition to the efforts to improve services for the children eligible for Medicaid and Title IV-E services, North Carolina has worked to increase the expanding and sharing of other funding streams, particularly Title IV-A, or Emergency Assistance (EA), which has been a badly underutilized

entitlement program. Thinking about this entitlement program was stimulated by bringing state agency staff and budget officers to a regional financing workshop held in New Orleans in August 1993 that was sponsored by the National Technical Assistance Center for Children's Mental Health at Georgetown University. After further study of Title IV-A (EA) possibilities, it became clear that this program could provide for reimbursement for services delivered to alleviate family emergencies.

Formerly, the EA program had been limited by the state legislature to a $300 cash payment for families experiencing emergencies. The service component had not been used and there was no dollar cap imposed on it; the federal reimbursement is 50% of cost and is the same for all states. Thus, three agencies, the Division of Social Services, the Division of Youth Services, and DMH/DD/SAS, came together to revise the state's Title IV-A (EA) plan to allow for the use of the service component and to allow equal access to these funds for the three agencies. The resulting plan provides for 50% reimbursement for any services to alleviate an emergency situation for which the family cannot pay, in whole or in part. The inability to pay is by declaration rather than by a test of the family's means. The definition of emergency includes natural perils and situations that could lead to a child's being removed from the home or becoming destitute if services were not provided. According to the state plan, an emergency could last up to 364 days.

Because of the desire to integrate the planning and delivery of emergency services and because of the federal requirement that a family be covered for only one emergency in a 12-month period, a multiagency, automated intake process was developed. Thus, regardless of the agency through which a family enters the service system, a multiagency service plan can be developed. Given the kinds of services covered, this entitlement program is applicable to a wide range of social services and treatment services for children. Their family members are also eligible for services to address the emergency situation, including services such as substance abuse treatment and treatment for episodes of mental illness. Needless to say, the use of Title IV-A (EA) has broadened the financial picture substantially.

Child Mental Health Services Program Demonstration

Although the expansion of Medicaid titles IV-A (EA) and IV-E has been of substantial benefit to services for children and families in North Carolina, this has involved primarily the Division of Social Services, the Division of Youth Services, and DMH/DD/SAS. There is a continued need to strengthen the cross-agency integration by bringing juvenile justice, health, and education into the picture. In 1994, DMH/DD/SAS implemented a child mental health demonstration program funded by the federal Center for Mental Health Services. The program, located in the eastern part of the state in Pitt, Edgecombe, and Nash counties, is a Public–Academic Liaison between the state office, the area programs, and East Carolina University, and is called the PEN-PAL Project. The focus of the project is to expand further the multiagency integration of services into a unified whole and to facilitate the cross-agency use of the entitlement programs. The staff participation by the agencies expands the matching funds available to draw down federal funds, and the joint planning for services uses the funding in creative, integrated ways. The role of the university is to take the community-based experience, including a priority role for the parent–professional partnership, and use these learnings to revamp the graduate education curriculum in child psychiatry, psychology, social work, nursing, special education, and marriage and family therapy.

State–Local Partnership

As North Carolina has developed plans to improve the use of federal entitlement programs, it has been important to address state–local issues. Because North Carolina is a state with a strong county government system and strong local agencies that are tied to county governments, it was recognized that 1) the strengths of these agencies should be enhanced rather than totally reconfigured, and 2) the planning needed to be integrated across the state and local levels rather than through a "top down" approach. Although the sophisticated local counterparts of the state agencies have recognized the importance of planning together around the needs of children and their families, there has been no required collaboration at the local level with regard to individual clients. Earlier, as collaborative planning moved forward within the Willie M. program, the infant and toddler programs, and the Robert Wood Johnson Children's Initiative, consideration was given to mechanisms to ensure that joint case planning was occurring and that this case planning served as the vehicle through which both the service plan and the funding for the plan would be developed. What has been essential in making refinancing a successful effort in North Carolina is the maximal use of the state–local partnership to design and implement change. The partnership has worked well over the years to effect change within the mental health system; as that system joins with other child-serving state agencies, bringing together the local agency counterparts and the parents of the children they serve becomes essential. The tasks to be undertaken in system building and in refinancing of those systems require an ongoing back-and-forth synergy to identify problems, to clarify processes, to recognize successes, and to plan for needed changes.

In restructuring financing, professionals in local agencies are asked to change the way they function in terms of either joint case planning, record keeping, or reporting. They need to understand the value of change and to receive some incentives to do so. Overall, it is anticipated that they will respond well to increased availability of funds for "their" children. Thus it is important to gain commitments, in advance, that increased revenues to the state will result in increased funding to local service programs. This enhancement activity cannot only be seen as a way for the state to get federal funds for state dollars already paid out; it also must be seen as a way to enhance the impoverished services that all three agencies are delivering. It seems that the failure to plow the funds back into the services is a major reason that revenue enhancement has not been effective in some states.

CONCLUSION

The issues discussed above in practice take time and patience to address. As North Carolina works toward the goals of successful restructuring of financing mechanisms and of ultimate improved collection of revenues, an important balance must be achieved. Planning and processing of plans is frequently best achieved through the joint efforts of the planners and the implementers. In this case, those efforts would involve the state-level planners, including both the program and budget staff and those at the local level who will be responsible for implementation of the new strategies. It does require time for all these state and local stakeholders to come to agreement and craft an acceptable course of action.

However, planning and processing can become delaying techniques in themselves. It takes secure and sophisticated participants to determine when it is time to stop planning and start doing. A review of the implementation of other major changes suggests that, essentially, planning never ends, even after implementation begins. Most important to a new way of doing business, then, is the built-in capacity to identify problems and to address them as the new programming and financing moves forward.

It is important to understand that financing cannot change the system out of context. It is only when financing mechanisms are restructured or created to support the vision, and the structure that follows from it, that they can reach their system change potential.

REFERENCES

Behar, L., Bickman, L., Lane, T., Keeton, W.P., Schwartz, M., & Brannock, E. (1995). The Fort Bragg child and adolescent mental health demonstration. In M. Roberts (Ed.), *Model practices in service delivery in child and family mental health.* Hillside, NJ: Lawrence Erlbaum Associates.

Cole, R.F., & Poe, S. (1993). *Partnerships for care: Systems of care for children with serious emotional disturbances and their families.* Washington, DC: Washington Business Group on Health.

Community Mental Health Center Act Amendments PL 94-63 (July 29, 1975). Title 42, U.S.C. 2689 et seq: (42CFR54). *U.S. Statutes at Large, 89,* 308.

DeWoody, M. (1994). *Making sense of federal dollars: A funding guide for social service providers.* Washington, DC: Child Welfare League of America.

Education for All Handicapped Children Act of 1975, PL 94-142. (August 23, 1977). Title 20, U.S.C. 1401 et seq: *U.S. Statutes at Large, 89,* 773–796.

Education of the Handicapped Act Amendments, PL 99-457. (October 8, 1986). Title 20, U.S.C. 1400 et seq: *U.S. Statutes at Large, 100,* 1145–1177.

Kirkpatrick, J.W., Knisley, M., Shear, L.L., & Blum, S.R. (1995). State-local partnership: Development of children's mental health services in Wake County. *Administration and Policy in Mental Health, 22,* 247–259.

Koyanagi, C., & Brodie, J.R. (1994). *Making Medicaid work.* Washington, DC: Bazelon Center for Mental Health Law.

Omnibus Budget Reconciliation Act, Title VI, Subtitle B, Section 6403: Medicaid Early Periodic Screening, Diagnosis and Treatment Amendments, PL 101-239. (December 19, 1989). Title 42, U.S.C. 1396 et seq: *U.S. Statutes at Large, 103,* 2258–2270.

Social Security Act, PL 74-271. (August 14, 1935). Title 42, U.S.C. 301 et seq: *U.S. Statutes at Large, 15,* 687–1774.

Stroul, B., & Friedman, R. (1986). *A system of care for children and youth with severe emotional disturbances* (rev. ed.). Washington, DC: Georgetown University Child Development Center, National Technical Assistance Center for Children's Mental Health.

Weil, M., Zipper, I.N., & Dedmon, S.R. (1995). Issues and principles of training for case management in child mental health. In B. Friesen & J. Poertner (Eds.), *Systems of care for children's mental health: Vol. 1. From case management to service coordination for children with emotional, behavioral, or mental disorders: Building on family strengths* (pp. 211–238). Baltimore: Paul H. Brookes Publishing Co.

Willie M. et al. v. James B. Hunt, Jr., et al., C-C-79-0294, slip op. (W.D.N.C. February 20; 1991; *See* 657 F. 2d 55, 4th Cir.; 1981).

CHAPTER 17

Measuring Outcomes in Systems of Care

Beth A. Stroul, Mary McCormack, and Susan M. Zaro

The rapid acceptance of the system of care concept and philosophy, and the rapid growth of systems of care across the nation, underscore the importance of documenting the experience and results of the evolving service delivery systems. Because systems of care are recent innovations, evaluation and research efforts to assess these systems are at early stages of development. Despite the infancy of efforts to measure the outcomes of systems of care, progress has been made in identifying appropriate outcome indicators, designing methodologies for evaluating systems of care, and analyzing the achievements of systems of care.

In order to determine the state of the art for outcome measurement in systems of care, a project was initiated by the National Technical Assistance Center for Children's Mental Health at Georgetown University (Stroul, 1993, 1994). The project involved collecting and analyzing available information from a sample of approximately 30 communities in which there have been demonstrable efforts to create comprehensive, coordinated, community-based systems. The sample of communities included sites funded by the Robert Wood Johnson Foundation to develop systems of care, sites included in a recently completed descriptive study of local systems of care (Stroul, Lourie, Goldman, & Katz-Leavy, 1992), and several additional communities identified by their respective state mental health agencies as having well-developed systems of care. The information collected from the communities included descriptive information about their systems of care (such as their major goals for system development, the population that they target for services, the service array that they developed, and the outcome indicators that they use to measure success) and actual information on the preliminary outcomes they have achieved through their system development efforts. This chapter summarizes this information and concludes with a description of the methodology designed to evaluate the newly emerging systems of care that are funded through the federal Child Mental Health Services Program.

INFORMATION ABOUT SYSTEMS OF CARE

Major Goals of System Development

System development initiatives are guided by broad goals that define the nature and purposes of the desired systems of care. Although specific goals vary from site to site, commonalities across communities were found with respect to the major goals of system development.

- *To develop and provide a full array of community-based services for children with serious emotional disturbances and their families.* Each of the communities has sought to develop a broad continuum of community-based services for youngsters and families moving well beyond the traditional outpatient and inpatient services found in most areas. These service capacities include intensive nonresidential as well as residential components, allowing the communities to provide more appropriate services and to achieve better outcomes for children and their families.
- *To reduce reliance on restrictive treatment environments and out-of-home placements.* A principal aim of all the communities is to provide services within the least restrictive environment and to reduce the historical pattern of overutilization of restrictive and expensive inpatient and residential treatment settings for the treatment of youngsters with emotional disorders. These communities have attempted to create an array of intensive community-based service alternatives that allow them to divert many youngsters from restrictive levels of care and serve them within their homes and communities. Thus reducing utilization of restrictive treatment settings and reducing unnecessary out-of-home care have been common purposes across communities.
- *To increase interagency coordination and collaboration in planning, developing, and delivering services.* A fundamental aspect of these system development initiatives is the emphasis on interagency collaboration in all aspects of planning and delivering of services in order to reduce the fragmentation that has characterized service delivery to children and families. These communities have brought together the agencies and systems that share responsibility for serving children with emotional disturbances for purposes including joint planning and service development, joint financing of services, system-level coordination and problem solving, and interagency treatment planning for individual youngsters.
- *To provide flexible, individualized services that are tailored to the unique needs of each child and family.* The communities have attempted to develop systems of care that are capable of providing individualized services. Individualized care has been defined as both a philosophy and a process by which services are delivered to youngsters and their families based

on their specific needs and are "customized" in accordance with an individualized service plan. Flexible funding, interagency service planning teams, "wraparound services," and case management are integral aspects of this approach. The communities have successfully used this approach for youngsters with the most serious disorders and have creatively designed services and supports (including many nontraditional approaches such as behavioral aides) to help them to remain within the community.

- *To contain costs and demonstrate the cost-effectiveness of systems of care for children and adolescents with emotional disturbances.* A central goal of system development has been to create organized systems of care that will contain or reduce the costs associated with caring for youngsters with emotional disorders and their families. The communities have attempted to demonstrate that a full continuum of services can be provided at the same or less cost than traditional service delivery approaches and that, even with expanded access to care, costs can be contained. Some communities have attempted to document the substantial cost avoidance that can be achieved by investing in systems of care—cost avoidance within the mental health system as well as within the child welfare, education, and juvenile justice systems.

Target Population

Most communities have targeted their systems of care to the children and adolescents considered "most in need" of services. Their target population definitions typically consist of such criteria as diagnosis, duration, functional impairments, and multiagency need. For example, eligibility for services provided through Kentucky IMPACT requires a psychiatric diagnosis; severe functional limitations in at least two areas, including self-care, interpersonal relationships, family life, self-direction, and education; disability for at least 1 year or high risk of continuing the disability for 1 year without intervention; and the need for service planning and coordination from two or more agencies.

Beyond such criteria, many communities have established priorities for service delivery based on risk status. In these areas, system of care services are targeted specifically to youngsters at high risk of out-of-home placements or those already in placements, such as psychiatric hospitals or residential treatment facilities. In three California counties that have been funded by the state legislature to develop systems of care based on the Ventura Planning Model (AB 377 counties; see Chapter 9), both clinical severity and risk status are used to define the target population. The Partners' Project in Oregon prioritizes youngsters whose emotional impairments put them at imminent risk of inpatient psychiatric hospitalization or long-term residential care.

An analysis of data describing the clients of the systems of care reveals more boys than girls in the client population, with boys comprising approximately two thirds or more of those served across sites. The predominant age group across sites appears to be early to midadolescents. The mean client age in the Virginia demonstration projects and in North Idaho is about 12.5, and the largest age categories across a number of sites is the 11–16 age group (Lubrecht, 1993; Virginia Deptartment of Mental Health, Mental Retardation, and Substance Abuse Services, 1992a).

With respect to diagnosis, by far the largest percentage of youngsters in most sites has a diagnosis in the disruptive disorders category (including attention-deficit/hyperactivity disorder, oppositional defiant disorder, and conduct disorder). In Kentucky IMPACT and Vermont's New Directions, about 56%–57% of the children served fall within this diagnostic grouping; in the Virginia demonstration projects, as many as 87% are diagnosed as having disruptive disorders (Illback, 1993; Vermont Deptartment of Mental Health and Mental Retardation, 1993; Virginia Deptartment of Mental Health, Mental Retardation, and Substance Abuse Services, 1992a). Anxiety and mood disorders comprise the next largest diagnostic categories for children served, although the percentages do not approach those for disruptive disorders. For example, youngsters with mood disorders account for 19% of the population serviced by Kentucky IMPACT (Illback, 1993). Across all sites, youngsters with psychotic disorders comprise an exceedingly small percentage of the client population, numbering about 3%–4% (Stroul, 1993). Multiple diagnoses are common in this population; the Family Mosaic Project in San Francisco reported that nearly half of the youngsters served have multiple diagnoses (Martinez & Smith, 1993).

The population served by these systems of care manifests a range of difficulties, suggesting that it is, in fact, an extremely high-risk population. Sites reported that the majority of youngsters (ranging from 60% to 82%) are behind educationally and are performing below the appropriate grade level. A substantial number qualify for special education services and placements—41% in the Virginia demonstrations and 88% in Wisconsin's Project FIND, for example (Virginia Deptartment of Mental Health, Mental Retardation, and Substance Abuse Services, 1992a; Wisconsin Deptartment of Health and Social Services, 1992). The majority have a history of psychiatric hospitalization. In Kentucky IMPACT, 60% of the youngsters have been hospitalized at least once in a psychiatric facility and 44% have exhibited behaviors considered dangerous to themselves or others (Illback, 1993).

A number of family risk factors also characterize the population served by these systems of care. A large proportion of the youngsters live in poverty (more than half in most sites), and a large proportion have divorced parents, live in single-parent households, or both. In the Virginia demonstration projects, as many as 68% of the children served live in single-parent households (Virginia Deptartment of Mental Health, Mental Retardation, and Substance Abuse Services, 1992a). Many of the children are in the custody of the child welfare agency; over 70% of the children served by Vermont's New Directions are in the custody of the Vermont Department of Social and Rehabilitation Services (Vermont Department of Mental Health and Mental Retardation, 1993). Additionally, a substantial proportion of the youngsters served have a history of physical or sexual abuse, estimated at one third by Kentucky IMPACT and by the Family Mosaic Project in San Francisco (Illback, 1993; Martinez & Smith, 1993). In addition, the families of many youngsters have histories of mental illness or substance abuse. In Kentucky IMPACT, more than one third of the youngsters' families have histories of mental illness and more than half have histories of chemical dependence (Illback, 1993).

Based on the multiple and complex needs of these youngsters, involvement with multiple agencies and services might be expected. In fact, the overwhelming majority of these youngsters (84% in the Virginia demonstration projects) have received services from more than one agency prior to involvement in the system of care (Virginia Department of Mental Health, Mental Retardation, and Substance Abuse Services, 1992a). Kentucky IMPACT reported that 87% of their youngsters had received mental health services, about two thirds had prior involvement with the child welfare and special education systems, and about one fourth had prior involvement with the juvenile justice system (Illback, 1993). Despite this history of prior involvement, service delivery systems generally had been unsuccessful in meeting the needs of this population of children with serious disturbances and multiple problems.

Service Array

In developing their systems of care, the communities have expanded existing service capacities and added new services. Each community has implemented a system offering a broad array of services, generally including some combination of residential and nonresidential services (Table 17.1). Some communities have developed the capacity to provide wraparound services that enable them to creatively construct a package of services and supports (formal and informal, traditional and nontraditional) to meet the needs of an individual child and family. In addition, some communities have added other service components, such as a preschool prevention program, an alternative education program, and a therapeutic summer program.

Many of these communities collect service utilization data that reflect the range of services used by the client population and, in some cases, patterns of service utilization. For example, the Oregon Partners' Project

Table 17.1.   Services included in many systems of care

Nonresidential Services
Assessment
Psychiatric services
Outpatient services (individual, family, and group)
Home-based services
Day treatment
Crisis services
After-school and evening programs
Therapeutic respite services
Behavioral aide services
Case management
Parent education and support services

Residential Services
Therapeutic foster care
Therapeutic group care
Crisis residential services
Residential treatment services
Inpatient hospital services

reported that, from 1992 to 1993, the services used most frequently included outpatient services (used by 70% of clients), respite services (40%), transportation (38%), day treatment (35%), recreation and recreation support (23.5%), education support (10.5%), and parent education (5.5%) (Oregon Partners' Project, 1993).

There are a number of important differences between the systems of care developed by these communities and traditional services systems for children with emotional disorders.

- *Expansion of "intermediate" services:* The communities have greatly expanded the availability of "intermediate" services, which are more intensive than traditional outpatient services and which can often be used as alternatives to hospitalization. These services can be highly treatment intensive, yet are offered in more normalized environments and have been shown to be effective in keeping youngsters within their homes and communities. The services that have been added to the continuum of care in these communities include home-based services, day treatment, therapeutic foster care, therapeutic group care, and respite care.
- *Use of individualized service approach:* The communities have adopted the philosophy of individualized care, with the types, mix, and duration of services dictated by the individual needs of each child and family. Service delivery is more flexible, and many communities have developed the capacity to provide wraparound services. Some sites have flexible funds available to case managers, interagency service planning teams, or both for this purpose.

- *Use of multidisciplinary and interagency teams:* The communities have greatly expanded the use of multidisciplinary and interagency teams. Some communities work on a two-tiered team approach, with a youth-specific team responsible for service planning and implementation and a higher-level interagency team to review more complex cases and to focus on system-level issues related to service delivery and interagency relationships. Service and treatment planning for youngsters with complex problems is often approached in these communities by the creation of a team involving representatives of the agencies involved with the child (and including the family). The team meets and works together over time to develop and implement a comprehensive, individualized service plan for the youngster and family.
- *Use of case management approaches:* The role of case managers or service coordinators includes a range of functions (planning, accessing, linking, advocating, monitoring, supporting, coordinating, brokering, educating, and others) that serve to integrate and maintain a network of services and supports for each child and family. Although the approach to case management varies across communities, each site has developed the capacity to fulfill these functions and to ensure that youngsters receive the array of services in a supportive, efficient, and cost-effective manner. Some communities have developed the capacity to provide an intensive form of case management, performed by highly skilled case managers, in response to the serious and complex challenges presented by the youngsters served by their systems of care.

Outcome Indicators

A number of indicators have been identified to assess the impact of systems of care for children and adolescents with emotional disorders and their families. These indicators address outcomes from multiple perspectives, including those of children, families, communities, and systems. Many communities have been collecting data relative to some combination of these indicators to assess the effectiveness of their systems of care. In addition to the increasing evaluation activities in states and communities, several carefully designed studies are underway to assess the outcomes of the systems of care developed in sites such as Fort Bragg, North Carolina; three California counties funded to develop systems of care (San Mateo, Santa Cruz, and Riverside); and communities involved in the AIMS Project in Tennessee. Both evaluation efforts and more rigorous research attempts have tended to focus on the following indicators:

- Effect on *out-of-home and out-of-community placements,* including reduction in out-of-home, out-of county, and out-of-state placements and increased stability of placements
- Effect on *utilization of restrictive service options,* including reduction in utilization and length of stay in inpatient and residential treatment

settings and increased use of less restrictive and more appropriate placements

- Effect on the *functioning of youngsters,* including improved functioning on specific behaviors, symptoms, or global levels of functioning
- Effect on the *educational status of youngsters,* including improved school attendance, performance, and placement status
- Effect on the *law enforcement status of youngsters,* including reduction in violations of the law, contacts with law enforcement, and incarceration and recidivism rates
- Effect on *family involvement,* including increased family participation and increased parent support
- Effect on *satisfaction with services,* including increased satisfaction of parents, youth, and providers
- Effect on *access to services,* including an increased proportion of the eligible population served
- Effect on *costs,* including comparisons of the costs of "traditional" or restrictive services with costs of community-based services for youngsters served, shifts in allocation of resources, and costs avoided by implementing a more comprehensive community-based service array

PRELIMINARY OUTCOMES OF SYSTEMS OF CARE

Out-of-Home and Out-of-Community Placements

A major objective of systems of care is to keep youngsters within their homes and communities to the greatest possible extent. Traditional patterns of service delivery emphasized removal of a child from the family and placement in a special setting for treatment, often distant from the child's home community and, in many cases, out of state. The communities with systems of care have emphasized the development of services and supports that maximize the likelihood of serving children within the context of their own families and communities and reduce the necessity for out-of-home and out-of-community placements.

In fact, emerging systems of care appear to be succeeding in this area. Vermont's New Directions, for example, found a nearly 20% increase in children living at home from the time of referral to approximately 1 year following service initiation (Vermont Department of Mental Health and Mental Retardation, 1993). Those communities with strong home-based service components have had particular success in averting out-of-home placements; in Ventura County, California, 85% of the children judged to be at imminent risk of placement remained at home for at least 6 months (Stroul, Lourie, Goldman, & Katz-Leavy, 1992).

In addition to keeping more youngsters at home, systems of care report favorable impacts on out-of-county and out-of-state placements. Communities reported reductions ranging from 42% to as much as 73% in out-of-county placements and reductions in out-of-state placements ranging from 38% to 100% in Bennington County, Vermont (Stroul, 1993). In the Mountain State Network of West Virginia, sites that have developed comprehensive systems of care had significantly lower rates of out-of-state placement than did comparison sites (Rugs, 1992). These declines are attributed to the development of a broader array of community-based services coupled with an explicit commitment to serve these children within the community.

Another indicator related to placement considers the effect on stability of placement. Many youngsters with emotional disturbances have experienced multiple placements, and such instability is known to have deleterious effects. Data from Kentucky IMPACT suggest that involvement in a system of care results in a decreased number of placements for youngsters as compared with their placement histories prior to involvement. The percentage of youngsters experiencing only one placement rather than multiple placements was increased from 35.7% in the year prior to involvement in the system of care to 50% in the year following involvement (Illback, 1993). Similarly, Vermont's New Directions succeeded in reducing the percentage of youngsters experiencing three or more placement changes by 59% from the year prior to enrollment in services to the year following enrollment (Vermont Department of Mental Health and Mental Retardation, 1993).

Utilization of Restrictive Service Options

Reducing reliance on restrictive service settings, such as hospitals and residential treatment centers, has been a goal universally shared by systems of care. In fact, a major premise of systems of care is that expanding the array of community-based services will decrease the likelihood of utilizing restrictive service options. It is within this area that the most extensive outcome information can be found. Evidence is building that systems of care do result in decreased utilization of such settings and that youngsters in communities with systems of care are less likely to be placed in inpatient and residential settings. Trends in these communities favor the use of less restrictive, more normalized service delivery approaches.

Findings from the Fort Bragg, North Carolina, demonstration reveal that children with serious emotional disturbances were five times more likely to be placed in an inpatient or residential setting at the comparison sites than were children with comparable levels of impairment at Fort Bragg. The percentage of clients served utilizing hospital and residential treatment settings decreased from 7% to less than 1.5% over the 2-year period from 1990 to 1992 (Behar, 1992a; Bickman, 1993).

Specifically with respect to inpatient utilization, data from a wide range of communities indicate substantial reductions. In Fort Bragg, the total number of bed days (12,199) and bed days per admission (49.6) were lower than at the comparison sites (21,488 and 57.0, respectively), which have approximately the same size population, and at Fort Hood (46,741 and 68.0, respectively), which has a smaller population. Only 3% of children at Fort Bragg were hospitalized, compared with 23% of children at the comparison sites (Behar, 1992a). When the client populations at Fort Bragg and the comparison sites were categorized by severity of impairment, it was found that comparison site clients had more hospital days at each level of severity (Bickman, 1993). Thus, even the youngsters with the most serious disturbances spent less time in hospital settings at the Fort Bragg demonstration site than at comparison sites without systems of care.

These findings are supported by data from other sites that indicate reductions in overall hospital admission rates as well as in total bed days. Lucas County, Ohio, for example, decreased hospital admissions by 46% and total inpatient days by 61% from 1988 to 1992 (Keros, 1993). The Children's Initiative in North Carolina succeeded in reducing inpatient days by 42% in 1992, at a time when inpatient utilization had been increasing statewide (Behar, 1992b).

Communities have been able to achieve particular reductions in the utilization of state hospitals and reported substantial declines in both admissions and average census. Augusta, Georgia, decreased state hospital admissions by 39% and Stark County, Ohio, and Ventura County, California, reduced their average daily census by 79% and 58%, respectively (Georgia Division of Mental Health, Mental Retardation, and Substance Abuse, 1992; Stroul, Lourie, Goldman, & Katz-Leavy, 1992). The three AB 377 system of care counties in California experienced lower state hospital utilization and expenditures than for the state as a whole (Rosenblatt & Attkisson, 1992a; Rosenblatt, Attkisson, & Mills, 1992).

In addition, two sites reported large reductions in Medicaid expenditures for psychiatric hospitalization: a one-third reduction in Kentucky IMPACT and a reduction of more than one half in Northumberland County, Pennsylvania (Illback, 1993; Stroul, Lourie, Goldman, & Katz-Leavy, 1992). Length of stay in inpatient settings also declined in many of these communities. Reported reductions in hospital average lengths of stay range from 24% to 56% (Stroul, 1993).

Similar findings were reported with respect to residential treatment centers (RTCs), with communities achieving substantial reductions in the number of youngsters in such placements. Fort Bragg decreased the number of children receiving RTC services by 68% from 1991 to 1992 (Behar, 1992a). Additionally, children at Fort Bragg spent an average of 40 total days in RTCs, as contrasted with an average of 130 days at the comparison sites, in the demonstration's first year of operation (Bickman, 1993). Similarly, Vermont's New Directions decreased the percentage of youngsters in RTCs from 45% at referral to 9% at a 1993 update (Vermont Department of Mental Health and Mental Retardation, 1993).

Experience in California provides additional evidence—in Ventura County and the three AB 377 counties, group home (i.e., RTC) placement rates per 10,000 population were significantly lower than for the state as a whole. Evaluators found that foster home and state hospital placements and expenditures were lower for the AB 377 counties than for the state as a whole and that special education placements were either comparable to the state rate or lower. Thus, these reductions in RTC placement were not achieved by shifting youngsters to other types of residential settings. Cumulative evidence in these counties led evaluators to conclude that they are utilizing restrictive levels of care at a lower rate than would be expected based on statewide utilization patterns (Rosenblatt & Attkisson, 1992a; Rosenblatt, Attkisson, & Fernandez, 1992; Rosenblatt, Attkisson, & Mills, 1992).

In addition to reducing the placement rate in RTCs, some sites have reduced length of stay in these settings by working closely with the centers and by offering services and supports that enable youngsters to return to the community. Fort Bragg, for example, has reduced the average length of stay in RTCs by 38%, from 105.1 days in 1991 to 68.5 days in 1992 (Behar, 1992a).

Evidence also is emerging to suggest that systems of care result in more appropriate placements. The Tennessee AIMS Project found that children in pilot areas were in significantly more appropriate and less restrictive placements at the end of a 6-month period than children in control areas, with only 9% of the children in pilot areas in the most restrictive placements, as compared with 17% in the control areas. In the pilot areas, restrictiveness of placement was more directly related to the child's level of psychosocial functioning than in the control areas, suggesting a better fit between the problem level of the child and the restrictiveness of the placement (Glisson, 1992).

Functional Improvements

Although other achievements of systems of care are important, the ultimate goal of such systems is to benefit the children served and to assist them in achieving meaningful improvements in their clinical status and levels of functioning. Therefore, it has been a priority for most communities to gather some type of evaluative information on functioning with respect to specific behaviors, symptoms, or global functioning measures. Many sites have found noteworthy improvements in a variety of areas.

Kentucky IMPACT, for example, used the Child Behavior Checklist (CBCL) to assess behavior at intake and at a 1-year follow-up (Achenbach, 1991a). Improvements were noted with respect to both internalizing problem behaviors (such as withdrawal, somatic complaints, anxiety, and depression) and externalizing problem behaviors (such as aggression and acting out) (Illback, 1993). Also based on administration of the CBCL, Tennessee's AIMS Project found improved functioning for children receiving services for 1 year. Furthermore, for children entering with higher levels of disturbance, more progress was made in the pilot areas than in the control sites (Glisson, 1992). North Idaho found improvements on the CBCL for 44 youngsters from the pretest to three subsequent test intervals (Lubrecht, 1993). The Children's Initiative in North Carolina administered the North Carolina Functional Assessment Scale at intake and at 1 year following service initiation and found that 38% of the children demonstrated moderate improvement and 18% showed substantial improvement in their global change scores (Behar, 1992b).

Ratings of various aspects of functioning have also been used by communities to assess progress in this area. Kentucky IMPACT found that ratings by parents, teachers, and children consistently indicated improvements in functioning from intake to 1 year following service initiation on domains including self-control, emotional adjustment, family relationships, peer relationships, and school adjustment (Illback, 1993). Connections, in Cleveland, Ohio, used progress ratings to assess improvements relative to specific presenting problems. High levels of improvement have been documented in such areas as decreases in alcohol or drug use, child abuse, suicidal thoughts and gestures, depressed mood, delusional behavior, hallucinatory behavior, and truancy (Hanna-Williams, 1993). Still other sites, such as Vermont's New Directions, have tracked negative behaviors and found reduced frequency of behaviors such as physical aggression, property damage, running away, sexual assault, and self-injury (Vermont Department of Mental Health and Mental Retardation, 1993).

Educational Status

An explicit goal of many communities is to improve the educational status of youngsters with emotional disturbances because they typically experience problems with school attendance and achievement. Some communities have demonstrated improvements in educational status as a result of involvement in their systems of care. For example, the Family Mosaic Project in San Francisco found sizable increases in school attendance based on a comparison of the year prior to and the year following enrollment (Martinez & Smith, 1993). Virginia's Local Interagency Service Projects also found an increased percentage of children attending school from the time of admission to the time of discharge, as well as reduced suspensions, expulsions, and dropout rates (Virginia Department of Mental Health, Mental Retardation, and Substance Abuse Services, 1992b). Evidence of improved school performance is provided by Ventura County, California, where youth involved in the specialized Phoenix School program (as well as receiving other services through the system of care) gained an average of 1.6 academic years after 1 year in the program (Stroul, Lourie, Goldman, & Katz-Leavy, 1992).

Law Enforcement Status

An important measure of the success of systems of care from both the child's and the community's perspective is the effect on youngsters' involvement with the juvenile justice system. Some communities have collected data in this area that suggest positive effects on law enforcement status. In the Mountain State Network in West Virginia, youngsters in system of care sites (Model A) had fewer contacts with the juvenile justice system than those in comparison sites (Rugs, 1992). Ventura County, California, the Family Mosaic Project in San Francisco, and the North Carolina Children's Initiative reported reduced incarceration and recidivism rates for youngsters served by their systems of care. For children with detention histories, the average days of detention was reduced by 40% from a period prior to involvement in the Family Mosaic Project to a period after involvement (Martinez & Smith, 1993). In Ventura County, the total days of incarceration for offenders participating in the project was reduced by 30% and the reincarceration rate for participating offenders was reduced by 56% (Stroul, Lourie, Goldman, & Katz-Leavy, 1992). For the seven-county area served by the North Carolina Children's Initiative, the average number of days spent by youngsters in secure detention was decreased by 30% and the total number of days of secure detention was decreased by 23% from 1989–1990 to 1991–1992 (Behar, 1992b).

Family Involvement

Although increasing family involvement and support are primary objectives of the majority of the systems of care, few systematically collect data to assess progress in this area. One exception is Kentucky IMPACT, which has gathered data regarding parents' perceptions of the support received from various providers. Based on an Inventory of Social Support administered at intake, 6 months, and 1 year following service initiation, increases were found in the amount of perceived support from providers, including service coordinators, respite providers, crisis counselors, recreation workers, in-home workers, and "total support" (Illback, 1993).

Satisfaction with Services

Consumer satisfaction with services is an important indicator of success, and several sites have mechanisms in place to assess parent satisfaction with services and, in one community, youth satisfaction. The data suggest that parents are indeed satisfied with services provided by the systems of care. In Fort Bragg, parents were significantly more satisfied with the services they received than parents at comparison sites, and they reported a higher level of confidence that the services children were receiving would ameliorate the problems they were experiencing (Behar, 1992a). Kentucky IMPACT found increased parent satisfaction at intervals of 6 months and 1 year following service initiation (Illback, 1993). Services in other communities (such as the Virginia demonstration project communities, North Idaho, and the area served by the North Carolina Children's Initiative) received consistently high parent satisfaction ratings.

Youth satisfaction was measured by New Directions in Vermont, where youngsters receiving services rated overall satisfaction an average of 4.17 on a 5-point scale, with 5 being "extremely satisfied" (Burchard et al., 1993). Virginia's demonstration projects measured provider satisfaction and found that more than two thirds of the providers in the demonstration communities were extremely satisfied with the impact of the system of care on their communities (Virginia Department of Mental Health, Mental Retardation, and Substance Abuse Services, 1992a). Similarly, a survey of providers from the range of child-serving agencies and systems in the area served by the North Carolina Children's Initiative revealed that 61% of the providers were very satisfied with the services their clients were receiving and 39% were moderately satisfied; no providers expressed dissatisfaction (Behar, 1992b).

Access to Services

There is some evidence that the development of systems of care has resulted in improved access to services by youngsters with emotional disorders. In Fort Bragg, for example, twice as many youngsters were served as compared with the comparison sites: 6% of the eligible population versus 3% at the comparison sites (Behar, 1992a). The AIMS Project in Tennessee also significantly increased the proportion of children in the pilot areas receiving mental health services (Glisson, 1992).

Cost Comparisons

One of the most important hypotheses of system development is that community-based systems of care can contain costs and provide efficient and cost-effective services. One way that communities have attempted to demonstrate this is by comparing the costs of "traditional" services with the costs of community-based services for youngsters served. Data suggest potential savings by implementing a system of care with an expanded array of community-based services.

A number of communities have documented lower costs with an array of community-based services than with more traditional services. They have approached this by comparing costs for the year prior to involvement in the system of care with the year following involvement or by comparing system of care costs with average costs for a more traditional mix of services, typically relying more heavily upon institutional environments. Kentucky IMPACT, using the former approach, found costs reduced by approximately $4 million in comparing the first year of services under Kentucky IMPACT with the prior year; in Franklin County, Ohio, 10% less was expended in a 6-month period through the system of care than in the 6 months prior to involvement (Illback, 1993; McCoard, 1993). When comparing average costs for traditional versus system of care service delivery configurations, Vermont's New Directions found that the average costs for 10 youngsters in out-of-state placements exceeded the average cost for 19 youngsters receiving individualized services in state for the same time period (Vermont Department of Mental Health and Mental Retardation, 1993).

Although cost reductions are reported consistently across sites, the reported average costs per client vary widely. These variations appear to be a function primarily of the nature of the population served by the system of care. Some systems serve only youngsters with the most serious and complex needs, resulting in relatively high per-client costs. Others may serve a more mixed population, such as Fort Bragg, which serves all youngsters with mental health needs, resulting in lower average costs. Variations also result from differences in computing the costs of services.

Increasing evidence indicates that systems of care with appropriate management of service delivery not only may contain costs but may result in shifts in the allocation of resources to the nonresidential service approaches utilized by the vast majority of service recipients. Such shifts in resource allocation have occurred at Fort Bragg. At the comparison sites, 95% of the resources are spent on hospital and residential care (which are utilized by a small minority of children), whereas, at Fort Bragg, only 47% of the resources are currently spent on hospital and residential care (Behar, 1992a). These changing patterns of resource allocation increase the likelihood that a greater proportion of youngsters in need will benefit from scarce mental health resources.

Additional evidence of the long-range fiscal benefits of systems of care is found in estimates of costs avoided by implementing more comprehensive community-based services. California provides convincing evidence to this effect. For example, the three AB 377 system of care counties have saved over $35 million in costs for group home residential care from 1989 to 1992 when compared with trends for the state. It has been estimated that the state of California could have saved a total of approximately $50 million in residential costs if the state had followed the trend of the AB 377 counties instead of the actual trend in the state for the same time period (Rosenblatt & Attkisson, 1992a, 1992b; Rosenblatt, Attkisson, & Fernandez, 1992; Rosenblatt, Attkisson, & Mills, 1992). Similarly, Ventura County, California, has documented not only cost avoidance within the mental health system but savings accrued by reducing youngsters' involvement in the child welfare, juvenile justice, and special education systems as well, primarily by reducing placement rates and lengths of stay (Stroul, Lourie, Goldman, & Katz-Leavy, 1992).

METHODOLOGY FOR EVALUATING SYSTEMS OF CARE

In order to promote the development of comprehensive systems of care, the federal Center for Mental Health Services (CMHS) initiated the Child

Mental Health Services Program in 1993. As of fiscal year 1994, the program funded 22 grantees at levels high enough to build the service array needed to adequately serve youngsters with serious emotional disorders and their families.

In conjunction with the services program, CMHS initiated an evaluation effort. The evaluation process began with a contract to Macro International, Inc., to develop an evaluation design; this was accomplished with input from an expert panel and the first four grantees. The evaluation was initiated in October 1994 by Macro in partnership with the University of South Florida and will proceed for a minimum of 3 years.

The purpose of the evaluation is to determine whether the initiative has reached its goals of expanding capacity at the local level, providing a broad array of services, and ensuring the full involvement of families. In addition, the evaluation will show whether there are detectable differences in client and system outcomes that can be linked to fully implemented systems of care. Findings from the evaluation will provide CMHS, other federal agencies, and the grantees empirical data on which to base policy and programmatic decisions and to improve the implementation of each system of care.

All grantees will participate in a core evaluation that will provide descriptive data about the clients served, client outcome data, and system outcome data. In addition, grantees may elect to participate in special studies designed to examine outcomes more comprehensively and focus in more detail on features of the system of care and the community that may affect outcomes. Although designed to evaluate grantees of this federal program, the methodology for the core evaluation has broad potential applicability for other states and communities interested in assessing the outcomes of their evolving systems of care.

As shown in Table 17.2, evaluation questions focus on three levels: the client descriptive level, the client outcome level, and the system level. On the client descriptive level, the evaluation seeks information on who is accessing the system of care, the types of behavioral and emotional problems they have experienced, and the array and costs of services they are receiving. The client outcome level focuses on the behavioral and affective changes that occur during the course of their involvement in the system of care; client and family satisfaction and empowerment also are examined.

On the system level, the evaluation profiles the development of systems of care over time. By focusing on the establishment and enhancement of systems of care, the evaluation will illuminate how the vision and philosophy of family-centered, community-based, child-focused, and culturally competent services are operationalized. This focus will lead to a better understanding of the factors that lead to the creation, maintenance, and enhancement of systems of care.

Table 17.2. Evaluation questions and measurement indicators

Evaluation questions	Indicators
Client Descriptive Level	
What are clients like?	• Gender
	• Race
	• Age
	• Educational level and placement
	• Socioeconomic status
	• Parents' employment status
	• Living arrangement
	• Presenting problem
	• Diagnosis
	• Level of functioning
	• Referral source
	• Risk factors for family and child
	• Case status
What services do they receive?	• Service setting and type
	• Duration/history
Client Outcome Level	
Has there been a reduction in symptoms?	• Number of positive behaviors
	• Number of problem behaviors
Has there been an increase in the level of client social functioning?	• Child ability to accomplish activities of daily living
	• Improved family relationships
	• Improved peer relationships
Has there been improvement in client functioning in law enforcement environment?	• Violations
	• Number of contacts with law enforcement
	• Number of incarcerations
Has there been improvement in client functioning in educational environment?	• School attendance
	• Expulsions, dropouts, suspensions
	• Academic performance
	• Restrictiveness of educational placement
Do children, families, and providers see progress resulting from the services and system of care and are families satisfied with the services provided?	• Child satisfaction
	• Parent or caregiver satisfaction
	• Child's perception of improvement
	• Parent or caregiver perception of child improvement
	• Family sense of support and empowerment
	• Child's perception of unconditional care and involvement
System Level	
Is care individualized?	• Active individualized service planning (ISP) process
	• Frequency of monitoring of ISP by case manager

(continued)

Table 17.2. (*continued*)

Evaluation questions	Indicators
Are services available and comprehensive?	• Availability of broad array of residential, intermediate, outpatient, and wraparound services
Are services community based?	• Availability and array of services at community level • Level of use of out-of-home, out-of-county, and out-of-state placements
Are services and the system of care accessible?	• Proportion of eligible population provided services • Time between identification of need and entry to system • Waiting lists for entry to system • Logistics and supports that encourage access
Is the system based on an interagency collaborative structure?	• Relevant agencies are participating in a collaborative way • Integration of staff, resources, functions, and funds • Interagency planning • Shared vision and goals
Is the system of care coordinated?	• Co-location of services of multiple agencies • Availability of case management/care coordination services • Case manager/care coordinator has broad responsibilities and active referral role • Integration and consistency in case management/care coordination across systems/agencies
Are services and system family centered?	• System and services involve parents or caregivers in developing individual client service plans • System and services involve parents or caregivers in overall system of care planning activities • System and services involve parents or caregivers in service delivery • System and services address needs of parents and caregivers for support

(*continued*)

Table 17.2. (continued)

Evaluation questions	Indicators
Are services offered in the least restrictive setting?	• Minimization of inpatient or residential treatment settings • Level of use of intermediate and outpatient services placements • Level of use of wraparound services • Stability and duration of placement • Level of use of mental health services in other settings
Are system and services culturally competent?	• Cultural diversity of the client population • Cultural diversity of provider population • Agency commitment to cultural competency • Culturally appropriate treatment of all clients
Is the system of care cost-efficient in comparison with traditional systems?	• Comparison of cost of services with traditional delivery system • Comparisons of costs using MIS data • Cost of each service unit • Comparison of cost of services over time • Increase in resources for nonresidential options

MIS, management information system.

Client descriptive data will be collected on all children who enter the system of care. Client outcome data will be gathered on either a census or a systematic sample of children at each site, depending on the size of the client population at the site. System-level data will be collected during annual site visits to each of the grantees.

Table 17.3 summarizes the strategies planned for gathering data. Most client descriptive indicators will be extracted from the grantee's management information system (MIS); most client outcome indicators will be measured with standardized instruments; and system-level indicators will be collected through semi-structured interviews, on-site observations, an interagency collaboration checklist, an index of system change, and focus groups with parents/caregivers.

For the national evaluation, data gathered through this protocol will yield both quantitative and qualitative information about the systems of care. The data present many opportunities for analysis both for individual grantees and across all grantee communities. Data will be analyzed sepa-

Table 17.3. Data collection strategies

Type of data	Instrument	Respondent	Periodicity
Client Descriptive Data			
Child-related data	MIS	Child or family as appropriate	At intake and then updated selectively during follow-up visits
Family-related data	MIS	Family	At intake
Client Outcome Data			
Functional assessment	Youth self-report (Achenbach, 1991b)	Child (only those 9 years old and older)	At intake, 6 months, 12 months, and annually thereafter
	Child Behavior Checklist (Achenbach, 1991a)	Child's parents/ caregiver	Same
	Child and Adolescent Functional Assessment Scale (Hodges, 1990/1994, 1994)	Child's provider	Same
Child satisfaction with system of care	Youth Satisfaction Questionnaire (Macro International, 1995c)	Child (only those 9 years old and older)	Same
Parent satisfaction with system of care	Family Satisfaction Questionnaire (Macro International, 1995a)	Child's parent/ caregiver	Same
Parent/caregiver sense of empowerment	Family Empowerment Scale (Portland State University, 1993)	Child's parent/ caregiver	Same
Restrictiveness of placement or living arrangements of child	Residential Living Environments Scale (Macro International, 1995b)	Child's provider	Same
System Data			
System descriptive data	• Site visit protocol • Provider and family focus group discussion guides • MIS	Providers and families	Annually
System outcome data	• Interagency collaboration instruments • MIS	Providers	Annually

MIS, management information system.

rately for each grantee so that it will be possible to draw specific conclusions about clients, about system development, and about client and system linkages in each community. Aggregate data analyses will be conducted at two levels: 1) sites at the same level of system development will be clustered together and their data will be analyzed jointly, and 2) all client data for all the grantees will be aggregated.

The evaluation protocol for the national evaluation potentially has broad applicability to other communities that are developing systems of care but that are not necessarily receiving federal funds. The evaluation questions, indicators, instrumentation, and periodicity of data collection can be adopted by interested communities. The methodology represents a major step toward the development of a consistent set of outcome indicators that can be broadly used to evaluate systems of care for children with emotional disorders.

DISCUSSION

Advocates for systems of care for children and adolescents with serious emotional disorders contend that such systems provide higher quality, more appropriate, and more cost-effective care. It is only through careful analysis of the outcomes of systems of care that these claims can be substantiated. Therefore, research and program evaluation activities designed to assess systems of care are critically important to shape future patterns of service delivery for this underserved and vulnerable population.

Because systems of care are fairly recent innovations, evaluation and research efforts related to them are in early stages of development. A report prepared by the Institute of Medicine (1989) documented the lack of research in the area of children's mental health, and a subsequent National Institute of Mental Health (NIMH) plan called for increased investment in this area, including research on services and systems of care. As a result, research on systems of care is increasing, with additional studies supported by NIMH and CMHS.

Although the need for additional research on systems of care is clear, there is increasing evidence emerging from a variety of sources that points toward the efficacy of the system of care approach. Some of this evidence is derived from rigorously designed studies and other information is derived from program evaluation activities undertaken by states and communities to assess their system-building initiatives. The methodology and quality of these data may be criticized in some cases, and much of the information must be considered preliminary. Nevertheless, some trends are becoming apparent with respect to the results of systems of care. Trends in data across systems of care suggest that

- Children receiving services within systems of care appear less likely to receive services in restrictive service environments such as hospitals and residential treatment centers, and, when they are admitted to these settings, they appear likely to remain for shorter periods of time.
- Children receiving services within systems of care appear less likely to be placed out of their homes and, when they are in out-of-home placements, appear less likely to be placed in treatment settings outside of their own counties and states.
- Children receiving services within systems of care appear to demonstrate improvements in functioning, including symptom reduction, reduction of negative behaviors, and improved overall functioning.
- Children receiving services within systems of care appear to demonstrate some improvements in school attendance and school performance.
- Children receiving services within systems of care appear to have fewer contacts with law enforcement, fewer episodes of incarcerations, and fewer days spent in juvenile detention facilities.
- Parents of children receiving services within systems of care appear to be more satisfied with services and with the support they receive.
- Costs of providing systems of care appear to be less than for traditional service delivery patterns, which rely more heavily on expensive treatment environments, and resources in systems of care shift so that a greater proportion are spent on nonresidential services.
- Systems of care appear to result in the avoidance of costs within the mental health, child welfare, education, and juvenile justice systems by reducing the use of facilities and programs paid for by these systems.

Continuing commitments to research and evaluation are needed in order to monitor and assess the results of systems of care as they evolve throughout the nation. Attention should be directed beyond the assessment of short-term outcomes for youngsters involved in such systems of care to determining long-term results over time for youngsters and their families. Despite methodological unevenness, this review suggests that many sites are beginning to focus on similar indicators for assessing the efficacy of their systems of care. As systems of care continue to develop nationwide, attention to a common set of outcome indicators would provide a framework for more systematic studies and multisite analyses. The methodology designed to evaluate the Child Mental Health Services Program grantees will provide an excellent vehicle for such multisite analyses and may be applied in communities regardless of whether or not they are receiving federal funds.

REFERENCES

Achenbach, T.M. (1991a). *Manual for the Child Behavior Checklist/4-18 and 1991 Profile*. Burlington: Department of Psychiatry, University of Vermont.

Achenbach, T.M. (1991b). *Manual for the Youth Self Report and 1991 Profile*. Burlington: Department of Psychiatry, University of Vermont.

Behar, L. (1992a). *Fort Bragg child and adolescent mental health demonstration project*. Raleigh: North Carolina Division of Mental Health, Developmental Disabilities, and Substance Abuse Services, Child and Family Services Branch.

Behar, L. (1992b). *The Children's Initiative, North Carolina Mental Health Services Program for Youth*. Raleigh: North Carolina Division of Mental Health, Developmental Disabilities, and Substance Abuse Services, Child and Family Services Branch.

Bickman, L. (1993). *The evaluation of the Fort Bragg demonstration project*. Nashville, TN: Vanderbilt University, Center for Mental Health Policy.

Burchard, J., Rosen, L., Heckman, T., Gendebien, M., Pandian, N., & Stith, A. (1993). *The role of youth satisfaction surveys in evaluating outcomes for children and adolescents receiving community-based, wraparound services*. Paper presented at the 6th Annual Research Conference, A System of Care for Children's Mental Health: Expanding the Research Base, Tampa, FL.

Georgia Division of Mental Health, Mental Retardation, and Substance Abuse. (1992). *A report on the August SED project*. Atlanta: Author.

Glisson, C. (1992). *The adjudication, placement, and psychosocial functioning of children in state custody*. Knoxville: University of Tennessee, College of Social Work.

Hanna-Williams, F. (1993). [Connections project data]. Unpublished raw data. Cleveland, OH: Cuyahoga County Community Mental Health Board.

Hodges, K. (1990/1994). *Manual for the Child and Adolescent Functional Assessment Scale*. Unpublished manuscript, Department of Psychology, Eastern Michigan University.

Hodges, K. (1994). *Child and Adolescent Functional Assessment Scale*. Ann Arbor, MI: Author.

Illback, R. (1993). *Evaluation of the Kentucky IMPACT program for children and youth with severe emotional disabilities, year two*. Frankfort, KY: Division of Mental Health, Children and Youth Services Branch.

Institute of Medicine. (1989). *Research on children and adolescents with mental, behavioral, and developmental disorders*. Washington, DC: National Academy Press.

Keros, J. (1993). [Lucas County, Ohio, hospitalization data]. Unpublished raw data. Toledo: Lucas County Mental Health Board.

Lubrecht, J. (1993). [North Idaho rural system of care evaluation data]. Unpublished raw data. Coeur d'Alene, ID: Region I Health and Welfare, Family and Children's Services.

Macro International. (1995a). *Family Satisfaction Questionnaire*. Atlanta: Author.

Macro International. (1995b). *Residential Living Environments Scale*. Atlanta: Author.

Macro International. (1995c). *Youth Satisfaction Questionnaire*. Atlanta: Author.

Martinez, M., & Smith L. (1993). *The Family Mosaic project, Report submitted to the Washington Business Group on Health*. San Francisco: Family Mosaic Project.

McCoard, D. (1993). *10 KIDS: An interprofessional managed care approach to returning SED youth placed out-of-county using nontraditional cross-system collaborative strategies*. Paper presented at the 6th Annual Research Conference, A System of Care for Children's Mental Health: Expanding the Research Base, Tampa, FL.

Oregon Partners' Project. (1993). [Partners' Project evaluation data]. Unpublished raw data. Portland, OR: Office of Child and Adolescent Mental Health.

Portlant State University. (1993). *Family Empowerment Scale*. Portland, OR: Research and Training Center on Family Support and Children's Mental Health.

Rosenblatt, A., & Attkisson, C. (1992a). Integrating systems of care in California for youth with severe emotional disturbance. I. A descriptive overview of the California AB377 evaluation project. *Journal of Child and Family Studies, 1*, 93–113.

Rosenblatt, A., & Attkisson, C. (1992b). Integrating systems of care in California for youth with severe emotional disturbance. III. Answers that lead to questions about out-of-home placements and the California AB377 evaluation project. *Journal of Child and Family Studies, 2*, 119–141.

Rosenblatt, A., Attkisson, C., & Fernandez, A. (1992). Integrating systems of care in California for youth with severe emotional disturbance. II. Initial group home expenditure and utilization finding from the California AB377 evaluation project. *Journal of Child and Family Studies, 1*, 263–286.

Rosenblatt, A., Attkisson, C., & Mills, N. (1992). *The California AB377 evaluation, three year summary report*. San Francisco: The University of California.

Rugs, D. (1992). *Mountain state network project*. Unpublished report, Florida Mental Health Institute, Department of Child and Family Studies, Tampa.

Stroul, B. (1993). *Systems of care for children and adolescents with severe emotional disturbances: What are the results?* Washington, DC: Georgetown University Child Development Center, National Technical Assistance Center for Children's Mental Health.

Stroul, B. (1994). Systems of care for children and adolescents with emotional disorders: What are the results? *Continuum, 1*(1), 29–49.

Stroul, B., Lourie, I., Goldman, S., & Katz-Leavy, J. (1992). *Profiles of local systems of care for children and adolescents with severe emotional disturbances*. Washington, DC: Georgetown University Child Development Center, National Technical Assistance Center for Children's Mental Health.

Vermont Department of Mental Health and Mental Retardation. (1993). *Vermont New Directions evaluation of children and adolescent services*. Waterbury, VT: Division of Mental Health.

Virginia Department of Mental Health, Mental Retardation, and Substance Abuse Services (1992a). *Demonstration project interim evaluation results*. Richmond, VA: Office of Research and Evaluation.

Virginia Department of Mental Health, Mental Retardation, and Substance Abuse Services (1992b). *Local interagency service projects initiative*. Richmond, VA: Office of Research and Evaluation.

Wisconsin Department of Health and Social Services. (1992). *Project FIND*. Madison, WI: Author.

CHAPTER 18

Research on Systems of Care

Implications of the Fort Bragg Evaluation

Leonard Bickman,
Wm. Thomas Summerfelt, and Michael Foster

The mental health system's response to children and adolescents with serious emotional disabilities and their families is in a period of transition. A shift in both conceptualization and practice is now in process. Recent changes include a recognition that generating empirically based knowledge can assist in the improvement of the service delivery systems for children and adolescents with serious emotional disorders and their families (Duchnowski & Kutash, 1993; Kutash, Duchnowski, & Sondheimer, 1994).

OVERVIEW OF RESEARCH ON LOCAL SYSTEMS OF CARE

The philosophies underpinning the system of care concept emphasize not only the need to develop community-based systems of care based on a set of values and principles, but that these systems should be guided by the best available research (Stroul & Friedman, 1986). In 1984, the National Institute of Mental Health (NIMH) launched a modestly funded program called the Child and Adolescent Service System Program (CASSP). The purpose of CASSP was to improve systems of care available at the community level for children and families. The influence of CASSP on service systems for children has been substantial and greater than anticipated, even by those who developed the initiative (Burns & Friedman, 1990; Knitzer, 1993). Although the focus of CASSP was primarily on the development of service delivery systems, funds also were made available for two research and

The authors would like to thank K. Kutash, D. Rugs, and D. Sondheimer for their assistance in preparing the section of this chapter entitled "Overview of Research on Local Systems of Care" and to B. Stroul for assistance with the section entitled "Issues Raised for Future Research on Systems of Care."

training centers. Through interagency agreements, NIMH and the National Institute on Disability and Rehabilitation Research established two centers to conduct research and training activities focused on this population, one located at the Florida Mental Health Institute of the University of South Florida and the other at Portland State University. One of the major accomplishments of the centers has been to increase the infrastructure of researchers focused on children's mental health services. Since 1988, the Florida center has hosted an annual research conference highlighting research on service systems for children and youth with serious emotional disorders.

While the foundation for the development of systems of care was being laid by CASSP activities, children with mental health needs were receiving additional attention from the U.S. Congress, which commissioned the Office of Technology Assessment to report on the status of children's mental health services (see Saxe, Cross, & Silverman, 1988; Saxe, Cross, Silverman, Batchelor, & Dougherty, 1987). Also, NIMH requested a report by the Institute of Medicine of the National Academy of Sciences (1989) on the available mental health research related to these children and adolescents. Both reports stressed the need to generate and utilize empirically based knowledge to improve service delivery to children and adolescents with serious emotional disorders and their families. The federal response has involved significant increases in the investment in research on children's mental health services and systems of care. Both NIMH and the Center for Mental Health Services have funded a variety of research projects focusing on various aspects of systems of care.

Despite the increase in effort, evaluations and research in children's mental health have only recently incorporated a systems approach (Morrissey, 1992; Morrissey, Tausign, & Lindsey, 1985). Recognizing that children with serious emotional disorders use an array of services, this approach views the delivery of services from a holistic perspective: Rather than studying individual components of the system, it focuses on the community-based system of care as the unit of analysis. To date, only a handful of studies incorporate a full-system focus. Four such studies include the California AB377 replication research (Rosenblatt & Attkisson, 1992), Tennessee's AIMS Project (Glisson, 1993; Glisson & James, 1992), the West Virginia Mountain State Network Project (Rugs, Warner-Levock, Johnston, & Freedman, 1994), and the Fort Bragg Evaluation Project (Bickman, Heflinger, Pion, & Behar, 1992). Given that the aim of all four studies was to document the effectiveness of community-based services for children and adolescents, they shared many common features. Each, for example, used some type of comparison group to examine the effects of the system of care. Each also used similar measures of outcome, such as level of restrictiveness of living environment or the differential use of family settings versus other settings (such as residential or inpatient hospital care) for the care of children and adolescents. However, there were marked differences in the types of comparison groups selected, the target populations studied, the method for selecting subjects, the outcome measures used, and how the implementation of systems of care was measured (Friedman, Rugs, & Cascardi, 1994).

Both the Tennessee and West Virginia studies found that communities that had implemented an integrated service delivery system could maintain youth in less restrictive living environments than could other communities. The California study focused on experimental, community-wide service delivery systems in three counties, with the remaining counties in the state serving as a comparison group. Results indicated that the three experimental counties stabilized the number of youths being placed in residential treatment settings as well as the expenditures for such placements. For the remaining counties in the state, placement rates and expenditures increased during the same time period (Rosenblatt & Attkisson, 1992).

One of the most extensive efforts to address the provision of a broad range of services (referred to as a "continuum of care") was funded by the Department of Defense and studied as a demonstration program in Fort Bragg, North Carolina. Through this program, the children and adolescents of military families in the catchment area were eligible to receive whatever types of mental health services were required, rather than being restricted to the traditional outpatient, inpatient, and residential treatment services (Behar, Macbeth, & Holland, 1993). The remainder of this chapter highlights the Fort Bragg study as one example of research on systems of care.

THE FORT BRAGG EVALUATION PROJECT[1]

Large expenditures for mental health services and quality of care, especially for children and adolescents, motivated Congress and the Department of Defense to fund a number of demonstrations of service delivery mechanisms. These included the Fort Bragg Demonstration Project, the first large-scale implementation of a continuum of care. The Fort Bragg Evaluation Project, which was initiated to assess the results of the demonstration, was among the first and largest attempts to study an innovative approach to service delivery for children and adolescents with mental health problems.

The Demonstration Project

The concept for the demonstration was developed by the North Carolina Department of Human Resources, Division of Mental Health, Developmental Disabilities, and Substance Abuse Services (DMH/DD/SAS). In 1989, the Department of the Army funded both the demonstration and an independent evaluation. The DMH/DD/SAS contracted with Cardinal Mental

---

[1]This section was adapted from the final report of the Fort Bragg Evaluation Project; for further information, the reader is referred to Bickman et al. (1995).

Health Group, a private, not-for-profit corporation located in Fayetteville, North Carolina, to implement and provide a continuum of care for the Fort Bragg catchment area, approximately a 40-mile radius surrounding the Army post. Over 42,000 child and adolescent dependents of military personnel in the Fort Bragg area were eligible for services. Cardinal contracted with individuals and agencies already providing traditional mental health services in the community. These services included outpatient therapy and acute inpatient hospitalization. Cardinal also provided intensive outpatient treatment and, for the intermediate level of the continuum, developed services that included in-home counseling, after-school group treatment services, day treatment services, therapeutic homes, specialized group homes, and 24-hour crisis management teams. These services were provided through the Major General James H. Rumbaugh, Jr., Child and Adolescent Mental Health Clinic. All children requesting demonstration services were to receive a comprehensive intake/assessment to determine the appropriate level of service to be provided.

Intermediate or more intensive clinical services were to be coordinated with other child-serving agencies and practitioners in the community. Services within the continuum and across other agencies were linked through case management and interdisciplinary treatment teams. Transportation and other services designed to provide individualized support also were provided.

The demonstration required no financial outlay for families; usual co-payments and deductibles were waived. Families seeking services for their children were required either to use the demonstration's free clinical services or seek and pay for services on their own. The demonstration was funded under a cost-reimbursement contract; therefore, theoretically no limits were placed on the types or costs of services to be offered as long as they were therapeutically appropriate. The demonstration was to provide the best possible services for children without typical limitations placed on providers by insurance companies or other public agencies. Thus, this was to be a test of the continuum of care mode, without the usual financial strictures.

Overview of the Evaluation Project

The Center for Mental Health Policy of the Vanderbilt Institute for Public Policy Studies at Vanderbilt University was awarded a subcontract by the North Carolina DMH/DD/SAS to conduct an independent evaluation of the demonstration project. The evaluation consisted of four substudies: 1) the implementation study, 2) the quality study, 3) the mental health outcome study, and 4) the cost/utilization study. The implementation and quality final reports were completed in 1993 (Bickman, Bryant & Summerfelt, 1993; Heflinger, 1993). The outcome and cost/utilization study final reports were completed in 1994 (Bickman et al., 1994).

The implementation and quality studies were devoted to documenting the demonstration's activities. The outcome study was longitudinal and involved a sample of 984 children and their families, 574 from the demonstration site and 410 from the comparison sites. Data were collected to determine the relative impact of the demonstration on child and adolescent psychopathology and psychosocial functioning as well as family well-being. Mental health outcome data were collected just after entry into the service system, with two additional follow-up waves (each was approximately 6 months apart). The cost/utilization study compared the actual use of services with the costs of those services for all children treated (including, but not limited to, those participating in the outcome study) at both the demonstration and comparison sites.

Because the evaluation project was unable to assign children to different systems of care randomly, the inclusion of comparison sites in this project was critical to the examination of the effectiveness of the demonstration (Bickman, 1992). The Army designated Fort Campbell, Kentucky, and Fort Stewart, Georgia, as comparison sites. In both places, children receive traditional care covered by the Civilian Health and Medical Program of the Uniformed Services, commonly known as CHAMPUS.

In 1991, CHAMPUS permitted up to 45 days of inpatient or hospital care, 150 days of residential treatment center (RTC) care, and 23 outpatient visits per year. Under unusual circumstances, additional treatment was allowed. CHAMPUS required a deductible of $150 per person and $300 per family. A copayment of 20% of allowable charges was required for outpatient services and a small daily fee or $25 per day, whichever was more, for inpatient services (Office of the CHAMPUS, 1992). Prior to 1991, no limitation on the number of covered RTC days existed. CHAMPUS is considered to be more generous than most private insurance. Most private insurance does not cover care in an RTC, and, unlike other insurers, no lifetime benefit or dollar limit is imposed by CHAMPUS (Baine, 1992).

Methods

The primary source of mental health outcome data was the project participants themselves. Children who received mental health services at the demonstration site or one of the comparison sites and their families participated in interviews designed to be comprehensive, providing information on a multitude of child and family variables; standardized, through use of established instruments and trained interviewers; and feasible, asking children and parents to provide adequate but not excessive amounts of information.

At the demonstration and comparison sites, mental health providers were asked to identify new child clients who were using CHAMPUS benefits. After providers identified potential participants, the child or adolescent or parents were told about the evaluation project and asked if they were interested in being contacted by evaluation project staff for more information. If they agreed, their names and phone numbers were recorded and forwarded to evaluation project staff. Face-to-face visits with each parent and child were then arranged to explain the project and obtain informed consent.

Interviews contained multiple measures in order to develop a comprehensive, multidimensional profile of each child. The project took a tripartite view of mental health, holding that three vantage points—those of the client, the mental health professional, and society—were important in considering mental health outcomes. The domains the project viewed from these vantage points were

- Psychopathology, where a decrease in symptomatology and severity of diagnosis are traditional goals in treatment
- Health functioning, with a focus on social competence
- Client satisfaction, as one measure of quality or "acceptability" of services

Each research participant was asked to participate in three data collection waves and was paid for participating in each wave, over a 1-year period. Wave 1 was within 30 days of entry into the mental health services and the evaluation project, wave 2 was 6 months after intake, and wave 3 was 12 months after the child entered treatment. Each wave of data collection included the following components: structured diagnostic interviews with parents, structured diagnostic interviews with children, behavioral checklists (including social competence scales, family well-being scales, and satisfaction with services scales), and demographic and background information.

Unlike mental health outcomes data, data on service utilization and costs were collected for all children treated within the catchment areas surrounding Forts Bragg, Stewart, and Campbell. The Rumbaugh Clinic's management information system (MIS) described all services provided by the demonstration. The MIS, however, recorded only services and not costs; thus, per-unit costs for those services were calculated by evaluation project staff. The primary source of utilization data for the comparison sites was information downloaded from the records of the CHAMPUS system, which provided information on all claims filed with CHAMPUS.

Findings

The Implementation Study The implementation study compared the program as implemented to the program as planned. It was evident that the demonstration had been implemented consistent with the expectations of the contract by implementing a single point of entry to services for the target population, meeting the terms of the contract regarding participant eligibility (e.g., age, beneficiary status, and diagnostic eligibility); and serving three times the number of children originally estimated. The continuum of care model proposed by the demonstration was implemented according to the expectations of the contract and program service philosophy through

- A comprehensive range of services, including the development of intermediate service levels (intensive outpatient and substance abuse services, in-home crisis stabilization, day treatment, therapeutic home services, and group homes)
- Case management and multidisciplinary treatment teams for clients in the most intensive levels of care
- A high level of coordination throughout the community of mental health services for military dependent children

The Quality Study The quality study focused on the two program components that were unique to the demonstration—intake/assessment and case management. Results showed that the intake/assessment component was of high quality in that

- Parents were satisfied with the intake/assessment services they received.
- Staff members were pleased with their jobs.
- Providers outside the Rumbaugh Clinic rated its intake process as being of high quality.
- An expert reviewer was able to find documented evidence of quality indicators within the clinical records.
- Intake/assessment at the demonstration was rated as the highest in adequacy and quality among all support services available.

The case management component of the quality study indicated that case management services at the Rumbaugh Clinic were strong for most clients, with a high degree of fidelity to the values of the stakeholders:

- There was a strong emphasis on planning and coordination of treatment plans, in keeping with the written expectations of the Army contract and the job description for case managers.
- Careful attention was paid to meeting standards for treatment reviews and level of care criteria.
- General positive satisfaction ratings by parents suggested that the above activities were carried out in a way that promoted client and family involvement.

Utilization of Services The demonstration had a dramatic effect on service utilization across a variety of dimensions. The *types* of services delivered changed:

- Seven of nine critical components of service utilization related to the intake and assessment process were found to demonstrate strong fidelity to the program model of the demonstration and were better at the demonstration than at the comparison sites.
- Intermediate services previously unavailable were used by large numbers of clients.
- A layer of services (treatment team services and clinical case management) was put in place to coordinate the various services.

The *mix* of services also changed:

- Individuals moved toward the middle of the continuum of care. A child treated at the demonstration site was less likely to receive care in a hospital or RTC but was also less likely to receive only outpatient services. This shift in service mix conformed to the prescriptions of the program theory underlying the demonstration. The "right" children seemed to receive the newly available intermediate services; those who were hospitalized were far more likely to receive intermediate services than those who were not.

The demonstration affected the *volume* of services as well: 1) the volume of intermediate services was quite large, and 2) clients receiving outpatient therapy had significantly more visits. The demonstration also affected the *timing* of services. Children at the demonstration site were far more likely to remain in treatment over time, and, when they were in treatment, they were less likely to experience a significant interruption in treatment. This improved *continuity* was reflected in the way services "fit together": On leaving a hospital or RTC, children at the demonstration site were far more likely to receive follow-up services in a less restrictive setting within 30 days than were children at the comparison sites.

It was also apparent that differences in service utilization between sites were not simply a manifestation of shifts in the type of child treated. Comparisons of the evaluation sample by site confirmed earlier results: Children with similar levels of problem severity received markedly different treatment.

Satisfaction with Services Two major components of care were examined separately for client satisfaction: intake/assessment and treatment. The intake/assessment process is an integral part of the continuum of care concept. One important feature of the demonstration model was a single point of entry into the continuum of care, allowing for a central and coordinated intake process. The Rumbaugh Clinic implemented such a single point of entry with fidelity to the model and high quality. In contrast, the comparison sites of Fort Campbell and Fort Stewart had neither a uniform single point of entry nor a standardized intake/assessment procedure. The demonstration site received higher ratings of parent satisfaction than the comparison sites on global ratings of the intake/assessment process and on 11 of 16 subscales measuring specific dimensions of satisfaction. These findings support the program theory that ease of access, reduced financial burden, and the individualized assessment process at the demonstration site should lead to increased consumer satisfaction.

The demonstration also received significantly higher ratings of parent satisfaction with all components of outpatient treatment. Adolescents rated two of the eight components more positively. Parents at the demonstration site reported significantly higher satisfaction with two components of inpatient and RTC services: access and convenience, and reduced financial charges. Both parents and adolescents at the demonstration site reported significantly higher global satisfaction with outpatient services than did respondents at the comparison sites. No statistically significant differences between sites were reported for global satisfaction with inpatient/RTC services.

Clinical and Family Outcomes   Extensive analysis of both child and family outcomes reported by parents and children indicated that children at both the demonstration and comparison sites improved. There was no clear superiority in mental health outcomes at the demonstration site. These results address the general demonstration hypothesis that children at the demonstration site, as a whole, would improve more than children treated at the comparison sites. The evaluation studied outcomes for the group as a whole as well as for particular subgroups of children. In each analysis, outcome was measured by 12 key outcome variables at wave 2 (6 months) and wave 3 (1 year). There were slightly more significant findings than expected by chance alone, several favoring the demonstration site and several favoring the comparison sites.

Cost of Services   Mental health services costs were explored at the system level and at the individual level. Analyses accounted for administrative costs, indirect costs, and cost shifts created by the two service delivery systems. It was concluded that, at the system level, instituting this continuum of care (under a cost-reimbursement contract) increased mental health expenditures for the Army relative to providing the usual CHAMPUS system of care. There were two reasons for the system-level differences: More children were treated at the demonstration site, and more money was spent per child at the demonstration site. Nearly 70% of the system-level cost differential is explained by differential access; the remainder is largely explained by the fact that a treated child received more services at the demonstration site, and unit costs rose at the demonstration site while unit costs fell at the comparison sites.

At the individual level, four factors seem to contribute to the higher cost: treatment duration, increased volume of services, use of intermediate services, and per-unit cost differences. The "typical" child at the demonstration site tended to have longer episodes of treatment, so that more services were provided, thus driving costs per child higher. Although hospital costs per child were lower at the demonstration site, these reductions were offset by the costs of intermediate services and of increased use of outpatient services. To a great extent, these costs reflect the fact that the duration of treatment was longer at the demonstration site.

Implications and Conclusions

- The demonstration increased access to services for children who needed treatment. At the comparison sites, the typical CHAMPUS system provided care to 2.7%–4.5% (in fiscal year 1993) of all children, in contrast to 8% that year at the demonstration site. The demonstration clearly increased access relative to the comparison.
- The demonstration successfully implemented a continuum of care in a federal–state partnership. There has been much discussion among mental health experts about the desirability of a continuum of care, yet none was ever documented to have been implemented before the Fort Bragg demonstration. This is a major accomplishment of the demonstration.
- The demonstration successfully treated children in less restrictive environments. Before the demonstration was implemented, there was concern that not placing children in institutional settings might have adverse effects. It had never been demonstrated that an extensive continuum of care that placed children in less restrictive settings would not harm children. The results of the demonstration clearly indicate that no adverse effects were associated with the use of less restrictive environments and that youngsters treated at the demonstration site did, in fact, improve.
- Parents and adolescents were more satisfied with the services provided at the demonstration. Extensive data were collected on the satisfaction of adolescents and parents with services. The demonstration showed significantly greater satisfaction, and more satisfaction was expressed at the demonstration site about services unique to the continuum of care model.
- No clear patterns of differences in clinical outcomes were found between the demonstration and comparison sites. The most surprising finding of the evaluation was the lack of a clear pattern of differences in clinical outcomes between the demonstration and comparison sites. Although the predicted clinical effects were not demonstrated within the time frame studied, it has been shown that the demonstration had a more systematic and comprehensive assessment and treatment planning approach, more parent involvement, better case management, more individualized services, fewer treatment dropouts, a greater range of services, enhanced continuity of care, increased length of treatment, and a better match between needs and services as judged by parents.

- Cost control through appropriate care was not effective. The theory of cost control tested in the demonstration was that clinicians and their managers, by placing children in the least restrictive and most appropriate care, would save money (because more expensive and restrictive services would not have to be used). This approach is called into question by the substantially higher costs per client at the demonstration site. These costs were primarily related to a longer duration of treatment and the use of more expensive intermediate-level services (which were not available in the comparison sites), without a sufficiently significant reduction in the use of traditional services (e.g., outpatient, hospital, and RTC).

- A continuum of care is not necessarily more expensive. Although costs per treated child were higher at the demonstration site, it should not necessarily be concluded that a continuum of care is more expensive than other treatment systems. The demonstration was not designed to control costs through the limitation of services (as was the CHAMPUS system at the comparison sites). Thus, it would be inaccurate to attribute the added costs of the demonstration solely to the continuum of care model.

- The evaluation project was a single study, with limitations. Although the demonstration and evaluation projects were well implemented, they still had limitations. For example, the cost of *not* providing services to children at the comparison sites is unknown. The project had no way of knowing how many children were placed in detention facilities or required special education, for example. Between-site comparisons could not include costs to society of not treating children at the comparison sites, and, because more children were treated at the demonstration site, these costs may have differed by site. It is also important to stress that clinical outcomes were studied only through a 1-year time period after entry into the study. Outcomes after longer periods of time may reveal differences between sites. Vanderbilt has received support from the NIMH to follow the participants in the outcome study for an additional period of time.

CHALLENGES IN CONDUCTING RESEARCH ON SYSTEMS OF CARE

The process of studying the Fort Bragg Demonstration Project has been instructive. The evaluation faced a variety of challenges that offer valuable lessons for future research. Dealing with these challenges was difficult for the Fort Bragg evaluation because, at the time the evaluation approach was developed, little prior evaluation work on systems of care existed to provide a base of experience. A number of these challenges are discussed below.

Measurement Challenges

The lack of a strong research base in the field of children's mental health complicated the measurement tasks. For example, research has not as yet elucidated optimal amounts of various services, and so it is difficult to evaluate whether the demonstration site (or comparison sites) provided enough of particular services. In addition, many terms used in the field have not as yet been operationalized. The theory of the continuum of care stipulates that more "appropriate" services will be delivered than in traditional care, yet no simple and agreed-on way of measuring appropriateness exists. The further definition of these terms provides fertile areas for future research (Bickman, Schut, Karver, & Salzer, 1995).

Unique to the systems perspective is the need to evaluate the system as an entity, with features and characteristics beyond the service components that comprise the system. A difficult challenge for evaluators was to provide evidence that such a system of care was successfully implemented at Fort Bragg. The evaluation team approached this problem by providing a detailed account of the implementation of the system and by the network analysis methodology (Heflinger, 1993). However, further developmental work is needed to determine how best to define and measure the existence of "systemness."

A further challenge stems from the fact that outcome measurement is not well developed in mental health. In the Fort Bragg evaluation, it was necessary not only to decide what was important to measure but also to find measures that were reliable, valid, and sensitive to change, particularly with such a diverse population. The selection of instruments was a particular challenge. Because of the time required for proper development, the evaluation team sought to avoid the creation of new measures. Consultation with experts and comprehensive literature reviews were helpful; however, the dearth of research in many areas (e.g., functioning and burden of care) compelled the evaluation team to modify existing instruments and develop new instrumentation. Because of the uncertainty surrounding measurement, the evaluators opted to use multiple measures of important constructs.

The measurement of program processes, such as assessment and treatment planning, also was difficult because there are no clear standards against which to judge these important activities. When evaluators find themselves in situations in which such standards do not exist, they often resort to the judgment of "experts" as a solution. Expert judgment was used in the Fort Bragg project, but subsequent research (Bickman et al., 1995) has indicated that such judgement may be unreliable. Thus, definitive conclusions about such intermediate outcomes as accuracy of assessment and the goodness of treatment planning could not be formed. This is typical in the mental health field (Dawes, 1994).

An additional measurement problem was the lack of a comprehensive methodology to describe and characterize patterns of care. Most research concerning mental health utilization has described utilization by producing a "box score" or a tally of the number of individuals receiving different types of services (e.g., Barkley, Anastopoulos, Guevremont, & Fletcher, 1991; Curtis, Millman, Struening, & D'Ercole, 1992; Halfon, Berkowitz, & Klee, 1992; Zahner, Pawelkiewicz, DeFrancesco, & Adnopoz, 1992). Although these box scores adequately describe the type and volume of services received, they do not address important service delivery issues such as the sequence of services and the continuity of care that have been underscored by the guiding principles of the system of care concept (Stroul & Friedman, 1986). Analyses of patterns of care have the potential to be more informative to service system research, system development, and public policy debates.

Measurement problems also affected the cost analyses. Original predictions were that direct expenditures on mental health services would be reduced by implementation of a continuum of care. As the demonstration developed (and its costliness became apparent), it was postulated that expenditures on mental health services may increase but that cost savings elsewhere may offset these increased costs. A major challenge to the evaluation, therefore, was to measure all the various areas where cost savings might be realized. Because the evaluation lacked data on all the sectors where individuals might receive mental health services specifically, or impose costs related to their emotional disorders more generally, measuring cost savings in other sectors was impossible.

Logistical Challenges

One of the major problems faced by evaluators in any evaluation is insufficient funds. Because this was the first comprehensive study of a system of care, estimating the cost of the evaluation was difficult. Fortunately, the contract allowed funding increases when judged appropriate, and the Army and the state of North Carolina provided supplementary funding. In addition, NIMH supported specific aspects of the project, such as the modification of the Child and Adolescent Functional Assessment Scale, the modification of the Child Assessment Schedule, and the study of family empowerment. In addition, NIMH is supporting an additional 3 years of data collection.

In a complex field study, the cooperation of many parties is required. In the Fort Bragg evaluation, children, their parents, mental health providers, the Rumbaugh Clinic, three military posts, the state of North Carolina, the Army, the Department of Defense, and the U.S. Congress all played significant roles. The ability of the evaluators to deal successfully with all of these groups was important to the completion of the project. Notably, during the evaluation, no political interference was experienced, even at the height of concerns and debate over health care reform.

Another resource that must be budgeted but is often overlooked is time (Hedrick, Bickman, & Rog, 1993), and it is clear that evaluations of systems of care take long periods of time to complete. First, participants do not receive services all at the same time; thus recruitment may take a year or two in order to obtain the numbers needed for sufficient statistical power. Moreover, studies of children and adolescents should be longitudinal. Although there is little research on the minimum time to assess outcome after entering treatment, it appears that at least a year may be required to detect the effects of treatment. As a result, these types of studies take at least 4 years to complete. A multiyear study of the Fort Bragg demonstration was planned, but the study took even longer than expected because of the difficulty in recruiting participants.

Because random assignment could not be used at the demonstration site, comparison data were collected from two similar army posts. Difficulties encountered in this aspect of the study included the staffing and maintaining of site offices, the recruitment of interviewers, and the development of relationships with the military medical personnel and the community mental health providers. In addition, the use of multiple sites required evaluators to keep a careful account of how services were provided at these sites and whether the provision of services changed over time. Although there were some unpredicted changes at the comparison sites, careful study indicated that they had little or no effect. However, it is critical that evaluators describe the services not only at the demonstration site but also at any comparison sites.

Other logistical problems affected the cost study in particular. Information on service use came from two sources: billing information from the records of the CHAMPUS system for the comparison sites and a MIS at the demonstration site. This doubled the time required to complete the fairly complex task of organizing service-level transactions into a description of individual service use. It also doubled the amount of negotiating necessary to obtain updates of the data and instructions as to how to interpret the information they contain. An added problem was that the MIS was not designed to track expenditures; it lacked any sort of cost information. As a result, the evaluation team had to develop per-unit costs from separate budgetary information. Obtaining this information created significant logistical problems.

Additional problems existed because the evaluators lacked control over some parameters of the demonstration and the evaluation. Although cooperation from the Army was good, the interests of the evaluation and those of the Army were, at times, in conflict. For example, some decisions made by the Army limited the ability of the evaluation to answer key questions. Copayments and deductibles were eliminated at the demonstration site over the objections of the evaluation. This change in parental cost-sharing confounds the effects of the continuum of care per se with those of changes in the financial arrangements under which care was provided. In addition, an ideal evaluation would also have included a catchment area epidemiological survey that would have provided some insight into the costs of illness and treatment among individuals not receiving mental health services. This would have provided valuable information as to whether increasing access at the demonstration site reduced the costs that untreated children impose on their parents and on society. This clearly was beyond the scope of this research project.

ISSUES RAISED FOR FUTURE RESEARCH ON SYSTEMS OF CARE

Since the completion of the Fort Bragg evaluation, investigators and reviewers have raised a number of issues. Although some of these issues were highligted by the Fort Bragg evaluation, others are intended to be reflective of the field in general. Some of the challenges and issues identified in this chapter will help to guide future research efforts to determine the effects of community-based systems of care on children with serious emotional disorders and their families.

Focus on Youngsters with Serious Disorders

Systems of care, as defined by Stroul and Friedman (1986), have a special focus on youngsters with serious emotional disorders and their families. As a result, research on systems of care should incorporate specific analyses of this group. The Fort Bragg demonstration, and therefore the evaluation, did not focus exclusively on children with serious disorders. However, subsequent analyses determined that about 65% of the evaluation sample could be classified as having serious emotional disturbance by the presence of a diagnosis and a Global Level of Functioning score of less than 61. Separate analyses of this group, and other relevant subgroups, again showed no clear pattern of differences between the demonstration and comparison sites on clinical outcomes. However, because clinical outcomes may differ if the focus is on subgroups of youngsters with serious problems rather than on broader groups of children, future research on systems of care should focus on these children or at least ensure that an adequate number of youngsters with serious emotional disorders participate.

Time Frame for Measurement of Impact

As noted previously, 6-month and 1-year intervals may be insufficient to assess the effectiveness of treatment for children and adolescents with serious disturbances. The Fort Bragg evaluation included data points at 6 months and 1 year in the final report. It appears that 6 months after intake may be a useful time frame for tracking progress but not for assessing impact, particularly because so many youngsters are still in treatment at that time. One year postintake also may prove to be too soon for assessing impact. It has been recognized that longer-term follow-up is important for the assessment of systems of care, and NIMH is providing support for continued data collection on the sample of youngsters involved in the Fort Bragg study. The use of multiple data collection points of less than 6 months that continue for a minimum of 1 year, and preferably longer, is suggested. This approach would afford researchers the opportunity to use the sophisticated methods that have recently been developed for longitudinal analyses.

Cost Assessment with Different Incentives

Assessing whether the continuum of care raised expenditures on mental health services is a complex undertaking. This is because care at the demonstration site was provided under different financial arrangements than at the comparison site. As discussed earlier, all services at Fort Bragg were provided free of copayments and deductibles and under a cost-reimbursement contract with providers. At the comparison site, however, services were provided by providers under typical fee-for-service arrangements; families receiving care paid copayments and deductibles. The demonstration site confounded—to some extent—differences in costs due to these factors with those due to the system of care per se.

The absence of any copayments or deductibles at the demonstration site might lead one to wonder whether higher expenditures there reflected an overuse of free services. The effect of eliminating cost-sharing by parents, however, was likely muted by the fact that the marginal cost to parents of obtaining services for their child was low at the comparison site. In addition, care was provided under a cost-reimbursement contract at the demonstration site. This might lead one to wonder whether care was provided inefficiently without regard to costs. There are indications, however, that efforts were made at the Rumbaugh Clinic to control costs through a utilization review/management process. Furthermore, the Army instituted increased cost controls after the first 2 years of the demonstration. The effects of these efforts are manifest in that the rate of increase in costs fell with each year of the demonstration.

Nonetheless, to some extent, differences between sites reflect these financial arrangements as well as differences in the service systems. Future research should assess systems of care that have various types of cost constraints; of particular interest would be those that combine the continuum of care with capitation.

Measurement of Cost Offsets in Other Child-Serving Systems

In assessing the cost-effectiveness of systems of care, one dimension to consider is the potential for cost savings in other child-serving systems. Youngsters receiving comprehensive services through a system of care may avoid high-cost services and placements that represent costs to the child welfare, education, juvenile justice, and health systems. The Fort Bragg evaluation obtained reports of service use from the parents of the children in the evaluation sample; analysis of these data did not suggest such savings for the demonstration. However, these potential cost offsets are an important area for exploration in future research on systems of care.

Use of Sensitive Measures

When research is done in community settings, the children and adolescents typically have a large variety of problems. This creates a special research and management challenge to identify measures of behavioral and emotional functioning that are reliable and yet sensitive to change in such a diverse population. Frequently, reliability and sensitivity to change over time are competing attributes of a measure. This is especially true regarding test–retest reliability, where stability over time is the goal of instrument development. Most measures used for systems and services research have been developed specifically for cross-sectional and not longitudinal analyses. Furthermore, finding sensitive measures that can be applied to a highly diverse population of youngsters is far more difficult than finding instruments to assess youngsters with depression or attention-deficit/hyperactivity disorder, for example. In this regard, some of the broader measures of overall functioning may be more useful for future research on systems of care than some of the more specific indicators of behavior. A key feature of the Fort Bragg evaluation was the use of multiple informants and several types of instruments to collect data in the same domain. For example, data about psychopathology were collected from teachers, parents, children, and adolescents using structured interviews and several checklists.

Measurement of the Quality of Service Delivery within Systems of Care

Another issue to be carefully considered in future research on systems of care is determining how to assess the quality of service delivery within a system of care. Although it is important to ensure that all of the infrastructure elements of a system of care are developed, and to implement the requisite array of services, the quality of interaction between the system and the children and families who use it is also important. Measurement of this quality represents a new area for research, and, therefore, measurement approaches have not yet been developed and refined. Some attempts have been made to use a case study methodology to capture information in this dimension. Without information establishing the quality of systems of care and of service delivery, it remains difficult to interpret outcome data as representing a true test of these systems. The Fort Bragg evaluation used a variety of techniques and informants to assess quality. A challenge for future research is to further define this concept and to develop useful measurement methods.

CONCLUSION

The Fort Bragg evaluation was the first large-scale study of a comprehensive, community-based continuum of care. As such, the study raised many questions, methodological concerns, and interpretive dilemmas. It will fall to future research efforts on systems of care to address some of these questions and concerns.

REFERENCES

Baine, D.P. (1992). Prepared statement to the Select Committee on Children, Youth and Families of the United States House of Representatives. In *The profits of misery: How inpatient psychiatric treatment bilks the system and betrays our trust* (GPO 1992-52-362). (pp. 172–194). Washington, DC: U.S. Government Printing Office.

Barkley, R.A., Anastopoulos, A.D., Guevremont, D.D., & Fletcher, K.E. (1991). Adolescents with ADHD: Patterns of behavioral adjustment, academic functioning, and treatment utilization. *Journal of the American Academy of Child and Adolescent Psychiatry, 30*, 752–761.

Behar, L.B., Macbeth, G., & Holland, J.M. (1993). Distribution and costs of mental health services within a system of care for children and adolescents. *Administration and Policy in Mental Health, 20*, 283–295.

Bickman, L. (1992). Designing outcome evaluations for children's mental health services: Improving internal validity. In L. Bickman & D.J. Rog (Eds.), *Evaluating mental health services for children (New Directions for Program Evaluation,* No. 54) (pp. 57–68). San Francisco: Jossey-Bass.

Bickman, L., Bryant, D., & Summerfelt, W.T. (1993). *Final report of the quality study of the Fort Bragg Evaluation Project.* Nashville, TN: Center for Mental Health Policy, Vanderbilt University.

Bickman, L., Guthrie, P., Foster, E.M., Lambert, E.W., Summerfelt, W.T., Breda, C., & Heflinger, C.A. (1994). *The final report of the outcome, cost, and utilization studies of the Fort Bragg evaluation project.* Nashville, TN: Vanderbilt University, Center for Mental Health Policy.

Bickman, L. Guthrie, P., Foster, E.M., Lambert, E.W., Summerfelt, W.T., Breda, C., & Heflinger, C.A. (1995). *Managed care in mental health: The Fort Bragg Experiment.* New York: Plenum Publishing.

Bickman, L., Heflinger, C.A., Pion, G., & Behar, L. (1992). Evaluation planning for an innovative children's mental health system. *Clinical Psychology Review, 12*, 853–865.

Bickman, L., Schut, J., Karver, M., & Salzer, M. (1995). *Conceptual and empirical approaches toward understanding appropriate care.* Symposium presented at Annual Research Conference, University of South Florida, Florida Mental Health Institute, Tampa.

Burns, B.J., & Friedman, R.M. (1990). Examining the research base for child mental health services and policy. *Journal of Mental Health Administration, 17*, 87–98.

Curtis, J.L., Millman, E.J., Struening, E., & D'Ercole, A. (1992). Effect of case management on rehospitalization and utilization of ambulatory care services. *Hospital and Community Psychiatry, 43*, 895–899.

Dawes, R. (1994). *House of cards: Psychology and psychotherapy built on myth.* New York: Macmillan.

Duchnowski, A.J., & Kutash, K. (1993). *Developing comprehensive systems for troubled youth: Issues in mental health.* Paper presented at Shakertown Symposium II: Developing Comprehensive Systems for Troubled Youth, Shakertown, KY.

Friedman, R.M., Rugs, D., & Cascardi, M. (1994). *Evaluating children's service delivery systems.* Tampa: University of South Florida, Florida Mental Health Institute.

Glisson, C. (1993). *The adjudication, placement, and psychosocial functioning of children in state custody.* Knoxville: University of Tennessee, College of Social Work.

Glisson, C., & James, L. (1992). The interorganizational coordination of services to children in state custody. *Administration in Social Work, 3/4*, 65–80.

Halfon, N., Berkowitz, G., & Klee, L. (1992). Mental health service utilization by children in foster care in California. *Pediatrics, 89*, 1238–1244.

Hedrick, T.E., Bickman, L., & Rog, D.J. (1993). *Planning applied social research.* Newbury Park, CA: Sage Publications.

Heflinger, C.A. (1993). *Final report of the implementation study of the Fort Bragg Evaluation Project* (Final Report No. Volume III: Appendix l). Nashville, TN: Vanderbilt University, Center for Mental Health Policy.

Institute of Medicine. (1989). *Research on children's and adolescents' mental, behavioral, and developmental disorders: Mobilizing a national initiative.* Washington, DC: National Academy of Sciences.

Knitzer, J. (1993). Children's mental health policy: Challenging the future. *Journal of Emotional and Behavioral Disorders, 1,* 8–16.

Kutash, K., Duchnowski, A.J., & Sondheimer, D.A. (1994). Building the research base for children's mental health. *Journal of Emotional and Behavioral Disorders, 2,* 194–197.

Morrissey, J.P. (1992). An interorganizational network approach to evaluating children's mental health service systems. In L. Bickman & D. Rog (Eds.), *Evaluating mental health services for children (New Directions for Program Evaluation, No. 54)* (pp. 85–89). San Francisco: Jossey-Bass.

Morrissey, J., Tausign, M., & Lindsey, M. (1985). *Network analysis methods for mental health service system research: Comparison of two community support systems.* Series BN No. 6, HHS Pub. No. (ADM) 85-1383. Washington, DC: U.S. Department of Health and Human Services.

Office of the Civilian Health and Medical Program of the Uniformed Services. (1992). *CHAMPUS Handbook (1992-675-578).* Washington, DC: U.S. Government Printing Office.

Rosenblatt, A., & Atkisson, C.C. (1992). Integrating systems of care in California for youth with severe emotional disturbance: A descriptive overview of the California AB377 evaluation project. *Journal of Child and Family Studies, 1,* 93–113.

Rugs, D., Warner-Levock, V., Johnston, A., & Freedman, G. (1994). *Adding system supports to children's service delivery: The impact on foster-care children in rural West Virginia.* Tampa: University of South Florida, Florida Mental Health Institute.

Saxe, L., Cross, T., & Silverman, N. (1988). Children's mental health: The gap between what we know and what we do. *American Psychologist, 43,* 800–807.

Saxe, L., Cross, T., Silverman, N., Batchelor, W., & Dougherty, D. (1987). *Children's mental health: Problems and treatment.* Durham, NC: Duke University Press.

Stroul, B.A., & Friedman, R.M. (1986). *A system of care for children and youth with severe emotional disturbances.* (rev. ed.) Washington, DC: Georgetown University Child Development Center, National Technical Assistance Center for Children's Mental Health.

Zahner, G.E.P., Pawelkiewicz, W., DeFrancesco, J.J., & Adnopoz, J. (1992). Children's mental health service needs and utilization patterns in an urban community: An epidemiological assessment. *Journal of the American Academy of Child and Adolescent Psychiatry, 31,* 951–960.

FAMILY INVOLVEMENT IN SYSTEMS OF CARE

CHAPTER 19

The Evolution of the Family Advocacy Movement

Scott Bryant-Comstock,
Barbara Huff, and John VanDenBerg

All major categorical service systems are under pressure to reform the way they deliver services to children and families with complex needs (Franz & Miles, 1994). Juvenile justice systems cannot afford to build more expensive detention centers. Mental health systems find themselves juggling between traditional practices and increasing demand from consumers for nontraditional services and supports other than outpatient and inpatient services. Child welfare systems are increasingly facing rising numbers of youth coming into state custody. Schools are struggling to meet sometimes contradictory requests for inclusion and exclusion of students with special needs. Alcohol and drug treatment agencies are recognizing that expensive facility-based treatment often does not generalize to the community environment. Public health systems are scrambling to deal with rising rates of teen pregnancy and the effects of poverty on the health of families. Legal advocates such as the American Civil Liberties Union are filing suit after suit against states and counties that refuse to change their methods of service delivery (Tucker, 1993). Finally, all systems are facing these pressures with declining funds and increasing calls for cost containment.

The title of a 1994 report on services to children and families, *All Systems Failure* (Koyanagi & Gaines, 1993), is a chilling but accurate depiction of the present situation. Public systems that are under particular pressure are those that have traditionally solved their problems related to children with complex needs by removing them from the community. Traditional categorical service delivery systems have been and remain inadequate, especially when used to serve individuals with complex needs that cut across many treatment jurisdictions.

Spurred by these and other pressures, some of these systems have been changing since the mid-1980s. These changes have been directed toward the organization of available cross-agency resources into seamless, individualized "systems of care" (Stroul & Friedman, 1986). A hallmark of these systems of care has been their focus on families. This family focus is seen in the emphasis on providing the services and supports needed to maintain the integrity and character of an intact family to the greatest possible extent. Furthermore, systems of care have emphasized involving families as full partners in the design, evaluation, and delivery of services. Along with reforms to improve service delivery systems and increase family involvement, there has been significant growth in family advocacy on behalf of children and adolescents with serious emotional and behavioral disorders. This has become known as the family advocacy movement.

The emphasis on family involvement is evident at federal and state levels. Grants provided by the federal Center for Mental Health Services (CMHS) to state mental health authorities to stimulate system of care development have included the involvement of families as a major objective. In addition, the community-level grants offered by CMHS to develop comprehensive systems of care require evidence of family involvement in the design, delivery, and evaluation of services. The federal government also has required states to involve family members in the development of statewide plans for providing child mental health services. Furthermore, the CMHS has provided direct support to facilitate the development of the family support and advocacy movement. Grants to family organizations have had a significant impact on the growth of these groups and on their ability to organize into statewide networks. By 1994, 28 states had received grants from the CMHS to establish statewide family support networks.

State-level governments, with encouragement from the federal level, have also begun to involve families more actively in policy-making decisions. Kansas, North Carolina, and Alaska are among the states whose mental health agencies have been on the forefront of involving families in the development of more effective and appropriate child mental health services. Many examples exist of states that have provided financial support for the development of family advocacy groups.

Two advocacy organizations with a primary focus on children and families who use mental health services have blossomed in recent years—the Federation of Families for Children's Mental Health and the National Alliance for the Mentally Ill Children and Adolescent Network. Both organizations represent strong voices for children and adolescents with emotional, behavioral, and mental disorders and their families. Policy makers at the state and national levels routinely involve these advocacy groups in discussions when considering legislation affecting the delivery of child mental health services. Increasingly, these organizations, particularly the Federation of Families for Children's Mental Health, with its focus on cross-system advocacy efforts, have become involved in policy-making discussions across service systems such as mental health, education, juvenile justice, and child welfare.

Family advocacy leaders recognize that, even with the phenomenal growth of the family advocacy movement, further improvement is needed in services for children and adolescents with serious emotional disorders and their families as well as in the area of family involvement. However, the progress achieved in the 1980s in family involvement and family advocacy has been dramatic.

GROWTH OF THE FAMILY ADVOCACY MOVEMENT

How did the family movement get to where it is today? To answer this question, it is necessary to reflect on the state of the child mental health service delivery system in the early 1980s. During this period, several key documents and federal activities contributed to the growth of the family advocacy movement. Two formative documents called for the involvement of families in systems of care for children and adolescents with emotional, behavioral, or mental disorders and their families. Knitzer's *Unclaimed Children*, published in 1982, took a scathing look at the state of mental health services across systems for children and adolescents with emotional, behavioral, or mental disorders and their families. Knitzer's study is widely recognized as one of the defining events that helped motivate child mental health service policy makers and providers to take a critical look at the state of the child mental health service delivery system. What they saw was unsettling. There was little in the way of leadership at the federal or state level, community-based services were all but nonexistent, and child-serving agencies tended to work in isolation from one another. Families were involved in most cases solely as recipients of services, with very little input into the design of those services, and advocacy efforts for children and adolescents with emotional, behavioral, or mental disorders and their families were minimal.

Stroul and Friedman followed with their monograph, *A System of Care for Children and Youth with Severe Emotional Disturbances*, in 1986. This monograph outlined in specific detail the necessary components needed in a system of care for children and adolescents with emotional, behavioral, or mental disorders and their families. Both documents called for increased family involvement and increased family advocacy. During this time, families themselves began to voice their concerns about their lack of involvement in designing the services that are delivered to their children.

Parents of children with developmental disabilities led the way in developing much of what is now known as the family advocacy movement. Beginning in the early 1960s, these parents began to influence state systems to improve services for their children. In many states, these groups of parents organized in Associations for Retarded Citizens, or ARCs. As a result, many state service systems for children and adults with developmental disabilities changed from inappropriate institution-based warehousing to viable home- and community-based services and support. In Alaska, parents working with professionals in organized groups brought remarkable reforms to the developmental disabilities system. Today, most Alaskan children and adults with developmental disabilities have truly individualized plans of care and a flexible budget to pay for needed services (Renfro, 1994).

Until recently, few advocacy groups similar to those in the developmental disabilities field existed for children and adolescents with emotional, behavioral, or mental disorders and their families. One notable exception was in Michigan, where a group of families organized the Michigan Association for Children with Emotional Disturbances in 1974. Another pioneering group of families advocating for children with emotional, behavioral, or mental disorders and their families was the Parents Involved Network of Pennsylvania, formed in 1984. This network is still effectively influencing state and national system of care development and providing support to Pennsylvania families. Beyond these and a few other organizations, families generally were not organizing to support one another or to advocate services for children and adolescents with serious emotional, behavioral, or mental disorders and their families.

Federal emphasis in this area began in 1984 when the National Institute of Mental Health Child and Adolescent Service System Program (CASSP) recognized the need for extensive family involvement in the design and implementation of a system of care for children who have serious emotional, behavioral, or mental disorders and their families. The CASSP program required its state grantees to address the need for family involvement and advocacy. As a result, states receiving CASSP funds began to attempt to gather families together into organized groups and to involve them in the implementation of service reform. Several of these state mental health programs funded the development of family organizations with money received from their CASSP grants.

In 1984, a joint effort between the National Institute of Mental Health and the National Institute on Disability and Rehabilitation Research resulted in the funding of a major technical assistance and research center located at Portland State University in Portland, Oregon. This center (the Research and Training Center on Family Support and Children's Mental Health) introduced the idea of parent–professional partnerships and family advocacy in a series of regional conferences entitled Families as Allies, the first of which was held in 1986. These conferences, and the literature derived from them, served to promote the idea of families as not only advocates for more and better services but also persons who, when directly involved with service delivery, could improve service design, implementation, and evaluation.

The Families as Allies experience was an important milestone in the growth of the advocacy movement for children and adolescents with serious emotional disorders and their families. For what may have been the first time in the history of the delivery of child mental health services, families were meeting face to face with professionals to discuss ways to improve services for them and for their children.

The initial meetings were simultaneously discomforting and exhilarating. For many family members, these meetings represented the first time they had been in a forum with mental health professionals where they felt on equal footing. Together, they discussed ways to improve the parent–professional relationship, with the larger goal of improving the array and method of delivery of services to children and adolescents with emotional, behavioral, or mental disorders and their families.

The natural outgrowth of these meetings was the recognition that families needed to organize. A national, family-focused advocacy organization would help to maintain a strong voice for the improvement of child mental health service delivery systems. It also would help to continue the serious discussion with professionals about how services could be better provided. The CASSP program helped this effort by inserting requirements for family involvement in its grant announcement. States began to talk more about the family perspective and struggled to figure out how to involve families.

By 1987, Families as Allies workshops had been conducted in each region of the United States, with technical assistance and consultation provided by the Research and Training Center at Portland State University. Families were increasingly finding opportunities to meet and discuss strategies for increasing their involvement in shaping the direction of child mental health services. A problem families quickly encountered was that the focus of the early work of the Families as Allies workshops was on the family–therapist relationship. Although this was helpful, families began to speak of reaching a plateau in terms of their ability to involve themselves beyond the family–therapist level.

State-level child mental health systems were slowly incorporating the idea of family involvement. By including family members on various councils, committees, and commissions, many state-level administrators thought they had met the federal requirement for family involvement. Family members, in contrast, were experiencing increasing frustration at not feeling that their input was either valued or listened to. Even family members appointed to state-level policy councils organized to create state child mental health plans began speaking of feeling as though they were acting out the role of "token" parent. Family members had achieved the visibility they had been asking for. Still, they did not feel their voices were being heard.

These were difficult times for the emerging family movement. On paper, many state-level child mental health systems could point to numerous examples of family involvement. As family members began to compare notes, consensus grew that a more visible presence for families was needed at state and national levels. The more families began to be present at national and state child mental health conferences, the more the awareness grew that child mental health services were in need of major reform. Family members felt that they knew best what some reform measures needed to be and that a strong national voice was needed to get their message across.

During this time of growing frustration at the lack of a national voice for families, the National Institute of Mental Health and the National Institute on Disability and Rehabilitation Research asked the Portland State University Research and Training Center to host a meeting to develop a 5-year plan for addressing key issues for families of children with emotional, behavioral, or mental disorders. Referred to as the "Next Steps" meeting, this event was held in December 1988, in Arlington, Virginia.

Significantly, this was one of the first national child mental health meetings to be designed, planned, and facilitated with full family involvement. Participants at the meeting heard from family members and state and national child mental health experts. The meeting focused on issues including family support services, access to appropriate educational services, relinquishing custody for obtaining services, and coordination of services at the individual family level, or case management (Thomas & Friesen, 1990). In addition, there was discussion about developing family organizations and building coalitions at the local, state, and national level.

Naomi Karp, then a Program Specialist with the National Institute on Disability and Rehabilitation Research of the U.S. Department of Education, captured the focus of the meeting in her address to the audience. She stated

> This meeting is intended to unite groups and individuals concerned about issues, policies, practices, regulations and laws that affect children and youth with emotional problems and their families. This meeting is to lay the groundwork for a cohesive, enduring coalition of groups and individuals who will consistently, articulately, and effectively speak with policy makers, professional organizations, legislators and the public about the needs of children with emotional problems and their families. We need a voice to speak for children and until we have that voice, [we] are always going to have problems in our agencies. Most importantly, families and children are going to have major problems. I don't think we want that and I don't want to be in a room like this in the year 2000, saying that we need to start planning. In the year 2000, we should be meeting to discuss accomplishments that began here today. (Thomas & Friesen, 1990, p. 38)

The Next Steps meeting was different from other child mental health meetings that had previously occurred. Besides the development of an elaborate agenda for improving child mental health services, something unplanned and spontaneous emerged during the wrap-up portion of the meeting. As participants reflected on the future of child mental health services, families began to stand up and come forward to the conference center microphone and speak out about the need for a national organization. They talked about an organization that would be led by families and could represent families around the country in their efforts to improve child mental health services at the state and national levels. Families repeatedly returned to the theme that adequate services would never be provided and their needs would never be given recognition without a separate organization to focus exclusively on children with emotional, behavioral, or mental disorders and their families. Furthermore, families were clear that such an organization should not be an extension of any federal or state agency. Many voiced the opinion that the organization should be family driven, but both family members and professionals should be a part of the organization. There was much discussion regarding the identification of the population that such an organization would be representing. Some believed that the organization should represent children and adolescents with all types of emotional, behavioral, or mental disorders and their families. Others preferred a focus primarily on children and adolescents with neurobiological mental disorders and their families.

By the end of the last session of the Next Steps meeting, some family members in the room volunteered to form a Steering Committee. The Steering Committee was comprised of families of children with emotional, behavioral, or mental disorders, representing 16 states. They produced the following motion:

> We move that a steering committee be appointed to develop a plan to establish a parent-run coalition to address the needs of children with emotional problems to promote their healthy development as children and in their transition to adulthood. (Thomas & Friesen, 1990, p. 44)

Family members in the audience approved the motion by a majority vote. The Steering Committee, made up of family volunteers, agreed to meet by March 1989.

The Next Steps conference was significant in the development of the family advocacy movement in that it represented the springboard for the formation of a new, family-driven organization devoted to improving services for children and adolescents with serious emotional disorders. Earlier in the year, the National Alliance for the Mentally Ill formed its Child and Adolescent Network, which adopted a focus of looking at ways to improve services for children with neurobiological disorders. The organization that emerged from the Next Steps conference was the Federation of Families for Children's Mental Health. Its emphasis was inclusive of all types of mental disorders and emotional and behavioral problems experienced by children and adolescents and their families. The Federation took the view that there needed to be a national organization that could include all families dealing with mental health issues across child and family serving systems. Since then, both organizations have flourished and have increased awareness of the needs of families significantly.

THE FEDERATION OF FAMILIES FOR CHILDREN'S MENTAL HEALTH

In February 1989, the Steering Committee that had formed at the Next Steps conference met and agreed that the time was long overdue for a national organization for families whose children had a range of emotional, behavioral, and mental disorders. The group recognized that, although there were many advocacy organizations that existed with specific focus areas (Children and Adults with Attention Deficit Disorders, National Alliance for the Mentally Ill, Autism Society, etc.), there did not seem to be an organization that was inclusive of a variety of emotional disorders and behavior problems. They also recognized that, to be successful, they would need to build an organization that welcomed both families and professionals and addressed issues across racial, economic, and service delivery boundaries. The group decided to organize and call itself the Federation of Families for Children's Mental Health. Their stated goal was to see every community have a range of state-of-the-art supports and services in place for children with emotional, behavioral, or mental disorders and their families by the year 2000.

Driving the Federation's vision of a brighter future for families were a set of value-based principles that outlined a vision for a family-centered system of children's mental health services. These principles were based on the belief that families and professionals together could make changes and inroads in archaic systems and attitudes that were keeping many families involved with the mental health delivery system as second-class citizens.

The Federation of Families for Children's Mental Health continues to operate on the philosophical underpinnings developed in 1989:

- Children must be seen as children first, with their special needs secondary.
- Families are not "dysfunctional." The inflexible policies and practices of service systems create unnecessary stress and overwhelming responsibilities for families. Professionals often may misperceive families as "dysfunctional" when they are experiencing normal reactions to a serious lack of appropriate, affordable, and accessible supports. The term "dysfunctional" is blaming and unnecessary and must not be used.
- Families must be viewed as experts about their children, and decisions should remain in control of the family. It is up to family members to become informed regarding options and choices for their children. Professionals have an obligation to provide families with up-to-date information about programs, services, and their rights.

- Families and professionals must respect the rights, strengths, and individuality of each child or adolescent, ensuring that she or he has a voice and a vote on any educational, mental health, or vocational rehabilitation decision making team. It is essential that self-determination be cultivated through the expression of choices and preferences.
- Services must emphasize the identification of strengths, based on a range of comprehensive assessment instruments that address social, cognitive, physical, and emotional capabilities.
- Services must be available, affordable, accessible, and appropriate, with the ultimate goal being to enable the young person to live, work, and play in his or her community. Funding mechanisms have to be flexible and individualized so that they are supportive of rather than destructive to families. Natural families are entitled to the same in-home supports, community-based supports and services that are provided for foster families.
- Families are entitled to supports that will help them keep their children at home rather than forcing them to seek out-of-home placements.
- Family units are a source of strength for children. When there is abuse or neglect, the child's safety and well-being must be first priority. Intensive support must be provided so that the child might safely remain with the family, and removal must be seen as the last resort. Reunification and family preservation must be the main goal after any move from the home takes place. When reunification is not possible, after all possible options have failed, another permanent family situation must be found.
- The location, quality, and frequency of services to the child and supports to the family must be based on need and not on the family's ability to pay.
- The training of professionals must be improved and expanded. There must be outreach to recruit, train, employ, and retain more qualified personnel, with special emphasis on members of different cultures. Professionals need exposure to more interdisciplinary and culturally sensitive training curricula and programs. Professionals need to receive support in their jobs, just as families need support in their homes. Families need training and information that will make them informed decision-makers.
- The greatest challenge to both families and professionals is that they must dare to dream and hope about what might be for children and adolescents with mental health disabilities. Families must recognize their strengths and their children's strengths and build on them. Professionals have to help families identify and capitalize on their strengths. Families and professionals must work together not only to improve services but to change the values and attitudes of society toward children with emotional, behavioral, and mental disorders. Families and professionals must

dare to challenge perceived limits and actual barriers that are erected by systems and society. Families and professionals must be willing to dream and take risks that will improve the quality of opportunities available. Without dreaming and risk-taking, full citizenship for this population of children and adolescents will not be achieved.

Throughout its history, the Federation of Families for Children's Mental Health has reminded its members that their purpose is to work collaboratively with professionals. The emphasis of this collaboration is to cause changes in attitudes, funding mechanisms, and policies so that children and adolescents with emotional, behavioral, and mental disorders will be able to live, play, and go to school in nonrestrictive settings. The organization advocates flexible policies and administrators, home-based service options, and integrated school programs. The Federation's position is that it is not acceptable for residential schools and hospitals to be considered the placement of first choice or for families to give up custody of their children in order to receive services. The Federation envisions the day when every community has services and supports that are tailored to each family's needs so that families are never forced to place their children outside their homes solely because they have no other options. The group wants national leaders who will truly listen to them and share their dreams, visions, and expectations for their children.

Since its inception, the Federation has positioned itself to be involved in state and national efforts that focus on improving services for children and adolescents with serious emotional disorders and their families. Beginning in 1989, the group held its first annual conference focusing on state-of-the-art advocacy efforts for families receiving mental health services for their children. The Federation's annual conference has become an important event each year. Families, children, and the professionals who serve them come together from throughout the United States to continue the quest for improved service delivery systems. The Federation has established two national awards that are presented at the national conference each year. The Claiming Children award is given to a family member who exemplifies the spirit and direction of the organization, and the Making a Difference award is given to a professional who has contributed significantly to the human services field in ways that benefit families.

Besides an annual national conference and the recognition of leaders in the family advocacy movement and professionals concerned with improving services, the Federation publishes a national newsletter, *Claiming Children*, that focuses attention on child mental health and family advocacy issues and provides updates on Federation activities. The Federation also has published two major works addressing family advocacy efforts and child mental health services. The publications, *All Systems Failure: An Ex-*

amination of the Results of Neglecting the Needs of Children with Serious Emotional Disturbance (published in collaboration with the National Mental Health Association) (Koyanagi & Gaines, 1993) and *Finding Help—Finding Hope* (Anderson, 1994), are used throughout the country by family advocacy groups, service providers, policy makers, and educators.

In a relatively short time, the Federation of Families for Children's Mental Health has become a national voice for children with emotional, behavioral, or mental disorders and their families. Whether through persistent lobbying efforts on Capitol Hill or providing input and guidance for federal activities, individual advocacy for families with state government officials, or one-on-one technical assistance to families interested in setting up family support groups, the Federation has maintained a high level of commitment to ensuring the betterment of services for children with emotional, behavioral, or mental disorders and their families.

In 1992, the Federation of Families for Children's Mental Health opened a national office in Alexandria, Virginia. The opening of the national office coincided with the receipt of a grant award from the Annie E. Casey Foundation to organize family networks in urban areas. The 5-year Casey Foundation effort seeks to demonstrate new ways of delivering culturally appropriate, family-sensitive mental health services in disadvantaged urban neighborhoods. The Federation serves as a catalyst to organize family networks for support, information sharing, and advocacy in these areas. The Federation remains involved in building family networks for mutual support, information, and advocacy in other communities and states. Additionally, the Federation is reaching out across the country and continues to include in its constituency families who are culturally and ethnically diverse and who represent all economic circumstances.

The Federation of Families for Children's Mental Health also has become involved in gathering and disseminating information about innovative ideas and best practices in the development of family organizations, the development and implementation of family support programs, and system change efforts. Specific areas receiving priority emphasis have included and continue to include how to involve families living in urban and rural areas, families who are poor, and minority families.

Through the national office, the board of directors, and an elaborate network of state and local chapters, the Federation has become a source of technical assistance and training for service providers across child-serving systems (child welfare, juvenile justice, education, and mental health). Since 1993, the Federation has been awarded funds to provide technical assistance and training to recipients of federal Statewide Family Network grants from the CMHS. These grants are designed to promote the development of statewide family advocacy organizations. By 1995, the Federation was providing technical assistance to grantees in 28 states, with plans for expanding its technical assistance capability to family advocacy organizations in all 50 states.

THE NATIONAL ALLIANCE FOR
THE MENTALLY ILL CHILDREN AND ADOLESCENT NETWORK

Another major national family advocacy organization that focuses on children's mental health issues is the National Alliance for the Mentally Ill Children and Adolescent Network. The National Alliance for the Mentally Ill (NAMI) was formed in 1979 by families of persons with long-term, serious mental illnesses. Over the years since its inception, NAMI became aware that the number of families in its ranks who had young children with neurobiological mental disorders was growing. By the late 1980s (close to the same time the Federation of Families for Children's Mental Health formed), several of these families formed groups that incorporated the NAMI philosophy but focused on serving families with children and adolescents. The National Alliance for the Mentally Ill Children and Adolescent Network (NAMI CAN) was formally established in 1988. NAMI CAN followed a rich tradition of advocacy set by the National Alliance for the Mentally Ill.

NAMI CAN modeled itself after its parent organization. Drawing parallels to NAMI's struggles in its infancy to disentangle mental illness from poor mental health,

> NAMI CAN is and remains fiercely independent and avoids options of joining coalitions of other organizations focused on a broader range of serious emotional disorders with class, race, and socioeconomic contributors to the overall well being of children and families. (Howe, 1995, p. 2)

NAMI CAN decided on its formation that it would welcome all families but place a primary emphasis on and specifically advocate for children with the following brain disorders: affective disorders, bipolar and unipolar depression, anxiety disorders, schizophrenia and schizo-affective disorders, obsessive–compulsive disorder, attention-deficit/hyperactivity disorder, Tourette syndrome, autism and pervasive developmental disorder, or other disorders characterized by demonstrable brain malfunctions. NAMI CAN believes that the services required by children with neurobiological mental disorders are different from those required by children and adolescents with other emotional disorders and children and adolescents whose emotional difficulties may either stem from or involve problems of violence, poverty, and other societal problems.

Since its inception, NAMI CAN has placed an emphasis on promoting additional research to better understand the causes of neurobiological mental disorders. "They want to know that the services for their children are the most appropriate and that those services will help their children to grow up to be as independent as their illness will allow" (Howe, 1995, p. 2). Although the clearly stated focus of NAMI CAN is on children with neurobiological mental disorders, the group recognizes that there are children with mental health or psychological problems that, from their perspective, are sociologically or environmentally caused problems. In addition, NAMI CAN recognizes a third group of children with serious disabilities—those with both a neurobiological mental disorder and a "mental health problem." The organization recognized that all children with severe disabilities need and deserve to have treatments and services geared to their specific disabilities, but crafted its mission and agenda around a subset of youngsters with mental health needs and their families.

The goals of NAMI CAN include

- The quest for a total range of individualized and appropriate educational, treatment, and rehabilitative services
- A comprehensive, community-based system of care available to every child and adolescent in need of such services
- An end to the practice of forcing parents to give up custody in order to obtain needed services
- An end to the practice of children with neurobiological disorders being placed in the juvenile justice system
- The rights of children and adolescents to a free, appropriate public education and related services as mandated by federal, state and local laws
- A change in public policy so that the needs of these children and adolescents are placed among the top priorities of the nation; full family participation in planning for education and treatment; full equity for children and adolescents with these disorders in the nation's health care and insurance systems; and research into causes
- Improved treatment, prevention, and cures for neurobiological disorders
- Research of the most effective educational strategies
- Improvement in the transition between adolescent and adult services (Howe, 1995, p. 2)

NAMI CAN states clearly that its emphasis on advocacy efforts for children and adolescents with neurobiological mental disorders represents the defining difference between itself and "other organizations that are focusing on the problems of poverty and other societal problems such as children who are abused, abandoned, and neglected or children who desperately need appropriate services for a variety of conditions" (Howe, 1995, p. 2).

As NAMI CAN looks toward the future, the group recognizes the need for more outreach across the systems that serve children with neurobiological mental disorders. The current focus of the organization, in addition to the continual press for more research into the causes of neurobiological mental disorders, is to develop strategies for educating faculty in the education system on how to recognize the signs of neurobiological mental disorders. NAMI CAN wants to bring scientific discoveries about mental illness into the classroom, presenting visible evidence of research studies on the brain, such as showing magnetic resonance imaging scans on which differences in the brain can be seen. According to Carolyn Sanger, President of NAMI CAN (personal communication, 1995), if educators understand how to recognize the signs of mental illness appropriately, they will be less likely to "misinterpret mental illness as bad and willful behavior" and will not rely solely on behavior management strategies as an intervention approach. Instead, they will be more likely to try strategies that include the perspective of mental health practitioners who understand mental illness and the use of psychopharmacological approaches when appropriate. The leadership of NAMI CAN hopes to take this education campaign into other child-serving agencies, including mental health, child welfare, and juvenile justice.

The most pressing concern of NAMI CAN at this time is that, from the organization's perspective, the language describing children with serious emotional disturbances in the Individuals with Disabilities Education Act of 1990 (PL 101-476) is too broad and includes too many other types of emotional problems, thus diminishing the focus they would like to see on children with neurobiological mental disorders. In testimony given before a Senate committee in the spring of 1994 (C. Sanger, personal communication, June 1995), representatives of NAMI CAN urged Congress to insert a new category in the reauthorization of PL 101-476 for children with neurobiological disorders. This is a position the organization continues to advocate strenuously.

The structure of the Children and Adolescent Network within NAMI currently is undergoing a transition. The organization is eliminating specialty networks, including the Children and Adolescent Network. However, the importance of issues regarding children and adolescents is being enhanced within the overall structure of NAMI by recruiting staff dedicated to these issues and through other strategies.

THE FAMILY ADVOCACY MOVEMENT TODAY

The family advocacy movement today is thriving but fragile. Two organizations have dominated advocacy efforts for children with emotional, behavioral, or mental disorders. NAMI CAN has operated under the umbrella of the firmly established organization, the National Alliance for the Mentally Ill. Like its parent organization, NAMI CAN has a strong interest in research in the hopes of finding answers for families who have children with neurobiological mental disorders. Its focus is on a subpopulation of children with mental health treatment needs. The Federation of Families for Children's Mental Health has relied primarily on its ability to secure grant funding from public and private sources and a growing membership willing to contribute time and dollars to ensure that the organization maintains a solid footing in the family advocacy movement. Because the federation considers its primary focus to be all families involved with the child mental health service delivery system, it finds its activities spread out in a variety of arenas, from mental health to juvenile justice to child welfare to education.

Both organizations are keenly aware that, as the 1990s come to a close, federal dollars for improving child mental health services are becoming limited. If the family advocacy movement is to thrive into the next century, advocacy groups will continually have to redefine who they are and how they can best serve their members. Examples are emerging of Federation of Families for Children's Mental Health chapters and NAMI CAN chapters exploring affiliation options and joint membership. Probably more at the state level, family advocates are beginning to recognize that a united front will be more effective when lobbying for dollars for child mental health services. Competition for funding reduces the chances of either group receiving funds or seeing funds secured for state child mental health services.

Still, fundamental differences remain at the national level about how and where to focus advocacy efforts. The combined agenda of the family organizations is to promote research into the causes of mental disorders as well as to promote the development of more integrated, family-friendly services for children and adolescents with a wide range of mental health problems and their families.

In the field of children's mental health services, one can now find pervasive evidence of family involvement in designing and evaluating services, setting policy, and providing services. As with any major change in systemic thinking, this process takes time, and the involvement of families in the mental health service delivery system is by no means complete. With the increasing trend toward privatization of mental health services and managed care, the inroads families have made into the public mental health service delivery system must be replicated in the private sector. The presence of families is being undeniably felt, however, and all indicators suggest that the family movement will be one of the defining forces in shaping the way services are provided to children and adolescents with emotional, behavioral, or mental disorders and their families in the future.

REFERENCES

Anderson, W. (1994). *Finding help—finding hope: A guidebook to school services for families with a child who has emotional, behavioral, or mental disorders*. Alexandria, VA: Federation of Families for Children's Mental Health.

Federation of Families for Children's Mental Health. (1989). *Philosophy statement of the Federation of Families for Children's Mental Health*. Unpublished manuscript.

Franz, J., & Miles, P. (1994, May). Scaling up: Looking to the wraparound process as an antidote for the collapse of our assembly-line human service industries. *The Calliope Journal*, pp. 1–7.

Howe, C. (1995).A History of NAMI CAN. *NAMI Advocate*, II(5), 2.

Individuals with Disabilities Education Act of 1990, PL 101-476. (October 30, 1990). Title 20, U.S.C. 1400 et seq: *U.S. Statutes at Large, 104*(Part 2), 1103–1151.

Knitzer, J. (1982). *Unclaimed children: The failure of public responsibility to children and adolescents in need of mental health services.* Washington, DC: Children's Defense Fund.

Koyanagi, C., & Gaines, S. (1993). *All systems failure: An examination of the results of neglecting the needs of children with serious emotional disturbance.* Alexandria, VA: National Mental Health Association.

Renfro, M. (1994, October). *Alaska's experience in individualization of services for persons who experience developmental disabilities.* Presentation at the Third Annual Wraparound Family Reunion, Burlington, VT.

Stroul, B., & Friedman, R. (1986). *A system of care for children and youth with severe emotional disturbances.* Washington, DC: Georgetown University Child Development Center, National Technical Assistance Center for Children's Mental Health.

Thomas, N., & Friesen, B. (1990). *Next steps: A national family agenda for children who have emotional disorders—conference proceedings.* Portland, OR: Portland State University, Research and Training Center on Family Support and Children's Mental Health.

Tucker, J. (1993). *R.C. vs Hornsby.* Unpublished paper, The Alabama American Civil Liberties Union, Montgomery, AL.

CHAPTER 20

A Family-Designed System of Care
Families First in Essex County, New York

Naomi Tannen

Working within the professional–client hierarchy is so ingrained in our service delivery systems that it is rarely questioned. It is assumed that doctors, lawyers, and therapists "know best," and that clients are the recipients of their expert advice and knowledge. Even the very best systems of care have been designed by professionals with little, if any, input from consumers. Families First in Essex County, New York, challenged this paradigm by implementing a system of care that was designed by families. This chapter describes the planning for the system, the implementation process, and how the vision of a parent-designed system of services has been maintained.

ESTABLISHING THE VISION

The goal of Families First has been to develop a system of services for families with children with serious emotional or behavioral problems in a rural area that has extremely limited resources. The initiative was designed to develop a system based on what families said they needed and wanted. On the surface, this hardly seems like a radical idea—just common sense. In actuality, making the assumption that families are the "experts" challenges deeply held convictions of the professional community. Rather than blaming parents for their children's emotional problems, the system is based on the belief that childhood mental illness results from a multiplicity of causes, including biochemical and genetic predisposition and severe en-

Families First in Essex County has been funded by the New York State Office of Mental Health Research Foundation for Mental Health through NIMH grant HD55M50736; Mary Evans, Principal Investigator, Mental Health Association in New York; Kelsey Trust; and Ben and Jerry's Foundation.

This chapter was written with parent contributions from Pam Haran, James Karr, Laurie Rafferty, Karen Robillard, Rebecca Santillo, Mary Stockwell, Betsey Thomas-Train, Dagne Trembley, Ginny Wood, and Anne Mancini. The youth contribution was provided by Skye Mancini.

vironmental and social pressures. The system is further based on the belief
that the great majority of parents love their children and are doing the best
they can to be adequate parents.

> "The main thing is for someone to really listen. We have had no say in anything
> that happens to us. How can anyone really know what we need if they haven't
> lived with our child 24 hours a day?"

> "In my 25 years of dealing with the system, not once has a professional asked
> me what I wanted or needed for my child."

The concept of developing a family-designed system of care was based
on the assumption that all families would have some shared basic needs,
regardless of differences in socioeconomic status, culture, race, ethnicity, or
sexual orientation. In addition, it was assumed that whatever services
evolved would have to be sensitive to cultural differences and the uniqueness of each family.

The Families First Planning Process

Initial Outreach and Funding Although a long-time resident of Essex
County in upstate New York, I had not been a part of the local service
system when I conceived of this project. It was therefore necessary to make
contact with the primary agencies and to garner their support for the concept. The goal was to cultivate a shared vision among all the service providers as well as a sense of ownership and pride in creating an innovative,
consumer-responsive system. The director of the Community Services
Board was supportive of the idea and was, fortunately, not threatened by
a "newcomer" with ambitious plans. With the director's encouragement, I
met with individuals on the state level to request support and funding and
wrote several foundation grants. Presentations were made to pertinent
groups in the community, including the Board of Supervisors, special educators, mental health clinicians, social service staff, and physicians. The
county Mental Health Association agreed to become the sponsor of the
project and supported Families First during its first year. (Families First has
since received its own nonprofit incorporation status; the board is composed of 12 individuals, three fourths of whom have family members who
have a serious emotional disturbance.)

Family Interviews Letters were written to all child-serving agencies,
including schools, requesting that they contact families who had children
with emotional, behavioral, or mental disorders to get their permission to
be interviewed. This required follow-up until the families were actually
contacted and permission was received so that I could interview them. In
all, 24 families were interviewed. Most of these interviews were conducted
in the families' homes and lasted approximately 2 hours. A group of parents
was interviewed together at a meeting of a chapter of the Association for
the Mentally Ill. The interviews consisted of asking people to tell their "stories," and then to answer three questions:

1. What has been most helpful to you?
2. What has not been helpful?
3. If you had a magic wand and could have any help you wanted, what would you like?

The interviews were tape recorded, and written notes were taken as well. There was overwhelming congruity in the families' responses. Parents expressed their pain at feeling rejected by the system, not being able to get the support services that would be most helpful, and feeling terribly isolated. Typical of their responses were the following:

"All the energy that I put into fighting the system I could use to help my family."

"I felt like I was being subjected to blame and shame."

"I want the sense that I am being believed, that there is someone who understands the stresses that I live with."

"I've never talked to another parent who had a child with problems like my child has."

"I had to be my own advocate. I fought every step of the way."

"I didn't give my son to social services. I just asked for help."

Parent Planning Committee   From among those interviewed, I invited parents to participate on a Parent Planning Committee. Parents were chosen who were articulate about their needs and indicated some awareness of system issues beyond their own situation; effort was made to ensure diverse representation. The core group that made a commitment to the process consisted of two fathers (one a single father) and three mothers (one adoptive and two biological). Two of the families were on public assistance. One parent was a mental health therapist; another of the participants was the parent director of the state Parent Support Network. The committee also had a "token" professional, the director of the county mental health clinic. Several other parents attended one to three meetings before dropping out of the group.

The committee met for eight 2-hour sessions. It seemed appropriate, given the belief that parents were experts, that they should be paid for their time. The parents were paid $25 per session plus mileage and child care reimbursement. Their task was to take the recommendations from the interviews and design a system of services, making specific recommendations for implementation.

Interagency Task Force   Simultaneous with this parent planning effort, a Families First Task Force was established consisting of representatives from all the child- and family-serving agencies in the county and interested community members, such as church leaders and retired social workers. The Task Force met monthly for 2 hours. The agenda for each meeting consisted of updates from attendees, discussion of a particular issue such as prioritizing the needs of families in the county, and a presentation from a parent of a child with serious emotional problems. Most of the parents who were invited to present were from out of the county, a strategy used to reduce the tendency of professionals to be defensive when parents conveyed their frustration and anger at the system.

Three subcommittees of the Task Force were formed. One addressed the lack of transportation, which the group believed to be a primary obstacle to service delivery; the second was to help the representative from the Housing Assistance Program to implement a mandate to establish a 5-year program to help families become financially independent; the third was a program and policy subcommittee. The latter committee was composed of the commissioner of social services, the clinical director of the Mental Health Center, the director of the Community Services Board, a special educator chosen to represent all the school districts, a person from the juvenile justice system responsible for diversion efforts, a Mental Health Association board representative, the Families First director, and seven parents.

> "I feel vindicated by sitting on the committee. It used to be that I felt like a victim at meetings, with professionals' goal to make me shape up. In this forum I'm taken seriously because I'm on an equal footing with the professionals."

Outcomes of the Families First Planning Process

Families' Priorities   There was almost total agreement among those interviewed as to the services considered most helpful. It is significant to note that the services requested by families tended to be support services that were less expensive and less intrusive than the programs for which professionals commonly advocate. When professionals design systems of care, those services that parents prioritized are typically not developed until more traditional components are in place. In many cases, they are not included in the range of services at all. The following clearly emerged as the highest priority needs of the 24 families interviewed:

- Respite

> "I was grief stricken when my child went into residential treatment. Our family was so exhausted that we felt that we didn't have an alternative. If only we could have had regular breaks, I know we could have maintained our child at home."

- An advocate

> "I needed somebody that we could talk to, who would listen, guide us. Someone who was in our corner."

> "We want someone to teach us how to maneuver through the system without disempowering us."

> "Sometimes I just don't know what to do for my child and I need someone to help me make decisions."

- Information and referral

  "Nobody explained schizophrenia to me until a year after my son's first schizophrenic episode."

  "You drag your child around from person to person telling your story over and over again, baring your soul in order to prove that you need services."

  "I desperately wanted someone to teach me the system."

- Parent and sibling support

  "I've never talked to another parent who had a child with problems like my child has."

  "Parents don't get to meet each other. Confidentiality is used as the excuse to keep us apart."

  "My other sons were so embarrassed on the school bus."

- Family center

  "It would be so wonderful to have a place to go that was safe and comfortable."

  "There are emergency telephone numbers for police and fire, but not for parents and kids who feel like they are going crazy."

- Community friend

  "My other kids have a social life, but J. has no friends, no experiences to talk about at the dinner table."

  "Being a single father, I want my girls to have a good female role model, like a big sister—someone they can talk to and do things with."

- Crisis services

  "In a crisis we need support and practical suggestions about what to do, and then a follow-up call."

  "I wished that someone could come into our house to help—maybe even a team, so someone could be with his brothers and sisters."

- Concrete assistance

  "I needed to call the hospital in the middle of the night. I banged on the neighbor's door to use their phone, but they wouldn't let me in."

  "The electricity was shut off, the water pipes froze, and all the kids were sick. Then they wonder why I feel depressed!"

Parent Planning Committee Recommendations The product of the eight sessions held by the Parent Planning Committee was a list of 32 specific recommendations for Families First programs and policies. These have become the blueprint for the project. The concepts in the recommendations have been reinforced by new parents who have become involved. The following are a sample of the challenging prescriptions that now form the foundation of Families First:

- All committees, including the board and steering committee, should have at least 50% parent representation.
- Preference should be given to parents of children with special needs for all staff positions.
- Parents should participate as trainers in the training of all staff and volunteers.
- Parents should establish criteria for family-friendly agencies and award those that meet the criteria a "Family Friendly Seal of Approval."
- Families should interview and "hire" those professionals and service providers working with them. Participants and service providers should have an agreement for a trial period after which either can decide to discontinue the contract. There should be scheduled periodic evaluations as part of every agreement to see if the match is successful and if the service suits the provider and the family.
- Families First should stress the importance of sensitivity to language that is respectful and inclusive of parents. Specifically, families should be referred to as "multistressed," never "dysfunctional." People using Families First services are "participants," not "clients." The term "advocate" should be used rather than "case manager."

"We are more likely to be open to working with someone who uses the more sensitive and accurate term. I can accept that my family is often multistressed, but we have never been dysfunctional. We have always functioned!"

"I am not resistant; I am cautious because of having been judged and blamed so many times in the past."

IMPLEMENTING THE VISION

Establishing Working Committees
It was considered essential for service providers and parents to have a sense of ownership of the project from the very beginning. Therefore, small subcommittees of the Task Force were established to hire staff, find and oversee a site, and purchase equipment. The Families First Steering Committee assumed responsibility for program planning. All the working committees had parent representation.

Hiring Staff
Advertisements for staff specified that preference would be given to parents of children with special needs. In the evaluation of applicants' qualifications, experience as a parent was weighted equally with academic and other work experience. The person who was hired to be the office manager and parent advocate has a bachelor's degree (B.A.) in Psychology and is the mother of a child with Tourette syndrome. The part-time bookkeeper is a parent of two children with special needs; the parent advocate hired to do

home visits has a master's degree in social work (M.S.W.) and is not a parent of a youngster with special needs. Having parents as well as professionals interview prospective staff enhanced the likelihood of hiring people who were respectful of families.

One of the first challenges that the personnel committee faced was the issue of whether a person with a B.A. and parenting experience should receive the same salary as an individual with a M.S.W. without parenting experience. It was decided that, if the expertise gained from living with a child with special needs was truly valued, the salaries should be equal.

Setting up the Center

Following parents' recommendations, the Facilities Subcommittee rented a house located in Elizabethtown, the county seat. The new office is in walking distance from other services such as mental health and social services. Fortunately, start-up costs were covered through a grant from the New York State Office of Mental Health. The front room was designed to look like a living room, with a couch, rocking chair, children's chair, and coffee table. The Family Support Coordinator works behind her desk, facing the entrance. One wall has floor-to-ceiling shelves for resources—books, pamphlets, cassettes, and videos for parents to use and borrow. First impressions are crucial; being welcomed warmly by a professional who is also a parent of a child with special needs, who is totally accessible and not behind any barriers of glass or walls, transmits a strong message to families.

Family members who cannot come into the office can use the toll-free telephone line and speak with the Family Support Coordinator. The coordinator frequently spends an hour on the phone or face-to-face in the office talking with families on their first contact.

> "When you walk in here you feel safe. You don't have to get your guard up because you think someone is going to challenge you and make you feel bad about yourself as a person and a parent."

> "Being given a book that tells me about my child's problems and what I can do about it makes me feel respected."

Improving Interagency Collaboration

> "There are so many people working with my family and nobody talks to anyone else."

> "Professionals are so concerned about their turf. When it comes to my child, it's *my* turf!"

A primary goal of Families First has been to create a family-friendly environment in the community, in which human services providers and families work as partners to improve the quality of life for families of children with serious emotional/behavioral problems. Providers in a very rural area with a dearth of services and little exposure to new ideas tend to be discouraged and stuck in old patterns of service delivery. Overworked and underpaid, their lack of hopefulness mirrors the discouragement of many of their clients.

Families First initiated many forums for interagency networking. The Families First Task Force meets monthly; there are two interagency teams that also meet monthly, one focused on individual children who are challenging to the system and the other focused on policy issues affecting families. In addition, individual treatment planning teams have been established for families needing intensive services. Parents play a central role in all of these forums. Families First never holds a meeting concerning a family without inviting the family to be there, as well as ensuring that the family sets the agenda, decides on who should attend (including members of their natural support system), and is in control of the meeting process. Meetings are frequently held in the family's home.

These structures and processes have resulted in significant improvements in the working relationships among the various child-serving agencies in the community. However, working with the system of providers is extremely challenging. As with any system work, it requires joining with the most positive forces and making efforts to entice reluctant and cautious members to participate. Furthermore, attempting a major system change, such as having professionals work with parents as full and equal partners, is a process that requires constant strategizing and a great deal of patience.

Developing Services

With limited funding, Families First has attempted to implement the parents' recommendations for services as rapidly as possible. There is a commitment to be responsive to everyone who contacts the project. Everyone can get something, even if it is simply a listening ear or a referral to another program. No one is told that they have to be placed on a waiting list. The Parent Support Coordinator who answers the telephone and greets drop-ins has been designated as the "red tape cutter." She has become knowledgeable about resources and will do the research necessary to obtain information for a family if the needed information is not readily available. Everyone can borrow books from the resource library and be put in contact with another parent for support.

Four parent support groups have been established in towns around the county. These are co-facilitated by parents who have received training; support is provided by the coordinator.

The social worker is available to conduct in-home assessments with families who cannot come to the office or who prefer a home visit. These are strengths-based assessments that are based on the families' perceptions of what they need and want. Ongoing support and advocacy are offered to the families in most need.

The approach used by the Families First staff involves strategizing with families to meet their particular needs. Discouragement is avoided by adhering to the concept of "creative use of existing resources." Natural support systems always are the first resources considered.

> "When I needed respite badly, Families First helped me make a plan for my sisters and my mother to each take one of the kids for the weekend."

Families First utilizes the concept of "wraparound services" in all its interventions. A small pool of flexible dollars permits the purchase of some individualized services and concrete items. The commitment is to find or develop the services that will allow children to remain at home and in their communities, in the least restrictive environment.

> "Two deputy sheriffs and a town cop came to drive him the three hours to the state hospital. It hurt real bad. I cried. L. cried. The sheriff wouldn't give me the hospital phone number. He said to look it up. I called L. every day he was there. I don't want to have to send him away ever again."

Two years after the inception of Families First, the county received funding for an intensive case manager (ICM). The position was assigned to Families First and is being implemented according to the project's values. Families are invited to all meetings; goals and plans are established by the family. The ICM interagency team has two parent representatives who contact the family prior to their consideration for eligibility and are available for support.

> "I called the parent and told them just what to expect at the meeting and that I would be there to support them."

The Respitality program is an example of the creative use of community resources. Fourteen inns and hotels in the county have agreed to provide free rooms to parents for respite, during off-peak times of the week and year.

> "Sally [another parent] drove me to the bed and breakfast and wouldn't even let me carry my suitcase. I felt like a princess sleeping in the canopied bed. Having time to myself was a spiritual experience for me."

With funds available to cover only four staff positions, Families First made a commitment to develop a corps of volunteers to deliver the services requested by families and to help maintain the project. Local newspaper and television spots, letters to schools and other agencies, posters, and direct requests to friends yielded some general assistance but few people who were interested in making a long-term commitment to a family. The project now has the funds to hire a part-time volunteer coordinator who we hope will recruit more volunteers and provide training and support to them.

Families First is convinced that an approach involving neighbors helping neighbors can be fruitful.

Program participants also are seen as a volunteer resource. When doing assessments, parents are always asked what they might like to contribute to the program, as well as what they would like to receive from the program. Participants have given their time for project activities such as being a representative at meetings, working on the Families First newsletter, and driving other participants to appointments.

Involving Youth

The initial planning process for a family-designed system of care relied on parents for input. Although youth were included in most of the interviews, the focus was on the adults. The process of family empowerment seems to follow a learning path that is not unique to Families First. Other forums are currently reaching a level of consciousness that is leading them to turn to the youth who have been diagnosed as having emotional, behavioral, or mental disorders for their input in program planning. Families First has established a Youth Advisory Committee that meets monthly and has been planning recreational activities as well as advising the staff on general issues. The committee is currently helping parents to design a crisis intervention component for the project and is working to establish support groups for youth.

"When things are tough, kids need a chance for respite, too."

"I hate it when teachers and others have meetings about me and don't tell me about it or include me in the meetings."

"Last night my son was very upset, throwing things against the wall. He called another member of the Youth Committee and talked for an hour. After that, his whole body was calm."

MAINTAINING THE VISION

Developing a parent-designed and -implemented system of services that strives for a true parent–professional partnership has been extremely challenging. Working in a rural area has meant confronting the isolation of both participants and professionals, the dearth of services, and the lack of a pool of trained and experienced staff. The lack of public transportation, long and harsh winters, and pervasive poverty also have made it difficult to enlist a substantial group of participants willing and able to assume responsibility for the program. Despite these difficulties, the project has remained totally committed to its values and has continued to grow and flourish. Services were offered to over 70 participants in the first year.

The following challenges will likely confront any project that undertakes the task of building a truly family-centered system:

- *Parents as providers*: When parents of children with serious emotional or behavioral problems become providers, they face complex challenges. For example, living with a child with an emotional disorder is extremely stressful, and there are inevitable crises that make it difficult to perform the job without special accommodations. Personnel policies must be flexible and "family friendly." It is recommended that the possible difficulties be articulated, as in the sample letter to parents shown in Figure 20.1.
- *Interagency collaboration*: Learning to share responsibility, planning, and resources is difficult for providers who are working under fiscal restraints and differing mandates. The challenge is magnified when they are asked to sit at the table with their clients as peers. Being asked to truly listen to recipients of service, and to work with them and their natural support systems as team members, can make traditional providers feel threatened and uncomfortable. When a plan is not working, it is an adjustment to ask how the team needs to change the plan, rather than to blame the family for being "unmotivated" or "resistant."
- *Blurring the boundaries*: Established wisdom is that families and systems function best when there are clear boundaries, such as maintaining professional distance between clients and service providers. In a parent-designed and -implemented system of care, this axiom is challenged as the boundaries between professionals and service recipients are deliberately blurred. Consumers are in charge of their own treatment plans, providers may be parents of children with serious emotional problems, parents train professionals, and services frequently are offered in the families' homes instead of in professionals' offices. Having families and providers working in a true partnership may be extremely productive and empowering, but it can also make both parties feel uncomfortable. Blurring the boundaries requires sensitivity, confidence, and a willingness to continually evaluate the process and articulate the new parameters.

CONCLUSIONS

Developing a system of care that is designed and implemented by families represents a new paradigm. The concept of basing services on what people say they want and need may appear to be the most obvious of ideas, but it challenges a traditional and deeply held belief system. Rather than assuming the superiority of professionals, and attributing "blame and shame" to supposedly "dysfunctional" families, it calls for consumers and providers to work as allies.

> "Since I've been on the Board of Families First, for the first time in eight years I don't feel ashamed of the fact that my daughter had serious emotional problems when she was a teenager."

We are very pleased that you are considering or have decided to work with Families First. We believe that the experience that you've gained living with a child who has emotional or behavioral problems is of tremendous value in your being able to be of help to other parents. Your expertise as a parent is also highly valuable in training and communicating with professionals. You know the realities of the day-to-day challenges, as well as the pleasures, of living with a child with special needs and strengths.

Families First is committed to giving preference to parents in hiring and to having parents be the primary designers and implementers of service. However, we have learned from experience that being a parent and working as a parent–provider are difficult roles to combine.

Some of the challenges parents have had and you might experience are:

1. *Boundary Issues*—When you are receiving service from Families First as well as delivering services, there may be times when you feel confused about your role. You also may find yourself interacting with professionals from other agencies with whom you have interacted as a client, while you are now in the role of a peer/worker. These overlapping roles can be confusing and stressful.
2. *Hope/Discouragement*—Part of your job with Families First is to help families feel hopeful in the face of discouragement. You can empathize with their frustration, but you want to help them appreciate the potential for things to improve. If you are going through a time of discouragement about your own child, it may feel very difficult to project hopefulness to others.
3. *Preoccupation with Your Own "Story"*—You may feel so absorbed with your own family challenges that it may be difficult at times to listen well to others' stories. Telling your story can be very helpful, especially in sensitizing professionals to families, but it is hard to share very painful and personal things with people you don't know well. Sometimes it is hard to know how much and what to share.
4. *Availability*—The stresses and inevitable crises that occur when living with a child with special needs make it hard to be consistently available. There are times when meeting work commitments will be difficult, both literally and emotionally.
5. *Anger at the System*—Your own anger and frustration with the system of providers may make it difficult to work cooperatively with professionals and to encourage other parents to work positively with them.
6. *Knowing Your Limits*—It may be hard to keep from getting overwhelmed by others' needs and overinvolved in their lives. Most parents of children with serious emotional problems are not psychotherapists or doctors (some are!), but it can be tempting to feel that you have to play those roles.

Knowing how challenging it is to work as a parent–provider, Families First will try to provide the clearest boundaries and expectations possible. We offer support and supervision and want to be responsive to the stresses in your life. We will try to be as flexible and accommodating as we can. If you feel that we are failing, please don't hesitate to let us know. "If in doubt, check it out!"

Everyone at Families First is hired for an agreed-on trial period. After the period is up, you will have a chance to discuss whether this is the right thing for you at this time in your life. If you would like to do an evaluation sooner, just ask for it.

Having parents work as providers is a new idea. We need your help to make it work. Don't hesitate to give us lots of feedback—positive and/or negative!

Figure 20.1. Letter to parents regarding work with Families First.

Providers and consumers have traditionally been in a hierarchical relationship. As in any grass roots movement in which the underclass demands more power, few of those who have held the power willingly give it up. For those who are engaged in making this transition, it is important to identify allies, to get support wherever one can, to recognize that change takes time, and to have faith in the process. It is crucial to instill hope in families and providers, so that they can form an alliance for change rather than succumb to despair.

If we are to move toward a system of care that families perceive as helpful rather than hurtful, those guiding the process of working with families to design the services must tenaciously maintain the vision. Systems, like families, are slow to change and require vigilant adherence to underlying values, patience, and creativity in strategizing to bring about change.

> "So the social worker said 'I'll go down and straighten things out at the school.' 'No,' I said, 'you come down and get me and we'll go together.' "

SUGGESTED READINGS

Agosta, J., Bradley, V., & Knoll, J. (1992). *Toward positive family policy: Components of a comprehensive family support system.* Cambridge, MA: Human Services Research Institute.

Byalin, K. (1990). Parent empowerment: A treatment strategy for hospitalized adolescents. *Hospital and Community Psychiatry, 41,* 81–90.

Castellani, P.J., Downey, M.A., Tausig, M.B., & Bird, W.A. (1986). Availability and accessibility of family support services. *Mental Retardation, 24,* 71–79.

Duchnowski, A.J., & Friedman, R.M. (1991). Children's mental health: Challenges for the nineties. *Journal of Mental Health Administration, 17,* 3–12.

Dunst, C.J., Trivette, C.M., & Cross, A.H. (1986). Mediating influences of social support. *American Journal of Mental Deficiency, 90,* 402–417.

Elizur, J., & Minuchin, S. (1989). *Institutionalizing madness: Families, therapy, and society.* New York: Basic Books.

Freud, E. (1989). *Family support programs for families who have children with severe emotional, behavioral or mental disabilities: The state of the art.* Cambridge, MA: Human Services Research Institute.

Freisen, B., Griesbach, J., Jacobs, J., Katz-Leavy, J., & Olson, D. (1988). Improving services for families and children. *Today, 17,* 18–22.

Friesen, B.J., & Koroloff, N.M. (1991). Family-centered services: Implications for mental health administration and research. *Journal of Mental Health Administration, 17,* 13–25.

Hutchinson, P., Lord, J., Savage, H., & Schnarr, A. (1985). *Listening to people who have directly experienced the mental health system.* Toronto: Canadian Mental Health Association.

Karp, N. (1993). Building collaborative partnerships with families: From rhetoric to reality. *Journal of Emotional and Behavioral Problems, 1,* 4.

Katz-Leavy, J.W., Lourie, I.S., Stroul, B.A., & Zeigler-Dendy, C. (1992). *Individualized services in a system of care.* Washington, DC: Georgetown University Child Development Center, National Technical Assistance Center for Children's Mental Health.

Knoll, J.A. (1990). Family support: A challenge for the 1990's. *Exceptional Parent, 20*(4), 28–30, 32, 34.

Knoll, J.A., & Bedford, S. (1989). *Becoming informed consumers: A national survey of parents' experience with respite services. Final project report.* Cambridge MA: Human Services Research Institute.

Lefley, H.P., & Johnson, D.L. (1990). *Families as allies in the treatment of the mentally ill: New directions for mental health professionals.* Washington, DC: American Psychiatric Press.

National Association of State Mental Health Program Directors Research Institute, Inc. (1992). Special issue on rural mental health services research. *Outlook, 2,* 3.

New York State Office of Mental Health. (1993, April). What makes a mental health program "user-friendly?" *OMH News, 5,* 2.

Portland State University, Research and Training Center on Family Support and Children's Mental Health. (1992). Parents as policy makers: Challenges for collaboration. *Focal Point, 6,* 1.

Ridgeway, P. (1988). *The voice of consumers in mental health systems: A call for change. A literature review.* Burlington: Center for Community Change for Housing & Support, University of Vermont.

Sawyer, D.A., Moreines, S.F., & Lumley, M.J. (1992). Strengthening the rural mental health network for children: Effective partnerships. *Rural Community Mental Health, 18,* 1.

Snyder, C.R., Irving, L.M., & Anderson, J.R. (1991). Hope and health. In C.R. Snyder & D.R. Forsyth (Eds.), *Handbook of social and clinical psychology: The health perspective* (pp. 285–305). Elmsford, NY: Pergamon Press.

Stroul, B.A., & Friedman, R.M. (1986). *A system of care for severely emotionally disturbed children and youth.* Washington, DC: Georgetown University Child Development Center, National Technical Assistance Center for Children's Mental Health.

Turnbull, H.R, Garlow, J., & Barbaer, P. (1991). A policy analysis for family support for families with members with disabilities. *University of Kansas Law Review, 39,* 739–783.

CHAPTER 21

Families and Professionals in Partnership

Neal DeChillo, Paul E. Koren, and Margaret Mezera

Collaboration provides the basis for many forms of human endeavor. In diverse activities ranging from surgery to bridge building to movie making, it is taken for granted that a variety of skills, talents, and perspectives are necessary for success. Beyond its pragmatic function, collaboration is also celebrated for the underlying interpersonal achievement that it represents. Great sports teams, musical groups, and business organizations are admired not only for their accomplishments but for their success in forging lasting partnerships that allow individuals to do something that they could not do alone.

Given this general affirmation of collaboration in the greater society, it is curious that collaboration in the field of children's mental health should be the source of so much apprehension and uncertainty. To an agency administrator, the mention of collaboration may cause concerns about how to coordinate services from multiple providers in the same community. To a practitioner, the term may cause uneasiness about redefining traditional notions of the professional–consumer relationship. To a parent, it may symbolize ambiguity about how to become involved in a decision-making process that is unfamiliar and perhaps viewed as unwelcoming. To each of these, the word "collaboration" may signify an idea that is intriguing but ill-defined and unspecified. Collaboration may be readily understood in other areas of everyday life, but in human services it has yet to truly come of age.

The reasons for this slowness in acceptance are not difficult to uncover. Mental health disciplines have long been dominated by theoretical approaches that emphasize deficits, pathology, and attribution of problems to individual or family characteristics or both (Caplan & Hall-McCorquadale, 1985; Wahl, 1989). Moreover, the widespread emulation of the traditional medical model has promoted a service delivery stance based on authority, privileged information, and labeling. These conditions have been slow to change because alternative approaches have only recently begun to be developed and persuasively articulated, and because of inertia in training curricula and practices. In many respects, the concept of collaboration in the human services is more developed as a value or principle than as a specific approach to the delivery of services. Nevertheless, sufficient progress has occurred to permit viewing the concept of collaboration as having a potentially profound influence on how human services are designed and delivered.

This chapter provides an overview of progress in the practice and study of collaboration. It begins with a discussion of the defining nature of collaboration and why it has become prominent at this point in time. Recent research and thinking on the topic are reviewed, and some principles are derived that may be used as general guidelines for those wishing to apply collaborative practices. Finally, areas for additional attention are outlined.

THE WHAT AND WHY OF COLLABORATION

Collaboration is commonly understood to mean two or more parties working together or joining in the pursuit of a common goal. In a sense, it may be viewed as a developmental refinement of what has traditionally been called the doctor–patient or professional–client relationship. Within the fields of health and mental health, the importance of this relationship has long been recognized. Certain qualities, such as trust, empathy, and genuineness, have generally been considered critical to the success of such relationships, and nearly everyone would agree that such qualities are necessary for successful collaboration as well. However, over roughly the past two decades there has been a significant shift in other aspects of the professional–client relationship that represents a radical departure from the traditional view. To an increasing degree, consumers (clients and family members) and some professionals have called for changing the power balance in professional–client relationships from an uneven one favoring professional status and knowledge to a more equal one based on mutual respect and recognition of unique roles, viewpoints, and experience.

Within the field of adult mental health, the interest in collaboration appears to have been instigated by families' longstanding dissatisfaction with services provided to them on behalf of their relatives with emotional disorders. Families have often felt blamed for the illness of a family member, alienated from the professionals providing treatment, and unrecognized as having a legitimate right to participate in decisions regarding their family members' needs (Grunebaum, 1984; Hatfield, 1982; McElroy, 1987; Spaniol, Jung, Zipple, & Fitzgerald, 1987). Within the field of children's mental health, the number of published reports in this regard is limited, but the findings are generally consistent with those in the adult field (Collins & Collins, 1990; Friesen, 1989; Tarico, Low, Trupin, & Forsyth-Stephens, 1989). Other important factors contributing to increased interest in collaboration include 1) the general rise in consumerism with its emphasis on empowerment and prerogative, 2) research evidence discrediting theories of family interaction as causative agents of emotional and mental disorders and supporting the biological etiology of the most severe disorders, and 3) the increasing recognition of the importance of social supports and the value of informal supports. These factors have sparked an increased interest in family–professional collaboration, based on the premise that the combined efforts of families and professionals will produce more satisfying working relationships and better outcomes for all concerned (Collins & Collins, 1990; DeChillo, 1993; Group for the Advancement of Psychiatry, 1986; Grunebaum, 1986; Hatfield & Lefley, 1987).

In discussing family–professional collaboration (in adult mental health), Bernheim (1990) provides a discussion of what family members and professionals working collaboratively may provide to each other. According to Bernheim, professionals may provide families with 1) a theoretical framework for understanding the client and his or her illness; 2) information about the client and his or her treatment, including medication; 3) linkages to supportive networks; and 4) skills for problem solving and behavior and stress management. Conversely, families may provide professionals with 1) historical information about the client and his or her treatment, including client-specific strengths and coping skills as well as signs and symptoms of regression or relapse; 2) information about the influence of environmental circumstances on the client; and 3) ongoing monitoring of the client's response to treatment, including medications. Finally, although not noted by Bernheim, because families often possess a broad view of the client's life, circumstances, and interests, this perspective can be utilized in developing a comprehensive assessment and treatment plan that goes beyond the narrow confines of traditional mental health and includes consideration of the social, recreational, and educational domains.

Is a collaborative relationship different from a good helping relationship in the traditional sense? Is not a skilled mental health practitioner collaborative in his or her dealings with consumers? These are questions that are sometimes asked by professionals who assert that collaboration is equivalent to good professional practice. They readily admit that this may not be the level or type of practice that consumers often experience, but it is the way professionals are supposed to practice.

As has been noted above, a distinguishing feature of collaboration is the idea of partnership. Implicit in this is the notion that no single person is an expert or has the answers to the issues at hand. This is a very different perspective than that of a traditional mental health practitioner, who may believe that the consumer's input is valuable but that in most cases it is only of value insofar as the information provided during assessment is processed by the professional. The professional then develops, implements, and evaluates the treatment plan. This is analogous to a client telling a physician his or her symptoms and the physician taking over. The client / consumer is not an active participant in the problem resolution. In a collaborative relationship, each party (professional and consumer) is essential to each of the phases of the helping process. Both have a unique perspective and knowledge essential to assessment, planning, implementation, and evaluation.

In a 1994 survey (Williams-Murphy, DeChillo, Koren, & Hunter, 1994), family members and professionals who had received training in collaboration were asked if they discerned a distinction between collaboration and "good practice." The majority believed that collaboration differs from "good practice" because collaboration requires partnership, reciprocity, and equality. Other respondents stressed that collaboration is of necessity a team concept, whereas a good mental health practitioner or therapist may or may not be a good team player.

Some also question the idea of partnership, which is central to collaboration. More than one professional has asked: "Does this mean that everything—all decisions, all responsibilities—are split 50/50 between family members and professionals?" Conversely, some parents think that collaboration means that they should always get their way. Both perspectives reflect an incomplete understanding of the notion of collaboration. In collaboration, as in any partnership, it is assumed that different participants will have different strengths and that these will be drawn on as required and appropriate. The notion of balance is crucial, much like that of a seesaw or teeter-totter, in which weight or responsibility shifts and adjusts as need changes.

SOME PRINCIPLES OF COLLABORATION

As with any emerging concept, there is general agreement about what collaboration generally means but substantial variation with respect to its constituent elements and qualities. Numerous authors have suggested distinguishing features of collaborative family–professional relationships. The majority of these suggestions are theoretically derived (Bernheim, 1990; Dunst & Paget, 1991; Grunebaum, 1986; Hatfield, 1979; Lamb, 1983; Spaniol, Zipple, & Fitzgerald, 1984; Vosler-Hunter, 1989), although efforts are increasingly being made to identify key characteristics of collaboration on an empirical basis (Cournoyer & Johnson, 1991; DeChillo, Koren, & Schultze, 1994; Dunst, Johanson, Rounds, Trivette, & Hamby, 1992; Friesen, 1989; Friesen, Koren, & Koroloff, 1992; Petr & Barney, 1993). The lists of characteristics or components of collaboration that have been suggested contain anywhere from 4 to 26 elements; however, the major characteristics consistently cited include 1) conveying a caring, nonblaming attitude toward the family; 2) sharing of information; 3) recognition of the family as a key resource; 4) recognition of limits and other responsibilities; and 5) shared responsibility and power in the relationship, including joint decision making and problem solving.

DeChillo and colleagues (1994) attempted to identify distinct behavioral components of collaboration by surveying 455 caregivers of children with emotional, behavioral, or mental disorders. Parents were asked to rate the extent to which a wide range of collaborative behaviors occurred in their experiences with professionals who provided services to their children. Through factor analysis of their responses, four empirically distinct elements of collaboration were identified:

1. The support and understanding shown by professionals in their relationships with family members (e.g., including families in decisions about the child and recognizing that families have responsibilities other than their child with a disorder)
2. The assistance given to families in the practical aspects of getting services for their child (e.g., helping families find, coordinate, and pay for services)
3. The clear and open exchange of information between families and professionals
4. The flexibility and willingness on the part of professionals to modify or change services based on parental feedback

These four broad categories sometimes subsumed finer distinctions between specific behaviors. For example, experiences related to trust, caring, and honesty occurred in tandem and were all included in the factor concerned with support and understanding.

The variety of findings and suggestions regarding components of collaboration underscores a key point about this concept—that it is less a matter of specific techniques and more a matter of values and principles. In other words, collaboration by its very nature precludes approaching any given situation with a specific sequence of activities in mind. Rather, collaboration allows activities to proceed according to the responsiveness of individuals to each other and according to evolving circumstances and needs. The governing principles that guide those activities are the distinguishing features of collaboration rather than the specific activities themselves. This is why collaboration is not necessarily characterized by an equal (i.e., 50/50) assignment of activities; rather, activities may be ostensibly unequal and still be collaborative if they occur by mutual consent and in a context of partnership.

In this spirit, the following principles of collaboration are offered, borrowing freely from the literature, previous studies, and ongoing discussions with parents and professionals. Because collaboration is a two-way street, these principles are discussed as they apply to both families and professionals.

1. All Assumptions Are Off.

Assumptions based on problem etiology, culture, class, roles, and history are the bane of collaborative relationships. As noted above, professionals are burdened by an extensive theoretical tradition of unproven assertions about the causes of problems that families face. In addition, recent discussions about the need for culturally competent service delivery (Cross, Bazron, Dennis, & Isaacs, 1989; Isaacs & Benjamin, 1991; Lefley & Pederson, 1986) illustrate the pervasiveness of other types of assumptions as well. On their part, family members who have had previous, negative experiences with professionals may bring their own sets of assumptions that hinder the formation of a working partnership. Unlike most other partnerships, collaboration in the human services often begins with participants having mixed or ambivalent viewpoints and expectations of each other. For this reason, it is especially important for all participants to examine their attitudes and put past negative experiences aside. Both family members and professionals need to try to "walk in the other's shoes" and avoid stereotypes. Forbearance and patience are critical.

2. Roles Are Permeable but Not Interchangeable.

A mistaken notion about the call for collaboration is that it implies a downgrading of professional competence and hence a diminishment of the professional role. On the contrary, true collaboration entails the explicit recognition of each individual's unique competence and contribution to the overall effort. If each individual did not bring unique talents and abilities to the task at hand, collaboration would be unnecessary and superfluous. In the human services, family–professional collaboration does involve a certain permeability in roles because all parties take on a more flexible approach to decision making and responsibility. At any given time, the professional may learn something from family members and vice versa, and each may play an influential role in judging the appropriateness and effectiveness of a particular service. Because this relationship is reciprocal and less one-sided than the traditional professional–client relationship, collaboration involves a reworking of the concept of professionalism. However, far from diminishing the professional role, such a reworking calls for augmenting professional skills as traditionally defined to include a new array of skills and abilities. These include the ability to promote inclusion of a wide variety of stakeholders, the flexibility to work with a broad array of service options and possibilities, and the capability of considering a range of issues that are made more complex because of the addition of multiple viewpoints and opinions.

Professionals should be prepared, thanks to the growing family support and advocacy movement, to encounter a growing number of families who are informed and assertive and who are strongly committed to the notion of family–professional partnerships. By the same token, families should be prepared to take on a more active and involved role in the decision-making process. All parties may feel some discomfort with the newfound influence gained by family members as well as some uncertainty about the responsibilities that accompany this shift in roles. Yet this discomfort and uncertainty can be put to good use if openly discussed as a relationship development process and recognized as an indication that new alignments are now possible.

Professionals and families can perhaps learn analogously from partnerships in other areas. Great song-writing teams have often described their creative efforts as a give-and-take process whereby sometimes the lyrics dictate the melody, and sometimes the melody suggests a certain approach to phrasing the lyrics. Typically, both the lyricist and composer are credited, because the final song reflects both influences. Their roles are not interchangeable, nor is one necessarily subservient to the other. Families and professionals may benefit by approaching collaboration in the same spirit.

3. Everyone Has Strengths.

Recognizing strengths is a key ingredient of collaborative relationships and is especially critical to the acknowledgment of everyone's unique role and contribution. The principle of emphasizing strengths in helping relationships has been widely discussed (Poertner & Ronnau, 1992). In essence, the principle states that all parties, no matter what their circumstances, have knowledge, insights, experiences, or abilities that can serve as valuable contributions to addressing the problem at hand. In a situation involving childhood emotional disability, family members may bring practical experience, historical perspective, and a deep level of commitment. Similarly, professionals may bring theoretical or technical knowledge about disability issues as well as a thorough understanding of resource options, financing mechanisms, and service system constraints. In ideal circumstances, the presence of such multiple strengths greatly facilitates establishing and maintaining a collaborative relationship. However, many circumstances are not ideal, and one challenge for families and professionals alike is to learn to recognize strengths that may not be immediately evident.

In recent discussions of the strengths perspective, a variety of guidelines have been suggested for meeting this challenge. These suggestions include taking a more holistic view of families' circumstances beyond the immediate problem (Kisthardt, 1992); reframing issues in nonblaming, more positive terms (Poertner & Ronnau, 1992); and explicitly noting competencies and skills. At the same time, it is perhaps equally important to recognize the factors that implicitly discourage taking a strengths approach. Weick, Rapp, Sullivan, and Kisthardt (1989), for example, discuss how the approach taken toward defining a problem can both constrain the identification of strengths and limit problem-solving efforts. That is, when attempts are made to define problems in precise causal fashion, the range of possible solutions and resources are limited in those terms. Overall, perhaps the most overriding advantage of taking the strengths approach is that it de-emphasizes the negative and sharpens the focus on abilities and competencies on which the family–professional relationship can build.

4. Everyone Has Constraints.

A corollary to recognizing strengths is the recognition of constraints. Collaboration does not occur in a vacuum but is contingent on the circumstances in which the family and professional find themselves. Family members face constraints in their lives brought about by economic factors, work responsibilities, and other family needs beyond those of the individual child (Koroloff, Elliot, Koren, & Friesen, 1994). For example, arranging for a child to receive multiple services may be difficult in the absence of reliable transportation, and job commitments may severely limit a parent's ability to attend planning meetings during working hours. Moreover, the stress of parenting a child with a serious emotional disorder and of futilely searching for the "right program" may lead some families to be overwhelmed and disorganized. Such constraints may have a pernicious effect by appearing to validate negative assumptions that professionals may hold about families. Missing an appointment may be due not to the family's lack of interest, but rather to other factors in the family's life that present serious obstacles.

Similarly, professionals working in organizations and within systems with limited resources and few supports for their efforts may at times be too stressed to express the concern and sensitivity that families warrant. Many of these professionals find themselves, like families, "in the trenches" and facing a variety of organizational and system constraints that discourage collaboration in subtle or blatant ways. Probably one of the biggest challenges for family members as they become participants in the collaborative process is to accept the fact that a variety of constraints combined with the limits of scientific knowledge make it unrealistic to expect professionals to necessarily "fix" their child. When the professional does not, in fact, work a miracle, it is unfair for the parents to place all the blame for the child's ongoing problems with the professional or the "system." In a partnership, expectations must be realistic or the continual disappointment will inevitably cause the partnership to fail.

5. Information Sharing Is Critical.

The old adage that information is power has particular relevance to relationships in which the power balance is inherently unequal. Because of the resource control, social status, and formal knowledge that professionals possess, parents typically find themselves in a "one-down" position when they initially seek services for their children. Professionals can redress this imbalance in a significant way by the open and forthright sharing of information. However, this process requires more than providing information for mere review and approval; instead, it requires information to be shared in a manner that allows parents to inform and shape the decisions that are made from the beginning.

In a similar vein, true collaboration requires that the gathering of information go well beyond simply using the family as informants in helping to fill out forms or develop an assessment. Parents are frequently asked to release very personal information to be shared by more than one professional, yet they often encounter difficulty in accessing their own records. An information-sharing process that is clothed in secrecy conveys a message that family members are not considered competent to understand their child's problems or the services designed to address them. Families will lose patience with professionals when information access is handled in a perfunctory manner or regarded as a one-way street.

On their part, family members also bear some responsibility for information sharing. True collaboration requires that they become adept at expressing their needs clearly and directly. They also must communicate any changes they observe in the functioning of their family or child quickly, so that all can stay on top of the situation. Family members must be willing to "tell their story," even if it seems as though they have done this many times and even if it is painful. This process is crucial in helping professionals develop empathy for the challenges that families face.

6. Support and Understanding Are Foremost.

Although the helping professions have devoted enormous attention to different therapeutic techniques and methods, the one key feature that transcends all of this is the supportive and caring quality of the professional–client relationship. Empathy, support, and concern appear to be essential to the success of such relationships, and this is no less true for family–professional partnerships. In a 1994 study of collaboration (DeChillo et al., 1994), professional activities that conveyed empathy, support, and understanding appeared to be the most preeminent feature of professionals' collaborative relationship with families. This notion is echoed repeatedly in conversations with families. The tendency to blame children's emotional problems on parents is so prevalent and pervasive, even in the form of self-blame, that any empathy and understanding provided by a professional can be a source of great comfort and relief.

Although the concept of support and understanding is common to most therapeutic and service delivery approaches, the collaborative approach differs from these in its emphasis on reciprocity. Family members bear partial responsibility for maintaining a mutually supportive relationship by acknowledging constraints affecting professionals. Family members may have to resist the temptation to act in an aggressive or contentious manner now that they are finally being given the opportunity to be equals in the decision-making process. This is especially true for parents who in the past have had to "demand" their rights and those of their child. Although many mental health professionals are committed to family involvement and collaboration, the development of new, mutually supportive relationships may proceed more slowly than some family members and advocates would like. Patience is especially needed here.

7. Support and Understanding Are Not Enough.

Support and understanding are necessary but not sufficient conditions for collaboration; that is, you can't do without them, but you need something else in addition. A fact of life for families who have children with serious emotional disabilities is that they often require multiple supports and services. This is primarily because of the many needs of their children and is greatly complicated by the fragmented nature of most service systems. At minimum, almost all such children are involved with the educational and mental health systems, but, to comprehensively address their needs, many children and families require a great deal more. This may include such diverse services as respite care, transportation, recreation, expensive medications, multiple assessments, and financial assistance. For some families, some or all of the needed services may be available. However, in many communities only the most traditional services (e.g., special education, individual psychotherapy) are available and, if other options exist, they may be beyond the financial resources of many families.

Given these realities, an important part of collaborating with families includes the instrumental or practical aspects of service planning and delivery. Here much depends on the role taken by the professional. For case managers, the areas of concern encompass almost all aspects of the child's and family's life. For professionals taking a more specialized role, such as assessment services, the areas of concern are more circumscribed. Regardless of the role, collaboration requires that attention be given to pragmatic details of service delivery that are important to families but possibly overlooked by professionals. Such details include arranging appointments that are manageable, giving sufficient attention to how services are paid for, and coordinating with different service providers to minimize impediments and barriers.

8. Attention to Language Is Essential.

Much recent attention has been devoted to understanding the nuances of communication and language. Especially when communicating verbally, there is an increased awareness that "what is said" is not as important as "what is heard." In this respect, sensitivity to the language used when professionals and family members communicate is essential to collaboration. This responsibility rests on both professionals and family members, but, because of a long history of pejorative labeling and diagnostic categorization, the responsibility rests more heavily on professionals. Family members often will react negatively to any language that suggests blaming or language that labels their family or child as dysfunctional. Moreover, such language provides little useful information about the specific circumstances of the family and child, the etiology of the child's disorder, or guidance regarding effective treatment strategies. As an alternative, people-first language (e.g., "person with schizophrenia" rather than "schizophrenic"), although at times awkward, is increasingly recognized as being more sensitive and accurate (i.e., the person is not the disease). Such sensitivity to language goes beyond "political correctness" because it serves the very pragmatic purpose of communicating attitudes and values. Nothing is lost except the blame.

9. The Best Goals Are Mutually Defined and Tailor Made.

Common sense dictates that persons working together toward an end should share an understanding of what they are trying to achieve and the means by which to achieve it. However, as has often been observed, common sense is not so common. Within the field of mental health, many professionals have kept consumers (clients or family members) in the dark about the purpose and methods of their work together. For example, families often spend numerous meetings with the staff of a residential or inpatient facility providing information about their child's functioning and their family but are never told the purpose for gathering the information. Collaboration requires that family members and professionals have a clear, mutually defined understanding about the purpose(s) of their work together. Such clarity and mutuality maximizes the likelihood that the participants will remain invested in the process and that their goals and objectives will be realized. To achieve this understanding, some writers recommend the use of service contracts as an important component of participatory decision making (Maluccio & Marlow, 1974; Seabury, 1979). The contract, according to Compton and Galaway (1994), is a means of establishing mutuality from the outset and maximizes the likelihood of consumer self-determination.

Also, establishing clear goals and objectives greatly facilitates the process of evaluating the effectiveness of services (Greene, 1989).

10. Evaluation Is Everyone's Job.

Good collaborative practice requires a willingness to work jointly toward solutions on an exploratory and incremental basis. This approach differs markedly from traditional efforts to routinely fit needs (child and family needs) into predefined treatment solutions. The notion of individualizing or tailoring services to specific needs and circumstances has been discussed in other contexts (Burchard & Clarke, 1990; VanDenBerg, 1992, 1993), but here emphasis is placed on the collaborative determination of whether or not it has been successfully accomplished. On the professional's part, this principle requires a spirit of flexibility and openness to change coupled with a willingness to put aside cherished beliefs about what services are effective. It also requires an evaluative stance that welcomes accountability and the prerogative of family members to make judgments about success or failure. Families are increasingly impatient with professionals who are not willing to listen when they recommend that a certain treatment approach should be abandoned because it has not proven effective.

By the same token, the collaborative approach to finding good service solutions requires a certain degree of flexibility and openness on the family's part. Expectations for immediate and effective generic solutions may meet with disappointment, and beliefs about what service approach works best may have to be revised in light of experience. This process can be made easier for family members if they are regularly asked for their opinions of service effectiveness and actively encouraged to provide timely feedback. Mechanisms such as meetings, phone calls, or self-report measures can be used for this purpose (Burchard et al., 1995). Such mechanisms not only facilitate the open exchange of evaluation-related information but also carry a clear message that family members are integral to the whole process of evaluation.

COLLABORATION AND THE BIGGER PICTURE

Our "top 10" principles provide some guidelines for what individual professionals and family members can do to promote collaboration at the interpersonal level. However, all family–professional collaboration takes place in a larger context, a context that often extends beyond the control of specific individuals. Recent efforts to apply collaborative principles in day-to-day service delivery have led to a greater appreciation of the importance of this context and how it may promote or impede collaboration. Recent developments in health care and system reform carry mixed omens for how well contextual factors will allow collaborative principles to be applied in the future.

When considering the bigger picture in which collaboration occurs, organizational and system factors are perhaps the most salient. Families and professionals frequently cite such factors as barriers to collaboration. For example, in a recent study of parents and professionals who were attempting to achieve collaborative relationships, high caseloads and insufficient administrative support were among the more frequently mentioned barriers to their efforts (Williams-Murphy et al., 1994). A key issue here is time. Like other significant human relationships, collaborative relationships take time to develop, and organizational or system factors that limit the amount of direct contact that is possible may have an inadvertent inhibiting effect. Another issue is organizational support. Professionals who wish to develop collaborative relationships may face disapproval from their peers, and this is compounded if administrators convey the same message. Both of these conditions may be considered to be outside the control of the individual professional and family, and both may have a profound influence on the degree of collaboration that is possible.

Organizational policies also can have an unintentionally chilling effect on collaboration. Two prime examples are policies existent in several states that require parents to give up custody to get state services (Cohen, Harris, Gottlieb, & Best, 1991; McManus & Friesen, 1989) and policies that prevent families from communicating with their child for several days or even weeks when he or she enters a residential treatment setting. Such policies perpetuate the traditional status of parents as blameworthy and even detrimental to their children's well-being, with obvious implications for the viability of any family–professional partnerships that might be possible. Although there are signs that custody policies and practices are being revised in a manner more favorable to families (Stubbee, 1990), policy debates are heating up on other fronts, and these are less encouraging. For example, recent discussions about limiting disability status to more narrowly defined categories threaten to exclude a large group of families who may be in particular need of mental health services. Policies that regard such families in this more punitive light would have a dramatically inhibiting effect on collaboration.

Yet another contextual factor affecting collaboration is the availability of services in a given community. DeChillo et al. (1994) found that the relative weight given to the different components of collaboration varied according to availability of services. For example, accessing services—simply finding resources—was found to carry relatively greater weight in circumstances in which services in the community were somewhat scarce. In contrast, information sharing, including discussions of various options, carried relatively more weight when resources were more available. There is no doubt that collaborative relationships in geographic areas with a profound scarcity of services—some rural areas, for example—present special challenges and require a high degree of creativity and cooperation. Yet, in such circumstances, the collaborative relationship takes on even more importance: It represents one of the few resources that the family has.

The importance of understanding the contextual basis of collaboration takes on a special urgency in light of recent developments that will set the stage for family–professional collaboration in the future. On the positive side, programs are being developed that explicitly promote and encourage collaboration as a routine matter. One example of such an undertaking is the Oregon Partners Project. This project was originally funded by the Robert Wood Johnson Foundation Mental Health Services Program for Youth (Beachler, 1990) and a consortium of state and local child-serving agencies in Multnomah County, Oregon. It was designed in accordance with system of care principles (Stroul & Friedman, 1986) to provide comprehensive, individualized, coordinated, and family-centered care in the least restrictive environment to children with serious emotional disturbances and their families. From its inception, a key component of the Partners Project was to actively involve families, along with all providers involved with the child, in the development and implementation of the plan of care for the child. These unified plans delineated the child's and family's objectives and specified the services and activities needed to meet those objectives and the responsibilities of the parties involved, including the family. The Partners Project is an example of an attempt to institutionalize family–professional collaboration and is illustrative of a number of innovative programs across the country (Cole & Poe, 1993).

The same social and fiscal pressures that prompted the Partners Project also portend major changes in mental health and health care systems nationwide, and, here, the future for collaborative practice may be less positive or at least more ambiguous. For example, the increasing emphasis on cost control and micromanagement of service delivery parameters may severely restrict the time and latitude in which families and professionals can build partnerships. Limits on the number of possible appointments, longer periods between contacts, higher caseloads, and narrower definitions of what constitutes a service are just a few of the possible constraints that the new managed care environment may place on mental health systems, and by extension, on family–professional partnerships. Conversely, this new environment may also bring about an increased emphasis on case management and a higher degree of service integration, both of which may be not only compatible with but conducive to family–professional collaboration. In the majority of cases, the experience and pragmatic expertise of family members are valuable resources, and a system designed to maximize resource utilization can no longer afford to downplay or ignore this. What ultimate effect the changing system context has on family–professional collaboration remains to be seen; however, this much is clear: Advocates must continually rethink how collaboration can be promoted and practiced in a changing environment.

COLLABORATION BEYOND THE INDIVIDUAL FAMILY

The possibilities for collaboration extend beyond the interpersonal level, and, although most discussions on this topic focus on the relationship between an individual service provider and family, mention should also be made of collaboration with respect to larger organizations, communities, and government. This collaboration can take place on many levels. It may range from involvement on advisory boards and governance committees that deal with day-to-day agency policies to opportunities to serve on committees that develop legislation.

By way of illustration, in 1989 Wisconsin families had an extraordinary opportunity to be involved in the development and eventual passage of an innovative piece of legislation, the Integrated Services Program for Children with Severe Disabilities Act (S.46.56), commonly referred to as the Children Come First Act. A strong partnership between family members and professionals made it all possible. The process began with a series of meetings attended by family members, state mental health personnel, mental health professionals, and advocates during which an integrated children's mental health system for Wisconsin was conceptualized. Next, a draft proposal was developed and refined, and strategies for the passage of the legislation were developed with the input of professionals who had a knowledge of the legislative process. All recognized that grass roots support was necessary if the legislation was to pass. Groundwork was laid for the passage of the legislation when parents testified at several legislative hearings about their dissatisfaction with the current system. Wisconsin Family Ties, a statewide family organization, sponsored regional conferences to discuss the proposed legislation, and information was also published in the organization's newsletter, *Family Ties*, encouraging parents to contact their legislators. The legislation was ultimately passed, funded, and signed by the governor. The family–professional partnerships that developed during this process are still strong today and continue to work for improving mental health services for Wisconsin's children.

Such large-scale opportunities for collaboration are not limited to issues involving legislation. They may also involve the development of training programs and curricula (Kelker, 1987; Raiff, Henry, & Dellmuth, 1995); service on policy and advisory boards (Koroloff, Hunter & Gordon, 1994); technical assistance to other organizations (Hunter, 1994); and the staffing of parent advocacy positions (Ignelzi & Dague, 1995).

COLLABORATION AND THE FUTURE

Some issues pertaining to the future of collaboration have been discussed, but a few points warrant explicit mention as topics needing more attention.

First, special efforts should be made to develop collaborative practice with families in especially difficult circumstances. A frequently heard comment is that collaboration is fine with "nice" families but not possible with families who have a history of child abuse, substance abuse, or other severe problems. This comment reflects a real concern that advocates of collaboration have yet to address well. Nevertheless, collaboration with such families, although challenging, is possible (Rooney, 1992). Much can be learned from efforts to apply collaborative practice to all families, even those who might have previously been labeled "unworkable." Such efforts may well reveal new insights and developments that would not otherwise be realized for lack of trying.

More attention should be directed toward developing measures of collaboration that can be used in evaluation and research. If collaboration is to become a common feature of service delivery, it must be specifically addressed in evaluations of service process and effectiveness. Some work has been done in developing a measure of collaboration from the perspective of family members (DeChillo et al., 1994) and practitioners (Johnson, Cournoyer, & Fisher, 1994), but more work is needed.

Finally, more research must be directed toward understanding how different conditions and circumstances affect the practice of collaboration. Practitioners and advocates will continue to call for more practical information on the implementation of collaborative practice; administrators and policy makers may ask how collaboration can be promoted in an environment of limited resources. Both sides are likely to intensify their demands in coming years as the service system framework continues to change. Systematic, well-designed studies offer one of the best approaches to meeting both needs.

These are only a few of many possible directions for further developing the concept of collaboration. This development is necessary, or collaboration faces the same fate of many ideas in the human services that have enjoyed brief recognition only to fade away for lack of refinement or maturation. The goal is to reach a point where the dominant question about collaboration is not "What?" or "Why?" but "Why not?" The goal is widespread recognition that, like great partnerships in other fields of human endeavor, success in children's mental health is best achieved by merging the unique talents, perspectives, and abilities of everyone who has a stake in the outcome. The future of collaboration depends on the common realization that, ultimately, all participants are advocates for the child.

REFERENCES

Beachler, M. (1990). The mental health services program for youth. *Journal of Mental Health Administration, 17,* 115–121.

Bernheim, K. (1990). Family-provider relationships: Charting a new course. In H.P. Lefley & D.L. Johnson (Eds.), *Families as allies in treatment of the mentally ill: New directions for mental health professionals* (pp. 99–113). Washington, DC: American Psychiatric Press.

Burchard, J.D., & Clarke, R.T. (1990). The role of individualized care in a service delivery system for children and adolescents with severely maladjusted behavior. *Journal of Mental Health Administration, 17*, 48–60.

Burchard, J.D., Hinden, B., Carro, M., Schaefer, M., Bruns, E., & Pandina, N. (1995). Using case-level data to monitor a case management system. In B.J. Friesen & J. Poertner (Eds.), *Systems of care for children's mental health: Vol. 1. From case management to service coordination for children with emotional, behavioral, or mental disorders: Building on family strengths* (pp. 169–187). Baltimore: Paul H. Brookes Publishing Co.

Caplan, P.J., & Hall-McCorquadale, I. (1985). Mother-blaming in major clinical journals. *American Journal of Orthopsychiatry, 55*, 345–353.

Cohen, R., Harris, R., Gottlieb, S., & Best, A.M. (1991). States' use of transfer of custody as a requirement for providing services to emotionally disturbed children. *Hospital and Community Psychiatry, 42*, 526–530.

Cole, R.F., & Poe, S.L. (1993). *Partnerships for care: Systems of care for children with serious emotional disturbances and their families. Interim report of the Mental Health Services Program for Youth.* Washington, DC: Washington Business Group on Health.

Collins, B., & Collins, T. (1990). Parent-professional relationships in the treatment of seriously emotionally disturbed children and adolescents. *Social Work, 35*, 522–527.

Compton, B.R., & Galaway, B. (1994). *Social work processes.* Pacific Grove, CA: Brooks/Cole.

Cournoyer, D.E., & Johnson, H.C. (1991). Measuring parents' perceptions of mental health professionals. *Research on Social Work Practice, 1*, 399–415.

Cross, T.L., Bazron, B.J., Dennis, K.W., & Isaacs, M.R. (1989). *Towards a culturally competent system of care.* Washington, DC: Georgetown University Child Development Center, National Technical Assistance Center on Children's Mental Health.

DeChillo, N. (1993). Collaboration between social workers and families of patients with mental illness. *Families in Society: The Journal of Contemporary Human Services, 74*, 104–115.

DeChillo, N., Koren, P.E., & Schultze, K.H. (1994). From paternalism to partnership: Family and professional collaboration in children's mental health. *American Journal of Orthopsychiatry, 64*, 564–576.

Dunst, C.J., Johanson, C., Rounds, T., Trivette, C.M., & Hamby, D. (1992). Characteristics of parent-professional partnerships. In S.L. Christenson & J.C. Conoley (Eds.), *Home school collaboration: Enhancing children's academic and social competence* (pp. 157–174). Silver Spring, MD: National Association of School Psychologists.

Dunst, C.J., & Paget, K.D. (1991). Parent-professional partnerships and family empowerment. In M.J. Fine (Ed.), *Collaboration with parents of exceptional children* (pp.25–44). Brandon, VT: Clinical Psychology Publishing Company.

Friesen, B.J. (1989). *Survey of parents whose children have serious emotional disorders: Report of a national study.* Portland, OR: Portland State University, Research and Training Center on Family Support and Children's Mental Health.

Friesen, B.J., Koren, P.E., & Koroloff, N.M. (1992). How parents view professional behaviors: A cross-professional analysis. *Journal of Child and Family Studies, 1*, 209–231.

Greene, G.J. (1989). Using the written contract for evaluating and enhancing practice effectiveness. *Journal of Independent Social Work, 4*(2), 135–155.

Group for the Advancement of Psychiatry. (1986). *A family affair—helping families cope with mental illness: A guide for professionals.* New York: Brunner/Mazel.

Grunebaum, H. (1984). Comments on Terkelson's "Schizophrenia and the family: II. Adverse effects of family therapy." *Family Process, 23*, 421–428.

Grunebaum, H. (1986). Families, patients, and mental health professionals: Toward a new collaboration. *American Journal of Psychiatry, 143*, 1420–1421.

Hatfield, A.B. (1979). The family as partner in the treatment of mental illness. *Hospital and Community Psychiatry, 30*, 338–340.

Hatfield, A.B. (1982). Commentary: Therapists and families: Worlds apart. *Hospital and Community Psychiatry, 33*, 513.

Hatfield, A.B., & Lefley, H.P. (Eds.). (1987). *Families of the mentally ill: Coping and adaptation.* New York: Guilford Press.

Hunter, R.W. (1994). *Parents as policy-makers: A handbook for effective participation.* Portland, OR: Portland State University, Research and Training Center on Family Support and Children's Mental Health.

Ignelzi, S., & Dague, B. (1995). Parents as case managers. In B.J. Friesen & J. Poertner (Eds.), *Systems of care for children's mental health: Vol. 1. From case management to service coordination for children with emotional, behavioral, or mental disorders: Building on family strengths* (pp. 327–336). Baltimore: Paul H. Brookes Publishing Co.

Integrated Services Program for Children with Severe Disabilities Act, S.46.56. (August 3, 1989). Wisconsin Act 31, Section 1101m.

Isaacs, M.R., & Benjamin, M.P. (1991). *Towards a culturally competent system of care. Volume II: Programs which utilize culturally competent principles.* Washington, DC: Georgetown University Child Development Center, National Technical Assistance Center for Children's Mental Health.

Johnson, H.C., Cournoyer, D.E., & Fisher, G.A. (1994). Measuring worker cognitions about parents of children with mental and emotional disabilities. *Journal of Emotional and Behavioral Disorders, 2,* 99–108.

Kelker, K.A. (1987). *Working together: The parent/professional partnership.* Portland, OR: Portland State University, Research and Training Center on Family Support and Children's Mental Health.

Kisthardt, W.E. (1992). A strengths model of case management: The principles and functions of a helping partnership with persons with persistent mental illness. In D. Saleebey (Ed.), *The strengths perspective in social work practice* (pp. 59–83). White Plains, NY: Longman.

Koroloff, N.M., Elliot, D.J., Koren, P.E., & Friesen, B.J. (1994). Connecting low-income families to mental health services: The role of the family associate. *Journal of Emotional and Behavioral Disorders, 2,* 240–246.

Koroloff, N., Hunter, R., & Gordon, L. (1994). *Family involvement in policy making: A final report on the Families in Action project.* Portland, OR: Portland State University, Research and Training Center on Family Support and Children's Mental Health.

Lamb, H.R. (1983). Families: Practical help replaces blame. *Hospital and Community Psychiatry, 34,* 893.

Lefley, H.P., & Pederson, P.B. (1986). *Cross-cultural training for mental health professionals.* Springfield, IL: Charles C Thomas.

Maluccio, A., & Marlow, W. (1974). The case for the contract. *Social Work, 19,* 28–36.

McElroy, E.M. (1987). The beat of a different drummer. In A.B. Hatfield & H.P. Lefley (Eds.), *Families of the mentally ill: Coping and adaptation* (pp. 225–243). New York: Guilford Press.

McManus, M.C., & Friesen, B.J. (1989). Barriers to accessing services: Relinquishing legal custody as a means of obtaining services for children with serious emotional disabilities. *Focal Point, 3*(3), 1–5.

Petr, C.G., & Barney, D.D. (1993). Reasonable efforts for children with disabilities: The parents' perspective. *Social Work, 38,* 247–254.

Poertner, J., & Ronnau, J. (1992). A strengths approach to children with emotional disabilities. In D. Saleebey (Ed.), *The strengths perspective in social work practice* (pp. 111–121). White Plains, NY: Longman.

Raiff, N.R., Henry, M., & Dellmuth, C. (1995). Parent-professional collaboration for public sector training for children's intensive case management: A case study. In B.J. Friesen & J. Poertner (Eds.), *From case management to service coordination for children with emotional, behavioral, or mental disorders: Building on family strengths* (pp. 239–255). Baltimore: Paul H. Brookes Publishing Co.

Rooney, R.H. (1992). *Strategies for work with involuntary clients.* New York: Columbia University Press.

Seabury, B. (1979). Negotiating sound contracts with clients. *Public Welfare, 37.*

Spaniol, L., Jung, H., Zipple, A., & Fitzgerald, S. (1987). Families as a resource in the rehabilitation of the severely psychiatrically disabled. In A.B. Hatfield & H.P. Lefley (Eds.), *Families of the mentally ill: Coping and adaptation* (pp. 167–190). New York: Guilford Press.

Spaniol, L., Zipple, A., & Fitzgerald, S. (1984). How professionals can share power with families: Practical approaches to working with families of the mentally ill. *Psychosocial Rehabilitation Journal, 8*(2), 77–84.

Stroul, B.A., & Friedman, R.M. (1986). *A system of care for severely emotionally disturbed children and youth.* Washington, DC: Georgetown University Child Development Center, National Technical Assistance Center for Children's Mental Health.

Stubbee, B. (1990). Relinquishing custody: Continuing the dialogue. *Focal Point, 4*(2), 1–2.

Tarico, V.S., Low, B.P., Trupin, E., & Forsyth-Stephens, A. (1989). Children's mental health services: A parent perspective. *Community Mental Health Journal, 25,* 313–326.

VanDenBerg, J.E. (1992). Individualized services for children. *New Directions in Mental Health Services, 54,* 97–100.

VanDenBerg, J.E. (1993). Integration of individualized mental health services into the system of care for children and adolescents. *Administration and Policy in Mental Health, 20,* 247–257.

Vosler-Hunter, R. (1989). *Changing roles, changing relationships: Parent-professional collaboration on behalf of children with emotional disabilities.* Portland, OR: Portland State University, Research and Training Center on Family Support and Children's Mental Health.

Wahl, O.F. (1989). Schizophrenogenic parenting in abnormal psychology texts. *Teaching of Psychology, 16,* 31–33.

Weick, A., Rapp, C., Sullivan, W.P., & Kisthardt, W. (1989). A strengths perspective for social work practice. *Social Work, 34,* 350–354.

Williams-Murphy, T., DeChillo, N., Koren, P.E., & Hunter, R. (1994). *Family/professional collaboration: The perspective of those who have tried.* Portland, OR: Portland State University, Research and Training Center on Family Support and Children's Mental Health.

CHAPTER 22

The Role of Family Members in Systems of Care

Nancy M. Koroloff,
Barbara J. Friesen, Linda Reilly, and Judy Rinkin

The nature and extent of family member involvement in children's mental health services has changed dramatically since 1984, when Congress approved the Child and Adolescent Service System Program (CASSP). This federal program, which was designed to assist states to improve services for children with serious emotional, behavioral, or mental disorders, has also provided leadership in stimulating full family participation in this reform. In less than two decades, the participation of parents and other family members who care for children with serious emotional disorders has expanded from limited "patient" or "client" roles (Friesen & Koroloff, 1990) to a wide range of planning, decision making, and evaluation roles (Koroloff, Hunter, & Gordon, 1995). It is no coincidence that the increased influence of family members has dovetailed with the emergence of more innovative ideas about how to shape the service delivery system and better serve children and families. As family members' roles expand and the range of family participation increases, so too will our vision of what the service delivery system can be.

In this chapter we trace the historical development of the role of parents and other family members at three levels: 1) families' involvement in organizing or providing services needed by their own children; 2) family

This chapter was partially developed with funding from the National Institute on Disability and Rehabilitation Research, United States Department of Education, and the Center for Mental Health Services, Substance Abuse and Mental Health Services Administration (NIDRR grant number H133B40021-94). The content of this publication does not necessarily reflect the views or policies of the funding agencies.

members' involvement in service planning, evaluation, and policy setting; and 3) family members as innovators and providers of services.

THE FAMILY AS CENTER OF THE CHILD'S CARE

Early Roles: Parents as Targets for Change

Until recently, the primary role of parents and other caregivers was as a target for change, often seen as equally or more needy than the child in question (Friesen & Koroloff, 1990; Knitzer, 1993). Within this conceptualization, the caregiver's major function was to provide information at the beginning of the treatment process. The process of assessment and evaluation might last for several sessions during which parents were expected to recite extensive details about the family, the child, and family relationships. Information provided by the family was often seen as suspect and needing corroboration from other sources. When overt reasons for the child's mental illness were not evident within the family, professionals were trained to dig deeper for hidden problems—problems such as child abuse or sexual difficulties between the parents. Within this perspective, parents and other caregivers were usually not involved in the development of the treatment plan nor were they asked for their input regarding service choices and implementation strategies.

With the family in the role of "patient" or "client," treatment plans tended to focus on "curing" the child, along with changing the deficits in his or her environment. The treatment of choice for children with serious emotional disorders was placement in residential treatment centers for long-term therapy, often lasting years (Wells, 1991; Whittaker, 1976). Long-term placement addressed two purposes. First, it allowed the therapist an extended period of time to address the child's difficult behaviors through building healthy relationships. It also removed the child from the family and community, which were thought to have caused the problems. Some residential treatment programs employed policies and practices that further isolated the child from family and community (Jenson & Whittaker, 1987). These included an orientation period of several weeks during which the child was not allowed contact with family, restricted visiting hours, and stringent rules about the frequency and lengths of home visits. Children attended school within the treatment center, and their recreation was often segregated from that of other community members.

The mental health problems of children were often considered shameful, and the overall goal of services was to restore children to mental health and return them to society, where no one would ever know that they had experienced an emotional disorder. The too-frequent result was that families were removed or removed themselves from their child's life. Sometimes families were told by well-meaning service providers that this separation was best for the child (Whittaker, 1976), but family members also pulled back in order to protect themselves from blame and criticism. Vestiges of these practices and attitudes toward the role of the family can still be found in mental health services today (Holten, 1990; Wahl, 1989).

Focus on the Family: Family Therapy

In the 1950s and 1960s, the technology of family therapy began to develop (Bateson, 1972; Johnson, 1986), and with it an expanded role of the family in the child's treatment. Within this framework, families were included actively as part of the therapeutic target systems. In fact, programs that employed family therapy often required the family to participate in family therapy and to attend family meetings—which usually had an educational agenda. The inclusion of all family members in treatment represented a positive step in that parents were no longer excluded from the treatment process. The emphasis on family systems approaches to treatment also contributed to taking a wider view of the needs of all members of the family, with an emphasis on problem solving. Some critics of family therapy, however, cautioned against the implementation of family therapy to the exclusion of other potentially useful interventions (Johnson, 1986).

As both adult and child mental health services move away from long-term care in institutions (Friesen & Koroloff, 1990; Stroul & Friedman, 1986), families have been once again called on to play a central role in their children's lives. Although the deinstitutionalization movement produced many positive results, until recently there has been a failure to recognize the gap between the resources and capacities of 24-hour institutions and the resources and capacities of families. Families have been expected to maintain children with serious emotional and behavioral problems at home after school, on weekends, and during program vacations, usually without support, respite care, or a plan for crisis. It has been assumed that an "involved and committed" family can find ways to accommodate the child's needs. At times, however, these needs are extreme and severely tax the resources of the family, as when a child with a sleep disturbance requires active adult management throughout the night.

Family Roles in Community Services

In the community, gaps and fissures between categorical service programs have also affected the roles that family members have played in services. Family members are often pressed into service as agents of transition; they serve as informal service providers who fill the gap when no categorical service fits. For example, for children in day treatment programs, parents provide transportation between home and program, between separate aspects of services, and to medical and dental appointments. Family members also often play coordinating roles, carrying information about the child between programs and service providers, and in some cases are the only persons who attempt to coordinate all of the pieces of a child's service plan. Some parents serve as couriers, carrying discharge summaries, histories, and medical and psychiatric reports between programs. Family members also circumvent barriers to interagency communication posed by restrictive confidentiality policies when they provide copies of reports and other information from their own files.

Family–Professional Collaboration

Within the reform efforts stimulated by CASSP, one attempt to expand the family's role with regard to the child's care involved an emphasis on parent–professional collaboration. This emphasis came out of a growing awareness of the extent to which family members viewed their relationships with service providers as problematic (Friesen, 1989b; Friesen, Koren, & Koroloff, 1992; Lipsky, 1985; Wasow & Wikler, 1983). In 1987, Working Together, a curriculum and training approach designed to improve parent–professional collaboration, was initiated through the Research and Training Center at Portland State University (Vosler-Hunter & Exo, 1988). The underlying premise of this training was that family members and professionals should be trained together to promote collaborative problem-solving, communication, and values clarification. An initial cadre of training teams, each consisting of a professional service provider and a family member, received intensive training, support, and assistance with curriculum and workshop design so they could train others to use this approach.

Between 1987 and 1989, a total of 87 pairs of trainers from diverse geographic locations were prepared to present the curriculum (Williams-Murphy, DeChillo, Koren, & Hunter, 1994). These teams trained hundreds of other family members and professionals throughout the United States over the ensuing years. An important result of this training was an increase in the number of both parents and professionals who viewed family members as resources in the planning and managing of their children's care. In addition, family members began to be recognized for the quality and depth they brought as co-leaders of training. This recognition was important to families who had felt stigmatized and blamed, had concerns about how they were being treated by professionals, or were frustrated with the lack of available services (Williams-Murphy et al., 1994). The issue of family-professional relationships is addressed in more depth by DeChillo, Koren, and Mezera in Chapter 21.

The Development of Advocacy Roles

Concurrent with the development of other roles, family members also assumed the role of advocate both for their own children and for other children and families (Friesen, 1989a; Friesen & Huff, 1990; Mayer, 1994). An important stimulus for advocacy at the individual child and family level was special education legislation that mandated parent involvement in the development of individualized education programs (Education for All Handicapped Children Act of 1975 [PL 94-142], Individuals with Disabilities Education Act of 1990 [PL 101-476]). Although there was no parallel legislation in mental health or child welfare, many family members learned about the need for advocacy through their experiences with regular and special education services. The special education law also provided a framework for advocacy; concepts such as children's rights, parents' rights, and the need for individualized services were first introduced to many families through the education system. In the mental health field, states such as Kansas and Kentucky hired the parent of a child receiving mental health services as a staff member within the state office of mental health with the specific purpose of providing an ombudsperson for families in that state. The Finger Lakes Family Support Program in New York State (Friesen & Wahlers, 1993), one of the first family support programs supported by federal and state funds, also included a child and family advocacy component.

More frequently, parents and other family members took on advocacy roles from positions outside the traditional service delivery system. Many parents acted individually, while others began to work together. A common scenario is as follows: Two mothers, both of whom have had a difficult time finding services for their children, meet and begin to talk. Because they have been successful in advocating for the provision of needed services (often from the schools), they become recognized as effective and knowledgeable regarding the ways of the service system. Other families begin to contact them when they have trouble, maybe referred by friendly professionals who do not know where else to turn. Sometimes a local support group is formed through these contacts; in other cases the two mothers form the center of an informal network of family members. Although the contacts are informal, the primary goal is to provide each other with hard-won information and emotional support.

Regular Lives and New Service Patterns

Increasingly family members articulate the wish to live "regular lives" (State of the Art Video, 1988), lives that are not continually buffeted and strained because they are responsibly trying to care for a child with a serious emotional disorder. Family members recognize that this is possible, encouraged by programs in other childhood disability fields (Castellani, Downey, Tausig, & Bird, 1986; National Center for Networking Community Based Services, 1987; Shelton, Jeppson & Johnson, 1987); and by a growing literature about family support in children's mental health (Anderson, 1994; Byalin, 1990; Federation of Families for Children's Mental Health, 1992; Fine & Borden, 1991; Friesen & Wahlers, 1993; Karp & Bradley, 1991). Recent studies (Dunst, Trivette, & Cross, 1986; Singer & Powers, 1993; Tracy & Whittaker, 1987) support the idea that addressing family needs requires a different mix of services and more emphasis on family support. The motto "whatever it takes" and the embracing of "wraparound" services are evidence of movement toward this goal.

The wraparound service philosophy (Burchard & Clarke, 1990; VanDenBerg, 1992, 1993) is enthusiastically embraced by many family members because it is highly compatible with their vision of a responsive service system. The wraparound approach emphasizes child and family participation in planning, strengths-based assessment, flexibility, and comprehensiveness. It may also include attention to the needs of all family members, thus increasing the family's ability to be a stable resource for the child with an emotional disorder. This approach to designing and implementing services for children with complex needs represents a more family-centered approach to service design and delivery than traditional mental health services that focus more narrowly on psychotherapeutic approaches. More extensive discussion of family-centered services is provided by Friesen and Huff (Chapter 3) and Tannen (Chapter 20).

FAMILIES AT THE POLICY LEVEL

In addition to expanded roles of family members in planning and service delivery for their own children, family members have also become increasingly involved in working to improve the service delivery system. The process of planning, financing, and evaluating services for all children is another arena where family members have taken on multiple and ever-expanding roles.

Exclusion and Tokenism

Until the early 1960s, families and consumers of all types, especially adult mental health consumers and the parents of children with emotional disorders, were excluded from serving on the committees and boards that governed most programs. Consumers of mental health services were thought to be biased, provincial, and too invested in their own concerns to make useful contributions (Cahn & Cahn, 1971; Cibulka, 1981; Windle & Cibulka, 1981). Even when the Community Mental Health Centers Act Amendments of 1975 (PL 94-63) required citizen input into the governing boards of community mental health centers, consumers and family members were regularly excluded from these positions (Cibulka, 1981).

The earliest policy-level involvement of parents whose children had mental health problems was token in nature. Individual parents, usually white, upper-middle-class women with little political experience, were invited to be the only nonprovider in a policy-making group. Although they expected to make an occasional comment, these early crusaders were generally expected to agree with the conclusions of the providers in the group. The anger that these individuals sometimes displayed and their insistence on telling stories about their children's problems and their difficulties in getting appropriate services shocked many professionals and led to a general myth that family members were "too emotional" to serve at the policy level. Or, when family members were included, their contributions were discounted. One family member described her experience this way (Koroloff et al., 1995):

> I went, just went and showed up the first time, because I was so infuriated by my problems and the problems of other parents that I had talked to. And I said, "Why does it take so long to get these kids placed?" and his answer was, "Parents say the darndest things." And that was it. (p. 16)

Many professionals believed that only a few, well-educated family members were really appropriate for appointment to governing boards and advisory committees. Comments of professionals made during focus groups exploring the issue of family member participation in policy making (Koroloff et al., 1995) included the following:

> And there's still the belief that professionals are the experts and parents don't really have a great deal to offer in terms of their own conceptions. (p. 16)

> I think a barrier in the system is that many administrators don't understand the viability of parents in groups or they don't want them on boards and commissions. One of the barriers is attitudes. (p. 16)

Family-Oriented Research

In the late 1980s, individual family members began to play a role with regard to informing service system planning. Although families and children with serious emotional disorders have traditionally been seen as research subjects, little formal attention had been paid to their opinions about the services they received or their ideas about how to change and improve the service system. In 1988, one of the first large-scale studies was done that examined the needs and experience of families with the service system (Friesen, 1989b). When asked about the most important issue they had to deal with, respondents mentioned the following broad categories:

- Problems with services
- Lack of services
- Problems with family–professional relationships
- Lack of public understanding and negative attitudes regarding emotional disorders
- Issues related to being a parent of a child with an emotional disorder
- Impact on the family
- Lack of emotional and social support
- Issues related to meeting the child's needs
- Parents' problems in coping with their children's behaviors
- Issues related to adoptive families
- Issues related to out-of-home placement

Family member respondents also clearly articulated four major unmet needs: financial assistance, parent support groups, support groups for brothers and sisters, and respite care. Other studies (Greenley & Robitschek, 1991; Kotsopoulos, Elwood, & Oke, 1989; Robin, 1989; Tarico, Low, Trupin, & Forsyth-Stephens, 1989) produced similar findings and identified some unique regional or state needs. Considerable needs assessment research was done as a part of the CASSP planning process that encouraged the broad scale involvement of family members in the development of service systems.

Families as Allies Conferences

Another set of activities that influenced the roles that family members played at the policy level were five regional Families as Allies conferences, regional conferences held throughout the nation between 1986 and 1988 (McManus & Friesen, 1986; Research & Training Center, 1987), followed by a number of state-level conferences utilizing a similar format. The purpose of these conferences was to bring child mental health professionals and parents together on equal terms to discuss issues within the children's services system. The conferences were designed to promote collaboration between parents and professionals at the case level, within the service delivery system, and in state-level decision making.

The format of the conference provided opportunities for family members and professionals to work together to develop plans and strategies for implementing ideas in their respective state and local communities. States brought delegations composed of representatives from the major service delivery systems (mental health, child welfare, juvenile justice, education), private service providers, and family members of children with serious emotional disorders. The conferences allowed family members from different states to meet together for the first time, served as a springboard for a number of initiatives driven by family members, and underscored and expanded the role of advocate that most parents occupy with regard to their child's plan of care. Another result of these conferences was that family members from the same state and town were brought together and discovered a commonly held commitment to changing the direction of the service system. In many instances, family support groups and advocacy organizations had their inception in this discovery of a shared commitment (see Chapter 19).

The Growth of Family Organizations

The growth and development of family support and advocacy organizations has been a major factor in the increase of family member involvement in planning and decision making at the system and policy levels. Family support and advocacy organizations may be distinguished from family support groups along a number of dimensions, although the boundaries between the two types of organizations are often blurred. Many family support and advocacy organizations began as support groups, and the activities of support groups and family support and advocacy organizations overlap considerably. Because the two terms are used to describe two different organizational forms, however, and because there is often confusion about the use of the two terms, a comparison of family support groups and family support and advocacy organizations is provided in Table 22.1.

Family Support Groups   These groups usually provide mutual assistance (i.e., support and information exchange among members), are small (3–15 regularly attending members), operate with little or no funding, and have no formal structure or governance mechanisms. The groups are relatively informal and tend to be self-limiting in terms of size because the needs of all members are difficult to address in meetings of more than 8–12 persons. In addition to providing support and information, family support groups often provide encouragement and support for family members' advocacy efforts on behalf of their own children and families.

Family Support and Advocacy Organizations   These organizations are composed of parents and other family members of children with serious emotional disorders who come together with three major purposes: 1) to provide tangible and emotional support to each other, 2) to gather and share information of interest to members, and 3) to advocate for the improvement of policies and services in the children's mental health field. Family support and advocacy organizations are more formal, having at least some staff, a budget, and a governance structure.

Many family support and advocacy organizations serve a statewide constituency, but some are regional or focus specifically on a large urban area. Family support and advocacy organizations are run by family members, although they may include mental health professionals and other noncaregivers on their governing boards. Usually the majority of the board members and most paid staff are experienced caregivers of children with emotional disorders. Often, the family support and advocacy organization is responsible for initiating and maintaining the support groups in a geographic region. The family support and advocacy organization may also sponsor conferences that bring together parents, family members, support group leaders, and interested professionals from throughout the state or region.

Within the family organization, advocacy occurs on many levels. Although much of the day-to-day activity is focused on helping individual caregivers obtain an appropriate array of services for their children, at the policy level family advocacy organizations have also had an impressive impact. Once a family advocacy organization becomes known to planners and service providers, family organization staff often receive multiple invitations to join various state-level advisory groups, special panels, and

Table 22.1. Comparison of family support groups and family support and advocacy organizations

Characteristics	Family support groups	Family support & advocacy organizations
Purpose	1. To provide *emotional* and sometimes *tangible support* to members, often through face–face contact. 2. To *gather and share information* among members.	1. To provide *emotional and tangible support* to those who request it. 2. To *gather and share information*. 3. To *advocate* for service system and policy change.
Size	*Small* (3–15 regularly attending members).	*Variable.* Core paid and/or volunteer staff who assist family members and professionals. Membership/constituency depends on membership/participant structure.
Auspices	*Variable. Often none.* Support groups form and exist independently, and/or with the sponsorship of other organizations.	*Variable.* May be independent organization, or may have fiscal or other relationship with sponsoring organization.
Funding	*Little or none.* Groups meet in homes or free meeting spaces such as agencies or churches; usually have no paid staff, no budget. May get in-kind assistance (postage, copying) from other organizations.	*Budget size varies.* Funding or in-kind assistance for basic operations (space, telephone, staff, supplies, etc.). Sources: federal grants, United Way, state mental health authorities, foundations, special events, etc.
Structure	*Informal.* May have a convener or leader, relatively simple means of communicating with members.	*Formal.* Have/are developing bylaws, boards of directors, personnel system, budget/fiscal control, and resource development mechanisms.
Governance	*None–little.* May elect officers or appoint leader.	*Board of directors or advisory committee.* Depending on structure.
Method of assistance	*Mutual aid.* Help is reciprocal, in that all members are expected to learn and benefit from activities.	*Service orientation.* Help provided by core staff/volunteers to those who request assistance; may sponsor support groups. Advocacy activities undertaken on behalf of entire constituency.

governing boards. The organization's staff and board may be asked to review and comment on pending legislation, administrative rules, and state plans for mental health and other services. Family members provide expert review for much of the policy activity within the formal system of care in some states and communities. These tasks are taken on either by staff or by parent volunteers who are willing and interested in having influence at that level. The individual (or several individuals) who attend these policy meetings are in a much more powerful position as representatives of a local or statewide organization than in the past, when they may have represented only themselves. Furthermore, the family support and advocacy organization can provide its representatives with information, support, and input that is difficult for an individual, unaffiliated parent to find. The individual family members on a policy-making body represent a wide constituency group through their association with the family support and advocacy organization.

Family organizations frequently collaborate with other organizations to address needed policy change. For example, the Oregon Family Support Network (a statewide family support and advocacy organization) worked with the Portland State University Research and Training Center on Family Support and Children's Mental Health and the state child welfare agency to address the problem of parents' having to relinquish custody of their children for the purpose of gaining access to state-funded residential services. The president of the Oregon Family Support Network located a state representative who was interested in this problem and willing to sponsor legislation to address it. Research and Training Center staff, who had previously conducted research about national practice in this area, worked with the Oregon Family Support Network to learn more about child welfare practice and the experiences of families in the state of Oregon. A work group consisting of representatives from the Oregon Family Support Network, the Research and Training Center, the state child welfare agency, and other interested individuals and organizations carefully defined the problem and outlined solutions. A smaller group worked to draft legislation and monitor its submission and refinement. Oregon Family Support Network staff, board, and members testified before the state legislature, and the bill was passed. Oregon Family Support Network staff and board members also worked closely with the state child welfare agency to design and conduct training related to the implementation of this new policy. This change process is described in detail by McManus, Reilly, Rinkin, and Wrigley (1993).

National Organizations In 1988–1989, family support and advocacy organizations across the country became connected through the establishment of two national family advocacy organizations: the Federation of Families for Children's Mental Health and the National Alliance for the

Mentally Ill Child and Adolescent Network. These two organizations have provided opportunities for families in different states to link with each other and learn from a variety of advocacy experiences. The influence of family members at the national level and in federal legislation has increased because of this national presence. Through their efforts, families of children with serious emotional, behavioral, and mental disorders have more of a common vision and a common goal for the system of care. Although there exist differences of opinion about priorities and specific policy changes, there is now more common energy focused on system change. In general, family members are much more knowledgeable, have a greater understanding of the political process, and are more effective participants at the policy level, whether local, state, or national, than when the current period of reform began in the early 1980s (Lourie, Katz-Leavy, & Jacobs, 1985).

Not only are family members better informed about the service delivery system and what to ask for, but they also better understand how policies and services can be changed and how to make their presence and constituency power known. Initiating legislation and changing administrative rules has been effective in some states, whereas, in other communities, family advocacy groups have resorted to using legal remedies such as grievances and lawsuits. In Pennsylvania, a class action lawsuit sponsored in part by the Parents Involved Network of Pennsylvania (PIN of PA) questioned the mechanisms for funding out-of-home care, with the result that all children, regardless of parents' income, became eligible for funding for residential treatment through a federal program, Early and Periodic Screening, Diagnosis and Treatment (EPSDT) (Margolis & Meisels, 1987). In Hawaii, a family organization, Hawaii Families as Allies, along with 16 other organizations, filed a successful lawsuit on behalf of children for whom there were no appropriate educational and mental health services. Hawaii Families as Allies also helped develop a strategic plan to address these problems (Briggs & Sinclair, 1995). Thus, from complaint to resolution, family members were key players in achieving system change.

Collaboration between family advocacy organizations and service providers has resulted in unique and positive solutions to service delivery issues and a growing appreciation of family member input and oversight. For example, staff from PIN of PA are now routinely included as members of program review teams that visit and evaluate all child-serving programs in Pennsylvania. In Louisiana and Virginia, family members are included as a part of all regional and local interagency planning teams.

FAMILIES AS SERVICE INNOVATORS

Gradually, family members' ideas and responses have made their way into the policy and service planning arena. Programmatic experiments have emerged slowly; in some cases they focus on family support and on what families need to survive and maintain their child at home. In other cases these programmatic innovations are new and better ways of serving the child within the family and community (Stroul & Goldman, 1990).

In some communities family members have developed a program or service and run it themselves because the service they needed was not available or because it was not delivered in a family-friendly fashion. Family members started parent-run support groups when professionally run support groups were not available or did not meet the families' need for information or shared emotional support. With the growth of family support and advocacy organizations, many have incorporated and expanded their staff so that they are able to experiment with innovative service ideas. For example, the Vermont Federation of Families helped to develop and now manages the respite care program for families of children with emotional disabilities (Sturtevant, 1992). This family organization was instrumental in the design of this innovative program. It developed and now delivers training to respite care workers and has been proactive in finding ways of making the respite program more family centered. The Finger Lakes Family Support Project in New York State provides an example of a family support program that is managed through a collaboration between professionals and family members in nine rural counties in the Finger Lakes region (Friesen & Wahlers, 1993). Family members participate in all of the decision making about the project, including its design, implementation, and evaluation. The project has developed three components: "family-support groups, child care and respite care, and conferences, family retreats, and other training opportunities" (p. 14). Services have evolved to fit the unique needs of the rural communities and are gradually leading to increased parent involvement in decision making about other components of the service system (Friesen & Wahlers, 1993).

Another example is found at the Sedgwick County Federation of Families for Children's Mental Health, which, in cooperation with the Mental Health Association of South Central Kansas, has begun a program that provides job training for parents who are receiving welfare benefits. Through a process that includes classroom training and on the job mentoring, parents of children with emotional, behavioral, and mental disorders are trained to become case management aides or educational advocates. Not only do the parent/trainees develop job skills, but they are also provided with extensive information and support regarding the services needed by their own children and families. This program was conceptualized and is directed by family members and has resulted in a triple win: 1) the community receives trained employees who are no longer dependent on public assistance, 2) the trainees get job skills and support for managing their child's disability, and 3) the family advocacy organization has an additional source of revenue and access to parents.

Family members are often able to push the boundaries of the traditional service system because their thinking is not bound by funding rules and policies. For example, in Oregon parents were told that a much-needed transition program for youth 16–25 years old could not be developed because programs for children and adults are paid for by different funding streams. The family members suggested, "Why not fund the adult and adolescent programs separately, but house them in the same space, and run them as one program?" Another mother asked, "Why must my adolescent son move to foster care because I can't always manage his behavior and because my employment makes it difficult for me to provide adequate supervision? Why not hire a foster parent to live with us so we can stay together?" As these examples illustrate, family members can provide a fresh perspective that, combined with service providers' expertise, creates innovative ways of meeting the needs of children and families.

CONCLUSION

As we review the progress that has been made since the mid-1980s, it is intriguing to speculate about what may come next. The following list of possibilities is proposed as a stimulus to further thought—not necessarily as recommendations but as areas that are likely to emerge throughout the 1990s and into the next century. These and other developments will need systematic examination as they unfold.

- Professional networks and family networks may begin to merge.

    Many family organizations report that the number of inquiries for information and assistance from professionals is increasing. Some professionals refer complex cases to family organizations because the family organizations are less constrained and more able to seek a cross-agency solution than employees in any given agency. An increasing number of family members are seeking professional training, and service systems are both hiring individual family members and contracting with family organizations to develop and provide services. The influence of these innovations on the configuration of "the system" could be considerable.

- Professional training will increasingly include information about family participation as a part of the core curriculum; thus, professionals should be better prepared to work collaboratively with families and family organizations.

    Currently, system of care concepts are taught and family members are included as a part of the educational process in some innovative programs

(Jivanjee, Moore, Schultze, & Friesen, 1995). A number of family organizations also provide training for professionals and have the goal of bringing family perspectives to professional education programs.

• Family groups and organizations will become more diverse in terms of race, culture, income, geography, and other factors.

These changes are evident in the work of the Federation of Families for Children's Mental Health through the Annie E. Casey Foundation's Urban Mental Health Initiative. An increasing number of family members of color attend national conferences about children's mental health and related topics each year, and outreach to families involved in the juvenile justice and child welfare systems is increasing because of foundation and federally supported initiatives. Youth who are mental health service recipients and their brothers, sisters, and friends have begun to organize and are increasingly included in service planning and decision-making bodies.

• Family members on task forces and planning bodies increasingly will be representatives of family organizations rather than lone individuals.

The effectiveness of family members who participate on planning bodies, task forces, interagency councils, and other planning and decision-making bodies appears to be enhanced by association with a family organization. Members of the family organization can provide support, prepare positions on issues, and provide backup for family members faced with a competing demand or crisis. The credibility and influence of family members who speak for many, rather than for themselves alone, are also increased (Koroloff et al., 1995).

• Family members' involvement in program evaluation and research will increase.

This activity is specifically encouraged at the federal level by the Child, Adolescent and Family Branch of the Center for Mental Health Services and the National Institute on Disability and Rehabilitation Research through requirements included in program announcements and grant review mechanisms. A growing number of individual researchers and research organizations include family members in the design, implementation, analysis, interpretation, and dissemination phases of their work. For example, the Research and Training Center on Family Support and Children's Mental Health at Portland State University sponsors an annual conference to bring together family members, researchers, service providers, and advocates; workshops and presentations feature many research efforts and programs that have solid family participation. In a cross-disability approach that includes mental health, the Beach Center on Families and Disability at the University of Kansas provides leadership in promoting family and consumer participation in all phases of research using a "Participatory Action Research" framework (Turnbull & Friesen, 1995).

The role of families has evolved from marginal to central in the quest for an effective, supportive system of care for children with emotional, behavioral, or mental disorders and their families. We look forward to accelerated progress as families and professionals continue to discover new and creative ways to work together toward mutual goals.

REFERENCES

Anderson, W.C. (1994). *Finding help—finding hope*. Alexandria, VA: Federation of Families for Children's Mental Health.

Bateson, G. (1972). *Steps to an ecology of the mind*. New York: Ballentine.

Briggs, H.E., & Sinclair, I. (1995). *Child and adolescent mental health strategic plan*. Honolulu: Hawaii Department of Health, Child and Adolescent Mental Health Division.

Burchard, J.D., & Clarke, R.T. (1990). The role of individualized care in a service delivery system for children and adolescents with severely maladjusted behavior. *Journal of Mental Health Administration, 17*, 48–60.

Byalin, K. (1990). Parent empowerment: A treatment strategy for hospitalized adolescents. *Hospital and Community Psychiatry, 41*, 89–90.

Cahn, E.S., & Cahn, J.C. (1971). Maximum feasible participation: A general overview. In E.S. Cahn & B.A. Passert (Eds.), *Citizen participation: Effecting community change* (pp. 9–65). New York: Praeger.

Castellani, P.J., Downey, N.A., Tausig, M.B., & Bird, W.A. (1986). Availability and accessibility of family support services. *Mental Retardation, 24*, 71–79.

Cibulka, J. (1981). Citizen participation in the governance of community mental health centers. *Community Mental Health Journal, 17*, 19–36.

Community Mental Health Centers Act Amendments of 1975. PL 94-63. (July 29, 1975). Title 42, U.S.C. 2689 et seq: *U.S. Statutes at Large, 89*, 308–334.

Dunst, C.J., Trivette, C.M., & Cross, A.H. (1986). Mediating influences of social support. *American Journal of Mental Deficiency, 90*, 402–417.

Education for All Handicapped Children Act of 1975, PL 94-142. (August 23, 1977). Title 20, U.S.C. 1400 et seq: *U.S. Statutes at Large, 89*, 773–796.

Federation of Families for Children's Mental Health. (1992). *Family support statement*. Alexandria, VA: Author.

Fine, G., & Borden, J.R. (1991). Parents Involved Network Project (PIN): Outcomes of parent involvement in support group and advocacy training activities. In A. Algarin & R.M. Friedman (Eds.), *A system of care for children's mental health: Expanding the research base* (pp. 25–29). Tampa, FL: University of South Florida, Florida Mental Health Institute, Research and Training Center for Children's Mental Health.

Friesen, B.J. (1989a). Parents as advocates for children and adolescents with serious emotional handicaps: Issues and directions. In R.M. Friedman, A.J. Duchnowski, & E.L. Henderson (Eds.), *Advocacy on behalf of children with serious emotional problems* (pp. 28–44). Springfield, IL: Charles C Thomas.

Friesen, B.J. (1989b). *Survey of parents whose children have serious emotional disorders: Report of a national study*. Portland, OR: Portland State University, Research and Training Center on Family Support and Children's Mental Health.

Friesen, B.J., & Huff, B. (1990). Parents and professionals as advocacy partners. *Preventing School Failure, 34*, 31–36.

Friesen, B.J., Koren, P.E., & Koroloff, N.M. (1992). How parents view professional behaviors: A cross-professional analysis. *Journal of Child and Family Studies, 1*, 209–231.

Friesen, B.J., & Koroloff, N.M. (1990). Family-centered services: Implications for mental health administration and research. *Journal of Mental Health Administration, 17*, 13–25.

Friesen, B.J., & Wahlers, D. (1993). Respect and real help: Family support and children's mental health. *Journal of Emotional and Behavioral Problems, 2*(4), 12–15.

Greenley, J.R., & Robitschek, C.G. (1991). Evaluation of a comprehensive program for youth with severe emotional disorders: An analysis of family experiences and satisfaction. *American Journal of Orthopsychiatry, 61*, 291–297.

Holten, J.D. (1990). When do we stop mother-blaming? *Journal of Feminist Family Therapy, 2*, 53–60.

Individuals with Disabilities Education Act, PL 101-476. (October 30, 1990). Title 20, U.S.C. 1400 et seq: *U.S. Statutes at Large, 104*(part 2), 1103–1151.

Jenson, J.M., & Whittaker, J.K. (1987). Parental involvement in children's residential treatment: From preplacement to aftercare. *Children and Youth Services Review, 9*, 81–100.

Jivanjee, P.R., Moore, K.R., Schultze, K.H., & Friesen, B.J. (1995). *Interprofessional education for family-centered services: A survey of interprofessional/interdisciplinary training programs.* Portland, OR: Portland State University, Research and Training Center on Family Support and Children's Mental Health.

Johnson, H.C. (1986). Emerging concerns in family therapy. *Social Work, 31*, 299–306.

Karp, N., & Bradley, V. (1991). Family support. *Children Today, 20*(2), 28–31.

Knitzer, J.E. (1993). Children's mental health policy: Challenging the future. *Journal of Emotional and Behavioral Disorders, 1*, 8–16.

Koroloff, N., Hunter, R., & Gordon, L. (1995). *Family involvement in policy making: A final report on the Families in Action Project.* Portland, OR: Portland State University, Research and Training Center on Family Support and Children's Mental Health.

Kotsopoulos, S., Elwood, S., & Oke, L. (1989). Parent satisfaction in a child psychiatric service. *Canadian Journal of Psychiatry, 34*, 530–533.

Lipsky, D.K. (1985). A parental perspective on stress and coping. *American Journal of Orthopsychiatry, 55*, 614–617.

Lourie, I.S., Katz-Leavy, J., & Jacobs, J.H. (1985). *The Office of State and Community Liaison (OSCL) Child and Adolescent Service System Program fiscal year 1985.* Washington, DC: National Institute of Mental Health.

Margolis, L.H., & Meisels, S.J. (1987). Barriers to the effectiveness of EPSDT for children with moderate and severe developmental disabilities. *American Journal of Orthopsychiatry, 57*, 424–430.

Mayer, J.A. (1994). From rage to reform: What parents say about advocacy. *Exceptional Parent, 4*(5), 49–51.

McManus, M.C., & Friesen, B.J. (1986). *Families as Allies conference proceedings.* Portland, OR: Portland State University, Research and Training Center to Improve Services to Emotionally Handicapped Children and Their Families.

McManus, M.C., Reilly, L.M., Rinkin, J.L., & Wrigley, J.A. (1993). *An advocate's approach to abolishing custody relinquishment requirements for families whose children have disabilities: The Oregon experience.* Salem, OR: Oregon Family Support Network.

National Center for Networking Community Based Services. (1987). *Family-centered health care for medically fragile children.* Washington, DC: Georgetown University Child Development Center.

Research and Training Center. (1987). Families as allies conferences. *Focal Point, 1*(2).

Robin, S.C. (1989). *Family-based services: "Success" as defined and experienced by families and providers.* Doctoral dissertation, University of Minnesota, Minneapolis.

Shelton, T.L., Jeppson, E.S., & Johnson, B.H. (1987). *Family-centered care for children with special health care needs.* Washington, DC: Association for the Care of Children's Health.

Singer, G.H.S., & Powers, L. (Eds.). (1993). *Families, disability, and empowerment: Active coping skills and strategies for family interventions.* Baltimore: Paul H. Brookes Publishing Co.

State of the Art Video. (1988). *Regular lives.* Washington, DC: Author.

Stroul, B.A., & Friedman, R.M. (1986). *A system of care for children and youth with severe emotional disturbances.* (rev. ed.). Washington, DC: Georgetown University Child Development Center, National Technical Assistance Center for Children's Mental Health.

Stroul, B.A., & Goldman, S.K. (1990). Study of community-based services for children and adolescents who are severely emotionally disturbed. *Journal of Mental Health Administration, 17*, 61–77.

Sturtevant, J. (1992). Respite for families with children with emotional disabilities. *Access to Respite Care & Help, 2*(3), 2–3.

Tarico, V.S., Low, B.P., Trupin, E., & Forsyth-Stephens, A. (1989). Children's mental health services: A parent perspective. *Community Mental Health Journal, 25*, 313–326.

Tracy, E.M., & Whittaker, J.K. (1987). The evidence base for social support interventions in child and family practice: Emerging issues for research and practice. *Children and Youth Service Review, 9*, 249–270.

Turnbull, A.P., & Friesen, B.J. (1995). *Forging collaborative partnerships with families in the study of disability.* Paper presented at the National Institute on Disability and Rehabilitation Research on Participatory Action Research, Washington, DC.

VanDenBerg, J.E. (1992). Individualized services for children. In E. Peschel, R. Peschel, C.W. Howe, & J.W. Howe (Eds.), *Neurobiological disorders in children (New Directions for Mental Health Services,* No. 54), (pp. 97–100). San Francisco: Jossey-Bass.

VanDenBerg, J.E. (1993). Integration of individualized mental health services into the system of care for children and adolescents. *Administration and Policy in Mental Health, 20*, 247–257.

Vosler-Hunter, R., & Exo, K. (1988). *Working together.* Portland, OR: Portland State University, Research and Training Center on Family Support and Children's Mental Health.

Wahl, O.F. (1989). Schizophrenogenic parenting in abnormal psychology textbooks. *Teaching of Psychology, 16*(1), 31–33.

Wasow, M., & Wikler, L. (1983). Reflections on professionals' attitudes toward the severely mentally retarded and the chronically mentally ill: Implications for parents. *Family Therapy, 10*, 299–308.

Wells, K. (1991). Long-term residential treatment for children: Introduction. *American Journal of Orthopsychiatry, 16*(3), 324–326.

Whittaker, J.K. (1976). Causes of childhood disorders: New findings. *Social Work, 21*, 91–96.

Williams-Murphy, T., DeChillo, N., Koren, P.E., & Hunter, R. (1994). *Family/professional collaboration: The perspectives of those who have tried.* Portland, OR: Portland State University, Research and Training Center on Family Support and Children's Mental Health.

Windle, C., & Cibulka, J.G. (1981). A framework for understanding participation in community mental health services. *Community Mental Health Journal, 17*, 4–18.

Service Delivery Within a System of Care

C H A P T E R   23

Individualized Services in a System of Care

Ira S. Lourie, Judith Katz-Leavy, and Beth A. Stroul

In 1986, Stroul and Friedman presented a conceptual framework for a "system of care," encompassing the full range of services and mechanisms required for the assurance of their appropriate delivery. In this model, the first core value was that a "system of care must be child-centered, with the needs of the child and family dictating the types and mix of services provided." The importance of tailoring services to the specific needs of the child and family was further emphasized in one of the 10 guiding principles for the system of care, which stated that "children should receive individualized services in accordance with the unique needs and potentials of each child, and guided by an individualized service plan" (p. 17). Although the concept of individualizing services has been widely accepted as a basic premise for systems of care, the actual power and potential of this approach have been developed beyond anything imagined in 1986 (Katz-Leavy, Lourie, Stroul, & Zeigler-Dendy, 1992).

It should be noted that, even before 1986, certain aspects of individualizing service planning were being implemented by practitioners. Friedman (1988) stated that, "Within particular service components, be it outpatient therapy, day treatment, or therapeutic foster care, for example, many clinicians have always tailored the service to meet the needs of each child and family" (p.10). Additionally, the push to expand the range of community-based services within the system of care was based on the recognition that more options needed to be available to adequately meet the unique needs of different children and families. Intensive case management is one service that is increasingly being utilized to individualize services. Intensive case managers with small caseloads work to customize services for each youngster and have "the independence, the knowledge, and the creativity to ensure that an individualized plan is developed and implemented" (Friedman, 1988, p. 10).

Another evolving aspect of individualizing services has been the provision of funds or staff resources in a flexible manner that permits case managers to wrap services around the needs of children and families rather than require the children and families to fit into existing programs (Friedman, 1988). The term "wraparound" was coined in North Carolina (Behar, 1985), and the approach has rapidly expanded to numerous states and communities throughout the country. This approach permits a case manager, treatment team, or service program to add new services, both traditional and nontraditional, specifically designed for individual youngsters and families to enable them to achieve the goals specified in a customized service plan. This chapter examines individualized services and their relationships to the concept and philosophy of a community-based system of care.

PHILOSOPHY AND VALUES UNDERLYING INDIVIDUALIZED SERVICES

The philosophy and values underlying individualized services are very similar to the philosophy for a system of care described by Stroul and Friedman (1986), which specifies that systems of care should emphasize the provision of services that are comprehensive, individualized, coordinated, provided in the least restrictive environment, and culturally competent, and involve families as full partners. Many communities currently are basing their developing systems of care on these values and principles. Within this overall value system, the individualized care approach emphasizes six major underlying values.

Focus on an Individual Child and Family

The first underlying value is that individualized services, as the designation suggests, are applied to one child and family at a time. This approach allows the creation of a service plan that is designed specifically to address the unique needs and strengths of each child and family. Tannen (1991) described the approach as highly child and family centered, with the goal of empowering each child and family so that they can effectively manage their lives. Burchard and Clarke (1990) stated that individualized care involves a "total commitment" to serve each child and family on an individual basis and to provide services for as long as there is a need. Thus, rather than only focusing on groups of youngsters within the confines of a specific agency or program, the focus in the individualized care approach is on meeting the needs of one child and family at a time.

Services Within the Most Normalized Environment

A second value emphasizes providing services within the most normative environment. All activities and services in the individualized care approach are geared toward enabling youngsters to remain in the least restrictive, most normalized environment and to live as normal a life as possible. The first option, always considered most preferable, is to enable the child to remain within his or her own family. If this is not possible, all efforts are made to enable the youngster to remain in the community in a family or family-like setting. Therapeutic foster homes or supported independent living for older adolescents often is the treatment environment of choice for youngsters who cannot reside with their own families. This value is based on the strong beliefs that youngsters should reside with their families or in family settings and that intensive treatment services can effectively be provided within these normative environments. VanDenBerg (1991) defined normalization as supporting lifestyles as similar as possible to the youngster's peers and emphasized that services and resulting lifestyles should be as culturally, ethnically, and age-appropriate as possible.

Partnership with Families

Inherent in the individualized care approach is the notion of creating a partnership with families. Because the entire process depends on addressing the child's and family's needs in a holistic manner, it would be impossible to plan and implement individualized services without a close collaborative relationship with the family. Individualized services are dependent on parent involvement during all phases of service delivery, including participating on the interagency service planning/treatment team, developing the individualized service plan, and monitoring and evaluating progress. As noted by Tannen (1991), the child and parents are included in every phase of individualized services and they are always listened to and treated with respect by professionals.

Strengths-Based, Ecological Orientation

Using a strengths-based, ecological orientation represents another underlying value of individualized care. A thorough assessment of the child's and family's strengths, needs, and desires forms a basis for the development of an individualized intervention plan. Although traditional assessments tend to emphasize pathology and service needs, assessments for individualized care emphasize the child's and family's assets as well as their deficits. As stated by Olson, Whitbeck, and Robinson (1991), the strengths-based orientation allows the child and family to be seen as individuals with unique talents, skills, and life histories as well as having specific unmet needs. This orientation recognizes the fact that even the most troubled youngsters and multistressed families have strengths, assets, and coping skills that can be built on when creating an intervention approach. Furthermore, the strengths-based assessment is not limited narrowly to the mental health domain, but takes an ecological approach to consider the child and family across all environments and life domains, including residential, family, social, educational, vocational, medical, psychological, legal, safety, and others. This strengths-based, ecological perspective not only drives the assessment but becomes the key factor in the development of the individualized service plan for the child and family.

Cultural Competence

Cultural competence is the fifth underlying value of individualized services. The need for culturally competent services was recognized as the system of care concept was developed; one of the guiding principles specifies that children should receive culturally competent services that are sensitive and responsive to cultural and ethnic differences. Although there has been discussion of the need for culturally competent services (Cross, Bazron, Dennis, & Isaacs, 1989; Isaacs & Benjamin, 1991), progress in this area has been slow. Individualized services, focusing on one child and family at a time, are uniquely able to take cultural and ethnic factors into consideration as the service plan is developed. VanDenBerg (1991) emphasized the importance of ensuring that services are culturally, ethnically, and age appropriate. The application of this value in planning and implementing services is facilitated by the strengths-based, ecological assessment, which allows the interagency service planning team to learn about the child's environment prior to planning and delivering services. The incorporation of cultural competency into this assessment of strengths and needs and design of the service plan means that efforts are made to learn about cultural and ethnic issues that impact the child and family and to understand and respect their values. The value further implies that providers work closely with referral agencies to ensure that children of color are appropriately identified and referred for services.

Unconditional Care

The final value of individualized care is that of unconditional care. This value has two primary components—an inclusive intake policy and a policy preventing punitive discharge. An inclusive intake policy specifies that no youngsters may be rejected or found ineligible for individualized services on the basis of the severity of their presenting problems. Thus, youngsters are eligible for services no matter how serious, complex, or difficult their problems. The second aspect of unconditional care holds that, once a youngster is found eligible for services, a long-term commitment is made to the child and family, and the providers do not give up on the child no matter what the child may do to jeopardize that commitment. Adherence to the value of "no punitive discharge" means that no youth is dropped, discharged, or ejected from services because of challenging or disturbed behaviors or other needs. Rather, the commitment of unconditional care obligates the providers to do "whatever it takes" to ensure that the youth receives clinically appropriate services within the least restrictive setting. Providers reconfigure services to meet crises and changing needs rather than dismissing youngsters or referring them elsewhere. Burchard (1988) noted that the commitment to unconditional care breaks the cycle of rejection that so many troubled youth experience.

Kaleidoscope, an agency founded in Illinois in 1973, adopted this philosophy of unconditional care, defining it to mean both "no reject" and "no eject" from services (Dennis, 1992). Kaleidoscope's founders and staff were determined to stick with the youngster no matter where he or she ended up. If the youth ended up in juvenile corrections or in jail, they would follow the youth there, and they would be there to offer support when the youth was released. This underlying value became a critical factor in hiring staff; a conscious effort was made to select only providers who believed in this kind of commitment and could accommodate to the flexibility such a commitment required. Unconditional care has become a cornerstone of individualized services and is a basic tenet of most individualized care efforts.

In describing the Alaska Youth Initiative, Dowrick (1988) wrote,

> The real reason that this works, the real key, is because someone takes the responsibility; someone stops the buck. There must be somebody who is in the position to say, "Yes, we will take care of these children, no matter what they do. If they try to kill themselves, try to kill each other, if they are sexually promiscuous, destroy things, set fire to buildings, assault one another, or generally drive people up the wall, we will take care of them nonetheless. One person will take responsibility." We will not say, "This person has a learning disorder, therefore, we can't deal with him. This person has mental retardation, that's not our population. This person is sixteen, she's too old. This person has a criminal record, that's for juvenile justice, and so on." We won't pass this child around anymore. We will take care of this child. (p. 60)

Dennis (1992) illustrated the underlying philosophy and principles of individualized services by describing the case of "Allen," a youth presenting serious and complex problems for whom Kaleidoscope successfully provided care using an individualized approach.

> Allen was a 16-year-old who had been rejected from several residential treatment centers. He was now being rejected from a correctional setting where he was considered too difficult to handle after tearing a door off an isolation cell. Everyone thought that he was incorrigible. Yet no matter where he was placed, no matter how far from his home and neighborhood, it was noted that his mother faithfully visited him twice a month. Based upon the strength of this apparent relationship, Kaleidoscope designed an individualized service plan for Allen.
>
> Despite the fact that she was extremely devoted to this son, Allen's mother was adamantly opposed to his return home; in fact, her state caseworker also counseled her not to let Allen come home. Undaunted by Allen's mother's resistance, Dennis prevailed upon her sense of hospitality to let him come in and play "a little game." This game was: "If he could wave his magic wand, what would it take for Allen to be able to come home?" If she would just do this for 10 minutes, then Dennis would leave and not return. Eager to get rid of this uninvited visitor, Allen's mother agreed to participate. With each wave of the wand, Allen's mother came up with another condition for her son's return:
>
> • Someone to come to their home and get Allen up for school.
> • Someone to be with Allen in school to help him control his temper.

- A therapist who would not be afraid of or give up on Allen even if it meant having a companion sit in on each session to help control Allen's violent outbursts.
- Someone to give her a few free hours of time each day when she came home from work.
- A 24-hour crisis plan for evenings, weekends, and holidays to ensure her safety when Allen became agitated.

Allen returned home the following week, but this time his mother had the support services she had helped to design. There were still crises, but they were anticipated, and everyone had agreed in advance how they would be handled. Ultimately, Allen was able to move into transitional community housing and participate in a supported work program.

This vignette illustrates a number of the underlying values of individualized services—focusing on the needs of one child and family, providing services in the most normal environment (the child's home), forming a meaningful partnership with families, and building an intervention plan using a strengths-based orientation. The Kaleidoscope staff knew that a major strength in this family was Allen's mother's love for him, but also knew that she needed meaningful support services if she was going to be able to cope with him. A program of support services was tailored to meet Allen's individual needs and those of his mother. It was designed around the strengths of both the youngster and his family, and it enabled him to return to his home and community.

THE PROCESS OF INDIVIDUALIZING SERVICES

The process of individualizing services includes four major features: interagency collaboration; case management/care coordination; wraparound services, including an array of traditional and nontraditional services; and flexibility of funding and services. It should be noted that these processes that characterize individualized services are the same processes that should characterize an effective, community-based system of care (Stroul & Friedman, 1986). The individualized care approach has further developed these processes and shown how they can be systematically applied to meet the needs of each child and family.

Interagency Collaboration

Interagency collaboration, the first of these features, appears to be an indispensable aspect of providing individualized care. In a recent nationwide survey of 15 different programs based on the individualized services approach, MacFarquhar and Dowrick (1993) asked the question, "What single factor contributes most to the success of your program?" (p. 170). The largest percentage of respondents (42%) indicated that an interagency team was the most important factor in the program's success. Of the programs surveyed, 93% used an interagency collaboration approach based on the use of some form of interagency service planning/treatment team. Programs using a team approach reported that decisions about service delivery were made as a team. Several communities worked on a two-tiered team approach. A youth-specific team was responsible for service planning and implementation and a higher level interagency team of some type reviewed more complex cases, approved unusual service or funding arrangements, and focused on system-level issues related to service delivery and interagency relationships. In addition, many states utilize a state-level interagency team to focus on broad system and policy issues related to service delivery and, in some situations, to review and resolve cases that cannot be resolved at the local level. It is the interagency youth-specific team that has been adopted almost universally by individualized service programs across the country.

The team approach appears to be helpful in a number of different ways. More complete information is obtained about the child and family because contributions are made by all involved parties, not just one or two agencies. Greater resources may become available by combining the staff and services of multiple agencies, and the workload and responsibility for time-consuming and complex cases are shared among multiple agencies. Furthermore, the creativity and energy of the group process are harnessed in planning for the child. A time-limited case conference format may be utilized to maximize utilization of staff time and to keep committee members focused. The benefits of using an interagency team were noted by Friedman (1988) when he wrote that,

> First, by convening a team of individuals who are knowledgeable about the child, including parents where possible, the likelihood of having a complete understanding of the child is enhanced. Second, since the individuals on the team may all be involved in implementing the service plan, the meeting is useful in providing all with an opportunity to give input and in gaining everybody's support for the plan. Third, the process of creative treatment planning can be facilitated by having a group of individuals with different perspectives rather than just one or two people (p. 57)

In addition, Burchard and Clarke (1990) wrote,

> Having an interdisciplinary care team allows for tracking services across agencies and makes individualized care easier to implement. It promotes shared ownership and makes it less likely that an individual or an agency will act without consensus. Communication is a critical function of the interagency team (p. 57)

An additional benefit is that team participants may begin to think more broadly about the functioning of the system of care in a community and often may initiate system improvements based upon their interactions relative to the needs of individual youngsters.

Case Management/Care Coordination

In all systems of care, some form of case management or care coordination plays a critical role in planning, orchestrating, monitoring, coordinating, and adjusting services. Behar (*Close to Home*, 1991) proposed that clinical case management is the "key to systemic success" in a complex system of services by virtue of providing consistent advocates for the client and family and by coordinating and monitoring all services throughout the course of treatment. Behar (1985) also stated that

> Case management, in its most positive sense, has emerged as: (a) the element of planning and coordination that has combined the workings of all agencies concerned with the child, (b) the energizing factor that has propelled the service plan into the reality of service delivery, and (c) the case advocacy strength that has sustained a commitment to each child and an optimism about each child's capacity to change" (p. 194)

For individualized services, case management plays an especially crucial role.

The case management/care coordination function has been described by a number of different terms. Young (1987) put forth a model of therapeutic case advocacy and described its usefulness in creating "an individualized system of care" for each child with an emotional disability and his or her family. North Carolina describes a program of clinical case management (Behar, *Close to Home*, 1991), and the Alaska Youth Initiative refers to an individualized services coordinator, also sometimes referred to as a youth-specific services coordinator, a family assistance coordinator, or a local coordinator (Alaska Department of Health and Social Services, 1989, 1990, 1991). The Vermont New Directions program, which was supported through a grant from the Robert Wood Johnson Foundation, refers to this concept as therapeutic case management (DeCarolis, 1992).

Although there is a diversity of terms to describe this function, it is clear, nevertheless, that some form of intensive case management plays an integral part in most individualized services for children with serious emotional or mental disorders and their families. In a number of sites, the case manager is responsible for conducting the ecological assessment and for bringing this preliminary work to the first meeting of the interagency team. In most cases, the case manager performs a facilitative role within the interagency team throughout the process of developing an individualized plan of services for a specific child and family. The case manager is then responsible for ensuring that the plan is implemented and that appropriate coordination across agencies occurs. The case manager also makes sure that mechanisms are in place to ensure frequent communication and to identify the need for changes in the plan if it is not meeting all of the life domain needs of the child or family, preferably before crises occur.

Wraparound Services

Individualized services draw on all available resources for children and families—formal and informal, traditional and nontraditional. The process of individualizing care incorporates the concept of wraparound services as an integral feature. Behar (1986) outlined a rationale for setting aside "flexible" dollars to pay for nontraditional services that often are needed to help troubled youth remain in the community and participate in traditional service programs. As an example, wraparound funds could be used to pay for respite services to give stressed parents a break, to allow a youth to pay apartment-related expenses, to enroll a youth in recreational activities, and to purchase otherwise unavailable items and services important to maintaining a specific child in his or her family or surrogate family in the community. The concept of wraparound services currently is applied more broadly to connote the creative combination of all types of services, resources, and supports that are needed by a youngster and his or her family.

The International Initiative on the Development, Training, and Evaluation of WrapAround Services (1992) defines wraparound services as interventions that are

> developed and/or approved by an interdisciplinary services team, are community-based and unconditional, are centered on the strengths of the child and family, and include the delivery of coordinated, highly individualized services in three or more life domain areas of a child and family. (p. 1)

As described by Burchard (1988), the underlying foundation of wraparound services "is to identify those children that are the most severely emotionally disturbed and wrap services around them to facilitate their adjustment in the mainstream" (p. 1). A thorough ecological assessment, completed by the case manager and interagency team, is used as the basis for identifying strengths and needs and for developing an individualized service plan that addresses all life domains and includes both existing services and other services and supports devised in response to specific needs.

MacFarquhar and Dowrick (1993) reported that all programs responding to their survey had the flexibility to design services and supports beyond traditional mental health programs. They provided some examples of wraparound services purchased with flexible dollars, including hiring foster parents with an apartment on their property that would allow a youth to move back and forth between foster care and independent living as necessary, and buying an auto part needed for repairs to provide transportation to therapy for a youth and family. Other examples consisted of providing a paid friend to supervise a youth in the community in order to promote socialization; providing a hotel room with supervised staff until appropriate placement was available after discharge from a psychiatric hospital; and purchasing a washing machine for a family whose child had enuresis. Programs across the country have used flexible dollars to wrap services around the child and family in areas including family support and sustenance, therapeutic services, school-related services, medical services, crisis services, independent living services, interpersonal and recreational skill development, vocational services, and reinforcers. The types of services and supports that can be provided to a child and family through this approach are constrained only by the limits of the creativity of the case manager and participants of the interagency service planning/treatment team.

Thus, in addition to capitalizing on and utilizing existing services and programs within the community's system of care as appropriate, individualized service plans are enriched by the addition of wraparound services that are used to ensure that the individualized service plan is able to appropriately address all of the child's life domains. It is the creative combination of services and supports of all types for a child and family that characterizes the individualized service approach and enriches a system of care, tremendously increasing its capacity to help troubled children.

Flexibility of Funding and Services

The fourth essential feature of the process of individualizing services is flexibility—flexible funding and flexible care. Individualized services cannot be provided without flexible funds that can be used to purchase or create the services specified in the individualized intervention plan. The concept of flexible funding requires that the money for purchasing the services follow the child in that it is available to serve the child regardless of the program the child is in.

> In terms of logistics this is the linchpin of individualized care. In order to provide care that is unconditional, child-and-family centered and flexible, it is essential that money is attached to the child for the purchase of services and not to a program for the delivery of services. (Burchard & Clarke, 1990, p. 57)

According to MacFarquhar and Dowrick (1993), this change in the way funding is conceptualized reflects a primary principle of individualized care. Monies are attached to each child to develop services and supports, and funding of services can be shifted as the treatment plan changes. Although flexible funding is considered an indispensable feature of individualized care, a substantial proportion of the programs included in MacFarquhar and Dowrick's survey (25%) indicated that funding is the most significant problem they face. The reported problems lie in acquiring adequate funding to provide individualized care as well as in the ability to use funds in a flexible manner. Many states and communities currently are experimenting with a variety of approaches to flexible funding. Strategies include creating a pool of blended funds from the various child-serving agencies that can be accessed by case managers, interagency teams, or both to pay for individualized intervention plans. Additionally, an increasing number of service programs across the country (such as home-based service, day treatment, and therapeutic foster care) are budgeting various amounts of flexible funds to purchase wraparound services and supports for participating youngsters and families.

Not only should funds be flexible, but services themselves must be flexible under an individualized care approach. "Flexible care requires services which can arrive when needed and then be increased and decreased in intensity, based on the needs of the child and family" (Burchard & Clarke, 1990, p. 51). Children with serious emotional or mental disorders move in and out of programs on a frequent basis, and their needs can fluctuate markedly on a weekly or even daily basis. If services are to be tailored to their needs, it is critical that the case manager have the resources and the authority to respond in a timely and flexible manner. Flexible care is based on the ability to change the service plan as frequently as necessary. In the individualized approach, if the child's and family's needs are not being met, the service plan is changed rather than expelling or rejecting the child. Implicit in the commitment to provide flexible services is a commitment to do whatever it takes to meet the needs of the child and family over the long term.

OPERATIONALIZING INDIVIDUALIZED SERVICES

In order to implement individualized services, decisions must be made in a number of key areas, including how to define the target population; how to organize and utilize interagency service planning/treatment teams; how to fulfill the case management/care coordination function; how to conduct assessments, plan, and provide services; and how to finance individualized services. Each of these issues is discussed below.

Defining the Target Population

The individualized service approach has been used extensively by many states and communities as a mechanism for facilitating the return of children from out-of-state residential treatment settings. During the mid- to late 1980s, several states launched initiatives to bring youngsters home from such out-of-state placements, relying on intensive, individualized services in the community as the alternative. For example, 39 youngsters were returned home from out-of-state facilities through the Alaska Youth Initiative (Alaska Department of Health and Social Services, 1990). A number of additional states have utilized or are currently in the process of utilizing the individualized service approach to return children who have been receiving treatment in out-of-state settings.

As the potential of individualized care has become more apparent, many states and communities have begun to expand its use to a broader population than children in out-of-state residential care. Based on a review of eligibility criteria across a range of communities, it appears that such criteria typically require that candidates for individualized services have a serious emotional or behavioral disturbance, functional impairment, and multiagency involvement. Two additional criteria appear to be most salient in defining candidates for individualized care:

1. Placement in, or risk of placement in, out-of-community residential treatment settings
2. Complex and difficult problems that are not being addressed within the framework of the existing service system

These criteria suggest that individualized services are being provided to those youngsters considered the most difficult to serve. This observation is confirmed by data collected by MacFarquhar and Dowrick (1993) indicating that programs were serving youngsters with multiple and severe problems that have a profound impact on their lives and whose prognosis is for long-term care and services. In the programs they surveyed, 71% of the youngsters being served were receiving special education and 64% were in state custody. Furthermore, across programs, the youngsters had an average of four prior psychiatric hospitalizations, some extremely long term, and an average of seven failed residential placements. Despite the high level of maladjustment among this client population, the respondent programs reported that these youths were successfully served with individualized services and that only a small percentage of youngsters were considered "too risky" to serve in the community. Tannen (1991) also noted that, in Vermont, some of the most difficult children have made remarkable progress through individualized care.

Although states and communities have tended to target a subset of youngsters with emotional disorders for individualized care, it is important to note that all youngsters could benefit from more individually tailored service approaches. A goal for many systems of care is to increase the population of youngsters targeted for individualized services as well as to ensure that all service programs within the system of care are provided in a more flexible, individualized fashion.

Using Interagency Service Planning/Treatment Teams

MacFarquhar and Dowrick (1993) found that interagency collaboration was the factor most frequently chosen by respondents as leading to the success of individualized services. In fact, 93% of the programs surveyed used an interagency team approach to providing services. This interagency team approach most often involves the creation of a team that is specific to each youth and family and is composed of the persons most involved and influential in the child's life. This team typically is organized by the case manager and includes the parents and the youngster themselves, depending on the child's age and maturity level. VanDenBerg (1993) specified that the team should include, at a minimum,

- The parent and/or surrogate parent (i.e., foster parent, therapeutic foster parent, or guardian)
- If the child is in custody, the appropriate representative of the state (social worker or probation officer)
- A lead teacher and/or vocational counselor
- If the child is in or should be in mental health treatment, the appropriate therapist or counselor
- A case manager or service coordinator (a person who is responsible for ensuring that the services are coordinated and accountable)
- An advocate of the child, parent, or both
- Any other person influential in the child's or parent's life who may be instrumental in developing effective services, such as a neighbor, a physician, a relative, or a friend
- The child, unless to do so would be detrimental to his or her development

The group may be expanded to include other professionals who are serving the child or who will potentially receive the child in a program.

Such teams have been given a wide range of labels, including service network, individual support team, interagency treatment team, core services team, family assessment and planning team, family service planning team, community support team, and creative community options team. Despite the wide range of labels, the role of the interagency service planning/ treatment team is remarkably consistent across states and communities. With the case manager playing a facilitative leadership role, the team meets and works together over time to develop and implement a comprehensive, individualized service plan for the youngster and family. The plan developed by the interagency team generally is holistic and addresses all of the child's life domains. The team meets as needed to monitor progress and to reconfigure the service plan and approaches based upon the child's changing needs. The team may meet more frequently during early phases of service delivery as the plan is being developed; subgroups may meet at times to resolve emerging problems. Thus, the emphasis for interagency service planning/treatment teams is on reaching consensus among the various participants on the complement of services and supports needed by the child and family and on working together to design, provide, monitor, and revise the package of individualized services and supports as changing needs dictate.

In some communities, an interagency team with a standing membership is used as the focal point for planning and implementing individualized services. This standing team may be composed of a core group of regular members who are supplemented by persons involved with the particular youngster under consideration at the time. Florida's family service planning teams, mandated statewide, are examples of standing interagency groups that are supplemented with individuals specific to the youth under consideration for purposes of developing and implementing an individualized service plan.

An alternative approach adopted by an increasing number of communities involves organizing a multitiered system of interagency collaboration that separates client-level functions from system-level functions in the community's system of care. Washington State, for example, uses an interagency coordinating mechanism comprised of administrators of each of the child-serving systems to provide system-level coordination. For each child, an individual support team is constituted to develop and adjust individualized "tailored" services (Olson et al., 1991).

In Vermont, child-specific interagency treatment teams are used to develop individualized plans for children. If funding, program, or policy problems impede the design or implementation of the plan, the case is referred to the second level—the local interagency team. Vermont's local interagency teams are responsible for individual case review as well as system-level issues such as improving local services, addressing and resolving policy and funding barriers, and improving interagency collaboration. On the rare occasion that cases cannot be resolved at this level, the State Interagency Team may be enlisted in problem solving (Katz-Leavy et al., 1992).

In Stark County, Ohio, a three-tiered system has been created for individualized case planning and review. A "creative community options" team is organized for each individual youngster and family to assess strengths and needs and develop an individualized service plan. If the creative community options group is unable to resolve difficult and complex barriers to serving a child and family effectively, a referral can be made to the second level of interagency service planning, the ACCORD (A Creative Community Options Review Decision). The ACCORD is a standing committee of midlevel managers who represent each of the major child-serving systems and who are empowered by their agencies to make decisions and commit resources to support creative individualized services. Cases that still cannot be resolved at the ACCORD level can be referred to the Stark County Interagency Cluster, a group comprised of executives of the child-serving agencies with the primary purpose of system-level planning and coordination (Stroul, Lourie, Goldman, & Katz-Leavy, 1992). As in Vermont, cases that cannot be resolved at the community level may be referred to the State Level Interdepartmental Cluster. The experience of a number of states and communities indicates that both child-specific interagency service planning teams and interagency entities focusing on system-level issues appear to be essential elements of effective systems of care.

The inclusion of the parents as full participants on the interagency team is essential for individualized service approaches. Unless precautions are taken, most parents find attending a service planning meeting with numerous professionals to be an intimidating experience. Steps can be taken to help parents feel more at ease at an interagency team meeting and to make their participation a positive experience. In several Florida communities, a parent volunteer who has previously attended interagency meetings contacts the parents prior to a scheduled meeting. The volunteer briefs the parents on the interagency process, explains what is expected of them, and answers questions. Other strategies involve sending written materials to parents prior to interagency team meetings and using the case manager to brief and prepare the parents. Involvement of parents in the interagency service planning process is critical for the development and implementation of a successful individualized care plan, although team members may show some initial resistance. In most instances, initial anxiety and resistance to parental involvement is reduced once individuals have participated in a few meetings involving parents.

In order to enhance the efficiency of the service planning process, some communities have developed specific formats or time frames to guide the activities of the interagency team. In Leon County, Florida, for example, approximately 20 minutes are devoted to presentations from the primary caseworker, staff, and family; 40 minutes are then devoted to identifying key issues and developing an individualized interagency plan (Stroul et al., 1992). In Stark County, Ohio, the Creative Community Options team outlines the history, prepares a "people map," and identifies strengths and problems, what works, what does not work, what the child needs, and options to meet needs (Stroul et al., 1992). Without some structure, a service planning meeting may become a lengthy and less productive process. All client and family information discussed or distributed at interagency team meetings is considered confidential. Typically, a single release form is used to obtain the consent of the parents for the exchange of information among the specific agencies involved on the interagency team.

Using Case Management/Care Coordination

Weil and Karls (1985) define case management as a set of logical steps and a process of interaction within a service network that assure that a client receives an array of services in a supportive, effective, efficient, and cost-effective manner. The role of case managers/care coordinators includes a range of functions (planning, accessing, linking, advocating, monitoring, supporting, coordinating, brokering, educating, and others) that serve to integrate and maintain a network of services and supports for each child and family. An individualized service approach requires a much more proactive and creative care coordination role than may be associated with a typical case manager. In fact, a more intensive form of case management, performed by highly skilled case managers, is required based on the challenges presented by the youngsters served and the complexity and uniqueness of their intervention plans. In addition, the individualized care approach needs one individual to function as the coordinator of the interagency service planning/treatment team; that individual most frequently is the case manager.

In describing therapeutic case management in Vermont, Santarcangelo (1990) indicated that the therapeutic case manager carries out all the usual functions of a case manager and some additional functions, most notably involving brainstorming with the treatment team to develop interventions and creative strategies to overcome obstacles and designing services when none are available through existing programs. These functions are essential for providing individualized services. Furthermore, case managers within the individualized care approach do provide high levels of support for the child and family as well as crisis intervention.

Case management for individualized care requires small caseloads because of the complexity of functions the case manager must perform. Vermont has reported that different phases of therapeutic case management require different levels of services as the child and family move through the process. The initial intake and treatment planning phases are usually the most intensive; services then generally stabilize somewhat as services and support are wrapped around the child and family in response to their needs. After a maintenance phase, the child and family finally make the transition into an inactive status. Santarcangelo (1990) reports that passage through these phases normally takes at least 2–3 years. The size of the caseload for therapeutic case managers would therefore depend on how many children were in the intensive phases and could range from a caseload of 5 to no more than 12 children and their families.

Providing Individualized Services

Because individualized services are based on the specific needs of the child and family, it follows that the process begins with an assessment and treatment planning phase. Rather than seeking a "slot" for the child in any available program, the approach involves assessing the strengths and needs of the child and family and building a program of services around them. The interagency service planning/treatment team, with leadership provided by the case manager, typically plays a central role in the assessment and planning process. Review of existing records, evaluations, and history are important sources of information for the assessment, as is information provided by the parents, child, professionals, and other key persons in the child's life.

Burchard and Clarke (1990) discuss the ecological nature of the assessment conducted for the purposes of providing individualized care. Instead of the traditional emphasis on personality characteristics and child deficits, they contend that "individualized care requires a shift to a more comprehensive, multilevel approach to assessment which examines the social ecology of behavior and attempts to understand youngsters by assessing the total environment in which they function" (p. 52). Burchard and Clarke propose four levels of assessment: analysis of the child and family's strengths; assessment of the broader social environment in which the child and family live; assessment of service needs and available community resources; and assessment, on an ongoing basis, of progress and needs. According to their framework, assessment represents a means to formulate and design specific, individualized treatment plans that better meet the needs of the child and family.

As noted, assessment and planning for individualized services use a strengths-based orientation that carefully considers and draws on the assets of the child and family as well as their needs. Reframing how the child and family are viewed may be helpful when identifying family strengths. For example, a child who is hyperactive may also be thought of as having a high energy level or an exuberant, outgoing personality, characteristics that may be valued more in the adult work world than they are in the classroom. Other examples of family strengths include a mother who visits her child regularly in each of his or her placements, a youth who is "street smart," a child who achieves a successful placement in a special education class, a child's budding skills in areas ranging from cooking to computers, and grandparents or other relatives who are interested in helping the family.

According to VanDenBerg (1993), needs should be defined in positive terms and might include a child's needs to express him- or herself in an art form or the need to continue to excel in school, as well as the need for remedial action, such as the parent's need to find employment or the child's need to stop hurting other children by learning appropriate interaction skills. The assessment and planning process for individualized care involves examining needs across all life domains. These include residential (a place to live); family or surrogate family; social (friends and contact with other people); educational and/or vocational; medical; psychological/emotional; legal (especially for children with juvenile justice needs); safety (the need to be safe); and other specific life domain areas, such as cultural/ethnic needs or community needs. VanDenBerg emphasizes that, in an individualized approach, the first question asked is, "What does this youth need so that he or she can get better?" The team then proceeds to construct a plan based on the identification of strengths and needs in all life domains. An essential aspect of the assessment and planning process is to ascertain the child's and family's own perspectives about their needs and what services and support they desire (Tannen, 1991). Friedman (1988) summarized the importance of a strengths-based, ecological assessment when he stated that only a thorough assessment—including ecologically oriented information that focuses not only on the child's problems but on strengths and interests—will enable a decision-making team to move away from a "placement" orientation and toward a "planning" orientation and to develop an individualized intervention plan.

Developing an individualized service plan involves creative thinking from the case manager and interagency team in order to address identified needs. Individualized services typically draw on all of the resources that the community may offer—including services that may exist within the community's system of care as well as a limitless range of creative, nontraditional approaches that may be designed to address specific needs. As stated by MacFarquhar and Dowrick (1993), the individualized assistance approach builds services around the needs of each child and family, attempting to tailor services to each youngster and adding new or innovative services where necessary. The term "wraparound services" is derived from the notion of surrounding the child and family with a full network of services and supports, in accordance with their wishes. Tannen (1991) emphasized that one of the major benefits of individualized services is that they do not require youngsters to conform to established institutional or programmatic rules, but rather respond to the changing needs and growth of the child.

The interagency team may determine that a particular program (such as home-based services, day treatment, or therapeutic foster care) is available in the community and can be used to address some of the identified needs for the child and family. Beyond the existing services within the system of care, the team may identify needs for which less traditional solutions are required. Flexible funds, with few if any categorical restrictions, may be used to provide wraparound services, which typically are not provided by community agencies. For example, a behavior aide may be hired to assist at home and school to prevent the out-of-home placement of the child. A family's utility bill may be paid so that the family can be kept intact; a car may be repaired so that the mother can continue to work and get her child to needed resources. Wraparound services and supports have been provided in a wide range of areas, including (Zeigler-Dendy, 1992)

- *Family support and sustenance:* providing emergency assistance for the child, paying for utilities, paying for repair of a car engine, paying for a telephone, paying for participation in Weight Watchers, and so on
- *Therapeutic services:* providing individual/family/group counseling, substance abuse services, a bilingual therapist, a therapist of color, respite care in or out of home, and so on
- *School-related services:* providing school consultation or an academic coach, utilizing behavioral aides or classroom companions at school,

paying for school insurance for a classroom companion, buying a chemistry set for Christmas, and so on

- *Medical services:* providing a needed medical evaluation, providing medical or dental care, paying for a tatoo removal, teaching sex education, teaching birth control, teaching medication management, and so on
- *Crisis services:* hiring a family member or friend to provide crisis support, utilizing a behavior aide in the child's home or therapeutic foster home, teaching crisis management skills, and so on
- *Independent living services:* helping to locate and rent an apartment, assisting a youngster to obtain Supplemental Security Income, hiring a professional roommate/mentor, providing a weekly allowance, teaching money management and budgeting, providing driving lessons, teaching meal preparation, teaching parenting skills, teaching housekeeping skills, purchasing a mobile home for a fire setter and providing 24 hour staff, and so on
- *Interpersonal and recreational skill development:* hiring a friend or finding a "big brother", teaching social skills and problem-solving skills; purchasing a membership in an exercise gym, a YMCA membership, horseback riding lessons, art or music lessons, summer camp registration, class trip, fishing license, bicycle, and so on
- *Vocational services:* providing job training, teaching good work skills, providing a job coach, finding an apprenticeship, providing a mentor at the apprenticeship or other program, paying someone to hire the youth for a job, conducting a vocational skills assessment, and so on
- *Additional reinforcers:* purchasing reinforcers, including items such as a radio, makeup, clothing, punching bag, skateboard, trips, dates or activities, photographs for teen magazine, and so on

Tannen (1991) warned that setbacks and crises are likely to occur during the course of implementing an individualized care plan. To prepare for this eventuality, the plan must include agreed-on approaches for handling crises. The inherent flexibility of individualized service approaches allows support to youngsters and caregivers to be quickly increased or decreased in response to changing needs. For example, an aide may be brought into the home or classroom during a crisis or particularly difficult period. Furthermore, based on the underlying value of unconditional care, individualized services are provided to children and families for as long as they are needed, regardless of youngsters' behavior or the challenges and complexities presented by their needs.

Financing Individualized Services

The availability of flexible funds to implement imaginative and resourceful intervention plans is a critical element of individualized care. Although expenditures of flexible funds may appear unusual, it is this ability that allows a package of services and supports to be tailored to the specific needs of the child and family. Olson et al. (1991) stressed that funding that is not preallocated to existing component services allows teams the freedom to create and implement a tailored program that can be responsive to the unique and changing needs of the child.

Although creating flexible funding mechanisms is particularly challenging, Tannen (1991) emphasized that, in order to provide creative, individualized services, expenditures cannot be expected to fit into current agency line item categories. In fact, categorical funding restrictions present a major barrier to the delivery of individualized services. Most state and federal funds have categorical restrictions that limit the ways in which the funds may be spent. For example, some state legislatures or agencies establish categorical funding streams that may be spent only on specific types of services, such as residential treatment; funds cannot be spent on services to prevent removing a child from his or her home. Flexible funds, with few if any categorical restrictions, are available in a limited (but steadily increasing) number of states and communities.

Several states have initiated policy changes at the state level that have eliminated some categorical funding restrictions and paved the way for the creation of flexible funds for individualized care. In West Virginia, for example, child welfare officials eliminated categorical funding restrictions by developing a policy that allows expenditure of residential funds for the development of services in the local community (C. Zeigler-Dendy, personal communication, 1992). If a child could be placed in a residential treatment facility at a cost of $75,000, the local interagency committee can spend up to that amount for delivery of individualized services in the local community. In Iowa, an initiative to decategorize the funding for services to youngsters and families in order to provide more individualized and responsive care has been implemented in four counties (Lourie, 1994). These types of policy changes represent clear shifts in incentives for local areas to serve youngsters within the community and to use individualized service approaches.

In addition to redirecting funds from residential or out-of-state care to community-based, individualized care, a number of states and communities are creating pools of blended funds from the various child-serving agencies as a mechanism to provide flexible funding. A legal agreement signed by the child-serving agencies in Stark County, Ohio, blends resources from multiple agencies that are then used to fund individualized service plans for multineed youngsters and their families (Stroul et al., 1992).

In some states and communities, legislators and administrators remain suspicious of flexible funding approaches. The fear that funds will be squandered and personnel will not be held accountable forms the basis for this attitude. Accountability mechanisms built into flexible funding procedures help to alleviate these concerns.

Although flexible funds have been called the "linchpin" of individualized care, many states have developed a wide array of Medicaid-billable services that allow for the provision of innovative and nontraditional services and supports. Recent revisions to the Medicaid Early Periodic Screening, Diagnosis, and Treatment (EPSDT) program offer one mechanism for expanding services to children with serious emotional problems, allowing for Medicaid reimbursement of all service needs identified during EPSDT screening (Koyanagi & Brodie, 1994).

Research on the cost-effectiveness of individualized services is needed. Reports from various states and communities indicate that, apparently, intensive, individualized services are less costly than institutional alternatives. Dowrick (1988) reported that the costs of out-of-state placements for youngsters in the Alaska Youth Initiative averaged $72,000 per year; the same children were cared for in state at an average cost of $47,000 per year. Burchard and Clarke (1990) stated that, in addition to the savings, it is believed that better services are being provided through the initiative. They contend that the cost-effectiveness of individualized care in the Alaska Youth Initiative, and other situations in which children are returned from residential placements, is demonstrated by using each child as his or her own control and showing that youngsters display good adjustment through less costly and less restrictive services. They acknowledge, however, that it is more difficult to demonstrate cost-effectiveness in situations in which individualized care is used to prevent residential treatment placement rather than to return youngsters from placements. In many cases, youngsters who have not as yet been placed in residential treatment are receiving few services prior to the initiation of individualized care, and, as a result, costs increase as individualized service plans are implemented. Comparison groups are needed to demonstrate cost-effectiveness across broader client populations. Although sufficient research to substantiate cost-effectiveness has not yet been completed, it appears that the individualized care approach potentially can effectively serve some of the most difficult-to-serve youngsters at costs that compare favorably to most residential treatment or hospital settings.

THE FUTURE OF INDIVIDUALIZED SERVICES IN SYSTEMS OF CARE

The compatibility of individualized services with the state-of-the-art concept and philosophy of a system of care is apparent in two major trends. First, many states and communities have incorporated individualized service approaches into their systems of care, particularly for the most difficult-to-serve, at-risk youngsters. These approaches, although reserved for a relatively small percentage of the target population, are receiving increasing resources and attention. They are being used to return youngsters from out-of-state and in-state residential placements as well as to prevent such placements; evidence regarding the cost-effectiveness of individualized care approaches in meeting these goals is mounting.

Second, the principles and processes that characterize individualized services are increasingly being applied to service programs or "components" within systems of care. For example, VanDenBerg (1989) describes the modification of "categorical" programs in Fairbanks, Alaska, to allow for the provision of unconditional care and wraparound services. As a result of added flexible funds and some program modifications, existing service programs in Fairbanks have been able to provide individualized services and reduce their rate of referral for inpatient hospitalization to the lowest in the state. Another example of a component program that has a history of individualizing service interventions is home-based services. Home-based service programs, both short- and long-term models, provide highly flexible interventions that are tailored creatively to the needs of each client family. Most home-based programs are committed to doing whatever it takes to assist a child and family, and many have flexible funds that can be used to purchase nontraditional services and supports (Stroul, 1988). Through the integration of individualized services principles and processes, the effectiveness of service programs is enhanced. Thus, the concept of individualized care, with its values and processes, is rapidly spreading throughout modern systems of care both in its "pure form" and as an enhancement or enrichment of existing component programs.

It is evident that individualized services and systems of care are mutually dependent at both conceptual and practical levels. Burchard and Clarke (1990) noted that a complete system of care continues to be necessary to provide component services, but that an individualized approach can greatly enhance the system's cost-effectiveness. Similarly, Duchnowski and Friedman (1990) emphasized that modern systems of care should incorporate the philosophy and process of individualized services. They stated that, within the context of a comprehensive system of care, the flexibility and creativity to ensure that an individualized treatment program is developed for each youth and his or her family are now considered imperative.

The ultimate goal for systems of care is that all interventions, in whatever organizational or programmatic form, be guided by the concept and values of individualized services. The process of assessing needs in an ecological, holistic manner, tailoring services to meet specific needs, involving families, using interagency strategies, and providing unconditional care should not be limited to the services provided to the most complex and challenging youngsters. Rather, this approach should permeate the entire system of care in a community—a goal that is consistent with, and established by, the current system of care philosophy.

The high level of interest and rapid growth in individualized services is apparent in the results of the MacFarquhar and Dowrick survey (1993); more than half of the programs studied were initiated within the past 3 years, revealing a significant trend toward increasing this type of approach nationally. One of the most difficult challenges to be faced by systems of care as they evolve throughout the 1990s may well be to achieve a viable balance between programmatic service components and individualized care approaches. Burchard and Clarke (1990) suggest that the future of individualized care will be determined by further research and development. However, they note that the approaches developed to date have been encouraging and suggest vast potential to improve services and systems of care for troubled children and their families.

REFERENCES

Alaska Department of Health and Social Services. (1989). *Status report: Alaska Youth Initiative.* Juneau: Alaska Department of Health and Social Services, Division of Mental Health and Developmental Disabilities.

Alaska Department of Health and Social Services. (1990). *Answers from AYI: Evidence of successfulness.* Juneau: Alaska Department of Health and Social Services, Division of Mental Health and Developmental Disabilities.

Alaska Department of Health and Social Services. (1991). *Annual report on the Alaska Youth Initiative.* Juneau: Alaska Department of Health and Social Services, Division of Mental Health and Developmental Disabilities.

Behar, L. (1985). Changing patterns of state responsibility: A case study of North Carolina. *Journal of Clinical Child Psychology, 14*(3), 188–195.

Behar, L. (1986, May-June). A state model for child mental health services: The North Carolina experience. *Children Today,* pp. 16–21.

Burchard, J.D. (1988). *Project Wraparound: Training clinical psychologists through a revised service delivery system for severely emotionally disturbed children and adolescents.* Burlington: University of Vermont, Department of Psychology.

Burchard, J.D., & Clarke, R.T. (1990). The role of individualized care in a service delivery system for children and adolescents with severely maladjusted behavior. *Journal of Mental Health Administration, 17,* 48–60.

Close to home: Community-based mental health for children, 102nd Congress, 1st Sess. 48–87 (1991; April 29) (testimony of Lenore Behar before the House Select Committee on Children, Youth, and Families).

Cross, T., Bazron, B.J., Dennis, K.W., & Isaacs, M.R. (1989). *Towards a culturally competent system of care: Vol. I. A monograph on effective services for minority children who are severely emotionally disturbed.* Washington, DC: Georgetown University Child Delevopment Center, National Technical Assistance Center for Children's Mental Health.

DeCarolis, G. (1992). *New directions: Implementing a comprehensive community-based system of care for Vermont's children, adolescents and their families. Final phase proposal submitted to the Robert Wood Johnson Foundation.* Waterbury: Vermont Department of Mental Health and Mental Retardation.

Dennis, K. (1992, April). Presentation at the First National WrapAround Conference, Pittsburgh, PA.

Dowrick, P.W. (1988). Alaska youth initiative. In P. Greenbaum, R. Friedman, A. Duchnowski, K. Kutash, & S. Silver (Eds.), *Children's mental health services and policy: Building a research base—Conference proceedings* (pp. 59–61). Tampa: University of South Florida, Florida Mental Health Institute, Research and Training Center for Children's Mental Health.

Duchnowski, A., & Friedman, R.M. (1990). Children's mental health: Challenges for the nineties. *Journal of Mental Health Administration, 17*(1), 3–12.

Friedman, R.M. (1988). Program update: Individualizing services. *Update—Improving Services for Emotionally Disturbed Children, 3,* 10–12 (Tampa: University of South Florida, Florida Mental Health Institute, Research and Training Center for Children's Mental Health).

International Initiative on the Development, Training, and Evaluation of WrapAround Services. (1992). *Definition of wraparound.* Pittsburgh: The Pressley Ridge Schools, Center for Research and Public Policy.

Isaacs, M.R., & Benjamin, M.P. (1991). *Towards a culturally competent system of care: Vol. II. Programs which utilize culturally competent principles.* Washington, DC: Georgetown University Child Development Center. National Technical Assistance Center for Children's Mental Health.

Katz-Leavy, J., Lourie, I., Stroul, B., & Zeigler-Dendy, C. (1992). *Individualized services in a system of care.* Washington, DC: Georgetown University Child Development Center, National Technical Assistance Center for Children's Mental Health.

Koyanagi, C., & Brodie J.R. (1994). *Making Medicaid work to fund intensive community services for children with serious emotional disturbances.* Washington, DC: Bazelon Center for Mental Health Law.

Lourie, I. (1994). *Principles of local system development for children, adolescents and their families.* Chicago: Kaleidoscope.

MacFarquhar, K.W., & Dowrick, P.W. (1993). Individualizing services for seriously emotionally disturbed youth: A nationwide survey. *Administration and Policy in Mental Health, 20*(3), 165–174.

Olson, D.G., Whitbeck, J., & Robinson, R. (1991). *The Washington experience: Research on community efforts to provide individualized tailored care.* Paper presented at "A System of Care for Children's Mental Health: Expanding the Research Base," Tampa, FL.

Santarcangelo, S. (1990). *Vermont's plan for statewide implementation of therapeutic case management for children and adolescents who have an emotional disturbance and their families.* Waterbury: Vermont Department of Mental Health and Mental Retardation.

Stroul, B.A. (1988). *Series on community-based services for children and adolescents who are severely emotionally disturbed: Vol. I. Home-based services.* Washington, DC: Georgetown University Child Development Center, National Technical Assistance Center for Children's Mental Health.

Stroul, B.A., & Friedman, R.M. (1986). *A system of care for children and adolescents with severe emotional disturbances* (rev. ed.). Washington, DC: Georgetown University Child Development Center, National Technical Assistance Center for Children's Mental Health.

Stroul, B., Lourie, I., Goldman, S., & Katz-Leavy, J. (1992). *Profiles of local systems of care for children and adolescents with severe emotional disturbances.* Washington, DC: Georgetown University Child Development Center, National Technical Assistance Center for Children's Mental Health.

Tannen, N. (1991). *Therapeutic case management: Guidelines for implementing an individualized care plan for children and adolescents with a severe emotional disturbance.* Waterbury: Vermont Department of Mental Health and Mental Retardation.

VanDenBerg, J. (1989). *Alaska Youth Initiative: Program background.* Juneau: Alaska Department of Health and Social Services, Division of Mental Health and Developmental Disabilities.

VanDenBerg, J. (1991). *Alaska Youth Initiative.* Juneau: Alaska Department of Health and Social Services, Division of Mental Health and Developmental Disabilities.

VanDenBerg, J. (1993). Integration of individualized services into the system of care for children and adolescents with emotional disabilities. *Administration and Policy in Mental Health, 20*(4), 247–258.

Weil, M., & Karls, J.M. (1985). *Case management in human service practice.* San Francisco: Jossey-Bass.

Young, T.M. (1987). Therapeutic case advocacy: A summary; Case management or care management. *Focal Point, 1,* 1–4.

Zeigler-Dendy, C. (1992). *Wraparound services.* Unpublished training material.

CHAPTER 24

Community-Based Service Approaches

Home-Based Services and Therapeutic Foster Care

Beth A. Stroul and Sybil K. Goldman

One of the significant changes in service delivery that has occurred since the 1980s is the recognition of the importance of an array of services for children and adolescents with serious emotional, behavioral, and mental disorders to meet the individual needs of these children and their families. Traditionally, this population of children, if they received services at all, received outpatient therapy in clinic and office settings or received treatment in inpatient hospitals or residential treatment centers. Services in these settings are critical components of a system of care for children. In the 1980s and 1990s, however, there has been a rapid development of new service modalities that are based on a number of key concepts: Children are best served in their own homes and with their families; if children cannot remain with their families for either brief or in some cases longer time periods, they need other family-like settings; children with serious emotional disorders need intensive treatment; and services provided in alternative settings can be more cost effective. Two of the service approaches that are based on these premises and have been widely developed are home-based services and therapeutic foster care.

To gain a better understanding of these service approaches, the National Technical Assistance Center for Children's Mental Health of the Georgetown University Child Development Center undertook a descriptive study of home-based services and therapeutic foster care (Goldman, 1988; Stroul, 1988, 1989). This study included several components: a survey of over 650 key organizations and individuals to identify programs across the country; a questionnaire sent to approximately 200 programs to gather more detailed information, with 80 programs in 36 states responding; site visits to a limited number of programs; and a literature review. A synthesis of this information provides the basis for this overview and description of each of these service modalities.

HOME-BASED SERVICES

Overview and Major Characteristics

Home-based services provide intensive counseling, support, and case management services on an outreach basis to children and families in their homes. These services have been given multiple designations, including in-home services, family-based services, intensive family services, and family preservation services. The Homebuilders Program in Tacoma, Washington, has been the prototype for many in-home programs that are crisis oriented and directed at preventing out-of-home placements. Other models work with families over an extensive period of time. Although there are variations among program characteristics, most home-based services represent an intensive method of service delivery that focuses on families rather than on individuals and is directed at strengthening families and preventing family dissolution (Hutchinson, Lloyd, Landsman, Nelson, & Bryce, 1983). The tenet of home-based services is that the family is most important to a child's well-being and that families should be supported and maintained whenever possible. Most home-based service programs strive to achieve three primary goals: 1) to preserve the integrity of the family and prevent unnecessary out-of-home placement, 2) to link the child and family with appropriate agencies and individuals to create an ongoing community support system, and 3) to strengthen the family's coping skills and capacity to function effectively in the community. In addition to intervening to prevent out-of-home placement, many home-based programs are used to assist children already in placement to reunify and reintegrate with their families. Home-based services can provide important supports to children who have been in residential treatment or psychiatric inpatient settings to assist with the adjustment period following their return home.

Child welfare agencies, mental health centers, hospitals, residential treatment centers, juvenile justice agencies, and other human services organizations all may be involved in providing home-based services. Despite the different auspices and organizational contexts, most home-based programs share similar characteristics. Based on the literature (Edna McConnell Clark Foundation, 1985; Family Empowerment Resource Network, 1987; Ginsberg, 1986; Kaplan, 1986; Lloyd & Bryce, 1984; and others) and the findings of this study, the following constitute the major features of home-based services:

- The intervention is delivered primarily in the family's home.
- Home-based services have a family focus, and the family unit is viewed as the client.

- The services have an ecological perspective and involve working with the community system to access and coordinate needed services and supports.
- Home-based service programs are committed to family preservation and reunification unless there is clear evidence that these are not in the best interest of the child.
- The hours of service delivery are flexible in order to meet the needs of families, and 24-hour crisis intervention is provided.
- The intervention is multifaceted and includes counseling and skill training as well as helping members of the family obtain and coordinate necessary services, resources, and supports.
- Services are offered along a continuum of intensity and duration based on the goals of the program and the needs of the family.
- Staff have small caseloads to permit them to work actively and intensively with each family.
- The relationship between the home-based worker and the family is uniquely close, intense, and personal.
- The programs are committed to empowering families, instilling hope, and helping families to set and achieve their own goals and priorities.

Variations

Although there are many commonalities across home-based interventions, there are also variations and some significant differences. The key variables among home-based service programs are intensity and duration. A distinguishing characteristic is whether a program is involved with a family for a short-term period of 4–6 weeks or longer term, up to a year or more.

Some home-based programs subscribe to the short-term, crisis intervention model of service provision. The goals of the crisis-oriented programs are to stabilize the family situation and reduce the risk of out-of-home placement, teach the family new coping skills, and connect the family with appropriate community resources for ongoing service needs. The short-term programs tend to provide intensive services to families (i.e., 10–20 or more hours per week for a 4- to 6-week period, often the equivalent of 2 years of traditional outpatient counseling). Because of the highly intensive nature of these services, workers carry extremely small caseloads, usually no more than two to three families at one time.

Short-term home-based programs are based on theories of time-limited crisis intervention. According to this intervention approach, in times of crisis individuals and families are particularly motivated to change, and home-based workers can capitalize on the family's increased willingness to accept help (Caplan, 1964). Time limits can be used constructively to further increase motivation. The pressure of the limited treatment time frame often can induce changes more quickly than they would occur otherwise. From the outset, families are made aware that services will be limited to a specified time period. Short-term programs are not intended to solve all of the family's problems. Generally, this model targets three to four selected goals as immediate priorities and expects the family to continue working on problems when the intervention is completed, with assistance from other community supports and resources.

Short-term interventions enable programs to serve a greater number of families over time and to control costs. Many home-based programs have been developed to serve more families in crisis and prevent out-of-home placements at less cost than residential or hospital options. Some advocates of time-limited models express concern that long-term interventions will not achieve the same cost savings.

Other home-based service programs stay involved with families for a much longer period than 4–6 weeks. Some long-term programs report an average duration of 9–18 months; others may remain involved with families for 3 years or more. The rationale for longer-term home-based services is that

- Families need consistency and support and can benefit from one person with whom they can form a strong relationship over time.
- It takes time to build trust and relationships with families, particularly those with difficult, longstanding problems who have been involved with multiple agencies and workers.
- In some cases, long-term treatment is required because of the family's needs. It may be counterproductive to terminate services or shift to another worker when an immediate crisis is alleviated, if a relationship has formed and the family is engaged in working on issues.

Thus, longer-term home-based programs extend the focus and goals beyond crisis intervention. They work with families over time to strengthen those families, build relationships, cope with problems, and address the needs of the children and adults within those families. Rather than refer families to other programs for ongoing assistance, these programs provide continuous support to families. The capacity to provide longer-term home-based assistance seems to be particularly important for those families for whom traditional service approaches do not work and in geographic areas where there is a lack of services and resources to provide ongoing treatment and support.

Short-term crisis intervention approaches may be particularly effective in communities with relatively comprehensive systems of care that can provide a range of follow-up resources for ongoing services. If a community has limited services, then brief, time-limited approaches may be insufficient to meet the needs of many families who have children with emotional disorders. Additional experience and research may be needed to determine the optimal length of home-based interventions or the optimal mix of intensity and duration for particular families. Currently, programs tend to base their decisions about the duration and intensity of services on their own programmatic focus and the requirements of their funding sources. Those decisions depend on whether programs define themselves as a crisis intervention service or a longer-term intervention alternative to more traditional mental health service approaches.

Services

Referrals to home-based service programs generally originate from a variety of child-serving agencies. In most cases, families are referred when a child is about to be removed from the home or is at high risk for out-of-home placement. The intervention or service delivery process for home-based programs can be divided into three phases: 1) engagement, assessment, and planning; 2) the actual interventions of counseling, skill building, and the brokering and coordinating of resources; and 3) termination and follow-up. The assessment and planning process involves clarifying issues of concern to the family, prioritizing these issues in order to focus the service delivery process, and assessing family strengths. Home-based programs do not attempt to solve all of a family's problems but rather try to set limited and specific goals that can be achieved within the time frame for service delivery. In addition, service delivery is guided by the two principles of "starting where the family is at" and emphasizing the achievement of small changes so that families can experience success.

Interventions are multifaceted. Counseling of various types is a major aspect of most home-based service programs, with a wide variety of techniques used, including structured exercises, family therapy, behavior therapy, and approaches to deal with depression, anxiety, and anger (Lloyd & Bryce, 1984). Skill teaching represents another essential element of home-based interventions. Programs work with families to improve a range of skills related to parenting and child management, communication and relationship-building, anger management and conflict resolution, problem solving, household management, assertiveness, and self advocacy. A third major aspect of service delivery is assisting families with obtaining needed resources and services from other agencies and systems and helping families link with informal or natural support systems in the community. The home-based worker often becomes the focal point for coordination because of the intense relationship with the family and the holistic approach to service delivery. In addition to these three major categories of interventions, some home-based services offer other services, such as respite care, liaison with the school, health services, and recreational activities. Flexible funds also enable programs to provide specialized services to meet the unique needs of families and individual family members.

Planning for termination of home-based services commonly begins when the case is opened, and termination occurs when the family has met the primary treatment goals and is linked with other service supports. In many of the programs of longer duration, termination is a gradual weaning process. As the family and child make progress, the worker naturally may visit less frequently. Many home-based programs remain a resource for the family following the termination of services. One of the most challenging issues for home-based programs is linking families with appropriate follow-up resources and services. Many programs struggle to find effective ways to support and monitor families following the termination of services without compromising current caseloads.

Staffing

Line staff are the most important resource for home-based programs, and the quality of staff is a major factor in a program's success. For that reason, many special considerations are involved in the selection, training, and support of home-based workers. The job of a home-based worker is far more demanding and stressful than traditional office-based counseling (Haapala & Kinney, 1979). Workers must be able to function well in unstructured, unpredictable, and potentially dangerous situations. They must be willing to work evenings, weekends, and holidays and must be highly flexible in order to respond to crisis situations that may arise at any time of day or night. They must be willing to do "hands-on" work with families and fulfill case management functions in addition to clinical work. Not surprisingly, the flexibility and variability that may make home-based work stressful and difficult for many persons are the very characteristics that make this type of work attractive to others.

One variable among home-based programs is whether the staff work individually with families or in teams. Many programs use two-person teams to deliver services to families based on the following advantages: Team members provide mutual support and assistance to each other in the context of demanding, unpredictable, and stressful work; professional objectivity is strengthened; service continuity and emergency coverage are enhanced; and the safety of workers is increased, particularly in inner city neighborhoods (Lloyd & Bryce, 1984). Although there are sound bases for using a team approach, there are also a number of reasons why programs opt for using individual workers with each family. Some home-based programs have found that the teams reduce the intimacy of the worker-family relationship. Logistical problems related to coordinating schedules and responsibilities may limit the workers' availability to families and responsiveness to needs. Also, for many programs, using two workers is not economically feasible.

Costs

There appears to be a wide range in the reported costs of home-based services. This variability appears to be due to a number of factors, including disparate service intensity and duration among programs, differences in staffing patterns, and salary differentials (Hutchinson et al., 1983). The difficulty in determining and comparing costs is also attributable to the different accounting methodologies and time frames used by programs. Hutchinson et al. report that the cost of home-based services ranges from $1,000 to $10,829 per family across all types of programs. Despite this disparity, two general conclusions can be made regarding the cost of home-based services: 1) the reported costs are incurred in serving an entire family rather than supporting one child in an out-of-home placement, and 2) the cost per average episode of out-of-home placement in any setting is far higher than the cost per average episode of home-based services.

Effectiveness and Evaluation Results

To date, the most frequently used measure of effectiveness of home-based services has been the prevention of out-of-home placements. Based on this indicator, programs have been reporting success rates of between 70% and 90% (Bryce & Lloyd, 1982; Hinckley & Ellis, 1985). Most programs are able to report the percentage of at-risk children remaining in their homes at the time that the case is closed. Some programs also obtain follow-up data at various intervals to determine whether the child is still in the home at 3 months, 6 months, or 1 year posttermination. Success rates tend to fall slightly at follow-up times but consistently remain over 60%.

It should be noted that the validity of these success rates has been questioned because of methodological shortcomings in much of the evaluation research (M. Jones, 1985; Tavantzis, Travantzis, Brown, & Rohrbaugh, 1986). First, as noted, figures on avoiding placement usually pertain only to the period during which services were provided, not to successive intervals posttermination. Second, few evaluations have included control families with comparable characteristics and problems for whom home-based services were not provided. Those studies that have employed controlled or comparison conditions support the effectiveness of home-based interventions but suggest more modest results (AuClaire & Schwartz, 1986, 1987; Bath & Haapala, 1994; Feldman, 1991; Fraser, Pecora, & Haapala, 1991; Jones, 1985; Schuerman, Rzepnicki, Littell, & Chak, 1993; Schwartz, AuClaire, & Harris, 1991; Wood, Barton, & Schroeder, 1988; Yuan, McDonald, Wheeler, Struckman-Johnson, & Rivest, 1990). Some of the studies found statistical differences between treatment and comparison groups in terms of placement rates at follow-up, as well as other advantages, including shorter, less restrictive placements; greater changes on standardized child and family adjustment measures; and lower costs. Three large state-initiated experimental studies found no differences in placement rates between experimental and control groups, but questions have been raised about the validity of these studies (Bath & Haapala, 1994). Also, some recent studies indicate that different client groups (e.g., age groups or neglect versus delinquency cases) have quite different outcomes resulting from home-based interventions (Bath & Haapala, 1994).

Despite methodological concerns, most researchers conclude that home-based services that include intensive counseling and concrete services can be effective in preventing, delaying, or reducing the length of placement and in enhancing the functioning of parents and children. Greater availability of these services will enable many troubled children to remain with their families and will ensure that residential treatment is more appropriately used. Data indicate that home-based services (brief, midrange, and long-term varieties) are successful with many families, and there is ample evidence to justify the use of home-based services as part of a comprehensive system of care.

Funding Opportunities

Many of the early home-based service programs were funded through foundation initiatives such as the efforts of the Edna McConnell Clark Foundation, but in the last decade the funding opportunities for home-based services have expanded dramatically. Many states and communities have redeployed dollars and engaged in refinancing strategies to capture federal revenues and shift resources to community-based services. As a result, a variety of federal and state funding streams are supporting home-based services. The Adoption Assistance and Child Welfare Act of 1980 (PL 96-272; Title IV-B) has played a major role in the development of home-based services by creating financial and other incentives for state efforts to prevent out-of-home placements and to ensure permanency for children. In 1993, Congress passed the Family Preservation and Support Services provisions of the Omnibus Budget Reconciliation Act, which strengthens the legislative mandate for family preservation and provides new federal dollars for preventive services and services to families at risk or in crisis as part of a comprehensive system of care. The Aid to Families with Dependent Children (AFDC) Emergency Assistance Program is another federal entitlement program that states have tapped into to support home-based services. Medicaid, through a variety of options, is increasingly being used as a funding source to reimburse for home-based services. As businesses and insurers are examining more cost-effective ways to provide treatment to children with emotional and behavioral disorders, more health insurance policies, particularly through managed care arrangements, are covering home-based service interventions.

THERAPEUTIC FOSTER CARE

Overview and Major Characteristics

Therapeutic foster care is considered the least restrictive option among the range of residential services for children and adolescents with serious emotional disturbances. Therapeutic foster care can be defined as a service that provides treatment for troubled children within the private homes of families with special training. This approach creates a therapeutic environment in the context of a nurturing family home by providing specialized treatment interventions in a home-based setting.

The recent proliferation of therapeutic foster care programs with a wide variety of characteristics and labels has made it difficult to reach agreement on a definition and on what therapeutic foster care should be called. Different labels include foster family-based treatment, specialized foster care, individualized residential treatment, treatment foster care, and professional foster care. Although there may be different terminology and definitions, there is strong agreement on the importance of distinguishing therapeutic foster care from traditional or regular foster care.

The primary function of regular foster care is to provide a substitute family environment for dependent children, whereas the primary function of therapeutic foster care is to provide a treatment environment for troubled children. This distinction is particularly important for policy makers and legislators to understand because they must pay more for therapeutic foster care than regular foster care services. The distinctions between the two are substantial and pertain to the types of persons recruited as parents, the payments they receive, the preparation required for the parenting role, and the assistance received in performing the parenting role (Cox & Cox, 1989). Foster parents for therapeutic foster care, often called treatment parents, are carefully selected based on their skills and motivation to handle the difficult challenges presented by children with serious disturbances. Thus, the payments to treatment parents are significantly higher than payments to regular foster parents to compensate for the enormous skill and commitment involved in treatment parenting. Extensive training and supervision are provided to support and equip treatment parents with the needed coping skills and intervention techniques. With therapeutic foster care, a professional staff person is in frequent contact with the treatment family, providing technical advice, support, encouragement, and crisis assistance for the treatment family and child. These differences underscore the basic premise that therapeutic foster care is designed to conduct therapeutic intervention programs with clearly stated intervention goals within the home environment of the foster family, not simply to provide substitute care and nurturance (Bryant & Snodgrass, 1989; Snodgrass & Campbell, 1981). It is the *treatment* aspect of therapeutic foster care that is its most distinguishing characteristic.

Therapeutic foster care programs serve children with a wide variety of symptoms, labels, and special needs. These children are in need of both out-of-home placement and specialized treatment related to their special needs and are at risk for more restrictive placements. They include children with serious emotional disturbances, youngsters who are delinquent, and those with substance abuse problems, physical disabilities, mental retardation, or severe medical problems. Programs have also been established to serve special populations such as infants and young children with acquired immunodeficiency syndrome (AIDS). Many programs report that they serve primarily adolescents and that individualized treatment approaches and family settings are highly effective with this group. Programs described in the literature and included in this study sample share a set of common characteristics:

- Therapeutic foster care provides a nurturant, family environment for one or two children with special needs; one child per home is considered ideal.
- Therapeutic foster care programs regard treatment parents as professional staff who are the primary agents of treatment for a child.
- Program staff provide frequent consultation, supervision, and support to treatment parents.
- Program staff have low caseloads to permit them to work actively and intensively with each treatment family, child, and natural family.
- Therapeutic foster care provides treatment services in the context of the treatment home; in most programs the treatment is highly goal directed and individualized.
- Therapeutic foster care programs provide 24-hour crisis intervention services to treatment families and children.
- Therapeutic foster care programs carefully select treatment parents and provide them with extensive training.
- Therapeutic foster care programs provide a variety of forms of support to treatment parents, including respite care and mutual support networks.
- Therapeutic foster care programs involve biological parents in the child's treatment to the extent possible and appropriate; however, the emphasis on the involvement of the biological parents does vary widely across programs and is considered one of the most challenging aspects of therapeutic foster care.
- Therapeutic foster care programs maintain active linkages with a variety of community agencies, particularly school systems.

Variations

Therapeutic foster care programs may differ with respect to such features as organizational auspices, program size, population served, and extent of involvement of biological parents in the treatment process. One significant variable concerns the uses of therapeutic foster care. Some programs define themselves primarily as alternatives to more restrictive treatment environments, whereas others are used as transitional or aftercare supplements to residential treatment. Furthermore, some programs consider it appropriate to use treatment homes as long-term placement options for children who cannot return home. Other programs regard their role more stringently as time-limited treatment and are reluctant to use their highly specialized treatment homes for long-term care. Some programs are specifically designed to provide short-term emergency placements for crisis intervention or acute care for children and adolescents with psychiatric problems (Bereika & Mikkelson, 1992). The average length of stay for youth in therapeutic foster care programs varies widely. In this study, the average length of stay of programs responding to the survey was approximately 18 months, ranging from 1 month to 5 years. Snodgrass and Bryant (1989) found that 73% of the programs in their survey allowed for the possibility of permanent placement with treatment families, contributing to the variance in length of stay data.

Beyond these differences in uses, the major variables among therapeutic foster care programs appear to center around two dimensions: treatment intensity and treatment approach. Therapeutic foster care programs vary along the dimension of treatment intensity, with some programs providing higher levels of active, systematic treatment interventions within the context of the treatment home than others. Hawkins (1987) identified a continuum of 10 variables that can be used to define the level of treatment intensity of a therapeutic foster care program:

- Parent qualifications
- Parent training by agency
- Support and supervision of parents by agency
- Intensity and generality of interventions directly with youth
- Intensity and generality of indirect interventions
- Case manager/staff qualifications
- Staff training by agency
- Support and supervision by staff
- Professional competencies of other staff
- Program accountability for process and outcome

According to this schema, the more rigorous and systematic a program is regarding each of these variables, the more treatment intensive it can be considered.

The second major variable is the treatment philosophy and approach espoused by the therapeutic foster care program. The salient issue appears to be the degree of reliance on the overall therapeutic milieu of the treatment home versus the degree of reliance on highly structured, primarily behavioral treatment approaches. By definition, all therapeutic foster care programs use the environment of a nurturing family as a critical component of the intervention. The difference lies in the *relative emphasis* placed on the therapeutic value of the family environment and on the use of structured interventions (Welkowitz, 1987). Some programs use highly structured, learning-based or behavioral treatment programs for all children in treatment homes; others emphasize the integration of the child into a supportive family and devote less attention to structured or behavioral treatment approaches. Still others adjust the degree of treatment structure and approach to meet the needs of the individual child.

Services

Once it is determined that a child is appropriate for therapeutic foster care, usually through a review committee, the process of matching begins— selecting a treatment family with the best combination of skills and characteristics to assist a particular child. Matching is considered one of the most critical steps in providing therapeutic foster care in that the success of the intervention is largely dependent upon the appropriateness of the treatment family for each individual child. Most programs develop an initial treatment plan based upon referral information; however, a more formal treatment plan is developed following the child's first several weeks in the treatment home. The plans commonly include a set of treatment goals to be achieved while the child is in the home; the long-term placement goal (whether the child can return home or needs long-term substitute care); educational, vocational, mental health, or other special services to be provided; goals and services for the biological family; and plans for the child's contact and visitation with the biological family (Meadowcroft, Hawkins, Grealish, & Weaver, 1989). Ideally the treatment plan is developed with the full involvement of the program staff, treatment parents, biological parents, involved caseworkers and therapists, and the child, if appropriate.

The actual services provided by therapeutic foster care programs fall within four broad categories: treatment services within the therapeutic foster care home, support services to the treatment home, ancillary services, and services to the biological family. As noted previously, the treatment services in the home include involving the child in a healthy family milieu; addressing troublesome behaviors, often using behavioral approaches; and teaching appropriate behaviors and community living skills. In order to enable treatment parents to fulfill their role, therapeutic foster care programs provide a range of supportive services to the treatment home. These services include consultation from program staff, in-service training, support groups, respite care, 24-hour crisis intervention, and parent aides. Children in therapeutic foster care receive a number of additional, ancillary services beyond the treatment provided within the context of the treatment home. These services may be provided by the program or agency but more often are "brokered" by the program and provided by other community agencies or systems. Two of the most significant of these services are mental health and special education services. An array of other ancillary services may be provided, including health, recreational, vocational, tutoring, and other extracurricular services.

For many therapeutic foster care programs, discharge planning is begun during the initial phases of the placement, when treatment goals are established indicating whether it is anticipated that the youngster will return to the biological family, progress to independent living, or require a long-term substitute care situation. Once youth are discharged from therapeutic foster care, follow-up or aftercare services may be provided to ensure a successful adjustment to the postdischarge placement and treatment continuity. Too often, however, the follow-up component is either limited or totally nonexistent, generally attributed to a lack of resources (Webb, 1988; Welkowitz, 1987). More typically, follow-up consists of occasional phone contacts or home visits made by program staff and treatment parents as well as the availability of crisis intervention services for a period of several months following discharge. The lack of more extensive follow-up services may have significant implications for the long-term effects of therapeutic foster care, because studies consistently have found that, regardless of the magnitude of the gains made in residential treatment programs, the postdischarge environment is a critical factor in determining successful long-term adjustment (Whittaker & Maluccio, 1989).

One of the most challenging aspects of therapeutic foster care involves working with the biological families of children in treatment homes. As noted previously, programs vary widely in the levels of effort and resources devoted to working with biological families and in their effectiveness in reaching out to and successfully involving biological families (Webb, 1988). In the last decade there has been growing recognition of the importance of working with biological families. It has been found that treatment in residential settings is more effective when programs involve parents (Sinanoglu, 1981). Whittaker and Maluccio (1989) stress that parental involvement in the helping process and continuing parent–child contact are among the most prominent variables affecting the ultimate outcome of therapeutic foster care services. They also acknowledge that there is likely to be a continuum of parental involvement in therapeutic foster care, with the degree, kind, and purpose of the involvement varying with the individual circumstances of each child and family.

Some of the approaches for involving and providing services to biological families include involvement of parents as active members of the treatment team, participating in the planning and delivery of services; ongoing contact between the child and family; counseling; casework services; parent education and skills training; parent support groups; and guidance and support from treatment parents.

Staffing

The key staff position in therapeutic foster care is the counselor, also called the case manager, program manager, or treatment parent supervisor. The counselor has direct supportive and supervisory responsibilities related to the treatment parents, children, and biological parents (Meadowcroft, Luster, & Fabry, 1989). This role involves providing the treatment parents with in-home supervision, training, consultation, and support through frequent visits and telephone contact as well as 24-hour crisis assistance. For children, the counselor is responsible for coordinating the development of the treatment plan, monitoring treatment implementation and progress, providing informal counseling and support, accessing and coordinating needed services, facilitating discharge planning, and providing follow-up care. The counselor's role with the biological parents involves providing counseling, education, assistance in accessing resources, and support. In addition to these duties, staff often have responsibility for the recruitment, selection, and training of treatment parents. Some programs use a team approach, with members of the team assuming different roles and responsibilities.

Because staff have multiple and varied responsibilities, caseloads for therapeutic foster care programs are typically small. In the Snodgrass and Bryant survey (1989), 79% of the respondent programs reported caseloads of fewer than 20 youths, with an average caseload of 12.5 youngsters per staff person. In an extensive survey of 321 treatment foster care programs in North America, Hudson, Nutter, and Galaway (1993) found that 89% of the programs set a caseload maximum and, of these, the maximum *client* caseload median was 10 (with a range from 2 to 25 clients) and the maximum treatment foster care *home* caseload median was 7 (with a range from 2 to 18 homes).

Many therapeutic foster care programs rely on bachelor's-level staff to fulfill the counselor's role. Although staff with advanced degrees such as a master's in social work, psychology, counseling, or special education may be preferred, programs typically do not offer salaries to attract higher paid professionals. In addition to minimum academic credentials, most programs require staff to have considerable previous experience working with troubled youngsters and families. Given the nature of the work, staff of therapeutic care programs must have personalities and life circumstances that are well suited to nontraditional schedules and roles.

The line counselors and supervisors in therapeutic foster care programs often are supported by a number of supplementary staff, such as educational specialists to serve as a liaison between the counselors and schools as well as psychiatrists and psychologists to assist in assessment and treatment.

Treatment Parents

It is obvious that the treatment parents are critical to the success of therapeutic foster care programs. The characteristics of treatment parents vary widely both within and among programs. In fact, there is no agreed-on set of "preferred" demographic characteristics for treatment parents. Programs have reported success with two-parent families, one-parent families of both sexes, and families with a wide range of social, economic, and ethnic backgrounds. Although some programs may recruit parents with college degrees and paid experience, others are equally adamant that formal credentials are not necessary. These programs contend that good basic parenting skills along with sincere desire and commitment are the key ingredients and that the skills and techniques for treatment parenting can be learned through the preservice and in-service training process. Many programs do require that one treatment parent not be employed outside the home or that couples have flexible schedules so that one parent can be available during the day for routine responsibilities as well as crises (Meadowcroft, 1988).

There can be no disputing the fact that successful recruitment of capable treatment parents is the key to establishing and maintaining an effective therapeutic foster care program. However, recruitment has been characterized as the most formidable obstacle facing programs, and programs face continuing struggles to attract and maintain pools of qualified treatment parents who are willing to cope with the difficult and complex problems manifested by children in therapeutic foster care (Gross & Campbell, 1989). Despite these difficulties, many programs report considerable success in locating treatment families. According to Meadowcroft (1988), difficulties in maintaining a sufficient pool of treatment parents do not result from a lack of interest within the community but rather from failure to devote sufficient energies to recruitment, failure to target the appropriate population in recruitment efforts, or failure to provide sufficient pay to attract treatment parents. Programs that are successful in recruiting a constant supply of treatment parents are those that consider recruitment to be an integral and ongoing function of program operations.

After recruitment efforts identify an array of interested individuals, programs typically use extensive screening and selection procedures designed to determine which candidates possess the appropriate mix of skills, personal characteristics and qualities, and family situation to become treatment parents. Once treatment parents are selected, all programs require them to participate in some combination of preservice and in-service training. Although the approach, breadth, duration, and content of training varies from program to program, the importance of training is not disputed.

In therapeutic foster care, treatment parents represent the "front line" (Bryant, 1981). Supervision, consultation, and support are provided by professionals, but treatment parents work directly with the child on a day-to-day basis and must be equipped with the knowledge and intervention skills needed to work with seriously disturbed youngsters.

The training provided by programs serves multiple purposes: continuing the screening and selection process, increasing treatment parents' knowledge of problem behavior and refining parenting and intervention skills, and preparing treatment parents for some of the difficulties they are likely to face in their work with troubled children. The design of preservice training varies widely among programs; Snodgrass and Bryant (1989) found that the number of preservice sessions required varies from 1 to 14, with an average of about 6 sessions. Training curricula for treatment parents usually combine didactic approaches, involving presentation of information, with experiential approaches involving learning and practicing specific skills. Programs serving children with emotional disorders tend to rely more heavily on skill-based training curricula (Snodgrass & Bryant, 1989). Most programs provide in-service training to enable treatment parents to continually enhance their skills and competence and to help them learn treatment strategies specific to the child currently in placement.

Costs

There is significant variability in the reported costs of therapeutic foster care. In large part, the variation in costs is attributable to the wide disparity in the level of payments made to treatment parents, which in turn is often related to the role of the therapeutic foster care program (long-term habilitation versus short-term acute psychiatric alternative to hospitalization) and the treatment parents' responsibilities in that role. It is estimated that more than half the cost of therapeutic foster care services represents treatment parent payments (Snodgrass & Bryant, 1989). The recent survey of 321 treatment foster care programs (Hudson et al., 1993) shows the lowest average monthly payment to treatment parents to be $808 and the highest average payment to be $1,037. It also is difficult to determine and compare costs across programs because of differences in accounting and costing methodologies. Programs compute and report costs for different time periods (e.g., per day, per month, per year, or per episode for each child). In addition, cost for special education, day treatment, therapy, and other adjunct services generally is not included in computing costs.

Despite the considerable range in costs of therapeutic foster care, it appears that even the most expensive programs are cost effective when compared with treatment in other group settings, such as group homes, residential treatment centers, or hospitals (Snodgrass & Bryant, 1989; Webb, 1988; Welkowitz, 1987). Snodgrass and Bryant (1989) reported that 92% of the programs responding to their survey reported costs to be lower than those of group home or institutional programs. According to Bereika and Mikkelson (1992), when psychiatric hospital inpatient admission rate and length of stay are prorated to be comparable to the average length of stay in an acute psychiatric treatment foster care program (16.8 days), cost of treatment foster care ($3,696) is less than half that of psychiatric hospitalization ($8,417).

Effectiveness and Evaluation Results

Evaluations of therapeutic foster care generally have relied on several measures to indicate effectiveness: discharge to a less restrictive setting, improvements in the child's functioning, and satisfaction with services. Although the evaluations of therapeutic foster care programs vary considerably in sophistication and methodological rigor, the outcomes based on these indices are positive. Data suggest that therapeutic foster care programs do have the potential to divert youngsters from more restrictive settings (Snodgrass & Bryant, 1989; Stroul, 1989). However, the data primarily reflect only the nature of the placement at the time of discharge from therapeutic foster care and do not address longer-term placement outcomes. The PRYDE Program in Pittsburgh, Pennsylvania, which collects follow-up information on discharged children on an annual basis, has found sustained positive outcomes over time, with more than 70% of the discharged children still living in less restrictive settings at 1 and 2 years postdischarge and 70% of the youths either attending school or being employed. Studies of behavioral and functional improvements of children in therapeutic foster care programs have also shown positive results (Bereika & Mikkelson, 1992; Bryant, 1981; Friedman, 1983; R. Jones, 1989; Maryland Department of Human Resources, 1987; Snodgrass & Campbell, 1981). Many programs have assessed satisfaction with services from a variety of perspectives, including those of youngsters, biological parents, and treatment parents and have documented favorable outcomes.

A number of studies have been conducted using comparison or control groups (Chamberlain, 1990; Chamberlain & Reid, 1991; Clark et al., 1993; Hawkins, Almeida, & Samet, 1989) comparing therapeutic foster care with other treatment settings, including group homes, residential treatment centers, and intensive treatment units in hospitals or correctional facilities. Findings indicate that therapeutic foster care is an effective alternative to residential treatment, psychiatric hospitalization, and correctional institutions. Research on the enduring changes produced by therapeutic foster care is promising. At least 7 months following discharge, children served by therapeutic foster care are more likely than those served in residential settings or intensive treatment units to be living in minimally restrictive settings (i.e., with their biological families, with adoptive families, or on their own) (Chamberlain, 1990; Hawkins et al., 1989; Meadowcroft, Thomlison, & Chamberlain, 1994).

Funding Opportunities

A range of funding sources are available to pay for therapeutic foster care programs. Title IV-E of the Social Security Act provides federal reimbursement to states for foster care maintenance payments for eligible children (i.e., children whose families received or were eligible for AFDC prior to court proceedings leading to removal). It also can subsidize foster care maintenance payments for up to 6 months for eligible children removed from their homes on the basis of voluntary placement agreements and for extended periods if a court rules that the placement is in the best interest of the child. Through this mechanism, a portion of the cost of therapeutic foster care (the maintenance portion) is financed by federal funds for some percentage of the population served. Other federal funds, such as the Title XX Social Services Block Grant, state funds, and county funds are used to finance therapeutic foster care services to varying degrees.

Some programs receive third-party reimbursements for services. These programs bill Medicaid and private insurers for portions of therapeutic care that can be covered—for example, individual and family therapy, psychiatric services, and case management. In addition, some programs indicate that they charge families fees based on a sliding scale; these fees generally comprise an insignificant percentage of program revenues.

CONCLUSION

Home-based services and therapeutic foster care are important components of a comprehensive, community-based system of care needed for children with emotional, behavioral, or mental disorders and their families. A comprehensive system of care for these youngsters ideally should include a range of nonresidential services (such as outpatient, home-based, day treatment, and crisis services) and a range of residential services (such as therapeutic foster care, group homes, residential treatment, residential crisis services, and inpatient services). The interdependence of these various service components is critical because the effectiveness of any one service component is related to the availability and effectiveness of all other components. Specifically, the effectiveness of both home-based services and therapeutic foster care is compromised without the availability of a range of service options to provide continuing services and support to the child and family as part of a holistic approach to serving children and families.

REFERENCES

Adoption Assistance and Child Welfare Act of 1980, PL 96-272. (June 17, 1980). Title 42, U.S.C. 601 et seq: *U.S. Statutes at Large, 94*, 500–535.

AuClaire, P., & Schwartz, I. (1986). *An evaluation of the effectiveness of intensive home-based services as an alternative to placement for adolescents and their families.* Minneapolis: University of Minnesota, Hennepin County Community Services Department and Hubert H. Humphrey Institute of Public Affairs.

AuClaire, P., & Schwartz, I. (1987). *Home-based services as an alternative to placement for adolescents and their families: A follow-up study of placement resource utilization.* Minneapolis: University of Minnesota, Hennepin County Community Service Department and Hubert H. Humphrey Institute of Public Affairs.

Bath, H., & Haapala, D. (1994). Family preservation services: What does the outcome research really tell us? *Social Service Review, 68*, 386–404.

Bereika, G., & Mikkelson, E. (1992). Individual residential treatment as an alternative to acute psychiatric hospitalization for children and adolescents. *Community Alternatives: International Journal of Family Care, 4*, 97–120.

Bryant, B. (1981) Special foster care: A history and rationale. *Journal of Clinical Child Psychology, 10*, 8–20.

Bryant, B., & Snodgrass, R. (1989). Therapeutic foster care: Past and present. In P. Meadowcroft & B. Trout (Eds.), *Troubled youths in treatment homes: A handbook of therapeutic foster care* (pp. 2–20). Washington, DC: Child Welfare League of America.

Bryce, M., & Lloyd, J. (1982). *Placement prevention and family reunification: A view from the child welfare sector* (rev. ed.). Iowa City: The University of Iowa School of Social Work, National Resource Center on Family Based Services.

Caplan, G. (1964). *Principles of preventive psychiatry.* New York: Basic Books.

Chamberlain, P. (1990). Comparative evaluation of specialized foster care for seriously delinquent youths: A first step. *Community Alternatives, 2*, 21–36.

Chamberlain P., & Reid, J. (1991). Using a specialized foster care community treatment model for children and adolescents leaving the state mental hospital. *Journal of Community Psychology, 19*, 266–276.

Clark, H., Boyd, L., Redditt, C., Foster-Johnson, L., Hardy, D., Kuhns, J., Lee, G., & Stewart, E. (1993). An individualized system of care for foster children with behavioral and emotional disturbances: Preliminary findings. In K. Kutash, C. Liberton, A. Algarin, & R. Friedman (Eds.), *Proceedings of the fifth annual research conference for a system of care for children's mental health* (pp. 365–370). Tampa: University of South Florida, Florida Mental Health Institute, Research and Training Center for Children's Mental Health.

Cox, R., & Cox, M. (1989). *Application of lessons from foster care research to the evaluation of foster family-based treatment.* Unpublished paper, University of Texas, Health Science Center, Austin.

Edna McConnell Clark Foundation. (1985). *Keeping families together: The case for family preservation.* New York: Author.

Family Empowerment Resource Network. (1987). *Definition of home-based services.* Middlebury, VT: Counseling Service of Addison County.

Feldman, H. (1991). *Assessing the effectiveness of family preservation services in New Jersey within an ecological context.* Trenton: New Jersey Division of Youth and Family Services, Bureau of Research, Evaluation, and Quality Assurance.

Fraser, M., Pecora, P., & Haapala, D. (1991). *Families in crisis: Findings from the Family-Based Intensive Treatment Project.* Hawthorne, NY: Aldine de Gruyter.

Friedman, R. (1983). *Therapeutic foster homes in Florida: A mid-1982 status report.* Tampa: University of South Florida, Florida Mental Health Institute, Child, Adolescent and Community Program.

Ginsberg, G. (1986). *A report on home-based family centered services.* Waterbury: Vermont Child and Adolescent Service System Program.

Goldman, S. (1988). *Series on community-based services for children & adolescents who are severely emotionally disturbed. Vol. II: Crisis services.* Washington, DC: Georgetown University Child Development Center, National Technical Assistance Center for Children's Mental Health.

Gross, N., & Campbell, P. (1989). Recruiting and selecting treatment foster parents. In P. Meadowcroft & B. Trout (Eds.), *Troubled youths in treatment homes: A handbook of therapeutic foster care* (pp. 35–50). Washington, DC: Child Welfare League of America.

Haapala, D., & Kinney, J. (1979). Homebuilders' approach to the training of in-home therapists. In S. Maybanks & M. Bryce (Eds.), *Home-based services for children and families: Policy, practice, and research* (pp. 248–259). Springfield, IL: Charles C Thomas.

Hawkins, R. (1987, August). *What is this thing? Defining foster care, special foster care and foster family-based treatment.* Paper presented at the First North American Treatment Foster Care Conference, Minneapolis, MN.

Hawkins, R., Almeida, C., & Samet, M. (1989). Comparative evaluation of foster-family–based treatment and five other placement choices: A preliminary report. In A. Algarin, R. Friedman, A. Duchnowski, K. Kutash, S. Silver, & M. Johnson (Eds.), *Proceedings of the Second Annual Research Conference* (pp. 98–119). Tampa: University of South Florida, Florida Mental Health Institute, Research and Training Center for Children's Mental Health.

Hinckley, E., & Ellis, F. (1985). An effective alternative to residential placement: Home-based services. *Journal of Clinical Child Psychology, 14,* 209–213.

Hudson, J., Nutter, R., & Galaway, B. (1993). Treatment foster care: North American developments. In C. Liberton, K. Kutash, & R. Friedman (Eds.), *Proceedings of the Sixth Annual Research Conference* (pp. 297–306). Tampa: University of South Florida, Florida Mental Health Institute, Research and Training Center for Children's Mental Health.

Hutchinson, J., Lloyd, J., Landsman, M., Nelson, K., & Bryce, M. (1983). *Family-centered social services: A model for child welfare agencies.* Iowa City: The University of Iowa School of Social Work, National Resource Center on Family Based Services.

Jones, M. (1985). *A second chance for families—five years later: Follow-up of a program to prevent foster care.* New York: Child Welfare League of America Research Center.

Jones, R. (1989) Evaluating therapeutic foster care. In P. Meadowcroft & B. Trout (Eds.), *Troubled youths in treatment homes: A handbook of therapeutic foster care* (pp. 143–182). Washington, DC: Child Welfare League of America.

Kaplan, L. (1986). *Working with multiproblem families.* Lexington, MA: DC Heath and Company.

Lloyd, J., & Bryce, M. (1984). *Placement prevention and family reunification: A handbook for the family-centered service practitioner* (rev. ed.). Iowa City: The University of Iowa, National Resource Center on Family Based Services.

Maryland Department of Human Resources. (1987). *Specialized foster care.* Baltimore: Department of Fiscal Services.

Meadowcroft, P. (1988). *Troubled youth in treatment homes.* Pittsburgh: The Pressley Ridge Schools.

Meadowcroft, P., Hawkins, R.P., Grealish, E.M., & Weaver, P. (1989). Providing services to children in therapeutic foster care. In P. Meadowcroft & B. Trout (Eds.), *Troubled youths in treatment homes: A handbook of therapeutic foster care* (p. 100–125). Washington, DC: Child Welfare League of America.

Meadowcroft, P., Luster, C., & Fabry, B. (1989). Professional staff and organizational structures. In P. Meadowcroft & B. Trout (Eds.), *Troubled youths in treatment homes: A handbook of therapeutic foster care* (pp. 100–125). Washington, DC: Child Welfare League of America.

Meadowcroft, P., Thomlison, B., & Chamberlain, P. (1994). Treatment foster care services: A research agenda for child welfare. *Child Welfare, LXXIII*(5), 565–581.

Omnibus Budget Reconciliation Act of 1993, PL 103-66. (August 10, 1993). Title 42, U.S.C. 629 et seq: *U.S. Statutes at Large, 107,* 649–658.

Schuerman, T., Rzepnicki, T., Littell, J., & Chak, A. (1993). *Evaluation of the Illinois Family First placement prevention program: Final report.* Chicago: Chapin Hall Center for Children at the University of Chicago.

Schwartz, I., Auclaire, P., & Harris, L. (1991). Family preservation services as the alternative to out-of-home placement of adolescents. In K. Wells & D. Biegel (Eds.), *Family preservation services: Research and evaluation* (pp. 33–46). Newbury Park, CA: Sage Publications.

Sinanoglu, P. (1981). Working with parents: Selected issues and trends as reflected in the literature. In A. Maluccio & P. Sinanoglu (Eds.), *The challenge of partnership: Working with parents of children in foster care* (pp. 3–21). New York: Child Welfare League of America.

Snodgrass, R., & Bryant, B. (1989). Special foster care and foster family-based treatment: A national program survey. In R.P. Hawkins & J. Breiling (Eds.), *Therapeutic foster care: Critical issues* (pp. 36–37). Washington, DC: Child Welfare League of America.

Snodgrass, R., & Campbell, P. (1981). *Specialized foster care: A community alternative to institutional placement.* Staunton, VA: People Places.

Stroul, B. (1988). *Series on community-based services for children & adolescents who are severely emotionally disturbed. Volume I: Home-based services.* Washington, DC: Georgetown University Child Development Center, National Technical Assistance Center for Children's Mental Health.

Stroul, B. (1989). *Series on community-based services for children & adolescents who are severely emotionally disturbed. Volume III: Therapeutic foster care.* Washington, DC: Georgetown University Child Development Center, National Technical Assistance Center for Children's Mental Health.

Tavantzis, T., Tavantzis, R., Brown, L., & Rohrbaugh, M. (1986). Home-based structural family therapy for delinquents at risk of placement. In M.P. Mirkin & S. Koman (Eds.) *Handbook of adolescent and family therapy* (pp. 69–87). New York: Gardner Press.

Webb, D. (1988). Specialized foster care as an alternative therapeutic out-of-home placement model. *Journal of Clinical Psychology, 17,* 34–43.

Welkowitz, J. (1987). *A report on therapeutic foster care.* Waterbury, VT: Department of Mental Health, Child and Adolescent Service System Program.

Whittaker, J., & Maluccio, A. (1989). Changing paradigms in residential services for disturbed/disturbing children: Retrospect and prospect. In R.P. Hawkins & J. Breiling (Eds.), *Therapeutic foster care: Critical issues* (pp. 81–102). Washington, DC: Child Welfare League of America.

Wood, S., Barton, K., & Schroeder, C. (1988). In-home treatment of abusive families: Cost and placement at one year. *Psychotherapy, 25,* 409–414.

Yuan, Y., McDonald, W., Wheeler, C., Struckman-Johnson, D., & Rivest, M. (1990). *Evaluation of AB 1562 in-home care demonstration projects: Final report.* Sacramento, CA: Office of Child Abuse Prevention.

CHAPTER 25

Culturally Competent Service Approaches

Marva P. Benjamin and Mareasa Isaacs-Shockley

Effective service delivery requires that service providers recognize the cultural complexity and rich diversity that exist among people of color (Benjamin, 1993; Cross, Bazron, Dennis, & Isaacs, 1989). Once these are recognized, however, service providers must also have the capacity to respond appropriately to the unique service delivery needs of populations that make up these complex and rich cultures.

Unfortunately, there are no blueprints to follow that automatically result in culturally competent services. However, there are programs and agencies in this country that have begun the developmental process of becoming more culturally competent (Isaacs & Benjamin, 1991). They have been able to do so by operationalizing a core set of principles and values that enhance their ability to implement their services within a cultural context. Indeed, these principles and values underlie the concept of cultural competence and therefore serve as guidelines for these programs to effectively implement culturally competent approaches to service delivery.

In an effort to provide concrete examples of programs that are striving to reach cultural competence in providing mental health and other services to children and families of color, Isaacs and Benjamin (1991) conducted a national survey and subsequently visited the sites of some of the programs included in the survey. Factors considered in identifying these programs were geographical diversity, population served, type of community, services provided, age range of clients, staff training on cultural competence issues, and the extent to which culturally competent principles are utilized at four different levels of service delivery: policy making, administrative, practitioner, and consumer levels.

During the site visits to these programs, a structured interview guide was utilized to ensure that a common set of issues was addressed in the interviews and that uniform information was gathered from each of the program sites. The site visit process included interviews, discussions, and group meetings with representatives from all levels of the organization, including administrative, clinical, program, and budget staff as well as board members. Interviews and discussions were also conducted with family members, child and adolescent clients, and other community agency representatives where appropriate. This chapter describes the principles and values shared by the programs included in the study as well as key characteristics and strengths that they demonstrated. In addition, specific strategies used to operationalize the cultural competence principles are described.

COMMON VALUES AND CHARACTERISTICS

In analyzing the results of the site visits, it was noted that the programs that were visited had begun to operationalize many of the core principles and values of a culturally competent system of care that had been identified by Cross and colleagues (1989) and Isaacs and Benjamin (1991), such as

1. The family as defined by each culture is the primary system of support and preferred intervention.
2. The system must recognize that minority populations must be at least bicultural and that this status creates a unique set of psychological/emotional issues to which the system must be equipped to respond (Gibbs & Huang, 1990).
3. The service system must sanction and, in some cases, mandate the incorporation of cultural knowledge into practice and policy-making activities.
4. Cultural competence involves working in conjunction with natural, informal support and helping networks within the minority community (e.g., neighborhood organizations, churches, spiritual leaders, healers, community leaders).
5. Individuals and families make different choices based on cultural forces; these choices must be considered if services are to be helpful.
6. Culturally competent services seek to match the needs and help-seeking behavior of the client population.
7. An agency staffing pattern that reflects the makeup of the potential client population, adjusted for the degree of community need, helps to ensure the delivery of effective services.
8. Community control of service delivery through minority participation on boards of directors, administrative teams, and program planning and evaluation committees is essential to the development of effective services.
9. Beyond services, culturally competent agencies recognize that they also have a role of advocacy and empowerment in relationship to their cli-

ents and the minority community in which they attempt to deliver highly responsive services.

In addition to emphasizing these values and principles, the programs that were visited tended to tailor their services to the specific needs and characteristics of the ethnic groups, the community, the service organizations, the attitudes and philosophies of the policy makers, and the political, economic, and social circumstances that shaped interactions in their area or community. Nevertheless, there were key characteristics and strengths that these programs had in common (Isaacs-Shockley, 1994).

Program Auspices

Most of the programs visited appeared to operate as private, nonprofit agencies, which seemed to provide greater latitude in assessing and implementing changes in services or policies. In addition, nonprofit agencies often operated with boards or advisory committees, which provided a mechanism for institutionalizing ongoing minority participation and involvement in evaluations of the agency.

Clear Program Philosophy and Policies

The selected programs had clearly articulated program philosophies and policies that were based on cultural dynamics and inclusion. Almost all had mission statements that expressly stated that cultural competence was a goal of the agency. The agency policies usually included a focus on effectively providing services to the minority community and on equal opportunity employment.

Name and Location of Programs

All of the selected programs were community based and highly accessible to the targeted minority community. The names of some of the programs, such as Roberto Clemente Family Guidance Center or Progressive Life Center, Inc., also reflected an attention to and awareness of cultural heroes, cultural strengths, or both. The facilities also had reading materials and decors that emphasized and reflected cultural values and achievements.

Types of Services Offered

The services offered by these programs were not unique in and of themselves; however, the amount of emphasis on certain types of interventions and modalities did tend to differ from that in more traditional programs. For instance, most programs focused on family or group interventions rather than focusing primarily on individual interventions. Greater attention was paid to outreach and education than is often seen in more traditional services. The interpersonal and social aspects of care were acknowledged and incorporated into the service delivery process such that opportunities for clients to engage in social activities with each other, with agency staff, or with both were provided. Food was often an important component and adjunct to services. Therapies that are more focused on the here-and-now, as well as more behaviorally oriented and interactive approaches, tended to predominate. Services and activities that have come to be associated with "case management" were also critical in serving minority populations because these families often encounter multiple problems across numerous agencies. Working with families to eliminate bureaucratic red tape and to become better advocates for their own needs is a critical component of culturally competent service agencies.

Emphasis on the Importance of Family

Without exception, the selected programs viewed the family as the primary source of intervention. This means that "family" must be defined by the families themselves and often includes persons who are not traditionally viewed as part of family systems by Eurocentric standards. These selected programs were built around the notion that family structures vary considerably in minority communities. Often, one of the major goals of service intervention is to rebuild and maintain the extended support network that has been a major source of strength and survival for many minority families. The roles played by various members are not assumed; rather, clients are asked to articulate their roles. For example, Nobles (1991) notes that the concept of family among African Americans appears to be based more on "eldership" rather than on "parents." In the Eurocentric model, family is conceptualized as the biological parents having ultimate authority and responsibility for the child. In African American and other ethnic communities, families tend to be built around eldership so that, even when parents are present, the ultimate authority may reside with a grandmother, an elder uncle, or others recognized by the family as having the greatest amount of wisdom and respect.

The role of the family in the service intervention process was also expanded in these agencies. Too often, service providers only see families when they wish to collect information or gain additional information about an individual client. In these culturally competent agencies, family members were viewed as collaborative partners with the agency and provided invaluable resources and advocacy, as well as information.

Recognition of the Need for Cultural Assessments

Each of the selected programs recognized the importance of understanding where the family or client fits on a cultural continuum and attempted to determine this point so as to better tailor services and agency worker assignments. It is also important to conduct a cultural assessment so that differentiations can be made between socioeconomic conditions and cultural values. Often, these programs utilized cultural assessments to focus on strengths rather than deficits and to develop interventions based on perceived strengths.

Ethnic-Specific Staffing Patterns and Recruitment/Retention Strategies

Staff who reflect the ethnic makeup of the client population was one of the greatest strengths of many of the programs selected. From their boards to administrators to direct services and support staff, these programs showed the ability to recruit and retain staff reflecting the ethnic makeup of their clients. This ability seemed to be directly related to several factors:

- The perception of the agency as a minority-oriented one with strong ties to the minority community
- The use of formal and informal networks and resources indigenous to the minority community for recruitment purposes
- The ability to provide an ethnic minority support network and to demonstrate visible role models for career mobility and advancement
- The use and reputation of the program as a training site for students and young professionals who are seeking expertise in meeting the needs of various ethnic minority populations
- The creative use of paraprofessionals
- The creative use of cultural consultants and other scarce resources
- The need for a critical mass of ethnic minority staff, which impacts on the program's success in recruitment efforts

Training and Education

Another strength of many of the selected programs was the strong emphasis and importance placed on training. In the orientation of new staff and training opportunities for seasoned staff, many of these programs provided ongoing, intensive, in-service training. Cultural issues were addressed and incorporated in aspects of the agency's functions and policies, thus creating a cultural milieu for staff as well as clients. In addition to an emphasis on training for their own staff, many of these programs offered training to other community agencies and government organizations. Many also provided consultation to hospitals, courts, police, schools, and other organizations experiencing problems in understanding the cultural components of behaviors and attitudes.

Service Linkages

The case management functions of these programs were usually very important. Staff in these programs spent considerable amounts of time understanding the entire ecology of the client or family; they often provided concrete services or assisted clients with solutions to the problems of daily living before they gained the trust and ability to delve into other levels of functioning. Therefore, it was critically important for the programs to establish and maintain linkages with other agencies that have an impact on the client's well-being. The programs also tended to be responsive to the perceived needs of the community and often developed new services around these needs.

Use of Natural Helpers and Community Resources

In addition to linkages with other agencies, these programs often maintained and utilized linkages with informal community resources, networks, and natural helpers. The strength of many of these programs lies in their knowledge of and ability to mobilize these informal networks and natural support systems for their clients. These programs were adept at identifying community leaders who are natural helpers and utilizing them as brokers between the formal and informal service delivery systems. Given the strong spiritual orientation of some ethnic minority groups, churches and spiritual leaders often become key allies in the service intervention process.

Furthermore, community centers, churches, and other community social settings are often used to deliver services to families. In relying on these natural resources, the programs come to be seen as community resources and an important component of the services available in the community. These programs often participated in or sponsored cultural activities that reinforce perceptions that they are true community resources.

Treatment Goals

The focus and end goals of the treatment process are not simply individual improvement or well-being. There is a recognition in most of these programs that larger external issues play a key role in the disabilities presented by their clients. Racism, discrimination, poverty, and lack of opportunity structures often constitute the context in which ethnic minority clients struggle. To address only the individual and "fix" him or her to fit into this context is neither desirable nor appropriate. Thus, the treatment goals in many of these programs also addressed the larger societal context in which they, and their clients, operate. Staff viewed themselves not only as treatment professionals but also as advocates and spokespersons for their clients. Furthermore, these programs often rallied against societal injustices or inequities that affect the well-being of their clients and their communities; they cannot separate themselves from political and social issues.

APPROACHES UTILIZED IN OPERATIONALIZING CULTURAL COMPETENCE PRINCIPLES

In reviewing some of the characteristics and strengths of the programs that were visited, it is abundantly clear that services provided are tailored to the specific needs of the ethnic group members served as well as to the political, economic, social, and cultural circumstances that shape interactions in a particular area or community. To further illustrate this point, the remainder of this chapter highlights some of the specific approaches and principles utilized by seven of these programs: Black Family Development, Inc.; the Roberto Clemente Family Guidance Center; the Asian/Pacific Center for Human Development; the Progressive Life Center, Inc.; the Soaring Eagles Program of the Indian Health Board of Minneapolis, Inc.; Roybal Family Mental Health Services, Utah Street School Co- Location Project; and the Santa Clara County Mental Health Bureau.

Defining the Family as the Primary System of Support and Intervention

Black Family Development, Inc. (Detroit) Black Family Development, Inc. (BFDI) pays careful attention to understanding the unique family structures in the African American community as defined by the culture of these families. For example, the initial assessment is extensive and includes obtaining identifying information, as well as a description of the presenting problems, from the perspectives not only of the referral source and BFDI counselors but also of the nuclear family, caregiver(s), extended family, friends, and significant others. Comprehensive information about family members, including an examination of the family support system, a review of use of leisure time of each family member, and an analysis of problem-solving approaches and parent–child relationships, is assessed from both the adult and the child perspectives. Family members are seen conjointly, individually, or both as needed, assuring a family focus and cultural sensitivity.

By working with families in their own homes, BFDI is able to operationalize a family-centered, culturally competent approach to service delivery. Such an approach provides an opportunity for staff to develop close working relationships with families, thus facilitating the development of trust and respect. BFDI utilizes the home-based service model, which stresses family preservation, because of the belief that children are best able to develop into healthy, productive adults when reared by their own families. Additionally, individual members benefit when the family is helped. BFDI believes that families can and must be empowered, and it is through such empowerment, enhancement, and preservation of the family that problems such as drug abuse, acquired immunodeficiency syndrome, child abuse, and teen pregnancy can be treated or prevented. This approach also empowers the African American family to seek solutions to family problems that fit within the context of their culture. In fact, the names of BFDI programs are indicative of the importance the agency places on empowering families. For example, Save a Family Through Empowerment (SAFE) and Families Abstaining with Commitment to Empowerment (FACE) are the names of two of the programs at BFDI.

Roberto Clemente Family Guidance Center (New York City) The Clemente Center strongly adheres to the cultural competence principle that the family, as defined by the culture, is the primary and preferred point of intervention. This emphasis on the family versus the individual is critical to maintaining the values and belief system of the Latino/Hispanic culture. Women and children often are not autonomous, independent beings but, rather, are defined by their roles and responsibilities to the family system.

It is of critical importance that significant males be included in the implementation of agency services because their sanction of treatment is extremely important. It is also important to allow the clients to define "family" in a way that makes sense to them. Often, this includes siblings, cousins, grandparents, friends, and others who provide support to the individual or family.

The goal of the therapeutic interventions at the Clemente Center is to stabilize, strengthen, and empower Latino/Hispanic families. Although mainstream mental health theories often hold that adolescence can, and often should, be viewed as a period of individuation from the family, Clemente Center staff believe that it is critical to treat Puerto Rican adolescents within the context of their families. The Puerto Rican family system views adolescence from an "apprenticeship" model, which differs substantially from the "individuation" model of American society.

Therefore, Clemente Center therapists have found the technique of "cultural reframe" very useful. In this technique, the experience or demand that a parent or adolescent makes is analyzed in relation to the cultural values that constitute the background for the demand or expectation. For example, a mother's request that her daughter interact less frequently with peers is viewed as expressing a value that the family takes priority over the individual. The adolescent's demand for greater peer contact is viewed as expressing a value of individuality over the family. Each value is understood to be functional, or adaptive, within its social context. Cultural reframe allows the therapist to shift the blame from the person to the acculturation process, which places different demands on the parent and adolescent generations. Once the problem is understood in the context of acculturation, the therapist may proceed to the next stage of therapy, which involves presenting an objective and impartial model for family progression through the states of adolescence. This model is based on the process of exchange and negotiation between parent and adolescent for greater freedom, trust, and responsibility.

Acknowledging Unique Issues of Bicultural/Bilingual Status

Asian/Pacific Center for Human Development (Denver) Because of language barriers, the Asian/Pacific Center for Human Development (A/PCHD) responds to access issues by providing bicultural/bilingual services. Based on a population study, the center recruits and hires bilingual/bicultural staff representing the client population. The major sources utilized for recruiting staff include community networking efforts, Asian-oriented newspapers, and staff who have connections in the Asian community. The A/PCHD provides services in 19 Asian languages and dialects, including Japanese, Chinese, Korean, Vietnamese, Cambodian, Laotian, Laotian/Hmong, Tagalog, Thai, Asian Indian, Samoan, and Indonesian. Because of the variety of subgroups that comprise the Asian American population, a variety of programs is necessary.

It is significant that the Asian community is experiencing an inevitable rise in the numbers of American-born or -reared children of Asian immigrant families, aggravating cultural differences between child and parent. With less exposure to the Asian traditions of extended family and authority, the child becomes more likely to identify with more permissive American family and societal structures. The confusion that this engenders for the Asian parent alienates parent and child and creates an intergenerational gap that is difficult to bridge. Because the staff speak the same language and are familiar with the culture, some of the barriers to utilizing mental health services are removed, making it easier for the children and their families to gain access to needed services.

Not only does the A/PCHD provide bilingual/bicultural services, but the center has also implemented an Interpreters Bank to ensure that refugees and recent immigrants lacking English proficiency receive quality care and equal treatment under the law. The bank is used as a community resource by the medical, legal, and general business community in providing assistance to refugees and recent immigrants. The Interpreters Bank may be accessed on a 24-hour basis, 7 days a week. It provides face-to-face interpretation and document translation services through 40 trained interpreters who speak any one of the languages available. This program assists service providers in effectively communicating with their clients.

Incorporation of Cultural Knowledge/Preferred Choices in Practice

Roberto Clemente Family Guidance Center One of the major strengths of the Clemente Center is the incorporation of knowledge about culture and preferred choices into the practice, therapeutic interventions, and policies of the center. The Clemente program philosophy is predicated on the major assumption that migration and acculturation, especially into another culture, create severe emotional distress and disorientation.

The conceptual approach to treatment used by Clemente Center staff recognizes the critical importance that culture and value orientations have on the behavior and belief systems of their clients. The program recognizes that values are influenced by the migratory experience of the group. For example, first-generation immigrants tend to uphold their culture of origin and its values when in the new host culture. In the new host environment, these immigrants often experience culture shock; they react to this culture shock by attempting to make the family a tighter unit and by holding more strongly to the values of their culture of origin. The second and third generations, starting in adolescence and preadolescence, must cope with and adapt to the language, culture, and values of the new environment. These constitute groundbreaking efforts where stress, failure, and defeat are not uncommon. Rather than attempting to change these values and belief systems, the center embraces and engages with clients regarding these values, thus allowing the development of therapeutic alliances and relationships that keep clients in therapy and assist them in redefining their problems and solutions.

Progressive Life Center, Inc. (Washington, D.C.)   The Progressive Life Center (PLC) philosophy and intervention techniques are based on a strong theoretical orientation that suggests that African cultural values and principles continue to be exhibited by African Americans today, and that these values and principles can be utilized to resolve some of the psychological and social conflicts that are presented by African American individuals and communities. This coherent philosophy, which permeates every aspect of the PLC's operation, provides a solid foundation from which to deliver services to the African American community. The PLC acknowledges and accepts that culture and cultural values are a predominant force in shaping behaviors, values, and institutions. Its outlook is based on the *"ntu"*[1] philosophy and *Nguzo Saba* principles of unity, self-determination, collective work and responsibility, cooperative economics, purpose, creativity, and faith. These seven principles of Nguzo Saba were developed by Dr. Maurana Ron Karengar (1977) as guidelines for healthy living. They enable the client as well as the practitioner to isolate and focus on specific behaviors relative to enhanced interpersonal functioning from an Afrocentric perspective. The *ntu* philosophy, as developed by the PLC, sets forth that optimal functioning is facilitated by a psychosocial environment in which the individual experiences and practices the principles of harmony, interconnectedness, authenticity, and balance.

This cultural framework has allowed the program to view mental health problems among African Americans as "interpersonal" rather than "intrapsychic." One can see that just this small shift results in a different definition of and orientation to mental health problems. Services are then developed that are compatible with the cultural patterns and rhythms of African Americans. Therefore, for example, interventions are more visual,

---

[1]"Ntu" (pronounced "in too") is a Bantu (central African) concept that loosely translates as "essence" of life and signifies a universal unifying force that touches on all aspects of existence. *Ntu* highlights the interrelatedness between the intrinsic (psyche and immaterial) and extrinsic (social and material) factors that affect a person's ability to both influence and respond to problems of daily living.

more action oriented, based more on interactions and relationships, and more spiritual. The normative structure for interventions becomes the family or group, not the individual. The goal becomes "healing" rather than "curing," and there is a shift away from the individual deficit model to a collective strength orientation. Many African Americans are very relationship oriented; the ability to bond and support each other (in extended families) has been a survival mechanism since the era of slavery.

Working with Natural Informal Support Systems

The Soaring Eagles Program of the Indian Health Board of Minneapolis, Inc. The Soaring Eagles Program of the Indian Health Board of Minneapolis (IHB) illustrates the cultural competence principle of viewing natural systems as primary mechanisms of support for minority populations. The program has based many of its activities on exposure to natural helpers and others in the Indian community who can teach the children about their culture and assist them in positive growth and development. The IHB also utilizes many cultural rituals as part of its ongoing program.

Medicine people often are involved in the healing process, and children frequently participate in activities such as powwows, sweats, and other Indian rituals/ceremonies that bring them into contact with traditional healers and helpers. In addition, natural helpers and other traditional Indian leaders often present lectures to the children or lead discussions about Indian values. Storytellers, traditional dancers, and those knowledgeable about ceremonial pipes and drums come to the program to impart these customs and traditions to the Soaring Eagles members. When the IHB moved into its new location several years ago, the executive director had one of the leading Indian spiritualists come and bless the building in a traditional ceremony. This gave sanction to the Indian community to use the building.

Although the mental health program is rather traditional in approach, its staff members have learned to modify their approach and interpretations to accommodate cultural differences. For example, a therapy group may open with the ceremonial pipe or with a drum ceremony before entering into more standard group therapy sessions.

The IHB has been quite successful in recruiting volunteers and soliciting support from various other resources within the community. In 1989, volunteers provided over 2,900 hours to the social center. The IHB has sponsored baby showers for pregnant mothers for which local retailers provided baby clothes, baby products, and clothing for the mothers. Many local businesses and private citizens have provided sponsorship for Soaring Eagles youth to attend community activities or to pursue their own interest areas. In 1989, over 83 businesses and civic organizations contributed food, clothing, toys, tickets, or other materials and goods to the Soaring Eagles and other programs. These contributions have been very important in enhancing the services available to the clients.

Progressive Life Center, Inc. Given their philosophy of collective responsibility and support, it should not be surprising that PLC staff participate in numerous community activities. They provide services to churches, participate in radio and television talk shows addressing subjects of interest to the African American community, and participate on community and government task forces. In addition, the center sponsors at least eight activities a year in which the larger community is invited. These include Kwanza celebrations, community picnics, lectures, and open houses. Rites of Passages ceremonies[2] are held in community churches and are attended by many community leaders and residents. Thus, the PLC and its staff are effectively integrated into the community.

These and other relationships increase the availability of resources for PLC clients. PLC staff have utilized ministers, psychic healers, astrologers, nutritionists, herbal experts, and other natural healers revered in the African American community when appropriate. They also have invited some of these persons to make presentations to staff or to serve the center in a consultative capacity.

Recognizing the Importance of Cultural Assessments

Roybal Family Mental Health Services, Utah Street School Co-Location Project (Los Angeles) The Roybal staff acknowledge the importance of understanding the client's level of acculturation and assimilation. The primary client base is that of Mexican Americans from a large working class community in East Los Angeles. Staff serving these clients must be bilingual/bicultural because it is believed that the benefits of therapy and other forms of intervention cannot be achieved through a translator.

When a child is referred to Roybal for an assessment, the clinic policy is that the family must call to make the appointment. In this way, the staff are given an opportunity to talk with key family members and to determine their attitudes regarding and knowledge of mental health care. These family meetings may be held at the school or at the Roybal clinic. This initial contact also provides an opportunity to elicit cultural information that is often missing in the assessments done by others. Level of acculturation, length of time in the country, country of origin, knowledge of the community, and use of other resources such as priests, curanderos (healers), and espiritualistas (spiritualists) are important components in the Roybal

---

[2]Participation in these ceremonies denotes that the youth has demonstrated a certain level of cultural and social maturity, as determined by parents, therapists, and other significant adults. It provides an opportunity for celebration of this accomplishment by everyone in the youth's psychosocial milieu. It also provides an opportunity for the youth to demonstrate newly acquired skills and abilities in a culturally and socially supportive setting.

assessment process. These components, along with an exploration of linguistic skills and belief systems within the family, provide the cultural context in which to understand and serve the child and family. If the family is found to have, for example, a high level of disenfranchisement, a community worker is assigned to the family to familiarize its members with services available and to assist them in understanding their rights. The community workers are usually paraprofessionals with a very strong knowledge of the resources and culture of the Los Angeles Latino/Hispanic community.

Providing Culturally Responsive Services

Roberto Clemente Family Guidance Center The Clemente Center meets the cultural competence principle of responsive services matched to the population being served through offering a culturally syntonic environment. This means that services show a respect for language and a respect for the values of the family. The Clemente Center requires that all staff be bilingual/bicultural and that services be offered in the language that the client finds most comfortable. Oftentimes, clients switch back and forth between English and Spanish, depending on the subject matter being discussed.

Because cultural beliefs cannot be mandated, the emergence of a culturally sensitive treatment program must come from within the structure itself. For example, the structure of the center's program contains the following features that are representative of and responsive to the culture of the clients: acceptance of spiritism and other natural helpers as an avenue to express conflict, acceptance and availability of food, and an understanding of the migratory experience and the acculturation process on mental health.

The center provides a supportive therapeutic environment that allows clients to express their beliefs without having negative interpretations placed on them. For example, a belief in "spiritism" is very common among clients. Instead of seeing this as something that must be shifted, a therapist, working within the described philosophical framework, would use the expression of these beliefs as a starting point for therapy. The authenticity of the client's belief system is never questioned. Spiritism is interpreted as a culturally specific vernacular that provides clients with an avenue for articulating their conflicts. It is discussed openly in sessions by clients without fear of the therapists imposing diagnoses or their own interpretations on these belief systems. The acceptability of spiritism creates an atmosphere that provides comfort and acceptance and encourages clients to attend therapy and express their own experiences in a way that is culturally familiar.

Food is also an integral part of the Latino/Hispanic culture. When one pays a visit to a Latino/Hispanic friend or family, it is often expected that the guest will be offered something to eat. Turning down food in this culture is considered impolite and rude. Food provides a means of connecting and welcoming others into one's home. Accordingly, food is present at most activities at the Clemente Center. It is an integral part of administrative meetings, staff meetings, and therapy sessions. By allowing the introduction of food, the Clemente Center enables clients to find acceptance and bonding in a setting where cultural values are similar to their own.

Although traditional modes of psychotherapy are utilized—individual, family, and group—the content and goals of treatment are very different. For example, the Clemente Center's group therapy program adheres to an educational psychotherapy model, based on the assumption that immigrant group populations need information and education as well as therapy. Additionally, the educational psychotherapy group for adolescents is a time-limited group experience focused on particular themes such as family and independence, sexuality, cultural identity, school issues, peers and peer pressure, and racism and discrimination. The 10-session educational psychotherapy group experience is designed to be a complete program in itself; however, it may also serve as an introduction to and preparation for continued therapy.

Other groups also have been developed to address the concerns of many Latino/Hispanic women. For example, there is a midlife crisis group for women experiencing the "empty nest" syndrome when their children leave the home. There are also groups for single parents and those that address sex roles and orientations in adjusting to American society.

Implementing Culturally Competent Staffing Patterns

Roybal Family Mental Health Services The Roybal Mental Health Clinic is staffed by Latino/Hispanic bilingual staff because it is believed that effective therapy and therapeutic relationships cannot be established when a translator is used. Although it is difficult to recruit Latino/Hispanic men as staff members in mental health settings, the male presence is extremely important in Latino/Hispanic cultures. Certainly the lack of adequate numbers of male staff in mental health programs is often a barrier, especially to reaching fathers and other key males in the family. Significantly, however, the project coordinator is a Latino/Hispanic male social worker.

The Roybal Clinic treatment philosophy dictates that staff must operate flexibly with respect to role definitions and functions. The needs of the clients define the types of services provided. Thus, sometimes staff must be advocates, interpreters, extended family members, educators, and negotiators in addition to carrying out their functions as therapists and case managers. Persons who find it difficult to live with such role diversity may find it difficult to be effective providers in this delivery system.

Progressive Life Center, Inc.   There has been a conscious decision on the part of PLC founders to hire only people who have advanced degrees and who are committed to working full time. These decisions were based on the fact that the PLC is operating out of a coherent philosophy and treatment approach that must be adopted by every staff person. The types of training and interventions to be learned were believed not to be as effective with part-time staff. The decision to hire only those with advanced degrees was viewed as a marketing tool; it also provided academic and professional legitimacy to the *ntu* therapeutic approach. It is important that PLC therapists be well trained and regarded as competent by the mainstream society and by other professional African Americans. PLC staff members have been trained in a variety of mental health models, including behavioral, psychoanalytic, cognitive, and humanistic. These different orientations make for interesting approaches to the overriding *ntu* philosophy.

The *ntu* philosophy leads to a different conceptualization of the role of "therapist." In the PLC, the therapist is viewed as a "guide" and "healer" rather than as a person who provides answers and stringent directions. The therapist is viewed as an enabler, someone who assists in empowering the individual to live and create a more positive and rewarding environment. In this regard, the treatment process is a participatory one, relying on action and activity rather than strictly on verbal communication and thoughts. PLC staff show the utmost respect to the clients and attempt to limit the "intrusive" aspects of therapy. In many ways, PLC staff become members of the extended family for clients.

Ensuring Minority Participation at All Organizational Levels

Santa Clara County Mental Health Bureau (San Jose, California)   The Santa Clara County Mental Health Bureau has sought to ensure that there is participation from ethnic minority groups at every level of the organization. The bureau has adopted a policy that supports these activities at the highest levels of its organization. The bureau also has engaged numerous ethnic minority professionals and involved them in decisions concerning its many planning activities associated with this effort. To coordinate these activities and to ensure that they remain on the agency's agenda, the bureau hired an Ethnic Population Program Specialist whose primary responsibility is to implement the minority initiatives.

The bureau has also established a planning process that includes significant and major input from persons within ethnic minority communities. The communities must develop and "buy in" to the planning process. In order to do so, they must be assured and guaranteed that the time and effort expended will result in a plan that will be vigorously implemented.

Externally, the major governance structures that affect the policies and programs of the Mental Health Bureau and other county agencies are the county executive and the five-member Board of Supervisors. The Board of Supervisors has very strong affirmative action planning and hiring policies. The board also appoints a 15-member Mental Health Advisory Board that includes physicians, psychiatrists, psychologists, social workers, consumers, and others involved in mental health programs and policies. This board advises the Director of Mental Health. It meets once a month and has some responsibility for program planning, the budgetary process, setting agency priorities, monitoring ongoing programs, and advocacy/legislative linkages. In addition, a Minority Advisory Committee was established to review issues specifically related to ethnic minority populations in the county.

Black Family Development, Inc. There are strong indications that BFDI adheres to the cultural competence principle that minority participation is essential in planning, governing, administering, and evaluating the development and implementation of services. The staffing patterns, membership on the governance board, clients and families served, needs assessment, and client satisfaction surveys are all testimony to the importance that BFDI places on the value of minority participation in its service delivery system.

The BFDI Board of Directors is an excellent example of a minority governing board that provides leadership and shapes policy for service delivery to a minority population/community. The board represents a broad and diverse cross section of the African American community, including attorneys, a banker, ministers, agency executives, legislators, police department personnel, judges, educators, physicians, social workers, and ordinary citizens. A slot on the board is reserved for a representative from the Detroit Association of Black Social Workers—the organization that established BFDI and that continues to serve as an advocacy group for the agency.

The Board of Directors sets policy for the agency, examines compliance with contracts, assumes fiscal accountability, and gets involved in the political arena by advocating for the interests of BFDI with elected officials in the state capitol in Lansing. Board members also meet with state agency executives as appropriate. The board sees itself as a "hands-on" board that is very committed to the African American community. It is organized into a number of committees, including public relations, program, finance, social issues, resource development, and long-range planning.

Because BFDI was established by a local professional African American organization and bases its policies and programs on community needs, it was, from the outset, sanctioned by the African American community. This means that BFDI has grass roots support and thus is able to generate a political climate conducive to providing effective services to African American families.

CONCLUSION

The programs described in this chapter demonstrate how the principles for culturally competent systems of care can be operationalized and their importance for providing effective services to minority populations. Thus, the importance of the family, location of services, the variety of services offered, community perceptions and images of the program, staffing patterns, cultural assessments, use of natural support systems, and minority participation in the planning, governing, and administration of programs are important considerations in culturally competent approaches to service delivery. Furthermore, based on the programs studied, it appears that the flexibility needed to establish and change program policies and practices toward greater cultural competence is enhanced when the agency is ethnic specific and operates under a nonprofit status. Additionally, it is critical that the program be viewed as a community resource.

REFERENCES

Benjamin, M. (1993). *Child and Adolescent Service System Program minority initiative research monograph*. Washington, DC: Georgetown University Child Development Center, National Technical Assistance Center for Children's Mental Health.

Cross, T. (in press). *Organizational self-study on cultural competence for agencies addressing child abuse and neglect*. Prepared for the People of Color Leadership Institute, Center for Child Protection and Family Support, Washington, DC.

Cross, T., Bazron, B., Dennis, K., & Isaacs, M. (1989). *Towards a culturally competent system of care: A monograph on effective services for minority children who are severely emotionally disturbed*. Washington, DC: Georgetown University Child Development Center, National Technical Assistance Center for Children's Mental Health.

Gibbs, J.T., & Huang, L.N. (1990) *Children of color: Psychological intervention with minority youth*. San Francisco: Jossey-Bass.

Karenga, M. (1977). *Kwanza: Origin, concepts, practice*. Los Angeles: Kawalda Publications.

Isaacs, M., & Benjamin, M. (1991). *Towards a culturally competent system of care: Programs which utilize culturally competent principles*. Washington, DC: Georgetown University Child Development Center, National Technical Assistance Center for Children's Mental Health.

Isaacs-Shockley, M. (1994). *Culturally competent service delivery systems*. Paper developed for the National HIV-STD Technical Assistance Project sponsored by the Association of Black Psychologists. Washington, DC: Progressive Life Center.

Nobles, W. (1991). *The African American perspective*. Paper presented at the Conference on Developing Cultural Competence in Health and Human Services—Imperative for the 90s, Chicago.

CHAPTER 26

Serving Youth with Mental Health and Substance Abuse Problems

Amelia T. Petrila,
Lynn Foster-Johnson, and Paul E. Greenbaum

Few comorbid disorders present as many challenges to practitioners as the assessment and treatment of alcohol and other drug (AOD) use co-occurring with mental health disorders among adolescents. These challenges spring not only from the clinical complexities inherent in this heterogeneous population, but from systemic conflicts that threaten adequate assessment and treatment. Although solutions to these problems have proven elusive, attention is needed to address the issues facing a population that is both troubling and endangered.

Growing empirical evidence supports the idea that co-occurrence of AOD use and mental health disorders is as prevalent among adolescents as it is among adults. Although methodological difficulties abound in obtaining valid prevalence data (Caron & Rutter, 1991; Greenbaum, Foster-Johnson, & Petrila, in press; McConaughy & Achenbach, 1994), the few existing studies of adolescents have found relatively high prevalence estimates for both disorders. Cohen and her colleagues (1993) found that, in their general population sample, at least half of the youths who had a substance use disorder as listed in the *Diagnostic and Statistical Manual of Mental Disorders* (American Psychiatric Association, 1987) also had a coexisting disruptive disorder. Boyle and Offord (1991), in a general population study of Canadian youth, found that those with conduct disorder were 3.5 to 6.5 times more likely to use substances, depending upon which substance was involved. Additionally, clinical studies have found that the prevalence of co-occurring disorders ranges from 21.8% to 82.0%—varying with age, specific combination of disorders, criteria for admission, definition of "caseness," and referral biases. Notwithstanding this wide variability, the prevalence cited most frequently in these studies was in the vicinity of 50%. Greenbaum and colleagues (in press) provide a more comprehensive review of studies estimating prevalence of co-occurring AOD and mental health disorders among adolescents. Given the high prevalence estimates for co-occurring AOD and mental health disorders, it is incumbent on systems of care to understand this population and design appropriate programmatic and therapeutic responses.

This chapter outlines a number of issues that are central to understanding adolescents with co-occurring AOD and mental health disorders. Included is a discussion of the differences between mental health and substance abuse systems and the difficulties that arise from these differences, and a discussion of assessment and treatment considerations that are important for this population. The chapter concludes with a description of programs that exemplify unique and innovative approaches to the needs of adolescents with both AOD and mental health problems.

SYSTEMS ISSUES

The approach of a particular program to treatment is based generally on a theoretical conceptualization of the causes of the problem and its treatment. Numerous models exist in both the mental health and AOD systems to guide the treatment of adolescents with co-occurring disorders. An understanding of these models, as well as the systemic differences that are associated with them, can help practitioners to develop flexible and individualized treatments for adolescents that integrate the most relevant elements of each system (Brower, Blow, & Beresford, 1989; Kaminer & Frances, 1991).

Schumacher, Duchnowski, and Algarin (1993) describe four treatment models that are useful in organizing treatment for persons with co-occurring emotional and AOD disorders: mental health, 12-step, relapse prevention, and criminal justice. They caution that these models are based on adult approaches and require adaptation for the developmental and individualized treatment needs of children and their families. Table 26.1 describes the key principles of these four models. These models form the basis for the development of programs and service systems that have basic differences in philosophy and orientation and that may be in conflict with each other.

Differences between substance abuse and mental health treatment systems often are cited by clinicians and researchers as negatively affecting service delivery to persons with co-occurring disorders. Differences include treatment philosophy, beliefs about etiology or causes of the disorder, licensure, staff training, and use of specific treatment techniques, including medication, therapeutic confrontation, group therapy, and 12-step groups (Center for Substance Abuse Treatment, 1993). These differences are summarized in Table 26.2.

Systemic differences between mental health and AOD systems have been identified as barriers to obtaining treatment for adolescents with dual

Table 26.1. Various models used by AOD and mental health systems

Model	Description
Mental health	Integrates biological, psychological, and social factors and focuses on correcting physiological deficiencies, building social support systems, improving family functioning, reinforcing positive behaviors, increasing functional abilities, encouraging rational thinking, and increasing awareness of feelings (Evans & Sullivan, 1990; Schumacher et al., 1993).
12-Step	Based on Alcoholics Anonymous and other self-help groups, requires the individual to accept his or her powerlessness over substances, to admit that life with substances is unmanageable, and to commit to seeking help from a higher power. Abstinence, regular attendance at meetings, peer support, "working the steps," sponsorship, and prayer are some of the defining characteristics of this approach (Schumacher et al., 1993).
Relapse prevention	Focuses attention on learning new skills to resist the attraction or urge to use substances. Key features include learning how to avoid situations where substance use is likely, identifying triggers to substance use, developing social skills and relationships with non–substance-using individuals, developing new interests and leisure activities, and learning coping skills for stress (Marlatt & Gordon, 1985).
Criminal justice	Views AOD abuse as a criminal violation. The primary focus is on detention, punishment, and deterrence. Use of substances is viewed as a matter of poor judgment rather than a symptom of a diagnosable and treatable disorder. The family and peer group are seen as negative influences from which the user must be removed. Although some criminal justice programs for youth are attempting to incorporate treatment into their philosophies, the overall approach is punitive (Schumacher et al., 1993).

diagnoses. The differences that create such barriers include rigid adherence to organizational boundaries, categorical funding, different licensure requirements, philosophical and training differences among staff, different approaches to assessment and diagnosis, and an insufficient array of appropriate services in either system (New York State Office of Mental Health, 1994; Ridgely, Goldman, & Willenbring, 1990; Thacker & Tremaine, 1989). These differences are discussed more fully below.

Organizational Issues

The administrative separation of AOD and mental health services at federal, state, and local levels continues to make it difficult to coordinate service delivery for adolescents who need assistance from both systems. This separation also can result in mental health and substance abuse programs competing with each other or with other children's programs (e.g., education or juvenile justice) for limited resources. The resulting "turf" disagreements can ultimately disrupt cooperative efforts undertaken by those who administer and deliver services to these youth (Behar, 1990a; Cooper, Brown, & Anglin, 1989; Menicucci, Wermuth, & Sorensen, 1988).

Table 26.2.   Differences in mental health (MH) and AOD programs

	MH system	AOD system
Philosophy	Shift from reliance on medical model/disease model to development of community supports and rehabilitation. Abstinence from substances is encouraged but not required.	Focus is on techniques to persuade and encourage abstinence by assertion of personal responsibility, interrupting belief systems, and involvement in activities that are drug free.
Etiology	MH disorders are generally viewed as brain diseases, although there is much debate among providers and consumers regarding the causes of MH disorders.	The premise that AOD abuse is a characterological deficit that can be overcome by exerting self-control is being replaced by the belief that AOD abuse and addiction are attributable to a combination of biological, psychological, and social factors.
Licensure/training	MH program staff, generally not trained to treat youth with AOD problems, instead refer youth to AOD programs for services. Licensure, admission criteria, and funding source may also prohibit serving youth with dual diagnoses.	AOD programs are similarly ill equipped to treat adolescents with MH problems.
Medication	Medications are considered important treatment components, with appropriate clinical assessment and oversight.	Medications, particularly those that are potentially addictive, are less common and may be prohibited.
Therapeutic confrontation	Minimal to moderate use, depending on setting, person, and problem.	Use is a central technique in treatment.
Group therapy	Central to treatment.	Central to treatment.
12-step groups	Historically underused, but use is growing.	Central to treatment.

Funding Issues

Funding for adolescents with co-occurring disorders also is problematic. In most states, providers are funded exclusively as either mental health or AOD treatment programs. Dollars are usually appropriated to provide specific units of services to a carefully defined population, often with specified, exclusionary diagnostic admission criteria. Combining or blending funds becomes an administratively complex task, requires creativity, and may involve some degree of risk to the provider.

There also are wide differences and limitations in insurance and other third-party reimbursement when providing services to adolescents with dual diagnoses, whose treatment is complex and often expensive. For example, the traditional reliance on inpatient facilities for treatment of adolescents with dual diagnoses is believed to be related to the availability of reimbursement for this level of care (Behar, 1990b; Butts & Schwartz, 1991). Until recently, many payors favored inpatient programs in hospitals rather than other residential or nonresidential alternatives, even though little research exists to suggest that inpatient care is more effective.

Licensure Issues

Administrative rules governing the licensure of programs and caregivers serving adolescents with dual diagnoses often are complex and inflexible. Providers usually are licensed separately by state mental health or AOD licensing agencies, and, unless program requirements are coordinated or a waiver process is in place to accommodate dual licensure, it becomes extremely difficult to serve individuals requiring multiple services. Typical licensure requirements that may conflict include space requirements, staffing credentials, staffing mix and number, admission criteria, treatment approaches, and frequency or type of service provided (New York State Office of Mental Health, 1994).

Philosophical and Training Issues

Philosophical differences among mental health and AOD staff occur within and across disciplines in both mental health and AOD programs. Disagreements result from a lack of mutual understanding as well as a lack of respect for the competencies of each field (Brown & Backer, 1988; Caragonne & Emery, 1987; Thacker & Tremaine, 1989). Common limitations in staff knowledge and skills related to dual diagnoses include lack of exposure to clinical needs of persons with either emotional or AOD problems, lack of training in necessary therapeutic skills, and lack of supervision and oversight. Cross-training has been an effective tool to expose staff from mental health and AOD programs to the similarities and differences in philosophies and treatments of each system, and has been shown to enhance the ability of programs to serve persons with co-occurring problems. Finally, the small number of professionals in both the mental health and substance abuse systems trained and credentialed to address developmental issues of youth is another major barrier to the appropriate care and treatment of adolescents.

Assessment/Diagnosis Issues

Assessment and diagnosis of adolescents are complicated by the isolation, dissimilarities, and lack of communication between AOD and mental health programs (Abram & Teplin, 1991; Thacker & Tremaine, 1989). Each system has its own criteria and methods for determining eligibility for receipt of services. Furthermore, differences in staff training and philosophy between the systems also result in differing diagnoses and treatment plans, which also affect access to programs.

Service Availability Issues

The types of services that are available for adolescents with dual diagnoses are often inappropriate, unavailable, or inaccessible, particularly to persons with limited ability to pay. In some areas, needed programs simply do not exist. Those programs that are available are often inaccessible to poor, uninsured adolescents or those covered by Medicaid. Additionally, many treatment services are designed for adults and are inappropriate for adolescents, particularly minority youth (Pires & Silber, 1991).

Amelioration of these systems issues involves a mutual commitment by both mental health and AOD systems to work together. Developing action plans and collaborative policies, committing resources or "blending" funding when needed, and instituting a cross-agency training program are just a few examples of concrete actions that can substantially improve services to this population. At a minimum, coordination of mental health and AOD services is enhanced by establishing cooperative case management programs or intersystem case conferences (M. Evans, Dollard, & McNulty, 1992; Fariello & Scheidt, 1989).

TREATMENT ISSUES

In addition to the systemic issues discussed above, a number of concerns related to the assessment and treatment of adolescents with co-occurring AOD and mental health disorders must be considered. These include the broad approach to treatment as well as considerations related to the special characteristics of adolescents.

Approach to Treatment

There are three commonly recognized approaches to treatment of adolescents with co-occurring disorders: sequential treatment, parallel treatment, and integrated treatment (Center for Substance Abuse Treatment, 1993). First, the traditional *sequential* approach, also known as "ping-pong treatment," involves referral back and forth between mental health and AOD systems. This approach has been shown to fail unless services are carefully coordinated, and some researchers assert that it may actually contribute to relapse and rehospitalization among some populations (Rosenthal, Hellerstein, & Miner, 1992). When responsibility is split between the two systems, adolescents and their families may have difficulty deciphering and complying with conflicting therapeutic messages. Follow-up on appointments and attendance at a variety of programs in different locations also is problematic with this approach. In addition, the general lack of coordination between systems may, paradoxically, contribute to the labeling of youth with both disorders as both noncompliant and resistant to treatment (Menicucci et al., 1988).

Parallel treatment, another approach to the treatment of dual diagnoses, involves adolescents being treated simultaneously by both mental health and AOD programs. For example, the adolescent may attend Alcoholics Anonymous and relapse prevention classes at an AOD program while also attending a medication clinic and group therapy at a mental health program. Coordination of services remains a concern with this approach and often is hard to achieve. Additionally, financial coverage and confidentiality laws often vary between systems, creating access and administrative deterrents (Center for Substance Abuse Treatment, 1993).

The third approach for adolescents with co-occurring disorders is *integrated treatment*, and there is general agreement in the literature that this approach is preferred because of its comprehensive and holistic features. Services traditionally provided by either mental health or AOD systems are combined in one program at one location. A unified and comprehensive program is developed with the adolescent and his or her family and carried out under the supervision of a trained case manager.

The system of care approach for children and adolescents with serious emotional disturbances proposed by Stroul and Friedman (1986) offers an excellent example of a philosophy and mechanism that integrates substance abuse services with an array of other services that are necessary for children and their families. In describing the system of care model, Stroul and Friedman (1986) provide a framework for states and communities to assess existing services and make improvements. They include guiding principles as well as a set of core values, including the need to assure that services are community based, culturally competent, and provided in a manner that respects the wishes, needs, and goals of the child and family.

Specific, interdependent components of the system of care are organized into eight dimensions, each representing an area of need. The service dimensions include mental health, social, educational, health, substance abuse, vocational, recreational, and operational services. Inclusion of substance abuse reflects the growing recognition of the effect of substance abuse on adolescents, and on youth with serious emotional problems in particular. It also reflects the belief that effective service systems require a wide range of services and close interagency collaboration and integration.

The advantages and disadvantages of sequential, parallel, and integrated treatment approaches are discussed in detail in a review completed by the Center for Substance Abuse Treatment (1993). Individual differences in dual diagnosis combinations, severity of symptoms, and degree of impairment affect the appropriateness of a specific treatment approach for each individual youngster. For example, sequential and parallel treatment are probably more appropriate for youth who have a very serious problem with one disorder but a mild problem with the other. In contrast, integrated treatment, because it is delivered in a setting designed to accommodate both problems, may better assure the recognition, assessment, and treatment of both disorders as they interrelate with each other.

Special Characteristics of Adolescents and Implications for Treatment

The special treatment needs of adolescents with co-occurring disorders must be addressed. These include 1) attention to developmental and other characteristics of adolescents, 2) a treatment focus that examines and involves the adolescent's social and familial networks, 3) the adaptation of clinical interventions for adolescents with dual diagnoses, and 4) the need for services to be coordinated and integrated across multiple systems and points of contact. Without attention to these issues, effectiveness of treatment for adolescents with co-occurring disorders is severely compromised. These issues and their impact on assessment and treatment are discussed below.

Developmental and Other Characteristics of Adolescents   A review of the literature indicates that adolescents require a range of developmentally appropriate assessment and treatment services that differ from those needed by adults (Center for Substance Abuse Treatment, 1993; Golden & Klein, 1988; Smith & Margolis, 1991). Adolescents, particularly those with serious co-occurring emotional and AOD disorders, require unique approaches corresponding to their age and developmental strengths and abilities.

For example, although the mental health and substance abuse fields are beginning to recognize the importance of developmental differences when evaluating adolescents, many current assessment instruments continue to consider adolescents as miniature adults. Assessment of adolescents in the substance abuse field continues to be based on a traditionally adult model. Compounding this problem, there is neither normative information nor agreement among professionals as to what constitutes AOD abuse or dependence (Halikas, 1990; Shedler & Block, 1990; Winters, 1990). Another issue is that AOD and mental health disorders often have similar symptoms or interact in a way that reduces the validity of the assessment results (Drake et al., 1990). Additionally, there are few psychometrically sound measures or proven methodologies available specifically for youth with AOD and mental health problems, either for assessing substance use or for determining the extent of co-occurrence with other disorders (Drake, Alterman, & Rosenberg, 1993; Farrow, Smith, & Hurst, 1993; Greenbaum et al., in press; Halikas, 1990; Winters, 1990).

A frequently used assessment approach has been to specify the sequence or severity of symptoms as primary or secondary. This method of assessment, which suggests that the disorder that manifests first is primary and must be served in a particular service system, has been viewed with controversy. Many believe that this approach artificially reduces diagnostic heterogeneity (Bukstein, Glancy, & Kaminer, 1992; Schuckit, 1989). In terms of assessment, this distinction may be important because different treatment routes are developed based on the results of initial assessments (Bean-Bayog, 1987). Furthermore, what may be a therapeutic program for some patients with dual diagnoses may be countertherapeutic for another group (Ford, Hillard, Giesler, Lassen, & Thomas, 1989). Others suggest that the use of the primary/secondary paradigm can obscure the variations in the prevalence of co-occurring disorders, and may even hide the true relationship between coexisting disorders (Bukstein, Brent, & Kaminer, 1989; Lehman, Myers, & Corty, 1989).

Clearly, developmental issues have serious implications for the sequence and methods of treatment (Bukstein et al., 1992; Menicucci et al., 1988; Schuckit, 1986). In fact, the traditional underutilization of outpatient alternatives for AOD-using adolescents recently has been attributed to the difficulties in identifying and diagnosing AOD abuse in adolescents.

A related issue is the timing of assessment, which may result in an inaccurate diagnosis of either AOD use or mental health disorders. In both substance abuse and mental health systems, assessment often occurs soon after admission into a hospital or a program. This practice may result in inaccurate diagnoses, because many side effects of AOD use mimic psychiatric symptoms, and because abstinence from substances, even while hospitalized, is often difficult to verify (Lehman et al., 1989; Stowell, 1991; Test, Wallish, Allness, & Ripp, 1989).

In addition to a developmental approach to assessment, a developmental, habilitative approach to treatment is recommended because it allows the adolescent to acquire or relearn coping skills to manage conflict and emotions (Ehrlich, 1987; Golden & Klein, 1988; Stowell, 1991). When adolescents abuse substances or are emotionally unstable, they miss opportunities to master age-specific skills that are critical for healthy, mature functioning. Developmental approaches offer an array of services that are age specific, including individual, group, and family therapy, vocational/educational therapy, developmental life skills training; and 12-step groups and specific education about substance abuse that is adapted to adolescents.

Social and Family Influences   Social and peer influences also are important factors to consider during treatment. Numerous researchers have found that peer associations are highly associated with drug use (Elliot, Huizinga, & Menard, 1989; Swaim, Oetting, Edwards, & Beauvais, 1989). Many recommend isolation from drug-using friends during treatment and suggest that treatment programs give more attention to the role of the peer group in both onset and maintenance of drug use. However, the need for isolation of adolescents from friends and family is hotly debated in the literature, and treatment decisions should be based on clinical symptoms and presentation. Those adolescents with more complex or serious problems may require inpatient or extended residential treatment, not because they should be isolated but based on the severity of their condition.

In fact, the exclusive use of residential settings for treatment of adolescents with co-occurring mental health and AOD disorders does not adequately address the needs of many youth for ongoing involvement with family, school, and community. The Center for Substance Abuse Treatment (1993) recently reported that evidence now suggests that many adolescents with co-occurring disorders can succeed with outpatient, nonresidential treatment approaches.

Furthermore, despite studies cautioning that the influence of peers must be addressed in AOD treatment, it is important to note that causality between peer group influence and AOD use has not been firmly established. It should not be surprising that adolescents associate with peers who reflect similar behavior. The question is whether or not substance use is caused by association with peers who also use, or whether the adolescent merely seeks a substance-abusing peer group because of the attraction that substances have for the adolescent.

The participation and support of the child's family in assessment and treatment also are important considerations for adolescents (Brown, Ridgely, Pepper, Levine, & Ryglewicz, 1989; Cooper et al., 1989; Weidman, 1985). In addition to the nuclear and extended family, significant others, friends, and social networks can yield critical insight. For example, an examination of the history of substance use and psychiatric disorders in the youth's family provides information about the risk for these disorders occurring in the adolescent. Additionally, determining availability and level of family support and presence of substance abuse in the home and within the context of the adolescent's life provides information valuable to treatment planning.

Family participation in treatment is critical to treatment success and has been neglected by many programs for adolescents (Elliot, et al., 1989; Polcin, 1992). Individual family therapy, multiple family therapy, psychoeducational approaches that utilize didactic interventions, and skill training all have been associated with positive treatment outcomes (Daley, Bowler, & Cahalane, 1992; Kaminer & Frances, 1991; Sciacca 1991). Families also have been shown to have a vital role in reducing drug abuse by teaching constructive values, monitoring, and by modeling behaviors that do not involve substance use (Bahr, Hawks, & Wang, 1993). Others call for family participation in the assessment, planning, training, and provision of treatment for children with emotional disorders (R.M. Friedman, Burns, & Behar, 1991; Stroul & Friedman, 1986).

Additionally, adolescents with substance abuse problems and their families tend to be racially and culturally diverse. Services must be relevant to the cultural background and ethnicity of the child and family. Diverse staff who reflect and understand the culture of the child's environment are needed, along with service delivery approaches that can be accepted and understood by the child and family (Stroul & Friedman, 1986).

Adaptation of Clinical Interventions for Adolescents A number of interventions commonly used with adults require adaptation for adolescents. These include engagement strategies, 12-step programs, medical detoxification, the use of medications, and attention to services to ease transition to adult programs. Each of these is discussed below.

Motivating individuals to enter treatment and engaging them in the treatment process is the key to treatment retention and positive outcomes for adolescents as well as adults (Lehman, Herron, Schwartz, & Myers, 1993). Techniques to engage an adolescent in treatment must recognize the common characteristics of adolescence (e.g., denial, poor frustration tolerance, and desire for immediate gratification) as well as the following concerns.

First, engagement strategies must initially focus on helping the adolescent to develop trust in adults and to acquire adequate communication skills. Behar (1990a) suggests individual treatment contracting and the use of strong positive reinforcers as a method of engagement. A number of researchers have found that ancillary services such as vocational counseling, housing supports, recreational opportunities, team sports, wilderness experiences, peer support groups, and family planning counseling were successful incentives that were positively related to treatment acceptance (Ehrlich, 1987; Friedman & Glickman, 1986). Others argue for nonjudgmental interventions, a supportive environment, and credible, age-appropriate educational materials to decrease defensiveness and encourage rapport, resulting in successful engagement (Golden & Klein, 1988; McKelvy, Kane, & Kellison, 1987).

Legal leverage or coercion to retain the adolescent in treatment while the therapeutic relationship is forming is another method suggested by some researchers (Lehman et al., 1993; Nikkel & Coiner, 1991). For example, courts may refer individuals to treatment as a condition for either sentencing or probation. These methods have been associated with improved treatment retention in adult populations and may prove to be useful with adolescents.

The use of 12-step programs with adolescents is another concern. Many questions have been raised about the suitability of such programs for persons with mental health disorders, and for adolescents in particular. Some clinicians believe that adolescents, particularly younger adolescents, lack the developmental ability or maturity to understand and accept the abstract concepts on which 12-step programs are based (Kaminer & Frances, 1991). Others believe that some of the basic tenets of 12-step programs, such as accepting powerlessness over substances and surrendering to a higher power, are incongruous with the normal developmental phases of adolescence (Ehrlich, 1987). However, useful ways of adapting the 12-step model to adolescents, presumably without sacrificing pivotal elements, also have been described (Chatlos, 1989; Ehrlich, 1987; Evans & Sullivan, 1990; Stowell, 1991).

Extensive medical detoxification is another concern and may not be required for most adolescents, because the long-term side effects of AOD use may not have had an opportunity to develop. However, a period of stabilization generally is recommended during which the adolescent's emotional state is observed and stabilized. Use of hospital-based or residential programs for the stabilization phase of treatment should depend on the severity of the problems and the desire and ability of the youth to abstain from substance use. Hospitalization or residential care should not necessarily be a prerequisite to treatment or the only option available.

The use of psychiatric medications for adolescents during detoxification or stabilization has been questioned for several reasons. Psychiatric medications often are utilized during detoxification of adults to alleviate severe withdrawal symptoms. With adolescents, withdrawal symptoms are less likely. Furthermore, the interactive effects of psychiatric medications on adolescents, particularly those who are substance abusers, is generally unknown (Geller, 1988). Finally, the adolescent's abstinence from substance use may be neither established nor certain to continue over time. Also, as with adults, AOD use can mimic, distort, or mask important clinical features that may clear when the adolescent becomes drug free. The prescription of any medication should always be preceded by a full psychological, medical, and substance use assessment, and should ideally follow a period of verified abstinence.

It is generally acknowledged in the literature that treatment is most effective when an array of clinical and concrete services is available in a variety of treatment settings (Kaminer & Frances, 1991; Ridgely, 1991). These services would ideally be chosen by matching the adolescent's assessed needs and motivation for treatment with the services considered most clinically appropriate and attractive to the adolescent (Lehman et al., 1993). The array of services critical to treatment of adolescents with co-occurring disorders includes crisis management, individual counseling, group therapy, family therapy, self-help and peer group support (including 12-step approaches), case management, educational interventions, home-based services, and relapse prevention and management.

A final area of concern for older adolescents is the transition to adult programs. Wagner (1993) discussed the multiple risks facing adolescents with emotional disorders after they leave high school. These risks include economic hardship, social isolation, difficulty obtaining affordable housing, and incarceration. A lack of coordinated services among the various child-serving agencies is a major contributor to transition difficulties. According to Clark and Foster-Johnson (Chapter 28), transition services need to support youth in their movement into adulthood and adult programs by offering comprehensive and individualized services that teach community skills, provide exposure to community life experiences, and respect the youths' self-determination.

Intersystem Coordination A critical feature for treatment of adolescents is coordination of services across numerous systems that serve children. Substance use disorders, in particular, have been strongly associated with other problem behaviors such as delinquency, precocious sexual behavior, deviant attitudes, and school dropout (Newcomb & Bentler, 1989). Coordination among program modalities within and among the education, social services, juvenile justice, health, and prevocational services systems is needed, because many of these programs lack adequate aftercare and continuity necessary for adolescents with co-occurring mental health and substance abuse disorders.

For example, occurrence of substance abuse or mental health disorders often interrupts the attainment of educational skills, resulting in low academic performance. Coordination with school authorities is necessary to assure that educational assessments are current, that needs are being identified, and that treatment services, if needed, are requested and accessible. Basic skill building and assessment for learning disabilities have been suggested in the literature (DeMilio, 1989; Kaminer & Francis, 1991). School-based services and supervised after-school activities are identified as needs of younger, school-age children (Trupin, Forsyth-Stephens, & Low, 1991).

Similarly, the juvenile justice system may be called on when attempts to place an adolescent into treatment during a crisis have failed. Adolescents with dual diagnoses may be arrested because they are considered "too bad" to be admitted to either substance abuse or mental health facilities (Abram & Teplin, 1991). Rigid eligibility requirements associated with many mental health and substance abuse programs place these youths at risk of arrest and incarceration. Crisis assessment and creative options are needed, including improved identification, assessment, and availability of treatment services in juvenile justice facilities.

PROGRAM MODELS: CAN IT BE DONE?

Despite the numerous issues and difficulties outlined above, a number of programs have been developed and identified by state authorities as innovative or unusual treatment approaches for adolescents with co-occurring mental health and AOD problems (Fleisch, 1991). The programs described below are arranged from least to most restrictive in terms of setting and are consistent with the distinguishing features outlined by the Center for Substance Abuse Treatment (1993) for outpatient and inpatient services for adolescents with co-occurring mental health and AOD disorders.

Nonintensive outpatient services are those in which regularly scheduled hours of service usually total less than 9 per week. These include school-based interventions and clinic treatment programs. Fleisch (1991) describes two programs that exemplify these types of outpatient programs. First, Matrix Community Services in Tucson, Arizona, is a school-based drug intervention program for adolescents facing multiple risks, such as parental substance abuse and poverty. It is designed to offer adolescents the opportunity to build positive peer relationships that do not involve alcohol and other drugs. This is accomplished by making it possible for young people to become active participants in their communities. Alternative recreational activities sponsored by Matrix are open to all students. Second, The Door—A Center of Alternatives, in New York City, is a clinic treatment program that is comprehensive and integrated, meeting the needs of adolescents with both emotional and substance abuse problems. The center's one-stop service delivery system provides a range of services staffed by physicians, mental health workers, nurses, family planning counselors, health educators, nutritionists, lawyers, social workers, artists, and physical education specialists. The elements are interconnected, and adolescents can receive or participate in any combination of services and activities. The goal is to help the child achieve psychological well-being and give up addictive substances.

Intensive outpatient programs are those providing treatment of 9–20 hours per week in a structured program. One example is the Mainstream Youth Program, Inc., in Portland, Oregon, an outpatient adolescent substance abuse treatment, education, and prevention program. What makes Mainstream's treatment program for African American adolescents unique is its insistence that the recovery process must be viewed as a cultural event. The program's role goes beyond the treatment session—the office is located in the heart of the community that it serves and is available to help the community members find solutions to problems (Fleisch, 1991).

A third type of outpatient service is *day treatment*, generally considered to be the most intensive outpatient service and consisting of more than 20 hours of treatment per week. The West Prep Adolescent Day Treatment Program in Valhalla, New York, is a unique day treatment program because of its focus on the dually diagnosed adolescent population. This program integrates aspects of the addiction model into the framework of adolescent mental health treatment. It also treats young people who need psychotropic medication to stabilize and function.

Inpatient and residential treatment includes short-term inpatient care, therapeutic communities, therapeutic foster care programs, and group home/halfway house programs. Fleisch (1991) provides examples of each type of program. First, the Manor House at Elmcrest in Portland, Connecticut, is a *short-term inpatient program* that is also part of a large child and adolescent psychiatric facility. Medical and nursing services, a sophisticated biofeedback clinic, and a secure setting for adolescents who are dangerous to themselves or others are accessible if needed. Manor House also offers a continuum of care ranging from intensive inpatient to outpatient therapy. Finally, the program is noteworthy in that it offers a strong vocational assessment and training component.

Therapeutic communities are residential programs in which adolescents generally are expected to stay from 6 months to 2 years. Amity, Inc., in Tuscon, Arizona, is an example of a therapeutic community designed for juveniles in correctional institutions with identified AOD problems. Amity has developed a holistic approach, including self-help techniques, vocational and special education, intense socialization, and strong peer modeling. Another therapeutic community, Pahl House in Troy, New York, is a longer-term residential and apartment program that teaches community skills to support a life of sobriety.

Morrison Center Breakthrough Program in Portland, Oregon, is a unique program for substance-abusing adolescents who are involved with the criminal justice system. The Breakthrough approach focuses on housing adolescents in "proctor" *foster homes* for the first 6 months of treatment. The proctor home provides a more natural living environment in which the youngsters live a 12-step lifestyle. The teens receive 56 hours per week of programs focusing not only on drug and alcohol addiction, but also on sexual abuse victim and offender issues, criminal thinking patterns, social and living skills education, and academic achievement.

CONCLUSION

The system of care approach would enable mental health and AOD systems and programs to address the multiple and complex needs of adolescents with both problems. In order to achieve this goal, at least three major steps must be taken. First, it is important to identify, describe, and evaluate existing programs that have integrated mental health and substance abuse services for adolescents, and disseminate this information to practitioners. Second, a large-scale epidemiological study of age-specific prevalence of mental health and substance use disorders among adolescents in the U.S. general population needs to be conducted. Third, a standardized methodology for assessing adolescents with mental health and AOD disorders must be developed. Information gathered would determine the level and types of services required by a clearly defined population.

Simultaneously, legislators, regulators, and providers must work together to establish the necessary program supports for adolescents with dual diagnoses. Most important, a reasonable funding formula is needed that encourages collaboration and integration of services on the local level. Finally, advocacy is needed to press legislators, health care providers, and others to establish appropriate programs for youth and their families who are so poorly served within the systems that now exist.

REFERENCES

Abram, K.M., & Teplin, L.A. (1991). Co-occurring disorders among mentally ill jail detainees: Implications for public policy. *American Psychologist, 46,* 1036–1045.

American Psychiatric Association. (1987). *Diagnostic and statistical manual of mental disorders* (3rd ed., rev.). Washington, DC: American Psychiatric Press.

Bahr, S.J., Hawks, R.D., & Wang, G. (1993). Family and religious influences on adolescent substance abuse. *Youth and Society, 24,* 443–465.

Bean-Bayog, M. (1987). Inpatient treatment of the psychiatric patient with alcoholism. *General Hospital Psychiatry, 9,* 203–209.

Behar, L.B. (1990a). *Addressing the service issues for adolescents with multiple diagnoses of emotional disturbance and substance abuse: A discussion for the practitioner.* Unpublished manuscript.

Behar, L.B. (1990b). Financing mental health services for children and adolescents. *Bulletin of the Menninger Clinic, 54,* 127–139.

Boyle, M.H., & Offord, D.R. (1991). Psychiatric disorder and substance use in adolescence. *Canadian Journal of Psychiatry, 36,* 699–705.

Brower, K.J., Blow, F.C., & Beresford, T.P. (1989). Treatment implications of chemical dependency models: An integrative approach. *Journal of Substance Abuse Treatment, 6,* 147–157.

Brown, V.B., & Backer, T.E. (1988). The substance abusing mentally ill patient: Challenges for professional education and training. *Journal of Psychosocial Rehabilitation, 12,* 43–54.

Brown, V.B., Ridgely, S.M., Pepper, B., Levine, I.S., & Ryglewicz, H. (1989). The dual crisis: Mental illness and substance abuse. *American Psychologist, 44,* 565–569.

Bukstein, O.B., Brent, D.A., & Kaminer, Y. (1989). Comorbidity of substance abuse and other psychiatric disorders in adolescents. *American Journal of Psychiatry, 146,* 1131–1141.

Bukstein, O.B., Glancy, L.J., & Kaminer, Y. (1992). Patterns of affective comorbidity in a clinical population of dually diagnosed adolescent substance abusers. *Journal of the American Academy of Child and Adolescent Psychiatry, 31,* 1041–1045.

Butts, J.A., & Schwartz, I.M. (1991). Access to insurance and length of psychiatric stay among adolescents and young adults discharged from general hospitals. *Journal of Health and Social Policy, 3,* 91–116.

Caragonne, P., & Emery, B. (1987). *Mental illness and substance abuse. The dually diagnosed client* (Series Clinical, No. 2), Rockville, MD: National Council of Community Mental Health Centers.

Caron, C., & Rutter, M. (1991). Comorbidity in child psychopathology: Concepts, issues and research strategies. *Journal of Child Psychology and Psychiatry, 32,* 1063–1080.

Center for Substance Abuse Treatment. (1993). *Guidelines for the treatment of alcohol- and other drug-using adolescents* (Treatment Improvement Protocol Series No. 4). Rockville, MD: US Department of Health and Human Services, Substance Abuse and Mental Health Services Administration.

Chatlos, J.C. (1989). Adolescent dual diagnosis: A 12-step transformational model. *Journal of Psychoactive Drugs, 21,* 189–201.

Cohen, P., Cohen, J., Kasen, S., Velez, C.N., Hartmark, C., Johnson, J., Rojas, M., Brook, J., & Streuning, E.L. (1993). An epidemiological study of disorders in late childhood and adolescence—I. Age and gender-specific prevalence. *Journal of Child Psychology and Psychiatry, 34,* 851–867.

Cooper, L., Brown, V.B., & Anglin, M.D. (1989). *Multiple diagnosis: Aspects and issues in substance abuse.* Unpublished document, Drug Abuse Information Monitoring Program, California Department of Alcohol and Drugs Program.

Daley, D.C., Bowler, K., & Cahalane, H. (1992). Approaches to patient and family education with affective disorders. *Patient Education and Counseling, 19,* 163–174.

DeMilio, L. (1989). Psychiatric syndromes in adolescent substance abusers. *American Journal of Psychiatry, 146,* 1212–1214.

Drake, R.E., Alterman, A.I., & Rosenberg, S. (1993). Detection of substance use disorders in severely mentally ill patients. *Community Mental Health Journal, 29,* 175–189.

Drake, R.E., Osher, F.C., Noordsy, D.L., Hurlbut, S.C., Teague, G.B., & Beaudett, M. (1990). Diagnosis of alcohol use disorders in schizophrenia. *Schizophrenia Bulletin, 16,* 57–67.

Ehrlich, P. (1987). 12-step principles and adolescent chemical dependency treatment. *Journal of Psychoactive Drugs, 19,* 311–318.

Elliot, D.S., Huizinga, D., & Menard, S. (1989). *Multiple problem youth: Delinquency, substance use, and mental health problems.* New York: Springer-Verlag.

Evans, K., & Sullivan, J.M. (1990). *Dual diagnosis: Counseling the mentally ill substance abuser.* New York: Guilford Press.

Evans, M., Dollard, N., & McNulty, T.L. (1992). Intensive case management for youth with serious emotional disturbance and chemical abuse. In *Progress and Issues in Case Management* (pp. 289–315). National Institute on Drug Abuse Research Monograph Series No. 127. Washington DC: National Institute on Drug Abuse.

Fariello, D., & Scheidt, S. (1989). Clinical case management of the dually diagnosed patient. *Hospital and Community Psychiatry, 40,* 1065–1067.

Farrow, J.A., Smith, W.R., & Hurst, M.D. (1993). *Adolescent drug and alcohol assessment instruments in current use: A critical comparison.* Olympia, WA: Division of Alcohol and Substance Abuse.

Fleisch, B. (1991). *Approaches in the treatment of adolescents with emotional and substance abuse problems* (DHHS Publ. No. ADM 91-1744). Rockville, MD: U.S. Department of Health and Human Services.

Ford, J., Hillard, J.R., Giesler, L.J., Lassen, K.L., & Thomas, H. (1989). Substance abuse/mental illness: Diagnostic issues. *American Journal of Drug and Alcohol Abuse, 15,* 297–307.

Friedman, A.S., & Glickman, N.W. (1986). Program characteristics for successful treatment of adolescent drug abuse. *Journal of Nervous and Mental Disease, 174,* 669–679.

Friedman, R.M., Burns, B.J., & Behar, L.B. (1991, January). *Major issues in improving mental health and substance abuse services for adolescents.* Tampa: University of South Florida, Florida Mental Health Institute, Department of Child and Family Studies.

Geller, B. (1988). Pharmacotherapy of concomitant psychiatric disorders in adolescent substance abusers. *NIDA Monograph Series, 77,* 94–112.

Golden, L., & Klein, K.M. (1988). Treatment as a habilitative process in adolescent development and chemical dependency. *Alcoholism Treatment Quarterly, 4,* 35–41.

Greenbaum, P., Foster-Johnson, L., & Petrila, A. (in press). Co-occurring substance use and mental health disorders among adolescents: Prevalence, assessment, and treatment. *American Journal of Orthopsychiatry.*

Halikas, J. (1990). Substance abuse in children and adolescents. In B.D. Garfinkel, G.A. Carlson, & E.B. Weller (Eds.), *Psychiatric disorders in children and adolescents* (pp. 210–234). Philadelphia: W.B. Saunders.

Kaminer, Y., & Frances, R.J. (1991). Inpatient treatment of adolescents with psychiatric and substance abuse disorders. *Hospital and Community Psychiatry, 42,* 894–896.

Lehman, A.F., Herron, J.D., Schwartz, R.P., & Myers, P. (1993). Rehabilitation for adults with severe mental illness and substance use disorders: A clinical trial. *Journal of Nervous and Mental Disease, 181,* 86–90.

Lehman, A.F., Myers, C.P., & Corty, E. (1989). Assessment and classification of patients with psychiatric and substance abuse syndromes. *Hospital and Community Psychiatry, 40,* 1019–1025.

Marlatt, G.A., & Gordon, J.R. (1985). *Relapse prevention.* New York: Guilford Press.

McConaughy, S.H., & Achenbach, T.M. (1994). Comorbidity of empirically based syndromes in matched general population and clinical samples. *Journal of Child Psychology and Psychiatry and Allied Disciplines, 35,* 1141–1157.

McKelvy, M.J., Kane, J.S., & Kellison, K. (1987). Substance abuse and mental illness: Double trouble. *Journal of Psychosocial Nursing, 25,* 20–25.

Menicucci, L.D., Wermuth, L., & Sorensen, J. (1988). Treatment providers' assessment of dual-prognosis patients: Diagnosis, treatment, referral, and family involvement. *International Journal of the Addictions, 23,* 617–622.

New York State Office of Mental Health. (1994). *Interim report to the legislature on mental illness and chemical abuse.* Albany, NY: Author.

Newcomb, M.D., & Bentler, P.M. (1989). Substance use and abuse among children and teenagers. *American Psychologist, 44,* 242–248.

Nikkel, R., & Coiner, R. (1991). Critical interventions and tasks in delivering dual-diagnosis services. *Psychosocial Rehabilitation Journal, 15,* 57–66.

Pires, S.A., & Silber, J.T. (1991). *On their own: Runaway and homeless youth and programs that serve them.* Washington DC: Georgetown University Child Development Center, National Technical Assistance Center for Children's Mental Health.

Polcin, D.L. (1992). A comprehensive model for adolescent chemical dependency treatment. *Journal of Counseling and Development, 70,* 376–382.

Ridgely, M.S. (1991). Creating integrated programs for severely mentally ill persons with substance disorders. In K. Minkoff & R.E. Drake (Eds.), *New directions for mental health services: Dual diagnosis of major mental illness and substance disorder* (pp. 29–41). San Francisco: Jossey-Bass.

Ridgely, M.S., Goldman, H.H., & Willenbring, M. (1990). Barriers to the care of persons with dual diagnoses: Organization and financing issues. *Schizophrenia Bulletin, 16,* 123–132.

Rosenthal, R.N., Hellerstein, D.J., & Miner, C.R. (1992). Integrated services for treatment of schizophrenic substance abusers: Demographics, symptoms, and substance abuse patterns. *Psychiatric Quarterly, 63,* 3–26.

Schuckit, M.A. (1986). Genetic and clinical implications of alcoholism and affective disorder. *American Journal of Psychiatry, 137,* 372–373.

Schuckit, M.A. (1989). *Drug and alcohol abuse* (3rd ed.). New York: Plenum Press.

Schumacher, J.E., Duchnowski, A., & Algarin, A. (1993). Services for youth with coexisting emotional and substance abuse problems. *Child and Adolescent Mental Health Care, 3,* 219–227.

Sciacca, K. (1991). An integrated treatment approach for severely mentally ill individuals with substance disorders. In K. Minkoff & R. Drake (Eds.), *New directions for mental health services: Dual diagnosis of major mental illness and substance disorder* (pp. 69–84). San Francisco: Jossey-Bass.

Shedler, J., & Block, J. (1990). Adolescent drug use and psychological health: A longitudinal inquiry. *American Psychologist, 45,* 612–630.

Smith, H.E., & Margolis, R.D. (1991). Adolescent inpatient and outpatient chemical dependence treatment: An overview. *Psychiatric Annals, 21,* 105–108.

Stowell, R.J.A. (1991). Dual diagnosis issues. *Psychiatric Annals, 21,* 99–104.

Stroul, B.A., & Friedman, R.M. (1986). *A system of care for severely emotionally disturbed children and youth* (rev. ed.). Washington, DC: Georgetown University Child Development Center, National Technical Assistance Center for Children's Mental Health.

Swaim, R.C., Oetting, E.R., Edwards, R.W., & Beauvais, F. (1989). Links from emotional distress to adolescent drug use: A path model. *Journal of Consulting and Clinical Psychology, 57,* 227–231.

Test, M.A., Wallish, L., Allness, D., & Ripp, K. (1989). Substance use in young adults with schizophrenic disorders. *Schizophrenic Bulletin, 15,* 465–476.

Thacker, W., & Tremaine, L. (1989). Systems issues in serving the mentally ill substance abuser: Virginia's experience. *Hospital and Community Psychiatry, 40,* 1046–1049.

Trupin, E.W., Forsyth-Stephens, A., & Low, B.P. (1991). Service needs of severely disturbed children. *American Journal of Public Health, 81*, 975–980.

Wagner, M. (1993). *Dropouts with disabilities: What do we know? What can we do?* Menlo Park, CA: SRI International.

Weidman, A.A. (1985). Engaging the families of substance abusing adolescents in family therapy. *Journal of Substance Abuse Treatment, 2*, 97–105.

Winters, K.C. (1990). The need for improved assessment of adolescent substance involvement. *Journal of Drug Issues, 3*, 487–502.

CHAPTER 27

Services for Runaway
and Homeless Youth

Sheila A. Pires and Judith Tolmach Silber

Runaway and homeless youth, despite their large numbers and growing visibility, are the most understudied and underserved subgroup among the homeless population, according to the Institute of Medicine (1989). Estimates of the number of homeless and runaway youth range from 730,000 to 1.3 million nationwide; determining a precise count is complicated not only by the transience of the population, but also by a lack of consensus on the definitions of "homeless" and "runaway." The federal government, for example, defines a homeless youth as a person without shelter who is away from home "without parental permission." This leaves out many youth whose families have rejected them or who literally have no families. National estimates are based entirely on youth 18 and under *who seek shelter*, leaving two major groups uncounted: older adolescents and young adults between the ages of 18 and 24, and street youth who do not seek shelter (Janus, McCormick, Burgess, & Hartman, 1987).

Studies indicate not only that homeless youth are increasing in number (in New York City, teenagers are the fastest growing group of homeless people), but also that their problems are increasing in severity (Pires & Silber, 1991; van Houten, 1992).

THE POPULATION

Changes in the Population
Homeless and runaway youth in the 1990s are profoundly different from the generation that informed development of the federal Runaway and Homeless Youth Act in 1974 (PL 96-509) and spawned the growth of alternative youth shelters in the 1960s and 1970s. At that time, it was assumed that most adolescents left home as a result of their own emotional turmoil and that, with the appropriate short-term assistance, they could return home (Speck, Ginther, & Helton, 1988). The act thus funded short-term

(15-day) emergency shelter, crisis intervention, and family reunification services. For an increasing number of youth in the 1990s, family reunification within 15 days is not a realistic goal.

Runaway and homeless youth today present a complex mixture of problems. The population includes youth who have left home to escape a dangerous, abusive environment; youth who, on their own, have left their home countries to seek refuge in the United States; so-called throwaway youth, who have been pushed out of their homes by their parents or legal guardians; long-term runaways, often called "street youth," who depend on prostitution and drug trafficking to meet their survival needs; youth (most often, boys over the age of 12) who have become homeless because their families were forced to take refuge in one of the many shelters that refuse to accept adolescents; teenagers who were pushed out of their homes when their families were forced to "double up" in an overcrowded apartment; and so-called system youth, who have been in the custody of the state because of child abuse, neglect, or mental illness and who have left state custody without a viable alternative placement or the ability to live independently.

Youth workers report that the percentage of runaway and homeless youth today who are truly without recourse to family support is increasing. For many youth, reconciliation of family issues and eventual independence may be the optimal outcome, rather than a return to families. Although some youth may be able to return home if intensive family preservation services are provided (and if the family is willing to participate in services), such youth still require interim housing, with support services, at least during the period that reunification is taking place—a period that extends well beyond the 15-day emergency shelter limit.

Today's homeless and runaway youth population reflects deep-seated structural changes in the American family, the economy, community support systems, and social institutions. Poverty, violence, and drugs characterize the homes and neighborhoods of many of these youth. More than any other adjective, "multiproblem" is used by researchers and practitioners to describe runaway and homeless youth, referring both to the environments from which they come and the problems they bring with them.

It is not surprising that today's youth require help with a wide range of problems, including serious educational and employment deficits, drug addiction, emotional and sexual trauma, severe depression, human immunodeficiency virus (HIV) infection, persistent health and dental problems, lack of housing and independent living skills, pregnancy, and parenthood. They require a comprehensive, integrated, and flexible array of services. Homeless and runaway youth programs struggle to provide long-term comprehensive solutions with short-term categorical funding. Short-term emergency shelter and crisis intervention services—the mainstays of the

Runaway and Homeless Youth Act—constitute a small part of the array of services that youth agencies now provide.

Despite their diversity with respect to age, race, gender, socioeconomic background, and life circumstances, today's youth present service providers with a consistent constellation of troubling characteristics. At the same time, these youth display an extraordinary resolve and ability to survive. Effective programs not only are responsive to the range of vulnerabilities of these youth but build on their strengths.

Characteristics of the Population

Older and Younger Today's homeless youth are both older and younger than they were in the 1980s. There are an increasing number of 18- to 24-year-olds seeking services at youth shelters. Many of these older adolescents had been in foster care, juvenile detention, or residential treatment but "aged out," "opted out," or were forced out of these placements. A recent nationwide survey conducted by the National Association of Social Workers (NASW) determined that one out of five youths who sought shelter came directly from a foster family or group home; 38% had been in foster care at some time during the previous year (NASW, 1991). Lacking a stable family to return to or the skills to live on their own, many older adolescents are in danger of becoming hardened street "survivors" (van Houten, 1992).

Homeless older youth often find refuge in adult shelters, a cause for concern among youth workers who contend that adult shelters unintentionally "enable" youth to continue living on the streets by meeting basic needs but failing to address the range of other problems these youth have. This concern has led to negotiations, collaboration, and new shelter intake policies between youth service agencies and adult shelters in a number of urban areas to try to divert youth to a broader range of services.

At the other end of the age spectrum are the 10- and 11-year-olds, many of whom come from families who have disintegrated under the assaults of poverty and drug abuse. Often such children become homeless when overburdened child welfare systems are forced to ignore their needs because limited resources must be expended on children who are even younger and more vulnerable.

The wide age spectrum among homeless and runaway youth requires an equally wide array of services, further straining the limited resources of homeless and runaway youth programs. It is this challenge that has inspired many agencies to collaborate in innovative ways. The LA Network in Los Angeles, for example, developed a computer-linked interagency service network.

More Substance Abuse Shelter staff report that 70%–90% of homeless and runaway youth abuse alcohol; 50%–75% abuse drugs, and nearly all of those who abuse drugs also use alcohol (Pires & Silber, 1991; Robertson, Doegel, & Ferguson, 1989). In addition, one fourth come from families where parents also abuse drugs, a factor that complicates reunification efforts (NASW, 1991).

The high rate of substance abuse among homeless and runaway youth is explained in part by the fact that drugs and alcohol are used as self-medication to dull both physical and emotional pain. Drug trafficking also provides necessary subsistence money. Drug abuse places homeless youth at extreme risk for HIV infection. The National Commission on Acquired Immune Deficiency Syndrome (1991) asserts that one third of all adolescent acquired immunodeficiency syndrome (AIDS) cases can be linked to drug abuse, caused by either the use of infected needles or unprotected sexual activity while under the influence of drugs.

More Pregnancy   As more adolescent girls seek shelter, more pregnancies are reported, as well as more pregnancies with a second child. Several factors contribute to the increased pregnancy rates among homeless youth: substance abuse, which makes the use of contraception less likely; prostitution as a means of earning subsistence money; and the failure of child welfare agencies (which formerly had responsibility for many homeless youth) to provide adequate sex education. Homeless pregnant teens, as a result of inadequate prenatal care and frequent drug and alcohol use during pregnancy, experience high rates of low birth weight infants and infant mortality (Robertson, Doegel, & Ferguson, 1989).

More Gangs, More Violence   Violent neighborhood gangs that actively recruit homeless and runaway youth can be found in every major metropolitan area (Pires & Silber, 1991). Fierce competition for new recruits has intensified the pressure on homeless youth and driven gang members to solicit younger members from a wider geographical area.

The increase in rival gangs has brought with it an increase in the use of weapons on the streets. Some of this upsurge in violence is an outgrowth of gang activity, but there is also increasing violence among nongang youth. Youth workers attribute the upsurge in violent behavior to the increased number of homeless and runaway youth who have themselves suffered physical and sexual abuse.

Increased violence has heightened the problem of security at youth shelters. Safety is of special concern to the teams of outreach workers who search the streets for homeless and runaway youth.

More Emotional Disturbance   Studies of homeless youth confirm consistently high rates of emotional disturbance (Robertson, 1989; Yates, MacKenzie, Pennbridge, & Cohen, 1989). One study concluded that "shelter users have a psychiatric profile largely indistinguishable from adolescents attending a psychiatric clinic" (Shaffer & Caton, 1984, p. 34). Homeless and runaway youth programs also report an influx of youth with a dual diagnosis of emotional disturbance and substance abuse. Some programs, such as Youthcare in Seattle, have expanded their capacity to provide in-house mental health treatment. However, youth suffering from suicidal or psychotic ideation, borderline personality disorder, or drug "flashbacks" require a structured treatment environment and psychiatric expertise that is not available at any program for homeless and runaway youth. In fact, appropriate public sector mental health treatment for adolescents, like drug treatment, is not available at all in many communities. The paucity of treatment options presents homeless and runaway youth programs with a difficult dilemma: to develop costly in-house expertise in mental health and substance abuse treatment or to provide less than adequate services to youth who are seeking their help.

More Cultural Diversity   As recently as the 1980s, youth shelters served mostly Caucasian, typically middle-class youth. Now, as minorities comprise a larger proportion of the total population, particularly the population that is poor and transient, homeless and runaway youth programs report an increased number of minority and immigrant (frequently non–English-speaking) youth (Wetzel, 1987). Similarly, minority youth who are overrepresented in the child welfare, juvenile justice, and mental health systems are also finding their way to the streets when those systems fail to prepare youth to return home or to achieve independence. The increase in cultural diversity poses new challenges to providers, who report having an inadequate number of staff of color or staff trained in cultural competence (Pires & Silber, 1991).

More School Dropouts   Two regional surveys completed in the 1980s revealed extremely high rates of school failure among homeless youth (Robertson, 1989; Shaffer & Caton, 1984). Many youth report that their decision to leave school precipitated the family conflict that preceded their leaving home. Observers contend that, in reality, the sequence is reversed: Family conflict is often a major cause of academic failure among junior high and high school students.

More Gay and Lesbian Youth   As more youth identify themselves as gay or lesbian, their risk of being forced from their homes increases. Incidences of depression and low self-esteem are unusually high among homosexual homeless youth; one study found that 53% of gay and lesbian youth had previously attempted suicide (Kruks, 1991).

More Health Problems   Living without housing, sanitation, or adequate rest or nutrition is a serious threat to health and well-being. In recent years, the additional threats of HIV infection, sexually transmitted diseases, tuberculosis, and highly addictive drugs have made street life even more dangerous. Many homeless youth lack access to health or dental care; a

Chicago study of homeless youth found that over two thirds had no access to medical insurance, nor could they receive standard treatments without parental permission (Chicago Coalition for the Homeless, 1993).

THE PROGRAMS

Changes in the Programs

To meet the challenge of providing a holistic spectrum of essential services for "multiproblem" youth, exemplary programs have evolved from small storefront shelters into complex collaborative service networks that link mainstream public and private agencies with alternative youth programs. Although each homeless and runaway youth program is shaped in part by the unique character of the youth and the community it serves, effective programs share many common practice principles, adopted in response to nationwide changes in the youth population and in the service environment:

- Programs have become more comprehensive, either by adding in-house service components or by developing partnerships and service networks with other agencies.
- Collaboration and contracting with mainstream agencies are increasing; "new morbidity" problems such as AIDS, adolescent pregnancy, drug abuse, and gang violence require collaboration with health care, juvenile justice, substance abuse, child welfare, and mental health systems.
- Youth workers have specialized skills in substance abuse, HIV education, mental health, and housing.
- Diverse public and private funding, requiring sophisticated fund-raising and fiscal management abilities, is a necessary corollary to service expansion.

Characteristics of Effective Programs

Effective programs typically incorporate several common principles governing service delivery. These programs are

- *Adolescent centered:* They adapt services to the adolescent, rather than expecting the adolescent to adapt to the services.
- *Community based:* They provide local, integrated, and coordinated services.
- *Comprehensive:* They recognize the multiple needs of these youth and ensure comprehensive services and holistic care.
- *Collaborative:* They draw on the resources of a community or work in coordination with other programs to provide a range of services, in-house or through interagency agreements.

- *Egalitarian:* They provide services in an environment and a manner that enhances the self-worth and dignity of adolescents, and they respect their wishes and individual goals.
- *Empowering:* They maximize opportunities for youth involvement and self-determination in the planning and delivery of services and foster a sense of personal efficacy that encourages youth to want to effect changes in their lives.
- *Inclusive:* They serve all runaway and homeless youth *or* provide and track referrals for those youth whom they are unable to serve.
- *Visible, accessible, and engaging:* They provide services that attract youth.
- *Flexible:* They incorporate flexibility in service provision and funding to support individualized services.
- *Culturally sensitive:* They work to provide culturally competent services.
- *Family focused:* They recognize the pivotal role that families play in the lives of high-risk adolescents.
- *Affirming:* They target strengths, not deficits, of youth and their families.

Effective homeless and runaway youth programs were forced to expand at a rapid pace in the 1980s. In almost every instance, expansion was the result of collaboration and cooperation between alternative youth programs and traditional public agencies. In Seattle, for example, teenage prostitutes are diverted from the public juvenile detention center to comprehensive services as a result of a partnership between the juvenile justice system and the alternative youth services agency; in San Diego, street youth attend school in an alternative classroom staffed and funded by the public schools; and in Boston, a nurse from the public hospital rides an outreach van nightly to help search for—and treat—homeless youth.

Effective programs intentionally blur the boundaries between various service components, such as mental health and substance abuse treatment. The Bridge in Boston, for instance, combines mental health and substance abuse treatment in its counseling program, which is staffed by counselors who are experts in both disciplines. By creating a seamless network of services, good programs enable youth to move into and out of a service component as their needs change. Often programs will utilize one service component to draw youth into another. At United Action for Youth in Iowa City, for example, a fully equipped recording studio and staff with musical skills are used to draw teenagers into drug counseling. Effective programs achieve this absence of internal fragmentation through communication and information sharing that is not accidental: Regular attendance at meetings and specified record keeping are required, as are structured supervision and in-service training. Case workers are encouraged to fashion a unique package of services tailored both to meet basic needs, such as food and medical care, and to encourage changes, such as drug counseling.

Holistic care is further strengthened by the practice of encouraging staff to work in various aspects of the program, which not only enlarges expertise but also alleviates burnout. In addition, effective programs foster a strong sense of "family" among staff. Through formal retreats and informal gatherings, staff are committed to nurturing one another; this strong internal bond minimizes the ability of youth to split staff into adversarial factions—a constant danger in programs that enroll troubled youth.

Essential Services

Street Outreach Homeless and runaway youth programs view outreach as the foundation for service delivery because it provides the necessary connection between frightened, distrustful youth and adults who want to help them to exit street life. Outreach takes a variety of forms, including street work, community organizing, public service announcements, telephone crisis lines, information fairs, posters, drop-in centers, peer counselors, and teen theater, as well as outreach to other city agencies, such as detention centers, housing projects, schools, and the police. A range of outreach styles is needed to reach the diverse population: youth who will never seek shelter but who will accept food, clothing, or medical care; those who can be convinced over time to seek shelter; and, finally, those youth who can be diverted from ever experimenting with street life.

Youth workers who staff outreach teams, drop-in centers, and roving vans are on the "front line," regularly confronting unpredictable situations that can jeopardize their personal safety or the agency's reputation. Effective programs provide outreach workers with preservice and in-service training, ongoing supervision, and detailed policy guidelines for handling emergencies. Interagency collaboration skills are essential for outreach staff, who must enlist the cooperation of police, local hospitals, community mental health centers, adult shelters, and others in order to link youth with essential resources in the community.

Outreach workers indicate that the success of drop-in centers and street outreach work depends on three essential attributes: 1) tangible services (food, showers, first aid, clothing) offered without obligation; 2) repeated opportunities to try out a program's trustworthiness, again without obligation; and 3) youth workers willing to listen and counsel without making legal or moral judgments (Pires & Silber, 1991).

To illustrate, The Bridge in Boston operates an outreach van that is fully equipped as a medical clinic. Staffed by volunteer nurses and doctors, The Bridge Free Medical Van makes regularly scheduled stops around the city each weeknight. By offering basic medical care and counseling to alienated youth, the van provides a safe and neutral gateway to additional services.

Substance Abuse Treatment and Education Substance abuse education and counseling permeates every aspect of the services provided at homeless and runaway youth programs; it is not considered a separate categorical "component" but is a crucial ingredient in every other intervention between youth and staff. Many programs have licensed drug counselors on staff; others provide extensive in-service training in substance abuse issues. For example, to improve the competence of its staff in dealing with substance abuse issues, The Bridge in Boston developed a 19-session curriculum for training all newly hired counselors. The *Drug Prevention and Education Training Manual for Runaway and Homeless Youth Service Providers* (developed with a grant from the U.S. Department of Health and Human Services) is an exhaustive review of all the complex issues that substance abuse education and counseling entails (Bridge Over Troubled Waters, Inc., 1991).

Even the best trained substance abuse counselors, however, cannot help addicted youth unless they have access to community-based detoxification and substance abuse treatment services that are appropriate for homeless and runaway youth. The need for specialized, comprehensive public-sector substance abuse treatment for adolescents has been well documented (Hawkins, Lishner, Jenson, & Catalano, 1987; Regier et al., 1990). What little treatment is available for adolescents exists mostly in for-profit facilities that are inaccessible to poor, uninsured adolescents. Many of the programs that do exist fail to address the close connection between drug dependence and its underlying causes: depression, family dissension, racism, neglect, and physical, sexual, and psychological abuse. They also may require family participation, which excludes many homeless youth.

The fact that substance abuse treatment services are unavailable, inaccessible, and inappropriate, combined with the increasing numbers of runaway and homeless youth who are involved with drugs, has created tension between alternative youth programs and the public-sector substance abuse agencies—the agencies that ostensibly have the public mandate and the expertise to provide treatment. Emergency shelters are faced with a difficult dilemma—allowing youth to come into the shelter high on drugs not only "enables" drug abuse but endangers staff and other youth; turning youth away, however, means abandoning them to the dangers of street life. San Diego Youth and Community Services, after years of struggling with this dilemma, developed its own day treatment program for addicted youth through a contract with the county drug abuse administration. Other programs have fostered "special relationships" with public and private detoxification programs in order to secure space in emergencies.

Mental Health Treatment The paucity of community-based mental health treatment for homeless and runaway adolescents is just one aspect of the general dearth of treatment for *all* children and adolescents. Runaway and homeless youth programs typically have staff who provide counseling, casework, or case management services; in addition, staff are able to identify youth who require immediate inpatient psychiatric evaluation. However, most youth workers, although they have years of valuable experience, are not trained mental health professionals.

As the mental health needs of runaway and homeless youth have increased in severity (and community resources remain scarce), effective programs have stretched their resources to fill the gap. Some programs have hired a clinical director to provide staff with ongoing supervision and in-service training; others use precious resources to hire master's level staff who can provide group, individual, and family therapy. Many programs have instituted a "therapeutic milieu" that provides youth workers with clear guidelines for establishing a relationship with troubled youth.

Huckleberry House in Columbus, Ohio, now provides intensive home-based "wraparound" services for youth in severe crisis. Using an interdisciplinary team (typically, a social worker, mental health counselor, advocate for the child, and case manager), services are tailored to the specific needs of the family. Team members sometimes move into the family home to provide stability and prevent a child (often a repeat runaway) from leaving home. As a result of its strong therapeutic component, Huckleberry House has established a close collaborative relationship with the local child welfare agency, the mental health board, the courts, and the police department, all of which refer youth to the program.

AIDS Education and Prevention Effective AIDS education and prevention programs are dependent on the availability of drug treatment, mental health treatment, transitional living facilities, alternative education, and job training options. When these services are not available, the choices available to street youth are severely reduced, increasing the likelihood of their engaging in "survival sex" and other high-risk behaviors. Despite the systemic social, economic, and psychological factors that sustain high-risk sexual and substance abuse practices, youth workers are diligent in their efforts to combat AIDS.

Much of the standard AIDS education literature and staff training curricula are not particularly relevant to street youth, many of whom have little capacity to think about consequences far into the future. What little material exists is particularly unsuited to minority and non–English-speaking youth. As a result, many runaway and homeless youth programs have developed their own curricula.

Four San Diego youth agencies (San Diego Youth and Community Services, San Diego YMCA, San Diego Youth Involvement, and South Bay Community Services) applied to the California Department of Health for funds to develop an AIDS education training manual. Using a train-the-trainers format, the curriculum has been used to train staff and volunteers from 11 local public and private programs, who, in turn, have trained several hundred other trainers (including youth).

To increase its AIDS outreach to Hispanic youth, Youth Development, Inc., in Albuquerque developed Project SIDA, an aggressive prevention program that utilizes bilingual street outreach workers, counseling, theatrical performances by former drug users, written materials in the form of comic books, and transportation to and from testing sites. To reach youth in the barrios, Project SIDA works closely with a fundamentalist church, Barrios for Jesus, that has been successful in working with intravenous drug users.

Youth workers cite a need for AIDS education efforts to be far more youth centered, using such techniques as peer outreach and youth theater and music groups (Pires & Silber, 1991). Youth workers agree that information and materials need to be frank concerning sexual issues and safe sex practices.

Programs differ in their attitudes toward HIV testing. Some programs do not encourage testing because it is believed that, whether the outcome is positive or negative, the effect on youth is detrimental. An HIV-negative result may encourage teens to continue engaging in high-risk behaviors; if results are HIV positive, there is a woeful lack of follow-up care in the community. Those programs that do encourage testing try to ensure appropriate follow-up support. Although there is a great deal of ambivalence toward the issue of testing, effective programs have policies in place to ensure youth have access to testing and to protect confidentiality of testing procedures and results.

Transitional Housing   Escalating poverty has caused the population of multiproblem older adolescents requiring short- and long-term housing to increase in recent years (Select Committee on Children, Youth and Families, 1989). This increase is reflected in the burgeoning population of older youth who are seen at homeless and runaway shelters. To prevent their emergency shelters from becoming permanently filled with youth who have nowhere to go, runaway and homeless youth programs have, in recent years, added transitional housing to their core services.

No one housing model can encompass the diversity of homeless youth. To create housing options tailored to particular life situations, effective programs struggle to develop a continuum of options, ranging from the most protected and structured to the most independent. These include emergency shelters, 15- to 45-day shelters, therapeutic group homes, transitional housing, cooperative apartment living, and independent living with follow-up care. Housing options must be adapted to the needs of special groups, such as teenage mothers and their infants, gay and lesbian youth, or former prostitutes.

The Bridge in Boston offers one example of an agency that has developed a housing continuum (The Bridge, Inc., 1985). Its Independent Living House provides up to 12 months of supervised housing for youth ages 16 to 21 who express a desire to leave street life. All residents must attend school, work after school, and participate in managing the house. Group activities are required, as is weekly group therapy; mental health treatment, which emphasizes issues of sexual abuse, sexuality, prostitution, drug and alcohol abuse, depression, self-worth, and vocational goals, is also mandatory. Residents open savings accounts and pay $50 per month in rent.

The Bridge also operates a cooperative apartment program. Two, three, or four residents share an apartment for 1 year; The Bridge subsidizes part of the rent, providing minimal supervision and access to services as needed. The Bridge also operates a group home for young mothers and their infants. The spectrum of housing options at The Bridge enables homeless and runaway youth to leave street life with the daily living skills, as well as the physical and psychological stamina, to achieve independence.

Employment and Training   Youth workers cite an urgent need for in-house employment and training components specifically tailored to runaway and homeless youth (Pires & Silber, 1991). Although there are some notable exceptions, most runaway and homeless youth programs provide only limited on-site job counseling and job development services, not comprehensive, structured employment and training programs. Some programs have arrangements to obtain employment and training services from other agencies in the community that specialize in this area.

The ingredients of successful employment and training programs for high-risk youth have been well documented (Act Together, Inc., 1983; DeLone, 1990; Taggart, 1981). They include

- An individualized, graduated approach
- The teaching of basic education and social and life skills, in addition to "world of work" preparation (some research also cites the importance of teaching specific vocational skills)
- Use of competency-based, computer-assisted basic skills curricula, which allow youth to proceed at their own pace while providing ongoing feedback
- A year-round program to prevent summer learning loss and to provide the time necessary to work intensively with high-risk youth
- A comprehensive focus that takes into account the multiple problems of high-risk youth and coordinates services with other agencies, particularly education and social services
- Use of job developers and job counselors to assist both employers and youth
- Competent, dedicated staff
- Stable funding

Many studies indicate that traditional employment and training programs are neither reaching most runaway and homeless youth (or most disadvantaged youth generally) nor meeting the needs of those whom they do reach. Robertson (1989), for example, found that homeless youth have little access to regular employment and training programs. Public/Private Ventures documented that less than 5% of eligible youth were served by the Job Training Partnership Act (JTPA) of 1982 (PL 97-300), the major federal employment and training program. Few of the youth JTPA did serve were the highest risk: Less than 30% of youth served by JTPA were school dropouts (whereas close to 75% of runaway and homeless youth are dropouts); less than 10% were single parents (an estimated 30% of homeless youth are pregnant or single parents); and less than 5% had limited or no English-speaking ability (whereas immigrant youth make up a growing proportion of the client population in a number of runaway and homeless youth programs) (Public/Private Ventures, 1990).

A major reason for the failure of traditional employment and training programs to reach high-risk youth is that these youth, and runaway and homeless youth in particular, have an array of problems that require comprehensive, coordinated intervention. Yet, as the Public/Private Ventures study notes

> [Y]outh employment programs have been either unwilling or unable to meet the multiple needs of at-risk youth . . . everything we have learned to date about how to affect the life chances of these youth indicates the need for longer-term and/or more intensive interventions that draw on a variety of resources and services. (Public/Private Ventures, 1990, p. 3)

Neither researchers nor runaway and homeless youth programs underestimate the difficulty of providing effective employment and training services to runaway and homeless youth. The suspicion with which street youth view services, their access to illegal sources of income, primarily through prostitution and drugs, as well as their multiple problems, pose formidable barriers. Public/Private Ventures, for example, notes that among the hardest youth to reach are those involved in underground economies of drugs and prostitution and those who, in addition, are homeless and have physical health, mental health, and substance abuse problems, a description that characterizes many street youth (Public/Private Ventures, 1990).

Education According to the National Coalition for the Homeless, more than 40% of homeless youth do not attend school (CD7 Reports, 1990). Runaway and homeless youth face numerous barriers to public school enrollment. Although Congress passed legislation in 1987 to exempt residency requirements for children whose families are living in shelters, emancipated teenagers are still turned away from school because they lack a permanent address, cannot meet school district residency requirements, fail to produce required school transcripts, or lack immunization records.

As a prerequisite for learning, youth first must find some refuge from the fear and anxiety that shadow them on the street. Also, many homeless youth need to be convinced that they have the ability to learn and that school is not necessarily a punitive, hostile place. To create a nurturing learning environment for youth who may be several grade levels behind in basic skills and need an opportunity to catch up without feeling embarrassed, effective programs, offered in collaboration with school districts, have created alternative classrooms or special schools for homeless youth. Along with a willingness to accommodate the anxiety, depression, low self-esteem, hunger, and physical exhaustion that homeless youth bring to school, these alternative education components utilize diagnostic and prescriptive teaching methods that enable teachers to design an individualized lesson plan for each student. Students proceed (and succeed) at their own pace.

Program staff, as well as researchers, emphasize that education programs, to be effective with runaway and homeless youth, also must incorporate basic reading and math skills acquisition and self-esteem building (Boyer, 1988). Schools that provide an independent living course, an alternative curriculum for homeless youth, and counselors who can link youth to community resources are also an essential source of survival skills training. For example, alternative education programs usually provide accurate AIDS prevention information. For homeless youth who are living on the street or with friends, this education component may be their only link to such life-saving information.

Medical and Dental Care   The health care system for adolescents generally is inadequate, fragmented, and inappropriate, and youth are the least likely of any age group to see a doctor (Children's Defense Fund, 1990). Current research attributes the lack of health care for adolescents to four principal barriers:

- Nearly one fifth of all children and youth under 18 have no health insurance, public or private (Children's Defense Fund, 1990).
- Teenagers and their families cannot afford to pay for health care. Even the poorest adolescents may be denied Medicaid eligibility in many states. Teens living on their own are frequently excluded from Medicaid if they cannot obtain parental permission or the required documentation, such as a birth certificate.
- Appropriate health care services for adolescents are in short supply. Particularly in many rural and inner city areas, there is a severe shortage of physicians willing to treat low-income patients, and there is a scarcity of adolescent age-appropriate services. Where such services are available, long waits for appointments, inconvenient hours, and an impersonal attitude toward patients often prevail, which deter teens from accessing services.
- Fragmented, categorically defined medical services fail to address the social, psychological, and environmental problems or the risk-taking behaviors that seriously endanger the health of adolescents.

The lifestyles and attitudes of homeless and runaway youth add other barriers to those already inherent in the health care delivery system. Many street youth are unfamiliar with and wary of medical procedures. For adolescents with a history of sexual abuse or exploitation, having to undress for a physical examination can be traumatic. Further resistance to medical treatment often occurs because street youth suspect that medical staff will report the results of an examination, their whereabouts, or information about their activities to their parents or to the police. Finally, any treatment protocol that requires more than one visit is jeopardized by the transient lifestyle of street youth (Pires & Silber, 1991). These barriers, coupled with an unrealistic sense of their own invulnerability, allow homeless youth to ignore even painful or disabling symptoms and to postpone prenatal care. Typically, teens convince themselves that health problems will eventually disappear.

There is little doubt that significant numbers of homeless teens suffer from severely impaired health. A Los Angeles study of street youth who were first-time patients at a free clinic revealed a high incidence of syphilis, pelvic inflammatory disease, trauma, rape, hepatitis, asthma, and scabies (Boyer, 1988). In a 1988 study of the health care needs of homeless and runaway youth, the Council on Scientific Affairs of the American Medical Association identified six major health problems of homeless youth and warned against "glossing over" the very different treatment needs of homeless youth and homeless adults. The Council identified the following major areas of concern: nutrition, substance abuse, mental health, physical health, sexual health, teen pregnancy, and victimization (Council on Scientific Affairs, 1989).

In some respects, dental services are even more inaccessible than medical care. Many insurance plans do not include dental coverage, and most states do not have an adequate system of public dental clinics.

The prevalence of death, sickness, and injury among homeless and runaway youth is unacceptably high, mostly as a result of health-damaging behaviors rather than disease. Traditional, specialized medical services are inadequate to meet the challenge of health problems that result from social, as opposed to biological, factors. Just as effective AIDS prevention must be comprehensive and include housing, adequate nutrition, medical care, education, and mental health treatment, recent evidence supports a holistic model of medical care capable of integrating all the related health needs of high-risk adolescents (Ooms & Herendeen, 1989b).

A number of runaway and homeless youth programs have developed alternative adolescent health components, where runaway and homeless youth are more likely to consent to medical care. In fact, at sites where there are alternative health clinics, medical services can be an "entree" to the comprehensive array of services that youth require (Boyer, 1988). Youth workers identify the following important features of holistic health services:

- Health professionals from all the relevant disciplines located at a single site or, if necessary, collaborative treatment relationships with other providers at several sites (staff caution that the more "stops" youth have to make to obtain health services, the less likely they are to receive care.)
- Health screening and treatment protocols that include all relevant social, psychological, and environmental factors that have an impact on teen health
- Staff who have the ability (and the time) to talk with teens about their life-styles in a nonjudgmental manner and who accord youth the same respect as they would adults
- Sensitivity to the special fears of sexually exploited youth
- Treatment that includes health education and family planning
- Evening clinic hours and scheduling flexibility that includes some "drop-in" clinic hours (Pires & Silber, 1991, p. 89)

WHERE DOES THE MONEY COME FROM?

In a survey of runaway and homeless youth programs, the National Network of Runaway and Youth Services found that over half of their funding came from state and county grants, 22% of the funding came from federal funds, and 24% came from the private sector. Although half of the agencies have a budget of $500,000 or less, they still provide an average of 14 different services (National Network of Runaway and Youth Services, 1990).

In recent years, the diminished availability of federal, state, and private foundation funding has coincided with an increased demand for services. State budgets in particular, which have contributed significantly to homeless and runaway youth programs, are facing steeper deficits in the 1990s. Such fiscal constraints force staff to perform their difficult work in a context of uncertainty. The most troubling aspects of this uncertainty include

- One-year funding cycles that make multiyear planning impossible
- The difficulty of securing funds for such "hidden costs" as follow-up services, staff training, or evaluation
- The inability to hire and retain competent staff when salary scales are low and future funding uncertain
- The categorical nature of state and federal grants that make holistic programming difficult

In addition to the instability of funding, program administrators are burdened with a multiplicity of grant applications and reporting requirements. Although funding diversity is a mainstay of healthy agencies, it is extremely labor intensive. The time and paperwork required to apply for federal grants is especially onerous, putting small agencies at a particular disadvantage. In some communities, agencies have pooled staff resources in order to apply jointly for a new resource. San Diego Youth and Community Services, for example, organized a consortium of five agencies that applied for state funds to set up a central volunteer recruitment and training center.

NECESSARY COLLABORATION

In the decade ahead, as limited resources continue to inhibit program expansion, the challenge of providing a holistic spectrum of services to high-risk youth will require extensive collaboration between public and private agencies. In a growing number of communities, juvenile justice and child welfare agencies are contracting with alternative homeless and runaway youth agencies for specialized services. For example, Youthcare's Threshold Program, a transitional living facility for young women at risk for or involved in prostitution, was set up to serve emancipated teenagers who are "system failures"—youth who have not succeeded in traditional foster homes. Other agencies, such as United Action for Youth in Iowa City and Youth Development, Inc., in Albuquerque, have contracts with local juvenile justice agencies to provide detention alternatives for first offenders charged with nonviolent delinquent acts.

Although interagency collaboration brings undeniable benefits to individual youth and to the community, it is not easy to accomplish. Collaboration takes time, energy, and effort; overworked youth workers cannot be expected to "find time" to meet with staff from other agencies unless such collaboration is sanctioned as an important part of their workload, not an extracurricular activity. Collaboration requires shared values and goals, a shared vocabulary, tact, and careful attention to the process by which agreements are reached (Boyer, 1988). It is important to acknowledge that not all disagreements can be resolved; sometimes the best tactic is to tolerate (and respect) differences. When collaboration is successful, the benefits are many, including

- An increased likelihood of obtaining funds when cooperation replaces competition
- The creation of a network of complementary, holistic services
- Opportunities to share the difficulty of serving multiproblem youth and to lessen feelings of helplessness
- The political strength of a broad-based advocacy group
- Opportunities to learn and adopt innovative strategies that have proved effective at other agencies
- Opportunities to share the expense of needed service components or of in-service training

These benefits, in addition to the complex and compelling service needs of their young clients, have inspired homeless and runaway youth programs across the country to seek new, creative, collaborative alliances.

REFERENCES

Act Together, Inc. (1983). *Employment and training for high risk youth.* Washington, DC: Author.

Boyer, D. (1988). *In and out of street life: A reader on interventions with street youth.* Portland, OR: Tri-County Youth Services Consortium.

The Bridge, Inc. (1985). *The Bridge House: A guidebook for designing and implementing an independent living residence for homeless youth.* Boston: Author.

Bridge Over Troubled Waters, Inc. (1991). *Drug prevention and education training manual for runaway and homeless youth service providers.* Boston: Author.

CDF Reports. (1990). *School barriers hamper efforts to educate homeless children.* Washington, DC: Children's Defense Fund.

Chicago Coalition for the Homeless. (1993). *Alone after dark: A survey of homeless youth in Chicago.* Chicago: Author.

Children's Defense Fund. (1990). *Improving health programs for low-income youths.* Washington, DC: CDF Clearinghouse Report.

Council on Scientific Affairs. (1989). Health care needs of homeless and runaway youths. *Journal of the American Medical Association, 262,* 1358–1361.

DeLone, R. (1990). *Replication: A strategy to improve the delivery of education and job training programs.* Philadelphia: Public/Private Ventures.

Hawkins, J., Lishner, D., Jenson, J., & Catalano, R. (1987). Delinquents and drugs: What the evidence suggests about prevention and treatment programming. In B. Brown & A. Mills (Eds.), *Youth at high risk for substance abuse.* Rockville, MD: National Institute on Drug Abuse.

Institute of Medicine. (1989). *Research on children and adolescents with mental, behavioral and developmental disorders.* Washington, DC: National Academy Press.

Janus, M., McCormick, A., Burgess A., & Hartman, C. (1987). *Adolescent runaways.* Lexington, MA: Lexington Books.

Kruks, G. (1991). Gay and lesbian homelessness. *Journal of Adolescent Health, 12,* 515–518.

National Association of Social Workers. (1991). *A summary of findings from a national survey of programs for runaway and homeless youth and programs for older youth in foster care.* Washington, DC: Author.

National Commission on Acquired Immune Deficiency Syndrome. (1991). *America living with AIDS.* Washington, DC: Author.

National Network of Runaway & Youth Services. (1990). *Fact sheet.* Washington, DC: Author.

Ooms, T., & Herendeen, L. (1989a). *Family Impact Seminar. Adolescent substance abuse treatment: Evolving policy at federal, state and city levels.* Washington, DC: American Association for Marriage and Family Therapy.

Ooms, T., & Herendeen, L. (1989b). *Integrated approaches to youths' health problems: federal, state and community roles.* Washington, DC: American Association for Marriage and Family Therapy, Family Impact Seminar.

Pires, S., & Silber, J. (1991). *On their own: Runaway and homeless youth and programs that serve them.* Washington, DC: Georgetown University Child Development Center, National Technical Assistance Center for Children's Mental Health.

Public/Private Ventures. (1990). *The practitioner's view: New challenges in serving high-risk youth.* Philadelphia: Author.

Regier, D.A., Farmer, M.E., Rae, D.S., Locke, B.Z, Keith, S.J., Judd, L.L., & Goodwin, F.K. (1990). Comorbidity of mental disorders with alcohol and other drugs. *Journal of the American Medical Association, 264,* 19.

Robertson, M. (1989, April). *Homeless youth: An overview of recent literature.* Paper presented at the National Conference on Homeless Children and Youth, Washington, DC (convened by Institute of Policy Studies, Johns Hopkins University).

Robertson, M.J., Doegel, P., & Ferguson, L. (1989). *Alcohol use and abuse among homeless adolescents in Hollywood: A report to the National Institute on Alcohol Abuse and Alcoholism.* Berkeley, CA: Alcohol Research Group.

Runaway and Homeless Youth Act of 1974, PL 96-509. (September 7, 1974). Title 45, U.S.C. 5701 et seq.

Select Committee on Children, Youth and Families. (1989). *No place to call home: Discarded children in America.* Washington, DC: United States House of Representatives.

Shaffer, D., & Caton, C.L.M. (1984). *Runaway and homeless youth in New York City: A report to the Ittleson Foundation.* Unpublished manuscript.

Speck, N., Ginther, D., & Helton, J. (1988, Winter). Runaways: Who will run again? *Adolescence, 13,* 92.

Taggart, R. (1981). *Fisherman's guide: An assessment of remediation and training strategies.* Kalamazoo, MI: W.E. Upjohn Institute for Employment Research.

Van Houten, T. (1992). *Underlying causes of youth homelessness: A final report to the Administration of Children, Youth, and Families, Department of Health and Human Services.* Unpublished manuscript.

Wetzel, J. (1987). *American youth: A statistical snapshot.* New York: The William T. Grant Foundation.

Yates, G., MacKenzie, R., Pennbridge, J., & Cohen, E. (1989). A risk profile comparison of runaway and non-runaway youth. *American Journal of Public Health, 78,* 820–821.

CHAPTER 28

Serving Youth
in Transition
into Adulthood

Hewitt B. Clark and Lynn Foster-Johnson

Young people with disabilities often experience difficulties making the transition from their lives at school to independent lives in the community. Many youth and young adults with disabilities encounter high levels of unemployment, dependence, economic hardship and instability, and social isolation when they exit the educational system (Johnson, Bruininks, & Wallace, 1992; Wagner, 1993).

This transition to adulthood may be particularly difficult for youth with emotional disturbances (Stroul & Friedman, 1986). The social and behavioral challenges experienced by these youth in their school years continue well into the transition years (Offord et al., 1992; Verhulst & van der Ende, 1992). Prange (1993) found that, for youth ages 15 through 18 with emotional/behavioral disturbances, the likelihood of their formal diagnoses (as derived from the *Diagnostic and Statistical Manual of Mental Disorders* [American Psychiatric Association, 1987]) persisting during a 3-year follow-up period was 88%. There also is growing evidence of accompanying difficulties with school and community life during these years. Wagner (1993) reported that students with emotional disturbances are more likely to drop out of school than youngsters in any other disability category, with almost 50% of these students leaving high school prior to graduation. The students

The Research and Training Center for Children's Mental Health at the Department of Child and Family Studies, Florida Mental Health Institute, University of South Florida was funded, in part, by the National Institute on Disability Rehabilitation Research and the National Institute of Mental Health through Grant #H133B90004-91, under which this chapter was written.

The authors wish to express their appreciation to Carol Taylor (Parent Advocate and Rehabilitation Specialist, State of Kansas) for her guidance in the preparation of Table 28.1 and to Elizabeth S. Stewart (Research Associate, University of South Florida) for her editorial suggestions.

with emotional disturbances in Wagner's sample also had the highest rate of absenteeism and the greatest probability of failing a course.

Postschool life for these youth may be demanding as well. Of the students with emotional disturbances who remain in school until graduation, only half obtain employment and acquire independence after leaving high school (Silver, Unger, & Friedman, 1995; Wagner, D'Amico, Marder, Newman, & Blackorby, 1992). Often, on exiting high school, these students develop relatively dependent lifestyles that are marked by job loss, economic hardship, social isolation, difficulty obtaining affordable housing, and incarceration (Wagner, 1993).

The hardships associated with transitioning of individuals with emotional disturbances into community life and employment may be linked to a number of programmatic and systemic factors. Traditionally, programs that have offered services to this population of youth have done so in a highly categorical fashion, limiting the range of services to one or two areas within employment or independent living (VanDenBerg, 1993).

These program limitations are only a reflection of even larger difficulties at the system level. Systemic limitations include the lack of coordinated services among the mental health, child welfare, educational, and rehabilitation systems (Knitzer, Steinberg, & Fleisch, 1990; Stroul & Friedman, 1986). Traditionally, the provision of services has been organized around one of three frameworks: geographic location of the individual, age of the recipient, or reported problem of the individual (e.g., mental health, substance abuse, juvenile delinquency) (Koroloff, 1990). These somewhat arbitrary boundaries have created a service provision mechanism that is static, inflexible, and often ineffective in meeting the transition needs of individuals with emotional disturbances.

The transition arena is further complicated by inconsistencies in state policies, confusion regarding bureaucratic authority over transition, and ambiguities in funding mechanisms (Koroloff, 1990). Traditionally, funding formulas with arbitrary age limitations and eligibility criteria were used to provide transition services for individuals with emotional disturbances, with most child welfare and mental health services being discontinued at age 18. This situation often leaves the youths and their families without the necessary supports and services to successfully and independently make the transition into community life and work (Koroloff, 1990). Accessing adult services may be difficult for individuals with emotional disturbances. Youth who are eligible for children's mental health services are not necessarily eligible for adult services (Modrcin, 1989). Even if a youth is eligible for adult services, programs are often fragmented, are often limited only to individuals with the most serious disturbances, and do not include programming specifically related to the transition process.

The complex challenges of the transition process and the unique needs of individuals with emotional disturbances present a compelling argument for designing transition systems around a solid framework of values and proven strategies. This tenet was first proposed by Stroul and Friedman (1986), in their seminal monograph on services for individuals with emotional disturbances. They state that a system of care represents more than a collection of service components; it should represent "a philosophy about the way in which services should be delivered to children and their families, . . . and should be guided by a set of basic values" (p. vi). The authors then go on to present a variety of core values and guiding principles for the system of care. Among these principles is the stipulation that children with emotional disturbances should be ensured smooth transitions to the adult service system as they reach maturity. Unfortunately, there are few programs in which these issues were explicitly considered in the development of transition services.

The purpose of this chapter is to describe core values and innovative strategies for facilitating the transition of youth and young adults with emotional disturbances into employment, educational opportunities, and independent living. Research findings regarding the values and best practices currently used by a number of transition programs will be employed to formulate guidelines and provide program examples for the development and maintenance of a community-based transition system.

TRANSITION SYSTEM DEFINED

A transition system prepares and supports youth and young adults in their movement into employment, educational opportunities, and independent living through a comprehensive, individualized process that 1) teaches community-relevant skills, 2) promotes exposure to community life experiences, 3) transcends the age barriers typical of child versus adult services, 4) focuses on community life functioning, and 5) respects consumer self-determination.

This definition of a transition system encompasses the features that have been emphasized in the evolution of the transition definition. For example, this definition is outcome oriented (Chadsey-Rusch, Rusch, & O'Reilly, 1991; Will, 1984), is focused on community integration (Modrcin, 1989; Wehman, 1988), and holds, as hallmarks of transition, self-determination (Olney & Salomone, 1992) and community adjustment (Halpern, 1989, 1993).

The definition also includes the four transition domains, comprising three setting-based domains (employment, educational opportunities, and independent housing) as well as the domain of community life, which involves activities and skills relevant across the other three. Figure 28.1 pres-

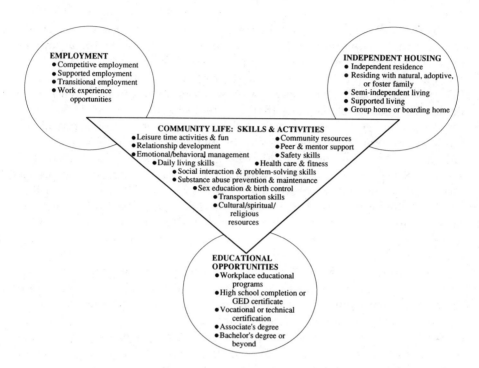

Figure 28.1. The four transition domains: three major setting-based domains and one community life domain that encompass skills and activities that are relevant across all of the domains. (Adapted from Clark, Unger, & Stewart [1993].)

ents the components of each of these four transition domains (Clark, Unger, & Stewart, 1993).

GUIDELINES FOR TRANSITION SYSTEMS

The following guidelines provide assistance to administrators, program coordinators, and other stakeholders with direction in developing and maintaining a successful transition system for individuals with emotional disorders. The guidelines were formulated based on studies of program values and best practices of transition programs for youth and young adults (Clark & Stewart, 1992; Clark et al., 1993); programs preparing youth for transition (Modrcin, 1989); policy issues related to transition (Koroloff, 1990), and consumer outcomes (Silver et al., 1995; Vander Stoep, Taub, & Holcomb, 1993). These six guidelines are intended to provide strategic and tactical assistance in developing and maintaining transition systems.

1. Transition Staff Must Be Consumer Centered.

Consumer Involvement A consumer-centered orientation means that program personnel encourage consumers' complete involvement in all aspects of planning and respect their opinions. Consumers are active partners in planning and decision making, with these processes being driven by their individual interests, cultural values, and strengths. A number of transition programs have embodied this value by actively seeking the opinions of their consumers in the operation of their programs. Social and leisure activities, work responsibilities, and club or program rules may be determined by the participants. Other programs have encouraged consumer investment and commitment by placing experienced youth in supervisory or mentoring roles. Consumers are encouraged to develop personal interests and set goals that then are used as a basis for actual educational opportunities, pre-employment experiences, and employment. One such program has incorporated this value by maintaining a philosophy of mutual support that states that staff and consumers will respect each other, provide support to one another, participate in activities, and keep the center safe and secure by following the rules of the program (Clark et al., 1993).

Early Intervention   There is a growing body of literature that emphasizes that transition planning should begin early for individuals with emotional disturbances (Koroloff, 1990; Modrcin, 1989). Fortunately, recent federal legislation (the Individuals with Disabilities Education Act of 1990; PL 101-476) mandates transition planning for students with disabilities who are 16 years and older. It may be that, for this planning to be effective with students with emotional disturbances, it must occur even earlier, which is permitted under this legislation.

Family Involvement and Family Role Resolution   Family involvement is one of the hallmarks of a successful system of care, and no less important for the transition process. A number of transition programs devote a substantial amount of time to communication and planning with families by utilizing case managers and family liaisons. This practice has enhanced transitions and assisted others involved in the transition process to be informed. Other programs have "home liaisons" who spend much of their time visiting families. In one program with a large rural catchment area, at least four visits were made annually to the consumer's home and, in some situations, the liaison worked with the families on a daily basis to support the consumer and parents during difficult periods (Clark et al., 1993).

Program personnel must also respect the wishes of older youth and young adults regarding the extent of parent involvement. For consumers over the age of 18, staff may need to help guide the process of family role resolution and provide assistance to the consumer in determining the level of family participation that is necessary for a successful transition experience. Relating to one's family while striving for greater independence involves a difficult balance, which may be particularly challenging for individuals with emotional disturbances.

2. Services Must Be Individualized and Comprehensive and Encompass All Transition Domains.

Transition Domains The transition process is conceptualized as encompassing three major setting domains—those of employment, education, and independent housing—and one community life domain that involves skills and activities that are relevant across all of the setting domains (Clark et al., 1993; Halpern, 1989). A transition system must provide a range of supports and services within each of these domains in order to accommodate consumers' individual needs (refer to Figure 28.1). For example, in the employment domain, it is helpful if a system has a variety of work opportunities with varying levels of support available, including work experience, transitional employment, supported employment, and competitive employment. Similarly, in the domain of community life, supports and services must be provided to assist consumers in learning new skills and in enhancing their competencies so that they can function in community settings. This domain is comprehensive and encompasses many of the skills and activities necessary for quality of life in the community. Of particular importance are social interaction and problem solving (e.g., accepting criticism, self-advocacy); relationship development (e.g., friendships, intimate relationships); leisure time activities and fun; substance abuse prevention; sex education and birth control; and cultural/religious resources.

Full Inclusion Another feature of this guideline stipulates that consumers operate in full-inclusion settings so that they are functioning alongside persons without disabilities. When this is not possible, the guiding rule should be that settings that provide the greatest experiential, therapeutic, and educational value in the least restrictive environment are matched to the consumers' interests and competencies. A number of transition programs have cooperative, contractual agreements with large companies that provide worksites for internships, training, and employment. Transition counselors are maintained at each site to coordinate job placements and provide job coaching services. The companies then provide student supervision and training through jobsite supervision and co-worker involvement. Another program provides a unique opportunity to allow individuals with psychiatric disabilities to pursue postsecondary educational goals. The program provides the individuals with support services as needed (Clark et al., 1993).

Individualization In order for consumers to be served in community settings, the transition system must provide individualized supports and services that can be "wrapped" around the individuals (Burchard & Clarke, 1990; VanDenBerg, 1993). This wraparound strategy is defined as an intervention that "is developed and/or approved by an interdisciplinary services team, is community-based and unconditional, is centered on the strengths of the child and family, and includes the delivery of coordinated, highly individualized services in three or more life domain areas of a child and family" (VanDenBerg, Burchard, & Dennis, 1992, p. 1). These individualized wraparound supports and services stand in brilliant contrast to the traditional services, which typically involve plugging a youth into an existing program, with the placement being based more on space availability than on the individual's needs.

Flexibility Creating an individualized and comprehensive transition system requires flexible supports and services that can be drawn from an array of resources and funding streams, including flexible funding. These supports and services must be coordinated by a consumer-centered case manager, so that they can be tailored to individuals' needs. The use of case managers is a common thread throughout many transition programs. Generally, a consumer is assigned a case manager on entry to a transition program. These case managers may visit schools, worksites, and homes to facilitate the transition process and coordinate services across settings and agencies (Clark et al., 1993).

Interagency Collaboration In order to provide quality services to consumers across all of the transition domains, interagency linkages and collaboration must be in place throughout the local transition system and should include extensive ties to the private sector of business/industry for internships, job training, and employment. A regional or state-level mechanism for coordinating interdepartmental resources and funding streams, and for resolving issues related to specific cases when local agencies have not been successful in their planning process, is also necessary (Koroloff, 1990).

Funding Funding is a necessary evil that must be addressed before any type of program is developed. The funding of a transition system is particularly challenging because of the idiosyncrasies of the funding sources and the various age criteria associated with these different sources. Table 28.1 provides a listing of transition-related funding mechanisms, with the purpose and source for each. These funding mechanisms vary by state and local regulation and are highly complex; furthermore, shifting federal policies make these mechanisms vulnerable to change. Also, each state and local area may have additional funding, service resources, or both that may be applicable to the transition needs of youth and young adults (e.g., summer work programs, scholarships for technical training programs, high school completion programs for young adults at a community college, adult education). Despite the variability and changing nature of funding sources, this information should be useful to administrators, program coordinators, and advocates as they target funding possibilities to develop or expand their transition systems.

Table 28.1.   Some funding mechanisms for transition services

Funding mechanism	Purpose and brief description	Responsible agent/source
Individuals with Disabilities Education Act (IDEA) (PL 101-476)	Promotes transition services for students (16 years and older) with disabilities by mandating that individualized education programs (IEPs) include transition goals related to adulthood.	Publicly funded schools and state department of vocational education
Carl D. Perkins Vocational Education Act (PL 98-524)	Provides funding of vocational education for an array of special groups, including students with disabilities and disadvantaged students, individuals with limited English proficiency, and adults in need of vocational retraining.	Publicly funded schools and state department of vocational rehabilitation
Independent Living Initiatives (PL 99-272) Independent Living Program	Provides for foster youth (16 years and older) to be assessed for possible training in preparatory skills related to employment, education, and community living and in other skill areas necessary to ensure self-sufficiency.	State department of child dependency
Subsidized Living Program	Provides for eligible foster youth to remain in their placement, or to reside in unlicensed but approved settings (e.g., their own or shared apartments, apartments with paid roommate mentors) until age 22.	State department of child dependency
Social Security Amendments of 1960 (PL 86-778)	Allows a minor child (under the age of 18) or an adult with disabilities, with a deceased, disabled, or retired parent to draw benefits based on that parent's previous contributions and the family's current size and income.	Social Security Administration

(continued)

Table 28.1. *(continued)*

Funding mechanism	Purpose and brief description	Responsible agent/source
Supplemental Security Income	Allows for Supplemental Security Income (SSI) benefits to be paid to children or adults with disabilities, even if these persons have never worked or contributed to Social Security. The benefit amount is based on other income.	Social Security Administration
PASS: Plan for Achieving Self-Support (PL 92-603)	Allows some SSI recipients to maintain their SSI monthly funding at current level while working for a period of time as designated within an approved plan designed to set aside funds to achieve work-related goals (e.g., establishing oneself in an occupation by receiving training or purchasing tools of the trade).	Social Security Administration
Rehabilitation Acts (PL 93-112) (PL 93-516)	Strengthens rehabilitation services through provisions such as 1) individualized written rehabilitation programs, similar to the IEPs required under IDEA; 2) training of individuals in integrated settings; and 3) supported employment and related services available to a broader array of individuals with varied disabilities.	State department of vocational rehabilitation

(continued)

Table 28.1. (*continued*)

Funding mechanism	Purpose and brief description	Responsible agent / source
Job Training Partnership Act of 1982 (PL 97-300)	Provides employment training opportunities (e.g., Job Corps for disadvantaged youth) and involvement of private business leaders in communities through the establishment of Private Industry Councils (PICs) to coordinate employment and training programs for disadvantaged youth.	State department of vocational rehabilitation
Other community and state resources	Includes other funding or service options, such as 1) summer job programs through the city, school district, or area PIC; 2) civic organization– sponsored job mentoring programs; 3) parent and professional advocacy organizations; 4) the U.S. Department of Housing and Urban Development Dollar-a-Lease Housing Program; and 5) other state and local programs available through mental health centers, community colleges, etc.	Private- and public-sector entities at local and state levels

3. The Transition System Must Focus on Consumers' Strengths and on the Development and Enhancement of Needed Skills as Related to Community-Relevant Settings.

Strengths-Based Assessment　As was discussed under the consumer-centered value, a transition assessment of consumers should place a primary focus on their competencies and capabilities across all four transition domains. Such strengths-based assessment should occur in the context of community settings, securing input from relevant persons from these settings and respecting the consumer's perspective (Duchnowski & Kutash, 1993).

Strengths-based assessment provides a profile for a plan that builds on the consumer's interests and strengths, and identifies and provides supports for possible limitations. For example, a streetwise girl with good verbal skills and an interest in working indoors was well matched to a part-time job in telephone solicitation. Although initially the employer did not want her to make sales for which she would have access to customers' credit card numbers, after several months of good work performance, she was promoted into the more lucrative area of telephone sales, where she was trusted to handle sensitive credit card information.

Another example of strengths-based assessment and planning is reflected in the situation of a 16-year-old boy in the foster care system who ran away from every foster home, group home, emergency shelter, and residential center placement he received, and had dropped out of school after a history of difficulty and poor performance. During his extensive runaway periods, he seemed to manage well in protecting himself and keeping out of serious trouble. A life coach and the wraparound team, to whom this youth was assigned, used a strengths-based assessment to identify his interests and competencies. They found that he related quite well to strong male figures and, although he had very limited reading and writing skills, he followed their instructions well. They also learned that he owned a bicycle that he kept in good repair, even though he lived on the streets. The plan they developed with him involved his getting a job at a bicycle shop, being mentored by one of the repairmen, and living on his own in a small apartment with his life coach working closely with him, teaching community life skills as necessary.

In both of these examples, it is interesting to note the attention that was given to matching the youth to settings that took advantage of individual interests and strengths. This is not to say that these initial plans addressed all aspects of these two consumers' needs, but the exposure and success with these life experiences set the stage for these youth to tackle other areas of skill development (e.g., her securing full-time employment in sales, his completing a general equivalency diploma with reading and writing competencies enabling him to attend vocational training in auto mechanics).

Curricular Modifications   Most youth and young adults with emotional disturbances have had extremely poor experiences related to school, with placements providing limited individualized supports and a curriculum that has little or no relevance to daily life (Knitzer et al., 1990). There is a growing body of literature demonstrating the importance of teaching skills in the context of activities that are functional and relevant to students (Dunlap et al., 1993; Dunlap, Kern-Dunlap, Clarke, & Robbins, 1991; Foster-Johnson, Ferro, & Dunlap, 1992; Horner, Sprague, & Flannery, 1993). This concept can be applied early in the transition years by teaching academic concepts using functional skills. For example, subtraction can be taught by having the youth use an actual bus schedule to determine the amount of time between bus arrivals at a local bus stop. When the student has determined the amount of time between arrivals, he or she can plan a trip to a local place of interest using the bus as transportation. This teaching strategy incorporates a number of functional, community-based skills (using the bus, reading the bus schedule) while meeting the state-mandated standards for academic competencies.

Providing opportunities for students to make choices of activities or materials and incorporating students' preferences into the classroom routine have been found to decrease behavior problems, increase skill acquisition, and enhance generalization to other settings (Dyer, Dunlap, & Winterling, 1991; Foster-Johnson, Ferro, & Dunlap, 1993). It is becoming more evident that consumers and their mentors (e.g., life coaches, teachers) can help identify the consumers' strengths, competencies, and skill deficits more easily when consumers are functioning in community settings of interest to them. As illustrated in the previous case examples, matching of consumers and settings may ameliorate many problem areas and set the stage for individuals to pursue relevant areas of growth, or at least to be more receptive to learning new skills (Elliott, Sheridan, Gresham, & Knoff, 1989).

Quality Teaching Methods   Staff can be more effective in their work with consumers if they are trained in quality teaching methods (Blase & Fixsen, 1987; MacDuff, Krantz, MacDuff, & McClannahan, 1988; McGee, Almeida, Sulzer-Azaroff, & Feldman, 1992) that focus on skill development and self-management (Agran, Fodor-Davis, & Moore, 1986; Kern-Dunlap et al., 1992). Quality teaching methods involve targeting of relevant skills, creating or catching opportunities for teaching, conducting in vivo instruction and practice, and recognizing individuals for their growth and accomplishments.

4.   Transition Staff Must Provide an Unconditional Safety Net of Support.

Unconditional Commitment   The value of providing an unconditional safety net of support encompasses many important features. The first of these is the unconditional commitment that personnel at all levels of the transition system must make to their youth and young adults. VanDenBerg et al. (1992) have defined this commitment as, "the team agrees to never deny services because of extreme severity of disability, to change services as needs of the child and family change, and to never reject the child or family from services" (p. 1).

Successes and Natural Consequences   Another feature of this guideline involves maximizing a consumer's likelihood of success while allowing him or her to experience the natural consequences of life. This feature is difficult for some child services personnel to accept because these professionals typically are oriented toward rescuing consumers from themselves, parents, the community, and realities of life.

A life coach can assist in maximizing a consumer's likelihood of success in ways such as developing a relationship with the individual, matching a consumer to appropriate settings, teaching relevant skills and self-management, and providing individualized supports and services. However, because of the nature of achieving independence and the restrictive histories that most of these individuals have had, they need to experience the natural consequences of trying something and failing. Often, difficult life experiences are the most powerful teachers. The value of unconditional commitment guides staff to ensure, to the extent possible, that consumers do not put themselves in life-threatening situations; to provide assistance to consumers when life experiences are too unpleasant or complex for the consumers to manage alone; and to assist consumers in dusting themselves off and getting refocused.

One program uses natural consequences quite effectively with the consumers who live in its residential facilities. Consumers are held responsible for the upkeep and care of their apartments and are responsible for any damages. If the consumer is evicted from the apartment, the next apartment in which he or she will be placed may not be as nice as the first apartment or may not be in his or her preferred living area (Clark et al., 1993).

Hopefulness   Another feature of this guideline is that staff express hopefulness and a positive affirmation of the consumers' worth and merit. This feature is evidenced by staff being positive and encouraging to consumers, speaking respectfully, involving consumers and parents as partners, respecting consumers' choices, and sharing a sense of humor.

Within most of the transition programs examined by Clark and his colleagues (1993), this value was embraced and reflected in staff respecting consumers for who they are and what they are working to become. Consumers were allowed to explore their work and social identities with guidance, support, and acceptance.

5.   The Transition System Must Provide Continuity from a Consumer's Perspective.

Continuity   The administrators of a transition system may think that their system and its components provide continuity. However, this attribute of the system must be judged from the "eye of the beholder." Systemic continuity, from a consumer's perspective, may be reflected in a practice such as ensuring that the consumer has easy access to one person who functions as a life coach, case manager, or mentor. Of course, having the same person readily available 24 hours a day, 365 days a year, is not feasible. Most transition programs use a team approach to ensure that, if the consumer's primary life coach is not available, another person who is known to the consumer, and knowledgeable about the case, is easily accessible.

Social Support   A feature that is indicative of the continuity guideline is to provide consumers with options for maintaining valued, positive relationships and opportunities for establishing sources of social support.

Many youth have difficulty trusting others, possibly as a result of their social, emotional, and behavioral challenges and the transient placements they have experienced. Some transition systems are assisting consumers by encouraging them to develop relationships with those individuals with whom they feel most comfortable (e.g., staff, relatives, mentors, peers). Thus, it is not mandatory that a consumer link exclusively with his or her assigned life coach. In fact, a transition system may assign each new consumer a primary and secondary life coach to ensure that a staff member is always available. Some programs provide as many as four other team members who are familiar with each case. This practice increases the level of continuity and provides the consumer with a number of qualified choices for his or her personal life coach. Based on the consumer's preferences, the team then modifies its assignments of primary life coaches (K. Dennis, personal communication, 1991).

Seamless System In order for life coaches to provide continuity and operate effectively on behalf of their consumers, the transition system must be value driven, with policies and procedures that provide a framework that supports the efforts of the coach (Koroloff, 1990). A transition system must be seamless, allowing access to public agency and private-sector resources throughout the community. Interagency agreements must exist so that access to resources can occur in a timely fashion and that disputes related to access and funding can be addressed at a community, regional, or state level.

6. The Transition System Must Operate with an Outcome Orientation.
This guideline related to outcome orientation emphasizes three features: consumer outcomes, system responsiveness, and system effectiveness (Friedman, 1991; VanDenBerg, Beck, & Pierce, 1993).

Consumer Outcomes This outcome orientation value must be applied to consumer progress and successes in the domains of employment, education, independent housing, and community life adjustment. The five previously discussed guidelines involve processes that can assist consumers in achieving successful outcomes across the transition domains. For each transition service and support provided, however, an outcome statement must be developed. For example, the third guideline, focusing on consumers' strengths and enhancing community-relevant skills, includes strengths-based assessment as well as planning centered around the consumers' functioning in relevant community settings. Transition plans related to the results of the assessment should be written with measurable objectives so that consumer progress on individualized goals can be tracked over time.

System Responsiveness System responsiveness refers to the extent to which the system is operating in accordance with the practices and values encompassed by the six guidelines presented in this chapter. Key process indicators of the transition system's responsiveness would involve such measures as

- Percentage of individuals with emotional disturbances who, by their 16th year, have a transition plan that has been signed by representatives from each of the relevant agencies
- Percentage of plans that were developed with the active involvement of the consumers and/or their guardians
- Proportion of consumers who are receiving individualized supports and services in each of the goals specified on their plans
- Percentage of consumers who, on a satisfaction survey, rate their life coaches (case managers, job coaches, mentors) with high marks on dimensions such as listening, problem solving, and supporting consumer efforts toward independence in work, school, and community life
- Percentage of consumers placed in full-inclusion settings for each domain

By periodically measuring key process indicators, system administrators can assess progress in improving the system's responsiveness to its consumers. This process information should assist stakeholders in identifying system strengths and weaknesses in order to guide them in modifying the system to enhance its responsiveness.

System Effectiveness The third feature of the outcome orientation guideline is system effectiveness. The effectiveness of the system can be assessed through key outcome indicators, based on consumer outcomes. For example, aggregation of data regarding individuals' employment goals allows for determination of the percentage of consumers who 1) are employed quarter-, half-, three-quarter-, and full time; 2) are earning a particular wage per hour; 3) have specific employer-paid benefits, such as sick leave, annual leave, and health insurance; and 4) are in a job that may be on a career track that the consumer wants to pursue. These types of key outcome indicators, if tracked over an extended period, can provide stakeholders and policy makers with valuable information on the system's outcome effectiveness.

CHALLENGES

The six guidelines described above should assist professionals in the development and expansion of a transition system for youth and young adults with emotional disturbances. However, these activities will require a tremendous advocacy effort—advocacy that can be conducted by individual consumers and parents as well as at an organizational level by involving parent advocacy groups, agency administrators, and other stakeholders. The advocacy effort may, at times, take the form of prodding, educating, demanding, persevering, and/or working collaboratively with other professionals and agencies to assist them in making the necessary changes to create an individualized transition system.

The advocacy effort in most communities and states will need to focus on four different arenas. The first is that of the education sector. Federal legislation is pushing the secondary education system to address transition planning and the high rate of dropouts among all students with disabilities. This initiative can be furthered by consumers, parents, professionals, and other groups to ensure that transitional assessments are occurring early, individualized transition plans are being formulated, and alternative education tracks and opportunities are available to all students (e.g., tutorial supports, practical work opportunities, vocational education tracks).

The second advocacy arena involves confronting the rigidity of some of the traditional public- and private-sector service agencies in mental health, child welfare, education, and rehabilitation. Advocacy for reform toward more individualized services must be undertaken at the consumer level (e.g., getting an agency to provide home-based services rather than placement in a residential treatment center) and at the system level (e.g., getting community agencies to enter into interagency agreements to collaborate on transition planning and the implementation of these plans).

The next major arena for advocacy is to involve business and industry in the transition process. Many leaders in the private business sector are interested in improving their communities and the caliber of education available. The availability of a skilled work force is essential to most every type of business and industry in today's society. Many communities have found it fruitful to undertake advocacy efforts focused on acquainting business leaders with the contribution that young people with disabilities can make to their enterprises, with support services that have proven to be valuable in integrating individuals with disabilities into work settings (e.g., supported employment), and with the role that business and industry can play in the preparation of youth for the work force (e.g., summer and after-school work experience, internships) (Fabian & Luecking, 1991).

The fourth arena will require continued advocacy efforts at the local, state, and federal levels to address the categorical nature of the policies and funding that drive the service systems. In the area of transition, the arbitrary age criteria and categorical funding mechanisms promote agency insularity. What is needed is policy and funding reform that will encourage states and communities to function on an interagency basis to provide an individualized system of care.

One of the greatest challenges in establishing an individualized transition system is to identify community leadership that can recognize the unique needs of individuals with emotional disturbances as they face this transitional period and share the values encompassed in the guidelines for developing and maintaining a transition system. Advocacy and educational efforts will be required to bring enlightened representatives together from the civic, business, provider agency and policy-making sectors. However, the benefits of such efforts can be powerful in the development of an individualized, consumer-centered system of services, as is being demonstrated in many communities.

REFERENCES

Agran, M., Fodor-Davis, J., & Moore, S. (1986). The effects of self-instructional training on job-task sequencing: Suggesting a problem-solving strategy. *Education and Training of the Mentally Retarded, 21,* 273–281.

American Psychiatric Association. (1987). *Diagnostic and statistical manual of mental disorders* (3rd ed. rev.). Washington, DC: Author.

Blase, K.A., & Fixsen, D.L. (1987). Integrated therapeutic interactions. *Journal of Child Care, 3*(1), 59–72.

Burchard, J.D., & Clarke, R.T. (1990). The role of individualized care in a service delivery system for children and adolescents who are severely emotionally disturbed. *Journal of Mental Health Administration, 17,* 48–60.

Carl D. Perkins Vocational Education Act of 1984, PL 98-524. (October 19, 1984). Title 20, U.S.C. 2301 et seq: *U.S. Statutes at Large, 98*(Part 3), 2435–2491.

Chadsey-Rusch, J., Rusch, F.R., & O'Reilly, M.F. (1991). Transition from school to integrated communities. *Remedial and Special Education, 12*(6), 23–33.

Clark, H.B., & Stewart, E.S. (1992). Transition into employment, education, and independent living: A survey of programs serving youth and young adults with emotional/behavioral disorders. In K. Kutash, C.J. Liberton, A. Algarin, & R.M. Friedman (Eds.), *Proceedings of the Fifth Annual Conference on A System of Care for Children's Mental Health: Expanding the Research Base* (pp. 189–198). Tampa: University of South Florida, Florida Mental Health Institute.

Clark, H.B., Unger, K.V., & Stewart, E.S. (1993). Transition of youth and young adults with emotional/behavioral disorders into employment, education, and independent living. *Community Alternatives: International Journal of Family Care, 5,* 20–46.

Duchnowski, A.J., & Kutash, K. (1993, October). *Developing comprehensive systems for troubled youth: Issues in mental health.* Paper presented at the Shakertown Symposium II: Developing comprehensive systems for troubled youth, Shakertown, KY.

Dunlap, G., Kern, L., dePerczel, M., Clarke, S., Wilson, D., Childs, K.E., White, R., & Falk, G.D. (1993). Functional analysis of classroom variables for students with emotional and behavioral disorders. *Behavioral Disorders, 18,* 275–291.

Dunlap, G., Kern-Dunlap, L., Clarke, S., & Robbins, R.F. (1991). Functional assessment, curricular revision, and severe behavior problems. *Journal of Applied Behavior Analysis, 24,* 387–397.

Dyer, K., Dunlap, G., & Winterling, V. (1991). Effects of choice making on the serious problem behaviors of students with severe handicaps. *Journal of Applied Behavior Analysis, 23,* 515–524.

Elliott, S.N., Sheridan, S.M., Gresham, F.M., & Knoff, H.M. (1989). Assessing and treating social skills deficits: A case study for the scientist-practitioner. *Journal of School Psychology, 27,* 197–222.

Fabian, E.S., & Luecking, R.G. (1991). Doing it the company way: Using internal company supports in the workplace. *Journal of Applied Rehabilitation Counseling, 22*(2), 32–33.

Foster-Johnson, L., Ferro, J., & Dunlap, G. (1992, November). *Does curriculum affect student behavior?* Paper presented at the 37th Annual Conference of the Florida Educational Research Association, Winter Park, FL.

Foster-Johnson, L., Ferro, J., & Dunlap, G. (1993, April). *The effect of student preference for curricular activities.* Paper presented at the meeting of the American Educational Research Association, Atlanta.

Friedman, R. (1991). The system of care. *Update, 3,* 13.

Halpern, A.S. (1989). A systematic approach to transition programming for adolescents and young adults with disabilities. *Australia and New Zealand Journal of Developmental Disabilities, 15,* 1–13.

Halpern, A.S. (1993). Quality of life as a conceptual framework for evaluating transition outcomes. *Exceptional Children, 59,* 486–498.

Horner, R.H., Sprague, J.R., & Flannery, K.B. (1993). Building functional curricula for students with severe intellectual disabilities. In R. VanHouton & S. Axelrod (Eds.), *Effective behavioral treatment* (pp. 47–71). New York: Plenum.

Independent Living Initiatives, PL 99-272. (April 7, 1986). Title 42, U.S.C. 31 et seq: *U.S. Statutes at Large, 100*(Part 1), 294–297.

Individuals with Disabilities Education Act of 1990, PL 101-476. (October 30, 1990). Title 20, U.S.C. 1400 et seq: *U.S. Statutes at Large, 104*(Part 2), 1103–1151.

Job Training Partnership Act of 1982, PL 97-300. (October 13, 1982). Title 29, U.S.C. 1501 et seq: *U.S. Statutes at Large, 96*(Part 1), 1322–1399.

Johnson, D.R., Bruininks, R.H., & Wallace, T. (1992, Fall). Transition: The next five years. *IMPACT: Feature Issue on Transition.* (University of Minnesota, Minneapolis). Vol. 5(3).

Kern-Dunlap, L., Dunlap, G., Clarke, S., Childs, K.E., Wilson, D., & White, R. (1992). Effects of a videotape feedback package on the peer interactions of children with serious behavioral and emotional challenges. *Journal of Applied Behavior Analysis, 25,* 355–364.

Knitzer, J., Steinberg, Z., & Fleisch, B. (1990). *At the schoolhouse door: An examination of programs and policies for children with behavioral and emotional problems.* New York: Bank Street College of Education.

Koroloff, N.M. (1990). Moving out: Transition policies for youth with serious emotional disabilities. *Journal of Mental Health Administration, 17,* 78–86.

MacDuff, G.S., Krantz, P.J., MacDuff, M.A., & McClannahan, L.E. (1988). Providing incidental teaching for autistic children: A rapid training procedure for therapists. *Education and Treatment of Children, 11,* 205–217.

McGee, G.G., Almeida, M.C., Sulzer-Azaroff, B., & Feldman, R.S. (1992). Promoting reciprocal interactions via peer incidental teaching. *Journal of Applied Behavior Analysis, 25,* 117–126.

Modrcin, M.J. (1989). Emotionally handicapped youth in transition: Issues and principles for program development. *Community Mental Health Journal, 25,* 219–227.

Offord, D.R., Boyle, M.H., Racine, Y.A., Fleming, J.E., Cadman, D.T., Blum, H.M., Byrne, C., Links, P.S., Lipman, E.L., MacMillan, H.L., Grant, N.I.R., Sanford, M.N., Szatmari, P., Thomas, H., & Woodward, C.A. (1992). Outcome, prognosis, and risk in a longitudinal follow-up study. *Journal of the American Academy of Child and Adolescent Psychiatry, 31,* 916–923.

Olney, M.F., & Salomone, P.R. (1992). Empowerment and choice in supported employment: Helping people to help themselves. *Journal of Applied Rehabilitation Counseling, 23,* 41–44.

Plan for Achieving Self Support (PASS), PL 92-603. (1972). Title 42, U.S.C. 1382 et seq.

Prange, M. (1993, January). *A longitudinal perspective of youth with conduct disorder problems.* Paper presented at the Conference on Rehabilitation of Children, Youth, and Adults with Psychiatric Disabilities, Tampa, FL.

Rehabilitation Act of 1973, PL 93-112. (September 26, 1973). Title 29, U.S.C. 701 et seq: *U.S. Statutes at Large, 87,* 355–394.

Rehabilitation Act Amendments of 1974, PL 93-516. (December 7, 1974). Title 29, U.S.C. 701 et seq: *U.S. Statutes at Large, 88*(Part 2), 1617–1634.

Silver, S.E., Unger, K.V., & Friedman, R.M. (1995). *Transition to young adulthood among youth with emotional disturbance.* Manuscript submitted for publication.

Social Security Amendments of 1960, PL 86-778. (September 13, 1960). Title 42, U.S.C. 423 et seq: *U.S. Statutes at Large, 74,* 924–997.

Social Security Disability Amendments of 1980, PL 96-265. (June 9, 1980). Title 42, U.S.C. 1305 et seq: *U.S. Statutes at Large, 94*(Part 1), 441–481.

Stroul, B.A., & Friedman, R.M. (1986). *A system of care for severely emotionally disturbed children & youth.* Washington, DC: Georgeotwn University Child Development Center, National Technical Assistance Center for Children's Mental Health.

VanDenBerg, J. (1993). Integration of individualized mental health services into the system of care for children and adolescents. *Administration and Policy in Mental Health, 20,* 247–257.

VanDenBerg, J., Beck, S., & Pierce, J. (1993). *The Pennsylvania outcome project for children's services.* Unpublished manuscript, Pressley Ridge School, Pittsburgh, PA.

VanDenBerg, J., Burchard, J.D., & Dennis, K. (1992, April). *WrapAround definition and related issues.* Paper presented at the First Annual WrapAround Conference, Pittsburgh.

Vander Stoep, A., Taub, J., & Holcomb, L. (1993). Follow-up of adolescents with severe psychiatric impairment into young adulthood. In C.J. Liberton, K. Kutash, & R.M. Friedman (Eds.), *Proceedings of the Sixth Annual Conference on A System of Care for Children's Mental Health: Expanding the Research Base* (pp. 373–380). Tampa: University of South Florida, Florida Mental Health Institute.

Verhulst, F.C., & van der Ende, J. (1992). Six-year developmental course of internalizing and externalizing problem behaviors. *Journal of the American Academy of Child and Adolescent Psychiatry, 31,* 924–931.

Wagner, M. (1993). *Dropouts with disabilities: What do we know? What can we do?* Menlo Park, CA: SRI International.

Wagner, M., D'Amico, R., Marder, C., Newman, L., & Blackorby, J. (1992). *What happens next? Trends in postschool outcomes of youth with disabilities.* Menlo Park, CA: SRI International.

Wehman, P. (1988). Supported employment: Toward zero exclusion of persons with severe disabilities. In P. Wehman & S. Moon (Eds.), *Vocational rehabilitation and supported employment* (pp. 3–16). Baltimore: Paul H. Brookes Publishing Co.

Will, M. (1984). Bridges from school to working life. *Programs for the Handicapped, 2,* 8–9.

CHAPTER 29

Meeting the Mental Health Needs of Young Children and Their Families

Jane Knitzer

As this book so clearly documents, the past decade has been a time of great activity in children's mental health. Parents have been assuming their rightful role as active participants in the helping process, becoming allies and partners with professionals. New service strategies have emerged that have challenged the customary use of out-of-home placements for serving seriously troubled children. It has been demonstrated that services such as in-home crisis intervention, behavioral aides, and respite care can be "wrapped around" the children and their families (including foster families)—in homes, in schools, and in community settings (Knitzer, 1993). Families across the country have been organizing to speak out on behalf of this group of children that for too long has lacked an effective parental advocacy voice (Friesen & Koroloff, 1990).

However significant these gains have been, they have focused primarily on older children and adolescents. Thus, the beneficiaries have primarily been children and families already worn down by years of searching for help, and often by years of unsuccessful treatment. Largely ignored in this effort have been the needs of younger children, especially those from birth to 6, and their families. The purpose of this chapter is to explore the needs of this younger population and their families, highlight some of the most promising mental health–related programmatic efforts to serve them, and identify the underlying values and critical issues that must be addressed if the mental health system, in partnership with families and other agencies, is to respond to this very vulnerable population at a point in time when careful interventions may have significant payoff. The chapter is based on preliminary findings from a national study being conducted by the author with support from the Annie E. Casey Foundation as well as from a study of promising program strategies in Head Start (Knitzer & Yoshikawa, 1995).

WHY FOCUS ATTENTION ON THE MENTAL HEALTH OF YOUNG CHILDREN AND THEIR FAMILIES?

Both experience and research data compel attention to mental health issues facing young children and their families. The need to focus on young children is compelling even in the face of the reality that public dollars are still not sufficient to meet the needs of older children and adolescents with emotional and behavioral disorders.

Reports from the Field

Field-based reports, some systematic and some anecdotal from teachers, child care providers, mental health professionals, and special education professionals, suggest there is increasing concern about the levels of problematic relationships, affect, and behaviors seen in young children. For example, a 1991 survey of 7,000 kindergarten teachers reported that 35% of their children were not ready for school, with 42% of the teachers reporting a worsening of the situation since the early 1990s (Boyer, 1991). A 1994 American Orthopsychiatric Association Task Force Report on Head Start and Mental Health found the Head Start community increasingly concerned about the challenging behaviors of children, the complex needs families experience, and the resulting strains on Head Start teachers and family service workers (American Orthopsychiatric Association, 1994). Parallel issues have also been reported by child care providers and administrators, particularly those involved with the federal child care subsidy programs. These reports suggest, not surprisingly, that low-income children and families are the most vulnerable, yet there are signs that other families with young children also are experiencing higher levels of stress (Love & Logue, 1992).

Specific concern is centered in four areas. First, there is a widespread sense that the children are entering into early childhood programs with more serious and challenging kinds of behaviors and needs than children had in the past. Unfortunately, there are no epidemiological data to confirm (or deny) this observation. Yet the perception is widespread, evident across the full spectrum of early childhood programs from Head Start to center-based programs to family day care. Reflecting the views of many, Edlefsen and Baird (1994), creators of a preschool mental health consultation service, note that "children arrive with fewer intellectual, social and emotional school readiness skills, [and] have a precocious knowledge of life issues that they lack the emotional and cognitive ability to understand and integrate" (p. 567). Also widespread is the sense of frustration in coping effectively with these children, dramatically underscored in disconcerting reports of young children being "expelled" from one or more child care centers. In one community, for example, 42 special education preschool teachers reported that 8% of the children in their classes had experienced at least one such expulsion and 1% had experienced two or more (Adolfi, Humenay, & Jeffries, 1995). Yet neither in this community nor in most others does this extreme marker of a serious problem trigger an offer of assistance to the family or the child care programs.

Also reported as a concern, particularly in the more comprehensive early childhood programs and in family support programs, is how to recognize and meet the multiple and complex needs of families, especially those affected by substance abuse, mental illness, or chronic depression. This wish for back-up help in finding effective ways to work with families whose lives appear to be disengaged or chaotic is evident in Head Start and other early childhood programs, in family support programs, and in home visiting programs.

A third widespread concern is how to cope with and help children and families cope with the effects of both familial and community violence. Violence is increasingly a part of the early childhood experience. Research on a sample of children under age 6 seen at Boston City Hospital indicated that 10% had witnessed a knifing or a shooting (Groves, Zuckerman, Marans, & Cohen, 1993). Reports from the Head Start community indicate similar concern (American Orthopsychiatric Association, 1994). The sequelae of exposure to violence affect individual young children, some of whom manifest posttraumatic stress disorder, and their families (Drell, Siegel, & Gaensbauer, 1993; Osofsky & Fenichel, 1994). Community violence also appears to be affecting programs. In some programs, for instance, recess is curtailed; in others, children are sent home early in order to be able to ride the elevators in public housing before gangs take them over (American Orthopsychiatric Association, 1994).

The fourth concern that is surfacing across the early child care and education community is related to the mental health of staff. With few exceptions, those who care for young children are poorly paid and not always well trained. Many face pressures not too different from the families with whom they work. Virtually all report great frustration and burnout when they must cope with children whose behavior is difficult and families whose needs they feel powerless to meet, including coping with violence. Paying attention to the mental health needs of staff is not part of the typical mental health paradigm. Yet the reality is that 56% of all mothers of infants, toddlers, and preschoolers work outside of the home (Brayfield, Gennis Deich, & Hoffereth, 1993), many children spend significant amounts of early childhood time in child care settings, and the quality of child care programs is of great concern. Thus, enhancing the staff's ability to understand children's behaviors, to build relationships with families, and to address their own needs for support is indirectly an investment in quality child care (American Orthopsychiatric Association, 1994).

Research Data

Research data also lend texture to the rationale for a greater focus on mental health–related issues for young children and families. Although a full review of these data is beyond the scope of this chapter, it is useful to highlight the lessons from several of these streams of work.

Perhaps the most powerful data are emerging from examinations of the role of risk and protective factors in the development of young children. That work is confirming and refining the initial dramatic evidence gathered by Rutter (1979) that not only is the presence or absence of risk factors related to subsequent emotional and behavioral problems, but the likelihood of problems increases as the number of risk factors increases. Thus, Rutter found that children exposed to two risk factors were four times as likely to have a psychiatric impairment as were children not exposed to any risk factor or only exposed to one risk factor. Children with exposure to four risk factors were 10 times as likely to have a psychiatric impairment as those with exposure to one or none. Rutter also found that the impact of risk factors was lessened for children who experienced "protective factors" (e.g., a warm, caring relationship with an adult). In Rutter's work, risk factors included marital discord, low socioeconomic status, large family size, parental criminality, maternal psychiatric disorder, and child welfare involvement. Subsequent efforts have examined the impact of combinations of biological and environmental risk factors, including, for example, lack of prenatal care, substance abuse during pregnancy, parental depression, poor temperamental fit between parent and child, substantiated abuse or neglect, and out-of-home placements. Not surprisingly, poverty itself also has been implicated as a risk factor, largely in relation to the stress it places on parent–child relationships (McLoyd, 1990). Taken together, the research leaves no doubt that, in combination, early and multiple risk factors can negatively affect the later emotional and academic well-being of children (Sameroff & Fiese, 1990; Sameroff & Seifer, 1983; Werner & Smith, 1992). Furthermore, the pattern holds regardless of the specific risk factors.

Implicit in these findings is a clear message for policy makers and service providers. Directing attention to both biological and environmental risk factors affecting young children may result in less educational and psychiatric impairment and hence lower public and private costs. Beyond this suggestive "pay now or pay more later" argument, however, the growing knowledge base about risk and protective factors also has direct program implications. A recent reanalysis of the efficacy of early childhood programs in preventing delinquency and related outcomes, such as conduct disorders, highlighted two such implications (Yoshikawa, 1994). First, the analysis suggests that high-quality early childhood programs may be powerful because they serve to buffer/protect children from the consequences of exposure to risk factors. It follows that the early childhood community might give explicit thought to building program strategies that deliberately enhance or create protective factors for children at risk of emotional or behavioral disorders. This, in turn, points toward the need for increased early childhood–mental health partnerships. Mental health skills, perspectives, and expertise can be used to tailor both program-level and individual-level strategies to enhance protective experiences for children exposed to multiple risk factors.

The second issue that Yoshikawa's work highlights is the importance of building program strategies that address not just the development and emotional well-being of children, but the developmental and family support needs of parents as well. In seeking to disentangle the differential effects of programs that focused primarily on the children, primarily on the families, or on both, Yoshikawa (1994) found that the most effective programs combined attention to both child and family needs. This parallels the lessons of a decade of reform in children's mental health. Intervention and support strategies must address not only the children but the families as well (Friesen & Wahlers, 1993).

Perhaps conceptually less groundbreaking, but also with very significant implications for designing early childhood–mental health partnerships, is the body of research related to maternal depression and its effects on children. Women in general, and poor women in particular, are especially vulnerable to depression (Belle, 1990; Institute of Medicine, 1994). In a study of one Head Start program, for instance, 47% of the parents reported poverty-related sadness, demoralization, and other indices of despair (Parker, Piotrkowsky, Horn, & Greene, 1995), a pattern repeated in other samples as well (Johnson & Walker, 1991). Furthermore, maternal depression has been linked to punitive parenting behaviors as well as anxiety and aggression in children (Constantino, 1992; Downey & Coyne, 1990; Lyons-Ruth, Botein, & Grunbaum, 1984; Piotrkowsky, Collins, Knitzer, & Robinson, 1994).

Although troubling, these data also represent a program opportunity—finding ways to support and help parents deal with chronic (often poverty-related) depression and mitigate its potential impacts on children. Unfortunately, from a research perspective, very few early childhood programs have assessed the impact of program involvement on parental depression. In two programs that have done such assessments, the results are provocative. In one instance, a highly respected child development–oriented program, parents showed clear gains (e.g., increased emotional responsiveness, knowledge of community resources, and decreased harsh attitudes about child rearing), but the high levels of depression originally identified in over half of both the intervention and control groups stayed constant in both groups (Johnson & Walker, 1991). In contrast, a program deliberately structured to address such high levels of depression, the Parent Services Program, did show demonstrable reductions in symptoms of depression in involved families (Stein & Associates, 1990). That program is, in fact, now being replicated in sites across the country.

A third cluster of research relevant to building early childhood–mental health partnerships is related to understanding the development of emotional and behavioral disorders (particularly conduct disorders) in children. This work is focused directly on understanding the antecedents of conduct disorders, seeking to show the connections between early experience and later outcomes as reflected in delinquency, emotional and behavioral disabilities, or other ultimately high-cost consequences (Constantino, 1992; Fischer, Rolf, Hasazi, & Cummings, 1984; Loerber, 1990). Other work is focusing on the pathways to violence, seeking to understand the mechanisms by which aggression occurs. Particularly relevant in this area is the research exploring the relationship between early abuse and later violence (Dodge, Bates, & Pettit, 1990).

Another body of research focuses directly on preschoolers manifesting emotional and behavioral disorders, exploring patterns and addressing issues related to screening and assessment (Neisworth & Fewell, 1991; Sinclair, Del'Homme, & Gonzalez, 1993). Also, significant is research highlighting the co-occurrence of communication problems and emotional and behavioral difficulties in young children (Prizant, Wetherby, & Roberts, 1993). This has implications not only for the training of speech and language therapists who work with young children but also for mental health practitioners. Additionally, it offers a valuable perspective on a well-known phenomenon, the reluctance to identify emotional and behavioral disturbances in young children and a tendency to "label down" such problems as speech and language problems. Nationally, for example, 67% of Head Start children identified as having a disability are diagnosed as having speech impairment, compared to 4% diagnosed as having an emotional or behavioral disability. However, in a pattern that appears to be typical, a functional assessment of 159 Head Start children identified as having disabilities found that 29% had serious emotional and behavioral disorders and 18% had speech impairments (Sinclair et al., 1993).

Finally, and of great significance, the 1990s have turned a particularly powerful lens on how infants and toddlers develop, yielding new understandings of the importance of the parent–infant relationship to the developmental process. These understandings have enormous implications for mental health perspectives and strategies. In particular, the research on infants and toddlers has highlighted the ways in which the rhythm of the parent–infant relationship can be disturbed and, increasingly, the ways it can be helped (Fenichel & Provence, 1993; Zeanah, 1993; Zero To Three, 1993). In an effort to move the field even further, Zero to Three (the National

Center for Clinical Infant Programs) has served as a catalyst for the development of a classification system for infant/toddler mental health issues (Zero to Three, 1994). From both a practice and a policy perspective, the new understandings about infant/toddler, family, and caregiver relationships and mental health point in two directions. First, they underscore the importance of ensuring that the formal mental health system has the capacity to respond to the needs of infants, toddlers, and their families where development is "in jeopardy" (Fenichel & Provence, 1993). Second, and of great consequence, they heighten the urgency of ensuring that all those concerned with the development of young children and families see that promoting positive infant/toddler–parent (and other caregiver) relationships should be integrated into the functions of the primary health care delivery system, infant and toddler child care, and the child welfare system and early intervention systems for infants and toddlers with disabilities (Carnegie Task Force on Meeting the Needs of Young Children, 1994; Szanton & Speirs, 1995).

Taken together, both experiential and research data not only frame a rationale for early childhood–mental health partnerships but also have clear implications for practice and policy. To that end, the following section considers promising program strategies and some existing but unexploited policy opportunities.

PROMISING PROGRAM STRATEGIES

As was true in the early 1980s with respect to older children and adolescents in need of mental health and related services and their families, the current program response to the mental health needs of infants, toddlers, and preschoolers and their families and other caregivers is spotty at best and, often, nonexistent (Knitzer, 1982). The system of care constructs (Stroul & Friedman, 1986) that have been so powerful for older children and adolescents have simply not been adapted to younger children; there is no place in the country where there is an early childhood mental health system of care. There are, however, approaches that suggest what such a system might look like.

Parents as Change Agents

One of the most powerful anchors of children's mental health reform since the mid-1980s has been the involvement of families as part of the service team. The Early Intervention Center (EIC) of the Positive Education Program in Cleveland has, at its core, a commitment to a parent-driven program; this commitment has resulted in the creation of a powerful intervention strategy. Modeled after the Regional Intervention Program in Tennessee (Timm, 1993), which in turn is based on the ecologically framed "reeducation" model, the EIC operates at two sites in Cleveland. What is particularly exciting about the EIC is that it is a parent-driven program. Parents not only provide support to one another, but they teach one another, modeling new ways of coping with challenging young children and circumstances. The program is a combination of individualized learning (largely for the parents), opportunities to participate in more formal "courses" as well as support groups (including specialized support groups for grandparents and fathers), and group experiences for the children that are staffed largely by parents whose own children have been through the program. Central to the program are the opportunities for parents to learn alternative strategies. Each parent must master, with his or her own child and with coaching from a parent mentor, a basic behavior management curriculum. After this, the parent gets help managing whatever situation he or she finds most difficult: having a 3-year-old throw cans off the grocery store shelf; being unable to talk on the phone; being terrorized by an aggressive, always-in-motion child; and the like. Parents learn first by rehearsing and role playing in the observation room and then by testing out new ways in the real world. The level of support that comes with this kind of "teaching," the opportunities for parents to give voice to their frequent helplessness and confusion, and the steady support from a skilled staff of both professionals and paraprofessionals mark this as a program of exceptional care and importance. Responding to increasing child welfare referrals, the EIC is developing a home-based component as a strategy to engage families with more complex problems. At the same time, as is true in programs across the country, staff are increasing their own skills and comfort in dealing with substance abuse and other related challenges.

As is often the case, the formal outcome data on the children who have moved through its doors are limited; the director informally estimates that only one third of the children must go on to specialized classes, although at intake two thirds are designated as special needs children. (A formal evaluation of the Regional Intervention Program found positive results from 3 to 9 years later for 40 children referred as preschoolers. The children could not be differentiated from their peers in terms of compliance with parental requests or in responding to teachers [Strain, Steele, Ellis, & Timm, n.d.].)

Community-Based Service Teams

Stark County, Ohio, which is well known as having one of the most effective systems of care for older children as well as a strong, collaborative governance structure through the Family Advocacy Council (composed of county-level executives of all child-serving agencies), has developed a special team that goes to where the children are. The roots of this team are interesting. Originally, the Stark County Children's Services Agency offered a traditional therapeutic day treatment program for preschoolers. As has been the pattern with day treatment programs for older children, the staff became concerned because the gains achieved in the center did not seem to translate back to other environments, particularly the child's family environment. In response, the decision was made to turn the program into a home- and community-based effort, drawing on the county's experience with an in-home program known as Family Ties (Knitzer & Cole, 1989). To that end, the Preschool Assertiveness Community Team (PACT) program was initiated. Instead of basing the "treatment" in a "pull-out" setting, the team went into the home. Experiencing success with this approach, Stark County went even further and brought the team into the community, testing out the model by working on-site in the county Head Start program. There, using a group of highly experienced paraprofessionals under the supervision of staff from the children's mental health center, the Head Start children identified as having, or at risk of having, emotional and behavioral problems were given individualized interventions, wrapping both classroom and home-based services around them and their families. In effect, Stark County translated the service strategies that have worked with older children and families into developmentally appropriate services for preschoolers. Stark County is planning to develop another specialized team to serve infants and toddlers in families experiencing serious relationship and/or developmental problems.

Managed Care and Early Childhood Systems Development

In 1993, the governor of North Carolina initiated Smart Start, an effort to enhance and expand child care services to children and to encourage more comprehensive services. Awarded a grant, a seven-county region in western North Carolina (which includes the Cherokee Nation) has recently joined forces with the Smoky Mountain Mental Health Center to strengthen the mental health services to young children and families. The mental health center is already known for its innovative participation in the Robert Wood Johnson Mental Health Services Program for Youth (MHSPY) (Beachler, 1990; Cole & Poe, 1993). Building on the fiscal and service expertise developed though MHSPY, the region made a commitment to reinvest part of the dollars saved from the avoidance of hospitalization for older children through its statewide Medicaid managed care initiative (Carolina Alternatives) to reach out to the early childhood community. Experience with some very young children who were inappropriately hospitalized and then subsequently helped through the MHSPY program not only paved the way for this new effort, but won credibility for the mental health center throughout the early childhood community. One of the center's key staff members for young children and families has been a strong partner in the planning of the entire Smart Start effort and a leader in framing the early childhood mental health component. Although just evolving, the effort already includes three early childhood consultants, one working exclusively with Head Start and the other two with child care centers. These consultants are available to assist staff and identify children needing specialized interventions. The positions are jointly funded by both mental health dollars and either Head Start dollars or funds from the Smart Start Partnership Board, the multiagency collaborative governing structure for the Smart Start initiative.

Consultants as Change Agents

Underscoring the fact that the impetus for enhancing an early childhood mental health focus can come from the early childhood community as well as the mental health community, San Francisco is building its initiative through a different strategy. The approach has involved capitalizing on the presence of the Infant–Parent Program, a mental health program for infants, toddlers, and their families based at the San Francisco General Hospital (Pawl, 1993), by adding a consultation component to its short-term, often home-based psychotherapy services. The consultants work with a range of child care programs, providing what is perceived as essential support and backup to the child care staff and, when necessary, orchestrating follow-up services for individual children and families. From a service perspective, the consultation approach is very powerful; the consultants establish a partnership with the child care staff and, through this partnership, are able to address what they view as the central issue—nurturing children through the child care relationships (Johnston, 1990). The program was originally funded with private dollars, but efforts are underway to maximize Medicaid funding for this very crucial mental health strategy. In fact, the approach has been so successful, and is so appreciated by the child care staff, that local public dollars made available for children's services as a result of a special referendum are now being used in similar ways. The city and county mental health agency also is exploring ways of funding a consultation model that would encompass children not identified as having emotional and behavioral disorders.

Head Start as a Laboratory

The required mental health component of Head Start has long been problematic (Cohen, Solnit, & Wohlford, 1979; Piotrkowsky et al., 1994). However, a recent search to identify current best practices suggests that, at the local level, albeit in a spotty fashion, innovation is occurring, sometimes in collaboration with individual mental health providers and often in collaborative partnerships with community mental health agencies. What marks these efforts as different from "business as usual" is an effort to infuse a mental health perspective into all aspects of the Head Start program, rather than viewing it as a stand-alone component largely involving referrals or even pull-out therapy. In Ventura County, for example, the long-established system of care serving older children has reached out to the Head Start community, helped pool resources to draw down additional Medicaid dollars, and stationed mental health professionals on site to provide backup and support to the family support workers and classroom teachers as well as direct services to the Head Start families.

Elsewhere, the mental health consultants working with a network of Head Start programs have joined with classroom teachers, family support workers, and often bus drivers and other Head Start staff (as well as families) into *classroom* teams, conferring frequently about the well-being of children and issues faced by the children and those who care for them. In a number of Head Start programs, members of the American Association of Marriage and Family Therapists serve as volunteers to Head Start programs. The role of these therapists involves in some instances supervising home visitors in home-based Head Start programs and in other instances working in centers (Knitzer & Yoshikawa, 1995). These strategies are truly grass roots, emerging largely without national leadership and clearly designed to be responsive to the children and families served by Head Start. They also carry a message for the larger field—that the traditional mental health paradigm and strategies are, as one informant said, "a turn off." Help must be offered in a way that is acceptable to the staff, children, and families, which means in their own settings and without the distance that traditional mental health provider–consumer relationships portend.

THE POLICY RESPONSE

From a policy perspective, meeting the mental health needs of young children and families has had no ownership; it has not been part of anyone's policy agenda—not mental health systems, not child care programs, not family resource networks. At some level, the reasons for omission are understandable. The larger mental health reform movement has been moving forward with a complex agenda, transforming the service paradigm and the infrastructure (Knitzer, 1993). The child care advocacy and policy community has been and remains focused on the most basic agenda: ensuring access, trying to ensure some levels of quality, and addressing cost issues. Family support/resource proponents have been working to solidify new ways of doing business with families and to seed what has been very much a neighborhood-based, grass roots movement. Yet each of these networks is increasingly alleging concern about the mental health and well-being of young children and families, setting the stage for a policy partnership and targeted effort.

As a context for exploring current and potential policy opportunities to create early childhood–mental health partnerships, it is appropriate to revisit the first targeted federal policy response to children's mental health,

Part F of the Community Mental Health Centers Act Amendments (PL 92-255). Enacted in 1972 during a time when fighting a "war on poverty" and giving young children a "head start" was at its height, grantees (either freestanding children's mental health programs or community mental health centers) were *required* to provide consultation and education to other community agencies, including agencies serving young children and families in child care and preschool settings. Part F (for still mysterious reasons) was repealed 2 years after its enactment. Because the awards were for 8 years, however, its effects were both positive and lasting (Knitzer, 1982; Meyers, 1985). Given the narrowing of public mental health services over the last decade to a focus entirely on children and adolescents with serious emotional and behavioral disorders, Part F represents an important contrasting policy vision, a commitment to early intervention and prevention.

Today, given the realities of budget cuts and the generally low priority that political leaders seem to place on ensuring young children a healthy start, a re-creation of the spirit of outreach and inventiveness that Part F spawned in the mental health community appears unlikely in the foreseeable future, particularly for young children. However, there may be opportunities at both state and federal levels to refocus attention on prevention and early intervention through managed care and the desire on the part of those holding the purse strings to control deep-end mental health costs (England & Cole, 1992).

State Opportunities

In this light, it is perhaps encouraging that, in a recent survey, 42 states officially endorsed the idea of early identification and intervention in their mental health system of care definitions. This suggests that the challenge lies in finding the mechanisms and opportunities, rather than in overcoming an unwillingness to stretch the boundaries of the current definition of children's mental health services (Davis, Yelton, & Katz-Leavy, 1995). It is also encouraging that at least two states, North Carolina and Nevada, have made a public commitment to respond to the mental health needs of young children and families, even in the context of many constraints.

In North Carolina, a multipronged, multiyear strategy with fiscal, service, and professional development components has evolved. The fiscal component has centered around the creation of a special category of Medicaid funding, "high-risk" funding. Any child under 3 found to have even one risk factor is eligible for a range of Medicaid services. Through this mechanism, the state is able to pay for a broad range of Medicaid mental health services to infants and toddlers who show "atypical development." The service component has centered around demonstration efforts in four parts of the state to enhance mental health services for infants and toddlers, particularly by supplementing local early intervention teams providing services through Part H of the Individuals with Disabilities Education Act

(IDEA) of 1990 (PL 101-476). To ensure personnel to deliver these services, the state established a credentialing program and made training available to mental health staff in the North Carolina network of community mental health centers. Although the spread of mental health services for infants and toddlers in North Carolina remains limited, the state has established a framework through which it can encourage centers to move forward. Also, as noted earlier, the state's innovative Medicaid managed care initiative also provides counties with the opportunity to include services to young children, particularly where they can demonstrate cost savings based on decreases in the utilization of hospitals and other high-cost placements.

In Nevada, the approach has been to develop a state-run early childhood mental health service system in the most populated part of the state. Known as Early Childhood Services, the unit is part of the Division of Child and Family Services that also includes responsibility for foster care and other child welfare services. The overall goal of the Early Childhood Services program is to improve parent–young child relationships using one of four program strategies, either alone or in combination. "Early counseling" focuses on working with parents and helping them develop social skills; it is provided in homes about 25% of the time. The therapeutic preschool program uses its six classrooms as a living lab for families and then works to integrate the children into child care settings. In addition, there are two intensive crisis programs. Family STAR (Supportive Treatment and Respite) uses a model of in-home services based on the Homebuilders family preservation model to prevent abuse and neglect. The Infant–Parent Outreach, with 24-hour-a-day availability for 2–4 months, is designed to strengthen disturbed attachment and bonding. Both programs have access to a crisis nursery on an as-needed basis, an important backup to any early childhood mental health strategy.

Federal Opportunities

Given the current state of flux of all federal policies for children and families, it is not known which if any of the opportunities highlighted here will survive in their current form. However, four points of opportunity that, to date, have only been exploited to the most limited extent on behalf of young children and families should be underscored.

Medicaid As was true in building systems of care for older children, Medicaid is a potentially powerful vehicle to provide responsive mental health services, either under the current system, through managed care, or through some combination. Many states have reimbursement mechanisms in place for flexible services; the services simply need to be tailored to the needs of young children and families.

Part H Part H is an opportunity waiting to be seized with respect to the mental health needs of infants and toddlers and their families, particularly in those instances in which relationship disturbances are already evident. As noted, Part H is the extension downward of IDEA. It requires a multisystem individualized family service plan (IFSP) for infants and toddlers rather than the individualized education program (IEP) required by IDEA for older children. (For preschoolers, states have the option of developing either IFSPs or IEPs.) Part H is an important point of entry in any effort to develop a system of mental health care for infants, toddlers, and preschoolers for three reasons. First, it is structurally consistent with the best principles of the children's mental health service system reform in that it calls for family-focused, multidisciplinary, and flexible services. Second, the legislation provides a clear directive to include infants and toddlers experiencing atypical development related to emotional and behavioral issues. Third, in theory, the legislation encourages states to serve infants and toddlers exposed to or experiencing factors that place them at risk of developmental delays (Benn, 1993). Although states have largely been unable (for fiscal reasons) to take advantage of this, Part H marks the clearest policy recognition of the body of research on risk and protective factors (Knitzer, 1993).

Children's Mental Health System of Care Initiatives   In 1993, Congress provided funds to support service development for systems of care to meet the mental health and related needs of children and adolescents with emotional and behavioral disabilities and their families (the Child, Adolescent, and Family Mental Health Services Program). As of 1995, this effort had seeded system of care efforts in 22 sites around the country. None, however, has systematically focused attention on developing collaborative partnerships with the early childhood community through these systems of care comparable to the partnerships that have developed with the schools, child welfare, and juvenile justice agencies. Nevertheless, the potential for building such partnerships focused on infants, toddlers, and preschoolers and their families is clear.

Opportunities Through Federal Child Care and Head Start Programs   Since the mid-1980s, Congress has put into place a series of new child development funding streams and shifted the child care paradigm of earlier decades, moving from support for program development to parental choice through vouchers for low-income children. Built into the child care subsidy system (and possible even under a block grant structure) is a set-aside for quality improvement funds that could be used either alone or in collaboration with mental health dollars to develop early childhood–mental health partnerships. Similarly, Head Start funds might also be reallocated (and matched with state or Medicaid mental health dollars) to build a base for a collaborative partnership. This partnership could create an Early Head Start program to stimulate the development of comprehensive services for infants, toddlers and their families, with an innovative and flexible structure that includes programming responsive to four "pillars" of development—child, family, community, and staff. This approach also represents an important new opportunity.

TOWARD THE FUTURE

The picture with respect to a response to the mental health needs of young children and families is bittersweet. The needs justify, and the knowledge base supports, a stronger, coherent response from all systems involved with young children and families. Furthermore, the service system reform efforts of the past decade, both within the children's mental health system and under other system reform auspices (Boyd, 1992; Bryant & Graham, 1993; Kahn & Kamerman, 1992; Knitzer, 1993), have created a level of community and policy understanding that suggests a readiness to move forward on this challenging agenda. At the same time, the recent and dramatic shift in the structure of federal support for children and the unraveling of commitment to use public policy as a tool to improve the lives of children (especially young, poor children) will make forward movement difficult. Yet even in the face of these unpleasant realities, the mental health of young children and their families can only be ignored at our societal peril. In order to move forward, attention must be devoted to building a vision, building the needed infrastructure at community and state levels, testing and refining service strategies, and training professionals and paraprofessionals with appropriate knowledge and skills.

Building a Vision

Building on the work that has already been done, there is a need to set forth a vision and frame the values that should undergird early childhood–mental health partnerships. The work that has already been done suggests some of these key core values:

- Young children and families should have access to family-centered mental health and related services and supports designed to support parents of young children *and other caregivers* to nurture and build caring relationships with young children.
- Young children and families should have access to mental health and related services and supports that are delivered in natural settings, including homes and child care programs.
- Young children and families should have access to mental health and related services and supports that respect developmental processes and are flexible and individualized to meet the needs of both children and parents.
- Young children and families should have access to mental health and related services and supports that are sensitive to the cultural and ethnic values of the families.

- Caregivers of young children and families in programs for infants, toddlers, and preschoolers, as well as family support workers, should have access to mental health program consultation, case consultation, and back-up support to address issues of burnout, cultural and workplace conflicts, and other staff issues that may interfere with their ability to provide responsive programs for young children and families.
- Vulnerable infants, toddlers, and preschoolers and their families in shelters, involved with courts, and in other high-risk settings should be the focus of outreach efforts and should have access to the early childhood mental health system of care.
- Young children, families, and programs experiencing crises related to violence, community disasters, or family-specific experiences should have immediate access to crisis intervention and support.

Building a Community and State Infrastructure

A mapping of the early childhood, family support, and mental health networks in communities suggests many potential points of leadership for building a strengthened community response to the mental health needs of young children and families. These include existing mental health–led system of care efforts, child care resource and referral programs, family resource programs, early intervention councils, early childhood planning groups and collaboratives, and Head Start. To mobilize this potential leadership, there must be formal opportunities for dialogue and seed money to support the time and organization necessary to develop a vision for, and take steps toward, a family-focused early childhood–mental health partnership.

Leadership will also be needed from states. Here, too, the catalysts will vary, although it is hoped that state children's mental health leaders will assume a key role, working with child care administrators, managed care planners, maternal and child health leaders, directors of Head Start/state collaboration projects, and children's policy advisors from the governor's office. For such officials, central infrastructure issues will include ensuring support for program consultation and staff support as well as ensuring access to appropriate interventions for young children and families at risk of emotional and behavioral disorders, in addition to those with diagnosable difficulties.

Testing Out, Refining, and Evaluating Service Strategies

Even the cursory review undertaken to date by the author and others of the status of current program efforts on behalf of young children and families reveals more activity and systematic attention to this issue than perhaps might have been expected. At the same time, there is a need to sharpen the focus and synthesize more carefully what we know, building a solid clinical and systems research agenda. Such an agenda must include significant attention to the actual and potential impacts of managed care on improving a range of mental health–related services to young children, their families, and other caregivers.

"Growing" the Field

Responding with sensitivity to the often complex and challenging mental health and other needs of infants, toddlers, preschoolers, and their families, and helping families navigate the multiple systems that provide services to them, requires a mix of knowledge and skills that is not easily attained. Required competencies include child development knowledge, clinical skills, family systems knowledge, multidisciplinary practice skills, and organizational savvy, to name a few. Therefore, in each state, within practice guilds and higher education institutions, and in both early childhood and mental health in-service training, efforts are needed to define and "grow" professionals and paraprofessionals with the right mix of skills and sensitivities.

CONCLUSION

Creating a responsive early childhood mental health system of care for young children and families is similar to, but also different from, creating a responsive system of care for older children. It is different because the developmental issues are different, the network of community agencies involved is different, working with caregivers and teachers is even more critical, and it is crucial to attend not just to "identified" children, but to high-risk children and, indeed, to all children and their families. Development of an early childhood system of care is similar to developing such a system for older children and adolescents because families are the center of any service delivery strategy and are called on as partners and sources of strength, services must be flexible and use a wraparound approach, and the process of collaborating with other agencies will require the same kind of shared leadership, vision setting, and time that has shaped mental health reform efforts for older children.

This chapter has argued that, if the mental health field is to respond in a systematic way (either with public resources or with public–private partnerships) to the needs of young children and their families, two central tasks must be addressed:

1. Mobilizing mental health knowledge and resources on behalf of younger children already showing signs of serious trouble
2. Reinventing a capacity to use mental health skills and strategies to support young children at risk of developing identifiable disorders,

whether they are at risk by virtue of poverty, homelessness, parental depression or other mental illness, exposure to violence, or any combination of factors

Research elucidates the factors that put young children at risk of developing disorders (especially conduct disorders), and analyses of program impacts suggest that early intervention in the context of family support can make a difference. The need, from the perspective of those who work with children and families, is urgent. Sound mental health services can strengthen developmentally appropriate early childhood programs and get families moving forward. Such services can also help to bring us closer to meeting important national goals—family self-sufficiency and readiness to learn. Recent progress has largely been limited to improvements in mental health services to children with the most serious disorders. For them, improvements have been significant. Yet it is perilous to continue this narrow focus. As we move toward the next century, investments of mental health dollars for young children, their families, and other caregivers must become an integral part of the children's mental health, early childhood, and family support agendas.

REFERENCES

Adolfi, B., Humenay, M., & Jeffries, H. (1995). Fairfax County Social Work Services, Preschool Special Education Programs Survey Results. Xerox. Falls Church, VA: Fairfax County Public Schools.

American Orthopsychiatric Association Task Force on Head Start and Mental Health. (1994). *Head Start and mental health: Pathways to quality improvement.* New York: American Association of Orthopsychiatry.

Beachler, M. (1990). The mental health services program for youth. *Journal of Mental Health Administration, 17,* 115–121.

Belle, D. (1990). Poverty and women's mental health. *American Psychologist, 45,* 385–389.

Benn, R. (1993). Conceptualizing eligibility for early intervention services. In D. Bryant & M. Graham (Eds.), *Implementing early intervention: From research to effective practice* (pp. 18–45). New York: Guilford.

Boyd, A. (1992). *Integrating systems of care for children and families: An overview of values, methods and characteristics of developing models.* Tampa: University of South Florida, Florida Mental Health Institute.

Boyer, E.L. (1991). *Ready to learn: A mandate for the nation.* Princeton, NJ: Carnegie Foundation for the Advancement of Teaching.

Brayfield, A.A., Gennis Deich, S., & Hoffereth, S.L. (1993). *Caring for children in low income families: A substudy of the National Child Care Survey, 1990.* Washington, DC: Urban Institute Press.

Bryant, D., & Graham, M. (Eds.). (1993). *Implementing early intervention: From research to effective practice.* New York: Guilford.

Carnegie Task Force on Meeting the Needs of Young Children. (1994). *Starting points: Meeting the needs of our youngest children.* New York: Carnegie Corporation of New York.

Cohen, D., Solnit, A., & Wohlford, P. (1979). Mental health services in Head Start. In E. Zyler &. J. Valentine (Eds.), *Project Head Start* (pp. 259–290). New York: Free Press.

Cole, R., & Poe, S. (1993). *Partnerships for care: Systems of care for children with serious emotional disturbances and their families.* Washington, DC: Washington Business Group on Health.

Community Mental Health Centers Act Amendments of 1972, PL 92-255. (June 30, 1972). Provisions were consolidated in the Omnibus Budget Reconciliation Act of 1981 (PL 97-35) and given as block grants from FY 1982–1984.

Constantino, J. (1992). On the prevention of conduct disorder: A rationale for initiating preventive efforts. *Infants and Young Children, 5*(2), 29–41.

Davis, M., Yelton, S., & Katz-Leavy, J. (1995). *State child and adolescent mental health: Administration, policies and laws.* Washington, DC: Georgetown University Child Development Center, National Technical Assistance Center for Children's Mental Health.

Dodge, K.A., Bates, J.E., & Pettit, G.S. (1990). Mechanisms in the cycle of violence. *Science, 250,* 1678–1683.

Downey, G., & Coyne, J.C. (1990). Children of depressed parents: An integrative review. *Psychological Bulletin, 108,* 50–76.

Drell, M.M., Siegel, C.H., & Gaensbauer, T.J. (1993). Post-traumatic stress disorder. In C.H. Zanah (Ed.), *Handbook of infant mental health* (pp. 291–304). New York: Guilford.

Edlefsen, M., & Baird, M. (1994). Making it work: Preventive mental health care for disadvantaged preschoolers. *Social Work, 39,* 566–573.

England, M.J., & Cole, R. (1992). Prevention as targeted intervention. *Administration and Policy in Mental Health, 19,* 179–189.

Fenichel, E., & Provence, S. (Eds.). (1993). *Development in jeopardy: Clinical responses to infants and families.* Madison, CT: International Universities Press, Inc.

Fischer, M., Rolf, J.E., Hasazi, J.E., & Cummings, L. (1984). Follow-up of a preschool epidemiological sample: Cross age continuities and predictions of later adjustment with internalizing and externalizing dimensions of behavior. *Child Development, 55,* 137–150.

Friesen, B., & Koroloff, N. (1990). Family-centered services: Implications for mental health administration and research. *Journal of Mental Health Administration, 17,* 13–25.

Friesen, B., & Wahlers, D. (1993). Respect and real help: Family support and children's mental health. *Journal of Emotional and Behavioral Problems, 2*(4), 12–15.

Groves, B., Zuckerman, B., Marans, S., & Cohen, D. (1993). Silent victims: Children who witness violence. *JAMA, 269,* 262–264.

Individuals with Disabilities Education Act of 1990, PL 101-476. (October 30, 1990). Title 20, U.S.C. 1400 et seq: *U.S. Statutes at Large, 104* (Part 2), 1103–1151.

Institute of Medicine. (1994). *Reducing risks for mental disorders: Frontiers for preventive intervention research.* Washington, DC: National Academy Press.

Johnson, D.L., & Walker, T.B. (1991). *Final report of an evaluation of the Avance Parent Education and Family Support Program.* New York: Carnegie Corporation.

Johnston, K. (1990, October 13). *Mental health consultation.* Paper presented at the Conference on Early Challenges: Caring for Children at Birth to Three, Infant Toddler Consortium of the San Francisco Psychoanalytic Institute, Haywood, CA.

Kahn, A., & Kamerman, S. (1992). *Integrating services integration: An overview of initiatives, issues and possibilities.* New York: National Center for Children in Poverty.

Knitzer, J. (1982). *Unclaimed children: The failure of public responsibility to children and adolescents in need of mental health services.* Washington, DC: Children's Defense Fund.

Knitzer, J. (1993). Children's mental health policy: Challenging the future. *Journal of Emotional and Behavioral Disorders, 1*(1), 8–16.

Knitzer, J. (1993). *Early intervention: State and federal system challenges.* Unpublished manuscript.

Knitzer, J., & Cole, E. (1989). *Family preservation services: The policy challenge to state child welfare and mental health systems.* New York: Bank Street College of Education.

Knitzer, J., & Yoshikawa, H. (1995). *Head Start and mental health and family support strategies: Lessons from the field.* Unpublished manuscript.

Loerber, R. (1990). Development and risk factors of juvenile antisocial behavior and delinquency. *Clinical Psychology Review, 10,* 1–41.

Love, J., & Logue, M.E. (1992). *Transitions to kindergarten in American schools: Executive summary* (U.S. DOE Contract No. LC88089001). (Available from Research Corp., 1000 Market St., Portsmouth, NH 03801.)

Lyons-Ruth, K., Botein, S., & Grunbaum, H.U. (1984). Reaching the hard to reach: Serving isolated and depressed mothers with infants in the community. In B. Cohler & J. Musick

(Eds.), *Intervention with psychiatrically disabled parents and their young children* (pp. 95–121). San Francisco, CA: Jossey Bass.

McLoyd, V.C. (1990). The impact of economic hardship on black families and children: Psychological distress, parenting and socioemotional development. *Child Development, 61,* 311–346.

Meyers, J. (1985). Federal efforts to improve mental health services for children: Breaking a cycle of failure. *Journal of Clinical Child Psychology, 14,* 182–187.

Neisworth, J.T., & Fewell, R.R. (Eds.). (1991). *Emerging trends for child behavior disorders.* Austin, TX: PRO-ED.

Osofsky, J., & Fenichel, E. (Eds.). (1994). *Caring for infants and toddlers in violent environments: Hurt, healing and hope.* Arlington, VA: Zero To Three/National Center for Clinical Infant Programs.

Parker, F.L., Piotrkowsky, C., Horn, W.F. , & Greene, S. (1995). The challenge for Head Start: Realizing its vision as a two-generation program. In S. Smith (Ed.), *Two-generation programs for families in poverty* (pp. 135–159). Norwood, NJ: Ablex Publishing.

Pawl, J. (1993). A stitch in time: Using emotional support, developmental guidance, and infant-parent psychotherapy in a brief preventive intervention. In E. Fenichel & S. Provence (Eds.), *Development in jeopardy* (pp. 203–229). Madison, CT: International Universities Press, Inc.

Piotrkowsky, C.S., Collins, R.C., Knitzer, J., & Robinson, R. (1994). Strengthening mental health services in Head Start: A challenge for the 1990's. *American Psychologist, 49,* 133–139.

Prizant, B.M., Wetherby, A.M., & Roberts, J.E. (1993). Communication disorders in infants and toddlers. In C.H. Zeanah (Ed.), *Handbook of infant mental health* (pp. 260–279). New York: Guilford.

Rutter, M. (1979). Protective factors in children's responses to stress and disadvantage. In M.W. Kent &. J.E. Rolf (Eds.), *Primary prevention of psychopathology: Vol. 3. Social competence in children* (pp. 49–74). Hanover, NH: University of New England.

Sameroff, A.J., & Fiese, B.H. (1990). Transactional regulation and early intervention. In S.J. Meisels &. J.P. Shonkoff (Eds.), *Handbook of early intervention* (pp. 119–149). New York: Cambridge University Press.

Sameroff, A.J., & Seifer, R. (1983). Familial risk and child competence. *Child Development, 54,* 1254–1268.

Sinclair, E., Del'Homme, M., & Gonzalez, M. (1993). Systematic screening for preschool behavioral disorders. *Behavioral Disorders, 18,* 177–188.

Stein, A., & Associates. (1990). *Parent services project evaluation. Final report of findings.* Fairfax CA: Parent Services Project.

Strain, P., Steele, P., Ellis, T., & Timm, M. (n.d.). *Long-term effects of oppositional child treatment with mothers as therapists and therapist trainers.* (Available from the author, Western Psychiatric Institute and Clinic, Pittsburgh, PA.)

Stroul, B., & Friedman, R. (1986). *A system of care for severely emotionally disturbed children and youth.* Washington, DC: Georgetown University Child Development Center, National Technical Assistance Center for Children's Mental Health.

Szanton, E.S., & Speirs, C.C. (1995). The politics of infancy in two countries. In K. Minde (Ed.), *Child and Adolescent Psychiatric Clinics of North America: Infant psychiatry,* 4(3), 701–718. Philadelphia: W.B. Saunders.

Timm, M. (1993). The Regional Intervention Program: Family treatment by family members. *Behavioral Disorders,* 19(1), 34–43.

Werner, E.E., & Smith, R.S. (1992). *Overcoming the odds: High risk children from birth to adulthood.* Ithaca, NY: Cornell University Press.

Yoshikawa, H. (1994). Prevention as cumulative protection: Effects of early family support and education on chronic delinquency and its risks. *Psychological Bulletin, 115,* 28–54.

Zeanah, C.H. (Ed.). (1993). *Handbook of infant mental health.* New York: Guilford.

Zero to Three. (1993). *Heart Start: The emotional foundations of school readiness.* Zero To Three/National Center for Clinical Infant Programs.

Zero to Three. (1994). *Diagnostic classification of mental health and developmental disorders of infancy and early childhood.* Arlington, VA: Zero to Three/National Center for Clinical Infant Programs.

C H A P T E R   30

Systems of Care for Children with Special Health Needs

Suzanne M. Bronheim, Marie L. Keefe,
Cappie C. Morgan, and Phyllis R. Magrab

Children with special health care needs are a diverse group with multiple needs. Technically, children with serious emotional disturbance are a subset of this group because they require highly specialized care not typically required by healthy young people. In our current system, however, mental health services are viewed as a separate system and are treated differently by third-party payers. Thus, when discussing the area of special health care needs, typically one is talking about the problems of children with non–mental health medical problems. Often there is an overlap between these two groups. Certainly, the issues of system coordination and development are critical to all children with special needs and their families. This chapter focuses on efforts to develop systems of care for this other set of children with special health care needs.

The group of children to be discussed is diverse. Children with illnesses that are chronic, life-threatening, or both, such as heart disease, diabetes, cancer, cystic fibrosis, seizure disorders, or asthma are included in this designation. In addition, children with musculoskeletal conditions such as cerebral palsy or muscular dystrophy, children with developmental disabilities, or those with genetic disorders also need specialized and often intense medical and therapeutic services. Finally, children who are the victims of accidents or violence may need long-term special care and become part of the group known as children with special health care needs. The commonality among these groups is their need for ongoing, specialized medical intervention over a long period of time.

The Need for Systems Development

The challenges in dealing with systems of care faced by families with children with special health care needs are, in many ways, quite similar to those encountered by families with children with serious emotional disturbances. The problems faced by families who have children with chronic illnesses or disabilities, however, have been, ironically, the result of successes in medical care. As medical technology and treatment leapt forward in the last half of this century, the medical outcomes for many children with chronic diseases and other conditions that require special medical care improved greatly. With this growth in types of treatments, types of specialists to provide those treatments, and highly technological equipment, families faced a real dilemma. On the one hand, they were thrilled that their children could be treated to increase their life span or to improve their functioning. On the other hand, for many life became a confusing and overwhelming dash from one appointment to another, from one agency to another, and from home to often distant special care centers. Meanwhile, parents often missed work, could not take care of other family members, and were confused by which professionals were responsible for providing what services. In effect, although medical science progressed, the delivery of care has not been systematically designed to support families.

Building Blocks of a System of Care

Although each family has its own story of how the system has (or has not) worked for it, over time four main areas have emerged as vital to a family-centered, coordinated system of care for children with special health care needs. First, there must be a way for *the child's problem to be identified and for the family to enter the system* of care. Second, *all of the needed services must be available*, as close to home as possible. These services must cover the multiple levels of medical care needed by many of these children, as well as nonphysician services and special therapies. In addition, families should not be barred from obtaining these services because of rules, regulations, overwhelming paperwork, costs, lack of transportation, or cultural barriers. Third, these *services must be coordinated* so that families do not have to deal with conflicting opinions, gaps or duplications in services, and lack of communication among service providers. Finally, systems must recognize the families' needs as well as their children's and provide *a way for families to have input to the planning and functioning of that system of care*.

System Change Efforts

As families and providers recognized these four basic features needed in systems of care for children with special health care needs, frustration with the existing system of care grew and finally gave rise to a call for change. At first this call for change was heard from only a few voices. Then two groups concerned with the health of children—one public and one private—took up the call. The Maternal and Child Health Bureau of the U.S. Department of Health and Human Services and the American Academy of Pediatrics began to work to resolve the problems that the system of care presented for families. By 1987, the issue had been so clearly defined that the Surgeon General of the United States, Dr. C. Everett Koop, established a national agenda for children with special health care needs.

In 1989, amendments were made to Title V of the Social Security Act—the federal law through which states receive money to provide services to children with special health care needs—to ensure changes in the Maternal and Child Health Block Grant. These amendments, in the Omnibus Budget Reconciliation Act (OBRA) of 1989, (PL 101-239), encouraged states to provide leadership in planning, promoting and coordinating health services. They were to work to improve access to health care that is comprehensive, coordinated, based in the child's community, and centered on the family. Finally, the focus shifted from simply creating more services to creating systems of care.

Communities Can Campaign

The process of consciously developing a system of care within a community was taking administrators, providers, and families into uncharted waters. The task seemed enormous, and there were very few guidelines to successful completion. To respond to this need for direction, the American Academy of Pediatrics and the Maternal and Child Health Bureau launched a project called the "Communities Can Campaign." The goal of this project has been to identify communities that have made substantial progress toward realizing the goal of a family-centered, coordinated system of care. Each community recognized had to be nominated by the state Director of Services for Children with Special Health Care Needs and the president of the state chapter of the American Academy of Pediatrics for having made substantial progress toward developing within the community effective ways to identify children in need of services, assure access to care and primary health care ("medical home"), coordinate care for families, and provide family support services/family involvement with the system of care—the four essential elements of a system. Having identified these communities, the project has studied these localities to learn how these goals were accomplished in order to help other communities realize that they, too, can develop family-centered, coordinated systems of care for their families.

To date, 14 charter communities have been involved in the Communities Can Campaign: Flagstaff/Coconino County, Arizona; Ukiah/Mendocino County, California; Naples/Collier County, Florida; Maui, Hawaii; Minneapolis, Minnesota; Wolf Point/Roosevelt County, Montana; Kearney, Nebraska; Toledo/Lucas County, Ohio; Berks County, Pennsylvania; Woonsocket, Rhode Island; San Antonio, Texas; Franklin County, Vermont; Fort Lewis, Washington; and Eau Claire, Wisconsin. These communities vary in size and shape because people's perceptions—not political and geographic boundaries—define communities. Thus, in Montana, a community to be served can include hundreds or thousands of square miles. A "neighbor" may be someone who lives 10 miles away. Families may be accustomed to driving long distances to shop, seek entertainment, go to worship, or see the doctor and thus have a broad geographic concept of community. In contrast, in Minneapolis, a few square blocks may define a family's community. Everything they do—shop, socialize, worship, see the dentist—may take place in a small area of their neighborhood. In Maui, Hawaii, a community is based on an island, separated from other parts of the state by miles of water. These different types of communities must, of course, develop very different kinds of systems of care to make sure that families of children with special health care needs feel that they are served within their communities.

LESSONS LEARNED FROM THE COMMUNITIES CAN CAMPAIGN

In studying these 14 communities and how they have been able to implement the four building blocks of systems of care, many common approaches became evident. Thus, although each community's solution might be unique, some universal strategies seemed to apply to all their efforts. Eight such "winning strategies" emerged that could be employed by any community seeking to implement a system of care for children with special health care needs.

1. *Implementing interagency collaboration.* Communities that have made substantial progress toward a family-centered, community-based, coordinated system of care have generally developed some means for different agencies and providers who serve children to work together. This working together may come at several levels, depending on the communities' needs. *Improved communication* among agencies; *shared planning*, either about services for a particular child and family or about the more general needs in the community; *joint programming*, such as multidisciplinary clinics or coordinated "child find" efforts; and *shared resources*, such as joint funding of personnel, use of common office or clinic space, or shared responsibility for various parts of a program or project, have all been important strategies noted by the Communities Can groups.

2. *Forming private–public partnerships.* Many times, the public sector is limited in its approaches to system building because of legislative or regulatory requirements about whom they serve or how they may spend money. As a result, there may be gaps in services, populations served, or resources to provide a truly coordinated set of services. The private sector often has far greater flexibility in how it operates or what it funds, but does not have the enormous resources that potentially exist in the public sector. Thus, successful communities have found ways to marry the private and public sectors to gain the advantages of each.

3. *Developing resources other than money.* Typically, when people begin to envision a system of care for their community, they come to a

halt at some point because there is "no funding" for a particular service or component. The above-mentioned 14 communities all reached that barrier; however, many were able to move beyond it by realizing that money is not the only resource that will make a project work. Donated space, phone lines, bits of personnel time, food, printing, volunteer time, and training are all examples of non-cash resources.

4. *Encouraging active participation by physicians in system development.* Generally, it is the medical system, and specifically physicians, who are the main contact point with a system of care for children with special health care needs and their families. Physicians have tremendous power within the medical system and prestige within their communities. They are also in an excellent position to know about the needs of these families. Thus, they can be leaders in a community with regard to systems development.

5. *Promoting active family involvement in system development.* The families of children with special health care needs are, in the end, the experts on what services are needed as well as how a system of care should work. They can have the interest, knowledge, and energy to keep system-building efforts on track, but only if families are seen as vital partners with agencies, providers, payers, and government.

6. *Building on existing programs rather than inventing new ones.* Many of the communities highlighted in this chapter work to maximize resources, including people's time and effort. Thus, they have built on existing efforts to collaborate for children when working to ensure an improved system of care for children with special health care needs. Some have used the local interagency council developed in response to federal early intervention legislation as a starting point.

7. *Developing generic systems of care to serve all children.* In the past, programs were frequently developed to serve children with a specific diagnosis, at a particular age, from a particular type of family background, or at a particular economic level. A number of communities have found that building "generic" systems to serve all children helps avoid duplicating services and ensures that all children have access to a coordinated system of care.

8. *Developing cultural competence in the system of care.* Services and systems cannot be successful if the families who need them find them inaccessible or unacceptable. Cultural differences between the families and the providers in the system are often a seemingly insurmountable barrier. The Communities Can system-building efforts have taken into account the cultural diversity of their communities. Extra efforts to develop competence in the system for reaching fam-

ilies from various cultures has paid off in multiple ways for these communities.

ACTUALIZING SYSTEMS OF CARE

The four building blocks and eight strategies only begin to make sense when one can see concrete examples. The material gained from the Communities Can Campaign provides just such real-life scenarios from the 14 charter communities. Although only a few examples are presented in relation to each of the four areas, the number of potential creative solutions is limited only by the particular needs, resources, and imagination of any given community.

A Way for the Family to Find and Enter the System of Care

A community can have a wonderful system of care—all the necessary services, funding for all of them, an effective way to coordinate—and yet still fail. If the children and families who need those services never get into the system, then the whole process is useless. Thus, the first essential component of any system of care that will truly help families is that it can identify and bring into the system all who need the care. Not surprisingly, this process is very complicated and must be approached from several angles.

Developing Community Awareness   One approach to helping the system and families find each other is to develop a high level of public awareness both in the general population and among providers in the community about where families can find help. In San Antonio, Texas, a private, nonprofit organization called Any Baby Can, Inc. (ABC) is the key link between families and the system of care. This private–public partnership approach provides a place where anyone can call with a concern about a child and be directed to appropriate services (either at the agency or in the community). They use a very simple motto—"Know a baby who needs help?"—that does not limit who can call to those who know their children's diagnosis or know what services they seek. Their logo is the Little Engine That Could, and they use this image to advertise on posters, on the backs of buses, on buttons, and on bumper stickers. They have enlisted help in the community from Pizza Huts, and now neon ABC signs light up their windows.

ABC also utilizes face-to-face contact. Peers are used to educate the professional community. For example, the neonatologist on the board is sent to speak at the area neonatologists' breakfast. ABC goes to all the school districts and holds mini-lunches to describe the programs.

Printed materials and other reminders also keep the community aware. ABC distributes literature in public libraries. Mugs with the ABC logo are left in emergency rooms and neonatal units to keep the program on the minds of staff. Mindful of the many Hispanic families in the San Antonio community, ABC is working to develop a Spanish brochure about the program. In a good example of private–public support and finding noncash resources, they are fortunate to have had the Hispanic advertising agency in town volunteer to translate, design, and produce the brochure for no cost.

Directed Outreach Efforts Public awareness, however, may not be the only effort needed to help families find and enter the system. In many instances, cultural and language differences, economic limitations, distrust of government, lack of transportation, and insufficient knowledge about their children's needs can prevent families from even trying to find or enter the system of care. Reaching out to families is another key approach that communities have devised to overcome these obstacles.

Flagstaff/Coconino County, Arizona, has a sizeable Native American population that has a strong skepticism about well-intentioned public policies. Traditional beliefs can be incompatible with the official concept of early intervention. In addition, human services workers who are not aware of cultural issues can be offensive to families and actually provide an additional barrier to families entering the system of care.

In order to ensure access to all children, the county needed to work in rural outreach. With Health Care Financing Administration money, they hired lay outreach workers of the same culture to go into homes on the reservation to find out what the families need, to make referrals, and to provide service coordination. Coconino County was able to save some time and effort by building on earlier efforts with similar models. There were three such programs already functioning in the state that were initiated to focus on prenatal care that served as examples. The person hired as coordinator had worked with a Native American tribe in the Phoenix area and serves as the coordinator for four part-time paraprofessionals who are Native Americans and who have received intensive training about health care issues and outreach.

Coconino County was able to develop this type of program through close interagency collaboration that existed as part of a countywide planning group for children's health. Although that group focuses on all children and all health issues, its broad base of representation allows it to tackle specific problems for children and families with special needs. A coalition of agencies is advancing this program by developing joint programming and sharing resources, including staff from the Health Department and Mental Health agency, among others. The area Health Education agency conducts the training, and the Community Health Center has provided free office space. This effort again demonstrates that not all resources are in the form of cash.

Child Find Efforts Another key approach to linking families with systems involves leaving nothing to chance. Some communities have worked to develop ways to systematically look for all the children and families who may need services and support from the system. Rather than trying to connect one by one, they create a way to find as many families as possible and see which ones need what kinds of help.

Wolf Point in Roosevelt County, Montana, has taken a systematic approach to finding children and families who need help from the system. Children and families were clearly not coming to the system, and individual agency and provider efforts to identify children who needed special supports also were ineffective. The school system, which had limited resources, had traditionally taken on this "child find" role; however, it was estimated that those efforts resulted in only 4% of the preschool population being screened. Thus, Wolf Point has developed a large communitywide screening effort that has been made successful by strong interagency collaboration, private and public cooperation, and identification of all types of resources, not just monetary support, for their efforts.

The solution that was developed involved the school and health department spearheading a highly collaborative child find effort that would result in a high turnout, low-cost, effective screening. By bringing in multiple components of the community, the screening effort could be larger and more effective without a major increase in expense. A local Native American economic enterprise donated the use of its bingo casino and volunteer labor to help provide meals for screening staff and to clean up. The school paid for advertising, provided secretarial support to take phone calls and register children, supplied paper products, and donated the special education teacher and the speech pathologist to conduct the screening of children over age 2 1/2. The local paper wrote feature articles and local radio stations provided public service announcements. Head Start programs, county nurses at well-child clinics, and school-employed family–school coordinators reminded parents of the screening. The actual screening was done by county nurses; staff from a private, nonprofit regional early intervention program; private providers under contract to the schools; and school personnel. The school notified parents of screening results.

Agencies now involved with planning and implementing the screening are the county schools; the regional Special Education Co-op; the county health department; Indian Health Services; Fort Peck Tribes; the Wolf Point Community Organization; the Women, Infants and Children program; Head Start; a private, nonprofit organization; private physicians and clinics; social services; the Bureau of Indian Affairs; and the state department of health and environmental services. Dental screening, transportation, and nutrition assessment have been added. As a result of the first of these collaborative efforts, 51% of the district's preschool children ages birth to 5 were screened over a 4-day period. Even with limited fiscal resources, this community has developed an approach that enables it to have a highly sophisticated and effective child find effort, the first stage in serving children with special health care needs.

Services that Are Available, Accessible, and Appropriate

For families with children with special health care needs, a major challenge is finding the many services needed within a reasonable distance that are actually usable, of high quality, and acceptable to the family's needs and values. The system of services for children with special health care needs has many levels and components. The ideal of health care for children is a well-organized system that consists of what are called primary, secondary, and tertiary levels of care. Most children who receive health care go to a doctor or clinic in their community for "well-child care" (immunizations, checking growth and development, screening for possible health problems) and for treatment of normal childhood problems such as ear infections, sore throats, flu, or chickenpox. The doctor or clinic gets to know the child and family and follows the health of the child over the years. This care, given by the family physician, pediatrician, general practitioner, or health clinic, is what is technically referred to as primary care.

Sometimes children need special care—to have a broken leg treated or have tonsils removed—or need to be in the hospital for a short time. The primary care doctor may be able to provide these services or a specialist may be asked to help with that particular problem. This type of special care is often called secondary care. The primary care doctor is still responsible for the long-term care, but specialists may help out from time to time.

A third level of care, called tertiary care, is sometimes needed. This type of care is highly specialized, and only a few specialist physicians in special centers or university hospitals may provide it.

When children have special health care needs, the system often gets turned on its head. Many children see only specialists—secondary or tertiary level doctors—because that doctor treats their special conditions. Thus, there may be no one who is following the health needs that every child has—immunizations, health education for child and parents, and monitoring of growth and development. In addition, these highly specialized physicians often do not practice in the child's community. Thus, every time the child has a cold or an earache, his or her family may have to travel a long distance to see a doctor whose specialty may not focus on these types of problems.

Building Primary Care Capacity Some of the Communities Can Campaign communities have found ways to address these problems. At the primary care level, the task has been to ensure that children with special health care needs have a "medical home" close to home. Many community-based primary physicians are not comfortable providing care to children with special health care needs. They often feel that they lack specialized knowledge about the child's condition or are concerned about the amount of time that caring for these children might take in a busy practice. In Maui, Hawaii, the Physician Involvement Project was developed in concert with the local chapter of the American Academy of Pediatrics with funding from the federal Maternal and Child Health Bureau. Although the project had many goals, increasing physician involvement in providing a medical home and care coordination for children with special health care needs was a major target.

Although most pediatricians recognize the need to serve these children and families, they typically wonder how they can accommodate these complex needs in a busy office practice. Medical school and residency training rarely prepares pediatricians for this challenge. The Hawaii training project filled that gap so that lack of understanding about the role of a medical home for children with special health care needs and lack of models to implement this service do not stand in the way of pediatricians adopting this important role.

The training program, a 6-hour series of continuing medical education workshops and accompanying handouts, is designed to assist the physician in assuring comprehensive care for optimal outcomes. It provides concrete illustrations of exemplary service and usable protocols to implement such care. It is composed of three modules, each of which involves 2 hours of training and covers a different aspect of optimal care. Not only has this training program been successfully implemented in Maui, but the Hawaii Academy of Pediatrics has worked with chapters in other states to provide this education in communities throughout the country. When pediatricians are helped to understand the importance of the medical home concept and learn how to incorporate it into a busy office practice, they are more open to providing the care leadership that children with special health care needs and their families require.

The Physician Involvement Project involved a number of other strategies in addition to the training of physicians. Interested physicians were recruited to become involved in child advocacy in the community. Efforts were also made to affect legislation and regulations that might enhance community physicians' ability to be involved in primary care for children with special health care needs. Collaboration with other child health efforts was also a key to the success of the project, helping direct families who needed a medical home to physicians who were ready to become involved.

Developing Specialty Services   A second part of a truly community-based system of medical care for children who have special needs is the availability of specialty care close to home. Many of these children need both secondary and tertiary levels of care, yet few communities can support a full range of specialty services. Ukiah, California, is one of those communities with no pediatric subspecialists. The community tackled this problem by establishing quarterly subspecialty outreach clinics in its local hospital, primarily using the resources of the California Pacific Medical Center in San Francisco and the Redwood Coast Regional Center. A variety of specialists come to the community on a periodic basis, thus reducing the need of families to go to San Francisco for this type of care, a time-consuming trip. The specialists who come to the clinic accept Medi-Cal payment for their services.

These subspecialty outreach clinics not only provide direct services in arenas such as pediatric gastroenterology, pediatric neurology, pediatric ophthalmology, developmental assessment, genetics, and child psychiatry, but they also provide opportunities for local physicians to learn from the visiting specialists. Each specialist provides continuing education presentations at each clinic in order to teach local providers about new diagnostic and intervention approaches. Local providers, especially pediatricians, have come to feel increasingly comfortable with highly specialized health problems because of the specialized support available through these on-site clinics as well as ready access to phone consultation with specialists. Thus, this infusion of specialty services also increases local physician knowledge and comfort, expanding access to primary care. In addition, occupational therapy, physical therapy, and speech personnel from the Ukiah school system are invited to specialty clinics and specialty training in order to make these therapies available and understandable and to help these specialists understand the overall intervention strategies for children with special needs. Thus, these clinics also serve as a mechanism for coordinating care.

Eliminating Paperwork Barriers   Even when services are available, the process of obtaining them can be overwhelming to families. Each service or agency requires an intake process, eligibility must be determined, and parents must spend valuable time running from office to office. In Fort Lewis, Washington, families at Madigan Army Medical Center no longer face these obstacles to care. In trying to simplify the process for families, it was suggested that workers at Madigan do an intake with a family, put the information in a database, and then produce an exact facsimile of each agency's form (because no agency could agree to give up its form). After much resistance by agencies, the Assistant Secretary of the State Department of Health became personally involved and directed state agencies to comply. With funding from the state to start the process, development of such a database was begun. From approximately 400 pieces of information, about 200 common data items were selected and entered into a standard computer database that served as the initial client interview. This database, along with a word-processing and forms-generation program, was able to generate very nearly exact copies of each agency form with about 50% of the required information filled in. Even though half the form remained blank, it still saved both families and agency staff time.

As part of this agreement for service coordination, the service coordinator at Madigan received formal training from each state agency involved and was given the authority to determine what services families will receive. Madigan's coordinator also will determine which agency will take responsibility for overall service coordination. The coordinator will complete the forms for specific services and will tell the family that they likely qualify for that service.

A Mechanism to Coordinate Services

Many of the Communities Can communities have developed an effective method of helping families pull together the pieces of the system so that services make sense and are delivered in a way that the family finds useful and supportive. There are many ways to accomplish this goal. In some communities, the system provides a person to work with each family in planning, seeking, and then coordinating services. Others have chosen to have a group of providers, agencies, and families that meet to coordinate care for each family. Finally, other communities have worked on ways to bring services together by providing them in one place, at the same time.

Use of Nurse Coordinators   In Collier County, Florida, the community uses specially trained nurse coordinators, funded through a state-level initiative to improve care for children, as the key to coordination of services. They coordinate efforts with local agencies to make sure that the children receive all needed medical, social, educational, and economic services for which they are eligible. They also enroll new clients, orient them to project procedures, provide education in basic child health care, and, as needed, supply instruction and help to those who must use special procedures or equipment to care for children at home. Nurse coordinators are active in identifying at-risk children. All children who are identified as potentially eligible are then visited so that the program can be explained to their parents. These nurses also are active in the local network of early intervention programs; they connect with the Foster Parents Association and counselors and interact with Medicaid case workers.

Another of the responsibilities of the nurse coordinators is to establish, maintain, and monitor individual care plans, notify parents of scheduled appointments and immunizations, and assist them in making contact with secondary care providers. As part of this coordination effort, the nurses act as advocates for children receiving these services, if necessary, and help families obtain entitlement and other nonmedical services. They coordinate health services with early intervention services, education services, social services, mental health services, and family-support services.

Parents and Providers Meet to Coordinate   In Eau Claire, Wisconsin, coordination of care is accomplished in a different manner. A program called Pathfinders can be set in motion by anyone in the system to bring together all those serving or potentially serving a family to assure a coordinated approach to care. Typically, a concerned professional contacts the family and all identified agencies to invite them to a coordination of services meeting. The concerned professional then arranges with the family prior to or at the meeting to have the release of information statement signed so verbal information about the family and child can be exchanged at the meeting and a written plan can be shared at its culmination. At the meeting, the concerned professional and parents present the basic information about the family and child. The family identifies their concerns, current needs, or both regarding their child. Then the committee (which includes the family) identifies any support systems that are needed by the family and any needed help in coordinating those systems. Of course, proposing solutions and, with the family, developing a coordinated plan are the ultimate tasks. At one meeting, a single medical, educational, and "family support" plan can be developed with the intent of maintaining the integrity of the family. The concerned professional responsible for bringing the committee together is responsible for recording, typing, and distributing the plan to everyone at the meeting, including the family, and providing the Family Support Coordinator at the Department of Human Services with a copy. One member of the team is then responsible for helping the family to implement the plan and for calling other meetings of the committee as the family's needs change. In effect, one person takes the lead for the group as a care coordinator with the family.

Co-location of Services In Kearney, Nebraska, coordination is taken right to the service provision level. Many communities believe that they can never bring the medical system together effectively with the other systems because physicians do not or will not come to team meetings, school conferences, and the like. In Kearney, a local private practice pediatrician and the other agencies involved have created a solution: Interdisciplinary evaluation clinics and team meetings take place in his and his partner's offices. The pediatricians, occupational therapist, physical therapist, nurse, social worker, teachers, and other school representatives can then all be involved with the family. Sometimes, specialists such as an orthopedist come to the meeting. Various professionals can examine the children together and can see six to eight children in a morning. They conduct assessments and work together to develop a plan, including a medical plan, that is then given to the family, the schools, and any treating therapists.

All children who qualify for state funding under Children with Special Health Care Needs must be seen by the team. The schools can also request such a team process for triennial evaluations, and parents can request a meeting of the team. The school system (when requested) pays consulting fees for the physician and nurse's time, and the physician pays the occupational and physical therapist. In other cases, Children with Special Health

Care Needs funds pay for the time of the professionals involved, and third-party payers are billed where appropriate.

Breaking down barriers to coordinated services can mean literally removing the walls that separate providers. Co-location of services and coordination of clinic times and other appointments can greatly ease the burden for families. This type of coordination requires collaboration between the private and public sectors and across many agencies. This level of collaboration takes effort and determination, but the payoff for families is enormous.

Coordinating the System   Sometimes it is not only the child's care that needs coordination, but the system itself that needs to become more effectively organized. In many communities, the same group that meets to work on individual care plans also takes on this role. In others, a broader planning effort may take place. In Woonsocket, Rhode Island, several collaboration-oriented ventures happened to come together at about the same time in the fall of 1992. For quite some time, the Child and Adolescent Service System Program (CASSP) had been a driving force behind coordinating mental health services in Rhode Island. In the Woonsocket area, a number of people had been talking about ways to achieve "wraparound services"—a package of individualized services in the home and community that would allow children with serious emotional disorders to remain in their own homes and communities. Woonsocket was also nominated for the Communities Can Campaign and had a group dealing with issues of coordinated services for children with special health care needs. Rhode Island is small enough that service providers asked to plan for any group of children are always the same people, who go from meeting to meeting, changing professional hats from time to time. As a result, they decided to create a global coordinating committee to pull the various service pieces together; this group would attempt to obtain some private funding. "Connecting for Children and Families" was established in late 1992. It combines CASSP, Communities Can, the YWCA and YMCA, parents, public and private social service agencies, school administrators, substance abuse agencies, legislators, business representatives, staff from developmental disabilities programs, and people from organizations representing minority groups. All in all, about 35 agencies and organizations are represented. The committee's mission is to bring coordinated services to families in northern Rhode Island, with Woonsocket being a special target.

Each agency or provider is contributing whatever resources it has, with cash being only one possible contribution. One agency is letting the committee have paper supplies; another provides meeting space. The group that has been part of Communities Can hopes to find some technical assistance to conduct a neighborhood assessment. The full committee meets once a month, and subcommittees (such as minority health and substance abuse) meet more frequently. This group has become the largest coalition in the area. Most of its members work out of Woonsocket, although they serve a larger district. The success of Connecting for Children and Families is due to the right set of forces converging at an opportune moment. Several parallel systems were talking about coordination, and opportunities for funding forced a community planning coalition that otherwise might not have been forged. This type of communitywide planning effort is one way that the system can begin to reshape itself, preventing the creation of multiple and duplicative coordination efforts and subsystems.

Recognition of Family Needs

Communities involve families at many levels in shaping the system. This type of involvement is more than asking for families' input regarding their own children's needs. It is recognizing that parents as well as providers of care and bureaucrats bring specialized knowledge and expertise to the process of planning and managing a community's system of care. Families not only bring the family-centered perspective to the process, but they may have greater knowledge about gaps and duplications in the system, how pieces of the system interrelate, and barriers to care than other members of the planning/management group, who may only see the system from one point of view.

Parents as Planners When Lucas County, Ohio, was developing its early intervention network, the leadership for the effort was determined to ensure that parents would have an equal role with professionals in building the system. In order to assure success, two parents co-chair the network with a third person who is a professional from the Office of Mental Retardation and Developmental Disabilities. By putting parents in this leadership role, there was a strong message about their centrality in the process. To further emphasize their value to the team, the parents were put on equal footing with the other members of the team by being paid for their time and contribution to the Network in Lucas County. The Department of Health employs the two parents, each of whom works 20 hours a week. There was initial resistance to parents playing significant roles, but persistence paid off.

Families as Educators In Vermont, parents have found another way to have an impact on the quality of care families receive. Parent to Parent of Vermont has developed two model programs with the University of Vermont to have families participate in the training of professionals who serve children with special needs. A family-centered philosophy is the focus of the Medical Education Project. The first session is a lecture about the concept, but this is quickly followed by a discussion for the group of about 12 medical students that guides them through understanding their own feelings, biases, and baggage that might ultimately affect how they care for children and families. A home visit with a family is then the learning experience for the students. Students are not there to interview, assess, or evaluate the family but to learn from them. Families direct the discussion during the home visit; therefore, each experience is unique. Some families may talk about their experiences getting the initial diagnosis for their children. Others may talk about how physicians could do a better job of sharing difficult information. All families work to help students understand that their children (the "patients") are first members of a family and a community. A final follow-up session gives students a chance to make sense of their experience and relate it to their personal experiences and to the lecture they heard in the first session.

Family Support Services   Too often systems that serve children forget that children are parts of families. When the child has difficulties, the family too has special stresses and needs. Thus, when families can give input to systems development, they make it clear that help for the entire family is critical to successfully treating children with special health care needs. Two critical parts of that help are emotional support and information, which comprise the basic components of the Kearney, Nebraska, Parent Assistance Network. Four collaborating agencies directly support the Parent Assistance Network: Good Samaritan Hospital, a 197-bed acute care hospital; Richard H. Young Hospital, an 80-bed psychiatric and chemical dependency facility; Kearney Public Schools, a Class A school district with an enrollment of over 4,000; and Educational Service Unit 10, which provides for children with developmental disabilities in nine counties. In addition, the four pediatricians at the Kearney Clinic are involved. The Parent Assistance Coordinator and secretary are employees of Good Samaritan Hospital but are housed in an office provided by Kearney Public Schools and furnished by both the hospitals and the school.

To ensure confidentiality, meeting notices are distributed through the school systems to students, who in turn share the information with their parents. Parents who wish to receive information directly ask to have their names placed on a mailing list. Numerous professionals from these collaborating agencies serve as speakers for the parent meetings. Three parent support groups based on the child's difficulties meet regularly and offer both emotional support and informational sessions. So that parents can more easily participate, child care is offered free of charge at the meetings. Students from Kearney State College studying to be special education teachers and high school students who are members of a teachers club at Kearney High School provide babysitting services. Parents may request information from the Parent Assistance Network Library, which currently contains approximately 200 books, periodicals, and audio and video cassettes with information on varied topics of interest to parents. A small "toybrary" with toys donated from a national foundation also is available for checkout to families and for use at the support group meetings. To enhance the community's understanding and acceptance of children with special needs, the Parent Support Network provides public education.

FROM LEARNING TO ACTION

The lessons learned from the Communities Can Campaign, and shared only in part in this chapter, are only a beginning. States, communities, providers, and families must begin to reassess the needs and possibilities available to them in developing systems of care for children with special health care needs that are based in the community, put the family at the center of the system, and provide a coordinated set of services. It is vital that all move beyond the "buzz words" of the laws and get past the enormity of ideas such as "systems building" to think about the concrete particulars of helping families and children. Families must join their voices, because, when they are heard, systems can change. (The entire process undertaken in Fort Lewis, Washington, was the result of family advocacy.) Professionals, particularly physicians, must look beyond the task of treating individual children to truly supporting changes in how services are delivered. In Kearney, Nebraska, Maui, Hawaii, and Franklin County, Vermont, private practice pediatricians have been leaders in system development. State agencies (as in Florida) and local governments (as in Flagstaff, Arizona; Wolf Point, Montana; and Eau Claire, Wisconsin) can also take a lead role in systems development. Private–public partnerships such as those formed in San Antonio have the flexibility and resources to spark change. Alternatively, all can work together in large communitywide planning efforts as in Woonsocket, Rhode Island. When any or all these potential players in the community understand the importance of developing systems of care for special health care needs that support families in the community, then the list of communities that can achieve this goal will be endless. Each community can learn from others but bring its own unique stamp to the system it develops, so that it best serves the families who live there. Finally, the systems that serve all children, whether their special health care needs primarily involve mental health providers or other medical specialists, can and must be integrated using these approaches.

REFERENCES

Bronheim, S., Keefe, M., & Morgan, C. (1993). *Communities Can: Vol. I. Building blocks of a community-based system of care: The Communities Can campaign experience.* Washington, DC: Georgetown University Child Development Center, National Technical Assistance Center for Children's Mental Health.

Omnibus Budget Reconciliation Act of 1989, PL 101-239. (December 19, 1989). Title 42, U.S.C. 6501(a)(1) et seq: *U.S. Statutes at Large, 103*, 2273.

Systems of Care in the Future

Beth A. Stroul, Robert M. Friedman, Mario Hernandez,
Linda Roebuck, Ira S. Lourie, and Chris Koyanagi

There has been, as demonstrated throughout this volume, extraordinary progress toward the development of community-based systems of care for children and adolescents with serious emotional disturbances and their families. Accomplishments are evident at national, state, and local levels, and span areas including the elucidation of the system of care concept and philosophy, the development of new services, the formation of an advocacy movement, the improvement of interagency collaboration, and the stimulation of research. Although gains have been substantial, great challenges lie ahead in the endeavor to develop systems of care. These challenges represent areas in which the field has not yet focused sufficient attention or achieved sufficient progress. They also take the form of changes in the environment in which systems of care are evolving, which necessitate attention and strategic responses to ensure continued movement toward system development goals. This chapter discusses a range of issues and challenges that will affect systems of care and their future development.

ISSUES AND CHALLENGES FACING
SYSTEMS OF CARE IN THE FUTURE

The future holds many challenges as we continue to pursue the goal of developing systems of care for troubled children and their families.

Achieving More Widespread Development of Systems of Care

Systems of care are emerging in many communities, and the progress that has been achieved in spreading this philosophy and approach to service delivery has been dramatic. Nevertheless, most communities in the nation remain without such systems of care. Many of the existing, and perhaps most advanced, systems of care are the results of special demonstrations or grants. Other communities are struggling to implement this approach but are deficient in either infrastructure, service capacity, or both; system development in many areas remains in rudimentary stages. A particular struggle has been the development of systems of care in large urban areas, where success in system development has been limited. Even systems of care with strong infrastructures have rarely had sufficient service capacity so that consumers do not have to be turned down for services or put on waiting lists. A major challenge for the future is to achieve more widespread system development so that more children with serious emotional disorders will be assured of having access to comprehensive, coordinated, community-based, family-focused, culturally competent systems of care.

Contemplation of the reasons that systems of care have not developed more broadly raises a number of questions: Is the system of care concept not yet universally understood or accepted? Are the incentives to actually implement systems of care inadequate? Is development thwarted by a lack of definitive research evidence that systems of care are, in fact, the optimal way to conceptualize and organize service delivery for this population? Is system development impeded by the lack of a pool of staff who are prepared with the philosophy and skills needed to work within a system of care context? Is there insufficient funding in mental health and other child-serving systems to accomplish system development or accomplish it well? It is likely that a combination of these and other factors explains the sluggish pace of system development in some states and communities.

One factor that has incontrovertibly impeded progress is resistance to change. The system of care movement is still relatively new, and the paradigm remains a dissonant one for many professionals (Friedman, 1993). It therefore can be expected to take a considerable amount of time to overcome such resistance and to change both attitudes and practices in the field.

In order to move toward more pervasive development of systems of care, attention to all of these factors will be imperative. The question of resource adequacy, however, is likely to be the most formidable obstacle to system development. The quantity of available resources may never be sufficient to achieve widespread development of systems of care with the infrastructure and rich service array envisioned. Particularly given the current fiscally conservative times, it is not unreasonable to question whether there will ever be a level of investment substantial enough to develop systems of care nationwide and, therefore, whether it is fiscally feasible to achieve the proposed vision. Although there are no clear answers to this question, it is clear that states and communities will be proceeding to develop systems of care in an atmosphere with an increasing focus on containing and reducing expenditures at all levels of government. Thus, system development will not proceed without the deliberate formulation of strategies to create, consolidate, or reallocate sufficient resources for this purpose (Center for the Study of Social Policy, 1994; Farrow, Watson, & Schorr, 1993; Friedman, 1994; Friedman, Burns, & Behar, 1992; Knitzer, 1993). At the same time, it is probable that, given the scarcity of resources, systems of care will be forced to direct available resources to better-defined target populations and to a narrower set of agreed-on outcomes. Similar to the approach used in Ventura County, California (see Chapter 9), this targeting of resources to specific populations and desired outcomes may be the most viable approach for systems of care in the future.

The need to develop a clear consensus about priority populations and the results that are sought was underscored recently in congressional testimony by Feltman (1994), the original architect of the Ventura County system of care. He emphasized that the first tasks of system development involve developing a vision for the system, defining the target populations, delineating the desired outcomes, identifying the services required in order to achieve those outcomes, and creating a strategy for developing those services. In order to capitalize on the fiscal opportunities available in this era of cost containment, planners must approach system development in this way, reaching agreement among key stakeholders as to the focus, priorities, outcomes, and activities deemed important for the system of care. Thus, although it is expected that gains in system development will continue throughout the nation's communities, systems of care in the future may be more narrowly focused and more targeted to specific populations and goals.

Coping with Managed Care and Other Financing Trends

Although health care reform efforts were unsuccessful at the national level, health care reform is proceeding at a rapid pace in the states. Health care reform at the state level typically is taking the form of implementing managed care approaches, initially focusing on state Medicaid programs. The changes related to managed care are likely to have profound implications for service delivery to children and adolescents with emotional disorders and their families. This is particularly true in view of the fact that Medicaid has been a major financing stream for community-based systems of care.

Managed care is a technology that has been widely implemented in the private sector, both for physical health and behavioral health (mental health and substance abuse) services. It is only within the past year that most state governments have been looking to managed care in an attempt to contain the runaway costs they are experiencing in their Medicaid programs. The translation of managed care to public-sector delivery systems is complex and challenging: the population served is more vulnerable; a larger proportion of the population requires extended care and supports beyond traditional medical services; multiple financing streams are involved; a large network of publicly funded agencies and providers exists to serve this population and has developed considerable expertise; and the public sector is seen as the safety net for those with serious health and mental health care needs—the provider of last resort.

The implementation of managed care involves both opportunities to enhance system of care development and threats to recent progress (Stroul, 1995). Much depends on the manner in which managed care is implemented and the goals it is intended to achieve. It is important to recognize that managed care is a set of tools, a technology that can be used to achieve the goals and vision of its implementers. Therefore, states are in the position to establish goals and desired outcomes for mental health service delivery as well as the values that will guide service system reform.

A primary goal of managed care is to achieve fiscal benefits resulting from improved efficiency and cost-effectiveness. However, if designed to be consistent with the values and goals of the system of care approach, managed care also presents potential opportunities to expand the service array, expand the covered population, reduce the use of high-cost services (inpatient and residential care), increase the appropriateness of services, increase coordination of services, increase accountability, and increase the focus on the measurement of both the quality and outcomes of service delivery. However, a number of risks or concerns have been identified that also may result from the implementation of managed care if a focus on children with emotional disorders and on systems of care is not incorporated. These potential negative impacts include

- A restricted range and level of services available
- Inadequate services to children with serious disorders because of the complexity and cost of serving this population
- Loss of an interagency focus in service delivery
- Reduced services to children with serious disorders who are not Medicaid eligible
- More limited availability of some types of providers and programs (particularly nontraditional providers)
- Increased fragmentation of service delivery with the introduction of new managed care organizations
- Decreased consumer and family input into the design, operation, and evaluation of service delivery systems

Historically, managed care has been used in the private-sector mental health arena primarily to contain costs by limiting access to services, limiting both the types and amounts of services that individuals could receive, or both. More recently, there has been some movement toward redefining the goal of managed care as the management of a full array of flexible, individualized services in order to achieve specific, desired outcomes as well as to contain costs. With this broad goal, the technologies of managed care can be used to enhance flexibility, coordination, quality, efficiency, and accountability in mental health services delivery—all of which are consistent with the system of care concept and philosophy. Thus, managed care is not inherently in conflict with the system of care philosophy; it is incumbent on states and communities to create their managed care approaches in a system of care context so that the values, goals, and philosophy of a system of care are reflected.

In order to accomplish this, persons who are knowledgeable about children's mental health and systems of care must be involved in the planning and design of managed care. Few individuals with managed care expertise have a substantial base of experience in designing, implementing, or operating a system of care. Consequently, those with system of care expertise must be "at the table" to ensure that managed care plans consider the needs of this population, maximize the potential positive impacts, and minimize potential negative effects. If this does not occur, the advent of managed care could devastate the progress achieved in system development over the last decade rather than being seized as an opportunity to further the system development agenda.

In addition to the adoption of managed care, other financing trends are likely to affect systems of care. One of these is the trend toward the consolidation of federal resources into block grants and similar mechanisms that have few specific requirements. This trend is evident in mental health, child welfare, education, and other funding streams. These types of mechanisms, particularly in mental health, are less likely to require the expenditure of certain amounts of funds for children or for system of care development. The lack of such requirements or set-asides may adversely affect systems of care in the future because, historically, states and communities did not make significant investments in these areas (Knitzer, 1982). A related trend is toward greater state discretion and control over spending and a similar transfer of greater control from states to the local level. It is important that this type of transition be accomplished carefully and thoughtfully and that control over resources not be turned over (from the federal to the state level, or from the state to the local level) without preparation, expectations, and accountability mechanisms.

The pace of change, particularly in the financing arena, is rapid and can be expected to continue to be rapid. Furthermore, financing of health and human services has become highly technical. Given the pace of change and the technical nature of financing policy, systems of care would be wise to commit resources to the development and maintenance of expertise in financing; these financing experts will be needed within systems of care to predict and adapt to changing political and economic circumstances. Although the future financial landscape for systems of care cannot be predicted, it can be predicted that systems of care will have to be much more astute and knowledgeable about financing services in the future.

Developing Human Resources for Systems of Care

Systems of care involve new ways of thinking about children, families, and services. The development of these systems will languish until more systematic attention is devoted to developing the human resources needed to administer them and to provide services. The challenge involves both developing preservice training programs that adequately prepare individuals for work within systems of care and developing mechanisms for preparing professionals who are already practicing in the field. Whether at the preservice or in-service stage, staff development efforts must focus on both the system of care concept and philosophy *and* the treatment technologies and approaches that are involved in systems of care. Large-scale investments in meeting the massive unmet need to develop staff for systems of care may be the next logical step to ensure the continued growth of systems of care in the future.

Changes in curricula at the university level to be consistent with the directions in the field are critically needed. A troubling obstacle has been that the training of providers in the traditional mental health disciplines (psychology, psychiatry, social work, counseling, and psychiatric nursing) has been rather inflexible and nonresponsive to changes in the service delivery arena, particularly in relation to the public-sector service system and the client populations with the most serious distrubances (K.E. Davis, 1990; Friedman & Duchnowski, 1990). Training does not prepare practitioners to provide family-focused, individualized services, nor does training provide them with the knowledge and skills needed to work with other agencies (or to even identify this as part of their responsibilities). Similar resistance to change is evidenced by the activities of some of the professional groups representing the interests of mental health professionals; many individuals and groups of mental health professionals seem wedded to the traditional private practice model.

Given the slow rate of change, the creation of some innovative, multidisciplinary programs may be warranted in order to prepare staff and provide them with opportunities to obtain the knowledge and skills needed to function within state-of-the-art systems of care. Other strategies to expose students to systems of care (such as courses taught by providers, internship and practicum opportunities, and joint programs between agencies and universities) will help to create a cadre of interested and skilled staff for the future (Friedman, 1993; Hanley, 1990; Taplin, 1990).

Many direct service staff already working in the field are not as yet well versed in the system of care philosophy or trained in the newer service approaches. Even if agency executives or program managers are committed to new ways of organizing and delivering services, these attitudes and skills do not necessarily filter down to those staff on the front lines (Stroul, Lourie, Goldman, & Katz-Leavy, 1992). Thus, in addition to the vast needs at the preservice level, there is an enormous unmet need for training of line staff. In order to address this need, a variety of strategies are necessary. For example, Pennsylvania has developed and funded a training institute to provide training to staff throughout the state on the system of care philosophy and service approaches. Whether state sponsored or at the initiative of local service systems, efforts to train direct service staff are crucial for the development of systems of care.

Of all aspects of the system of care, those that have received the most attention with respect to curriculum development and training have been case management and home-based services. It is likely that these modalities have commanded such attention because they are fairly new roles, quite dissimilar to traditional psychotherapy. Furthermore, these approaches are not tied to a particular mental health discipline and require additional skills and training regardless of the individual's professional discipline or degree level. Training in these approaches, home-based services in particular, also has received the support of private foundations such as the Edna McConnell Clark Foundation. Continued efforts in these areas will be needed for systems of care in the future, as well as training efforts focused on other aspects of system functioning.

One of the most important federal roles in the area of human resource development may be in the development and testing of training methodologies and curricula that are transportable and that might be applied in university settings as well as in practice settings in the field. The federal role also might encompass stimulating and supporting the development of multidisciplinary professional training programs for systems of care.

Enhancing Cultural Competence

Attaining cultural competence is an area in which many communities lag, even those with the most well-developed systems of care (Stroul et al., 1992). Although most communities recognize that cultural competence is an important goal for their service delivery systems, they generally have great difficulty in operationalizing the concept of cultural competence and in determining how to approach the challenge.

One of the barriers to achieving cultural competence has been the paradigm within which mental health systems have tended to operate. Guided by the "medical model," service systems have focused primarily on the identified "patient." More recently, this focus has enlarged to embrace families as well. However, in order for service systems to become culturally competent, the community culture in which children and families live also is an important consideration in the design and delivery of services. The challenge for systems of care in the future is to enhance their cultural competence by learning about the communities they serve and incorporating this knowledge into their framework for providing services.

Moving toward cultural competence, then, will involve two levels of attention. The first, and most basic, involves the requirement that the system of care learn about the culture of the community it serves and perhaps reconceptualize the very nature of the services it offers to be more attuned to the community culture. It has been well documented that culture has a powerful effect on the way in which individuals define problems and on their help-seeking behavior (Scapocznik & Kurtines, 1993; see also Chapter 25). Studying a community would yield valuable information about how individuals perceive and explain mental health problems, how they normally go about getting help, and how they think about mental health care. Accordingly, this examination may lead the system of care to provide services in completely different ways in order to be synchronized with the community and the children and families within it. Neglecting this step will prevent systems of care from becoming truly culturally competent, regardless of other actions they may take.

The second level of attention involves the more specific activities needed to move toward greater cultural competence. Systems of care will be most successful if they develop a "cultural competence master plan" (Bernard, 1992) that specifies the agencies and organizations within the system of care, the areas needing attention, and the goals and strategies to be implemented. The plan should cover four major domains: 1) policy and administration, including attention to mission, policies, procedures, and the like; 2) human resources, including staff recruitment, retention, education, and training; 3) client and family services, including outreach, assessment processes, translation of forms and services, and environment; and 4) research and evaluation, including such items as cultural competence program reviews and a focus on minority populations in evaluations.

A beginning step for systems of care involves thinking geographically, in terms of community. Data on service utilization can be analyzed by "geo code," revealing where in the area children receiving services come from, whether they cluster in certain communities, and whether there appear to be patterns. Such analysis also will reveal whether there are glaring gaps, particular areas or communities that the system of care is not reaching. This type of analysis lays the groundwork for additional study about why the system of care may be connecting better with certain communities than with others, and what steps might be necessary to address problems that have been identified. It may be necessary for systems of care to break down their service areas into smaller geographic regions (e.g., segments of a city or county or neighborhoods) for organizing services. This may make it easier to understand the community, its attitudes toward deviant behavior, and its help-seeking behavior.

Systems of care in the future also will need to do a better job of linking with informal supports in the community, such as self-help organizations, naturally occurring leaders, churches, clubs, and community organizations. In addition to formal agencies, these new partners should be drawn in to help design services and to teach service systems how to better connect people in the community with these services (Hernandez, 1995). This reaching out to communities may be the next stage of evolution of systems of care, enabling them to proceed further toward the goal of cultural competence.

Enhancing Family Involvement

Enormous change has occurred with respect to the role of families of children with emotional disorders (Duchnowski, Berg, & Kutash, 1995; Friesen & Koroloff, 1990; see also Preface). Families were often viewed as part of the problem, the cause of the problem, resistant, incompetent, or dysfunctional. Increasingly, families are now seen as the most important resource for their children, and it is recognized that even the most troubled families have strengths that can be built on in the helping process. Stemming from this profound shift in the way families are viewed has been the recognition that families of youngsters with emotional disorders should be partners in all aspects of systems of care—both in the planning, delivery, and evaluation of services for their own children and in planning and overseeing services at the system level. Significant progress has been achieved in many communities in involving families both at the level of the individual child and, albeit with somewhat less consistency, at the system level. Another area of progress has been in the development of family organizations at the local, state, and national levels that are serving as a much-needed advocacy voice for youngsters with serious emotional disturbances (see Chapter 19).

Despite this progress, there is still much to be done to fully involve families as partners in systems of care, and this represents a vital challenge to systems of care in the future. A major aspect of this challenge involves continuing to bring the message of families to professionals—the new way of viewing families as well as the importance of family involvement in services and systems of care. Many practitioners, and the agencies in which they work, do not yet view families as allies. They remain uneducated about these issues, and their attitudes regarding families and family involvement still have not shifted. In order to continue the process of attitude change, universities will have to incorporate into professional training curricula new attitudes toward families and new ways of working with families as partners. Similarly, child-serving agencies will have to utilize training, supervision, and other means to foster new ways of relating to families among staff. One obvious beginning would be for families of youngsters with emotional disorders to routinely be speakers in the training programs for agency personnel and for students of the various mental health disciplines. Thus, systems of care must continue to educate direct service workers in their agencies and in universities about the new paradigm with respect to families.

A second major aspect of this challenge is to continue to develop, strengthen, and support the organized family movement. Efforts are needed to keep the momentum of this fledgling movement going at local, state, and national levels. Support for family organizations can come from government and nongovernment sources and can take many forms. However, an important source of support has come from the federal Center for Mental Health Services (CMHS), providing resources to assist family organizations to develop into statewide networks. Such financial support is crucial for the survival and ongoing viability of family organizations as support groups, providers of services, and advocates for children with serious emotional disturbances. With or without federal resources, systems of care must find ways of strengthening and supporting family organizations in their communities and states.

Finally, the development and evolution of systems of care is occurring at a time when societal trends indicate that families are increasingly stressed (Annie E. Casey Foundation, 1994). Compounding the growing economic and social stresses is the fact that families do not have the supports (e.g., extended families, neighbors, and others) that were once available. An ongoing dilemma for systems of care and the family movement is how to support families in which there are a tremendous number of problems, such as high levels of poverty, substance abuse, and neglect. Systems of care inevitably are strongly affected by these social trends and must recognize and assist in addressing them.

Utilizing Appropriate Governance Structures

An issue receiving increasing attention and debate is that of "governance" of systems of care. The term "governance" has been used to refer to the focal point for planning, administering, and coordinating a system of care, with all of the functions attendant to this management role. At issue are both the *level* at which such governance or oversight should be vested and the *type* of structure best suited to oversee and administer systems of care.

With respect to the level at which system management should be ensconced, there has been much discussion about the roles of different levels of government, the relationship between them, and the level of government that should have system management authority. Some recommend organizing and administering systems of care in small communities or geographic areas where services are closer to the people, whereas others (such as states and managed care organizations) emphasize that a larger population base or sufficient "covered lives" are needed to support a system of care and suggest moving to more regional governance for service systems. Thus, there may be competing pressures for smaller service areas on the one hand and larger, regional configurations on the other.

In addition to debate about the level of system governance, the type of structure needed for this purpose has been the subject of debate. It is widely agreed that systems of care need some type of structure for interagency coordination and that some entity (whether existing or newly created) must become the focal point for management of the system of care. It is not yet clear, however, what types of organizational structures are required to fulfill these functions and whether some are more effective than others. The management structures used in various communities include regional boards, county agencies, councils of government, private nonprofit corporations, regional branches of state agencies, and interagency councils. In addition to the lack of clarity on the optimal types of governance structures, the specific types of responsibilities the structures should have and the extent to which they should control the resources and services in a system of care remain open to discussion.

What is becoming increasingly clear is the realization that the solution to the governance dilemma differs from place to place. Both the role and character of system oversight may vary from state to state and from community to community. Some systems may not need to create a new structure but may utilize or adapt existing entities. In other areas, a new type of configuration may be needed to fulfill the management and coordination functions envisioned for the system. In all cases, both the form and functions conceived for governance should be related to the vision for the system of care. Because there is no prescribed formula for system governance that can be applied everywhere, systems of care will have to experiment with various types of management/coordination structures. It is likely that a variety of types of structures will be found to be effective in different communities in assuming local control over systems of care.

Integrating with Other System Reforms

As mental health systems are undergoing major reforms, other child-serving systems also are in the process of attempting major reforms of their systems. Notably, most systems (including mental health, child welfare, education, juvenile justice, and health) appear to be moving in similar directions—toward community-based, family-focused services provided in the least restrictive, most appropriate setting. Additionally, the values and principles espoused by these systems are remarkably consistent. Although it is encouraging that the directions are compatible across systems, it is nevertheless important to consider the implications for systems of care of the reforms emerging within the major child-serving systems that share responsibility for youngsters with emotional disorders and their families. Furthermore, it is important to consider how these reforms can be integrated.

One of the first tasks in addressing this challenge is to determine how the various systems can become involved in the planning and implementation of reforms in each other's systems. This type of joint planning must occur at national, state, and local levels. Most of the deliberations regarding directions for the various child-serving systems are "parallel," rather than occurring with reciprocal efforts to obtain the involvement and input from the other systems. Input from the other child-serving systems should be an integral part of planning, particularly when one considers the fact that changes in one system often have direct effects on the operation and costs of other systems.

At the level of local systems of care, close integration among the various systems becomes even more critical, particularly in planning for and implementing system reforms. Although basic values across the systems appear to be converging, differences among systems remain, as they should, with respect to their specific mission and population served. Although there is considerable overlap among systems in the populations of concern, basic differences in agenda and target population priorities must be acknowledged and reconciled in planning for integrated systems of care. For example, the mental health system currently is focusing most of its resources on children with serious emotional disorders and has prioritized this group (which historically has been underserved); the child welfare system is concerned with a broader population of youngsters who are "at risk" and may push the mental health system to broaden its target population definition to achieve greater consistency. The special education system may see itself as focusing on a narrower target population than mental health, those youngsters with serious emotional disorders that have an adverse impact on their ability to succeed in school. In some commuities, school systems are perceived as taking this requirement to an extreme, and perhaps underidentifying children with serious emotional disorders for special education services. These potential differences in agenda and priorities may complicate system development efforts in a community and may create a dynamic tension between systems.

Given this context of both similarities and differences among the child-serving systems, a basic task for systems of care involves bringing together the key service systems in the community to reach agreement on where their missions do and do not overlap, what priorities for service delivery should be established jointly, and what resources can be applied to the collaborative system of care. This process acknowledges that the various systems can legitimately have their own purview, mission, and priorities, but that there is a joint mission for which they come together. In most communities, the joint mission of the child-serving systems centers around the group of youngsters with very serious problems that are likely to endure for an extended period of time and that require services from a variety of agencies. It is this population in particular that requires the close collaboration of the child-serving systems and for which joint service strategies can be created. At the same time, agencies can work jointly to create capacities in the community to meet the needs of those youngsters who may only require certain elements of the array of services included in a system of care.

Thus, the development of systems of care will be advanced by the fact that the various child-serving systems are engaged in system reforms based on compatible values and principles. However, in order to integrate these reforms, agencies must find opportunities to contribute to the planning and implementation of each other's reforms. Furthermore, systems of care in the future must recognize and acknowledge the different agendas of the participating systems and identify those joint priorities to be collectively addressed.

Developing Systems of Care in a Privatized Environment

The future appears to bode changes in the distinction between the public and private sectors. As a result of health care reforms, most involving managed care, it has been predicted that the distinction between the public and private sectors will become increasingly blurred and that the two systems will eventually merge, resulting in a largely privatized (and for-profit) service delivery system operating under government contracts. The trend toward privatization also is spurred by a general assumption that public-sector agencies generally cannot get the job done well and that contracting out services to the private sector will result in greater efficiencies and a better likelihood of success.

As noted with respect to managed care, there may be some advantages and opportunities in the trend toward privatizing services, but there also are some concerns related to this trend. Opportunities can be found in the ability of private-sector agencies and organizations to change more rapidly. Many would argue that public systems have been notoriously intractable and slow to change and that innovations in service delivery may flourish and grow more easily in a private context. Concerns, however, center around ensuring that the public-sector mission and commitment to meeting the needs of children with serious emotional disabilities and their families, and to being the provider of last resort, are not compromised as they are blended with the management technologies and cost-containment philosophy of the private-sector world. Anxiety about what will happen to the larger mission of the public sector in a privatized system is not unreasonable.

A related concern is that the quality and effectiveness of services may diminish as the bottom line becomes the dollar. Although there is clearly room within service systems for greater efficiency and cost-effectiveness, safeguards will be needed to ensure that quality is not lost to concerns about cost in systems of care in the future. Furthermore, the private sector is not well versed in the system of care philosophy or in nontraditional service approaches. It will take a great deal of education and cross-fertilization to ensure that the philosophy and technologies developed in public-sector systems of care are maintained and further developed in the context of privatized service delivery systems.

Generating Public Awareness and Support

Of all of the afflictions of children, emotional and behavioral disorders are probably the least well understood. The lack of understanding of these disorders among the general public as well as among decision makers at various levels has made it difficult to secure resources for services and supports for this population. The public perception of many youngsters with emotional disturbances is that they are "bad" rather than sick; the children themselves, or in many cases the parents, are blamed for the problems.

The lack of understanding of these youngsters underscores the necessity for concerted efforts to more clearly and more widely convey the message about who these youngsters are and what interventions they require. Public education efforts must highlight the population of concern, emphasizing that systems of care are not focusing on youngsters with normal developmental problems or with mild, transitory distress. Rather, the youngsters needing services through such systems have profound problems that are likely to last over time and that interfere with their functioning.

The federal CMHS is sponsoring a public awareness campaign for this purpose. The campaign is designed to enhance public awareness and understanding of children with serious emotional disturbances and of systems of care. It involves the development of media kits and close work with a number of CMHS grantees in local communities with the goal of public education. Focus groups in these local sites were used to determine how best to "package" the message so that people will understand and accept it. It will be important to study and build on this groundbreaking work by CMHS in the future. Systems of care will need to focus considerable energy and resources on the challenge of generating public awareness and support; such support is likely to be crucial for the survival and future development of systems of care.

Building in Accountability, Evaluation, and Research

The future development and survival of systems of care will depend, in large part, on the information generated about them that documents the functions that they fulfill and the results they achieve. Information is needed both by system managers, who make ongoing decisions about the continuing operations of systems of care, and by policy makers, who make decisions about the approaches that should be taken to address various societal and health problems as well as about resource allocation.

The first level of information needed by systems of care falls under the rubric of "accountability." Effective operation of systems of care requires the ongoing collection of systematic data that reflect how well the system is performing. Use of this type of data is the only way that leaders can make knowledge-based decisions as they administer systems of care; without collection of such data on a regular basis, systems are severely handicapped in their ability to assess their performance and to self-correct when necessary. Accountability processes are not the same as formal evaluations, but rather are practical, manageable systems to track both progress and outcomes. The basic information that a system of care needs for accountability purposes includes who is being served, what services are provided, and what has changed. A challenge for systems of care is to develop such practical, ongoing tracking mechanisms.

For accountability purposes, it is suggested that systems of care focus on a tracking system that includes a reasonable amount of information on the children and families served and on the services provided, coupled with a simple set of repeatable outcome measures that are consistent with the goals of the system of care and are easy to obtain and interpret (Young, Gardner, Coley, Schorr, & Bruner, 1994). A streamlined set of outcome measures can be selected from four domains of outcome (clinical outcomes, functional outcomes, system outcomes, and consumer/family satisfaction). The process of identifying which outcomes to include in an accountability system is in itself a healthy activity for a system of care in that it brings key stakeholders together to reach consensus on what the system is trying to accomplish.

As a first step, it may be judicious for systems to focus on some very basic outcomes for which information can be regularly collected and effort can be sustained. Efforts to create accountability systems have failed as a result of being too ambitious, complex, and costly and not sustainable over time. Many may argue that the information obtained in this way is not objective, scientific evidence of system effectiveness. Yet managers are making decisions regularly that involve billions of dollars with minimal information about the populations served, services provided, and outcomes achieved. Although accountability systems may not provide rigorous, scientific information, they are indispensable tools for the management and future development of systems of care.

Evaluation goes beyond the global indicators and benchmarks included in accountability systems and, in a more precise and scientific fashion, attempts to answer questions about the effectiveness of systems of care. Although evaluation is seen as a more objective and scientific process, there is movement in the field away from seeing evaluation as a process removed from system operation and toward new models of participatory evaluation (Weiss, 1995; Weiss & Greene, 1992; Whyte, 1991). In this new framework, evaluators are viewed partly as consultants, part of a team who help to raise questions and issues and gather information that will guide system change.

As systems of care evolve, it is important that we avoid the temptation to conduct formal evaluations prematurely. It is suggested, for example, that perhaps systems of care should not be formally evaluated on how well they are serving children until they have been in operation for a period of time and have been able to develop and refine their infrastructure and services. There is a tendency across human services to rush to conduct formal evaluations before developmental work is completed and service delivery approaches are fine tuned. Rather than devoting much effort and resources to evaluating the start-up phase, it may be well advised to postpone full-scale evaluations until systems have reached some minimal level of maturity; earlier evaluations might focus more on implementation issues.

The appropriateness of the use of comparisons in the evaluation of systems of care is an issue that has aroused considerable debate. It is suggested that comparisons are appropriate after systems of care have been in operation for a period of time, and after accountability and quality assessment mechanisms indicate that the system of care is, in fact, one that is well developed and of high quality. Comparison of the results of a poor-quality system of care at one location with those for another community or group of youngsters will not yield any useful or valid information on the effectiveness of the system of care approach. Furthermore, if comparison sites are used, evaluators must ensure that the populations served are comparable across sites. Evaluations must focus on the population for which the system of care concept was designed—youth with *serious* emotional disturbances. Measures of functional impairment provide the mechanism for separating out youngsters with serious disorders from those with less serious disorders.

An additional challenge for the evaluation of systems of care lies in exploring new ways to measure the quality of services or the extent to which they conform to system of care values and principles and to standards of practice where they exist. Furthermore, developmental work is needed to design strategies for assessing the benefits to other child-serving systems resulting from systems of care.

Beyond evaluation, other types of research must be built into systems of care in the future. Although some may advocate randomized studies in children's mental health, both logistical and ethical concerns make it unlikely that this type of scientific rigor can be applied to research on community-based services or systems of care. The use of randomized field studies, which has its roots in agricultural research, in other human service fields (such as delinquency or substance abuse) has met with limited success (Weiss, 1995). In addition, youngsters with serious emotional disorders represent a complex population, most of whom do not have a pure diagnosis. With this caveat, further research is needed to increase our knowledge in two major areas related to systems of care: 1) to continue to assess the effectiveness of various treatments and interventions for children with serious emotional disorders (Rivera & Kutash, 1994), and 2) to continue to enhance our understanding of emotional and behavioral disorders in children, with a focus on exploring developmental pathways as well as risk factors and protective factors at various stages of development. Most clinical research has taken place in academic settings or other specialized settings with selected populations. To advance the field, there is a need for clinical research in more "real-world" settings, community settings more akin to those used as service settings for systems of care.

For all types of evaluation and research initiatives, it is important to remember that, for systems of care, the goal is not to assess individual service components or modalities apart from the context of the overall system. Rather, it is the *synergy* of the various components, and the coordination among them, that is postulated to lead to enhanced outcomes in systems of care. Finally, an ongoing challenge for systems of care is to translate the results of evaluation and research into service delivery.

Responding to the Effects of Violence

It is only in the last few years that the system of care movement has focused attention on the issue of violence. The effects of violence on children, families, and neighborhoods is perhaps the most striking and worrisome aspect of increasing poverty and urban distress. Violence affects not only the perpetrators and victims but also children exposed to violence, because exposure to violence is a known risk factor for the development of emotional disturbances (American Psychological Association, Commission on Violence and Youth, 1993; National Mental Health Association, 1995). Furthermore, escalating violence in society has implications for systems of care. To respond, systems of care must examine 1) assessment and treatment approaches to ensure that children suffering from the consequences of violence are correctly identified, 2) the training of staff to ensure that they have the requisite skills in this area, and 3) the agencies and community leaders with whom the system is connected in order to participate in addressing violence in the community and its effects.

We are only now learning about the profound effects of exposure to violence. The challenge to systems of care in the future involves developing appropriate responses for individual youngsters and their families as well as participating at the community level in working toward solutions.

Increasing the Priority on Children

Enormous progress has been made within mental health systems since the mid-1980s with respect to children. There is evidence, within most states, of dramatic changes in the attention focused on children in terms of policy, legislation, and resource commitments at both administrative and service delivery levels (M. Davis, Yelton, Katz-Leavy, & Lourie, 1995). In fact, whereas other areas have remained stable or been reduced, children's services have represented an area of growth in the mental health systems in most states.

However, despite this noteworthy progress, in many situations children still are not receiving the attention and priority that is warranted. In some situations, the needs of children remain an afterthought, and planners and policy makers have only a minimal understanding of the special needs of children and the service considerations that distinguish them from adults. For example, in the implementation of managed care, some state Medicaid and mental health agencies are proceeding with planning and implementation without sufficient input from those with expertise in children's mental health services and systems. The systems that are designed, then, are not likely to be attuned to the special needs of children's systems, particularly in the degree to which they are dependent on interrelationships with other child-serving systems. These are areas that will need correcting as implementation proceeds.

A related problem is that, within mental health bureaucracies, those representing children's issues still are not uniformly at high levels, positioned so that they can be a part of major policy debates and decisions. It is important that, organizationally, those with expertise in children's mental health systems have the ear of the director and are at the table for deliberating critical issues that will have major ramifications for children's systems. A continuing challenge for systems of care will be to advocate increased priority on children within local, state, and federal bureaucracies.

The need to increase the priority on children does not fall solely within mental health systems but is true within society at large. Society at this time is struggling to find solutions to problems that seem to be increasing in both magnitude and severity, such as poverty, family disorganization, community disorganization, crime, violence, substance abuse, illiteracy, and teen pregnancy. Data from the Kids Count project of the Annie E. Casey Foundation (1994) and the Children's Defense Fund (1992) show that children and youth are faring worse today than they were only a decade ago. Some of these problems seem so overwhelming that the mental health needs of children seem almost insignificant in comparison. Yet the interrelationship between these problems and emotional disorders in children and adolescents has been demonstrated empirically (Friedman, in press; Schorr, 1988; see also Chapter 4), and these problems create great strains on human service resources and systems of care. Regardless of how mental health interventions and concerns are interwoven, society must provide greater supports to children and families to address these pervasive and devastating problems.

Systems of care cannot take responsibility for addressing all of these needs; in fact, systems of care in the future are likely to become even more targeted in their focus in order to achieve significant outcomes within ever-increasing resource constraints. However, systems of care in the future will be operating within the context of increased prevalence of many different problems that are interrelated and create strains on families, schools, communities, and service systems. They can make contributions by participating in planning, community development, system reform activities, and early intervention efforts to address some of these problems. The participants in systems of care also will need to become an active part of broader advocacy movements on behalf of children and families.

In short, if we do not address the needs of children and families better as a society, there is likely to be a "flood" of children needing services, and even the best developed systems of care will be unable to meet the need. Furthermore, until we establish the overall well-being of children and families as a societal priority, and invest resources in the future of children and families accordingly, mental health problems will continue to be only one of many sources of suffering that will need increased attention.

CONCLUSION

All of the issues and challenges discussed above must be viewed through the lens of a thorough understanding of the population of concern. Systems of care are developing in a climate with tremendous pressures to provide short-term interventions and to contain costs. The pressures in these directions stand in stark contrast with the realization that children with serious emotional disorders and their families are likely to need services and supports on a long-term basis and that services and supports for this group are likely to be costly. The youngsters being served through systems of care are not those who have only a mental health disorder; they are those with a diagnosis *plus* significant impairment of functioning. Our concern about these youngsters does not stem solely from the personal distress experienced by them and their families, but stems also from the fact that the impairment of their day-to-day functioning creates significant costs for public systems such as schools, juvenile justice, and health. Research suggests that, as adults, these youngsters have difficulty holding jobs, unstable personal relationships, substance abuse problems, antisocial behavior, and higher utilization of psychiatric services (Schorr, 1988; Silver, Unger, & Friedman, 1994; see also Chapter 4). Therefore, they represent significant costs to public systems, both in the present and predictably in the future.

A problem in assessing the cost-effectiveness of systems of care is that the cost savings from such systems are more likely to be seen in other systems than in the mental health system. Investments in system development, therefore, must be weighed against benefits that may be achieved across the various child-serving systems, not only in the mental health or health arenas. In addition, such investments must be balanced against both current and future costs that can be anticipated in responding to the variety of real-life problems typically experienced by youngsters with serious emotional disorders. In the long run (and looking beyond just the mental health system), investment in systems of care and in long-term services and supports for this population is likely to be a prudent and cost-effective approach.

A final challenge for systems of care is to truly actualize the values and guiding principles that we advocate. This will involve going beyond the rhetoric of principles such as individualized care, family involvement, and cultural competence. The challenge is to find meaningful ways of implementing these values, not just talking about them and then doing business in the old way. For example: Are we going to say that we provide individualized services but continue to move youngsters from program to program if they do not fit the services offered? Are we going to say that we believe in family involvement but continue to exclude parents from our advisory boards and boards of directors? Are we going to say that we believe in preserving family integrity but continue to force parents to relinquish custody for their child to receive needed residential treatment? Are we going to say that we believe in comprehensive, coordinated services but continue to focus on specialized mental health services apart from all of the other services and supports needed by a child and family? Are we going to say that we believe in cultural competence but continue to function without minority staff, training, and outreach to minority communities? Are we going to say that we believe in system integration but continue to guard our own agency's resources and resist a joint commitment to a system of care? Are we going to say that we are committed to community-based care but continue to send youngsters out of county or even out of state for treatment? It is only when we truly actualize our values and principles that we will have effective systems of care.

As we move to the next stage of system development, it is important for the field to consolidate what we have accomplished and learned about the development of systems of care. At the same time, it is important, as a field, to remain flexible and open to changes in both philosophy and approach based on what we learn as systems of care continue to evolve.

REFERENCES

American Psychological Association, Commission on Violence and Youth. (1993). *Violence and youth: Psychology's response: Vol. I. Summary report of the American Psychological Association Commission on Violence and Youth.* Washington, DC: Author.

Annie E. Casey Foundation. (1994). *Kids count data book: State profiles of child well-being.* Baltimore: Annie E. Casey Foundation.

Bernard, J. (1992). *Ventura County's Cultural Competence Master Plan.* Unpublished manuscript, Ventura County Department of Mental Health, Ventura, California.

Center for the Study of Social Policy. (1994). *Financing reform of family and children's services: An approach to the systematic consideration of financing options.* Washington, DC: Author.

Children's Defense Fund. (1992). *State child poverty data.* Washington, DC: Author.

Davis, K.E. (1990). Collaboration between public mental health systems and universities. *Community Support Network News, 7,* 8–9.

Davis, M., Yelton, S., Katz-Leavy, J., & Lourie, I. (1995). Unclaimed children revisited: The status of state children's mental health service systems. *Journal of Mental Health Administration, 22,* 147–166.

Duchnowski, A., Berg, K., & Kutash, K. (1995). Parent participation in and perception of placement decisions. In J.M. Kauffman, J.W. Lloyd, T.A. Astuto, & D.P. Hallahan (Eds.), *Issues in the educational placement of pupils with emotional or behavioral disorders.* Hillsdale, NJ: Lawrence Erlbaum Associates.

Farrow, F., Watson, S., & Schorr, L. (1993). A framework for improving outcomes for children and families. *Family Resource Coalition Report, 12,* 13–15.

Feltman, R. (1994). Testimony before the Subcommittee on Labor-Management Relations, Committee on Education and Labor, U.S. House of Representatives, Hearings on Health Care Reform, Washington, D.C.

Friedman, R.M. (1993). Preparation of students to work with children and families: Is it meeting the need? *Administration and Policy in Mental Health, 20,* 297–310.

Friedman, R.M. (1994). Restructuring of systems to emphasize prevention and family support. *Journal of Clinical Child Psychology, 23*(Suppl.), 40–47.

Friedman, R.M. (in press). Child mental health policy. In B.L. Levin & J. Petrila (Eds.), *Mental health services: Public health perspective.* New York: Oxford University Press.

Friedman, R.M., Burns, B., & Behar, L. (1992). Improving mental health and substance abuse services for adolescents. *Administration & Policy in Mental Health, 19,* 191–206.

Friedman, R.M., & Duchnowski, A.J. (1990). Service trends in the children's mental health system: Implications for the training of psychologists. In P.R. Magrab & P. Wohlford (Eds.), *Improving psychological services for children and adolescents with severe mental disorders: Clinical training in psychology* (pp. 35–42). Washington, DC: American Psychological Association.

Friesen, B., & Koroloff, N. (1990). Family-centered services: Implications for mental health administration and research. *Journal of Mental Health Administration, 17,* 13–25.

Hanley, J. (1990). State mental health needs and adequacy of personnel to meet these needs. In P.R. Magrab & P. Wohlford (Eds.), *Improving psychological services for children and adolescents with severe mental disorders: Clinical training in psychology* (pp. 43–48). Washington, DC: American Psychological Association.

Hernandez, M. (1995). *Developing cultural competence master plans: Linking mental health systems of care with community cultures.* Unpublished manuscript, Florida Mental Health Institute, University of South Florida, Tampa.

Knitzer, J. (1982). *Unclaimed children: The failure of public responsibility to children and adolescents in need of mental health services.* Washington, DC: Children's Defense Fund.

Knitzer, J. (1993). Children's mental health policy: Challenging the future. *Emotional and Behavioral Disorders, 1,* 8–16.

National Mental Health Association. (1995). *Voices vs. violence.* Alexandria, VA: Author.

Rivera, V.R., & Kutash, K. (1994). *Components of a system of care: What does the research say?* Tampa: University of South Florida, Florida Mental Health Institute, Research and Training Center for Children's Mental Health.

Scapocznik, J., & Kurtines, W.M. (1993). Family psychology and cultural diversity: Opportunities for theory, research, and application. *American Psychologist, 48,* 400–407.

Schorr, L.B. (1988). *Within our reach: Breaking the cycle of disadvantage.* New York: Anchor.

Silver, S.E., Unger, K.V., & Friedman, R.M. (1994). *Transition to young adulthood among youth with emotional disturbance.* Unpublished manuscript, Florida Mental Health Institute, University of South Florida, Tampa.

Stroul, B. (1995). *Opportunities and risks presented by managed care for children's mental health services and systems of care.* Washington, DC: Georgetown University Child Development Center, National Technical Assistance Center for Children's Mental Health.

Stroul, B., Lourie, I., Goldman, S., & Katz-Leavy, J. (1992). *Profiles of local systems of care for children and adolescents with severe emotional disturbances.* Washington, DC: Georgetown University Child Development Center, National Technical Assistance Center for Children's Mental Health.

Taplin, J.R. (1990). Training clinical child psychologists to serve SED youth: Delaware's prospects and hopes. In P.R. Magrab & P. Wohlford (Eds.), *Improving psychological services for children and adolescents with severe mental disorders: Clinical training in psychology* (pp. 185–190). Washington, DC: American Psychological Association.

Weiss, H.B. (1995). New directions in program evaluation. Presentation to the Annual Conference on System of Care Research in Children's Mental Health, Florida Mental Health Institute, University of South Florida, Tampa.

Weiss, H.B., & Greene, J.C. (1992). An empowerment partnership for family support and education programs and evaluations. *Family Science Review, 5,* 131–148.

Whyte, W.F. (Ed.). (1991). *Participatory action research.* Newbury Park, CA: Sage.

Young, N., Gardner, S., Coley, S., Schorr, L., & Bruner, C. (1994). *Making a difference: Moving to outcome-based accountability for comprehensive service reforms.* Falls Church, VA: National Center for Service Integration.

Index

Page numbers followed by "f," "t," or "n" indicate figures, tables, or footnotes, respectively.